DOWN HOME COOKING

THE NEW, HEALTHIER WAY

READER'S DIGEST

DOWN HOME COOKING

THE NEW, HEALTHIER WAY

Reader's
Digest

The Reader's Digest Association, Inc.
Pleasantville, New York/Montreal

DOWN HOME COOKING

◆◆◆

CONTRIBUTORS

Editorial Director	Beth Allen
Art Editor	Joan Mazzeo
Photographer	Spencer Jones
Illustrators	David Cain
	Karin Kretschmann
	Beth Krommes
Food Stylist	Andrea Swenson
Asst. Food Stylist	Karen Hatt
Prop Stylist	Deborah E. Donahue
Recipe Developers	Louise Burbidge
	Georgia Chan Downard
	Claudia Gallo
	Jean Galton
	Sandra Rose Gluck
	Helen Taylor Jones
	Kathleen Kaliban
	Carol Prager
	Sarah Reynolds
	Diane Simone Vezza
	Marianne Zanzarella
Recipe Tester	Michelle Gurdon
Text Researcher	Judith Blahnik
Photo Researcher	Marion Paone
Copy Editor	Lynne Eppel
Indexer	Catherine Dorsey

STAFF

Project Editor	Gayla Visalli
Senior Art Editor	Henrietta Stern
Art Associate	Eleanor Kostyk

CONSULTANTS

Nutrition	Annette B. Natow Ph.D., R.D.
	Jo-Ann Heslin, M.A., C.H.E., R.D.
Computer	Michael Callery
	David Schoen

READER'S DIGEST GENERAL BOOKS

Editor in Chief	John A. Pope, Jr.
Managing Editor	Jane Polley
Executive Editor	Susan J. Wernert
Art Director	David Trooper
Group Editors	Will Bradbury
	Sally French
	Norman B. Mack
	Kaari Ward
Group Art Editors	Evelyn Bauer
	Robert M. Grant
	Joel Musler
Chief of Research	Laurel A. Gilbride
Copy Chief	Edward W. Atkinson
Picture Editor	Richard Pasqual
Head Librarian	Jo Manning

Library of Congress Cataloging in Publication Data

Down home cooking the new, healthier way.
     p.   cm.
     At head of title: Reader's digest.
     Includes index.
     ISBN 0-89577-646-4
     1. Cookery. I. Reader's Digest Association. II. Reader's digest. III. Title: Reader's digest down home cooking the new, healthier way.
TX714.D69 1994
641.5—dc20   94-13511

ABOUT THIS BOOK

♦♦♦

Within these pages you can take a trip back to days when children brought friends home from school for freshly baked cookies and milk, or relive heartwarming Sunday suppers that featured a roast and perhaps Mom's blue-ribbon apple pie. Whatever your own fond memories of food happen to be, you'll find some of their tastes and sweet smells in DOWN HOME COOKING THE NEW, HEALTHIER WAY. Here are more than 450 recipes and 75 variations, gathered from all over America, from cookbooks written generations ago, and from families who represent every culinary tradition brought to this country. They are just as scrumptious as ever but have been updated by professional recipe developers and nutrition experts to accommodate today's nutritional guidelines and busier lifestyles. Each one appears in an easy-to-follow step-by-step format, accompanied by nutrition counts and preparation and cooking times. Just for the fun of it, every chapter presents two or three recipes in their traditional form, alongside a newer version. And a "Back to Basics" chapter features cooking techniques and tips and winning ways with garnishes.

There's much more, however, all making DOWN HOME COOKING just as delightful to read as to use. You'll come with us to food fests and state fairs, into diners and family cafés, to a strawberry farm, a cheese factory, and an old-fashioned soda fountain. There you'll meet folks who are busy preserving food traditions for the generations to come. You'll also enjoy gems of information about the recipes' origins, ingredients, unusual preparation methods, and treasured traditions. So rediscover the familiar, fabulous foods of yesteryear, brought to life again with the cooking know-how of today—the new, healthier way.

•CONTENTS•

A SPRINKLE AND A DASH

❖❖❖

When you cut fat and salt from favorite recipes, one way to make up the difference in flavor is to use more herbs and spices. Look for fresh herbs at your greens market, and dried herbs at a supermarket or specialty food store, then experiment to your taste's delight.

Allspice, appropriately named, tastes like a blend of cinnamon, cloves, nutmeg, and pepper. Steep the whole berries in hot cider, marinades, and pickling liquids. Sprinkle the ground form into sauces and stews.

Anise seeds have a strong licorice flavor. Use them to flavor plain butter cookies. Add a teaspoonful to the water when steaming or poaching shrimp, crabs, or mild-flavored fish such as cod.

Basil, an herb with minty flavor and clove-like aroma, enlivens tomato-based Italian-style sauces, salads (especially tomato), and dishes made with mozzarella. It's a must in every summer garden.

Bay leaf adds a pungent, woodsy flavor to stews, marinades, and poaching liquids. Always remove it from a dish before serving.

Cardamom has a gingery flavor and perfume-like aroma. Add the ground seeds to curries and Scandinavian breads and cookies.

Chili powder is a mixture of ground dried chilies, oregano, cumin, garlic, and sometimes allspice and cloves. It's an essential ingredient in classic Tex-Mex recipes, and also adds zip to Western egg and vegetable dishes.

Cilantro (also called Chinese parsley) is the leafy part of the coriander plant. It contributes a pungent flavor to many Southwestern recipes and traditional Chinese dishes. Use it sparingly.

Cinnamon, in its ground form, imparts a warm, spicy flavor to baked goods and stews. The stick adds a spicy overtone if infused in hot chocolate or punch, a pickling mixture, or a poaching syrup.

Cloves have a sweetish, peppery taste. Dot baked ham with whole cloves. Use the ground form in stews, mashed winter squash, sweet potato pie, and cookies.

Coriander seeds have a lemony, orange flavor. Add the crushed whole seeds to pickling mixtures, the ground seeds to breads, stews, fruit pies, and compotes.

Cumin is an earthy flavored spice favored in Indian, Mexican, and Native American dishes. Add the ground seeds to guacamole or vinaigrette dressings. Mix with yogurt to garnish chili or tacos.

Curry powder is a mixture of several spices, including cardamom, cloves, cumin, coriander, ginger, and turmeric. To mellow its flavor, warm the powder in a skillet or sauté it with an ingredient in the recipe, such as onions or garlic. Add a dash to mayonnaise when making chicken salad.

Dill adds a refreshing, sweetish flavor to sour-cream dips and cucumber or tomato salads. Chop and stir it into oil or softened butter to flavor grilled or poached fish, such as salmon. Look for it fresh or dried (called dill weed).

Fennel has a delicate licorice flavor and aroma. Sprinkle snipped fresh leaves into a pasta salad or over poached fish. Add the seeds to Italian sauces, coleslaw, or a poaching liquid for salmon or sole.

Ginger has a pungent, peppery flavor that works well with both savory and sweet dishes. Add the fresh root to stir-fries, marinades, and stews; use the dried ground form in fruit-poaching liquids, ham glazes, cookies, and cakes.

Mace (the lacy covering of the nutmeg kernel) gives a nutmeg-like flavor to foods. Use it sparingly, either grated or ground.

Marjoram has a delicate flavor, reminiscent of sage and mint. It's sold in fresh bunches and as dried leaves, whole or ground. Add to meat loaf as well as lamb, pork, and chicken dishes. Sprinkle over such vegetables as yellow squash, green beans, lima beans, snow peas, and sugarsnap peas.

Mint, a fresh-tasting, fragrant herb, has many varieties, including peppermint and orange. It is a fine addition to lamb, carrots, peas, tomatoes, and fruit salads. The leaves may be infused in tea or in syrup for flavoring chocolate sauce or sorbet. Fresh leaves have more intense flavor than dried.

Mustard seeds are often used when pickling vegetables. A pinch of the ground form adds zest to salad dressings, cheese sauces, and deviled eggs.

Nutmeg is a pungent spice used in eggnog, puddings, baked goods, meat pies, and creamy pasta sauces. You can buy a whole kernel and freshly grate it yourself, or purchase it already ground.

Oregano is an herb known for its slightly bitter, evergreen flavor with spice and thyme accents. Use it sparingly, especially when ground. Add fresh or dried leaves to tomato sauces, marinades, and salad dressings. Sprinkle on pizza, grilled meats, and chicken too.

Paprika usually has a mild peppery flavor, though there is a hot Hungarian type, and the Spanish variety has an earthy overtone. Use paprika to enhance fish, pork and beef stews, vegetables, and salad dressings. For extra color as well as flavor, sprinkle it on eggs, cheese dishes, and baked chicken.

Parsley is available in a curly-leaf as well as the more pungent flat-leaf Italian variety. It's often used as a garnish, but also adds a fresh flavor. Mix chopped parsley with minced garlic and grated lemon rind, then add the mixture to eggs, pastas, vegetables, salads, sauces, fish, stews, and soups.

Pepper comes in the milder, green form, the mature, more pungent black, and the hulled white, also hotter. (Ground red pepper, or cayenne, and red pepper flakes are from dried red chili peppers.) Use whole peppercorns in marinades and pickling and poaching liquids. Sprinkle (preferably freshly) ground pepper on meat, pastas, soups, salads, and sauces

Rosemary has an intense evergreen flavor and aroma. Add chopped fresh or crumbled dried leaves to meat (especially lamb), poultry, fish, marinades, potatoes, beans, salad dressings, and pizza.

Sage has a woodsy, evergreen flavor. Add chopped fresh leaves or the rubbed or ground dried form to stuffings for pork or poultry, and to chowders, stews, beans, and cheese dishes. Use it sparingly.

Savory is an aromatic herb that makes a wonderful substitute for salt, especially in salads and egg dishes. The summer variety is the mildest and the easiest to use.

Sesame seeds (known as benne seeds in the South) have a rich, nutty flavor when toasted. Use on top of breads and rolls and in coatings for chicken.

Tarragon is an anise flavored herb that's best for chicken and fish dishes, tartar sauce, and salad dressings. Use it sparingly.

Thyme is an herb that adds a bright, spicy flavor to stuffing, marinades, salad dressings, eggs, fish, vegetables, stews, and soups. Look for fresh bunches and dried whole or ground leaves.

Turmeric is a spice with an earthy flavor that softens with cooking. Use it to flavor relishes, cauliflower, curries, and marinades, and to add a yellow color to food.

BITS, BITES & SIPS

♦♦♦

Entertaining in America—
sharing good times and good food with family
and friends—has evolved from the campfire
meetings, church suppers, barn raisings, and
ice cream socials of yesteryear, to the tailgate
picnics, tree trimmings, family reunions, and
video parties of today.

We've collected some favorite bits, bites,
and sips often served at such gatherings, then
streamlined them to lower the fat and calories.
Angels on Horseback (actually, oysters and
bits of bacon) are made with less and leaner
bacon than the original; Sausage Bites contain
reduced-fat cheese; and crispy, coated fresh
vegetables are baked rather than fried. We've
stuffed mushrooms with vegetables (instead
of sausage), used much less butter to pot
shrimp, and created Cajun Popcorn from real
popcorn instead of deep-fried crawfish. Our
Hot Chocolate is made with low-fat milk and
our old-fashioned sodas with low-fat ice
cream, but they're still as memorable as ever.

Many recipes can be prepared ahead, for
example, Nancy's Curry Dip, Church Supper
Deviled Eggs, Pickled Shrimp, and the tortilla chips for Tex-Mex Nachos. Of course,
when enjoying these tempting tidbits, keep in
mind that moderation is the key to snacking
and entertaining the healthier way.

CLAMS CASINO
◆◆◆

When patrons of gambling houses were reluctant to lose their places at the tables, these clams were often brought to them in the casino.

12 cherrystone clams in their shells	2 tablespoons finely chopped sweet green pepper
Coarse rock salt or aluminum foil	1 tablespoon minced parsley
2 slices lean bacon, diced	½ teaspoon lemon juice
1 tablespoon unsalted butter or margarine	¼ teaspoon black pepper
3 tablespoons finely chopped shallots or green onions	⅛ teaspoon salt

PREP TIME: 15 MIN. / COOKING TIME: 10 MIN.

1 Buy the clams the day you plan to cook. Ask your fishmonger to shuck them, leaving them on the half shell and reserving the liquor. Cover the clams and liquor and refrigerate.

2 Preheat the broiler. To keep the clams upright during broiling, line a broiling or shallow baking pan with the rock salt or crushed foil.

3 In a small skillet, bring 2 inches of water to a boil over moderately high heat. Add the bacon and cook for 2 minutes. Using a slotted spoon, transfer the bacon to a paper towel and discard the water. In the same skillet, melt the butter. Add the shallots and green pepper and sauté for 5 minutes. Stir in the parsley, lemon juice, black pepper, and the ⅛ teaspoon of salt.

4 Place the clams in their shells on the prepared pan. Drizzle each clam with about 1 teaspoon of clam liquor, then top with about 1 teaspoon of shallot mixture and a few pieces of bacon. Broil 4 inches from the heat for 2 minutes or until the clams curl at the edges. Makes 12 appetizers.

1 clam: Calories 44; Saturated Fat 1 g; Total Fat 2 g; Protein 4 g; Carbohydrate 1 g; Fiber 0 g; Sodium 95 mg; Cholesterol 14 mg

OYSTERS ROCKEFELLER
◆◆◆

Created by Chef Jules Alciatore of the famous Antoine's restaurant in New Orleans, this dish is known for being "as rich as Rockefeller himself."

12 oysters in their shells	½ cup finely chopped fresh spinach leaves
Coarse rock salt or aluminum foil	1 tablespoon plain dry bread crumbs
2 tablespoons unsalted butter or margarine	½ teaspoon lime juice
3 tablespoons finely chopped green onions, with tops	¼ teaspoon dried tarragon leaves
	¼ teaspoon salt
2 tablespoons finely chopped celery	3 drops hot red pepper sauce

PREP TIME: 15 MIN. / COOKING TIME: 6 MIN.

1 Buy the oysters the day you plan to cook. Ask your fishmonger to shuck them, leaving them on the half shell and reserving the liquor. Cover the oysters and liquor and refrigerate.

2 Preheat the broiler. To keep the oysters upright during broiling, line a broiling or shallow baking pan with rock salt or crushed foil.

3 In a small skillet, melt the butter over moderately high heat. Add the green onions and celery and sauté for 2 minutes. Stir in the spinach and sauté 1 minute longer or until vegetables are tender. Remove from the heat and stir in the bread crumbs, lime juice, tarragon, the ¼ teaspoon of salt, and the red pepper sauce.

4 Place the oysters in their shells on the prepared pan. Drizzle each oyster with 1 teaspoon of oyster liquor, then top with 1 tablespoon of spinach mixture. Broil 4 inches from the heat for 3 minutes or until the oysters curl at the edges. Serve immediately. Makes 12 appetizers.

1 oyster: Calories 30; Saturated Fat 1 g; Total Fat 2 g; Protein 1 g; Carbohydrate 1 g; Fiber 0 g; Sodium 68 mg; Cholesterol 13 mg

A taste of old New Orleans: spicy Oysters Rockefeller, served with frosty Planter's Punch (page 37)

ANGELS ON HORSEBACK

❖❖❖

Oysters curl as they cook, resembling angel wings.

12 oysters in shells	1 clove garlic, minced
Coarse rock salt or aluminum foil	¼ cup dry white wine (with or without alcohol)
3 slices lean bacon	12 drops hot red pepper sauce
2 tablespoons minced parsley	

PREP TIME: 15 MIN. / COOKING TIME: 3 MIN.

1 Buy the oysters the day you plan to cook. Ask your fishmonger to shuck them, leaving them on the half shell and reserving the liquor. Cover the oysters and liquor and refrigerate.

2 Preheat the broiler. Line a broiling or shallow baking pan with the rock salt or a layer of crushed foil. Cut each slice of bacon in half crosswise, then lengthwise. In a small bowl, mix the parsley with the garlic.

3 Place the oysters in their shells in the prepared pan. Top each oyster with a piece of bacon, then about ½ teaspoon of the parsley mixture. Top each oyster with a little white wine, oyster liquor, and a drop of red pepper sauce. Broil 4 inches from the heat for 3 minutes or until the oysters curl at the edges and the bacon browns. Serve immediately. Makes 12 appetizers.

1 oyster: Calories 23; Saturated Fat 0 g;
Total Fat 1 g; Protein 2 g; Carbohydrate 1 g; Fiber 0 g;
Sodium 45 mg; Cholesterol 9 mg

STUFFED MUSHROOMS
•••

*Not until the 1920's were
mushrooms widely cultivated in America.*

Nonstick cooking
spray

1½ pounds medium-size
mushrooms, with
stems, rinsed

3 tablespoons extra-
virgin olive oil

½ cup finely chopped
yellow onion

2 cloves garlic, minced

1 teaspoon chopped
fresh thyme or
¼ teaspoon dried
thyme leaves

2 cups shredded
unpeeled zucchini

¼ cup finely chopped
sweet red pepper

½ teaspoon salt

¼ teaspoon black
pepper

½ cup plain dry bread
crumbs

2 tablespoons minced
parsley

5 tablespoons freshly
grated Parmesan
cheese (1¼ ounces)

PREP TIME: 30 MIN. / COOKING TIME: 25 MIN.

1 Preheat the oven to 375°F and coat a large shallow baking pan with the cooking spray. Remove the mushroom stems and chop them coarsely. Arrange the mushroom caps on the pan, cavities facing up; brush the insides and edges with 2 tablespoons of the oil.

2 In a 12-inch nonstick skillet, heat the remaining 1 tablespoon of oil over moderately high heat. Add the onion, garlic, and thyme and sauté for 2 minutes or until soft. Stir in the mushroom stems, zucchini, red pepper, salt, and black pepper. Sauté for 6 minutes or until most of the liquid has evaporated. Stir in the bread crumbs, parsley, and 2 tablespoons of the cheese.

3 Using a teaspoon, mound the filling into the mushroom caps, pressing it down gently with your fingers. Sprinkle the mushroom caps with the remaining 3 tablespoons of cheese. Bake for 15 minutes or until tender and lightly browned. Serve immediately. Makes about 30 appetizers.

---

*1 mushroom: Calories 32; Saturated Fat 0 g;
Total Fat 2 g; Protein 1 g; Carbohydrate 3 g; Fiber 0 g;
Sodium 69 mg; Cholesterol 1 mg*

CRUNCHY BAKED GARDEN VEGETABLES
•••

*For this healthier, yet appealing
version of deep-fried vegetables, use broccoli or
cauliflower florets, carrot sticks, small
mushrooms, sweet green or red pepper sticks,
yellow squash or zucchini slices.*

Nonstick cooking
spray

½ cup reduced-calorie
mayonnaise

¼ cup finely chopped
yellow onion

1 tablespoon Dijon
mustard

4 cups assorted cut-up
fresh vegetables

1 cup Italian seasoned
dry bread crumbs

¼ cup freshly grated
Parmesan cheese
(1 ounce)

PREP TIME: 30 MIN. / COOKING TIME: 10 MIN.

1 Preheat the oven to 425°F and spray 2 baking sheets with the cooking spray. In a large bowl, blend together the mayonnaise, onion, and mustard. Add the vegetables and toss to coat.

2 In a large self-sealing plastic bag, toss the bread crumbs with the cheese. Put the coated vegetables in the bag, ½ at a time, shaking until they are well covered. Transfer the vegetables to the baking sheets, spreading them in single layers. Bake for 10 minutes or until the vegetables are tender and golden brown. Serve with toothpicks. (This recipe may easily be doubled.) Makes 12 appetizer servings.

---

*⅓ cup: Calories 79; Saturated Fat 1 g;
Total Fat 4 g; Protein 3 g; Carbohydrate 9 g; Fiber 0 g;
Sodium 120 mg; Cholesterol 5 mg*

CHINESE CHICKEN SESAME

Ever since the first Chinese immigrants landed in San Francisco in 1847, Americans have been discovering the wonders of cooking Chinese.

½ cup reduced-sodium soy sauce

2 green onions, with tops, finely chopped (¼ cup)

3 tablespoons sesame seeds

1 clove garlic, minced

1 teaspoon dark sesame oil

½ teaspoon dry mustard

¼ teaspoon ground ginger

1 pound skinned and boned chicken breasts, cut into 4- x 1- x ½-inch strips

Nonstick cooking spray

2 tablespoons orange marmalade

2 tablespoons fresh orange juice

Optional garnishes:

Green onion fans (page 366)

Kumquats

PREP TIME: 15 MIN. / MARINATING TIME: 2 HR. COOKING TIME: 8 MIN.

1 In a self-sealing plastic bag, mix ¼ cup of the soy sauce with the green onions, sesame seeds, garlic, oil, mustard, and ginger. Add the chicken and seal the bag tightly. Refrigerate for at least 2 hours, turning the bag over occasionally.

2 Preheat the oven to 425°F. Spray 2 baking sheets with the cooking spray. Thread each chicken strip onto a 6-inch skewer and place on a baking sheet. Reserve the marinade. Bake the chicken, uncovered, for 8 minutes or until golden, turning and basting frequently with the marinade.

3 In a small bowl, whisk the remaining ¼ cup soy sauce with the marmalade and orange juice. Arrange the chicken on a serving platter, garnish with green onion fans (page 366) and kumquats if you wish, and serve with the sauce. Makes about 16 chicken pieces and ⅓ cup sauce.

1 chicken strip and 1 teaspoon sauce: Calories 52; Saturated Fat 0 g; Total Fat 1 g; Protein 8 g; Carbohydrate 3 g; Fiber 0 g; Sodium 297 mg; Cholesterol 17 mg

Chinese Chicken Sesame, reminiscent of the snacks served in San Francisco's Chinatown

The more the merrier; the fewer, the better fare.

—*John Palsgrave*

FLASH UN KAS

◆ ◆ ◆

Many German food customs in America got their roots in the Pennsylvania communities where Germans from the Rhineland settled. These appetizers resemble the German Fleisch und Kase, which means "meat and cheese."

For the pastry:

- 2 cups all-purpose flour
- Pinch salt
- 2 packages (8 ounces each) Neufchâtel cream cheese
- ½ cup (1 stick) unsalted butter or margarine
- 2 tablespoons cold water

For the filling:

- 1 tablespoon unsalted butter or margarine
- 2 green onions, with tops, finely chopped (¼ cup)
- 2 large shallots, finely chopped (¼ cup)
- 1 pound skinned and boned chicken breasts, cooked and cubed (about 2¾ cups)
- ⅓ cup chopped baked ham (2 ounces)
- ¼ cup low-fat (1% milkfat) milk
- ¼ cup minced parsley
- ¾ teaspoon black pepper
- ¼ teaspoon salt
- Nonstick cooking spray
- 1 large egg white
- 1 teaspoon cold water

PREP TIME: 30 MIN. / CHILLING TIME: 1 HR.
COOKING TIME: 26 MIN.

1 To prepare the pastry: In a large bowl, combine the flour and salt. Using a pastry blender or 2 knives, cut in the cream cheese and butter until coarse crumbs form. Stir in the water to form a dough, then wrap and chill for 1 hour.

2 To prepare the filling: In a small skillet, melt the butter over moderately high heat. Add the green onions and shallots and sauté for 5 minutes or until tender. Spoon into a food processor with the chicken, ham, milk, parsley, pepper, and salt. Process 1 minute or until smooth.

3 Preheat the oven to 375°F and spray 2 baking sheets with the cooking spray. On a floured surface, roll out the chilled pastry dough, ½ at a

A Pennsylvania Dutch treat: Flash un Kas, homemade pastries filled with meat and cheese

time, into a 16-inch circle, ⅛ inch thick. Using a 2½-inch fluted round cutter, cut the dough into 48 circles. Spoon 1 tablespoon of filling on half of each pastry circle, then fold the pastry over, forming a semi-circle. Using the back of a fork, seal the edges, and place on the baking sheets. (If making ahead, refrigerate at this point.) In a cup, beat the egg white and water; brush on the pastries with a pastry brush. Bake for 20 minutes or until crisp. Serve hot. Makes 48 appetizers.

1 flash un kas: Calories 82; Saturated Fat 2 g; Total Fat 5 g; Protein 5 g; Carbohydrate 4 g; Fiber 0 g; Sodium 73 mg; Cholesterol 28 mg

PIGS-IN-A-BLANKET

◆◆◆

American pancake houses introduced us to Pigs-in-a-Blanket. Those pigs were sausage links and their blankets were pancakes. This version features miniature bites of lean franks wrapped in thin strips of flaky dinner-roll dough.

1	8-ounce package refrigerated crescent dinner-roll dough	1	teaspoon Worcestershire sauce
2	tablespoons Dijon mustard with seeds	8	lean frankfurters, cut into thirds

PREP TIME: 20 MIN. / COOKING TIME: 10 MIN.

1 Preheat the oven to 375°F and set out 1 ungreased baking sheet. On a lightly floured surface, spread out the dough and separate into 8 triangles. In a small cup, combine the mustard and Worcestershire sauce. Using a pastry brush or a small spoon, spread 1 teaspoon of the sauce mixture over each triangle. Starting at the point, cut each of the 8 triangles with scissors into three smaller triangles, making 24.

2 Place one frankfurter piece on the wide end of each dough triangle. Roll up each triangle, starting from the wide end. Place the triangles, point-side-down, on the baking sheet and press down lightly to seal. (If making ahead, refrigerate until a few minutes before serving time.) Bake for 10 minutes or until puffy and golden brown. Serve immediately. Makes 24 appetizers.

1 pig-in-a-blanket: Calories 81; Saturated Fat 0 g; Total Fat 6 g; Protein 3 g; Carbohydrate 4 g; Fiber 0 g; Sodium 271 mg; Cholesterol 0

◆ On Entertaining ◆

Entertaining should be enjoyable, not only for your guests but you too. It's all in the planning. "When you are entertaining, keep it simple and single-focused," advises Lawrence Harvey, Executive Director of Catering for The Plaza Hotel in New York City. "Choose a menu, set a mood and create an evening that expresses your personality and succeeds in telling your guests they are very special. Above all, plan ahead and prepare as much in advance as you can, so you spend less time in the kitchen and more time with your guests."

Whether you are planning an informal Sunday supper or a formal wedding reception for 100, here are a few of Mr. Harvey's tips to keep in mind:

• Select a theme. It might be Hawaiian, if you have just returned from the isles ... or trim-the-tree to decorate for Christmas ... or Southwestern for a backyard barbecue. Then, everything else flows easily—from invitations, to foods, china, linens, the decorations, even the music.

• Set a mood. It could be as simple as lighting a roaring fire for a wintry night supper, filling a room with candlelight for a formal dinner, or playing Spanish music for a paella party.

• Choose a menu that matches your lifestyle. Consider featuring dishes that have been in your family for years, ones that reflect your nationality, or that relate to a region where you grew up.

• Select foods that can be prepared ahead of time, such as stews which need only rewarming, appetizers you can pop into the oven at the last moment, and frozen or bake-ahead desserts.

• Use recipes that you know work—ones that are your specialties. Never choose a recipe for entertaining that you have not tried before!

• Consider going back to the basics, such as serving a perfectly prepared pot roast and mashed potatoes, barbecued chickens hot off the grill, or roasted turkey with dressing. Such comfort foods make guests feel right at home and very welcome.

• Leave time to enjoy your guests—and have fun. You will soon realize your guests are enjoying the party too!

SWEDISH MEATBALLS

◆◆◆

1 large egg	8 ounces lean ground pork
⅓ cup plain dry bread crumbs	1 cup low-fat (1% milkfat) milk
3 tablespoons chopped yellow onion	1 medium-size all-purpose potato, peeled, cooked, and mashed (½ cup)
¾ teaspoon salt	2 tablespoons olive oil
¾ teaspoon brown sugar	3 tablespoons all-purpose flour
¾ teaspoon ground nutmeg	1 cup Beef Stock (page 74) or low-sodium beef broth
½ teaspoon each ground allspice, cloves, and ginger	Sprigs of fresh dill
1 pound lean ground beef	

PREP TIME: 30 MIN. / COOKING TIME: 35 MIN.

1 In a large bowl, whisk the egg, then stir in the bread crumbs, onion, salt, sugar, nutmeg, allspice, cloves, and ginger. Mix in the beef, pork, ¼ cup of the milk, and the mashed potato. Form the meat mixture into 60 balls, 1 inch in diameter.

2 In a 12-inch nonstick skillet, heat the oil over moderately high heat. Cook the meatballs, in batches if necessary, for 4 minutes or until browned, turning occasionally. Using a slotted spoon, transfer them to a bowl and keep warm.

3 Pour off all but 2 tablespoons of the pan drippings. Whisk in the flour, then the stock and the remaining ¾ cup of milk, scraping to loosen the browned bits. Bring the mixture to a simmer and cook, uncovered, for 2 minutes, stirring constantly, until slightly thickened. Stir the meatballs into the sauce, along with any juices that have collected, and simmer for 3 minutes or until the meatballs are heated through. Place in a chafing or shallow dish, garnish with sprigs of dill, and serve with toothpicks. Makes 60 meatballs.

1 meatball and 1 teaspoon sauce: Calories 45; Saturated Fat 1 g; Total Fat 3 g; Protein 3 g; Carbohydrate 1 g; Fiber 0 g; Sodium 44 mg; Cholesterol 13 mg

---

DOWN HOME TRADITION

When Europeans first settled in the South, they ate what the Native Americans ate — corn, squash, beans, turkey, fish, and deer. But they soon established herds of pigs, and pork became one of the mainstays of their diet. In fact, early Southerners regarded the preservation of pork an important survival skill. Smokehouses sprang up, and homemade sausages with plenty of sage and spice were common. During plantation days, Southern gatherings often featured sausage specialties — and it's still true today.

◆ Sausage Balls ◆

2 cups buttermilk biscuit mix
1 pound country pork sausage, crumbled
2 cups shredded Cheddar cheese (8 ounces)
¼ cup heavy cream

PREP TIME: 30 MIN. / COOKING TIME: 15 MIN.

1 Preheat the oven to 375°F and grease 2 baking sheets. In a large bowl, using a fork or your hands, mix the biscuit mix, sausage, and cheese until well blended.

2 Add the cream and blend thoroughly, then roll the mixture into 72 balls, 1 inch in diameter. Arrange the balls on the prepared baking sheets and bake for 15 minutes or just until golden brown. Serve hot with toothpicks. Makes 72 appetizers.

1 sausage ball: Calories 41; Saturated Fat 2 g; Total Fat 3 g; Protein 2 g; Carbohydrate 1 g; Fiber 0 g; Sodium 106 mg; Cholesterol 9 mg

Swedish Meatballs: A Scandinavian tradition,
typically featured at smörgåsbord feasts in the Midwest

SAUSAGE BITES

◆◆◆

You can still dine in traditional Southern style, yet stay healthy too. These tiny sausage balls have that old-fashioned flavor but less fat.

Nonstick cooking spray

2 cups buttermilk biscuit mix

1 pound reduced-fat country pork sausage, thawed if frozen, crumbled

1 cup shredded Monterey Jack cheese with jalapeño peppers (4 ounces)

½ cup shredded reduced-fat Cheddar cheese (2 ounces)

3 tablespoons low-fat (1% milkfat) milk

PREP TIME: 30 MIN. / COOKING TIME: 20 MIN.

1 Preheat the oven to 375°F and spray 2 baking sheets with the cooking spray. In a large bowl, using a fork or your hands, mix the biscuit mix, sausage, and cheeses until well blended. Add the milk and blend thoroughly, then roll the mixture into 72 balls, 1 inch in diameter. Arrange the balls on the baking sheets and bake for 20 minutes or just until golden brown. Serve hot with tooth-picks. Makes 72 appetizers.

1 sausage bite: Calories 30; Saturated Fat 1 g; Total Fat 2 g; Protein 2 g; Carbohydrate 1 g; Fiber 0 g; Sodium 77 mg; Cholesterol 6 mg

TEX-MEX NACHOS

◆◆◆

The nachos first made in Mexico were simply tiny tostadas topped with a little cheese. Today many resemble Mexican pizzas.

3 **8-inch flour tortillas**	1 **medium-size fresh or pickled jalapeño pepper with seeds, finely chopped (1½ teaspoons)**
1½ **cups shredded Monterey Jack cheese (6 ounces)**	
2 **tablespoons finely chopped green onions, with tops**	1 **large lime, thinly sliced**

PREP TIME: 15 MIN. / COOKING TIME: 12 MIN.

1 Preheat the oven to 450°F. Cut the tortillas into 8 wedges each, making 24. Arrange the wedges on 2 ungreased baking sheets and bake for 5 minutes. Turn the wedges over and bake 5 minutes longer or until crisp and golden.

2 Sprinkle each wedge with 1 tablespoon cheese and 2 or 3 pieces of green onion and jalapeño pepper. Return to the oven and bake for 2 minutes or until the cheese melts. Transfer to a platter, garnish with the lime slices and serve piping hot. Makes 24 appetizers.

1 nacho: Calories 39; Saturated Fat 1 g; Total Fat 2 g; Protein 2 g; Carbohydrate 3 g; Fiber 0 g; Sodium 41 mg; Cholesterol 6 mg

◆

Cheesy Nachos with Beans

Prepare and bake the tortilla wedges as for Tex-Mex Nachos. Meanwhile, rinse and drain **1 can (10½ ounces) red kidney beans**. Using the back of a wooden spoon, crush the beans until they are mashed but not puréed. Stir in **2 cloves minced garlic**. Spread about 2 teaspoons of beans on top of each wedge, sprinkle with the cheese, green onions, and jalapeño pepper, and bake as directed. Makes 24 appetizers. *1 nacho: Calories 50; Saturated Fat 1 g; Total Fat 2 g; Protein 3 g; Carbohydrate 5 g; Fiber 0 g; Sodium 81 mg; Cholesterol 6 mg*

QUESADILLAS

◆◆◆

In Spanish, quesadilla means "a little something made of cheese," which is exactly what these wonderful snacks are.

8 **8-inch flour tortillas**	4 **teaspoons minced cilantro (coriander) or 4 teaspoons minced parsley plus ½ teaspoon dried cilantro**
¾ **cup shredded Monterey Jack cheese (3 ounces)**	
2 **tablespoons finely chopped green onions, with tops**	**Optional garnish:**
1 **small fresh or pickled jalapeño pepper with seeds, finely chopped (1 teaspoon)**	**Chunky salsa**

PREP TIME: 15 MIN. / COOKING TIME: 5 MIN.

1 Preheat the oven to 350°F. Arrange 4 tortillas on an ungreased baking sheet. Top each with 3 tablespoons cheese, 1½ teaspoons green onions, ¼ teaspoon jalapeño pepper and 1 teaspoon cilantro. Cover each one with a second tortilla, pressing down lightly to form a sandwich.

2 Bake for 5 minutes or until the cheese melts and the tortillas are crisp. Cut each Quesadilla into 8 wedges and top each wedge with a spoonful of salsa if you wish. Makes 32 appetizers.

1 quesadilla: Calories 44; Saturated Fat 1 g; Total Fat 2 g; Protein 2 g; Carbohydrate 4 g; Fiber 0 g; Sodium 30 mg; Cholesterol 5 mg

For many Southwesterners... the tortilla is the staff of life.

—from American Food by Evan Jones

GUACAMOLE
◆◆◆

1 cup plain low-fat yogurt

1 large ripe tomato, peeled, cored, and finely diced (1 cup)

½ cup finely chopped white onion

1 large fresh or pickled jalapeño pepper with seeds, finely chopped (1 tablespoon)

2 tablespoons minced cilantro (coriander) or 1 teaspoon dried cilantro

1 tablespoon fresh lime juice

½ teaspoon salt

2 ripe avocados, peeled, pitted, and coarsely mashed

Optional garnishes:

Tomato wedges

Strips of sweet red and yellow peppers

Cucumber slices

Cilantro leaves

PREP TIME: 25 MIN. / STANDING TIME: 30 MIN.

1 Line a strainer with cheesecloth or paper towel and place over a bowl. Spoon in the yogurt and let it drain for 30 minutes. Discard the liquid.

2 While the yogurt drains, in a medium-size bowl, combine the tomato, onion, jalapeño pepper, cilantro, lime juice, and salt. Fold in the drained yogurt and the avocado. Garnish with the tomato wedges, pepper strips, cucumber slices, and cilantro if you wish, and serve with tortilla chips. Makes 3 cups.

1 tablespoon: Calories 17; Saturated Fat 0 g; Total Fat 1 g; Protein 0 g; Carbohydrate 1 g; Fiber 0 g; Sodium 29 mg; Cholesterol 0 mg

Guacamole or "avocado sauce," made the healthier way with low-fat yogurt

Many's
the long
night I've
dreamed of
cheese,
toasted,
mostly.

—*Robert Louis Stevenson*

DOWN HOME TRADITION

Colonists from England brought their love of Cheddar and Cheshire cheeses to America and for some time ate the varieties imported from their homeland. However, after the Revolution, when exorbitant taxes were placed on English cheeses, Americans began developing their own cheese-making talents. In the South, where the sultry climate made the ripening of cheese difficult, the product was brought in from the northern colonies and was considered a luxury to be saved for celebrations. Southern buffet tables often included delicacies like these Cheese Pennies. They are still popular at Southern celebrations today.

◆ Cheese Pennies ◆

1 cup shredded sharp Cheddar cheese (4 ounces),
at room temperature

1 cup unsifted all-purpose flour

1 teaspoon salt

½ teaspoon dry mustard

¼ teaspoon ground red pepper (cayenne)

6 tablespoons (¾ stick) unsalted butter or margarine, softened

Paprika

PREP TIME: 25 MIN. / CHILLING TIME: 30 MIN. / COOKING TIME: 15 MIN.

1 In a medium-size bowl, mix together the cheese, flour, salt, mustard, and red pepper. Using a pastry blender or fork, cut in the butter just until the mixture is moist and resembles coarse crumbs. (To keep the pennies flaky and tender, avoid overmixing.) Press the dough into a ball, roll in plastic wrap, and refrigerate for 30 minutes.

2 Preheat the oven to 350°F and set out 2 ungreased baking sheets. On a lightly floured surface, roll the dough into an 18- x 12-inch rectangle, about ¼ inch thick. Using a 1½-inch round cutter, preferably a fluted one, cut the dough into 30 circles and place them 2 inches apart on the baking sheets. Using the back of a fork, lightly flatten each circle twice, making a criss-cross pattern, until the dough resembles a coin about ⅛ inch thick.

3 Bake for 15 minutes or just until crisp, but not browned. Using a spatula, transfer the pennies to wire racks, dust lightly with paprika, and let cool. Store in an air-tight container for up to 2 weeks or in the freezer for up to 3 months at 0°F. Makes about 30 appetizers.

*1 penny: Calories 51; Saturated Fat 2 g; Total Fat 4 g; Protein 1 g;
Carbohydrate 3 g; Fiber 0; Sodium 95 mg; Cholesterol 10 mg*

CHEESY PENNY WAFERS

◆◆◆

*These flaky wafers are lower in fat,
and cholesterol than their traditional cousins,
thanks to the use of reduced-fat cheese.*

1 **cup shredded reduced-fat Cheddar cheese (4 ounces)**	1 **cup unsifted all-purpose flour**
3 **tablespoons unsalted butter or margarine, softened**	½ **teaspoon dry mustard**
3 **tablespoons vegetable oil**	¼ **teaspoon ground red pepper (cayenne)**
	Paprika

PREP TIME: 20 MIN. / CHILLING TIME: 30 MIN.
COOKING TIME: 15 MIN.

1 In the bowl of a food processor, process the cheese and butter for about 30 seconds or just until combined. With the machine running, slowly pour in the oil through the feed tube. Then add the flour, mustard, and red pepper. Process for 30 seconds or just until the mixture resembles coarse crumbs. (To keep the wafers flaky and tender, avoid overprocessing.) Remove the dough, press into a ball, roll in plastic wrap, and refrigerate for 30 minutes.

2 Preheat the oven to 350°F and set out 2 ungreased baking sheets. Shape the dough into 40 balls, ½ inch in diameter, and place them 2 inches apart on the baking sheets. Using the back of a fork, lightly flatten each ball twice, making a criss-cross pattern, until the dough resembles a coin about ⅛ inch thick.

3 Bake for 15 minutes or just until crisp, but not browned. Transfer to wire racks, dust lightly with paprika, and let cool. Store in an airtight container for up to 2 weeks or in the freezer for up to 3 months at 0° F. Makes about 40.

*1 wafer: Calories 37; Saturated Fat 1 g;
Total Fat 2 g; Protein 2 g; Carbohydrate 3 g; Fiber 0;
Sodium 14 mg; Cholesterol 5 mg*

Perfect for snacking: Melt-in-your-mouth Cheddar cheese bites, shaped into penny wafers and fancy straws

◆

Vermont Cheddar Straws

Make dough for Cheesy Penny Wafers, using only ⅛ **teaspoon ground red pepper (cayenne).** Chill for 30 minutes, then roll out on a lightly floured surface to ⅛ inch thick. Using a serrated pastry cutter or a sharp knife, cut into thirty-six 3- x ½-inch sticks. Place on ungreased baking sheets, dust lightly with grated Parmesan cheese if you wish, and bake at 350°F for 15 minutes or just until crisp. Makes about 36. *1 straw: Calories 41; Saturated Fat 1 g; Total Fat 3 g; Protein 1 g; Carbohydrate 3 g; Fiber 0; Sodium 16 mg; Cholesterol 5 mg*

The all-American party starter: A creamy Cheese Ball rolled in fresh herbs and nuts

CHARLESTON BENNE SEED WAFERS

◆◆◆

*Benne seeds, another name for sesame seeds,
came to the Southern states from Africa during the
slave-trading days. Use them to make these thin
biscuits, often called wafers in the South.*

½ cup benne (sesame) seeds	½ teaspoon baking soda
Nonstick cooking spray	3 tablespoons unsalted butter or margarine
2 cups sifted all-purpose flour	3 tablespoons vegetable shortening
2 teaspoons baking powder	¾ cup buttermilk
¾ teaspoon salt	6 ounces thinly sliced sugar-cured baked ham (optional)

PREP TIME: 30 MIN. / COOKING TIME: 24 MIN.

1 Preheat the oven to 350°F. In a shallow baking pan, spread out the benne seeds in a single layer. Bake for 12 minutes, tossing the seeds frequently until light golden; allow to cool. Increase the oven temperature to 425°F. Spray 3 baking sheets with the cooking spray.

2 Meanwhile, in a medium-size bowl, stir the flour with the baking powder, salt, and baking soda. Using a pastry blender or 2 knives, cut in the butter and shortening until the mixture resembles coarse crumbs, then stir in the toasted benne seeds. Make a well in the center of the mixture and pour in the buttermilk, then stir quickly with a fork, just until a dough forms.

3 Turn the dough onto a lightly floured surface and knead 8 times. Using a lightly-floured rolling pin, roll out the dough until ⅜ inch thick. Using a 1-inch round cutter (preferably a fluted one), cut into biscuits, re-rolling the scraps as you go. Place the biscuits 1 inch apart on the baking sheets and bake for 12 minutes or until golden, but not browned. Serve hot, stuffed with tiny bites of ham if you wish. Makes about 9 dozen.

*1 wafer: Calories 19; Saturated Fat 0 g;
Total Fat 1 g; Protein 0 g; Carbohydrate 2 g; Fiber 0;
Sodium 27 mg; Cholesterol 1 mg*

CHEESE BALL
◆◆◆

Cheese has been included at many American celebrations over the years. In 1802, President Jefferson was presented with a 1,235-pound Cheshire cheese at the White House. Surprisingly, it had come from Cheshire, Massachusetts, not England.

3 tablespoons finely chopped pecans	¼ teaspoon hot red pepper sauce
1 package (8 ounces) Neufchâtel cream cheese, at room temperature	¼ teaspoon minced garlic
	1 cup shredded sharp Cheddar cheese (4 ounces)
3 green onions, finely chopped, with tops (⅓ cup)	¼ cup minced parsley
1 teaspoon Dijon mustard	

PREP TIME: 15 MIN. / COOKING TIME: 8 MIN.
CHILLING TIME: 15 MIN.

1 Preheat the oven to 350°F and spread out the pecans in a small pan. Bake, tossing once, for 8 minutes or until toasted. Meanwhile, in a small bowl, place the cream cheese, onions, mustard, red pepper sauce, and garlic. With an electric mixer at moderate speed, beat for 3 minutes or until well blended. Stir in the Cheddar cheese. Wrap the mixture in plastic wrap, shape into a 4-inch ball, and chill for 15 minutes.

2 On wax paper, toss the toasted pecans with the parsley. Unwrap the cheese ball and carefully roll it in the parsley mixture, coating it completely. Re-wrap in plastic wrap and refrigerate until time to serve. Place the ball on a serving platter and surround with an assortment of crackers. Makes about 24 servings.

1 tablespoon: Calories 50; Saturated Fat 2 g; Total Fat 4 g; Protein 2 g; Carbohydrate 1 g; Fiber 0; Sodium 72 mg; Cholesterol 12 mg

POTTED SHRIMP
◆◆◆

To preserve shrimp, our ancestors often "potted" them by cooking and sealing them with plenty of fat, usually butter. Today, thanks to refrigeration, we can "pot" shrimp by using only a little butter.

1 pound peeled and deveined medium-size shrimp with tails removed	1 teaspoon Worcestershire sauce
¼ cup finely chopped white onion	¼ teaspoon hot red pepper sauce or to taste
2 tablespoons unsalted butter or margarine, melted	¼ teaspoon ground mace
2 tablespoons fresh lemon juice	**Optional garnishes:**
2 tablespoons reduced-calorie mayonnaise	Curly strips of lemon zest (colored part of the rind)
	Sprigs of parsley

PREP TIME: 25 MIN. / COOKING TIME: 8 MIN.
CHILLING TIME: 1 HR.

1 Half-fill a large saucepan with water and bring to a boil over high heat. Add the shrimp, lower the heat, and cook, uncovered, for 3 minutes or until pink. Drain; rinse with cold water. Set aside 3 of the largest shrimp for garnish.

2 In a food processor or blender, process the remaining shrimp for 30 seconds or until coarsely chopped, then add the remaining ingredients. Process for 1 minute or just until the mixture is chopped and blended but not puréed.

3 Spoon the shrimp mixture into a small serving "pot" or dish and top with the 3 reserved shrimp. Cover with plastic wrap and refrigerate for 1 hour or until thoroughly chilled. Garnish with the strips of lemon zest and sprigs of parsley if you wish. Serve cold with an assortment of crackers. Makes 1½ cups.

1 tablespoon: Calories 28; Saturated Fat 1 g; Total Fat 2 g; Protein 3 g; Carbohydrate 0 g; Fiber 0; Sodium 36 mg; Cholesterol 31 mg

CHILI CON QUESO
◆◆◆

Believe it or not, chili peppers originated in America. Columbus found them cultivated by Indians and held in great esteem. On his return to Spain, he introduced the chili pepper to his countrymen.

2 large poblano chilies (8 ounces)	½ cup low-fat (1% milkfat) milk
4 8-inch flour tortillas	½ cup shredded sharp Cheddar cheese (2 ounces)
1 tablespoon vegetable oil	½ cup shredded Monterey Jack cheese (2 ounces)
1 large yellow onion, chopped (1½ cups)	1 small tomato, seeded and chopped (½ cup)
1 clove garlic, minced	
1 tablespoon all-purpose flour	

PREP TIME: 30 MIN. / COOKING TIME: 32 MIN.

1 Preheat the broiler. Place the chilies on an ungreased baking sheet and broil 5 inches from the heat, turning frequently, for about 10 minutes or until evenly charred. Place in a paper bag or covered dish and let stand for 15 minutes. Wearing rubber gloves and using a sharp knife, remove the stems, peel off the skins, and cut the chilies into 1- x ¼-inch strips, reserving the seeds.

2 While the peppers are standing, preheat the oven to 450°F. Cut the tortillas into 8 wedges each, making 32. Bake on ungreased baking sheets for 5 minutes, turn the wedges over and bake 5 minutes longer or until crisp. Using a spatula, transfer the wedges to a rack to cool.

3 In a 10-inch nonstick skillet, heat the oil over moderately high heat. Stir in the onion and garlic and sauté for 5 minutes or until tender. Add the flour and the chilies with their reserved seeds and cook 1 minute longer, stirring constantly. Pour in the milk and bring to a boil, stirring briskly. Lower the heat and simmer, uncovered,

for 2 minutes, stirring frequently, until slightly thickened. Remove from the heat, add the cheeses, and stir until melted. Pour into a serving dish, garnish with the tomato and serve with the tortilla chips. Makes 2 cups of dip and 32 chips.

1 teaspoon dip and 1 chip: Calories 35; Saturated Fat 1 g; Total Fat 2 g; Protein 2 g; Carbohydrate 4 g; Fiber 0 g; Sodium 30 mg; Cholesterol 4 mg

PIMIENTO CHEESE SPREAD
◆◆◆

From the Houston Junior League Cookbook, comes this velvety cheese spread, flavored with both sweet and hot peppers.

2 cups shredded sharp Cheddar cheese (8 ounces)	¼ teaspoon ground red pepper (cayenne), or to taste
½ cup reduced-calorie mayonnaise	⅛ teaspoon salt
¼ cup grated white onion	1 jar (4 ounces) pimientos, drained well and chopped

PREP TIME: 10 MIN.

1 In a medium-size bowl, with an electric mixer at low speed, blend the cheese, mayonnaise, onion, red pepper, and salt.

2 Increase the speed to high and beat for 2 minutes or until light and creamy, then fold in the pimientos. Spoon into a small serving bowl, cover with plastic wrap, and chill until serving time, up to 6 hours if you wish. Serve with an assortment of crackers. Makes 2 cups.

1 tablespoon: Calories 40; Saturated Fat 2 g; Total Fat 3 g; Protein 2 g; Carbohydrate 1 g; Fiber 0 g; Sodium 56 mg; Cholesterol 9 mg

TEXAS CAVIAR

◆◆◆

*Texans consider black-eyed peas a
great delicacy—especially pickled and chilled.*

⅓ cup red wine vinegar

¼ cup vegetable oil

¼ cup finely chopped
   yellow onion

½ small fresh or
   pickled jalapeño
   pepper with seeds,
   finely chopped
   (½ teaspoon)

1 clove garlic, minced

½ teaspoon salt

¼ teaspoon black
   pepper

3 cups cooked or
   canned black-eyed
   peas, rinsed and well
   drained

PREP TIME: 10 MIN. / MARINATING TIME: 2 HR.

1 In a medium-size bowl, whisk the vinegar
with the oil. Stir in the onion, jalapeño pepper,
garlic, salt, and black pepper until blended.

2 Gently stir in the black-eyed peas and refrigerate, covered, for at least 2 hours. Many
Texans recommend marinating the Caviar for
2 days to a week. Serve well chilled as an
appetizer spread or a relish. Makes 3½ cups.

*1 tablespoon: Calories 18; Saturated Fat 0 g;
Total Fat 1 g; Protein 0 g; Carbohydrate 2 g; Fiber 0 g;
Sodium 20 mg; Cholesterol 0 mg*

Chili con Queso: A traditional Tex-Mex dip, served with homemade chips

PICO DE GALLO

◆◆◆

*The name of this salsa party dip
comes from its bright red color, similar to that
of a rooster's beak. Translated,
Pico de Gallo means "peck of the cock."*

8	8-inch flour tortillas
4	large ripe tomatoes (2 pounds), peeled, cored, and diced (4 cups)
1	medium-size red onion, diced (1 cup)
1	extra-large fresh or pickled jalapeño pepper with seeds, finely chopped (4 teaspoons)

1	clove garlic, minced
1	cup finely chopped cilantro (coriander) or 1 cup minced parsley mixed with 2 tablespoons dried cilantro
2	tablespoons fresh lime juice
1	tablespoon olive oil
½	teaspoon salt

PREP TIME: 20 MIN. / COOKING TIME: 10 MIN.
MARINATING TIME: 30 MIN.

1 Preheat the oven to 450°F. Cut the tortillas into 8 wedges each, making 64. Bake on ungreased baking sheets for 5 minutes. Turn the wedges over and bake 5 minutes longer or until crisp and golden. Using a spatula, transfer the chips to a rack to cool.

2 Meanwhile, in a medium-size serving bowl, gently stir together the remaining ingredients. Cover and refrigerate for at least 30 minutes to allow the flavors to blend. Serve with the tortilla chips. This dip will keep for up to 3 days in the refrigerator, the chips for up to 3 days at room temperature in an airtight container. Makes 4 cups of salsa and 64 chips.

---

*1 tablespoon salsa and 1 chip: Calories 18; Saturated Fat 0 g;
Total Fat 1 g; Protein 1 g; Carbohydrate 3 g; Fiber 0 g;
Sodium 37 mg; Cholesterol 0 mg*

GOLDEN GATE AVOCADO DELIGHT

◆◆◆

*This layered dip from the Junior League of San
Francisco blends the Spanish and Mexican
influences commonly found in the region.*

2	large avocados, peeled, pitted, and cut into chunks (3 cups)
2	teaspoons fresh lemon juice
1	cup reduced-fat sour cream
2	tablespoons reduced-calorie mayonnaise
1	package (1¼ ounces) taco seasoning mix (1¼ teaspoons)

1	cup shredded sharp Cheddar cheese (4 ounces)
1	cup shredded Monterey Jack cheese (4 ounces)
1	pound tomatoes, diced (2¼ cups)
1	cup sliced pitted black olives, drained
4	green onions, with tops, finely chopped (½ cup)
½	cup chunky picante sauce

PREP TIME: 30 MIN. / CHILLING TIME: 30 MIN.

1 Set out a 12-inch round flan dish or large, deep platter. In a blender or food processor, whirl the avocados with the lemon juice for 30 seconds or just until smooth, then spread evenly in the bottom of the dish.

2 In a small bowl, stir together the sour cream, mayonnaise, and taco seasoning mix until blended, then spread evenly over the avocado mixture. Layer the remaining ingredients, one at a time, over the sour cream mixture, as follows: Cheddar cheese, Jack cheese, tomatoes, olives, and green onions. Top with the picante sauce. Cover with plastic wrap and refrigerate for at least 30 minutes or up to 4 hours. Serve with tortilla chips. Makes 24 servings.

---

*1 tablespoon: Calories 79; Saturated Fat 3 g;
Total Fat 6 g; Protein 3 g; Carbohydrate 4 g; Fiber 0 g;
Sodium 131 mg; Cholesterol 12 mg*

Curry Dip: Perfect with vegetables fresh from the garden

NANCY'S CURRY DIP
◆◆◆

This dip comes from Nancy Eppel of Martha's Vineyard, who describes it as her "exotic, mysterious replacement" for the familiar onion dip.

1 teaspoon curry powder	2 drops hot red pepper sauce
½ cup reduced-fat sour cream	1 teaspoon grated white onion
½ cup reduced-calorie mayonnaise	Pinch salt
	Basil leaves, garnish

PREP TIME: 10 MIN. / CHILLING TIME: 1 HR.

1 In an 8-inch skillet, heat the curry powder over moderate heat, stirring, for about 30 seconds or just until fragrant; stir in the next five ingredients. Spoon into a small serving bowl, cover,

and chill for at least 1 hour (will keep for up to 2 days). Garnish with the basil and serve with a basket of assorted fresh vegetables. Makes 1 cup.

1 tablespoon: Calories 34; Saturated Fat 1 g; Total Fat 3 g; Protein 0 g; Carbohydrate 2 g; Fiber 0 g; Sodium 86 mg; Cholesterol 2 mg

LOUISIANA HOT CRAB DIP
◆◆◆

Ever since our forefathers first discovered crabs, "goin' crabbing" has been a favorite pastime, especially in Louisiana.

Nonstick cooking spray	2 tablespoons prepared white horseradish, drained
2 packages (8 ounces each) Neufchâtel cream cheese, at room temperature	2 teaspoons Worcestershire sauce
12 ounces fresh crabmeat or 2 cans (6 ounces each), drained and picked through for shells	¼ teaspoon hot red pepper sauce
	¼ cup dry white wine (optional)
1 small white onion, finely chopped (½ cup)	1 tablespoon plain dry bread crumbs
	⅛ teaspoon paprika

PREP TIME: 15 MIN. / COOKING TIME: 20 MIN.

1 Preheat the oven to 350°F and coat the inside of a 1-quart round baking dish with the cooking spray. In a medium-size bowl, beat the cream cheese with a wooden spoon until smooth. Fold in the crabmeat, onion, horseradish, Worcestershire sauce, red pepper sauce, and wine if you wish, then spoon into the baking dish.

2 In a small bowl, toss the bread crumbs and paprika, then sprinkle on top of the crabmeat mixture. Bake, uncovered, for 20 minutes or until bubbly and hot. Serve immediately with an assortment of crackers. Makes 3 cups.

1 tablespoon: Calories 30; Saturated Fat 1 g; Total Fat 2 g; Protein 2 g; Carbohydrate 1 g; Fiber 0 g; Sodium 99 mg; Cholesterol 10 mg

Gorp for your backpack:
A sustaining mix of nuts, dried fruits, and seeds

CAJUN POPCORN
❖❖❖

*Authentic Cajun Popcorn isn't corn at all,
but deep-fried crawfish tails, seasoned with peppery
Cajun spices. We've created our own healthier
version using popped corn instead.*

½ cup popping corn	½ teaspoon each dried basil and thyme leaves
2 tablespoons vegetable oil	
1 teaspoon salt	½ teaspoon paprika
¾ teaspoon each ground cumin and garlic powder	¼ teaspoon each black pepper and ground red pepper (cayenne)

PREP TIME: 15 MIN. / COOKING TIME: 10 MIN.

1 Using a hot-air popping machine, pop the corn into a large serving bowl and cover with foil to keep it hot. In a small saucepan, heat the oil over moderate heat for 1 minute. Add the

remaining ingredients. Cook, stirring constantly, for 1 minute, then drizzle over the hot popcorn. Makes 4 quarts or sixteen 1-cup servings.

*1 cup: Calories 41; Saturated Fat 0 g;
Total Fat 2 g; Protein 1 g; Carbohydrate 5 g; Fiber 0 g;
Sodium 134 mg; Cholesterol 0 mg*

GORP
❖❖❖

*The name of this popular hiker's
snack comes from the first letters of its original
ingredients: Good Old Raisins and Peanuts.
Now it often contains other dried fruits, seeds,
nuts, and sometimes even chocolate.*

2 cups whole natural almonds with skins, coarsely chopped	1 cup candy-coated chocolate candies (optional)
2 tablespoons sesame seeds	½ cup banana chips
	½ cup roasted cashews
Nonstick cooking spray	½ cup golden or dark raisins
¼ cup hulled unsalted pumpkin seeds	¼ cup hulled unsalted sunflower seeds
3 cups assorted dried fruits, cut into bite-size pieces	

PREP TIME: 15 MIN. / COOKING TIME: 14 MIN.

1 Preheat the oven to 350°F. In a shallow baking pan, scatter the almonds and sesame seeds. Bake for 8 minutes or until golden, stirring several times. Transfer to a large serving bowl.

2 Meanwhile, coat the inside of an 8-inch skillet with the cooking spray. Add the pumpkin seeds and stir over moderate heat for 6 minutes or until all of the seeds are toasted and popped. Add to the almond mixture. When the mixture has cooled, add the remaining ingredients and toss until mixed. Makes about 8 cups.

*¼ cup: Calories 125; Saturated Fat 1 g;
Total Fat 7 g; Protein 3 g; Carbohydrate 15 g; Fiber 1 g;
Sodium 4 mg; Cholesterol 0 mg*

TEXAS TRASH

"Y'all come!" has long been a favorite party invitation in the South. Once you arrive, you are likely to find a giant-size bowl of Texas Trash.

4 cups mixed bite-size cereal squares (corn, rice, and wheat)	3 tablespoons vegetable oil
2 cups old-fashioned rolled oats, uncooked	3 tablespoons Worcestershire sauce
2 cups pretzel sticks	2 tablespoons melted bacon drippings or butter
1 cup Cheddar-flavored goldfish crackers	¾ teaspoon salt
1 cup dry-roasted mixed nuts	½ teaspoon black pepper
	¼ teaspoon hot red pepper sauce

PREP TIME: 10 MIN. / COOKING TIME: 20 MIN.

1 Preheat the oven to 350°F. In a large shallow roasting pan, toss the cereals with the oats, pretzel sticks, crackers, and nuts. In a small bowl, whisk the remaining ingredients and drizzle over the cereal mixture. Toss quickly to mix well. Bake for 20 minutes or until crisp and golden, stirring several times. Makes 10 cups.

¼ cup: Calories 69; Saturated Fat 1 g; Total Fat 4 g; Protein 1 g; Carbohydrate 8 g; Fiber 0 g; Sodium 149 mg; Cholesterol 1 mg

"BIG D" PECANS

Native pecans seem to be bigger and better in Texas-- especially when spiced the way the folks serve them in that "Big D" city of Dallas.

1 tablespoon unsalted butter	1 teaspoon salt
1 tablespoon vegetable oil	½ teaspoon ground cinnamon
2 cups pecan halves	½ teaspoon hot red pepper sauce
1 tablespoon Worcestershire sauce	¼ teaspoon garlic powder
2 teaspoons sugar	

PREP TIME: 5 MIN. / COOKING TIME: 30 MIN.

1 Preheat the oven to 300°F. In a 13" x 9" x 2" baking pan, combine the butter and oil and heat in the oven until the butter melts. Stir in the pecans, tossing until coated with the butter mixture. Bake, uncovered, for 15 minutes.

2 In a small bowl, stir together the remaining ingredients. Drizzle over the pecans and toss until coated. Return the pecans to the oven and bake 15 minutes longer or until crisp, stirring several times. Makes 2 cups.

1 pecan half: Calories 18; Saturated Fat 0 g; Total Fat 2 g; Protein 0 g; Carbohydrate 1 g; Fiber 0 g; Sodium 25 mg; Cholesterol 0 mg

Texas cooking is as rich and distinctive as the state itself.

—from Tastes & Tales From Texas ...With Love by Peg Hein

PICKLED SHRIMP

◆◆◆

"Shrimp boats are a-coming" used to be a familiar cry throughout Southern plantation towns. Not surprisingly, this recipe comes from a Colonel Harris' family in the town of Smithfield, Virginia.

1	small whole white onion, peeled	1	medium-size red onion, thinly sliced (1 cup)
¼	cup chopped celery leaves	⅓	cup vegetable oil
2	tablespoons pickling spices	⅓	cup white wine vinegar
5	bay leaves	1½	tablespoons drained capers
1	clove garlic, minced	1	teaspoon celery seeds
1	pound peeled and deveined large shrimp with tails left on	¼	teaspoon hot red pepper sauce

PREP TIME: 20 MIN. / COOKING TIME: 8 MIN.
MARINATING TIME: 2 HR.

1 Half-fill a large saucepan with cold water and add the white onion, celery leaves, pickling spices, 1 of the bay leaves, and the garlic. Bring to a boil over high heat and stir in the shrimp. Lower the heat and cook, uncovered, for 3 minutes or until the shrimp turn pink.

2 Using a slotted spoon, spread the shrimp in a single layer in a large shallow dish, then top with the remaining 4 bay leaves and the red onion. Discard the cooking liquid and vegetables.

3 In a small bowl, whisk the oil with the vinegar, capers, celery seeds and red pepper sauce. Drizzle over the shrimp, then cover and refrigerate for at least 2 hours, preferably overnight, turning the shrimp occasionally. Remove the bay leaves and serve with toothpicks. Makes about 2 dozen pickled shrimp.

1 shrimp: Calories 33; Saturated Fat 0 g; Total Fat 2 g; Protein 4 g; Carbohydrate 1 g; Fiber 0 g; Sodium 37 mg; Cholesterol 29 mg

SHRIMP COCKTAIL

◆◆◆

Ask any true Cajun the way to boil shrimp. The answer is likely to be: "Start off by adding several spoonfuls of crab boil spices to the water." You can find them in the spice section of the supermarket.

⅔	cup low-sodium ketchup	3	cups water
¼	cup chili sauce	4	teaspoons crab boil or pickling spices
2	teaspoons prepared white horseradish, drained	1	pound peeled and deveined large shrimp with tails left on
¼	teaspoon hot red pepper sauce		Crushed ice

PREP TIME: 20 MIN. / COOKING TIME: 12 MIN.
CHILLING TIME: 30 MIN.

1 In a small serving bowl, mix the ketchup, chili sauce, horseradish, and red pepper sauce until well blended. Cover and refrigerate.

2 In a large saucepan, bring the water and crab boil to a boil over high heat and continue boiling, uncovered, for 5 minutes. Stir in the shrimp, lower the heat, and cook, uncovered, for 3 minutes or just until the shrimp turn pink. Drain in a colander, cool under cold running water, and transfer to a shallow dish. Cover with plastic wrap and refrigerate for at least 30 minutes or until cold. (These can be prepared up to 8 hours in advance.)

3 To serve, place the bowl of cocktail sauce in the center of a large serving platter and float a few shrimp on the sauce for garnish. Line the platter with the crushed ice, then attractively arrange the shrimp with tails pointing toward the edge of the platter. Serve immediately. Makes about 24 shrimp and 1 cup of sauce.

1 shrimp and 2 teaspoons sauce: Calories 21; Saturated Fat 0 g; Total Fat 0 g; Protein 3 g; Carbohydrate 2 g; Fiber 0 g; Sodium 111 mg; Cholesterol 29 mg

CHURCH SUPPER DEVILED EGGS

◆◆◆

Basket socials once were popular ways to raise money for the church. The ladies brought beautifully decorated supper baskets, and the men bid for their supper. They often found delicious deviled eggs tucked inside.

12 large eggs
2 green onions, with tops, finely chopped (¼ cup)
¼ cup finely chopped sweet red pepper
¼ cup finely chopped dill pickle
¼ cup reduced-calorie mayonnaise

1 teaspoon curry powder
¼ teaspoon hot red pepper sauce, or to taste

Optional garnishes:
Paprika
Finely chopped parsley

PREP TIME: 30 MIN. / COOKING TIME: 20 MIN.

1 Place the eggs in a large saucepan, cover with cold water, and bring to a full boil over high heat. Remove from the heat, cover, and let stand for 15 minutes or until hard-cooked. Cool eggs immediately under cold running water and peel. Slice the eggs in half lengthwise, then remove the yolks. Refrigerate 6 half yolks for another use.

2 Arrange 18 of the egg white halves on a serving platter. Place the remaining 6 egg white halves and the 18 egg yolk halves in a large bowl. Using a fork or a pastry blender, mash the eggs, then blend in the remaining ingredients.

3 Spoon or pipe the mixture into the 18 egg white halves. Sprinkle with the paprika and parsley if you wish. Cover and refrigerate for up to 6 hours. Makes 18 appetizers.

½ egg: Calories 51; Saturated Fat 1 g; Total Fat 4 g; Protein 4 g; Carbohydrate 1 g; Fiber 1 g; Sodium 66 mg; Cholesterol 108 mg

Church Supper Deviled Eggs: Guaranteed to be a star at every social gathering

PLAZA TEA SANDWICHES

At your next party, or afternoon get-together with friends, serve these traditional tea sandwiches from New York's Plaza Hotel.

12 slices thinly sliced whole-wheat bread	1 bunch watercress, leaves only (2 cups)
12 slices thinly sliced white bread	3 hard-cooked eggs (page 363), peeled and chopped
6 tablespoons unsalted butter or margarine, at room temperature	4 tablespoons mayonnaise
6 slices ripe tomato	2 medium-size cucumbers
¼ teaspoon salt, or to taste	Optional garnishes:
¼ teaspoon black pepper, or to taste	Radish slices
	Sprigs of fresh dill

PREP TIME: 30 MIN.

1 On a clean, dry bread board, lay out all of the bread slices. Using a spatula, spread one side of each slice with the butter.

2 To prepare the tomato sandwiches: Arrange 2 slices of tomato on the buttered side of each of 3 slices of whole-wheat bread. Sprinkle with a pinch each of the salt and pepper, or to taste. Cover with a second slice of whole-wheat bread, buttered side down. Cover with a damp towel.

3 To prepare the watercress sandwiches: In a small bowl, toss together the watercress leaves, ⅓ of the chopped eggs, 1 tablespoon of the mayonnaise, plus a pinch each of the salt and pepper. Let stand for 5 minutes or just until the leaves start to wilt. Spread ⅓ of this mixture on the buttered side of each of 3 slices of white bread. Top with a second slice of white bread, buttered side down. Cover with a damp towel.

4 To prepare the egg sandwiches: In a small bowl, mix the remaining ⅔ of the eggs with the remaining 3 tablespoons of mayonnaise and a pinch each of the salt and pepper until well blended. Spread ⅓ of this mixture on the buttered side

Taking Tea—with a plate of dainty sandwiches and a steaming cup of the freshly brewed beverage

of each of 3 slices of whole-wheat bread. Top with a second slice of whole-wheat bread, buttered side down. Cover with a damp towel.

5 To prepare the cucumber sandwiches: Cut the cucumbers lengthwise into 9 thin slices, about ⅛ inch thick. Arrange 3 slices of cucumber on the buttered side of each of 3 slices of white bread. Sprinkle lightly with the remaining salt and pepper. Top with a second slice of white bread, buttered side down.

6 To serve, make 3 stacks consisting of one of each sandwich: tomato, watercress, egg, and cucumber. Using a serrated knife, carefully trim off the crusts evenly. Cut each stack in half diagonally, making 2 servings each of 4 different triangular sandwiches. Place a serving on each plate and garnish with radish slices and a sprig of dill if you wish. Makes 6 servings.

1 serving: Calories 359; Saturated Fat 6 g; Total Fat 18 g; Protein 11 g; Carbohydrate 40 g; Fiber 2 g; Sodium 608 mg; Cholesterol 112 mg

CITRUS ICED TEA

◆◆◆

Serving icy pitchers of tea dates as far back as the 1860's in America. Neighbors, especially in the South, have often shared tall glasses of iced tea, whatever the season.

5   cups cold water
¼   cup loose black or orange pekoe tea in tea ball, or 10 tea bags
6   whole cloves
2   strips each of lemon and orange zest (colored part of the rind), 3 inches long
½   cup sugar
½   cup fresh orange juice
¼   cup fresh lemon juice
¼   cup packed fresh mint leaves
    Ice cubes
1   large unpeeled lemon, thinly sliced
1   large unpeeled orange, thinly sliced
1   long curly strip of orange zest, about 8 inches long
    Sprigs of fresh mint

PREP TIME: 20 MIN. / COOKING TIME: 5 MIN.
STANDING TIME: 1 HR.

1 Bring 4 cups of the water to a boil. Combine the tea, cloves, and the 3-inch strips of lemon and orange zest in a heatproof bowl. Cover with the boiling water and steep for 5 minutes. Remove the tea ball, then stir in the sugar, orange and lemon juices, and mint leaves. Cover, let stand for 30 minutes, strain into a 2-quart pitcher, and stir in the remaining 1 cup of water. Chill.

2 To serve, fill the pitcher with ice cubes and stir in the lemon and orange slices. Garnish with the curly strip of orange zest and sprigs of mint. Pour in tall glasses filled with ice. Makes about 1¼ quarts or six 6-ounce servings.

1 serving: Calories 74; Saturated Fat 0 g; Total Fat 0 g; Protein 0 g; Carbohydrate 20 g; Fiber 0 g; Sodium 6 mg; Cholesterol 0 mg

◆ Tea Time ◆

Take a break to enjoy tea time at the Plaza Hotel in New York City. Outside lies bustling Fifth Avenue. But in the Plaza's Palm Court, soft music is playing and smiling waiters are welcoming guests to an authentic English tea. Tables with pink cloths and fresh flowers in elegant surroundings invite one to relax here with friends.

"We begin with a steaming pot of tea accompanied by freshly made scones, jams, and thickly clotted cream," explains Executive Chef Bruno Rene Tison. "An assortment of delicate tea sandwiches comes next, all attractively arranged on a doily-lined plate, garnished with a tiny radish rose and a sprig of fresh dill. And for the perfect ending, there's a plate filled with petite pastries.

"Whatever one chooses to serve at tea time should be delicate and light, just enough to complement the subtle flavors of the tea, without overpowering them. For this reason, we make our tea sandwiches with very thinly sliced white and whole-wheat breads, spread them with the thinnest coating of sweet butter, then add simple fillings, seasoned only lightly with salt and pepper."

The Perfect Cup of Tea

Here is how Chef Tison recommends that you brew tea to obtain the best flavor. Fill your teapot, preferably of earthenware or glazed china, with hot water and let it stand. (This warming keeps the tea water at boiling point when it hits the tea leaves, extracting optimum flavor.) Bring cold water to a boil in a teakettle. Meanwhile, fill a tea ball with your favorite tea, using one heaping teaspoon per cup and one for the pot. Or use tea bags, one per cup. The minute the water comes to a full boil, place the tea in the empty warmed pot, pour in the water, and top with the lid. (Avoid letting the water boil a long time; it loses oxygen and may cause the tea to become bitter and cloudy.)

Cover the teapot with a tea cozy or towel, then let the tea steep for 3 to 5 minutes or until it reaches the strength you wish. Remove the ball or bags and pour the tea into your finest cups. Offer a choice of serve-alongs: white and brown sugars, warm milk and light cream, and slices of fresh orange and lemon.

HOMEMADE LEMONADE

Step back to yesteryear, when summer afternoons were just made for sipping homemade lemonade on the back porch or beneath the old oak tree. An icy glassful can take you back.

1½ cups sugar

3 cups cold water

1½ cups fresh lemon juice (8 large lemons)

1 tablespoon grated lemon zest (colored part of the rind)

½ cup fresh mint leaves (optional)

Ice cubes

Garnishes:

3 large lemons, thinly sliced

Sprigs of fresh mint (optional)

PREP TIME: 15 MIN. / COOKING TIME: 8 MIN.
STANDING AND CHILLING TIME: 2½ HR.

1 In a medium-size saucepan, bring the sugar and 2 cups of the water to a boil over high heat, stirring until the sugar dissolves. Boil, uncovered, for 5 minutes. Stir in the lemon juice, lemon zest, and mint leaves if you wish. Remove from the heat, cover, and let stand for 30 minutes.

2 Pour the lemonade through a strainer into a 2-quart pitcher, then stir in the remaining 1 cup of water. Cover with plastic wrap and chill for 2 hours or overnight. To serve, fill the pitcher almost to the top with the ice cubes, stir in the lemon slices, and garnish with the mint sprigs if you like. Pour into tall glasses filled with ice. Makes about 1¼ quarts or six 6-ounce servings.

1 serving: Calories 206; Saturated Fat 0 g; Total Fat 0 g; Protein 1 g; Carbohydrate 59 g; Fiber 0 g; Sodium 6 mg; Cholesterol 0 mg

Fresh-squeezed Lemonade for sale—only 5 cents a glass!

◆

Limeade

Prepare as for Homemade Lemonade, substituting **1 cup fresh lime juice (from 5 large limes) plus ½ cup fresh lemon juice (from 3 large lemons)** for the lemon juice and **1 tablespoon grated lime zest** for the lemon zest. Garnish with **3 thinly sliced large limes** instead of lemon slices, plus mint sprigs if you like. Makes about 1¼ quarts or six 6-ounce servings. *1 serving: Calories 206; Saturated Fat 0 g; Total Fat 0 g; Protein 1 g; Carbohydrate 57 g; Fiber 0 g; Sodium 5 mg; Cholesterol 0 mg*

SANGRIA
◆◆◆

Originating in Spain, this wine and fruit drink grew in popularity after being served in the Spanish Pavillion at the 1964 New York World's Fair.

2 bottles (750 ml. each) dry red wine (with or without alcohol), chilled	2 medium-size unpeeled oranges, thinly sliced
2 cups fresh orange juice, chilled	1 large unpeeled lemon, thinly sliced
¼ cup superfine sugar	1 cup club soda, chilled
4 large peaches (2 pounds), peeled and thinly sliced	2 tablespoons Spanish brandy (optional)

PREP TIME: 20 MIN. / CHILLING TIME: 1 HR.

1 In a large pitcher, stir together the wine, juice, sugar, peaches, oranges, and lemon. Cover and refrigerate for at least 1 hour or overnight. To serve, stir in the club soda plus the brandy if you wish. Pour into tall glasses filled with ice. Makes about 2 quarts or ten 6-ounce servings.

1 serving: Calories 210; Saturated Fat 0 g; Total Fat 0 g; Protein 2 g; Carbohydrate 29 g; Fiber 1 g; Sodium 13 mg; Cholesterol 0 mg

PLANTER'S PUNCH
◆◆◆

Originating in Jamaica, these beverages became favorites on Southern plantations. Each planter added his own extras to suit his taste.

¼ cup fresh lime juice	2 ounces (¼ cup) dark rum (optional)
3 tablespoons superfine sugar	Crushed ice (about 4 cups)
2 teaspoons grenadine syrup or frozen cranberry juice concentrate	Optional garnishes:
½ teaspoon Angostura bitters	Fresh lime and orange slices
1 quart (4 cups) fresh orange juice	Fresh pineapple wedges
	Maraschino cherries

PREP TIME: 15 MIN.

1 In a 2-quart pitcher, stir the lime juice, sugar, grenadine, and bitters until the sugar dissolves. Pour in the orange juice and rum if you wish, then fill with crushed ice. Garnish with the fruits threaded on bamboo stirrers if you wish. Makes about 1¼ quarts or six 6-ounce servings.

1 serving: Calories 106; Saturated Fat 0 g; Total Fat 0 g; Protein 1 g; Carbohydrate 26 g; Fiber 0 g; Sodium 3 mg; Cholesterol 0 mg

CHAMPAGNE RECEPTION PUNCH
◆◆◆

Since Colonial days, a punch of Champagne and fruit has been a favorite for "very proper receptions."

5 pints (10 cups) fresh strawberries	¾ cup superfine sugar
1½ cups pineapple juice, chilled	1 bottle (⅘ quart) Champagne or sparkling wine (with or without alcohol), chilled
¾ cup fresh lemon juice	

PREP TIME: 15 MIN. / FREEZING TIME: 6 HR. CHILLING TIME: 2 HR.

1 To make the strawberry ice cubes: At least 6 hours before party time, wash the berries. Place 1 small, pretty berry (with leafy hulls attached) in each compartment of 2 standard-size ice cube trays, then fill with water and freeze.

2 To prepare the punch: Remove the hulls from the remaining berries and place them in a food processor. Process for 2 minutes or until puréed, then transfer to a punch bowl. Stir in the pineapple juice, lemon juice, and sugar; cover and refrigerate. Just before serving, pour in the Champagne and float the strawberry ice cubes on top. Makes eighteen 4-ounce servings.

1 serving: Calories 92; Saturated Fat 0 g; Total Fat 0 g; Protein 1 g; Carbohydrate 17 g; Fiber 0 g; Sodium 1 mg; Cholesterol 0 mg

HOT CHOCOLATE
◆◆◆

What could be more welcome on a cold winter's day than a steaming cup of hot chocolate? This recipe calls for low-fat milk, yet still has that old fashioned goodness.

2 squares bittersweet or semi-sweet chocolate (2 ounces), chopped	1 quart low-fat (2% milkfat) milk
2 tablespoons sugar	2 cinnamon sticks, 3 inches long
½ cup cold water	Optional garnish: Miniature marshmallows

PREP TIME: 5 MIN. / COOKING TIME: 10 MIN.
STANDING TIME: 10 MIN.

1 In a large saucepan, stir the chocolate, sugar, and water over low heat until the chocolate melts. Stir in the milk and cinnamon sticks, increase the heat to moderate, and bring just to a simmer, stirring constantly. Do not let boil.

2 Remove from the heat, cover, and let stand for 5 minutes, then remove the cinnamon sticks. Pour into mugs and garnish with the marshmallows if you wish. Makes six 6-ounce servings.

1 serving: Calories 105; Saturated Fat 2 g; Total Fat 5 g; Protein 5 g; Carbohydrate 13 g; Fiber 0 g; Sodium 62 mg; Cholesterol 9 mg

◆

Hot Cocoa

Prepare the chocolate-sugar-water mixture as for Hot Chocolate, substituting ⅓ **cup unsweetened cocoa** for the bittersweet chocolate and increasing the **sugar to ¼ cup.** Whisking constantly, bring the mixture to a boil over moderate heat and boil for 1 minute, then proceed as directed. Makes six 6-ounce servings. *1 serving: Calories 90; Saturated Fat 2 g; Total Fat 3 g; Protein 5 g; Carbohydrate 14 g; Fiber 0 g; Sodium 64 mg; Cholesterol 9 mg*

MULLED CIDER
◆◆◆

In Elizabethan England, someone said: "They are more stengthen'd for hard work by Cyder than the very best beer." Not surprisingly, when English colonists came to America, mulled cider became a favored drink here.

2 quarts sweet apple cider	1 teaspoon whole cloves
½ cup firmly packed brown sugar	1 teaspoon whole allspice berries (about 16)
½ cup fresh lemon juice	1 cup apple brandy
3 cinnamon sticks, 3 inches long	Additional cinnamon sticks, for stirrers

PREP TIME: 10 MIN. / COOKING TIME: 15 MIN.

1 In a large saucepan, bring the cider, sugar, lemon juice, 3 cinnamon sticks, cloves, and allspice to a boil over high heat. Lower the heat and simmer, uncovered, for 10 minutes.

2 Remove from the heat and stir in the apple brandy. Strain into a heatproof pitcher. Serve immediately in mugs with cinnamon stick stirrers. Makes about 2 quarts or eight 8-ounce servings.

1 serving: Calories 218; Saturated Fat 0 g; Total Fat 0 g; Protein 0 g; Carbohydrate 17 g; Fiber 0 g; Sodium 4 mg; Cholesterol 0 mg

◆

Sweet Spiced Cider

Prepare as for Mulled Cider, using only ⅓ **cup fresh lemon juice and 1 extra cup of sweet apple cider** instead of the apple brandy. Makes about 2 quarts or eight 8-ounce servings. *1 serving: Calories 184; Saturated Fat 0 g; Total Fat 0 g; Protein 0 g; Carbohydrate 47 g; Fiber 0 g; Sodium 12 mg; Cholesterol 0 mg*

FLAMING CAFÉ BRÛLOT
◆ ◆ ◆

*The Cajuns, who arrived in New Orleans
in the mid-1700's, came from southern France
via the Acadian colony of Nova Scotia.
Many of their foods, such as this Café Brûlot,
are French. (Café is coffee, and
brûlot refers to the burning brandy.)*

4 whole allspice berries	Zest from ½ large lemon, slivered
4 whole cloves	8 sugar cubes or 8 teaspoons sugar
1 cinnamon stick, 3 inches long, broken	4 cups hot, strong coffee
Zest from 2 large oranges (colored part of the rind), slivered	½ cup brandy
	¼ cup Curaçao or other orange-flavored liqueur

PREP TIME: 15 MIN. / COOKING TIME: 5 MIN.

1 Make a spice bag by placing the allspice, cloves, and cinnamon pieces in the center of a small piece of cheesecloth. Bring up the corners, and tie securely with cotton string. Set aside 8 slivers of the orange zest for garnish.

2 In a brûlot bowl, chafing dish, or medium-size saucepan, combine the remaining orange zest with the lemon zest, sugar cubes, and spice bag. Stir in 1 cup of the coffee, plus the brandy and Curaçao. Simmer, uncovered, over moderately low heat for 5 minutes, stirring and mashing the zest and sugar cubes until the sugar dissolves and the mixture is hot. Using a slotted spoon, remove and discard the spice bag and zest.

3 Standing away from the coffee mixture, carefully ignite it with a wooden match. Stir in the remaining 3 cups of coffee, ladle into brûlot or demitasse cups, and garnish with the orange zest. Makes 8 demitasse (4-ounce) servings.

*1 serving: Calories 73; Saturated Fat 0 g;
Total Fat 0 g; Protein 0 g; Carbohydrate 7 g; Fiber 0 g;
Sodium 3 mg; Cholesterol 0 mg*

The big warm-up: A steaming cup of Hot Chocolate

◆

Orange Café Brûlot

For non-alcoholic brûlot, place 1 of the sugar cubes in a small dish and pour over **1 teaspoon of orange or lemon extract**. Prepare as for Flaming Café Brûlot, using the remaining 7 sugar cubes in the coffee mixture and omitting the brandy and Curaçao. Just before pouring in the 3 cups of coffee, place the soaked sugar cube in a long-handled spoon, hold over the bowl, and ignite. Pour in the coffee and serve. Makes 8 demitasse (4-ounce) servings. *1 serving: Calories 40; Saturated Fat 0 g; Total Fat 0 g; Protein 0 g; Carbohydrate 5 g; Fiber 0 g; Sodium 3 mg; Cholesterol 0 mg*

SYLLABUB:
THE NEW-FASHIONED WAY

◆◆◆

The egg white meringue that tops this light wine punch is cooked with hot sugar syrup to the safe stage of at least 160°F.

4	cups cold low-fat (1% milkfat) milk
1	cup cold whole milk
2	cups dry white wine (with or without alcohol), chilled
1½	cups sugar

¼	cup grated lemon zest
¼	cup cold water
4	large egg whites
	Ground nutmeg (preferably freshly grated)

PREP TIME: 15 MIN. / COOK TIME: 15 MIN.

1 In a large bowl, stir together the low-fat milk, whole milk, wine, 1 cup of the sugar, and the lemon zest. With an electric mixer set on high, beat for 3 minutes or until frothy, then transfer to a punch bowl, cover, and chill.

2 In a small heavy saucepan, combine the remaining ½ cup of sugar with the water. Bring to a boil over high heat, stirring until the sugar dissolves. Wash the sides of the saucepan with a brush dipped in cold water. Lower the heat and simmer, uncovered, without stirring, for about 10 minutes, until the syrup reaches the soft ball stage (238°F) or until ½ teaspoon of the mixture dropped into a saucer of cold water forms a soft ball. Remove from the heat.

3 In a large bowl, with an electric mixer set on high, beat the egg whites until soft peaks form. With the mixer running, add the hot sugar syrup in a slow steady stream, beating until the egg whites stand in stiff peaks. Top the wine mixture with dollops of egg white, sprinkle with nutmeg, and ladle into punch cups. Makes about 2 quarts or sixteen 4-ounce servings.

1 serving: Calories 128; Saturated Fat 1 g; Total Fat 1 g; Protein 3 g; Carbohydrate 22 g; Fiber 0 g; Sodium 54 mg; Cholesterol 5 mg

For a toast to the holidays: Syllabub, a creamy yet light version of the traditional wine punch

DOWN HOME TRADITION

Borrow a tradition from our forefathers: Toast in the holidays with syllabub. It looks, even tastes, something like eggnog, but is based on white wine or cider, instead of a strong liquor such as bourbon or rum. Once considered by some as "too weak a potion for men to drink," syllabub was generally regarded as a woman's beverage. One old recipe says: "Sweeten a quart of cyder with refined sugar and a grating of nutmeg, then milk your cow into your liquor until you have the amount you consider proper, then top it off with about a half a pint of the sweetest, thickest cream." Traditionally, syllabub was whipped with willow twigs or a flat whisk or rod until a froth of cream stood on top, and served with cookies, especially at Christmas time.

◆ Syllabub ◆

3 cups very cold whole milk
2 cups very cold heavy cream
2 cups dry white wine (with or without alcohol), chilled
1½ cups sugar
¼ cup grated lemon zest (colored part of the rind)
¼ cup cold water
4 large egg whites
Ground nutmeg (preferably freshly grated)

PREP TIME: 15 MIN. / COOKING TIME: 15 MIN.

1 In a large bowl, stir together the milk, cream, wine, 1 cup of the sugar, and the lemon zest. With an electric mixer set on high, beat for 3 minutes or until frothy, then transfer to a punch bowl, cover, and chill.

2 In a small heavy saucepan, combine the remaining ½ cup of sugar with the water. Bring to a boil over high heat, stirring until the sugar dissolves. Wash the sides of the saucepan with a brush dipped in cold water. Lower the heat and simmer, uncovered, without stirring, for about 10 minutes, until the syrup reaches the soft ball stage (238°F) or until ½ teaspoon of the mixture dropped into a saucer of cold water forms a soft ball. Remove from the heat.

3 In a large bowl, with an electric mixer set on high, beat the egg whites until soft peaks form. With the mixer running, add the hot sugar syrup in a slow steady stream, beating until the egg whites stand in stiff peaks. Top the wine mixture with dollops of egg white, sprinkle with nutmeg, and ladle into punch cups. Makes about 2 quarts or sixteen 4-ounce servings.

1 serving: Calories 224; Saturated Fat 8 g; Total Fat 13 g;
Protein 3 g; Carbohydrate 22 g; Fiber 0 g; Sodium 49 mg; Cholesterol 47 mg

Wassaile
the trees,
that they
may beare
You many
a plum
and many
a peare.

—*Olde English
Christmas Carole*

◆ An Old Fashioned Soda Shoppe ◆

Step through the door of Eddie's Sweet Shoppe in New York City's borough of Queens, and you step into small-town America around the beginning of the 20th century. Those were the days when children and grown-ups alike could be found in ice cream parlors on a lazy afternoon, licking ice cream cones or sipping frosty sodas through a straw.

Even today, when you're sitting at this soda fountain, you forget that it's not the early 1900's, when Eddie's first opened its doors. In the years since, Eddie's hasn't changed much. It still has its stained glass window, painted cast iron ceiling, white-and-blue tile floor, and antique chandeliers. And naturally, there is the original marble counter, complete with small wood and brass stools that do spin around and around! In the back, customers sip their fountain treats at tables. Rich mahogany woodwork with inlay trim abounds.

Eddie's present owners, Connie and Giuseppe (Joe) Citrano, bought the shoppe in 1968. Almost every day since, Joe has been making real old-fashioned ice cream (at least 20 different flavors) and whipping up as many as 50 quarts of cream on a hot summer's day, in his kitchen beneath the soda fountain. Many of the ice cream flavors—for example, vanilla, chocolate, strawberry, pistachio, and even tutti-fruitti—never change. But others, such as peach and blueberry, are seasonal, available only when the fruits are juicy-ripe and plentiful.

Behind the counter, Joe whirls a thick chocolate malted, stirs a black and white soda, or carefully arranges a tri-colored banana split. Everything that goes into his creations is home-made, including the hot fudge toppings and most of the syrups. When asked the secret to his success, Joe says simply: "It's the quality that counts. I really care about serving the very best." Every spoonful of ice cream and every sip of soda proves that fact ... down to the very last, scrumptious bite.

New York Chocolate Egg Cream
◆◆◆

Egg creams were first served at soda fountains around New York in the 1930's. Contrary to popular belief, they contain neither egg nor cream, just syrup, milk, and seltzer. When the drink is mixed correctly, a foam rises to the top that looks like whipped egg whites.

3 tablespoons chocolate syrup (in supermarket beverage-mix section)	½ cup very cold whole milk Chilled seltzer (about ⅔ cup)

PREP TIME: 5 MIN.

1 Into a tall, chilled soda glass, spoon the syrup, then stir in the milk. Holding the seltzer bottle about 12 inches above the top of the glass, slowly pour in the seltzer until the high foam reaches the rim. Using a long-handled spoon, stir the egg cream quickly one time, being careful not to overflow the foam. Serve immediately. Makes one 12-ounce serving.

1 serving: Calories 198; Saturated Fat 3 g; Total Fat 5 g; Protein 5 g; Carbohydrate 39 g; Fiber 0; Sodium 147 mg; Cholesterol 17 mg

◆

Double Divine Chocolate Egg Cream

In a blender, place ⅓ **cup very cold whole milk, 2 tablespoons chocolate syrup**, and **1 scoop of low-fat chocolate ice cream**. Blend for 30 seconds or until smooth, then pour into a tall glass. Using the method for the New York Chocolate Egg Cream, fill to the top with about ⅔ **cup of chilled seltzer**. If you wish, add **an additional scoop of low-fat chocolate ice cream**. Makes one 12-ounce serving. *1 serving: Calories 190; Saturated Fat 2 g; Total Fat 4 g; Protein 5 g; Carbohydrate 36 g; Fiber 0; Sodium 137 mg; Cholesterol 12 mg*

CHOCOLATE MALTED MILK

◆◆◆

Often called simply a malted, this soda fountain favorite contains malted-milk powder, created in 1887 by William Horlick in Racine, Wisconsin. The powder, made from dried milk, malted barley, and wheat flour, can be found usually in the beverage-mix section of a supermarket.

2 small scoops low-fat chocolate ice cream or frozen yogurt (¼ pint)	2 tablespoons chocolate syrup
¾ cup very cold low-fat (1% milkfat) milk	2 tablespoons malted milk powder

PREP TIME: 5 MIN.

1 In a blender or food processor, whirl all ingredients until thick and smooth. Serve immediately in a tall glass. Makes one 12-ounce serving.

1 serving: Calories 429; Saturated Fat 1 g; Total Fat 7 g; Protein 9 g; Carbohydrate 48 g; Fiber 0 g; Sodium 153 mg; Cholesterol 15 mg

STRAWBERRY MILK SHAKE

◆◆◆

First mentioned in print in 1889, the milk shake probably contained whiskey, but by the turn of the century it had become a wholesome milk drink. Today, the milk shake travels under several names, such as cabinet in Rhode Island and thick shake in the Midwest.

2 small scoops low-fat strawberry ice cream or frozen yogurt (¼ pint)	½ cup fresh strawberries or dry-pack unsweetened frozen strawberries
⅓ cup very cold low-fat (1% milkfat) milk	1 tablespoon strawberry syrup

A frosty, fresh Strawberry Milk Shake—just made for sipping through a straw

PREP TIME: 5 MIN.

1 In a blender or food processor, whirl all ingredients until thick and smooth. Serve immediately in a tall glass. Makes one 12-ounce serving.

1 serving: Calories 221; Saturated Fat 3 g; Total Fat 5 g; Protein 6 g; Carbohydrate 39 g; Fiber 0 g; Sodium 67 mg; Cholesterol 18 mg

BLACK AND WHITE SODA

In the early 1900's, the person behind the soda fountain was constantly jerking on the soda spigots to fill the glasses. He became known as a soda jerk.

2 tablespoons chocolate syrup	¾ cup chilled soda water (club soda)
1 small scoop low-fat vanilla ice cream or frozen yogurt (⅛ pint)	1 small scoop low-fat chocolate ice cream or frozen yogurt (⅛ pint)

PREP TIME: 5 MIN.

1 In a tall soda glass, stir together the chocolate syrup and vanilla ice cream until smooth. Gradually pour in about ½ of the soda water until the glass is half full. Add the chocolate ice cream and fill to the top with soda water. Stir and serve immediately. Makes one 12-ounce serving.

1 serving: Calories 233; Saturated Fat 0 g; Total Fat 2 g; Protein 5 g; Carbohydrate 54 g; Fiber 0; Sodium 147 mg; Cholesterol 3 mg

BROWN COW

In the 1940's and '50's, root beer stands were familiar sights along our highways and byways. The Brown Cow was almost always offered.

3 tablespoons chocolate syrup	¾ cup (6 ounces) chilled root beer
2 small scoops low-fat vanilla ice cream (¼ pint)	Whipped topping (page 365), optional

PREP TIME: 5 MIN.

1 In a tall soda glass, stir together the chocolate syrup with 1 scoop of the ice cream until smooth. Gradually pour in about ½ of the root beer until the glass is half full. Add the remaining scoop of ice cream and fill to the top with root beer. Add whipped topping if you wish and serve immediately. Makes one 12-ounce serving.

1 serving: Calories 320; Saturated Fat 0 g; Total Fat 3 g; Protein 5 g; Carbohydrate 77 g; Fiber 0; Sodium 139 mg; Cholesterol 4 mg

Reminiscent of the 1930's and 1940's: The Shirley Temple, fruity and refreshing

ORANGE SORBET FREEZE

◆◆◆

2 small scoops orange sorbet or sherbet (¼ pint)

½ cup very cold low-fat (1% milkfat) milk

½ cup ice cubes

3 tablespoons frozen orange juice concentrate

PREP TIME: 5 MIN.

1 In a blender or food processor, whirl all ingredients until thick and smooth. Serve immediately in a tall glass. Makes one 12-ounce serving.

1 serving: Calories 251; Saturated Fat 2 g;
Total Fat 3 g; Protein 6 g; Carbohydrate 46 g; Fiber 0 g;
Sodium 110 mg; Cholesterol 12 mg

SHIRLEY TEMPLE

◆◆◆

Like its namesake, this drink
represents the essence of innocence.

8 teaspoons grenadine syrup or frozen cranberry juice concentrate

2 cups (16 ounces) chilled ginger ale

Garnishes:

4 maraschino cherries with stems

4 strips lemon zest

4 wedges fresh orange

PREP TIME: 5 MIN.

1 In each of four 6-ounce cocktail or saucer-style champagne glasses, spoon 2 teaspoons of grenadine and fill to the rim with the ginger ale. Stir, then drop 1 cherry and 1 strip of lemon zest into each glass. Cut a small slit in the center of each orange wedge and place on the rim of each glass. Makes four 4-ounce servings.

1 serving: Calories 94; Saturated Fat 0 g;
Total Fat 0 g; Protein 0 g; Carbohydrate 24 g; Fiber 0;
Sodium 20 mg; Cholesterol 0 mg

RASPBERRY SHRUB

◆◆◆

Shrubs, originally fruit-based
drinks with brandy or rum, have been a part
of our country's heritage since Colonial
days. This version is whirled from fruits and
fresh juices, making it great to serve
to guests of all ages.

1 package (10 ounces) frozen raspberries in light syrup, thawed

2 cups fresh orange juice

⅓ cup fresh lime juice

Crushed ice (about 2 cups)

Optional garnish:

4 sprigs fresh mint, each 4 inches long

PREP TIME: 15 MIN.

1 Set aside 4 of the raspberries for garnish. In a blender or food processor, whirl the remaining raspberries and the syrup until smooth and liquid. Strain into a 1-quart pitcher, discarding the seeds. Stir in the orange and lime juices.

2 Pour into 4 short tumblers filled with crushed ice. Garnish each drink with a reserved raspberry and a sprig of fresh mint if you wish. Serve immediately. Makes four 6-ounce servings.

1 serving: Calories 134; Saturated Fat 0 g;
Total Fat 0 g; Protein 2 g; Carbohydrate 33 g; Fiber 2 g;
Sodium 6 mg; Cholesterol 0 mg

Shake one
brown cow!

—A soda-fountain jerk
(early 1900's)

FROM THE SOUP POT

◆◆◆

Soups have long been an important part of America's culinary history. Native Americans simmered them over open fires, putting in almost anything available, including corn, squash, and lima beans. New England colonists created chowders chock full of clams or lobsters, and Southern plantation owners proudly served gumbos featuring chicken and sausage. Philadelphia gave us its pepper pot, Kentucky its burgoo, and the United States Senate its own bean soup.

Across the country we've found countless other down-home favorites, among them a famous Manhattan-style clam chowder and a beef-vegetable soup, the latter recipe handed down for generations in a Wyoming family.

We've re-created many a traditional recipe with lower fat, fewer calories, and less sodium by using our own low-fat, low-salt stocks, And we've revised popular cream soups by incorporating low-fat milk or more stock than cream. Those who like a soup that is both healthful and hearty enough for a complete meal will find several, including Turkey Vegetable Soup, Golden Cheese Soup, Fish Muddle, and Beef Barley Soup. Whatever your choice—"Soup's on!"

CREAM OF ASPARAGUS SOUP
◆◆◆

2 tablespoons unsalted butter or margarine	1½ pounds asparagus, washed, woody ends snapped off, cut into 1-inch pieces
1 large yellow onion, finely chopped (1½ cups)	½ teaspoon salt, or to taste
1 tablespoon all-purpose flour	¼ teaspoon ground white pepper
4 cups Chicken Stock (page 74) or low-sodium chicken broth	1 cup low-fat (2% milkfat) milk

PREP TIME: 15 MIN. / COOKING TIME: 25 MIN.

1 In a large saucepan, melt the butter over moderately high heat. Add the onion and sauté for 5 minutes or until tender. Add the flour and cook until bubbly, stirring constantly. Whisk in the stock. Stir in the asparagus, salt, and pepper and bring to a boil. Lower the heat, cover, and simmer for 15 minutes or until the asparagus is very tender. Using a slotted spoon, remove ½ cup of the asparagus to a plate.

2 In a food processor or blender, in batches if necessary, purée the soup for 45 seconds or until smooth. Return soup to the saucepan, add the milk, and cook, uncovered, over moderate heat until hot, stirring frequently. (Do not let it boil.) Ladle soup into bowls and garnish with the reserved asparagus. Makes six 1-cup servings.

1 serving: Calories 126; Saturated Fat 5 g; Total Fat 7 g; Protein 6 g; Carbohydrate 13 g; Fiber 1 g; Sodium 265 mg; Cholesterol 19 mg

Beautiful soup, so rich and green, waiting in a hot tureen!

—Lewis Carroll

FRUIT SOUP
◆◆◆

As Scandinavians immigrated to America, they brought with them traditional food customs, such as beginning a meal with a tart cold fruit soup.

6 cups cranberry-apple juice	½ teaspoon grated orange rind
1 large tart green apple, peeled, cored, and diced (1½ cups)	3 tablespoons instant tapioca
¾ cup pitted prunes, quartered	2 tablespoons sugar
¾ cup dried apricots, quartered	For the yogurt topping:
¼ cup each dark and golden raisins	1 cup plain low-fat yogurt
1 cinnamon stick, 3 inches long	2 teaspoons sugar
	½ teaspoon vanilla extract

PREP TIME: 15 MIN. / COOKING TIME: 25 MIN.
CHILLING TIME: 2 HR.

1 In a large saucepan, bring 4 cups of the juice, the apple, prunes, apricots, raisins, cinnamon stick, and orange rind to a boil over high heat. Lower the heat and simmer, uncovered, for 15 minutes or until the fruits are tender.

2 In a small saucepan, stir together the remaining 2 cups of juice, the tapioca, and sugar. Let stand for 5 minutes, then cook over moderate heat until the mixture boils and turns translucent. Stir into the fruit mixture, cover, and chill for 2 hours or until cold. Remove the cinnamon stick.

3 To make the yogurt topping: While the soup chills, line a strainer with cheesecloth or a paper coffee filter and place over a bowl. Spoon in the yogurt, cover, and chill for 30 minutes. Discard the liquid. Transfer the yogurt to a small bowl, then stir in the sugar and vanilla. Spoon the soup into small bowls and garnish each with a swirl of topping. Makes six 1-cup servings.

1 serving: Calories 343; Saturated Fat 0 g; Total Fat 1 g; Protein 4 g; Carbohydrate 85 g; Fiber 1 g; Sodium 41 mg; Cholesterol 2 mg

Avocado Soup

◆ ◆ ◆

Because the avocado once grew only in areas where alligators lived, such as Florida, it is also called the alligator pear. This Southwestern soup combines it with Mexican spices and a French velouté, or white sauce made with stock.

2 tablespoons unsalted butter or margarine

1 medium-size yellow onion, chopped (1 cup)

2 large fresh or pickled jalapeño peppers with seeds, minced (2 tablespoons)

2 tablespoons all-purpose flour

3½ cups Chicken Stock (page 74) or low-sodium chicken broth

½ cup cold water

½ cup plain low-fat yogurt

2 medium-size ripe avocados (1 pound), peeled, pitted, and halved

¼ cup chopped cilantro or ¼ cup minced parsley plus 2 teaspoons dried cilantro

Fresh lemon juice to taste

Optional garnishes:

3 6-inch corn tortillas

2 tablespoons vegetable oil

¼ teaspoon chili powder

PREP TIME: 25 MIN. / COOKING TIME: 25 MIN.
CHILLING TIME: 1 HR.

A perfect beginning: Frosty Scandinavian Fruit Soup

1 In a large heavy saucepan, melt the butter over moderately high heat. Add the onion and jalapeño peppers and sauté for 5 minutes or until tender. Stir in the flour and cook until bubbly, stirring constantly. Whisk in the stock and water and bring to a boil. Lower the heat and simmer, covered, for 15 minutes. Strain the stock into a large bowl, reserving the vegetables. Return the stock to the saucepan.

2 Cut 1½ avocados into chunks; dice and set aside the remaining half. In a food processor or blender, purée the vegetables, yogurt, and avocado chunks for 45 seconds or until smooth.

3 Over moderate heat, bring the stock to a simmer. Whisk in the avocado purée and heat through. (Do not let it boil.) Remove from the heat, stir in the cilantro and diced avocado and season to taste with lemon juice. Ladle into small bowls and refrigerate until cold.

4 About 15 minutes before serving, prepare the tortilla chips if you wish. Preheat the oven to 400°F. In a cup, mix the oil with the chili powder and brush on both sides of the tortillas. Using scissors, cut each tortilla into 8 wedges and bake on an ungreased baking sheet for 10 minutes or until crisp and golden. Garnish the soup with the tortilla chips. Makes six ¾-cup servings.

*1 serving: Calories 193; Saturated Fat 4 g;
Total Fat 14 g; Protein 4 g; Carbohydrate 12 g; Fiber 2 g;
Sodium 118 mg; Cholesterol 17 mg*

Soup
is cuisine's
kindest
course.

—Anonymous

Tomatoes were first cultivated in North America in the late 18th century. Among those who raised them was Thomas Jefferson. But most people believed the tomato was an exotic fruit or vegetable to be cooked with caution and eaten sparingly. The earliest recipes for tomatoes, which appeared in American cookbooks during the 19th century, often suggested that they be cooked for at least three hours to rid them of their raw taste. It was considered unhealthy to eat them raw. At that time, Americans began using tomatoes in preparing recipes like this old fashioned favorite.

◆ Cream of Tomato Soup ◆

2 tablespoons unsalted butter
1 medium-size yellow onion, chopped (1 cup)
3 cloves garlic, minced
2 cans (28 ounces each) whole, peeled tomatoes, undrained
½ cup Beef Stock (page 74) or beef broth
1 teaspoon sugar
1 teaspoon salt
¼ teaspoon baking soda
¼ teaspoon each black pepper and ground mace or nutmeg
1½ cups heavy cream
Garnishes:
1 medium-size tomato, finely chopped (1 cup)
Minced parsley
Heavy cream (optional)

PREP TIME: 20 MIN. / COOKING TIME: 25 MIN.

1 In a large saucepan, melt the butter over moderate heat. Add the onion and garlic and sauté for 5 minutes or until tender. Stir in the tomatoes and their juices, the stock, sugar, salt, baking soda, pepper, and mace. Bring to a boil, then lower the heat and simmer, uncovered, for 10 minutes.

2 In a food processor or blender, purée the soup for 1 minute or until smooth. Return the soup to the saucepan and stir in the cream. Heat over moderately low heat for about 5 minutes or just until heated through. (Do not let it boil.) Ladle the soup into bowls and garnish with the tomato and parsley, plus an extra swirl of cream if you wish. Makes six 1-cup servings.

1 serving: Calories 322; Saturated Fat 16 g; Total Fat 27 g; Protein 5 g;
Carbohydrate 19 g; Fiber 2 g; Sodium 882 mg; Cholesterol 93 mg

Fresh from the tomato patch: Steaming Rosy Tomato Soup made the healthier way

ROSY TOMATO SOUP
◆◆◆

Here is a modern version of cream of tomato soup, just as good as the old-fashioned recipe, but much lower in fat, cholesterol, and sodium. The touch of baking soda rounds out the flavors by neutralizing the acid.

1 tablespoon vegetable oil

1 medium-size yellow onion, chopped (1 cup)

3 cloves garlic, minced

2 tablespoons all-purpose flour

1 can (28 ounces) low-sodium whole, peeled tomatoes, undrained

1 cup Beef Stock (page 74) or low-sodium beef broth

1 teaspoon sugar

½ teaspoon salt

¼ teaspoon baking soda

¼ teaspoon each black pepper and ground mace or nutmeg

3 cups low-fat (2% milkfat) milk

Garnishes:

1 medium-size tomato, finely chopped (1 cup)

2 tablespoons snipped fresh chives

Plain low-fat yogurt (optional)

PREP TIME: 20 MIN. / COOKING TIME: 25 MIN.

1 In a large saucepan, heat the oil over moderate heat. Add the onion and garlic and sauté for 5 minutes or until tender. Stir in the flour and cook, stirring constantly, until bubbly. Add the tomatoes, their juices, the stock, sugar, salt, baking soda, pepper, and mace. Bring to a boil; lower the heat and simmer, uncovered, for 10 minutes.

2 In a food processor or blender, purée the soup for 1 minute or until smooth. In the saucepan, warm the milk over moderate heat just until it begins to bubble. Stir in the puréed tomato mixture and heat through. (Do not let it boil.) Ladle the soup into bowls and garnish with the tomato and chives. For a special touch, top each serving with a swirl of yogurt if you wish. Makes six 1-cup servings.

1 serving: Calories 142; Saturated Fat 2 g; Total Fat 5 g; Protein 7 g; Carbohydrate 18 g; Fiber 1 g; Sodium 311 mg; Cholesterol 11 mg

CHICKEN BOOYAH

◆◆◆

Belgian by origin, booyah stands for bouillon, which is the base for this Midwestern stew-like soup of beef, pork, and chicken.

1	stewing chicken (about 4 pounds), giblets removed	6	medium-size all-purpose potatoes, peeled and cut into ½-inch cubes
2½	pounds meaty cross-cut beef shanks, 1 inch thick	1½	cups bite-size pieces fresh or frozen green beans
1½	pounds bone-in pork shoulder	1	can (14½ ounces) whole tomatoes, drained
7	cups water	1½	teaspoons salt
3	cups Chicken Stock (page 74) or low-sodium chicken broth	1	teaspoon dried rosemary leaves
4	cloves garlic, 3 whole, 1 minced	½	teaspoon each black pepper and dried thyme leaves
2	bay leaves	½	cup frozen peas
1	tablespoon vegetable oil	1½	teaspoons grated lemon rind
2	medium-size yellow onions, chopped (2 cups)		Hot red pepper sauce to taste
3	large carrots, peeled and sliced (1½ cups)	½	cup minced parsley
2	stalks celery, chopped (1 cup)		

PREP TIME: 45 MIN. / COOKING TIME: 2½ HR.

1 In an 8-quart stockpot, bring the chicken, beef, pork, water, stock, the 3 whole garlic cloves, and the bay leaves to a boil over high heat, skimming off any foam. Lower the heat, cover, and simmer for 2 hours or until the chicken and meats are tender. Uncover the pot for the last 40 minutes of cooking.

2 Remove the chicken and meats from the pot. When cool enough to handle, pull the chicken and meats from their bones, cut into bite-size pieces, and set aside. Strain and measure the stock, setting aside 8 cups for the soup, adding water if necessary. Discard the skin, bones, and bay leaves.

A down-home supper of Chicken Booyah, served traditionally with Beth's Buttermilk Biscuits (page 306)

3 In the same stockpot, heat the oil over moderately high heat. Add the onions, carrots, celery, and minced garlic. Sauté for 5 minutes or until tender. Add the reserved stock, the potatoes, green beans, tomatoes, salt, rosemary, pepper, and thyme and bring to a boil. Lower the heat and simmer, uncovered, for 10 minutes or until the potatoes and green beans are tender.

4 Add the peas, reserved chicken and meats, and the lemon rind; season with the red pepper sauce. Simmer 5 minutes longer or until the peas are tender. Ladle into large soup bowls; garnish with the parsley. Makes twelve 1½-cup servings.

1 serving: Calories 282; Saturated Fat 2 g; Total Fat 6 g; Protein 30 g; Carbohydrate 27 g; Fiber 2 g; Sodium 467 mg; Cholesterol 76 mg

CHICKEN-CORN CHOWDER
◆◆◆

Typical of New England chowders, this one is hearty, creamy, and chock full of chicken and vegetables. Although many penny-wise New Englanders would use the less expensive chicken wings and backs, this recipe calls for the leaner breasts instead.

3 strips lean bacon, diced

1 large yellow onion, chopped (1½ cups)

1 stalk celery, chopped (½ cup)

4 medium-size all-purpose potatoes, peeled and cut into ¼-inch cubes (4 cups)

3 cups Chicken Stock (page 74) or low-sodium chicken broth

3 cups low-fat (2% milkfat) milk

12 soda crackers, crumbled (⅔ cup)

3 cups fresh corn kernels (from 6 ears) or frozen kernels

3 skinned and boned chicken breast halves (12 ounces), cut into bite-size pieces

½ teaspoon salt, or to taste

¼ teaspoon paprika

PREP TIME: 30 MIN. / COOKING TIME: 30 MIN.

1 In a 6-quart Dutch oven, sauté the bacon over moderately high heat for 3 minutes or until crisp, then transfer to paper towels to drain. Pour off all but 2 teaspoons of the bacon drippings.

2 Add the onion and celery; sauté for 5 minutes or until tender. Stir in the potatoes and stock and bring to a boil. Lower the heat and simmer, uncovered, for 10 minutes or until the potatoes are tender.

3 Meanwhile, in a medium-size bowl, stir the milk with the crackers and let stand for 5 minutes or until the crackers are thoroughly soaked. Stir this cracker mixture into the chowder, then add the corn, chicken, salt, and paprika. Cook for 10 minutes or until the chicken is cooked through. Ladle into large soup bowls and garnish with the bacon. Makes six 1½-cup servings.

1 serving: Calories 346; Saturated Fat 2 g; Total Fat 5 g; Protein 25 g; Carbohydrate 50 g; Fiber 1 g; Sodium 464 mg; Cholesterol 51 mg

COCK-A-LEEKIE SOUP
◆◆◆

Jennifer Cowden Manley of New Jersey proudly makes this cock (chicken) and leek soup that she remembers from her Scottish childhood.

1 stewing chicken (3 to 4 pounds), giblets removed

8 cups cold water

6 large leeks, with tops, washed and sliced, (6 cups)

1 bay leaf

½ teaspoon salt, or to taste

½ teaspoon black pepper

½ cup uncooked long-grain white rice

¼ cup minced parsley

PREP TIME: 20 MIN. / COOKING TIME: 2½ HR.

1 In a 6-quart Dutch oven or stockpot, bring the chicken, water, 3 cups of the leeks, the bay leaf, salt, and pepper to a boil over high heat, skimming off any foam. Lower the heat, cover, and simmer for 2 hours or until the chicken is very tender and falls away from the bone; skim the surface occasionally.

2 Using a slotted spoon, transfer the chicken to a plate. When cool enough to handle, tear the chicken into shreds, discarding the skin and bones, and return to the soup.

3 Add the remaining 3 cups of leeks and the rice. Bring to a boil, lower the heat, and simmer, covered, for 20 minutes or until the rice is tender. Discard the bay leaf and stir in the parsley. Makes six 1½-cup servings.

1 serving: Calories 250; Saturated Fat 1 g; Total Fat 4 g; Protein 23 g; Carbohydrate 30 g; Fiber 2 g; Sodium 375 mg; Cholesterol 59 mg

CHICKEN NOODLE SOUP

Comforting and delicious, this soup for some brings back memories of many a lunch shared with friends in school lunchrooms.

8 cups Chicken Stock (page 74) or low-sodium chicken broth	1 cup (2 ounces) uncooked, fine egg noodles
¾ teaspoon salt, or to taste	2 cups diced cooked chicken (12 ounces)
3 large carrots, peeled and thickly sliced (1½ cups)	1 cup frozen peas
1 stalk celery, diced (½ cup)	1 tablespoon minced parsley
¼ teaspoon black pepper	1 tablespoon snipped fresh dill

PREP TIME: 20 MIN. / COOKING TIME: 25 MIN.

1 In a large saucepan, bring the stock and salt to a boil over high heat. Add the carrots, celery, and pepper, then lower the heat and simmer, uncovered, for 10 minutes.

2 Stir in the noodles and simmer 8 minutes longer, stirring occasionally, until the noodles are tender. Add all of the remaining ingredients; cook, uncovered, for 5 minutes or until heated through. Makes six 1½-cup servings.

1 serving: Calories 192; Saturated Fat 0 g; Total Fat 2 g; Protein 18 g; Carbohydrate 15 g; Fiber 1 g; Sodium 445 mg; Cholesterol 55 mg

Soup is better the second day in cool weather.

— *Thomas Jefferson*

MATZO BALL SOUP

Eating matzo (unleavened bread) and the matzo meal made from it is traditional for Passover, the Spring holiday that celebrates the liberation of Jews from slavery in Egypt, millennia ago.

2 large egg whites	¾ teaspoon salt, or to taste
1 large egg	¼ teaspoon black pepper
1 tablespoon vegetable oil	6¼ cups Chicken Stock (page 74) or low-sodium chicken broth
¼ cup unflavored seltzer	
⅔ cup matzo meal	
2 tablespoons minced parsley	

PREP TIME: 15 MIN. / CHILLING TIME: 30 MIN.
COOKING TIME: 40 MIN.

1 In a medium-size bowl, whisk together the egg whites, egg, and oil, then whisk in the seltzer. Add the matzo meal, 1 tablespoon of the parsley, the salt, and pepper, stirring until smooth. Cover and refrigerate for 30 minutes.

2 While the matzo mixture chills, half-fill a large saucepan with cold water and bring to a boil over high heat. Using your hands, roll the matzo mixture into 1-inch balls (about 22) and drop them into the boiling water. Lower the heat, cover, and simmer for 40 minutes or just until the matzo balls are cooked through.

3 In another large saucepan, bring the stock to a boil over high heat, adding additional salt to taste if you wish. Using a slotted spoon, transfer several matzo balls from the boiling water to each soup bowl, then ladle over the hot stock. Garnish with the remaining 1 tablespoon of parsley. Makes six 1¼-cup servings.

1 serving: Calories 132; Saturated Fat 0 g; Total Fat 3 g; Protein 6 g; Carbohydrate 14 g; Fiber 0 g; Sodium 391 mg; Cholesterol 43 mg

Homey and soothing: Chicken soup with matzo balls

TURKEY VEGETABLE SOUP

◆◆◆

Making soup from the rest of the Thanksgiving turkey is as traditional as the dinner itself.

2	tablespoons unsalted butter or margarine
3	cups sliced fresh mushrooms
1½	cups chopped yellow onions
1	cup sliced carrots
1	cup sliced celery
3	cloves garlic, minced
10	cups Turkey Stock (page 74) or low-sodium chicken broth
⅔	cup uncooked long-grain white rice
1	bay leaf
1	teaspoon salt, or to taste

½	teaspoon black pepper
1	tablespoon each chopped fresh thyme and rosemary or ½ teaspoon each dried thyme and rosemary leaves
2	cups diced white turnips
2	cups bite-size pieces fresh or frozen green beans
2	cups diced cooked turkey (12 ounces)
2	tablespoons fresh lemon juice
¼	cup minced parsley

PREP TIME: 45 MIN. / COOKING TIME: 40 MIN.

1 In an 8-quart stockpot, melt the butter over moderately high heat. Add the mushrooms, onions, carrots, celery, and garlic and sauté for 5 minutes or until the vegetables are tender.

2 Add the stock, rice, bay leaf, salt, pepper, thyme, and rosemary. Raise the heat to high and bring to a boil. Lower the heat and simmer, uncovered, for 20 minutes, stirring and skimming the surface occasionally.

3 Add the turnips and green beans and simmer for 7 minutes. Stir in the turkey and simmer another 5 minutes or until the vegetables are tender. Discard the bay leaf and stir in the lemon juice and parsley. Makes ten 1½-cup servings.

1 serving: Calories 181; Saturated Fat 1 g; Total Fat 3 g; Protein 13 g; Carbohydrate 19 g; Fiber 1 g; Sodium 359 mg; Cholesterol 34 mg

RUTH'S SHRIMP GUMBO

Celebrations at Ruth Dorman's in Houston, Texas, often center around the gumbo pot. Her secrets: make the roux by browning dry flour, and use both fresh and dried shrimp.

¼ cup all-purpose flour	3 cups cold water
4 thick slices lean bacon, diced	1 bay leaf
1 pound fresh or frozen okra, sliced	1 teaspoon dried thyme leaves
1 cup each chopped onion and chopped celery	½ teaspoon black pepper
½ cup chopped sweet green pepper	4 pounds medium-size fresh shrimp, shelled and deveined
2 cloves garlic, minced	1 cup (4 ounces) dried shrimp (optional)
1 can (28 ounces) low-sodium whole tomatoes, undrained	¼ cup minced parsley
3 cups mixed vegetable juice	1 teaspoon hot red pepper sauce
	4 cups cooked long-grain white rice

PREP TIME: 30 MIN. / COOKING TIME: 2 HR.

1 To prepare the roux: In a 6-inch skillet, stir the flour constantly over moderate heat for 5 minutes or until brown. Remove from the heat.

2 To prepare the gumbo: In a 6-quart Dutch oven, cook the bacon over moderately high heat for 3 minutes or until crisp, then transfer to paper towels. Add the okra; sauté for 10 minutes. Stir in the onion, celery, green pepper, and garlic and sauté 5 minutes longer or until tender.

3 Add the roux, tomatoes and their juices, the mixed vegetable juice, water, bay leaf, thyme, and black pepper. Bring to a boil; add the shrimp, parsley, and red pepper sauce. Lower the heat. Simmer, uncovered, for 1½ hours or until the gumbo turns a rich brown. Discard the bay leaf. Ladle the gumbo over the rice and sprinkle with the bacon. Makes eight 1½-cup servings.

1 serving: Calories 391; Saturated Fat 1 g; Total Fat 5 g; Protein 42 g; Carbohydrate 42 g; Fiber 1 g; Sodium 708 mg; Cholesterol 286 mg

◆ King Gumbo ◆

Meet John Noel, gumbo king extraordinaire. He is from Bridge City, Louisiana, a proud Cajun community, nestled among plantations and magnolias, that lies just west of New Orleans. In Bridge City, Gumbo Capital of the World, citizens like John Noel and their teams prepare 1,500 gallons of gumbo for the annual Gumbo Festival, held the second weekend of October. This fund raiser for a local church has become a Louisiana tradition, drawing over 130,000 visitors yearly.

"In three days, we cook up about 1,600 pounds of small shrimp, 40 gallons of oysters,

400 pounds of crabmeat, 1,400 pounds of chickens, 700 pounds of andouille (a Cajun smoked pork sausage), 700 pounds of country sausage, 50 gallons of roux, plus plenty of fresh vegetables. It all goes into making two authentic Cajun gumbos: one with chicken and sausage, the other with fresh seafood. The first gumbo pots (each holds 400 gallons!) are set to cook at 5:00 a.m. Judging follows, then the eating begins!"

Gumbos are a perfectly balanced blend of several ethnic influences. Included are the Spanish love of rice and spices and the African fondness for okra. The French added to the pot their method for making roux, Caribbeans contributed their special way of combining seasonings, and the Choctaw Indians gave the secret of thickening gumbo with filé powder, made from sassafras leaves (which was omitted from these recipes because it is difficult to find).

But the real secrets are in the slow cooking and the seasonings. A good gumbo is judged by its flavor and spice—so don't be shy with the hot red pepper sauce!

CHICKEN-SAUSAGE GUMBO

◆◆◆

*Gumbo King John Noel advises:
"Stir your roux constantly so it doesn't
stick and keep stirring until it turns
a deep mahogany brown."*

For the roux:

- ¼ cup vegetable oil
- ½ cup flour

For the gumbo:

- 1 tablespoon vegetable oil
- 4 pounds chicken parts, skinned
- ¾ teaspoon black pepper
- ¼ teaspoon salt
- 2 cups chopped onions
- 1 cup each chopped celery and sweet green pepper
- 3 cloves garlic, minced
- 8 cups cold water
- 1 pound andouille or other smoked sausage, cut diagonally into ½-inch slices
- ½ teaspoon ground red pepper (cayenne)
- ½ teaspoon dried thyme leaves
- 2 cups okra, cut into 1 inch pieces or a 10-ounce package sliced frozen okra
- 2 tablespoons sliced green onions
- ¼ cup minced parsley
- Hot red pepper sauce to taste
- 4 cups cooked long-grain white rice

PREP TIME: 30 MIN. / COOKING TIME: 2 HR.

1 To prepare the roux: In a heavy 6-inch skillet, heat the oil over moderately low heat. Add the flour and cook, stirring constantly, for 10 minutes or until it is deep brown. Remove from the heat.

2 To prepare the gumbo: In a 6-quart Dutch oven or stockpot, heat the oil over moderately high heat. Season the chicken with ¼ teaspoon each of the pepper and salt. Brown the chicken for 4 minutes on each side or until golden, then transfer to a platter.

3 To the Dutch oven, add the onions, celery, green pepper, and garlic. Cook, stirring occasionally, for 5 minutes or until tender. Stir in the roux and heat until bubbly. Gradually whisk in the water, mixing until smooth.

A Cajun specialty: Chicken-Sausage Gumbo
served with rice and freshly baked Corn Pone (page 301)

4 Add the chicken and sausage, the remaining ½ teaspoon of black pepper, the ground red pepper, and thyme. Bring to a boil, then lower the heat and simmer, uncovered, for 1½ hours, skimming the surface occasionally. Stir in the okra and green onions; cook 10 minutes longer. Stir in the parsley and season to taste with the red pepper sauce (don't be timid!). Ladle the gumbo over the rice. Makes eight 1½-cup servings.

*1 serving: Calories 538 ; Saturated Fat 9 g;
Total Fat 31 g; Protein 43 g; Carbohydrate 40 g; Fiber 2 g;
Sodium 743 mg; Cholesterol 142 mg*

Want some
sea food,
mama!
Shrimpers
and rice, that's
very nice!

—Fats Waller

Americans have been stirring up bisques — cream soups based on shellfish or vegetables — since at least 1896, when Fannie Farmer published her first cookbook. A bisque is usually puréed just before serving. But here, we have taken the liberty of adding the fresh shrimp after puréeing, so there are bits of shrimp in almost every bite.

◆ Creamy Shrimp Bisque ◆

2 tablespoons unsalted butter

1 medium-size onion, finely chopped (1 cup)

1 stalk celery, finely chopped (½ cup)

⅓ cup finely chopped carrot

2 tablespoons all-purpose flour

2 cups Fish Stock (page 75) or chicken broth

1 can (14½ ounces) whole tomatoes, drained and chopped (1 cup)

½ cup dry white wine or Fish Stock

1 bay leaf

1 teaspoon dried marjoram

⅛ teaspoon ground nutmeg

1 pound medium-size shrimp, shelled, deveined, and cut into ½-inch pieces

2 cups heavy cream

½ teaspoon salt

2 tablespoons fresh lemon juice

PREP TIME: 25 MIN. / COOKING TIME: 30 MIN.

1 In a large saucepan, melt the butter over moderately high heat. Stir in the onion, celery, and carrot and sauté for 5 minutes or until tender. Add the flour and cook, stirring constantly, until bubbly. Stir in the stock, tomatoes, wine, bay leaf, marjoram, and nutmeg and bring to a boil. Lower the heat and simmer, covered, for 15 minutes, then discard the bay leaf.

2 In a food processor or blender, purée the soup, in batches if necessary, for 45 seconds or until smooth. Return the soup to the saucepan. Add the shrimp and cook, uncovered, over moderate heat for 1 minute. Blend in the cream and cook about 2 minutes longer or just until the soup is heated through and the shrimp are firm and pink. Remove from the heat and season with the salt and lemon juice. Makes six 1-cup servings.

1 serving: Calories 449; Saturated Fat 21 g; Total Fat 35 g; Protein 20 g; Carbohydrate 11 g; Fiber 1 g; Sodium 538 mg; Cholesterol 270 mg

A luscious, light, and elegant beginning for any dinner: Fresh Shrimp Bisque

FRESH SHRIMP BISQUE

♦♦♦

*This lighter version of a bisque substitutes
fish stock and milk for most of the heavy cream.*

1 tablespoon unsalted
butter

1 tablespoon vegetable
oil

¾ cup finely chopped
yellow onion

½ cup finely chopped
celery

⅓ cup finely chopped
carrot

2 tablespoons all-
purpose flour

3 cups Fish Stock
(page 75) or low-
sodium chicken broth

1 can (14½ ounces)
low-sodium whole
tomatoes, drained
and chopped (1 cup)

½ cup dry white wine
or Fish Stock

1 bay leaf

1 teaspoon dried
marjoram

⅛ teaspoon ground
nutmeg

1 pound medium-size
shrimp, shelled,
deveined, and cut
into ½-inch pieces

1 cup low-fat
(1% milkfat) milk

2 tablespoons heavy
cream or low-fat
milk

½ teaspoon salt

2 tablespoons fresh
lemon juice

Sprigs of fresh
marjoram (optional)

PREP TIME: 25 MIN. / COOKING TIME: 30 MIN.

1 In a large saucepan, heat the butter and oil over moderately high heat. Stir in the onion, celery, and carrot and sauté for 5 minutes or until tender. Add the flour and cook, stirring constantly, until bubbly. Stir in the stock, tomatoes, wine, bay leaf, marjoram, and nutmeg and bring to a boil. Lower the heat and simmer, covered, for 15 minutes, then discard the bay leaf.

2 In a food processor or blender, purée the soup, in batches if necessary, for 45 seconds or until smooth. Return the soup to the saucepan. Add the shrimp and cook, uncovered, over moderate heat for 1 minute. Blend in the milk and cream and cook 2 minutes longer or just until the soup is heated through and the shrimp are firm and pink. Remove from the heat and season with the salt and lemon juice. Garnish with sprigs of marjoram if you wish. Makes six 1-cup servings.

*1 serving: Calories 218; Saturated Fat 4 g;
Total Fat 8 g; Protein 20 g; Carbohydrate 11 g; Fiber 1 g;
Sodium 434 mg; Cholesterol 166 mg*

THE OYSTER BAR'S MANHATTAN CLAM CHOWDER

Since 1913, New York's Oyster Bar and Restaurant in Grand Central Terminal has been serving clam chowder—presently more than 240 gallons every day!

2	dozen fresh chowder or cherrystone clams
	Bottled clam juice as needed
1	dozen fresh cherrystone clams, unshucked (optional)
1	bay leaf
½	teaspoon each dried oregano and thyme leaves
2	tablespoons vegetable oil
1	medium-size yellow onion, finely chopped (1 cup)
2	medium-size all-purpose potatoes, peeled and diced (2 cups)
4	large tomatoes, peeled and coarsely chopped (2 cups)
1	large carrot, peeled and finely chopped (½ cup)
1	stalk celery, finely chopped (½ cup)
1	small sweet green pepper, cored, seeded, and finely chopped (½ cup)
½	cup cold water
1	small leek, white part only, finely chopped (¼ cup)
½	cup tomato purée
¼	teaspoon each salt and black pepper, or to taste

PREP TIME: 30 MIN. / COOKING TIME: 1¼ HR.

1 Shuck all of the chowder clams (page 362), reserving the liquor, and coarsely chop them (you should have about 2 cups). Strain the clam liquor, adding enough bottled clam juice, if necessary, to make 1½ cups. Scrub the unshucked cherrystone clams if using. Cover and refrigerate all of the clams and liquor.

2 To make a bouquet garni: On a 4-inch square of cheesecloth, place the bay leaf, oregano, and thyme. Pull up the corners of the cheesecloth and tie them tightly with a cotton string.

3 In a large saucepan or 6-quart Dutch oven, heat the oil over moderately high heat. Add the onion and sauté for 5 minutes or until tender.

Authentic Manhattan Clam Chowder, chock full of clams, tomatoes, and other fresh vegetables

Stir in the reserved clam liquor, potatoes, tomatoes, carrot, celery, green pepper, water, leek, tomato purée, salt, black pepper, and bouquet garni. Bring to a boil. Lower the heat and simmer, uncovered, for 30 minutes, stirring occasionally.

4 Add the chopped clams and continue to cook, uncovered, 15 minutes more. Add the cherrystone clams in their shells if you wish. Continue cooking 15 minutes more or until the clams and vegetables are tender. Discard the bouquet garni and any clams that did not open. Using a slotted spoon, divide the unshucked clams among 4 soup bowls, then ladle the chowder over them. Makes four 1½-cups servings.

1 serving: Calories 357; Saturated Fat 2 g; Total Fat 9 g; Protein 25 g; Carbohydrate 46 g; Fiber 3 g; Sodium 524 mg; Cholesterol 52 mg

SEAFOOD CHOWDER

♦♦♦

*The original recipe for this chowder made
Sara Hayden Okolotkiewicz a winner in the
Seafood Festival in Charlestown, Rhode Island.
Now lighter, this version is still a winner.*

3 tablespoons unsalted butter or margarine

2 tablespoons all-purpose flour

4 ounces mushrooms, sliced (1¼ cups)

⅓ cup finely chopped white onion

1½ cups low-fat (1% milkfat) milk

12 ounces fresh, canned, or thawed frozen crabmeat, picked over for bits of shell (1½ cups)

8 ounces medium-size fresh or thawed frozen shrimp, shelled and deveined (page 362), halved (¾ cup)

1 cup half-and-half

¼ teaspoon salt, or to taste

¼ teaspoon white pepper

¼ cup minced parsley

3 tablespoons dry sherry (optional)

PREP TIME: 25 MIN. / COOKING TIME: 23 MIN.

1 In a large heavy saucepan, melt the butter over moderate heat. Stir in the flour and cook, stirring constantly, until bubbly. Add the mushrooms and onion and sauté for 5 minutes or until tender. Add the milk, lower the heat, and simmer, uncovered, for 10 minutes.

2 Stir in the crabmeat, shrimp, and half-and-half. Simmer 5 minutes longer or just until the shrimp are cooked through. Season with the salt and pepper. Stir in the parsley, plus the sherry if you wish. (This recipe may easily be doubled.) Makes six 1-cup servings.

*1 serving: Calories 226; Saturated Fat 7 g;
Total Fat 13 g; Protein 18 g; Carbohydrate 9 g; Fiber 0 g;
Sodium 460 mg; Cholesterol 122 mg*

SALMON CHOWDER

♦♦♦

*Salmon's popularity in the Pacific
Northwest began with local Indians, for whom the
words fish and salmon were synonymous.*

1 tablespoon vegetable oil

1 large yellow onion, finely chopped (1½ cups)

1 clove garlic, minced

2 medium-size all-purpose potatoes, peeled and diced (2 cups)

1 cup canned crushed tomatoes, undrained

½ fish bouillon cube or 1 teaspoon fish bouillon granules

3 cups cold water

12 ounces boned and skinned fresh or canned salmon fillets, cut into ½-inch pieces (2 cups)

2 tablespoons snipped fresh dill or 2 teaspoons dried dill weed

¼ teaspoon each salt and black pepper

2 cups low-fat (2% milkfat) milk

2 teaspoons fresh lemon juice

PREP TIME: 20 MIN. / COOKING TIME: 25 MIN.

1 In a large, heavy saucepan, heat the oil over moderately high heat. Add the onion and garlic and sauté for 5 minutes or until tender. Stir in the potatoes, tomatoes, bouillon cube, and water and bring to a boil. Lower the heat, cover and simmer, stirring occasionally, for 15 minutes or until the potatoes are tender.

2 Stir in the salmon, dill, salt, and pepper. Simmer, uncovered, for 3 minutes or just until the salmon is opaque. Stir in the milk and simmer 2 minutes longer or until heated through. Remove from the heat and stir in the lemon juice. Makes six 1¼-cup servings.

*1 serving: Calories 177; Saturated Fat 2 g;
Total Fat 6 g; Protein 13 g; Carbohydrate 19 g; Fiber 1 g;
Sodium 582 mg; Cholesterol 16 mg*

Chowder is an American tradition.

*— The Early American Cookbook
by Hyla O'Connor*

BILLI BI

◆◆◆

This recipe substitutes milk and light cream for the heavy cream used traditionally. The resulting soup is lower in fat, yet still creamy.

4 pounds mussels in their shells	1 bay leaf
1 tablespoon dry mustard	2 cups light cream or whole milk
1½ cups dry white wine, Fish Stock (page 75), or clam juice	2 cups whole milk
	¼ teaspoon each salt and turmeric
⅓ cup finely chopped, washed leeks, white parts only	⅛ teaspoon ground red pepper (cayenne)
2 tablespoons minced parsley	1 large egg yolk
	1 tablespoon cornstarch
1½ teaspoons fresh thyme or ½ teaspoon dried thyme leaves	2 tablespoons fresh lemon juice
	Paprika to taste

PREP TIME: 25 MIN. / STANDING TIME: 15 MIN.
COOKING TIME: 15 MIN.

1 Scrub the mussels thoroughly with a stiff brush, remove their beards by tugging on them, and discard any opened mussels. Place the mussels in a large bowl, cover with cold water, and stir in the mustard, which helps them disgorge any sand. Let stand for 15 minutes. Drain and rinse the mussels with cold running water.

2 In a covered 6-quart Dutch oven, bring the mussels, wine, leeks, parsley, thyme, and bay leaf to a boil over high heat. Lower the heat and steam, covered, for 5 minutes or until the mussels open; discard any that do not.

3 Line a large strainer or colander with cheesecloth and place it over a large heat-resistant bowl. Pour the broth mixture through the strainer, catching the mussels. Remove and discard the bay leaf. Shuck the mussels and cover to keep them warm; discard the shells. Return the broth to the Dutch oven and stir in 1½ cups of the cream, the milk, salt, turmeric, and ground red pepper. Bring just to a simmer over moderate heat, stirring often.

4 Meanwhile, in a medium-size bowl, whisk the egg yolk and cornstarch with the remaining ½ cup of cream. Whisk in about 1 cup of the hot soup, then, whisking constantly, pour the yolk mixture into the soup. Continue cooking, stirring constantly, for 5 minutes or until the soup thickens slightly. (Do not let it boil.) Season to taste with the lemon juice. Divide the mussels among 6 large heated soup plates, ladle in the soup, and sprinkle with a touch of paprika. Makes six 1-cup servings.

1 serving: Calories 351; Saturated Fat 12 g; Total Fat 21 g; Protein 17 g; Carbohydrate 15 g; Fiber 0 g; Sodium 386 mg; Cholesterol 142 mg

◆ Billi Bi ... or Billy By? ◆

Back in 1925, French Chef Louis Barthe created this velvety soup in Deauville, France, for one of his regular American customers, William Brand. He named the recipe with the diminutive of the patron's first name and the initial of his last. One sometimes sees the anglicized version, "Billy By."

His creation resembles *mouclade*, the popular soup of Normandy that contains fresh mussels. But, Mr. Brand wanted a soup with mussel flavor – and no mussels! So when Billi Bi was created, the mussels were removed just before serving. Breaking with tradition, we stir them back in.

The famous cream of mussel soup called Billi Bi, made with less cream and whole mussels

FISH MUDDLE

◆◆◆

Order fish stew for supper in North Carolina and what you're likely to be served is called a fish muddle (or mixture). But to quote a North Carolinian: "Never, oh never put milk in the pot!"

1	teaspoon vegetable oil
2	strips reduced-salt bacon, diced
6	green onions, with tops, sliced (¾ cup)
1	medium-size sweet green pepper, cored, seeded, and chopped (1 cup)
1	large carrot, peeled and chopped (½ cup)
2½	cups Fish Stock (page 75) or low-sodium chicken broth
2	medium-size all-purpose potatoes, peeled and cut into bite-size pieces (2 cups)
1	medium-size tomato, chopped (1 cup)
½	teaspoon dried thyme leaves
8	ounces cod or scrod fillets, cut into 2-inch chunks
8	ounces sea scallops, trimmed and halved
3	tablespoons minced parsley

PREP TIME: 30 MIN. / COOKING TIME: 30 MIN.

1 In a large saucepan, heat the oil over moderately low heat. Add the bacon and sauté for 2 minutes or just until the bacon sweats. Stir in the green onions, green pepper, and carrot. Cover and cook for 5 minutes or until all the vegetables are tender, stirring once.

2 Add the stock, potatoes, tomato, and thyme. Increase the heat to high, and bring to a boil. Lower the heat and simmer, uncovered, for 15 minutes or until the potatoes are tender. Stir in the fillets and scallops. Cover and cook for 5 minutes or just until the seafood turns opaque. Stir in the parsley. Makes four 1½-cup servings.

*1 serving: Calories 251; Saturated Fat 1 g;
Total Fat 4 g; Protein 25 g; Carbohydrate 22 g; Fiber 1 g;
Sodium 254 mg; Cholesterol 48 mg*

VEGETABLE BEEF SOUP

◆◆◆

This recipe for homemade Vegetable Beef Soup comes from the family of Adele Kaffer, one of the first women settlers in Wyoming.

2 tablespoons vegetable oil	1 teaspoon each dried oregano, marjoram, and thyme leaves
3½ pounds meaty cross-cut beef shanks or oxtails, 1 inch thick	2 medium-size all-purpose potatoes, peeled and diced (2 cups)
6 large carrots, peeled and sliced (3 cups)	2 medium-size parsnips, peeled and diced (1½ cups)
4 stalks celery, sliced (2 cups)	3 medium-size white turnips, peeled and diced (1½ cups)
2 medium-size yellow onions, coarsely chopped (2 cups)	1 pound green beans, trimmed, cut into bite-size pieces
3 cloves garlic, minced	1½ cups fresh corn kernels
12 cups cold water	1 cup fresh peas
2 cans (28 ounces each) crushed tomatoes, undrained	¼ cup minced parsley
1 teaspoon salt, or to taste	
½ teaspoon black pepper	

PREP TIME: 35 MIN. / COOKING TIME: 3¼ HR.

1 In an 8-quart stockpot, heat the oil over moderately high heat. Add the beef shanks and cook, turning frequently, for 10 minutes or until browned. Transfer the shanks to a plate.

2 Add the carrots, celery, onions, and garlic to the stockpot and sauté for 15 minutes or until tender. Stir in the water, tomatoes, salt, pepper, oregano, marjoram, and thyme.

3 Return the shanks to the pot, raise the heat to high, and bring to a boil. Lower the heat and simmer, uncovered, for 2½ hours or until the meat is tender, stirring and skimming the surface occasionally. Using a slotted spoon, transfer the beef shanks to a cutting board. When cool enough to handle, cut the meat into bite-size pieces and return to the soup. Discard the bones.

All the makings for a steaming stockpot of old-fashioned Vegetable Beef Soup

4 Add the potatoes, parsnips, turnips, and green beans and simmer, uncovered, for 10 minutes. Stir in the corn and peas and simmer 5 minutes longer or until the vegetables are tender. Stir in the parsley. Makes sixteen 1½-cup servings.

1 serving: Calories 225; Saturated Fat 2 g; Total Fat 5 g; Protein 21 g; Carbohydrate 23 g; Fiber 2 g; Sodium 404 mg; Cholesterol 42 mg

BEEF BARLEY SOUP

❖❖❖

- 4 pounds meaty cross-cut beef shanks, about 1 inch thick
- ¾ teaspoon each salt and black pepper
- ¼ cup all-purpose flour
- 3 tablespoons vegetable oil
- 8 cups cold water
- 1 pound mushrooms, sliced (6 cups)
- 3 large carrots, peeled and thinly sliced (1½ cups)
- 1 large yellow onion, chopped (1½ cups)
- 1 stalk celery, chopped (½ cup)
- 3 cloves garlic, minced
- 3 cups Beef Stock (page 74) or low-sodium beef broth
- 3 cups Chicken Stock (page 74) or low-sodium chicken broth
- 1 can (14 ounces) low-sodium whole tomatoes, undrained
- ⅓ cup medium pearl barley
- 1 bay leaf
- 1 teaspoon chopped fresh thyme or ¼ teaspoon dried thyme leaves
- ¼ cup minced parsley

PREP TIME: 30 MIN. / COOKING TIME: 2¼ HR.

1 Season the beef shanks with the salt and pepper, then coat with the flour, shaking off any excess. In a 6-quart Dutch oven, heat 2 table-spoons of the oil over moderately high heat. Add the beef shanks and cook, turning occasionally, for 10 minutes or until evenly browned. Add the water, increase the heat to high, and bring to a boil. Lower the heat, cover partially, and simmer for 1½ hours, skimming the surface occasionally.

2 In a large heavy skillet, heat the remaining 1 tablespoon of oil over moderately high heat. Add the mushrooms, carrots, onion, celery, and garlic and sauté for 5 minutes.

3 To the Dutch oven, add the vegetables, beef and chicken stocks, tomatoes and their juices, barley, bay leaf, and thyme. Raise the heat to high and return to a boil, stirring to break up the tomatoes. Lower the heat and simmer, uncovered, for 45 minutes or until the beef is tender.

4 With a slotted spoon, transfer the beef to a cutting board. When cool enough to handle, cut the meat into bite-size pieces and return to the soup, discarding the bones. Reheat the soup until steaming. Discard the bay leaf and stir in the parsley. Makes ten 1½-cup servings.

1 serving: Calories 341; Saturated Fat 4 g; Total Fat 11 g; Protein 38 g; Carbohydrate 19 g; Fiber 1 g; Sodium 319 mg; Cholesterol 83 mg

SCOTCH BROTH

❖❖❖

From Douglas Boller, a Scotsman now living in New Jersey, comes his mother's flavorful version of this traditional, heart-warming soup.

- 8 cups cold water
- 1 pound boneless lamb shoulder, trimmed and cut into ¾-inch cubes
- 2 large leeks, with tops, washed and sliced (2 cups)
- 2 large carrots, peeled and chopped (1 cup)
- 1 cup peeled, chopped yellow turnip (rutabaga)
- 1 stalk celery, finely chopped (½ cup)
- ¼ cup dried green split peas
- 2 tablespoons medium pearl barley
- ¾ teaspoon salt, or to taste
- ½ teaspoon black pepper
- ¼ cup minced parsley

PREP TIME: 20 MIN. / COOKING TIME: 1¾ HR.

1 In a 6-quart Dutch oven or stockpot, bring the water, lamb, leeks, carrots, yellow turnip, celery, split peas, barley, salt, and pepper to a boil over moderately high heat. Lower the heat and simmer, covered, for 1½ hours or until the lamb and split peas are tender. Stir in the parsley. Makes six 1½-cup servings.

1 serving: Calories 179; Saturated Fat 1 g; Total Fat 4 g; Protein 18 g; Carbohydrate 18 g; Fiber 2 g; Sodium 346 mg; Cholesterol 45 mg

To make
a good soup,
the pot
must only
simmer, or
"smile."

—French Proverb

DOWN HOME TRADITION

The Cheddar cheeses enjoyed by the colonists were mostly imported from England. But after the Revolution, high tariffs on imported cheeses made them delicacies which were eaten only for such special occasions as holidays. Thanks to techniques developed by Englishman Joseph Harding during the 19th century, American Cheddars became widely available and more reasonably priced. In fact, they were sold in almost every New England grocery as store cheeses. Vermont, especially, became famous for its Cheddar.

◆ Vermont Cheddar Cheese Soup ◆

3 tablespoons unsalted butter

1 stalk celery, chopped (½ cup)

6 green onions, thinly sliced (¾ cup)

1 small yellow onion, chopped (½ cup)

3 tablespoons all-purpose flour

⅛ teaspoon each ground nutmeg and black pepper

2 cups Chicken Stock (page 74)
or low-sodium chicken broth

2 cups light cream

2 cups whole milk

¾ teaspoon salt

⅛ teaspoon ground red pepper (cayenne)

12 ounces sharp Cheddar cheese, shredded (3 cups)

PREP TIME: 20 MIN. / COOKING TIME: 30 MIN.

1 In a large saucepan, melt the butter over moderately high heat. Add the celery, ½ cup of the green onions and the yellow onion. Sauté for 5 minutes or until tender. Stir in the flour, nutmeg, and black pepper and cook for 2 minutes, stirring constantly.

2 Whisk in the stock and bring to a boil. Lower the heat, cover, and simmer for 15 minutes, stirring occasionally. Stir in the cream, milk, salt, and ground red pepper. Heat just until the soup begins to bubble.

3 Add the cheese, one handful at a time, and whisk constantly until melted. (Do not let it boil.) Ladle into bowls and garnish with the remaining ¼ cup of green onions. Makes six 1-cup servings.

1 serving: 522 Calories; Saturated Fat 27 g; Total Fat 43 g; Protein 20 g; Carbohydrate 13 g; Fiber 0 g; Sodium 730 mg; Cholesterol 143 mg

A New England favorite: Golden Cheese Soup, high in cheese flavor, but much lower in fat

GOLDEN CHEESE SOUP
◆◆◆

This healthier version of cheese soup calls for less cheese and more chicken stock, plus low-fat milk in place of cream and whole milk.

2 tablespoons unsalted butter or margarine	2 cups Chicken Stock (page 74) or low-sodium chicken broth
1 stalk celery, chopped (½ cup)	1 quart (4 cups) low-fat (1% milkfat) milk
6 green onions, thinly sliced (¾ cup)	
1 small yellow onion, chopped (½ cup)	⅛ teaspoon ground red pepper (cayenne)
3 tablespoons all-purpose flour	8 ounces sharp Cheddar cheese, shredded (2 cups)
⅛ teaspoon each ground nutmeg and black pepper	

PREP TIME: 20 MIN. / COOKING TIME: 30 MIN.

1 In a large saucepan, melt the butter over moderately high heat. Add the celery, ½ cup of the green onions, and the yellow onion. Sauté for 5 minutes or until tender. Stir in the flour, nutmeg, and black pepper and cook for 2 minutes.

2 Whisk in the stock and bring to a boil. Lower the heat, cover, and simmer for 15 minutes, stirring occasionally. Stir in the milk and ground red pepper and heat just until the soup bubbles.

3 Gradually add the cheese and whisk constantly until melted. (Do not let it boil.) Ladle into bowls and garnish with the remaining ¼ cup of green onions. Makes six 1-cup servings.

1 serving: Calories 290; Saturated Fat 11 g; Total Fat 18 g; Protein 16 g; Carbohydrate 14 g; Fiber 0 g; Sodium 356 mg; Cholesterol 60 mg

SPLIT PEA AND HAM SOUP

◆◆◆

*Split peas are just what their
name implies: peas that have been dried
until they split in two.*

6 cups cold water	2 cups dried green split peas, sorted and rinsed
1 medium-size yellow onion, peeled and studded with 3 whole cloves	2 stalks celery, finely chopped (1 cup)
1 medium-size yellow onion, chopped (1 cup)	3 cloves garlic, minced
1 meaty smoked ham hock (about 1 pound)	1 bay leaf
	¼ teaspoon salt, or to taste
4 large carrots, peeled and chopped (2 cups)	¼ teaspoon hot red pepper sauce
	Carrot curls (page 367)

PREP TIME: 20 MIN. / COOKING TIME: 1½ HR.

1 In a 6-quart Dutch oven, combine the water, both of the onions, the ham hock, carrots, split peas, celery, garlic, and bay leaf, and bring to a boil over moderately high heat. Lower the heat, and simmer, covered, for 1¼ hours or until the split peas are tender.

2 Using a slotted spoon, transfer the ham hock to a cutting board. When cool enough to handle, cut the meat into bite-size pieces and stir back into the soup, discarding the bone. Discard the bay leaf and whole onion. Stir in the salt and red pepper sauce and garnish with the carrot curls. Makes eight 1-cup servings.

*1 serving: Calories 216; Saturated Fat 0 g;
Total Fat 2 g; Protein 17 g; Carbohydrate 35 g; Fiber 2 g;
Sodium 314 mg; Cholesterol 9 mg*

A great winter's eve supper: a crock of Split Pea and Ham Soup with crusty French bread

U.S. SENATE BEAN SOUP

◆◆◆

A resolution was passed that requires bean soup to be served every day in the U.S. Senate Dining Room. Several recipes exist, but we like this one best.

1	pound dried navy or great Northern beans, sorted, soaked overnight, and drained (page 361)	3	cups chopped onions
		2	cups chopped celery
		1	cup mashed potatoes
		3	cloves garlic, minced
12	cups cold water	½	teaspoon black pepper
2	meaty smoked ham hocks (2 pounds)	½	cup minced parsley

PREP TIME: 15 MIN. / SOAKING TIME: 8 HR.
COOKING TIME: 2 HR.

1 In an 8-quart stockpot, bring the beans, water, and ham hocks to a boil over high heat. Lower the heat and simmer, covered, stirring occasionally and skimming the surface, for 1 hour or until the beans are almost tender.

2 Stir in the onions, celery, mashed potatoes, and garlic. Raise the heat to high and bring to a boil. Lower the heat and simmer, covered, for 1 hour or until the vegetables are tender, stirring occasionally. Season with the pepper.

3 Using a slotted spoon, transfer the ham hocks to a cutting board. When cool enough to handle, cut the meat into bite-size pieces, discarding the bones, and stir back into the soup with the parsley. Makes six 1½-cup servings.

*1 serving: Calories 394; Saturated Fat 1 g;
Total Fat 4 g; Protein 27 g; Carbohydrate 65 g; Fiber 7 g;
Sodium 626 mg; Cholesterol 25 mg*

The Senate stands for many things... One is its bean soup.

—*Bernard Clayton, Jr.*

PHILADELPHIA PEPPER POT SOUP

◆◆◆

Over the years in Philadelphia, this cry, by women selling soup from carts, was heard in the streets: "Pepper pot, pepper pot! Makes backs strong; makes lives long. All hot! Pepper pot!"

1	tablespoon unsalted butter or margarine	½	teaspoon each crushed red pepper flakes and dried thyme leaves
1	tablespoon vegetable oil		
1½	cups chopped sweet green pepper	⅛	teaspoon each ground allspice and cloves
1	cup chopped onion	8	ounces skinned and boned chicken breasts or cooked tripe, cut into 1-inch pieces
½	cup chopped celery		
2	cups diced potatoes		
2	tablespoons all-purpose flour	½	cup light cream (optional)
5½	cups Chicken Stock (page 74) or low-sodium chicken broth	¼	teaspoon black pepper, or to taste
1	bay leaf	¼	cup minced parsley
½	teaspoon salt		

PREP TIME: 20 MIN. / COOKING TIME: 35 MIN.

1 In a large heavy saucepan, heat the butter and oil over moderately high heat. Stir in the green pepper, onion, and celery and sauté for 5 minutes or until tender. Stir in the potatoes and flour and cook until bubbly. Stir in the stock, bay leaf, salt, crushed red pepper, thyme, allspice, and cloves and bring to a boil. Lower the heat and simmer, covered, stirring occasionally, for 20 minutes or until the potatoes are tender.

2 Add the chicken and cream if you wish and simmer, covered, stirring occasionally, for 5 minutes or until the chicken is cooked. Discard the bay leaf. Season to taste with the pepper and stir in the parsley. Makes six 1½-cup servings.

*1 serving: Calories 178; Saturated Fat 3 g;
Total Fat 7 g; Protein 15 g; Carbohydrate 17 g; Fiber 1 g;
Sodium 299 mg; Cholesterol 35 mg*

VIRGINIA PEANUT SOUP

◆◆◆

George Washington Carver gets the credit for first creating soup from peanuts in the early 1900's. Today, this soup is a prized specialty, particularly throughout Virginia.

1 tablespoon unsalted butter or margarine	1 cup unsalted creamy peanut butter
1 large carrot, peeled and chopped (½ cup)	⅓ cup chopped dry-roasted peanuts
1 stalk celery, chopped (½ cup)	2 tablespoons fresh lemon juice
1 small onion, chopped (½ cup)	¼ teaspoon celery seeds
1 clove garlic, minced	¼ teaspoon salt
⅓ cup all-purpose flour	⅛ teaspoon black pepper
6 cups Chicken Stock (page 74) or low-sodium chicken broth	⅛ teaspoon hot red pepper sauce, or to taste

PREP TIME: 20 MIN. / COOKING TIME: 40 MIN.

1 In a large saucepan, melt the butter over moderately high heat. Add the carrot, celery, onion, and garlic and sauté for 5 minutes or until tender. Stir in the flour and cook 2 minutes longer. (Do not allow to brown.)

2 Gradually whisk in the stock and bring to a boil. Lower the heat and simmer, uncovered, for 30 minutes. Whisk in the peanut butter, peanuts, lemon juice, celery seeds, salt, and pepper and heat through. Season with the red pepper sauce. Makes eight ¾-cup servings.

1 serving: Calories 307; Saturated Fat 5 g; Total Fat 23 g; Protein 14 g; Carbohydrate 14 g; Fiber 2 g; Sodium 204 mg; Cholesterol 14 mg

CURRIED SQUASH SOUP

◆◆◆

A favorite food of Native Americans was the squash, which they found growing wild. It's from the Narraganset name for it, asquatasquash, that our own word is derived.

3 tablespoons unsalted butter or margarine	1 tablespoon curry powder, or to taste
1 medium-size yellow onion, chopped (1 cup)	½ teaspoon ground ginger
1 large butternut squash (about 2½ pounds), peeled, seeded, and cut into ½-inch pieces (8 cups)	¼ teaspoon ground allspice
	4 cups Chicken Stock (page 74) or low-sodium chicken broth
2 large red cooking apples, such as McIntosh or Rome Beauty, peeled, cored and diced (3 cups)	Garnish:
	½ cup plain low-fat yogurt

PREP TIME: 15 MIN. / COOKING TIME: 50 MIN.

1 In a 6-quart Dutch oven, melt the butter over moderate heat. Add the onion and sauté for 5 minutes or until tender. Stir in the squash, apples, curry, ginger, and allspice and cook, uncovered, for 10 minutes, stirring occasionally.

2 Stir in the stock, raise the heat, and bring to a full boil. Lower the heat and simmer, covered, for 30 minutes or until the squash is tender.

3 In a food processor or blender, purée the soup, in batches if necessary, for 45 seconds or until smooth. Return the soup to the Dutch oven and reheat over moderate heat, stirring frequently, for 5 minutes or until heated through. Ladle into bowls and garnish each serving with a tablespoon of yogurt. Makes eight 1-cup servings.

1 serving: Calories 182; Saturated Fat 3 g; Total Fat 5 g; Protein 4 g; Carbohydrate 32 g; Fiber 3 g; Sodium 65 mg; Cholesterol 17 mg

PUMPKIN SOUP

◆◆◆

Pumpkin was one of the first foods introduced to colonists by the American Indians. Throughout the country's history, pumpkin dishes have remained a part of our tradition.

1 tablespoon unsalted butter or margarine

1 tablespoon vegetable oil

1 cup diced onion

½ cup diced celery

½ cup sliced, washed leeks, with tops

1 clove garlic, minced

1 tablespoon minced fresh ginger or 1 teaspoon ground ginger

4 cups Chicken Stock (page 74) or low-sodium chicken broth

3 cups peeled pumpkin chunks or 2 cups plain puréed canned pumpkin

½ teaspoon salt

2 teaspoons light brown sugar

⅛ teaspoon freshly grated or ground nutmeg

Garnish:

6 tablespoons plain low-fat yogurt or reduced-fat sour cream, for garnish

PREP TIME: 25 MIN. / COOKING TIME: 35 MIN.

1 In a large heavy saucepan, heat the butter and oil over moderately high heat. Add the onion, celery, leeks, garlic, and ginger and sauté for 5 minutes or until tender.

2 Add the stock, pumpkin, and salt and bring to a boil. Lower the heat, cover, and simmer for 20 minutes or until the soup has thickened and the flavors are blended.

3 In a food processor or blender, purée the soup, in batches if necessary, for 45 seconds or until smooth. Return the soup to the saucepan and stir in the sugar and nutmeg. Reheat over moderately high heat, stirring occasionally, for 5 minutes or until heated through. Ladle into soup bowls and garnish each serving with a tablespoon of yogurt. Makes six 1-cup servings.

1 serving: Calories 117; Saturated Fat 2 g; Total Fat 5 g; Protein 3 g; Carbohydrate 14 g; Fiber 1 g; Sodium 263 mg; Cholesterol 11 mg

Healthy, hearty Pumpkin Soup, decorated for company with a star burst of creamy yogurt (page 367)

◆

Sweet Potato Soup

Prepare as for Pumpkin Soup, adding **one 3-inch cinnamon stick** and a **pinch of ground cloves** along with the vegetables and ginger and substituting **3 cups peeled and cubed sweet potatoes** for the pumpkin. Before puréeing the soup, remove the cinnamon stick with a slotted spoon. For the brown sugar, substitute **1 teaspoon maple syrup**. Makes six 1-cup servings. *1 serving: Calories 271; Saturated Fat 3 g; Total Fat 5 g; Protein 6 g; Carbohydrate 49 g; Fiber 8 g; Sodium 284 mg; Cholesterol 11 mg*

KENTUCKY BURGOO

◆◆◆

From Owensboro, Kentucky, comes this
recipe featuring the three burgoo basics: beef,
mutton or lamb, and chicken.

1 tablespoon vegetable oil	1 bag (20 ounces) frozen baby lima beans
2 pounds meaty cross-cut beef shanks, 1 inch thick	3 medium-size yellow onions, chopped (3 cups)
2 pounds meaty cross-cut lamb shanks, 1 inch thick	½ cup low-sodium ketchup
14 cups cold water	⅓ cup tomato purée
1 stewing chicken or fowl (4 pounds)	1½ tablespoons Worcestershire sauce
1½ teaspoons salt	1¼ teaspoons hot red pepper sauce
½ teaspoon black pepper	½ teaspoon crushed red pepper flakes
1 large green cabbage, shredded (6 cups)	2 packages (10 ounces each) frozen corn kernels
6 large russet potatoes (3 pounds), peeled and diced (6 cups)	3 tablespoons cider vinegar
1 can (28 ounces) low-sodium whole tomatoes, undrained	2 tablespoons fresh lemon juice

PREP TIME: 30 MIN. / COOKING TIME: 4 HR.

A Kentucky favorite: A thick stew-like soup called Burgoo

1 In a heavy 12-inch skillet, heat the oil over moderately high heat. Working in batches, add the beef and lamb shanks and cook for 3 to 4 minutes or until browned, turning frequently.

2 Transfer the shanks to an 8-quart stockpot and add the water, chicken, salt, and pepper. Bring to a boil over high heat, skimming off any fat. Lower the heat and simmer, uncovered, for 2 hours or until the chicken and meats are tender. Remove the shanks and chicken and let cool.

3 To the stock pot, add the cabbage, potatoes, tomatoes, lima beans, onions, ketchup, tomato purée, Worcestershire, red pepper sauce, and crushed red pepper and bring to a simmer. Meanwhile, skin and bone the chicken and pull the meats from their bones. Cut all the chicken and meat into bite-size pieces and add them to the burgoo pot; discard the skin and bones.

4 Simmer the burgoo for 2 hours, uncovered, stirring occasionally. Stir in the corn, vinegar, and lemon juice; simmer 10 minutes more or until heated through. Makes fourteen 1¼-cup servings.

1 serving: Calories 276; Saturated Fat 2 g;
Total Fat 6 g; Protein 33 g; Carbohydrate 25 g; Fiber 2 g;
Sodium 283 mg; Cholesterol 82 mg

◆ Burgoo ... Bird Stew or Barbeque? ◆

The town is Owensboro, Kentucky—right in the heart of burgoo country, out in the Western farmlands of Kentucky. "We may be small, but each year thousands of people visit our International Barbecue Festival, which is held on the Saturday before Mother's Day," says winning team member John Kaelin. By profession, he's a computer technician. But his friends also know him as a burgoo aficionado, just as his father and grandfather were before him.

"Burgoo has been around for generations, beginning as a soup of leftover squirrel, rabbit, or possibly wild game—whatever happened to be on hand that day. But now most of the recipes are carefully created, especially by the Kentuckians who live in and around Owensboro."

At one time, burgoo may have been a mispronunciation of the word barbecue, or even bird stew. But today, it's a unique dish, just plain burgoo.

Every year at the festival in Owensboro over 80,000 cups of burgoo are served. "It's a celebration that actually starts weeks before, as teams collect the makings for 2,000 gallons of burgoo, plus barbecued chicken and mutton too.

"On festival day, the teams begin working around 5 a.m. stewing and boning chickens, sawing and simmering sides of beef and mutton, then pulling the cooked meat from the bones and putting them in the soup pot. Numerous fresh vegetables are added too, such as corn, cabbage, tomatoes, onions, potatoes, and lima beans. Then the real art of preparing the burgoo begins, as we each add our own special seasonings. Finally, we simmer the burgoo pots, stirring them (we call it raking) with large oar-like paddles for at least four hours over open fires.

"Shortly after noon, the judging begins. Then the selling and tasting gets into full swing, ending, finally, late in the night, with empty burgoo pots and substantial proceeds for local charities."

The tradition continues, year after year—just for the fun and fund-raising of it all.

LENTIL PREACHING SOUP

◆◆◆

Among the Pennsylvania Dutch, serving this hearty soup between their two Sabbath services has satisfied both preacher and the faithfully gathered.

1 tablespoon vegetable oil	4 cups cold water
2 medium-size yellow onions, chopped (2 cups)	1 pound lentils, sorted and rinsed
3 large leeks, white parts only, sliced (1 cup)	12 ounces baked ham, cut into bite-size pieces (2 cups)
3 cloves garlic, minced	4 large carrots, peeled and chopped (2 cups)
1 tablespoon ground cumin	2 stalks celery, chopped (1 cup)
2 teaspoons fresh thyme or ½ teaspoon dried thyme leaves	1 bay leaf
½ teaspoon black pepper	¼ cup minced parsley
5 cups Chicken Stock (page 74) or low-sodium chicken broth	2 tablespoons cider vinegar
	¼ teaspoon salt, or to taste

PREP TIME: 30 MIN. / COOKING TIME: 1¼ HR.

1 In a 6-quart Dutch oven, heat the oil over moderately high heat. Add the onions, leeks, garlic, cumin, thyme, and pepper and sauté for 10 minutes or until the vegetables are tender.

2 Stir in the stock, water, lentils, ham, carrots, celery, and bay leaf. Raise the heat to high and bring to boil. Lower the heat and simmer, partially covered, stirring occasionally, for 1 hour or until the lentils are tender. Discard the bay leaf and stir in the parsley, vinegar, and salt. Makes eight 1¼-cup servings.

*1 serving: Calories 340; Saturated Fat 1 g;
Total Fat 5 g; Protein 26 g; Carbohydrate 47 g; Fiber 6 g;
Sodium 673 mg; Cholesterol 27 mg*

BEEF STOCK

◆◆◆

*Here's a great technique for adding
extra flavor to a stock: roast the vegetables
before putting them in the stockpot.*

3	pounds beef bones	14	cups cold water
1½	pounds meaty cross-cut beef shanks, 1 inch thick	1½	cups low-sodium tomato-vegetable juice
1	pound boneless beef chuck, cut into large chunks	1	can (1 pound) whole tomatoes, undrained
1	extra-large unpeeled yellow onion, quartered	2	large leeks, with tops, washed and thickly sliced (2 cups)
1	large white turnip, peeled and cut into 1-inch cubes (2 cups)	1	stalk celery with leaves, thickly sliced (½ cup)
		8	sprigs parsley
3	large carrots, scrubbed and coarsely chopped (1½ cups)	4	cloves garlic, crushed with the flat of a knife
1	large parsnip, peeled and thickly sliced (1 cup)	2	sprigs fresh thyme, or 1 teaspoon dried thyme leaves
		2	bay leaves

PREP TIME: 30 MIN. / COOKING TIME: 6 HR.

1 Preheat the oven to 500°F. In a large shallow roasting pan, arrange the beef bones, shanks, and chuck. Roast for 45 minutes or until well browned, turning occasionally, then transfer to an 8-quart stockpot. Stir the onion, turnip, carrots, and parsnip into the pan juices. Roast for 15 minutes or until browned, stirring occasionally, then transfer to the stockpot.

2 Pour 2 cups of the water into the roasting pan, stirring to loosen the browned bits. Transfer to the stockpot, along with the remaining 12 cups of water and the other ingredients. Bring to a boil over high heat, skimming off any foam. Lower the heat and simmer, uncovered, for 5 hours, skimming the surface occasionally.

3 Strain the stock through a large sieve into a heatproof bowl and discard the meat, bones, and vegetables. When the stock has cooled, cover and refrigerate until cold. Scrape any fat from the surface. Use refrigerated stock within 3 days, frozen stock within 3 months. Makes 3 quarts.

*1 cup: Calories 63; Saturated Fat 0 g;
Total Fat 1 g; Protein 5 g; Carbohydrate 9 g; Fiber 1 g;
Sodium 171 mg; Cholesterol 10 mg*

CHICKEN OR TURKEY STOCK

◆◆◆

4	whole cloves	2	large carrots, scrubbed and coarsely chopped
2	medium-size yellow onions, peeled		
6	quarts cold water	6	cloves garlic, peeled
5	pounds chicken or turkey parts, on bones (preferably dark meat)	4	sprigs fresh thyme, or 2 teaspoons dried thyme leaves
		2	bay leaves
3	stalks celery with leaves, coarsely chopped (1½ cups)	12	sprigs parsley
		12	black peppercorns
		½	teaspoon salt

PREP TIME: 15 MIN. / COOKING TIME: 3¼ HR.

1 Insert 2 cloves into each onion. In a 10- or 12-quart stockpot, bring the water and chicken to a boil over high heat, skimming off any foam. Stir in the onions and the remaining ingredients and return to a boil. Lower the heat and simmer, uncovered, for 3 hours.

2 Strain the stock through a large sieve into a heatproof bowl and discard the meat, bones, and vegetables. When the stock has cooled, cover and refrigerate until cold. Scrape any fat from the surface. Use refrigerated stock within 3 days, frozen stock within 3 months. Makes 5 quarts.

*1 cup: Calories 35; Saturated Fat 1 g;
Total Fat 2 g; Protein 3 g; Carbohydrate 2 g; Fiber 0 g;
Sodium 91 mg; Cholesterol 8 mg*

Homemade soup stocks: An essential for every fine cook

FISH STOCK
◆◆◆

6 pounds heads and bones from lean white fish, such as flounder, haddock, halibut, sea bass, cod, or sole, rinsed	4 stalks celery with leaves, coarsely chopped (2 cups)
14 cups cold water	2 cups dry white wine or additional cold water
4 medium-size unpeeled yellow onions, coarsely chopped (4 cups)	16 sprigs parsley
	16 whole black peppercorns
	2 bay leaves

PREP TIME: 10 MIN. / COOKING TIME: 30 MIN.

1 In an 8-quart stockpot, bring all the ingredients to a boil over high heat, skimming off any foam. Lower the heat and simmer, uncovered, for 30 minutes. Strain the stock through a large sieve into a heatproof bowl and discard the bones and vegetables. When the stock has cooled, cover and refrigerate until cold (do not freeze). Scrape any fat from the surface. Makes 4 quarts.

1 cup: Calories 47; Saturated Fat 0 g;
Total Fat 0 g; Protein 4 g; Carbohydrate 3 g; Fiber 0 g;
Sodium 27 mg; Cholesterol 9 mg

VEGETABLE STOCK
◆◆◆

2 tablespoons vegetable oil	3 stalks celery with leaves, coarsely chopped (1½ cups)
3 large leeks, with tops, washed and sliced (3 cups)	2 medium-size parsnips, peeled and thickly sliced (1½ cups)
2 large carrots, scrubbed and coarsely chopped (1½ cups)	10 sprigs parsley
1 medium-size onion, peeled and coarsely chopped (1 cup)	1½ tablespoons minced fresh ginger
4 cloves garlic, crushed with the flat of a knife	2 bay leaves
	¾ teaspoon dried marjoram
8 ounces mushrooms, halved (3 cups)	14 cups water
1 small celery root (5 ounces), peeled and sliced (2 cups)	3 tablespoons tomato paste
	½ teaspoon salt

PREP TIME: 30 MIN. / COOKING TIME: 1¼ HR.

1 In a 6-quart stockpot, heat the oil over moderately high heat. Add the leeks, carrots, onion, and garlic. Cook for 10 minutes or just until the vegetables are tender, stirring occasionally.

2 Stir in the remaining ingredients. Raise the heat to high, and bring to a boil. Lower the heat and simmer, uncovered, for 1 hour. Strain the stock through a large sieve into a heatproof bowl and discard the vegetables. When the stock has cooled, cover and refrigerate. Makes 3 quarts.

1 cup: Calories 70; Saturated Fat 1 g;
Total Fat 2 g; Protein 2 g; Carbohydrate 12 g; Fiber 1 g;
Sodium 151 mg; Cholesterol 0 mg

It is on a good stock...
That excellence in cookery depends.

— Isabella Beeton

PLEASE PASS THE MEAT

◆◆◆

Meat has played a significant role in our country's cooking heritage: pig roasts in the South, for example, steakouts on Western ranches, chili cook-offs in the Southwest, and backyard barbecues everywhere. Of course, special occasions have always brought meat to our tables: beef roast for Saturday-night company, leg of lamb for Sunday dinner, baked ham for Easter, and corned beef and cabbage for St. Patrick's Day, whether you're Irish or not.

Now you can continue these traditions but in a healthier way. We've chosen the leanest cuts of meat, then cooked them as your grandmother (and probably her mother too) used to do—while making a few changes along the way. We've trimmed fat and made sauces with low-fat milk, stock, or fruit juice instead of cream. We've also cut back on pan drippings in gravy. Finally, we've sliced meat thinner and served a little less than in years past. And the results are better than ever. Try a few of these—Yankee Pot Roast, Country Style Ribs, Kansas City Strips, Smorgasbord Meatballs, Red Flannel Hash, Apricot-Glazed Pork Loin—and see for yourself.

PEPPER-CRUSTED TENDERLOIN ROAST

◆ ◆ ◆

*"Company's coming," often means
bringing out the family's best china and silverware
and serving extra-special dishes, like this
roasted tenderloin of beef.*

1 whole trimmed beef tenderloin (4 pounds)	4 shallots, minced (½ cup)
1 tablespoon black peppercorns	¼ teaspoon black pepper
4 cloves garlic, minced	2½ cups Beef Stock (page 74) or low-sodium broth
1 tablespoon chopped fresh thyme or 1 teaspoon dried thyme leaves	½ cup dry white wine or beef stock
1 tablespoon balsamic or red wine vinegar	1 tablespoon tomato paste
¾ teaspoon salt	1 bay leaf
1 tablespoon unsalted butter	¼ cup reduced-fat sour cream
8 ounces shitake or white mushrooms, sliced (3 cups)	1 tablespoon cornstarch
	½ cup cold water
	2 tablespoons minced parsley

PREP TIME: 20 MIN. / MARINATING TIME: 2 HR.
COOKING TIME: 40 MIN.

1 Tuck the thin end of the meat under the roast and tie with clean cotton string at 1½-inch intervals. Using a rolling pin or the bottom of a heavy saucepan, crush the peppercorns between 2 sheets of paper towel. In a small bowl, mix the peppercorns, 2 cloves of the garlic, ½ of the thyme, and the vinegar. Rub this paste over the entire roast, place on a plate, cover with plastic wrap, and marinate in the refrigerator for 2 hours.

2 Preheat the oven to 450°F. Sprinkle the meat with ½ teaspoon of the salt, then place it on a rack in a shallow roasting pan. Roast, uncovered, until the meat is the way you like it (for rare, 35 minutes or until an instant-read thermometer inserted into the center reads 135°F; for medium, 45 minutes or 155°F). Remove to a cutting board, cover with foil, and let stand for 5 minutes.

3 While the meat is roasting, prepare the sauce. In a large saucepan, melt the butter over moderately high heat. Stir in the mushrooms, shallots, the remaining 2 cloves of garlic, the remaining ¼ teaspoon of salt, and the pepper and sauté for 5 minutes or until tender. Add the stock, wine, tomato paste, the remaining thyme, and the bay leaf; bring to a boil. Lower the heat and simmer, uncovered, for 20 minutes.

4 In a small bowl, blend the sour cream and cornstarch and stir into the sauce. Simmer 5 minutes more, stirring constantly, until slightly thickened. Discard the bay leaf.

5 Transfer the meat to a cutting board and remove the strings. Place the roasting pan with the drippings over moderately-high heat; add the water and boil for 3 minutes, scraping up all of the browned bits. Strain this liquid into the sauce and stir in the parsley. Slice the meat 1 inch thick, arrange on a warm serving platter, and spoon the sauce around it. Serve with Farmhouse Horseradish Cream (page 261) if you wish, and baked potatoes. Makes 10 servings.

*1 serving: Calories 317; Saturated Fat 5 g;
Total Fat 13 g; Protein 37 g; Carbohydrate 10 g; Fiber 1 g;
Sodium 294 mg; Cholesterol 109 mg*

Roast Beef, Medium, is not
only a food. It is a philosophy...
Roast Beef, Medium, is safe
and sane, and sure.

—Edna Ferber

Yankee Pot Roast: A one-dish meal, New England style

YANKEE POT ROAST

❖❖❖

The method of braising meat in a pot came to America with the English, French, and Dutch settlers. In Colonial days, the pot hung low over the coals in the fireplace and one day contained venison, another bear or beef.

¼ cup all-purpose flour

1 teaspoon salt

¼ teaspoon black pepper

1 boneless beef rump or chuck roast, trimmed (4 pounds)

2 tablespoons vegetable oil

2 medium-size yellow onions, coarsely chopped (2 cups)

4 cloves garlic, crushed

¾ teaspoon dried thyme leaves

1 bay leaf

3 cups cold water

1 pound small white onions, peeled (about 16)

5 large carrots, peeled and cut into 2-inch chunks (2½ cups)

3 medium-size parsnips, peeled and cut into 2-inch chunks (2 cups)

1 pound all-purpose potatoes, peeled and cut into 1-inch chunks (2 cups)

PREP TIME: 25 MIN. / COOKING TIME: 3 HR.

1 In a small bowl, combine the flour, ¼ teaspoon of the salt, and the pepper and rub into the roast, coating it well. In a 6-quart Dutch oven, heat the oil over moderate heat. Add the roast and cook for 8 minutes or until browned, turning it several times. Remove the roast, add the yellow onions and garlic, and sauté for 10 minutes or until the onions are lightly browned. Stir in the thyme, bay leaf, and remaining ¾ teaspoon salt.

2 Return the roast to the pot, pour in the water and bring to a boil. Lower the heat and simmer, covered, for 1½ hours, turning the roast over once. Stir in the white onions, carrots, parsnips, and potatoes and bring to a boil over high heat. Lower the heat and simmer, covered, 1 hour longer or until the meat and vegetables are tender, skimming the surface occasionally. Remove the bay leaf. Makes 10 servings.

1 serving: Calories 491; Saturated Fat 6 g; Total Fat 16 g; Protein 58 g; Carbohydrate 26 g; Fiber 4 g; Sodium 327 mg; Cholesterol 147 mg

PLANKED STEAK AND VEGETABLES

Planking—presenting broiled meat or fish and vegetables on a hardwood board—is an old American custom. A well-oiled board should be used, preferably of oak or hickory, with a groove for catching the juices. (An ovenproof platter can also be used instead.)

4 large baking potatoes, peeled, cooked, and drained

2 tablespoons unsalted butter or margarine, melted

1 large egg white, lightly beaten

¾ teaspoon salt

¼ cup snipped fresh chives or green onions

1 bunch broccoli, cut into flowerettes

1 pound baby carrots, trimmed and peeled

½ teaspoon each garlic salt and black pepper

1¾ pounds boneless beef sirloin steak, 1½ inches thick, well trimmed

½ pound fresh mushrooms, fluted (page 366)

1 pint cherry tomatoes, washed and stemmed

1 tablespoon olive oil

2 tablespoons fresh lemon juice

1 tablespoon chopped fresh thyme or 1 teaspoon dried thyme leaves

PREP TIME: 30 MIN. / COOKING TIME: 30 MIN.

1 Pre-soak and oil a large hardwood board, about 1 inch thick, for planking (page 363) or set out an ovenproof platter. In a medium-size bowl, mash the potatoes and beat in 1 tablespoon of the butter, the egg white, ½ teaspoon of the salt, and the chives.

2 In a large saucepan over high heat, bring the broccoli, carrots, and 1 inch of cold water to a boil. Lower the heat and simmer, covered, for 3 to 5 minutes or until crisp-tender, then drain.

3 Preheat the broiler. In a cup, mix the garlic salt and pepper and sprinkle on the steak. On a broiling pan, broil the steak 4 inches from the heat for 5 minutes. Arrange the mushrooms and tomatoes alongside and broil 3 minutes longer.

A grand presentation: Beefsteak, potatoes, and vegetables beautifully arranged on a wooden plank

4 In a small bowl, combine the remaining tablespoon of butter, the olive oil, lemon juice, thyme, and the remaining ¼ teaspoon of salt.

5 Using a pastry bag, fitted with a fluted tip, or a spoon, arrange the potatoes around the edge of the plank. Place the steak in the center, uncooked-side-up, and surround with the vegetables. Drizzle the vegetables with the lemon-thyme butter. Broil 5 minutes longer for medium-rare or until the steak is the way you like it. Makes 6 servings.

1 serving: Calories 477; Saturated Fat 9 g; Total Fat 20 g; Protein 36 g; Carbohydrate 38 g; Fiber 5 g; Sodium 582 mg; Cholesterol 105 mg

SHARON'S BEST RIB-EYE STEAKS

◆◆◆

This spicy recipe won Sharon Bickett of Chester, South Carolina, a chance to compete in the National Beef Cook-Off. "I finally came up with this concoction, which everyone seems to love!"

4	boneless beef rib-eye steaks, 1½-inches thick, trimmed (2 pounds)	1½	teaspoons black pepper
1	tablespoon olive oil	1	teaspoon salt
1	tablespoon paprika	1	teaspoon lemon-pepper seasoning
1	tablespoon garlic powder or 2 large cloves garlic, minced	1	teaspoon ground red pepper (cayenne)
2	teaspoons each dried thyme and oregano leaves		**Garnishes:** Thin unpeeled orange slices, halved Parsley sprigs

PREP TIME: 10 MIN. / MARINATING TIME: 1 HR.
COOKING TIME: 10 MIN. / STANDING TIME: 5 MIN.

1 Brush the steaks on both sides with the oil. In a small bowl, mix the remaining ingredients and rub on both sides of the steaks. Place the steaks in a shallow glass dish, cover with plastic wrap, and marinate in the refrigerator for 1 hour.

2 Heat the grill or preheat the broiler. Grill the steaks over medium coals or broil 4 inches from the heat until the steaks are the way you like them, 5 or 6 minutes on each side for medium-rare. Transfer the steaks to a cutting board, let them stand for 5 minutes, then thinly slice crosswise on an angle. Arrange on a warm serving platter and garnish with the orange slices and parsley sprigs. Serve with 'Tater Boats (page 229) and steamed carrot sticks. Makes 8 servings.

1 serving: Calories 275; Saturated Fat 6 g; Total Fat 15 g; Protein 32 g; Carbohydrate 2 g; Fiber 0 g; Sodium 348 mg; Cholesterol 91 mg

LONDON BROIL

◆◆◆

Although this dish carries the name of an English city, the first recipe for it appeared in America in 1946 and seems to be thoroughly American in origin. Flank steak was popular for it then, but round steak is more commonly used today.

½	teaspoon salt	½	teaspoon dried thyme leaves, crumbled
2	cloves garlic, minced		
2	teaspoons olive oil	1½	pounds boneless beef round steak, trimmed
1	teaspoon whole black peppercorns		

PREP TIME: 10 MIN. / MARINATING TIME: 1 HR.
COOKING TIME: 10 MIN. / STANDING TIME: 5 MIN.

1 Sprinkle the salt over the garlic on a cutting board. Using the flat side of a chef's knife, scrape and mash the garlic and salt together to make a paste. Transfer to a cup and stir in the oil.

2 Using a rolling pin or the bottom of a heavy saucepan, crush the peppercorns between 2 sheets of paper towels and stir them and the thyme into the garlic paste. Rub the paste into both sides of the steak. Cover the steak with plastic wrap and marinate in the refrigerator for 1 hour.

3 Heat the grill or preheat the broiler. Grill the steak over medium coals or broil 4 inches from the heat until the steak is the way you like it, 5 to 6 minutes on each side for medium-rare. Transfer the steak to a cutting board, let it stand for 5 minutes, then thinly slice crosswise on an angle. Serve with Long Island Parsleyed Potatoes (page 232) and grilled eggplant. Makes 6 servings.

1 serving: Calories 251; Saturated Fat 5 g; Total Fat 13 g; Protein 31 g; Carbohydrate 1 g; Fiber 0 g; Sodium 271 mg; Cholesterol 76 mg

◆ Y'all Come to a Barbecue! ◆

"**B**arbecue means something different everywhere you go," states Jim Quessenberry, International Barbecue Champion from Cherry Valley, Arkansas. "In Kansas City, barbecue is done over charcoal and slathered with a sauce that's heavy on the tomatoes and the liquid smoke. They often begin there by rubbing meats and poultry with a dry spice rub before placing them on the grill, then mop on the sauce only during the last half hour.

"In the Great Lakes states, folks cook over fires seasoned with chips of fruitwood and baste with sauces containing more sweetness than spice.

"Throughout California and Washington too, the locals often barbecue with Oriental sweet and sour sauces, which may include such Polynesian ingredients as pineapple.

"Down in the back country in the Carolinas, the sauces are mostly spicy vinegar concoctions—no tomato at all. Day-long barbecue feasts called pig pickin's are common there. They slowly roast a whole hog over a pit until the meat is almost falling off the bone, then pull it off with long hooks and pile it high on freshly baked buns.

"On the plains and ranches of Texas, barbecues are often a community affair. Friends and families gather round the chuck wagons for abundant eating and possibly a square dance too. The barbecue pits are fired up with a mixture of charcoal and sticks of pecan, hickory, or oak. Beef briskets and ribs are usually on the menu and they're generously mopped with a thick sauce that's described as 'the spicier, the better!'

"And in New England, where the winters are cold, barbecue commonly refers to any food that is smothered with a smoky sauce, then cooked in the oven."

All around the country, barbecue times frequently mean "y'all come" times, with lots of good food and plenty of fun too.

KANSAS CITY STRIPS

◆◆◆

Chef Paul Kirk of Shawnee Mission, Kansas, shares here one of his favorite steak recipes.

2 cloves garlic, minced
¾ teaspoon salt
2 teaspoons sugar
¼ teaspoon low-salt beef bouillon powder
1 tablespoon fresh lemon juice
1 teaspoon paprika

½ teaspoon black pepper
2 teaspoons prepared horseradish
2 Kansas City strip steaks (boneless beef sirloin), 1 inch thick, trimmed (12 ounces each)

PREP TIME: 15 MIN. / MARINATING TIME: 1 HR.
COOKING TIME: 10 MIN. / STANDING TIME: 5 MIN.

1 In a small bowl, mix the garlic with the salt until it forms a thick paste. Blend in the sugar, bouillon powder, lemon juice, paprika, pepper, and horseradish. Spread the mixture on both sides of the steaks, cover with plastic wrap, and marinate in the refrigerator for 1 hour, turning once.

2 Prepare the grill or preheat the broiler. Grill the steaks directly over medium-hot coals, or broil 4 inches from the heat, for 5 to 6 minutes on each side for medium-rare, or until the steaks are the way you like them. Transfer the steaks to a cutting board, let stand for 5 minutes, then slice diagonally across the grain. Serve with Oven-Fried Onion Rings (page 225) and Corn Roasted on the Grill (page 219). Makes 4 servings.

1 serving: Calories 315; Saturated Fat 6 g;
Total Fat 15 g; Protein 40 g; Carbohydrate 4 g; Fiber 0 g;
Sodium 317 mg; Cholesterol 113 mg

ARKANSAS SLABS OF RIBS
◆◆◆

*Jim Quessenberry, grand prize winner
in the Memphis in May World Championship
Barbecue Cooking Contest, slowly smokes pork
ribs on a barbecue for several hours. For faster
cooking, roast them in the oven, then
finish them on the grill.*

For the spice rub:
- ½ cup sugar
- 2 tablespoons dry mustard
- 2 tablespoons paprika
- 1 tablespoon dried basil leaves
- 1 tablespoon garlic powder
- 1 tablespoon onion powder
- 1 teaspoon black pepper
- 1 teaspoon ground red pepper (cayenne)
- 2 racks pork spareribs or baby back ribs, trimmed (about 6 pounds)

For the basting sauce:
- ½ cup cider vinegar
- ½ cup cold water
- 1½ teaspoons hickory smoked salt

PREP TIME: 12 MIN. / SLOW SMOKE: 4½ HR.
OVEN/GRILL: 50 MIN.

1 To make the spice rub: In a small bowl, combine all the spice-rub ingredients, then rub on both sides of the ribs, coating them well. If you wish, cover and refrigerate for up to 8 hours. To make the basting sauce: In another small bowl, whisk together the vinegar, water, and salt.

2 Slow smoke cooking method: Prepare the grill by heating the coals at one end. Place the ribs on the other end of the rack, away from the coals. Cover the grill and vent slightly. Smoke for 4½ to 5 hours or until tender, brushing occasionally with the basting sauce.

3 Oven/grill cooking method: Preheat the oven to 350F°. Place a rack in a large shallow roasting pan and pour in 1 inch of hot water. Arrange the ribs on the rack and cover with foil. Roast for 15 minutes, baste with the sauce, turn over, then roast 15 minutes longer. Preheat the

**Arkansas Slabs of Ribs from the
back country—succulent and high on the spice**

grill or broiler. Grill the ribs, covered, directly over medium-hot coals, or broil 4 inches from the heat, for 10 minutes on each side or until browned, basting frequently with the sauce. Serve with generous helpings of Fourth of July Potato Salad (page 254). Makes 8 servings.

*1 serving: Calories 623; Saturated Fat 19 g;
Total Fat 48 g; Protein 35 g; Carbohydrate 11 g; Fiber 0 g;
Sodium 423 mg; Cholesterol 159 mg*

REAL TEXAS BARBECUE

Texan Coleman Hudgins Locke slowly smokes a brisket of beef over charcoal and pecan wood until it is black on the outside yet still juicy inside. If you don't have a smoker, use our oven/grill method.

1 **whole boneless beef brisket (12 pounds)**	1½ **teaspoons celery salt**
½ **cup fresh lemon juice**	1 **teaspoon each garlic salt and seasoned salt**
2 **teaspoons lemon pepper or black pepper**	½ **teaspoon meat tenderizer**
2 **teaspoons dried oregano leaves**	1 **cup Worcestershire sauce**

PREP TIME: 15 MIN. / MARINATING TIME: 30 MIN.
SLOW SMOKE: 14 HR. / OVEN/GRILL: 3 HR.

1 Using a small brush or basting mop, coat the brisket on all sides with ¼ cup of the lemon juice. In a small bowl, combine the lemon pepper, oregano, the celery, garlic and seasoned salts, and the meat tenderizer. Coat the meat with ½ of this mixture, cover, and refrigerate for 30 minutes.

2 To make a basting sauce: In a small bowl, mix the Worcestershire with the remaining lemon juice and seasoning mixture.

3 Slow-smoke cooking method: Prepare a charcoal smoker according to the manufacturer's directions, adding a stick of green pecan to the charcoal. Place the brisket on the rack and smoke, covered, over indirect heat for 14 to 18 hours or until juicy and tender, brushing the meat generously with the sauce every 3 hours.

4 Oven/grill cooking method: Preheat the oven to 350° F. Place the brisket on a rack in a large roasting pan. Coat it well with half of the basting sauce, cover with foil, and bake for 2½ hours, turning and basting once with the sauce. Preheat the grill or broiler. Grill the brisket, covered, directly over medium coals or broil 4 inches from the heat for 30 minutes or until tender, basting frequently with the remaining sauce.

Chow-time at the Big Horn Ranch—featuring Cowboy Steak simmered in a slow cooker

5 Transfer the brisket to a cutting board and diagonally slice across the grain, ¼ inch thick. Serve with Texas Barbecue Sauce (page 278) if you wish and a large bowl of Ranch Hand Beans (page 211). Makes 16 servings.

1 serving: 378 Calories; Saturated Fat 8 g; Total Fat 21 g; Protein 44 g; Carbohydrate 1 g; Fiber 0 g; Sodium 344 mg; Cholesterol 139 mg

COWBOY STEAK
◆◆◆

Mardie Hanson of the Big Horn Ranch in Cowdrey, Colorado, frequently makes this dish for her cowboys. To quote them about the secret to cooking good beef: "Don't mess with it—the simpler, the better!"

2¼ pounds boneless beef round or chuck steak, trimmed and cut into 1-inch pieces

1 teaspoon black pepper

¼ teaspoon salt, or to taste

1 medium-size yellow onion, thinly sliced

4 medium-size all-purpose potatoes, peeled and cut into bite-size pieces (2 pounds)

6 large carrots, peeled and sliced diagonally ½ inch thick (3 cups)

1 stalk celery, chopped (½ cup)

8 ounces green beans, trimmed and cut into 2-inch pieces (2 cups)

2 cans (14½ ounces each) low-sodium stewed tomatoes, undrained

1 can (10¾ ounces) tomato soup, undiluted

2 tablespoons quick cooking tapioca

PREP TIME: 25 MIN. / COOKING TIME: 5 HR. ON HIGH OR 9 HR. ON LOW

1 On a piece of wax paper, toss the steak with the pepper and salt. Place in a 5-quart electric slow cooker. Layer the onion, then the potatoes, carrots, celery, and green beans on top.

2 In a medium-size bowl, stir together the tomatoes, soup, and tapioca and pour over the meat and vegetables. Cover the pot and cook on High for 5 to 6 hours or on Low for 9 to 10 hours or until the beef and vegetables are tender; stir once during the last hour of cooking. Serve with freshly baked Corn Pone (page 301). Makes 8 servings.

1 serving: Calories 365; Saturated Fat 2 g; Total Fat 7 g; Protein 34 g; Carbohydrate 42 g; Fiber 2 g; Sodium 423 mg; Cholesterol 159 mg

COUNTRY STYLE RIBS
◆◆◆

Farmers Karen and Don Gingerich of Parnell, Iowa, grill almost year round. Their recipe for barbecued ribs (the meaty kind) is typically Midwestern. The slightly sweet sauce has a tomato base, with just a little hot spice added.

2 racks (3¼ pounds) country-style pork spare ribs, trimmed

1½ cups reduced-sodium ketchup

3 tablespoons Worcestershire sauce

2 tablespoons brown sugar

2 tablespoons prepared yellow mustard

⅛ teaspoon black pepper

Pinch ground red pepper (cayenne)

PREP TIME: 10 MIN. / COOKING TIME: 30 MIN.

1 Preheat the grill or broiler. Place the ribs in a 6-quart Dutch oven, add enough cold water to cover, and bring to a boil over high heat. Lower the heat and simmer, uncovered, for 10 minutes. Using tongs, transfer the ribs to paper towels.

2 To prepare the sauce: In a small saucepan, stir together the remaining ingredients and bring to a boil over moderate heat. Lower the heat and simmer, uncovered, for 1 minute.

3 Grill the ribs directly over medium-hot coals or broil 4 inches from the heat for 15 minutes, turning and brushing with the sauce every 5 minutes or until the ribs are glazed. Serve with Sunshine Salad (page 256). Makes 6 servings.

1 serving: Calories 449; Saturated Fat 10 g; Total Fat 27 g; Protein 31 g; Carbohydrate 6 g; Fiber 0 g; Sodium 325 mg; Cholesterol 128 mg

◆

Rocky Mountain Ribs

Prepare as for Country Style Ribs increasing the ground red pepper to ½ **teaspoon** and adding **1 tablespooon liquid smoke**. *1 serving: Calories 449; Saturated Fat 10 g; Total Fat 27 g; Protein 31 g; Carbohydrate 6 g; Fiber 0 g; Sodium 325 mg; Cholesterol 128 mg*

SWISS STEAK

◆◆◆

The name of this dish comes from the English term "swissing," which means to smooth and flatten meat before cooking.

1¼ pounds boneless beef chuck steak, 1½ inches thick	1 clove garlic, minced
½ teaspoon black pepper	¼ teaspoon each ground cinnamon, ginger, and nutmeg
¼ teaspoon salt, or to taste	1 can (16 ounces) whole tomatoes with purée
2 tablespoons all-purpose flour	1¼ cups cold water
1 tablespoon olive oil	1 bay leaf
1 large yellow onion, sliced	2 tablespoons chopped fresh basil or 2 teaspoons dried basil leaves
1 small sweet green pepper, cut in strips	¼ cup minced parsley
	1 teaspoon fresh lemon juice

PREP TIME: 20 MIN. / STANDING TIME: 30 MIN.
COOKING TIME: 1½ HR.

1 Sprinkle the steak on both sides with the pepper and salt. With a meat mallet or the bottom of a small heavy skillet, pound the flour into both sides of the steak until the steak is ½ inch thick; let stand for 30 minutes.

2 In a deep, 12-inch nonstick skillet, heat the oil over moderately high heat. Brown the steak for 3 minutes on each side; transfer to a plate. Add the onion, green pepper, garlic, and spices and sauté for 5 minutes. Return the steak to the skillet with the tomatoes, water, and bay leaf and bring to a boil. Lower the heat, cover, and simmer, stirring occasionally, for 1 hour or until the steak is tender.

3 Discard the bay leaf; stir in the basil, parsley, and lemon juice. Diagonally slice the steak across the grain, ¼ inch thick; spoon on the sauce. Serve with egg noodles or rice. Makes 4 servings.

1 serving: Calories 360; Saturated Fat 5 g;
Total Fat 14 g; Protein 45 g; Carbohydrate 13 g; Fiber 2 g;
Sodium 399 mg; Cholesterol 129 mg

GRILLADES AND GRITS

◆◆◆

Grillades, Creole specialties, are thin steaks that are fried in lard, then slowly simmered with onions and tomatoes until tender. We have used a little oil instead of lard and shortened the cooking time.

4 boneless beef cubed minute steaks (top round), ¼ inch thick (1 pound)	2 cloves garlic, minced
	½ teaspoon dry mustard
¼ teaspoon salt, or to taste	1 teaspoon dried thyme leaves
4 tablespoons all-purpose flour	⅛ teaspoon ground red pepper (cayenne)
1 tablespoon vegetable oil	1 cup Beef Stock (page 74) or low-sodium beef broth
¾ cup finely chopped sweet green peppers	1 cup canned crushed tomatoes, undrained
¾ cup finely chopped yellow onion	1 bay leaf
½ cup chopped celery	4 cups cooked grits

PREP TIME: 25 MIN. / COOKING TIME: 45 MIN.

1 Season the steak with the salt and coat with 2 tablespoons of the flour. In a heavy 12-inch nonstick skillet, heat the oil over moderately high heat. Brown the steak for 3 minutes on each side, then transfer to a plate.

2 Add the remaining 2 tablespoons of flour to the skillet and stir for 3 minutes or just until golden. Add the vegetables, spices, and herbs and sauté for 5 minutes or until tender. Add the stock, tomatoes, bay leaf, and steak and bring to a boil.

3 Lower the heat, cover, and simmer, stirring occasionally, for 30 minutes or until the steak is tender; discard the bay leaf. Diagonally slice the steaks across the grain, ¼ inch thick. Transfer the slices to a platter, surround with the grits, and ladle the sauce on top. Serve with Creole Okra and Tomatoes (page 223). Makes 4 servings.

1 serving: Calories 389; Saturated Fat 2 g;
Total Fat 9 g; Protein 32 g; Carbohydrate 44 g; Fiber 2 g;
Sodium 255 mg; Cholesterol 65 mg

SHAKER FLANK STEAK

◆◆◆

*Arriving from England in the late 18th
century, the Shakers lived celibate, communal lives
and dined on wholesome, simple foods.*

1 tablespoon all-purpose flour	½ cup finely chopped sweet yellow pepper
¾ teaspoon dried thyme leaves	½ cup finely chopped celery
½ teaspoon black pepper	½ cup diagonally sliced green onions
¼ teaspoon salt	½ cup finely chopped carrot
1 pound boneless beef flank steak, trimmed	⅓ cup low-sodium ketchup
1 tablespoon vegetable oil	¼ cup cold water
½ cup finely chopped sweet red pepper	1 tablespoon fresh lemon juice

PREP TIME: 25 MIN. / COOKING TIME: 1¼ HR.

1 On a sheet of wax paper, mix together the
flour, ½ teaspoon of the thyme, ¼ teaspoon of
the pepper, and the salt. With a sharp knife, lightly score both sides of the steak, then coat both
sides with the flour mixture.

2 In a heavy 12-inch skillet, heat the oil over
moderately high heat. Brown the steak for
5 minutes on each side, then transfer to a plate.

3 Add the sweet peppers, celery, green onions,
carrot, the remaining ¼ teaspoon of thyme and
¼ teaspoon of pepper and sauté for 5 minutes or
until tender. Add the browned steak, ketchup,
water, and lemon juice and bring to a boil.

4 Lower the heat, cover, and simmer for 1 hour
or until the steak is tender. Diagonally slice
the steak across the grain, ¼ inch thick, then
arrange on a platter; spoon on the sauce. Serve
with Potato Rolls (page 297). Makes 4 servings.

*1 serving: Calories 328; Saturated Fat 4 g;
Total Fat 10 g; Protein 33 g; Carbohydrate 7 g; Fiber 0 g;
Sodium 329 mg; Cholesterol 80 mg*

Grillades is like gumbo...
Everyone has his own recipe.

—Chef Paul Prudhomme

A skillet of Southern-Fried Steak: The source of many wonderful memories

SOUTHERN-FRIED STEAK

◆◆◆

*With less fat in the batter, the skillet,
and the gravy too, this recipe is healthier than the
original, yet still traditional in flavor. To cut
the fat even more, you can substitute whole
milk for the half-and-half.*

1 pound boneless
beef round steak,
trimmed, cut into
4 pieces, and
pounded ¼ inch
thick, or 1 pound
cubed beef steaks

½ teaspoon black
pepper

¼ teaspoon salt, or to
taste

1 large egg

1 large egg white

¼ cup low-fat
(1% milkfat) milk

½ cup all-purpose flour

2 tablespoons
vegetable oil

For the gravy:

1 tablespoon unsalted
butter or margarine

2 green onions, with
tops, sliced (¼ cup)

1 cup low-fat
(1% milkfat) milk

2 tablespoons all-
purpose flour

½ cup half-and-half or
whole milk

1 teaspoon
Worcestershire
sauce

⅛ teaspoon each salt
and ground red
pepper (cayenne)

PREP TIME: 20 MIN. / COOKING TIME: 15 MIN.

1 Season the steaks with the pepper and salt. In a small shallow bowl, beat the whole egg, egg white, and milk. Dip the steaks into this mixture, then into the flour, shaking off any excess.

2 In a heavy 12-inch skillet, heat the oil over high heat. Add the steaks and cook for 3 minutes on each side or until golden brown. Transfer to a warm platter and cover with foil.

3 To prepare the gravy: In the same skillet, melt the butter over moderately high heat. Add the green onions and sauté for 3 minutes. In a small bowl, whisk the milk and flour until smooth, add the mixture to the skillet with the remaining ingredients, and bring to a boil, stirring constantly. Lower the heat and simmer, uncovered, for 3 minutes or until the gravy has thickened slightly, then spoon over the steaks. Serve with Cajun Corn (page 219). Makes 4 servings.

*1 serving: Calories 400; Saturated Fat 8 g;
Total Fat 20 g; Protein 34 g; Carbohydrate 20 g; Fiber 1 g;
Sodium 354 mg; Cholesterol 140 mg*

DOWN HOME TRADITION

Chicken frying is a scrumptious Southern way of tenderizing less tender cuts of meat. Traditionally, Southern cooks begin with beef round steaks, pounded thin, or minute steaks. Then they dip them in egg batter, dredge them with seasoned flour, and fry them very crisp, usually in hot lard or butter in a heavy iron skillet. They rarely discard the skillet drippings. Instead they use them to make a rich cream gravy to ladle over all.

◆ Chicken-Fried Steak ◆

1 pound boneless beef round steak, cut into 4 pieces
and pounded ¼ inch thick, or 1 pound cubed beef steaks

½ teaspoon each salt and black pepper

2 large eggs

¼ cup whole milk

½ cup all-purpose flour

¼ cup vegetable oil

For the gravy:

2 tablespoons bacon drippings

1¼ cups heavy cream

1 tablespoon all-purpose flour

1 teaspoon Worcestershire sauce

½ teaspoon salt

⅛ teaspoon ground red pepper (cayenne)

PREP TIME: 20 MIN. / COOKING TIME: 12 MIN.

---

1 Season the steaks with the salt and pepper. In a small shallow bowl, beat the eggs with the milk. Dip the steaks into this mixture, then into the flour, shaking off any excess.

2 In a heavy 12-inch skillet, heat the oil over high heat. Add the steaks and cook for 3 minutes on each side or until golden brown. Transfer to a warm platter and cover with foil. Reserve the drippings in the skillet.

3 To prepare the gravy: Heat the bacon drippings in the skillet over moderately high heat. In a small bowl, whisk the cream and flour until smooth, add to the skillet with the remaining ingredients, and bring to a boil, stirring constantly. Lower the heat and simmer, uncovered, for 3 minutes or until the gravy is smooth and thickened. Surround the steak with Beaten Biscuits (page 307) and ladle the gravy over all. Makes 4 servings.

---

1 serving: Calories 694; Saturated Fat 25 g; Total Fat 55 g; Protein 33 g; Carbohydrate 16 g; Fiber 1 g; Sodium 671 mg; Cholesterol 281 mg

---

No Texas cookbook can claim authenticity without including a chicken-fried steak.

—from Tastes &Tales from Texas...with love by Peg Hein

HUNGARIAN GOULASH

◆◆◆

Over the years, many American families have enjoyed some variation of this satisfying stew.

1 pound boneless beef chuck, trimmed and cut into 1½-inch cubes	2 cloves garlic, minced
½ teaspoon black pepper	½ teaspoon caraway seeds
¼ teaspoon salt	½ teaspoon dried marjoram leaves
2 tablespoons olive oil	1¼ to 1¾ cups Beef Stock (page 74) or low-sodium beef broth
1 large yellow onion, thinly sliced (1½ cups)	8 ounces red-skinned potatoes, scrubbed and cut into ¾-inch cubes (2 cups)
1 tablespoon all-purpose flour	
1 tablespoon sweet Hungarian paprika	4 ounces mushrooms, quartered (1½ cups)
1 tablespoon tomato paste	2 tablespoons minced parsley
1 tablespoon red wine vinegar	½ teaspoon grated lemon rind

PREP TIME: 25 MIN. / COOKING TIME: 1¾ HR.

1 Season the beef with the pepper and salt. In a 5-quart nonstick Dutch oven, heat 1 tablespoon of the oil over moderately high heat. Sauté the meat for 6 minutes, then transfer to a plate.

2 Add the onion to the Dutch oven and sauté for 5 minutes or until lightly browned and tender. Stir in the browned beef and any juices that have collected on the plate, the flour, paprika, tomato paste, vinegar, garlic, caraway seeds, and marjoram; cook for 3 minutes, stirring constantly.

3 Stir in the stock; bring to a boil. Lower the heat, cover, and simmer for 1 hour. Add the potatoes and more stock if needed. Simmer, uncovered, for 25 minutes or until the beef and potatoes are tender.

4 While the stew simmers, heat the remaining 1 tablespoon of oil in an 8-inch skillet over moderately high heat. Add the mushrooms and sauté for 6 minutes or until browned, then stir into the Goulash with the parsley and lemon rind. Serve

with egg noodles and Cheesy Biscuits (page 307). Tip: This recipe doubles easily. Any extra will keep in the freezer for up to 1 month. Makes 4 servings.

---

1 serving: Calories 381; Saturated Fat 4 g; Total Fat 15 g; Protein 39 g; Carbohydrate 22 g; Fiber 3 g; Sodium 313 mg; Cholesterol 103 mg

SKILLET LIVER AND ONIONS

◆◆◆

Stationary lunch wagons, or diners, in the shape of railroad cars began appearing in late-19th-century America. Back then (and still today), liver with onions was almost always a staple.

1 teaspoon unsalted butter or margarine	1 teaspoon black pepper
2 tablespoons vegetable oil	1 pound calf's liver, trimmed and cut into slices, ½ inch thick
5 cups thinly sliced Spanish onions	
4 cups thinly sliced red or yellow onions	½ teaspoon salt
	¼ cup all-purpose flour

PREP TIME: 15 MIN. / COOKING TIME: 40 MIN.

1 In a heavy 12-inch nonstick skillet, melt the butter and 1 tablespoon of the oil over moderate heat. Add the Spanish and red onions; cook, uncovered, stirring occasionally, for 30 minutes or until browned and very soft. Season with ½ teaspoon of the pepper, transfer to a warm platter, and keep warm.

2 Season the liver with the salt and remaining ½ teaspoon of pepper and coat with the flour. In the same skillet, heat the remaining 1 tablespoon of oil over moderately high heat. Sauté the liver for 3 minutes on each side or until the liver is the way you like it, then arrange on the platter with the onions. Serve with a generous helping of Mashed Potatoes (page 361). Makes 4 servings.

---

1 serving: Calories 407; Saturated Fat 5 g; Total Fat 14 g; Protein 28 g; Carbohydrate 44 g; Fiber 2 g; Sodium 362 mg; Cholesterol 405 mg

BEEF POT PIE

◆◆◆

The English colonists brought their love of pot pies to America. This one has a Southern touch; instead of the traditional pie crust dome, it is topped with buttermilk biscuits.

Beef Pot Pie, hearty and wholesome

2 pounds boneless beef chuck, trimmed and cut into ¾-inch cubes

¼ cup all-purpose flour

1 tablespoon vegetable oil

1 cup chopped onion

3 cloves garlic, minced

3 cups Beef Stock (page 74) or low-sodium beef broth

1 tablespoon tomato paste

½ teaspoon dried thyme leaves

½ teaspoon each salt and black pepper

4 large carrots, peeled and cut into ¼-inch rounds (2 cups)

1 large all-purpose potato, peeled and cut into ½-inch cubes (1½ cups)

2 medium-size parsnips, peeled and cut into ½-inch cubes (1 cup)

For the biscuit topping:

1½ cups all-purpose flour

1¾ teaspoons baking powder

½ teaspoon sugar

½ teaspoon dried thyme leaves

¼ teaspoon each salt and baking soda

¼ cup (½ stick) cold unsalted butter or margarine, cut up

¾ cup low-fat buttermilk

PREP TIME: 35 MIN. / COOKING TIME: 1¾ HR.

1 Preheat the oven to 350°F. Coat the beef with the flour. In a 6-quart nonstick Dutch oven, heat the oil over moderately high heat. Sauté the meat, turning frequently, for 5 minutes or until browned, then transfer to a bowl.

2 Add the onion and garlic and sauté for 5 minutes or until tender. Stir in the beef and any juices that have collected, along with the stock, tomato paste, thyme, salt, and pepper. Bring to a boil over high heat, then cover, transfer to the oven, and bake for 30 minutes. Stir in the vegetables and bake, covered, 40 minutes longer or until the meat is tender.

3 To make the biscuit topping: In a large bowl, combine the flour, baking powder, sugar, thyme, salt, and baking soda. Using a pastry blender or two knives, cut in the butter until the mixture resembles coarse crumbs. Using a fork or your hands, mix in the buttermilk just until a dough forms. On a lightly floured surface, pat the dough into a circle, ½ inch thick. Using a floured 2-inch biscuit cutter, cut out about 16 biscuits and place on top of the beef mixture. Bake, uncovered, for 15 minutes or until the biscuits are golden brown. Serve with Warm Spinach-Bacon Salad (page 257). Makes 8 servings.

1 serving: Calories 453; Saturated Fat 7 g; Total Fat 16 g; Protein 40 g; Carbohydrate 35 g; Fiber 4 g; Sodium 309 mg; Cholesterol 119 mg

Guaranteed to cure hunger pains: A bowl of Doc's "Secret Remedy" Chili on steaming rice

SESPE CREEK CHILI

◆◆◆

Californian Jim Beaty cooked his way to the top at the 1986 World's Championship Chili Cookoff with this hearty pot of chili.

2 tablespoons vegetable oil

2½ pounds boneless beef sirloin, trimmed and cut into ⅜-inch cubes

1⅓ cups Chicken Stock (page 74) or low-sodium chicken broth

1⅓ cups Beef Stock (page 74) or low-sodium beef broth

2 medium-size white onions, chopped (2 cups)

1 small yellow onion, chopped (½ cup)

½ cup plus 2 teaspoons chili powder

2 teaspoons ground cumin

1 teaspoon dried oregano leaves

½ cup canned low-sodium tomato sauce

5 cloves garlic, mashed into a paste (about 2 teaspoons)

¾ teaspoon seasoned salt, or to taste

⅛ teaspoon ground coriander (optional)

1 teaspoon hot red pepper sauce

PREP TIME: 25 MIN. / COOKING TIME: 2 HR.

1 In a 12-inch nonstick skillet, heat the oil over moderately high heat. Sauté the sirloin for 3 minutes or until browned, turning frequently and transferring to a 6-quart Dutch oven as you go.

2 To the Dutch oven, add the chicken stock, ⅔ cup of the beef stock, the white and yellow onions, ½ cup of the chili powder, the cumin, and oregano. Bring to a boil over high heat. Lower the heat and simmer, partially covered, for 1½ hours or until the sirloin is tender.

3 Stir in the tomato sauce, garlic, the remaining 2 teaspoons of chili powder, the seasoned salt, and coriander if you wish. Simmer, uncovered, for 20 minutes. Stir in the remaining ⅔ cup of beef stock and the hot pepper sauce. Serve over rice. Any extra chili may be frozen for up to 1 month. Makes 8 to 10 servings.

1 serving (for 8): Calories 275; Saturated Fat 3 g; Total Fat 11 g; Protein 34 g; Carbohydrate 11 g; Fiber 4 g; Sodium 340 mg; Cholesterol 77 mg

Doc's "Secret Remedy" Chili

6 ounces country-style bulk pork sausage

1 tablespoon olive oil

3 pounds boneless beef sirloin, trimmed and cut into ½-inch cubes

2 cups Beef Stock (page 74) or low-sodium beef broth

1 can (8 ounces) low-sodium tomato sauce

1 can (6 ounces) spicy or plain tomato juice

½ teaspoon Worcestershire sauce

¾ cup (6 ounces) beer (with or without alcohol)

6 to 11 tablespoons chili powder

1 tablespoon onion powder

1 teaspoon garlic powder

2 teaspoons hot red pepper sauce

1 tablespoon ground cumin

½ teaspoon salt

10 to 12 cups cooked long-grain white rice

PREP TIME: 15 MIN. / COOKING TIME: 2¼ HR.

1 In an 8-quart Dutch oven, sauté the sausage over moderately high heat for 3 minutes or until browned. Using a slotted spoon, transfer the sausage to a plate. Heat the oil in the Dutch oven, add the beef, in batches if necessary, and cook for 3 minutes or until browned, turning frequently.

2 Return all the meat, and any juices that have collected, to the Dutch oven. Stir in the stock, tomato sauce, tomato juice, Worcestershire, beer, as much chili powder as you dare, the onion and garlic powders, and 1 teaspoon of the hot pepper sauce; bring to a boil. Lower the heat and simmer, covered, for 1½ hours or until the beef is tender.

3 Stir in the cumin, the remaining 1 teaspoon of red pepper sauce, and the salt. Cook, partially covered, 30 minutes longer or until the flavors are well blended. For each serving, place a heaping spoonful of rice in a soup plate and ladle chili on top. Serve with Hush Puppies (page 299). Makes 10 to 12 servings.

1 serving (for 10): Calories 561; Saturated Fat 4 g; Total Fat 14 g; Protein 41 g; Carbohydrate 64 g; Fiber 4 g; Sodium 583 mg; Cholesterol 88 mg

◆ Chili Champion ◆

"Chili should be a blend of just the right amount of meat and spice—not too mild, but not so hot that it makes your eyes water." Such are the words of advice from chili champion Dr. Ed Pierczynski. This skilled family practitioner from Carson City, Nevada, should know. His Doc's "Secret Remedy" Chili won him in 1992 the Best of the Best first prize ($25,000!) at the International Chili Society's World's Championship Chili Cookoff, a contest that has been affectionately dubbed, by those in the know, the "Chili Olympics."

Ed's Secret Remedy is the true Texas chili, that is, chili without beans. (Although he admits that red beans can taste great in it too).

"Begin with some of the best beef you can find, such as the juicier end of the sirloin called tri-tip beef, or culotte steaks, in some areas. Chuck steak makes an excellent chili too, but you need to let the pot simmer long enough to tenderize it. Be sure to cut the meat into pieces that are small enough to cook into tender bites, yet not so small that they fall apart in the pot during cooking. Half-inch chunks seem to work best.

"Browning the meat adds extra flavor. Then, I strain any extra fat from the pan drippings before adding the other ingredients to the pot."

Finding that perfect blend of hot flavors and spices for the chili pot is Ed's all-important secret. "Some seasonings, like hot pepper sauce, give an instant hot heat at the first-bite. Chili powder made with sweeter and milder Chimayo chilies gives a hotness while you're eating, and chili powder made from jalapeño peppers adds a hot and spicy ending."

Knowing when the chili is ready is important too. "Simmer the pot long enough so that it's not too watery nor too thick. If a spoon can stand up in the pot, the chili's ready for eating!"

TEX-MEX FAJITAS

◆◆◆

These tortilla roll-ups resemble the ones made throughout the Southwest from grilled beef skirt steaks. Here, we've made them the faster way with a more tender sirloin steak.

2 tablespoons vegetable oil	4 8-inch flour tortillas
¼ cup fresh lime juice	¼ teaspoon salt
2 cloves garlic, minced	1 extra large yellow onion, cut into thin strips (3 ½ cups)
1 bay leaf	
½ teaspoon dried oregano leaves	½ recipe Guacamole (page 21)
¼ teaspoon black pepper	2 plum tomatoes, chopped (¾ cup)
1 pound boneless beef sirloin steak, 1 inch thick	

⏱ PREP TIME: 30 MIN. / MARINATING TIME: 30 MIN.
COOKING TIME: 18 MIN.

1 In a large shallow glass dish, mix 1 tablespoon of the oil with the lime juice, garlic, bay leaf, oregano, and pepper. Add the steak, turning to coat with the marinade. Cover and marinate in the refrigerator for 30 minutes, turning once.

2 Preheat the grill or broiler and broiler pan. Wrap the tortillas in foil and place on the edge of the grill or in the oven. Season the steak with the salt; discard the marinade. Grill the steak over medium-hot coals, or broil 4 inches from the heat, for 5 to 6 minutes on each side for medium-rare. Slice across the grain, ¼ inch thick.

3 In a 10-inch skillet, heat the remaining oil over moderately high heat. Add the onion and sauté for 5 minutes or until browned. Fill the tortillas with the steak and onions, roll up, and place seam-side-down on a warm platter. Top with the Guacamole and sprinkle with the tomatoes. Serve with Sangria (page 37). Makes 4 servings.

1 serving: Calories 472; Saturated Fat 5 g; Total Fat 22 g; Protein 32 g; Carbohydrate 40 g; Fiber 3 g; Sodium 362 mg; Cholesterol 61 mg

◆

Chicken Fajitas

Prepare as for Tex-Mex Fajitas, substituting **1 pound skinned and boned chicken breast halves** for the beef. Grill or broil for 3 to 4 minutes on each side or until the juices run clear. *1 serving: Calories 422; Saturated Fat 4 g; Total Fat 18 g; Protein 28 g; Carbohydrate 40 g; Fiber 2 g; Sodium 362 mg; Cholesterol 53 mg*

CHIPPED BEEF

◆◆◆

Chipped, or dried, beef was once a staple in America. Its name comes from the early English meaning of chip:"to strip, or pare away, a crust." This dish is a classic Sunday supper in New England.

1 tablespoon unsalted butter or margarine	2¼ cups low-fat (1% milkfat) milk
5 ounces dried beef, rinsed, patted dry, and coarsely chopped	¼ teaspoon each black pepper and paprika
	⅛ teaspoon ground red pepper (cayenne)
3 tablespoons all-purpose flour	4 slices whole-wheat bread, toasted

⏱ PREP TIME: 5 MIN. / COOKING TIME: 12 MIN.

1 In a 12-inch nonstick skillet, melt the butter over moderate heat. Add the beef and sauté for 1 minute. Stir in the flour until the beef is well coated. Gradually stir in the milk, then the black-pepper, paprika, and ground red pepper.

2 Cook, uncovered, stirring frequently, for 10 minutes or until thickened. Spoon over the toast. Serve with a fresh green salad tossed with Roasted Tomato Vinaigrette (page 263) and hot Portland Popovers (page 310). Makes 4 servings.

1 serving: Calories 270; Saturated Fat 4 g; Total Fat 7 g; Protein 19 g; Carbohydrate 34 g; Fiber 1 g; Sodium 1209 mg; Cholesterol 46 mg

BEST BEEF STROGANOFF

◆◆◆

This dish was one of First Lady Jacquelin Kennedy's favorite recipes for White House dinners.

1 tablespoon olive oil	8 ounces fresh mushrooms, sliced ¼ inch thick (3 cups)
1½ pounds beef tenderloin, trimmed, cut into 3" - x 1"- x ¼" strips	
	½ cup Beef Stock (page 74) or low-sodium beef broth
½ teaspoon salt	
¼ teaspoon black pepper	⅔ cup reduced-fat sour cream
1 tablespoon unsalted butter or margarine	¼ cup cognac or brandy (optional)
1 small yellow onion chopped (½ cup)	3 tablespoons minced parsley

PREP TIME: 15 MIN. / COOKING TIME: 10 MIN.

1 In a 12-inch nonstick skillet, heat the oil over high heat. Brown the beef for 1 to 2 minutes, transfer to a warm platter, and season with ¼ teaspoon of the salt and the pepper.

2 Melt the butter in the skillet over moderate heat. Add the onion and sauté for 2 minutes or until tender, then stir in the mushrooms, cover, and cook for 3 minutes. Uncover and stir in the remaining ¼ teaspoon of salt and the stock. Bring to a boil, stirring to scrape up any browned bits, and boil, uncovered, for 2 minutes.

3 Remove the skillet from the heat and whisk in the sour cream until smooth. Stir in the beef and any juices that have collected on the platter. Place over low heat and stir constantly just until heated through (don't let the sauce boil).

4 If you wish, heat the cognac in a small skillet over moderate heat. Remove from the heat. Tilting the pan away from you, ignite the cognac with a wooden match and shake gently until the flame is almost out. Pour over the Stroganoff, then sprinkle with the parsley. Serve with noodles and a tossed green salad. Makes 6 servings.

1 serving: Calories 521; Saturated Fat 7 g; Total Fat 17 g; Protein 34 g; Carbohydrate 7 g; Fiber 1 g; Sodium 307 mg; Cholesterol 105 mg

Set for company: Beef Stroganoff and hot noodles with poppy seeds

BEEF-STUFFED PEPPERS

◆◆◆

4 large sweet green, red, or yellow peppers

For the stuffing:

1 tablespoon olive oil

1 small yellow onion, chopped (½ cup)

1 stalk celery, chopped (½ cup)

1 clove garlic, minced

8 ounces each lean ground beef and ground pork

1 cup cooked and drained brown or white rice

1 cup canned low-sodium, crushed tomatoes

2 tablespoons minced parsley

2 tablespoons chopped fresh basil or 2 teaspoons dried basil leaves

½ teaspoon salt, or to taste

½ teaspoon black pepper

Pinch ground red pepper (cayenne)

For the tomato sauce:

2 teaspoons vegetable oil

2 tablespoons chopped onion

1 clove garlic, minced

2 cups canned low-sodium, crushed tomatoes

⅛ teaspoon each salt and black pepper

PREP TIME: 30 MIN. / COOKING TIME: 1 HR.

1 Half-fill a large saucepan with cold water and bring to a boil over high heat. Trim the top ½ inch off of each sweet pepper; remove the seeds and ribs, being careful not to cut through the bottoms. Slide the peppers into the boiling water and simmer, uncovered, for 5 minutes. Remove with tongs or a slotted spoon and drain upside-down.

2 To prepare the stuffing: Preheat the oven to 350°F; lightly grease an 8-inch round baking dish. In a 12-inch nonstick skillet, heat the oil over moderately high heat. Add the onion, celery, and garlic and sauté for 5 minutes or until tender. Add the beef and pork and cook, stirring frequently, for 8 minutes or until no longer pink. Stir in the remaining stuffing ingredients.

3 Bring to a simmer, then remove from the heat. Spoon this mixture into the sweet peppers, and stand them upright in the baking dish. Bake, uncovered, for 40 minutes or until tender.

Ready for baking: A colorful group of Beef-Stuffed Peppers

4 To prepare the tomato sauce: In a medium-size saucepan, heat the oil over moderate heat. Add the onion and garlic; sauté for 5 minutes or until tender. Stir in the remaining ingredients and bring to a boil. Lower the heat, cover, and simmer for 10 minutes or until the flavors are blended, then spoon over the peppers. Serve with Minted Green Peas (page 226) and Fresh Fruit Salad with Poppy Seed Dressing (page 250). Makes 4 servings.

1 serving: Calories 393; Saturated Fat 6 g; Total Fat 20 g; Protein 26 g; Carbohydrate 29 g; Fiber 4 g; Sodium 438 mg; Cholesterol 79 mg

TAMALE PIE

◆◆◆

The tamale, originally an Aztec favorite of seasoned meat enclosed by cornmeal and rolled in a cornhusk, was sold by street vendors in the early days of Texas. In the early 20th century, this casserole version became popular.

For the cornmeal crust:
- 1½ cups yellow cornmeal
- 4 cups cold water
- 1 tablespoon unsalted butter or margarine
- ½ teaspoon each salt and black pepper

For the filling:
- 2 pounds lean ground beef
- 1½ cups chopped yellow onion
- 1½ cups chopped sweet green peppers
- 2 cups canned crushed tomatoes, undrained
- 2 tablespoons chili powder
- 3 cloves garlic, minced
- 1 tablespoon ground cumin
- 1 tablespoon chopped fresh oregano or 1 teaspoon dried oregano leaves
- ¼ teaspoon salt, or to taste
- 2 cups fresh or frozen corn kernels
- 2 tablespoons chopped fresh or pickled jalapeño peppers with seeds
- 1 tablespoon white wine vinegar
- ¼ cup loosely packed slivered cilantro or 1 teaspoon dried cilantro (optional)
- ½ cup pitted black olives, sliced (optional)

For the topping:
- 1½ cups shredded Cheddar cheese (6 ounces) (optional)

🕐 PREP TIME: 30 MIN. / COOKING TIME: 1¼ HR. STANDING TIME: 10 MIN.

1 To make the cornmeal crust: In a small bowl, mix the cornmeal with 1 cup of the water. In a medium-size saucepan, bring the remaining water to a boil and stir in the cornmeal mixture, butter, salt, and black pepper. Lower the heat; simmer, covered, for 35 minutes, stirring occasionally. Remove from the heat and keep warm.

2 Meanwhile, to prepare the filling: In a 6-quart Dutch oven over moderate heat, sauté the beef for 10 minutes or until browned. Using a slotted spoon, transfer to a bowl. Pour off all but 1 tablespoon of the drippings.

3 Add the onion and green peppers to the Dutch oven and sauté for 5 minutes or until crisp-tender. Return the meat to the pan, along with any juices that have collected, and stir in the tomatoes, chili powder, garlic, cumin, oregano, and salt. Bring to a boil, then lower the heat and simmer, uncovered, for 20 minutes, stirring occasionally. Stir in the remaining filling ingredients and remove from the heat. (The filling may be made the day before, then refrigerated. Reheat, stirring, over moderate heat, before assembling the pie.)

4 Preheat the oven to 400°F. Grease a deep 12-inch ovenproof skillet or 13" x 9" x 2" baking dish. Using a rubber spatula, spread half of the cornmeal mixture on the bottom and up the sides of the skillet, then carefully spoon the meat filling into the crust. Spread the remaining cornmeal on top and sprinkle with the cheese if you wish.

5 Bake for 30 minutes or until the top is golden brown and bubbling. Let the pie stand for 10 minutes before cutting. Serve with a salad of mixed greens tossed with Buttermilk Dressing (page 260). Makes 10 servings.

---

1 serving: Calories 389; Saturated Fat 6 g; Total Fat 16 g; Protein 26 g; Carbohydrate 36 g; Fiber 2 g; Sodium 523 mg; Cholesterol 74 mg

Beef is the soul of cooking.

—Marie Antoine Caréme

New England Boiled Dinner

In years past, this one-dish meal was put on to cook after Sunday breakfast, then served at noonday following church services. Any leftovers were traditionally turned into Red Flannel Hash (opposite page).

1	**corned beef brisket (4 to 5 pounds), rinsed and trimmed**
4	**medium-size beets (1 pound), scrubbed and trimmed**
1	**medium-size green cabbage (2 pounds), cut into 6 wedges and cored**
12	**small red-skinned potatoes (1¾ pounds), scrubbed and halved**
10	**small white onions (1 pound), peeled**
6	**large carrots (1 pound), peeled and cut into chunks**
4	**large white turnips (1 pound), peeled and quartered**
1	**tablespoon unsalted butter or margarine**
2	**tablespoons all-purpose flour**
1	**tablespoon red wine vinegar**
½	**cup reduced-fat sour cream**
2	**tablespoons Dijon mustard with seeds**
	Prepared horseradish (optional)

PREP TIME: 25 MIN. / COOKING TIME: 2¼ HR.

1 Place the corned beef in a 6-quart Dutch oven and add enough cold water to cover it by 2-inches. Bring to a boil over high heat, skimming the surface occasionally. Lower the heat, cover, and simmer for 2 hours.

2 While the corned beef is cooking, place the beets in a medium-size saucepan, add cold water to cover, and bring to a boil over high heat. Lower the heat and simmer, uncovered, for 30 minutes or until tender. Drain the beets, rinse with cold water, then peel. Return to the saucepan, cover, and keep warm.

3 Add the cabbage, potatoes, onions, carrots, and turnips to the pot with the corned beef and return to a boil over high heat. Lower the heat, cover, and simmer, for 20 minutes or until the vegetables are tender. Remove the beef to a

◆ An Old Yankee Tradition ◆

About the name of Red Flannel Hash, stories abound. Some believe that it comes from its likeness (in color) to red flannel underwear. Others suggest it was named by members of the Yale Club because the reddish hue reminded them of the crimson battle colors of their rival university, Harvard.

Whatever its origin, Red Flannel Hash almost always is made from beets plus other vegetables and meat. Most people agree that it was first invented as a creative way to use up the leftovers from New England boiled dinner.

When making this dish, take a tip from a Yankee gentleman: "Chop all the ingredients instead of grinding them, then cook the hash until it's crisp and evenly browned."

In Rhode Island, it's traditional to top each serving with a poached egg. Most New Englanders suggest passing chili sauce on the side.

warm serving platter, reserving 1½ cups of the cooking liquid. Surround the meat with the beets and other vegetables and keep warm.

4 In a small saucepan, melt the butter over moderate heat. Whisk in the flour and cook, stirring constantly, for 1 minute, or until bubbly, then add the reserved cooking liquid and the vinegar. Bring to a boil and cook, stirring frequently, for 4 minutes or until slightly thickened. Remove from the heat and whisk in the sour cream and mustard. Carve the corned beef and serve with the vegetables and sauce, plus the horseradish if you wish. Serve with Boston Brown Bread (page 302). Makes 8 servings.

1 serving: Calories 455; Saturated Fat 7 g; Total Fat 23 g; Protein 25 g; Carbohydrate 34 g; Fiber 2 g; Sodium 824 mg; Cholesterol 90 mg

RED FLANNEL HASH

◆◆◆

3 medium-size russet
   potatoes, scrubbed
   (1½ pounds)

3 small beets,
   scrubbed (8 ounces)

1 large yellow onion,
   root end removed

½ teaspoon black
   pepper

⅛ teaspoon ground red
   pepper (cayenne), or
   to taste

8 ounces cooked
   corned beef, cut into
   ½-inch pieces
   (2 cups)

2 tablespoons unsalted
   butter or margarine

PREP TIME: 15 MIN. / COOKING TIME: 1 HR.

1 Preheat the oven to 450°F. Line a 13" x 9" x 2" baking pan with foil. Wrap the potatoes in foil. Arrange the potatoes, beets, and onion in the pan. Roast for 45 minutes or until the vegetables are tender. Let cool, then peel, dice, and place in a large bowl. In a cup, mix the black and ground red peppers, then sprinkle on the vegetables. Stir in the corned beef.

2 Preheat the broiler. In a 12-inch nonstick skillet, melt the butter over moderate heat. Spread the hash in the skillet; cook, uncovered, for 10 minutes or until the underside is browned. Wrap the skillet handle with foil. Broil the hash, 4 inches from the heat, for 5 minutes or until brown and crisp. Serve with Portland Popovers (page 310) and slices of fresh tomatoes, sweet green peppers, and cucumbers. Makes 4 servings.

*1 serving: Calories 361; Saturated Fat 6 g;
Total Fat 15 g; Protein 14 g; Carbohydrate 42 g; Fiber 1 g;
Sodium 642 mg; Cholesterol 66 mg*

New England Boiled Dinner: A Yankee version of corned beef and cabbage

100

A taste of the foods eaten by some Native Americans: Indian Corn Stew

INDIAN CORN STEW

Pueblo Indians often simmered large pots of meat stew over an open fire, adding fresh vegetables such as corn and squash to the pot.

- 1 tablespoon vegetable oil
- 1½ pounds lean ground beef
- 1½ cups sweet green peppers, cored, seeded, and chopped
- 1 large yellow onion, chopped (1½ cups)
- 2 cloves garlic, minced
- 8 large ears of corn, kernels cut off, or 4 cups frozen corn
- 1 can (14 ounces) crushed tomatoes
- 4 teaspoons Worcestershire sauce
- ½ teaspoon each black pepper and chili powder
- ¼ teaspoon salt
- ⅛ teaspoon ground red pepper (cayenne), or to taste
- 1 medium-size zucchini or yellow summer squash, thinly sliced crosswise (2 cups)

PREP TIME: 20 MIN. / COOKING TIME: 35 MIN.

1 In a 6-quart Dutch oven, heat the oil over moderately high heat. Add the beef and cook, stirring frequently, for 8 minutes or until browned. Lower the heat, stir in the green peppers, onion, and garlic and simmer, uncovered, for 5 minutes or until tender, stirring occasionally.

2 Stir in the corn, tomatoes, Worcestershire, black pepper, chili powder, salt, and red pepper and bring to a boil. Lower the heat, cover, and simmer for 15 minutes; add the squash, then simmer 5 minutes longer or until the vegetables are tender. Serve with slices of Anadama Bread (page 293). Tip: Any extras may be frozen for up to 1 month. Makes 6 servings.

1 serving: Calories 397; Saturated Fat 6 g; Total Fat 18 g; Protein 27 g; Carbohydrate 37 g; Fiber 1 g; Sodium 337 mg; Cholesterol 70 mg

THIS IS IT! MEAT LOAF

◆◆◆

*This stick-to-the-ribs meat loaf is
adapted from the one that Craig Josephs mixes
at a down-home Texas eatery in Houston
called This Is It! Bar and Grill.*

1 tablespoon vegetable oil	2 large eggs, beaten
1 cup finely chopped celery	1 tablespoon all-purpose flour
1 cup finely chopped yellow onion	¾ teaspoon salt, or to taste
1 cup finely chopped sweet green pepper	¼ teaspoon black pepper
2 cloves garlic, minced	4 strips lean bacon (optional)
1 tablespoon finely chopped fresh or pickled jalapeño pepper with seeds	1 can (8 ounces) low-sodium tomato sauce (1 cup)
2 pounds lean ground beef	1 small tomato, finely chopped (½ cup)

PREP TIME: 20 MIN. / COOKING TIME: 1½ HR.
STANDING TIME: 10 MIN.

1 Preheat the oven to 350°F and lightly grease a 13" x 9" x 2" baking dish. In a 12-inch nonstick skillet, heat the oil over moderately high heat. Add the celery, onion, green pepper, garlic and jalapeño pepper and sauté for 5 minutes or until tender. Transfer to a large bowl.

2 Add the beef, eggs, flour, salt, and black pepper. Using your hands, mix well, then put the mixture in the baking dish and shape into a 9- x 6-inch loaf. If you wish, drape the bacon diagonally on top. In a small bowl, combine the tomato sauce and the tomato, then pour over all.

3 Bake, uncovered, for 1¼ hours or until an instant-read thermometer inserted in the center registers 160°F. Transfer to a warm platter; let stand for10 minutes. Slice and serve with Hash Browns (page 226). Makes 8 servings.

*1 serving: Calories 279; Saturated Fat 6 g;
Total Fat 17 g; Protein 33 g; Carbohydrate 7 g; Fiber 0 g;
Sodium 337 mg; Cholesterol 109 mg*

18 CARATS HASH

◆◆◆

*In 1850, diners at the Eldorado Hotel
in Hangtown, California, often found two types of
hash on the menu: Low Grade Hash for
75 cents and the top-quality choice of
18 Carats Hash for $1.00.*

1 tablespoon vegetable oil	½ cup plus 2 tablespoons Beef Stock (page 74) or low-sodium beef broth
1 small yellow onion, chopped (½ cup)	¼ teaspoon each salt and black pepper
1¼ pounds cooked roast beef, cut into ½-inch cubes (about 3 cups)	½ teaspoon Worcestershire sauce
3 medium-size all-purpose potatoes, peeled, cubed, and cooked (3 cups)	2 tablespoons minced parsley

PREP TIME: 15 MIN. / COOKING TIME: 17 MIN.

1 In 12-inch nonstick skillet, heat the oil over moderately high heat. Sauté the onion for 5 minutes or until tender. Stir in the roast beef, potatoes, ½ cup of the stock, the salt, pepper, and Worcestershire, and cook for 5 minutes, stirring. Lower the heat, add the remaining stock and the parsley, stirring to scrape up any browned bits.

2 Preheat the broiler. Wrap the skillet handle with foil and broil the hash, 5 inches from the heat, for 5 minutes or until browned and crisp. Serve with steamed spinach and San Francisco Sourdough (page 290). Makes 4 servings.

*1 serving: Calories 443; Saturated Fat 6 g;
Total Fat 17 g; Protein 47 g; Carbohydrate 22 g; Fiber 1 g;
Sodium 258 mg; Cholesterol 136 mg*

◆

Today's Hash

Prepare as for 18 Carats Hash, adding ¾ **cup each chopped, cooked sweet green pepper and carrots** with the potato. *1 serving: Calories 458; Saturated Fat 6 g; Total Fat 17 g; Protein 48 g; Carbohydrate 26 g; Fiber 3 g; Sodium 273 mg; Cholesterol 136 mg*

SHEPHERD'S PIE

This British dish, adopted long ago by Americans, is a meat and vegetable combination baked under a "crust" of mashed potatoes.

- 4 large all-purpose potatoes, peeled, cooked, and drained
- 1 tablespoon unsalted butter or margarine, melted
- ¼ cup low-fat (1% milkfat) milk
- ¼ cup minced parsley
- ¾ teaspoon salt
- ½ teaspoon black pepper
- 1½ pounds lean ground beef or lamb
- 1 large clove garlic, minced
- 1 tablespoon vegetable oil

- 4 large carrots, peeled and chopped (2 cups)
- 4 ounces fresh mushrooms chopped (1½ cups)
- 1 large yellow onion, chopped (1½ cups)
- 1 tablespoon chopped fresh thyme or 1 teaspoon dried thyme leaves
- 1 cup Chicken Stock (page 74) or low-sodium chicken broth
- 1 tablespoon all-purpose flour
- 1 package (10 ounces) frozen corn, thawed

PREP TIME: 30 MIN. / COOKING TIME: 1 HR.

1 Preheat the oven to 375°F and set out a 2-quart round baking dish or deep 9-inch pie plate. Mash the potatoes, mixing in the butter, milk, parsley, ½ teaspoon of the salt, and ¼ teaspoon of the pepper. Set aside.

2 In a 12-inch nonstick skillet, sauté the beef and garlic over moderately high heat for 10 minutes or until browned; transfer to a bowl.

3 In the same skillet, heat the oil and sauté the carrots, mushrooms, and onion for 5 minutes. Stir in the thyme and the remaining ¼ teaspoon each of salt and pepper.

4 In a cup, stir the stock and flour until smooth; stir into the skillet. Bring to a boil, lower the heat, and simmer, uncovered, stirring occasionally, for 10 minutes or until thickened slightly. Add the corn, beef, and any juices that have collected in the bowl; spread the mixture in the baking dish.

A deep-dish Shepherd's Pie—
topped with a piping of fluffy mashed potatoes

5 Using a pastry bag fitted with a large rosette tip, pipe the potato mixture in diagonal strips on top of the pie, or use a small spoon to make a ring of rosettes. Bake, uncovered, for 30 minutes or until bubbly. Serve with Chopped Tomato Salad (page 256). Makes 6 servings.

1 serving: Calories 529; Saturated Fat 11 g; Total Fat 28 g; Protein 26 g; Carbohydrate 44 g; Fiber 6 g; Sodium 380 mg; Cholesterol 89 mg

SALISBURY STEAK
◆◆◆

*This broiled patty of beef was named
for Dr. J. H. Salisbury who, in the late 1800's,
advocated eating beef three times
a day for health reasons.*

1	pound lean ground beef round or sirloin	½	teaspoon black pepper
¼	cup chopped yellow onion	¼	teaspoon salt
2	tablespoons minced parsley	2	strips lean bacon, cooked crisp, drained, and crumbled

PREP TIME: 15 MIN. / COOKING TIME: 8 MIN.

1 Preheat the broiler and line a broiling pan with foil. In a large bowl, using your hands or a spoon, mix all the ingredients except the bacon. Form the mixture into 4 oval patties, each about 1 inch thick. Place on the broiler pan.

2 Broil the patties 3 inches from the heat for 5 minutes; turn and press the bacon into the uncooked side. Broil 3 minutes longer or until the meat is the way you like it. Serve with Steak Fries (page 230). Makes 4 servings. Tip: For 8 servings, just double the recipe.

*1 serving: Calories 238; Saturated Fat 6 g;
Total Fat 15 g; Protein 22 g; Carbohydrate 1 g; Fiber 0 g;
Sodium 244 mg; Cholesterol 73 mg*

Ground, chopped,
minced, or hashed beef
grew up with
the United States.

—*James Beard*

SMORGASBORD MEATBALLS
◆◆◆

*Made with a soft paste (panade) of bread,
milk, and egg, these meatballs resemble the ones
made by Norwegian Americans.*

1	large egg	¼	teaspoon each salt and black pepper, or to taste
1	cup ½-inch cubes white bread (2 slices)	1	pound lean ground beef
2	tablespoons low-fat (1% milkfat) milk	1	tablespoon vegetable oil
2	tablespoons finely chopped onion	1	cup Beef Stock (page 74) or low-sodium beef broth
2	tablespoons snipped fresh dill or 2 teaspoons dried dillweed	1	cup reduced-fat sour cream
½	teaspoon ground nutmeg		Paprika

PREP TIME: 30 MIN. / COOKING TIME: 30 MIN.

1 In a large bowl, beat the egg lightly, then mix in the bread cubes and milk. Let stand for 10 minutes to form a smooth paste. Stir in the onion, dill, nutmeg, salt, and pepper. Using your hands or a spoon, mix in the beef just until blended, then roll into 20 meatballs, 1½ inches in diameter.

2 In a 12-inch nonstick skillet, heat the oil over moderate heat. Add the meatballs and cook, turning often, for 10 minutes or until browned. Add the stock and bring to a boil, then lower the heat and simmer, uncovered, for 5 minutes, stirring occasionally. With a slotted spoon, transfer to a warm platter, leaving the drippings in the skillet.

3 Whisk the sour cream into the skillet, add the meatballs, and stir constantly over low heat for 3 minutes or just until heated through (don't let the mixture boil). Sprinkle with paprika, plus extra nutmeg if you wish. Serve over hot egg noodles tossed with poppy seeds. Makes 4 servings.

*1 serving: Calories 379; Saturated Fat 9 g;
Total Fat 23 g; Protein 27 g; Carbohydrate 16 g; Fiber 0 g;
Sodium 391 mg; Cholesterol 138 mg*

APPLE-STUFFED PORK CHOPS

◆◆◆

*Eating "high on the hog" has long been an
American tradition; pork was the most widely eaten
meat here until the early 20th century. Now
being bred with less fat, it is gaining
in favor once again.*

1 tablespoon unsalted butter or margarine	½ teaspoon salt, or to taste
2 stalks celery, finely chopped (1 cup)	¼ teaspoon ground nutmeg
1 small yellow onion, chopped (½ cup)	4 loin pork chops with bone, 1 inch thick (8 ounces each)
1 Granny Smith apple, peeled, cored, and chopped (1 cup)	1 tablespoon olive oil
1 cup ½-inch cubes white bread (2 slices)	2 cups cold water
¼ cup chopped walnuts	¼ cup all-purpose flour
¼ cup dark raisins	**Optional garnishes:**
1 tablespoon packed light brown sugar	1 unpeeled Granny Smith apple, cored, and cut into thin slices
1 teaspoon cider vinegar	Parsley sprigs

PREP TIME: 30 MIN. / COOKING TIME: 1 HR.

1 In a 12-inch nonstick skillet, melt the butter over moderate heat. Add the celery and onion and sauté for 5 minutes or until crisp-tender. Stir in the apple and cook 2 minutes longer or until lightly browned. Mix in the bread cubes, walnuts, raisins, sugar, vinegar, ¼ teaspoon of the salt, and the nutmeg, then remove from the heat.

2 With a sharp pointed knife, horizontally cut a pocket in each chop, cutting towards the bone. Stuff the pockets with the apple mixture and close tightly with toothpicks. Sprinkle the chops with the remaining ¼ teaspoon of salt.

3 In the same skillet, heat the oil over moderately high heat. Brown the chops for 5 minutes on each side. Add 1¾ cups of the water, bring to a boil, lower the heat, cover, and simmer for 35 minutes or until tender. Transfer the chops to a warm platter, reserving the pan drippings; remove the toothpicks.

4 In a cup, whisk the flour and remaining ¼ cup of water. Stir the mixture into the pan drippings, bring to a boil, and cook, uncovered, for 2 minutes, then spoon over the chops. Garnish with the apple slices and parsley sprigs if you wish. Serve with Sweet Potato Fries (page 231). Makes 4 servings.

*1 serving: Calories 395; Saturated Fat 7g;
Total Fat 21 g; Protein 21 g; Carbohydrate 31 g; Fiber 1 g;
Sodium 535 mg; Cholesterol 67 mg*

CIDER-BAKED PORK CHOPS

◆◆◆

*"Here's a terrific all-purpose marinade for pork
roasts as well as chops," writes Esther Ver Meer.*

½ cup sweet apple cider or apple juice	1 clove garlic, minced
4 teaspoons fresh lemon juice	⅛ teaspoon black pepper
4 teaspoons reduced-sodium soy sauce	4 loin pork chops with bone, 1 inch thick (8 ounces each)
2 teaspoons honey	

PREP TIME: 10 MIN. / MARINATING TIME: 2 HR.
COOKING TIME: 25 MIN.

1 In a large shallow glass baking dish, mix the cider, lemon juice, soy sauce, honey, garlic, and pepper. Arrange the chops in a single layer and turn to coat. Cover with plastic wrap and marinate in the refrigerator for at least 2 hours or overnight, turning the chops several times.

2 Preheat the oven to 400°F. Drain off all but ¼ cup of the marinade and reserve. Bake the chops, uncovered, turning once and basting frequently with the reserved marinade, for 25 minutes or until the way you like them. Serve with 'Tater Boats (page 229). Makes 4 servings.

*1 serving: Calories 252; Saturated Fat 4 g;
Total Fat 13 g; Protein 24 g; Carbohydrate 3 g; Fiber 0 g;
Sodium 123 mg; Cholesterol 83 mg*

APRICOT-GLAZED PORK LOIN
◆◆◆

Esther Ver Meer and her husband Owen own a 375-acre farm in Leighton, Iowa, where they raise hogs, corn, and oats. "Cooking with pork is second nature to me. I always do a pork roast inside a cooking bag to keep it moist."

2	cloves garlic, minced
1½	teaspoons salt
1½	teaspoons chopped fresh rosemary or ½ teaspoon dried rosemary leaves
¾	teaspoon chopped fresh thyme or ¼ teaspoon dried thyme leaves
½	teaspoon paprika
¼	teaspoon black pepper
1	boneless pork loin roast (4 pounds), trimmed and tied

1	oven cooking bag (14 x 20 inches) with a nylon tie
1	tablespoon all-purpose flour

For the apricot glaze:

1	jar (12 ounces) apricot preserves
¼	cup light corn syrup
2	tablespoons cider vinegar
½	teaspoon dry mustard
1	recipe Curried Fruit Medley, page 271 (optional)

PREP TIME: 15 MIN. / MARINATING TIME: 30 MIN.
COOKING TIME: 2 HR.

1 In a small bowl, combine the garlic, salt, rosemary, thyme, paprika, and pepper, then rub into the roast, coating it completely. Cover tightly with plastic wrap and refrigerate for 30 minutes.

2 Preheat the oven to 325°F and set out a 13" x 9" x 2" baking pan. Spoon the flour into the cooking bag and shake to coat the inside. Unwrap the roast, place it in the bag, secure the opening with the nylon tie, then place in the pan. Using scissors, cut six ½-inch slits in the top of the bag. Roast for 1½ hours.

3 To prepare the apricot glaze: In a small saucepan, combine the glaze ingredients; stir over moderately low heat until the mixture begins to bubble, then simmer for 1 minute.

Apricot-Glazed Pork Loin: Simple yet elegant fare, presented with hot curried fruits

4 Remove the roast from the oven, cut the bag open, and fold down the sides, being careful of the steam. Pour the glaze over the roast. Cook, uncovered, 30 minutes longer or until an instant-read thermometer inserted in the center registers 160°F. Transfer the roast to a large warm platter, remove the ties, and surround with Curried Fruit Medley (page 271). Serve with the pan juices if you wish and Wild Rice with Pecans (page 207). Makes 12 servings.

1 serving: 342 Calories; Saturated Fat 4 g; Total Fat 11 g; Protein 33 g; Carbohydrate 26 g; Fiber 0 g; Sodium 374 mg; Cholesterol 95 mg

SWEET AND SOUR PORK

Chinese culinary influences in America, such as combining sweet and tart flavors in main dishes, date back to the mid-19th century, when Chinese housemen cooked in California homes.

12 ounces boneless pork loin, trimmed and cut into 1-inch cubes	1 each large sweet green and red pepper, cored, seeded, and cut into thin strips
1 tablespoon sherry or orange juice	1 medium-size yellow onion, coarsely chopped (1 cup)
⅛ teaspoon each salt and black pepper	2 cups fresh or canned and drained pineapple chunks
1 large egg white, lightly beaten	¾ cup cold water
3 tablespoons cornstarch	¼ cup ketchup
2 tablespoons olive oil	2 tablespoons sugar
1 clove garlic, minced	2 tablespoons red wine vinegar
1 teaspoon minced fresh ginger or ½ teaspoon ground ginger	1 tablespoon low-sodium soy sauce
2 small carrots, peeled and thinly sliced on the diagonal (1 cup)	4 cups hot cooked long-grain white rice

PREP TIME: 35 MIN. / STANDING TIME: 15 MIN.
COOKING TIME: 15 MIN.

1 In a medium-size bowl, combine the pork, sherry, salt, and black pepper and let stand for 15 minutes. In a small bowl, mix the egg white and 2 tablespoons of the cornstarch until smooth. Add the pork mixture and toss until well combined.

2 In a wok or heavy 12-inch skillet, heat 1 tablespoon of the oil over moderately high heat. Add the pork and stir-fry for 4 minutes or until golden. Using a slotted spoon, transfer to a plate and keep warm.

3 Heat the remaining 1 tablespoon of oil in the wok. Add the garlic and ginger and sauté for 30 seconds or until fragrant. Add the carrots, sweet peppers, and onion. Stir-fry for 5 minutes

A favorite Chinese-American dish:
Sweet and Sour Pork over steaming hot rice

or until crisp-tender, then stir in the pineapple. Cook 1 minute more or until heated through. Using a slotted spoon, transfer to a plate.

4 In a small bowl, stir a little of the water with the remaining 1 tablespoon of cornstarch until smooth. Stir in the remaining water, ketchup, sugar, vinegar, and soy sauce. Pour the mixture into the wok, bring to a boil, and cook for 2 minutes or until slightly thickened. Stir in the pork, any juices that have collected, and the vegetables. Bring to a boil and cook 1 minute longer or until heated through. Spoon over the rice. Follow this course with orange segments and fortune cookies. Makes 4 servings.

1 serving: Calories 610; Saturated Fat 4 g; Total Fat 14 g; Protein 27 g; Carbohydrate 93 g; Fiber 5 g; Sodium 443 mg; Cholesterol 54 mg

CHOP SUEY

◆◆◆

2 tablespoons vegetable oil	1½ cups sliced fresh mushrooms
1 pound boneless pork loin, trimmed and cut into thin strips	1 cup canned sliced water chestnuts
4 cups shredded green cabbage	1 cup fresh, or canned and drained, bean sprouts
2 medium-size yellow onions, thinly sliced	1 cup Chicken Stock (page 74) or low-sodium chicken broth
1½ cups sliced celery	3 tablespoons reduced-sodium soy sauce
2 cups sweet red pepper strips	2 tablespoons rice wine (sake) or Chicken Stock
1 tablespoon minced fresh ginger or 1 teaspoon ground ginger	2 tablespoons cornstarch
2 cloves garlic, minced	6 cups hot cooked long-grain white rice
¼ teaspoon black pepper	

PREP TIME: 30 MIN. / COOKING TIME: 15 MIN.

1 In a wok or deep 12-inch skillet, heat 1 tablespoon of the oil over moderately high heat. Add the pork and stir-fry for 5 minutes. Using a slotted spoon, transfer to a plate and keep warm.

2 Heat the remaining 1 tablespoon of oil in the wok; add the cabbage, onions, celery, sweet red pepper, ginger, garlic, and black pepper. Stir-fry for 5 minutes or just until the cabbage starts to wilt. Add the mushrooms, water chestnuts, and bean sprouts and stir-fry 3 minutes more, then stir in the cooked pork.

3 In a small bowl, whisk the stock with the soy sauce, wine, and cornstarch; stir the mixture into the wok. Increase the heat to high, bring to a boil, and cook, uncovered, for 1 minute or until the sauce thickens. Place the rice in a large shallow bowl and spoon the Chop Suey on top. Serve with Tomato Aspic (page 258) Makes 6 servings.

1 serving: Calories 510; Saturated Fat 3 g; Total Fat 11 g; Protein 26 g; Carbohydrate 75 g; Fiber 5 g; Sodium 386 mg; Cholesterol 48 mg

◆

Chicken Chop Suey

Prepare the Chop Suey, substituting **1 pound of boned and skinned chicken breasts, cut into thin strips,** for the pork loin. *1 serving: Calories 473; Saturated Fat 1 g; Total Fat 7 g; Protein 27 g; Carbohydrate 75 g; Fiber 5 g; Sodium 385 mg; Cholesterol 27 mg*

Chop Suey with Shrimp

Prepare the Chop Suey, substituting **1 to 1½ pounds of shelled and deveined medium-size shrimp** for the pork loin. *1 serving: Calories 470; Saturated Fat 1 g; Total Fat 6 g; Protein 25 g; Carbohydrate 76 g; Fiber 5 g; Sodium 448 mg; Cholesterol 116 mg*

Chopped Up Odds 'n Ends

Many of the meals for the gangs of workmen, who helped build the transcontinental railroad in the 1800's, were prepared by male Chinese cooks. These men often created concoctions of meats and vegetables, which became known as Chop Suey.

Although no such dish existed in China, the name given to it here possibly derived from the Mandarin words *tsa sui,* meaning "chopped up odds and ends." When spoken by Americans, these words might easily have sounded like chop suey.

Honey Baked Ham—Dressed up for Easter Sunday with a garland of fresh spring vegetables

HONEY BAKED HAM
◆◆◆

As in years past, many Southerners still gather around a Sunday dinner table that features a luscious hickory-smoked ham.

1	**fully-cooked smoked whole ham with bone (12 to 16 pounds), trimmed**
3	**tablespoons whole cloves**
1½	**cups firmly packed light brown sugar**
2	**tablespoons all-purpose flour**

2	**tablespoons each honey and fresh orange juice**
2	**tablespoons orange marmalade**
1	**tablespoon Dijon mustard with seeds**
1	**teaspoon each ground cinnamon and ground nutmeg**

PREP TIME: 15 MIN. / COOKING TIME: 2¼ HR.
STANDING TIME: 15 MIN.

1 Preheat the oven to 325°F. Place the ham, fat side up, on a rack in a large roasting pan. Using a small sharp knife, score the fat into diamonds and stud with the cloves. Pour 1 inch of hot water into the pan and bake, uncovered, 1¾ hours for a 12-pound ham, 2¼ hours for a 16-pound ham.

2 While the ham is baking, mix the remaining ingredients in a small bowl until smooth. Remove the ham from the oven and with a sharp pointed knife, carefully remove the tough skin from the shank end. Using a spatula, spread the glaze over the ham. Continue baking 30 minutes longer or until the outside is browned and glazed.

3 Transfer to a warm platter, remove the cloves, and let stand for 15 minutes before slicing. If you wish, surround with Sweet Potato Puffs in orange cups (page 361), steamed baby carrots, and cherry tomatoes; serve Beth's Buttermilk Biscuits (page 306) too. Makes 24 to 30 servings.

*1 serving: Calories 263; Saturated Fat 3 g;
Total Fat 8 g; Protein 29 g; Carbohydrate 19 g; Fiber 0 g;
Sodium 1657 mg; Cholesterol 72 mg*

SCHNITZ-UN-GNEPP

◆◆◆

In Pennsylvania Dutch land, schnitz has evolved to mean dried apples, which are often served with gnepp (dumplings), as in this hearty fare.

8 ounces dried apples (2 cups)	2 cups sifted all-purpose flour
3 cups boiling water	1 tablespoon baking powder
1 fully-cooked smoked ham shank with bone (5 to 7 pounds)	¼ teaspoon salt
	1 large egg, beaten
1½ quarts sweet apple cider (6 cups)	1 cup low-fat (1% milkfat) milk
2 tablespoons light brown sugar	2 tablespoons unsalted butter or margarine, melted

PREP TIME: 30 MIN. / COOKING TIME: 1¾ HR.

1 Put the dried apples in a medium-size bowl. Pour in the boiling water, cover, and let stand for 10 minutes. Drain and set the apples aside.

2 Meanwhile, place the ham in an 8-quart stockpot, cover with cold water, and bring to a boil over high heat. Lower the heat, cover, and simmer for 1 hour. Carefully discard the cooking liquid, then add the cider, apples, and brown sugar and bring to a boil over high heat. Lower the heat, cover, and simmer for 30 minutes. Transfer the ham to a platter, surround with the apples, and keep warm.

3 To prepare the dumplings: In a large bowl, stir the flour, baking powder, and salt. In a small bowl, whisk the egg, milk, and butter, then pour into the flour mixture and stir just until blended. Drop the dumplings by heaping tablespoons into the simmering cooking liquid. Cover and simmer for 10 minutes or until cooked in the center (page 363). Using a slotted spoon, transfer the dumplings to the serving platter; ladle the cider over the top. Serve with steamed snap peas. Makes 12 to 16 servings.

1 serving (for 12): Calories 390; Saturated Fat 5 g; Total Fat 13 g; Protein 29 g; Carbohydrate 59 g; Fiber 1 g; Sodium 951 mg; Cholesterol 89 mg

HAM AND RED-EYE GRAVY

◆◆◆

As the legend goes, Andrew Jackson once asked his whiskey-drinking cook to "bring some ham and gravy as red as your eyes." And that's how the pan gravy from country ham was named.

1 cup quick-cooking hominy grits	1 tablespoon instant espresso coffee powder
1 center-cut ham steak, ½ inch thick, trimmed (1 to 1¼ pounds)	1 cup boiling water

PREP TIME: 5 MIN. / COOKING TIME: 25 MIN.

1 Prepare the grits according to the package directions. While the grits are cooking, heat a heavy 12-inch skillet (preferably a cast iron one) over moderately high heat until a droplet of water sizzles when added to the skillet. Add the ham steak and cook for 5 minutes on each side or until browned. Remove to a warm platter.

2 Stir the coffee powder into the boiling water, then into the skillet. Simmer for 1 minute, stirring constantly to get up all the browned bits. Spoon the grits next to the ham steak and pour the red-eye gravy over all. Serve with Creole Okra and Tomatoes (page 223) and a basketful of Hush Puppies (page 299). Makes 4 servings.

1 serving: Calories 349; Saturated Fat 4 g; Total Fat 11 g; Protein 29 g; Carbohydrate 32 g; Fiber 0 g; Sodium 1704 mg; Cholesterol 67 mg

Fried Ham and Red-Eye Gravy is a breakfast institution.

—from *The Smithfield Cookbook* by the Junior Women's Club of Smithfield, Virginia

STIR-FRY PORK

Ellen Hankes a farmer and a home economist in Fairbury, Illinois, combines pork with the popular Chinese technique of stir-frying.

2 tablespoons vegetable oil	3 tablespoons reduced-sodium soy sauce, or to taste
1 pound pork tenderloin, cut into ½-inch strips	2 tablespoons cornstarch
2 cloves garlic, minced	8 ounces fresh, or frozen and thawed, snow peas, trimmed (2 cups)
2 stalks celery, thinly sliced on the diagonal (1 cup)	
1 medium-size yellow onion, thinly sliced	1 pint cherry tomatoes, stemmed and halved (2 cups)
1 tablespoon grated fresh ginger or 1 teaspoon ground ginger	1 cup sliced, canned water chestnuts
1½ cups cold water	3 cups hot cooked long-grain white rice

PREP TIME: 25 MIN. / COOKING TIME: 10 MIN.

1 In a wok or 12-inch nonstick skillet, heat the oil over high heat. Add the pork and stir-fry for 2 minutes or just until no longer pink. Using a slotted spoon, transfer the pork to a plate. Add the garlic, celery, onion, and ginger. Stir-fry for 3 minutes or until almost tender.

2 In a measuring cup, whisk together the water, soy sauce, and cornstarch; add to the wok with the snow peas, tomatoes, and water chestnuts. Cook 2 minutes longer or until the sauce thickens and the vegetables are crisp-tender.

3 Return the pork to the wok with any juices that have collected on the plate, then heat 1 minute longer or until hot. Serve as a one-dish meal over the rice, followed by a dessert of assorted fresh fruits such as orange sections, strawberries, and pineapple spears. Makes 4 servings.

1 serving: Calories 493; Saturated Fat 2 g; Total Fat 11 g; Protein 33 g; Carbohydrate 65 g; Fiber 3 g; Sodium 409 mg; Cholesterol 74 mg

CITY CHICKEN

During the Depression of the 1930's, pork was less expensive than chicken. This dish became a favorite—and still is today, especially in Pennsylvania. If you prefer, substitute 1 pound boned and skinned chicken thighs for the veal.

8 ounces boneless pork loin, cut into 1-inch cubes	2 teaspoons snipped fresh rosemary or 2 teaspoons dried rosemary leaves
8 ounces boneless veal loin, cut into 1-inch cubes	½ teaspoon black pepper
1 large egg	1 tablespoon unsalted butter or margarine
1 tablespoon cold water	1 tablespoon olive oil
¾ cup seasoned dry bread crumbs	¾ cup Chicken Stock (page 74) or low-sodium chicken broth

PREP TIME: 15 MIN. / COOKING TIME: 20 MIN.

1 Preheat the oven to 350°F. Alternately thread cubes of pork and veal onto eight 9-inch skewers (preferably wooden ones). In a pie plate or shallow dish, whisk the egg with the water. On a piece of wax paper, mix the bread crumbs, rosemary, and pepper. Roll the skewered meat in the egg mixture, then in the crumbs, pressing gently to coat completely.

2 In an ovenproof 12-inch skillet or a shallow 2-quart casserole, heat the butter and oil over moderately high heat. Brown the skewered meat, turning frequently, for 6 minutes or until golden-brown on all sides.

3 Wrap the skillet handle with foil. Pour in the stock, cover, and bake for 13 minutes or just until the juices no longer run pink. Serve with O'Brien Potatoes (page 227), and Carrot-Raisin Slaw (page 253). Makes 4 servings.

1 serving: Calories 309; Saturated Fat 5 g; Total Fat 14 g; Protein 29 g; Carbohydrate 15 g; Fiber 1 g; Sodium 269 mg; Cholesterol 142 mg

Shashlik on Rice Pilau (page 203): An American cook-out with a Slavic accent

Shashlik

◆◆◆

Brought to America by Russian immigrants, Shashlik is their version of Shish Kebab.

1 cup dry red wine (with or without alcohol)

¼ cup olive oil

4 cloves garlic, minced

3 tablespoons red wine vinegar

3 bay leaves

1 tablespoon chopped fresh oregano or 1 teaspoon dried oregano leaves

½ teaspoon black pepper

2 pounds boneless leg of lamb or beef sirloin, cut into 1½-inch cubes

2 medium-size tomatoes, cut in 1-inch wedges

1 medium-size eggplant (1 pound), cut in ½-inch pieces (3½ cups)

1 large yellow onion, cut into ½-inch wedges (1½ cups)

10 medium-size fresh mushrooms (2 cups)

¾ teaspoon salt

 PREP TIME: 25 MIN. / MARINATING TIME: 1 HR.
COOKING TIME: 10 MIN.

1 In a medium-size glass bowl, whisk the wine with the oil, garlic, vinegar, bay leaves, oregano, and pepper. Add the lamb cubes and toss to coat. Cover with plastic wrap and marinate in the refrigerator for at least 1 hour, or overnight.

2 Let the lamb stand at room temperature in the marinade for 1 hour before cooking. Preheat the grill or broiler. Alternately thread the lamb and vegetables onto eight 12-inch skewers, brush with the marinade, and sprinkle with the salt.

3 Grill the shashlik over medium-hot coals or broil 5 inches from the heat, turning and basting often with the remaining marinade until the lamb is the way you like it (about 10 minutes for medium-rare) and the vegetables are tender. Serve with Rice Pilau (page 203). Makes 8 servings.

1 serving: Calories 243; Saturated Fat 3 g;
Total Fat 12 g; Protein 20 g; Carbohydrate 9 g; Fiber 1 g;
Sodium 320 mg; Cholesterol 57 mg

SUNDAY DINNER LEG OF LAMB
◆◆◆

1 whole leg of lamb, trimmed (7 pounds)	½ cup plus 1 tablespoon cold water
8 large cloves garlic, slivered	3 pounds unpeeled red-skinned potatoes, cut into 1-inch chunks
4 teaspoons snipped fresh rosemary or dried rosemary leaves	1 pound baby carrots, peeled
1 tablespoon minced fresh mint or 1 teaspoon dried mint leaves	2 tablespoons olive oil
	3 cups cooked fresh or thawed frozen peas
2 teaspoons dry mustard	1 cup dry red wine or low-sodium beef broth
1½ teaspoons salt	2 tablespoons cornstarch
¼ teaspoon black pepper	½ cup red currant jelly

PREP TIME: 30 MIN. / COOKING TIME: 2 HR.

1 Preheat the oven to 350° F. Place the lamb, fat side up, on a rack in a large roasting pan. Using a small pointed knife, insert the garlic slivers into the meat. In a small bowl, combine 3 teaspoons of the rosemary with the mint, mustard, 1 teaspoon of the salt, the pepper, and 1 tablespoon of the water, then spread over the lamb.

2 Insert a meat thermometer into the thickest part, avoiding the bone. Roast, uncovered, basting with the drippings, for about 2 hours or until the meat is the way you like it (155°F for medium).

3 After the lamb has been roasting for about 15 minutes, toss the potatoes with the carrots, olive oil, the remaining 1 teaspoon of rosemary, and ½ teaspoon of salt in a 13" x 9" x 2 " baking pan. Roast, uncovered, in the same oven with the lamb for 1½ hours. Stir in the peas and roast 10 minutes longer. When the lamb and vegetables are done, arrange on a platter and keep warm.

4 Pour the drippings from the lamb into a small saucepan; skim the fat. In a cup, stir the wine, the remaining ½ cup of water, and the cornstarch; add to the drippings with the jelly. Bring to a boil over moderate heat and boil for 1 minute, whisking constantly. Pour into a gravy boat and serve with the lamb, vegetables, and hot Parker House Rolls (page 296). Makes 10 servings.

1 serving: Calories 517; Saturated Fat 4 g; Total Fat 13 g; Protein 42 g; Carbohydrate 52 g; Fiber 2 g; Sodium 255 mg; Cholesterol 115 mg

LAMB CHOPS WITH MINT
◆◆◆

With the first burst of spring, many Americans enjoy lamb chops, hot-off-the-grill.

6 loin lamb chops with bone (4 ounces each), trimmed	¼ cup chopped green onions, with tops
½ teaspoon each salt and black pepper	⅓ cup Chicken Stock (page 74) or low-sodium chicken broth
1 tablespoon olive oil	2 tablespoons balsamic or wine vinegar
1 tablespoon unsalted butter or margarine	2 tablespoons chopped fresh mint

PREP TIME: 10 MIN. / COOKING TIME: 15 MIN.

1 Preheat the grill or broiler. Sprinkle the lamb chops with the salt and pepper. Grill directly over medium-hot coals, or broil 4 inches from the heat, for 4 to 5 minutes on each side for medium-rare or until the chops are the way you like them. Transfer to a serving platter and keep warm.

2 In a small saucepan, heat the oil and butter over moderately high heat. Add the green onions and sauté for 2 minutes or until tender. Add the stock and vinegar and simmer, uncovered, 2 minutes longer or until slightly thickened. Stir in 1 tablespoon of the mint, pour over the chops, and sprinkle with the remaining 1 tablespoon of mint. Serve with Honey-Spiced Carrots (page 216) and a lettuce salad. Makes 6 servings.

1 serving: Calories 217; Saturated Fat 4 g; Total Fat 11 g; Protein 26 g; Carbohydrate 2g; Fiber 0 g; Sodium 210 mg; Cholesterol 83

MULLIGAN STEW
◆◆◆

In early 20th-century America, mulligan was the slang word used in hobo camps for a stew made with whatever was available.

2	pounds boneless lamb shoulder or beef chuck, trimmed and cut into 1-inch cubes	1¼	teaspoons dried thyme leaves
3	tablespoons all-purpose flour	½	teaspoon salt, or to taste
2	tablespoons olive oil	¼	teaspoon black pepper
1	large yellow onion, chopped (1½ cups)	2½	pounds medium-size all-purpose potatoes, peeled and quartered
3	cloves garlic, minced	6	large carrots, peeled and cut into 2-inch chunks
1½	cups cold water		
1	can (28 ounces) low-sodium whole tomatoes, drained and chopped	4	medium-size white turnips, peeled and quartered
1	bay leaf	2	cups frozen peas

PREP TIME: 30 MIN. / COOKING TIME: 2 HR.

1 Preheat the oven to 350°F. Coat the lamb with the flour. In a 6-quart Dutch oven, heat the oil over moderate heat. Add the lamb and sauté for 5 minutes, then transfer to a bowl.

2 Add the onion and garlic and sauté for 5 minutes or until tender. Stir in the water, tomatoes, bay leaf, thyme, salt, pepper, and lamb. Bring to a boil, cover, and transfer to the oven.

3 Bake for 40 minutes; stir in the potatoes, carrots, and turnips. Bake 1 hour longer or until tender, skimming the surface often. Stir in the peas and bake 5 minutes more. Discard the bay leaf. Serve with slices of Country Loaf (page 288). Tip: This recipe may be doubled. Leftovers will keep, frozen, for up to 1 month. Makes 8 servings.

1 serving: Calories 415; Saturated Fat 3 g; Total Fat 12 g; Protein 29 g; Carbohydrate 51 g; Fiber 6 g; Sodium 295 mg; Cholesterol 75 mg

All-American grill-out: Lamb Chops with Mint, served with Honey-Spiced Carrots (page 216)

Candlelight Supper: Veal Cordon Bleu, an old favorite revived

VEAL CORDON BLEU

◆◆◆

*This Swiss method of stuffing veal
cutlets can also be used for chicken cutlets.*

4 veal cutlets (4 ounces each), ⅛ inch thick	¼ teaspoon black pepper
4 thin slices boiled or baked ham (2 ounces)	⅛ teaspoon salt, or to taste
4 slices reduced-fat Swiss cheese (4 ounces)	1 large egg
	½ cup plain dry bread crumbs
3 tablespoons all-purpose flour	2 teaspoons olive oil
	2 teaspoons unsalted butter or margarine
	2 lemons, thinly sliced

PREP TIME: 20 MIN. / COOKING TIME: 9 MIN.

1 Lay the veal on a work surface and top each
cutlet with 1 slice each of the ham and cheese.
Using scissors, trim the ham and cheese to the
shape of the cutlets. Fold each cutlet in half,
making a semi-circle, and close with 3 toothpicks.

2 On a piece of wax paper, mix the flour with
the pepper and salt. In a pie plate or shallow
dish, whisk the egg until frothy. Spread the bread
crumbs on another plate. Coat each cutlet with
the flour mixture, then the egg, and then the
bread crumbs, pressing gently to coat completely.

3 In a 12-inch nonstick skillet, heat the oil and
butter over moderately high heat. Brown the
cutlets for 4 minutes on each side or until golden
brown and the cheese melts. Using a slotted
spatula, carefully transfer the cutlets to a warm
platter, remove the toothpicks, and garnish with
the lemon slices. Serve with generous helpings of
hot buttered noodles and fresh asparagus spears,
topped with a lemon-butter sauce. If you wish,
garnish each serving with a ham rose (page 366).
Makes 4 servings.

*1 serving: Calories 374; Saturated Fat 7 g;
Total Fat 14 g; Protein 41 g; Carbohydrate 17 g; Fiber 0 g;
Sodium 464 mg; Cholesterol 171 mg*

VEAL PARMESAN

½ cup grated Parmesan cheese (2 ounces)

1 large egg

1 large egg white

1 tablespoon cold water

¾ cup plain dry bread crumbs

6 veal cutlets (3 ounces each), ⅛ inch thick

2 tablespoons olive oil

1 small yellow onion, chopped (½ cup)

2 cloves garlic, slivered

1¾ cups crushed canned tomatoes, undrained

2 tablespoons chopped fresh basil or 2 teaspoons dried basil leaves

½ teaspoon sugar

¼ teaspoon salt

4 ounces part-skim mozzarella cheese, thinly sliced

PREP TIME: 30 MIN. / COOKING TIME: 26 MIN.

1 Preheat the oven to 425°F and set out an 11" x 17" x 2" baking dish. On a piece of wax paper, spread the Parmesan cheese. In a pie plate, whisk the whole egg, egg white, and water until frothy. Spread the bread crumbs on another plate. Coat each cutlet with the Parmesan, then the egg mixture, and then the bread crumbs.

2 In a 12-inch nonstick skillet, heat 1 tablespoon of the oil over moderately high heat. Brown the veal for 2 minutes on each side or until golden brown, then drain on paper towels.

3 In the same skillet, heat the remaining 1 tablespoon of oil over moderately high heat. Add the onion and garlic and sauté for 5 minutes. Stir in the tomatoes with their juices, the basil, sugar, and salt. Lower the heat and simmer, uncovered, for 5 minutes.

4 Spread ½ of the tomato sauce in the baking dish, top with the veal, the remaining sauce, and the mozzarella cheese. Bake, uncovered, for 10 minutes or until bubbly. Serve with helpings of Peppered Pasta (page 199). Makes 6 servings.

1 serving: Calories 352; Saturated Fat 6 g; Total Fat 15 g; Protein 37 g; Carbohydrate 16 g; Fiber 0 g; Sodium 675 mg; Cholesterol 142 mg

MICHAEL'S VEAL SURPRISE

This special meatloaf comes from Michael Callery, computer consultant and host extraordinaire in New York City.

3 slices white bread, crumbled (1½ cups)

½ cup low-fat (1% milkfat) milk

1 tablespoon olive oil

1 medium-size yellow onion, chopped (1 cup)

3 cloves garlic, minced

½ cup each finely chopped carrots and sweet green pepper

2 pounds ground veal

1 large egg, beaten

¼ cup minced parsley

1 tablespoon fresh lemon juice

1½ teaspoons poultry seasoning

¾ teaspoon salt

½ teaspoon black pepper

3 large eggs, hard-cooked and peeled (page 363)

6 small whole gherkin pickles

PREP TIME: 45 MIN. / COOKING TIME: 1¼ HR. STANDING TIME: 15 MIN.

1 Preheat the oven to 350°F and grease a 9" x 5" x 3" loaf pan. In a large bowl, soak the bread in the milk. In a 12-inch nonstick skillet, heat the oil over moderately high heat. Add the onion, garlic, carrots, and green pepper; sauté for 5 minutes or until tender; transfer to the large bowl.

2 Add the veal, beaten egg, parsley, lemon juice, poultry seasoning, salt, and pepper. Using your hands, mix until thoroughly combined.

3 Press ½ of the meat mixture into the bottom of the pan. Arrange the three cooked eggs, lengthwise end to end, down the center, then the pickles lengthwise alongside. Top with the remaining meat, covering the eggs to form a loaf.

4 Bake, uncovered, for 1¼ hours or until browned. Let stand for 15 minutes before removing from the pan. Makes 8 servings.

1 serving: Calories 261; Saturated Fat 4 g; Total Fat 11 g; Protein 26 g; Carbohydrate 13 g; Fiber 0 g; Sodium 457 mg; Cholesterol 194 mg

A Chicken in Every Pot

◆◆◆

A presidential campaign slogan of the 1928 election promised "a chicken in every pot," expressing the hope that all families would soon have ample food on the table. Anyone who could afford chicken in those days served it as a treat, mainly on Sunday, and had turkey Thanksgiving Day and Christmas only. Today chickens are plentiful, and turkey is available year-round. In their many guises—broiled, poached, roasted, barbecued, simmered with vegetables, baked in pies, and stewed with dumplings—these birds have become all-American traditions.

To enjoy poultry at its most healthful, you should serve it skinless: A chicken breast without the skin contains at least 50 percent less fat than one with skin. Consider too that white meat has about half the fat and less cholesterol than dark meat. Of all domestic fowl, chicken and turkey contain the least fat, goose and duck the most; so reserve the latter two for special occasions. You can follow our recipe directions for skimming fat while poultry simmers, making sauces lighter, and sautéing or baking with a little fat instead of frying. Then sit down to an old-fashioned meal with a new-healthy touch and wonderful taste.

Roasted chicken, stuffed with wild rice and ready for family Sunday dinner

Roast Chicken with Wild Rice Stuffing

◆◆◆

½ cup each uncooked wild rice and long-grain white rice

1 tablespoon olive oil

1½ cups sliced mushrooms

½ cup each chopped carrot, celery, onion, and shallots

½ cup Chicken Stock (page 74) or low-sodium chicken broth

¼ cup toasted slivered almonds (page 365)

¼ cup minced parsley

½ teaspoon dried thyme leaves

½ teaspoon each salt and black pepper

1 roasting chicken (5 pounds), giblets removed

PREP TIME: 30 MIN. / COOKING TIME: 2¾ HR.
STANDING TIME: 10 MIN.

1 Cook the wild rice and white rice separately per package directions, drain, and place in a large bowl. In a 12-inch nonstick skillet, heat the oil over moderate heat. Stir in the mushrooms, carrot, celery, onion, and shallots and sauté for 5 minutes or until tender. Add to the rice mixture with the stock, almonds, parsley, thyme, and ¼ teaspoon each of the salt and pepper; toss well.

2 Preheat the oven to 425°F. Season the inside of the chicken with the remaining salt and pepper; stuff it, truss (page 363), and insert a roasting thermometer in its thigh. Roast on a rack in an open roasting pan, for 30 minutes.

3 Lower the temperature to 350°F roast, basting with the pan drippings, 1½ hours longer or until the thermometer registers 180°F. Let the chicken stand for 10 minutes; carve it, discarding the skin. Serve with Candied Cranberry Sauce (page 281) and fresh beans. Makes 6 servings.

*1 serving: Calories 404; Saturated Fat 3 g;
Total Fat 12 g; Protein 54 g; Carbohydrate 17 g; Fiber 1 g;
Sodium 328 mg; Cholesterol 146 mg*

◆

Stuffed Chicken Breasts

Prepare rice stuffing as directed. Use to stuff **four 6-ounce, skinned, bone-in chicken breast halves**, inserting it between the flesh and bone. Line a buttered 13" x 9" x 2" baking dish with any remaining stuffing; arrange the stuffed breasts on top, meat side up. Cover with foil and bake at 350°F for 25 minutes. Makes 4 servings. *1 serving: Calories 247; Saturated Fat 1 g; Total Fat 7 g; Protein 31 g; Carbohydrate 17 g; Fiber 1 g; Sodium 279 mg; Cholesterol 69 mg*

CHICKEN WITH SAGE-ONION STUFFING

◆◆◆

Perhaps nothing is so evocative of down-home days than the wonderful smell of roasting chicken.

2 tablespoons unsalted butter or margarine	⅓ cup minced parsley
1 cup chopped celery	½ teaspoon rubbed sage
1 cup chopped onion	¾ teaspoon salt
5 cups day-old bread cubes (10 slices)	½ teaspoon black pepper
1⅓ cups Chicken Stock (page 74) or low-sodium chicken broth	1 roasting chicken (5 pounds), giblets removed

PREP TIME: 30 MIN. / COOKING TIME: 2¼ HR.
STANDING TIME: 10 MIN.

1 In a 12-inch skillet, melt the butter over moderate heat. Add the celery and onion; sauté for 5 minutes or until tender. Transfer to a large bowl. Stir in the bread, stock, parsley, sage, ½ teaspoon of the salt, and ¼ teaspoon of pepper.

2 Preheat the oven to 425°F. Season the inside of the chicken with the remaining ¼ teaspoon each of salt and pepper. Stuff the chicken with the bread mixture, truss (page 363), and insert a roasting thermometer in its thigh. Transfer the rest of the stuffing to a buttered au gratin dish, cover tightly with foil, and refrigerate.

3 Roast the chicken on a rack in an open roasting pan for 30 minutes. Lower the temperature to 350°F and roast, basting with the pan drippings, 1½ hours longer or until the thermometer registers 180°F. Bake the extra stuffing, covered, during the last 30 minutes. Let the chicken stand for 10 minutes, then carve it, discarding the skin. Serve with Green Beans Amandine (page 220). Makes 6 servings.

1 serving: Calories 402; Saturated Fat 5 g;
Total Fat 12 g; Protein 53 g; Carbohydrate 15 g; Fiber 1 g;
Sodium 461 mg; Cholesterol 157 mg

DENVER BARBECUED CHICKEN

◆◆◆

Colorado barbecue sauces blend influences from different regions: tomato from Kansas City, vinegar from North Carolina, honey from the Midwest, and hot spice from Texas. Cooks there broil marinated chicken on the edge of the grill—not directly over the coals—to avoid over-browning.

2½ to 3 pounds chicken pieces, skin removed	3 tablespoons honey
1 tablespoon unsalted butter or margarine	2 tablespoons light brown sugar
¼ cup minced onion	1 tablespoon each Worcestershire sauce and low-sodium soy sauce
3 cloves garlic, minced	
1 can (6 ounces) tomato paste	1 teaspoon each dry mustard and pepper
¾ cup cider vinegar	½ teaspoon hot red pepper sauce
¼ cup cold water	

PREP TIME: 30 MIN. / COOKING TIME: 1 HR.

1 In a large shallow dish, arrange the chicken in a single layer. In a medium-size saucepan, melt the butter over moderate heat. Add the onion and garlic and sauté for 5 minutes or until tender.

2 Whisk in the remaining ingredients and bring to a boil. Lower the heat and simmer, stirring, for 20 minutes or until thickened. Brush the sauce on the chicken, coating it completely, cover, and refrigerate for at least 30 minutes, turning once.

3 Meanwhile preheat the grill to medium hot. Heap the coals in the center and arrange the chicken around the edge of the rack. Cover the grill (keeping the vents open) and cook the chicken, brushing occasionally with the sauce, for 20 minutes on each side or until the juices run clear when a thigh is pricked with a fork. Arrange the chicken over the coals, and grill 5 minutes more on each side or until browned. Serve with 'Tater Boats (page 229). Makes 4 servings.

1 serving: Calories 229; Saturated Fat 2 g;
Total Fat 6 g; Protein 38 g; Carbohydrate 3 g; Fiber 0 g;
Sodium 288 mg; Cholesterol 109 mg

DOWN HOME TRADITION

Originally, the French created delicate and creamy fricassée dishes with chicken or veal. Then, in New Orleans at the turn of the 20th century, Creole cooks prepared their own version of Chicken Fricassée, first by dredging the chicken in flour, then browning it in hot fat to create a rich brown roux. When they added onions and other vegetables to the skillet — plus parsley, bay leaf, thyme, and stock — a rich chicken and gravy dish resulted and a Creole tradition was born.

◆ Chicken Fricassée ◆

½ cup all-purpose flour

½ teaspoon each salt and black pepper, or to taste

¼ teaspoon ground red pepper (cayenne)

1 large broiler-fryer chicken (3½ to 4 pounds), cut into 8 pieces

¼ cup butter

2 tablespoons vegetable oil

1 large yellow onion, chopped (1½ cups)

2 large carrots, peeled and chopped (1 cup)

2 stalks celery, chopped (1 cup)

2 cups chicken stock or broth

⅔ cup heavy cream

½ cup whole milk

1 teaspoon chopped fresh thyme or ¼ teaspoon dried thyme leaves

1 bay leaf

2 tablespoons fresh lemon juice

4 cups hot, cooked wide egg noodles (8 ounces)

¼ cup minced parsley

PREP TIME: 25 MIN. / COOKING TIME: 1 HR.

1 On a piece of wax paper, mix the flour with the salt and both of the peppers. Coat the chicken with this mixture, reserving any extra flour. In a 12-inch skillet, heat the butter and oil over moderately high heat. Add the chicken and brown for 4 minutes on each side; transfer to a plate with a slotted spoon.

2 Add the onion, carrots, celery, and the remaining seasoned flour to the skillet and sauté for 5 minutes or until the vegetables are tender. Return the chicken, along with any juices that have collected, to the skillet; add the stock, cream, milk, thyme, and bay leaf and bring just to a boil.

3 Lower the heat, cover, and simmer for 45 minutes or until the juices run clear when a thigh is pricked with a fork. Discard the bay leaf. Remove the chicken from the heat and stir in the lemon juice. Line a serving platter with the noodles and arrange the chicken on top. Ladle the gravy over all and sprinkle with the parsley. Serve with Fried Greens (page 222). Makes 4 servings.

1 serving: Calories 764; Saturated Fat 20 g; Total Fat 42 g; Protein 60 g; Carbohydrate 32 g; Fiber 1 g; Sodium 511 mg; Cholesterol 260 mg

Louisiana Chicken

◆◆◆

*This version of a traditional
Creole dish keeps its homemade flavor, while
saving on fat and calories.*

1 tablespoon vegetable oil	1 bay leaf
1 broiler-fryer chicken (3 pounds), skinned and cut into 8 pieces	4 cups hot, cooked wide egg noodles (8 ounces)
1 large yellow onion, chopped (1½ cups)	1½ tablespoons unsalted butter or margarine
2 large carrots, peeled and chopped (1 cup)	3 tablespoons all-purpose flour
2 stalks celery, chopped (1 cup)	1 cup low-fat (1% milkfat) milk
2 cups Chicken Stock (page 74) or low-sodium chicken broth	2 tablespoons fresh lemon juice
1 teaspoon chopped fresh thyme or ¼ teaspoon dried thyme leaves	½ teaspoon each salt and black pepper, or to taste
	¼ cup minced parsley

PREP TIME: 25 MIN. / COOKING TIME: 1 HR. 5 MIN.

1 In a 12-inch nonstick skillet, heat the oil over moderately high heat. Add the chicken and cook for 4 minutes on each side or until browned, then transfer to a plate with a slotted spoon.

2 Add the onion, carrots, and celery to the skillet and sauté for 5 minutes or until tender. Return the chicken, along with any juices that have collected, to the skillet; add the stock, thyme, and bay leaf and bring to a boil.

3 Lower the heat, cover, and simmer for 45 minutes or until the juices run clear when a thigh is pricked with a fork. Discard the bay leaf; reserve the cooking liquid, skimming off any fat. Line a warm serving platter with the noodles and arrange the chicken on top. Cover with aluminum foil to keep warm.

4 In the same skillet, melt the butter over moderate heat. Add the flour and cook for 1 minute or until bubbly. Whisk in the milk and

Louisiana Chicken, richly browned, then gently simmered with fresh vegetables in a flavorful sauce

the cooking liquid from the chicken. Cook for 3 minutes or until thickened, then remove from the heat. Stir in the lemon juice, salt, and pepper. Ladle the gravy over the chicken and top with the parsley. Serve with Chopped Tomato Salad (page 256). Makes 4 servings.

*1 serving: Calories 543; Saturated Fat 8 g;
Total Fat 19 g; Protein 53 g; Carbohydrate 35 g; Fiber 1 g;
Sodium 492 mg; Cholesterol 176 mg*

Chicken Indienne, a taste of elegant dining from the trains of yesteryear

CHICKEN INDIENNE

◆◆◆

Passengers riding the Southern Pacific Railroad in the 1920's might have dined on this curried chicken dish, adapted from the 1927 handbook, "Special Recipes for Guidance of Chefs on Dining Cars."

4 tablespoons all-purpose flour	1 tablespoon unsalted butter or margarine
1 tablespoon curry powder	1 large unpeeled cooking apple, such as Rome Beauty, cored and cut into 8 wedges
½ teaspoon salt	
4 chicken breast halves with bones (about 6 ounces each), skinned	½ cup whole milk or half-and-half
1 tablespoon vegetable oil	3 cups hot cooked white rice
1 cup water	¼ cup coconut, toasted

PREP TIME: 15 MIN. / COOKING TIME: 30 MIN.

1 On a piece of wax paper, combine 3 tablespoons of the flour, the curry powder, and salt, then coat the chicken with this mixture.

2 In a deep 12-inch nonstick skillet, heat the oil over moderately high heat. Add the chicken and brown for 4 minutes on each side. Add the water and bring to a boil. Lower the heat, cover, and simmer for 10 minutes or until the juices run clear when the flesh is pricked with fork. Using a slotted spoon, transfer to a warm platter and cover with foil. Reserve the drippings in the skillet.

3 Meanwhile, in a 10-inch nonstick skillet, melt the butter over moderate heat. Add the apple and sauté for 5 minutes or until lightly browned.

4 To prepare the gravy: In a cup, whisk the milk and remaining 1 tablespoon of flour. Whisk into the drippings in the 12-inch skillet and bring to a simmer over moderate heat, whisking constantly. Simmer, whisking 2 minutes longer or until the gravy is slightly thickened. To serve, arrange the chicken on the rice, ladle the gravy on top, and sprinkle with the coconut. Spoon the apples alongside; serve with chutney and steamed green beans. Makes 4 servings.

1 serving: Calories 470; Saturated Fat 6 g; Total Fat 12 g; Protein 31 g; Carbohydrate 60 g; Fiber 1 g; Sodium 369 mg; Cholesterol 74 mg

SOUTHERN PACIFIC'S CHICKEN OF THE DAY

Dining Car Chef Roscoe White cooked on board the Southern Pacific Railroad for more than 45 years. His chicken-in-wine dishes were some of the passengers' favorites.

3	tablespoons all-purpose flour
½	teaspoon black pepper
1	broiler-fryer chicken (2½ to 3 pounds), skinned and cut into 8 pieces
1	tablespoon olive oil
1	tablespoon unsalted butter or margarine
4	ounces fresh mushrooms, sliced (1½ cups)
1	large onion, finely chopped (1½ cups)

1	clove garlic, minced
½	cup dry white wine or low-sodium chicken broth
½	teaspoon salt
2	tablespoons minced parsley

For the croutons:

2	teaspoons unsalted butter or margarine
2	teaspoons olive oil
4	slices white bread, cut into ½-inch cubes (2 cups)
⅛	teaspoon garlic powder

PREP TIME: 25 MIN. / COOKING TIME: 45 MIN.

1 On a piece of wax paper, mix the flour and pepper, then use to coat the chicken. In a 12-inch nonstick skillet, heat the oil over moderately high heat. Add the chicken and brown for 4 minutes on each side, then transfer to a platter.

2 In the same skillet, melt the butter. Add the mushrooms, onion, and garlic and sauté for 5 minutes or until tender. Add the chicken, wine, and salt and bring to a boil. Lower the heat, cover, and simmer, stirring often, for 30 minutes or until the juices run clear when a thigh is pricked with a fork. Transfer to a warm platter and cover with foil.

3 Meanwhile, prepare the croutons: In a 10-inch nonstick skillet, heat the butter and oil over moderately high heat. Add the bread cubes and garlic powder and stir for 4 minutes or until

◆ All Aboard! ◆

In the heyday of railroad travel in America (about 1890-1950), a long trip by train was usually highlighted by memorable meals. "Railway dining cars were some of the best restaurants in the USA," explains Robert Andrade, a chef with the Southern Pacific Railroad. "Each line had its specialties—barbecued chicken on the Louisville & Nashville, prime steaks on the Union Pacific, crab cakes on the Baltimore & Ohio, French toast on the Sante Fe, and strawberry shortcake on the Pullman Company line.

"The early cars duplicated Victorian drawing rooms, with mahogany walls, plush velvet seats, and gilded trimmings, while cars of the 1930's represented art deco at its best. Passengers then were pampered with seven-course dinners that were prepared with the best ingredients America had to offer—Iowa pork, Wisconsin cream, Florida oranges, Washington apples—and served with fine linens, silver, and china.

"Since galley and oven space were limited, menus had to contain dishes that could be baked or roasted at the same temperature. And due to the train's motion, baking cakes, soufflés, and yeast breads was unreliable. So we usually picked up bread from our commissaries and baked pies instead."

A passenger motto might have been: "Dinner in the diner, nothing could be finer!" The recipes from those meals were special and should remain a part of our culinary tradition. It was a time well worth remembering.

the croutons are browned. Spoon on top of the chicken and sprinkle with the parsley. Serve with steamed broccoli spears. Makes 4 servings.

1 serving: Calories 422; Saturated Fat 6 g; Total Fat 17 g; Protein 41 g; Carbohydrate 19 g; Fiber 1 g; Sodium 444 mg; Cholesterol 122 mg

AUTO-TRAIN SPECIAL

Chef Eric Sims has served aboard Am Track's Auto Train, which takes passengers and their cars to sunny Florida. Here's one of his chicken specials, adapted to a home kitchen.

1 broiler-fryer chicken (2½ to 3 pounds), skinned and cut into 8 pieces	1½ cups sliced fresh mushrooms
1 teaspoon garlic salt	1½ cups sliced onions
½ teaspoon black pepper	1½ cups sweet green pepper strips
1 tablespoon unsalted butter or margarine	½ cup chopped celery
1 tablespoon olive oil	1 can (15 ounces) low-sodium tomato sauce
	8 ounces spaghetti, cooked and kept hot

PREP TIME: 20 MIN. / COOKING TIME: 48 MIN.

1 Preheat the oven to 350°F. Sprinkle the chicken with the garlic salt and pepper. In a 12-inch nonstick skillet, heat the butter and oil over moderately high heat. Add the chicken and cook for 4 minutes on each side or until browned. Transfer to a large shallow roasting pan.

2 To the same skillet, add the mushrooms, onions, green pepper, and celery and sauté for 5 minutes or until tender. Stir in the tomato sauce and cook for 4 minutes. Pour over the chicken and bake for 30 minutes or until the juices run clear. Serve over the spaghetti. Makes 4 servings.

---

1 serving: Calories 434; Saturated Fat 4 g; Total Fat 13 g; Protein 44 g; Carbohydrate 34 g; Fiber 1 g; Sodium 654 mg; Cholesterol 117 mg

◆

Pork Conquistador

Prepare as for Auto-Train Special, substituting **four 5-ounce, ½ inch thick, bone-in lean pork chops** for the chicken. Makes 4 servings. *1 serving: Calories 439; Saturated Fat 7 g; Total Fat 20 g; Protein 30 g; Carbohydrate 34 g; Fiber 1 g; Sodium 624 mg; Cholesterol 89 mg*

HUNTER'S CHICKEN

This longtime American favorite was inspired by the Italian dish, Pollo alla Cacciatore.

1 broiler-fryer chicken (2½ to 3 pounds), skinned and cut into 8 pieces	2½ cups chopped fresh tomatoes
½ cup all-purpose flour	½ cup dry red wine (with or without alcohol) or low-sodium chicken broth
2 tablespoons olive oil	
1 medium-size yellow onion, chopped (1 cup)	2 teaspoons chopped fresh thyme or ½ teaspoon dried thyme leaves
2 cloves garlic, minced	
12 ounces fresh mushrooms, quartered (4½ cups)	1 teaspoon chopped fresh rosemary or ¼ teaspoon dried rosemary leaves
1 large sweet red pepper, cored, seeded, and cut into 1-inch cubes (1 cup)	¼ teaspoon salt, or to taste
	¼ teaspoon black pepper

PREP TIME: 20 MIN. / COOKING TIME: 1 HR.

1 Coat the chicken with the flour, shaking off the excess. In a deep, 12-inch nonstick skillet, heat 1 tablespoon of the oil over moderately high heat. Cook the chicken for 4 minutes on each side or until browned, then transfer to a plate.

2 Add the remaining 1 tablespoon of oil, the onion, and the garlic to the pan. Sauté for 5 minutes or until tender. Stir in the mushrooms and red pepper and sauté 5 minutes longer.

3 Add the chicken, along with any juices that have collected, and the remaining ingredients. Bring to a boil, then lower the heat, cover, and simmer for 15 minutes. Turn the chicken over, then simmer, covered, 15 minutes longer or until the juices run clear when a thigh is pricked with a fork. Serve with steamed rice and broccoli florets. Makes 4 servings.

---

1 serving: Calories 394; Saturated Fat 3 g; Total Fat 13 g; Protein 43 g; Carbohydrate 22 g; Fiber 2 g; Sodium 478 mg; Cholesterol 109 mg

Suppertime at the Patchwork Quilt Country Inn, in Middlebury, Indiana: Time for Arletta's Buttermilk Pecan Chicken

BUTTERMILK PECAN CHICKEN

Arletta Lovejoy, founder of the Patchwork Quilt Country Inn, won first place in the 1970 National Chicken Cooking Contest with this recipe.

3 tablespoons unsalted butter or margarine	2 broiler-fryer chickens (2½ to 3 pounds each), skinned and cut into 16 pieces
¾ cup low-fat buttermilk	
1 large egg	14 pecan halves (optional)
1 cup all-purpose flour	**For the tomatoes:**
1 cup ground pecans (about 4 ounces)	1 tablespoon unsalted butter or margarine
¼ cup sesame seeds	1 pint cherry tomatoes, stemmed (2 cups)
1 tablespoon paprika	
¾ teaspoon salt, or to taste	¼ teaspoon sugar
⅛ teaspoon black pepper	⅛ teaspoon salt

PREP TIME: 25 MIN. / COOKING TIME: 1 HR. 5 MIN.

1 Preheat the oven to 375°F. Place the butter in a large shallow roasting pan and put in the oven to melt. Meanwhile, in a pie plate, whisk the buttermilk and egg. On a piece of wax paper, toss the flour, with the ground pecans, sesame seeds, paprika, salt, and pepper.

2 Dip the chicken pieces into the buttermilk mixture, then coat with the pecan mixture. Roll the chicken in the melted butter, then arrange in a single layer in the roasting pan. Top each piece with a pecan half if you wish.

3 Bake the chicken, uncovered, without turning, for 1 hour or until golden and the juices run clear when a thigh is pricked with a fork.

4 Meanwhile, prepare the cherry tomatoes: In a 12-inch nonstick skillet, melt the butter over moderately high heat. Add the tomatoes, sugar, and salt. Stir and shake the skillet for 4 minutes or just until the tomatoes are heated and their skins start to wrinkle. Arrange the chicken on a platter and surround with the tomatoes. Serve with Succotash (page 236) and large helpings of Mashed Potatoes (page 361). Makes 8 servings.

1 serving: Calories 393; Saturated Fat 6 g; Total Fat 16 g; Protein 43 g; Carbohydrate 18 g; Fiber 1 g; Sodium 367 mg; Cholesterol 149 mg

CHICKEN PUDDING

◆◆◆

This hearty dish, one of President James Monroe's favorites, comes to the table under a puffy pudding-like topping.

1⅔ cups all-purpose flour	2 large egg whites
½ teaspoon each salt and black pepper	1 cup low-fat (1% milkfat) milk
1 broiler-fryer chicken (2½ to 3 pounds), skinned and cut into 8 pieces	3 tablespoons unsalted butter or margarine, melted
1 tablespoon olive oil	3 tablespoons minced parsley
4 cups Chicken Stock (page 74) or low-sodium chicken broth	1 teaspoon chopped fresh thyme or ¼ teaspoon dried thyme leaves
1 large egg	

PREP TIME: 30 MIN. / COOKING TIME: 1 HR.

1 On a piece of wax paper, combine ⅓ cup of the flour, ¼ teaspoon of the salt, and the pepper. Coat the chicken with this mixture. In a deep, 12-inch nonstick skillet, heat the oil over moderately high heat. Add the chicken and cook for 4 minutes on each side or until browned. Add the stock and bring to a boil. Lower the heat, cover, and simmer for 15 minutes. Transfer to a buttered 13" x 9" x 3" baking dish, reserving the stock.

2 Preheat the oven to 425°F. In a large bowl, whisk the egg and egg whites. Whisk in the milk, 1 tablespoon of the butter, and the remaining ¼ teaspoon of salt, then whisk in 1 cup of the flour until smooth. Pour over the chicken and bake, uncovered, for 15 minutes. Reduce the oven temperature to 350°F and bake 20 minutes longer or until the topping is puffed and golden.

3 Meanwhile, in a medium-size saucepan, heat the remaining 2 tablespoons of butter over moderate heat. Add the remaining ⅓ cup of flour and cook until bubbly. Whisk in 3½ cups of the reserved cooking liquid and bring to a boil. Lower the heat and simmer for 5 minutes, stirring frequently. Stir in the parsley and thyme. Drizzle about ½ of the gravy over the chicken. Serve with the remaining gravy and a leafy green salad tossed with Buttermilk Dressing (page 260). Makes 4 servings.

1 serving: Calories 603; Saturated Fat 9 g; Total Fat 21 g; Protein 51 g; Carbohydrate 45 g; Fiber 0 g; Sodium 528 mg; Cholesterol 197 mg

A Presidential Favorite: Monroe's Chicken Pudding

◆ Shaker Food Ways: Simple, Hearty, Wholesome ◆

Take a stroll through Hancock Shaker Village in Pittsfield, Massachusetts, for a taste of simple, unpretentious farm living, 19th-century style. "The official gathering (or founding) of the village began in 1790 with three farming families. At first, food was scarce and the few inhabitants lived on a "souply" fare of broth and bread. But

gradually, the village grew and even prospered.

"Shaker cooking was pure vernacular cuisine at its finest," explains Cheryl Anderson, Coordinator of Crafts and Domestic Industries at Hancock Shaker Village. "It was plain and simple, using foods from the region, the technology of the time, and food preparation techniques of the period. As in other New England farm areas, the Shaker diet was rich in cream, butter, meats, and sweets—all believed necessary for the strenuous, farming lifestyle. But unlike other farmers, the Shakers ate a wide variety of foods, many brought back by their trustees, who traveled widely.

"Generally, menus varied with the season, according to what was plentiful and ready for harvest. The first asparagus of spring and the fresh, juicy fruits of summer called for celebration, especially after a long winter of smoked and salted meats, root vegetables, and dried fruits.

"Eating whole grains became a way of life for the Shakers in the mid-1800's, when it was promoted by the creator of the graham cracker, Sylvester Graham. Poultry was eaten mostly in the fall, to avoid having to care for the birds over the winter.

"The typical Shaker breakfast usually included such hearty foods as Rye Indian Bread (made from

cornmeal and rye flour) and fish, shellfish, or meat that was generally fried and served with a rich gravy, and often sweet potatoes. Breakfast sweets were favored too: pancakes drenched in butter, strawberry cakes, and apple pie, real New England treats.

"Not surprisingly, the most substantial meal was served at noon, and included not only meat and vegetables, but also brown bread, potato cakes, more apple pie, gingerbread, spoon cakes, pickles, cream cheese, and even doughnuts."

Whatever the season, a Shaker meal was a wholesome feast, served in the simplest way, but never prepared on Sunday, for that always was the day of rest.

SHAKER CHICKEN IN CIDER AND CREAM
◆◆◆

1 broiler-fryer chicken (2½ to 3 pounds), skinned and quartered	2 tablespoons unsalted butter or margarine
1 teaspoon black pepper	¾ cup apple cider
¾ teaspoon salt	½ cup light cream
	1 tablespoon grated lemon rind

PREP TIME: 10 MIN. / COOKING TIME: 45 MIN.

1 Season the chicken with ½ teaspoon of the pepper and ¼ teaspoon of the salt. In a 12-inch nonstick skillet, melt the butter over moderately high heat. Add the chicken and cook for 4 minutes on each side or until browned. Lower the heat and cook, covered, for 30 minutes or until the juices run clear when a thigh is pricked with a fork. Remove the chicken to a warm serving platter and cover with foil to keep warm.

2 Into the same skillet, whisk the cider, cream, lemon rind, and remaining ½ teaspoon each of pepper and salt. Bring to a simmer over moderate heat, whisking to scrape up the browned bits. Cook for 3 minutes or until slightly thickened; pour over the chicken. Serve with Glazed Acorn Squash (page 234). Makes 4 servings.

1 serving: Calories 350; Saturated Fat 9 g; Total Fat 17 g; Protein 39 g; Carbohydrate 7 g; Fiber 0 g; Sodium 508 mg; Cholesterol 145 mg

DOWN HOME TRADITION

From the North Union Shaker Village in Ohio comes this rich chicken pot pie, topped with a creamy mushroom sauce. Like much of Shaker cooking, it features typical fresh farm ingredients, such as chicken, butter, eggs, and cream.

◆ Sister Clymena's Chicken Pie ◆

Pastry for a double-crust pie (page 368)
2 broiler-fryer chickens (3 pounds each), quartered
1½ teaspoons salt
2¾ cups heavy cream
3 large eggs
1 cup chopped yellow onion
⅓ cup minced parsley
¼ cup finely chopped chervil or 1 teaspoon dried chervil leaves
1½ teaspoons black pepper
¾ teaspoon sugar
½ cup (1 stick) unsalted butter or margarine
1 pound fresh mushrooms, finely chopped (6 cups)
¼ cup all-purpose flour
½ cup whole milk

PREP TIME: 45 MIN. / COOKING TIME: 2 HR.

1 Prepare the pastry, roll tightly in plastic wrap, and chill. In an 8-quart stockpot, place the chicken, enough cold water to cover, and ½ teaspoon of the salt. Cover and bring to a boil over high heat. Lower the heat and simmer for 1 hour or until the chicken is fork-tender. When cool enough to handle, remove the skin and bones and cut the meat into bite-size chunks. Reserve the cooking liquid.

2 In a large bowl, whisk 2 cups of the cream, the eggs, ½ cup of the onion, the parsley, chervil, 1 teaspoon of the pepper, ½ teaspoon of the sugar and ½ teaspoon of the remaining salt. Stir in the chicken and ¼ cup of the cooking liquid.

3 Preheat the oven to 425°F. On a lightly floured surface, roll out ½ of the dough; fit into a 12-inch deep dish pie plate. Fill with the chicken mixture. Roll out the remaining dough and place over the filling, crimping the edges. Cut a few steam holes in the top. Bake for 40 minutes or until golden brown.

4 To prepare the mushroom sauce: In a 12-inch skillet, melt the butter over moderate heat. Add the mushrooms and remaining ½ cup of onion and sauté for 8 minutes or until tender. Add the flour and cook until bubbly. Whisk in the remaining ¾ cup of cream, the milk, ½ cup of the chicken cooking liquid, and the remaining ½ teaspoon each of salt and pepper and ¼ teaspoon of sugar. Cook, stirring, for 4 minutes or until slightly thickened. Serve with steamed Brussels sprouts. Makes 8 servings.

1 serving: Calories 1124; Saturated Fat 40 g; Total Fat 77 g; Protein 51 g;
Carbohydrate 58 g; Fiber 1 g; Sodium 618 mg; Cholesterol 367 mg

A perfect
fall supper: Deep-
Dish Chicken
Pot Pie

DEEP-DISH CHICKEN POT PIE

*Bake a pot pie the lighter way
by using only a top crust and no cream.*

Pastry for a single-crust pie (page 368)	2 **large carrots, peeled, thinly sliced, and cooked (1 cup)**
1 **broiler-fryer chicken (2½ to 3 pounds), quartered**	1 **cup fresh or frozen corn kernels, cooked**
½ **teaspoon salt**	1 **cup fresh or frozen lima beans, cooked**
2 **tablespoons unsalted butter or margarine**	1 **cup fresh or frozen peas, cooked**
6 **tablespoons all-purpose flour**	4 **ounces diced cooked ham (½ cup)**
1 **cup low-fat (1 % milkfat) milk**	¼ **teaspoon black pepper**

PREP TIME: 45 MIN. / COOKING TIME: 1½ HR.

1 Prepare the pastry, roll in plastic wrap, and chill. In a 6-quart stockpot, place the chicken, enough cold water to cover, and ¼ teaspoon of the salt. Cover and bring to a boil over high heat, skimming the surface. Lower the heat; simmer for 1 hour or until the chicken is fork-tender. Cool, then remove the skin and bones and cut the meat into bite-size chunks. Reserve the cooking liquid.

2 In a medium-size saucepan, melt the butter over moderate heat. Whisk in the flour and cook until bubbly. Gradually whisk in 2 cups of the reserved cooking liquid and the milk and cook, whisking occasionally, for 10 minutes or until thickened. Stir in the chicken, carrots, corn, lima beans, peas, ham, pepper, and the remaining ¼ teaspoon of salt. Cook for 3 minutes or until hot, then spoon into a 10-inch deep-dish pie plate or round baking dish.

3 Preheat the oven to 425°F. On a lightly floured surface, roll out the dough to ¼ inch thick. Using a leaf cookie cutter or a round biscuit cutter (preferably fluted), cut out about 12 decorations and arrange on top of the chicken filling. Bake, uncovered, for 12 minutes or until bubbly. Serve with Cranberry Orange Conserve (page 280). Makes 6 servings.

*1 serving: Calories 615; Saturated Fat 11 g;
Total Fat 26 g; Protein 40 g; Carbohydrate 54 g; Fiber 1 g;
Sodium 485 mg; Cholesterol 116 mg*

A fireside supper for friends: Brunswick Stew, similar to one that our forefathers enjoyed

BRUNSWICK STEW FROM CHOWNING'S TAVERN

◆ ◆ ◆

According to legend, Brunswick stew originally contained squirrel. Today, chicken is used instead. This stylish version comes from Chowning's Tavern in Colonial Williamsburg, Virginia.

2 broiler-fryer chickens (3 pounds each), skinned and cut into 16 pieces

2 quarts cold water

1 teaspoon salt, or to taste

2 large yellow onions, sliced (3 cups)

1½ pounds potatoes, peeled and diced (3 cups)

1 can (28 ounces) low-sodium chopped tomatoes, undrained

1 tablespoon sugar

1 teaspoon black pepper

4 cups fresh corn kernels or 2 packages (10 ounces each) frozen corn kernels

2 cups shelled fresh lima beans or 1 package (9 ounces) frozen lima beans

2 cups sliced fresh okra or 1 package (10 ounces) frozen cut okra

PREP TIME: 30 MIN. / COOKING TIME: 1¼ HR.

1 In an 8-quart Dutch oven, bring the chicken, water, and ½ teaspoon of the salt to a boil over high heat. Lower the heat and simmer, uncovered, for 45 minutes or until the chicken is tender, skimming the surface. Using a slotted spoon, transfer the chicken to a platter to cool.

2 Add the onions, potatoes, tomatoes, sugar, pepper, and the remaining ½ teaspoon of salt. Return to a boil. Lower the heat, cover, and simmer for 15 minutes. Add the corn and lima beans, cover, and simmer 5 minutes longer.

3 Remove and discard the chicken bones and cut the meat into bite-size pieces. Stir the okra and chicken into the pot, cover, and simmer 5 minutes longer or until the okra is tender and the chicken is heated through. Serve with slices of Country Loaf (page 288). Makes 10 servings.

1 serving: Calories 389; Saturated Fat 1 g; Total Fat 6 g; Protein 42 g; Carbohydrate 44 g; Fiber 2 g; Sodium 364 mg; Cholesterol 114 mg

CHICKEN AND DUMPLINGS

◆◆◆

1 broiler-fryer chicken (2½ to 3 pounds), skinned and cut into 8 pieces	½ cup whole milk
¼ teaspoon each salt and black pepper	1 teaspoon fresh lemon juice
1 tablespoon olive oil	3 tablespoons minced parsley
2 cups chopped leeks	**For the dumplings:**
1½ cups chopped carrots	1¾ cups all-purpose flour
½ cup chopped celery	½ teaspoon baking soda
½ teaspoon each dried marjoram and thyme	¼ teaspoon salt
¼ cup all-purpose flour	3 tablespoons vegetable shortening
5½ cups Chicken Stock (page 74) or low-sodium chicken broth	⅔ to ¾ cup low-fat buttermilk

PREP TIME: 30 MIN. / COOKING TIME: 50 MIN.

1 Sprinkle the chicken with the salt and pepper. In a deep, nonstick 12-inch skillet, heat the oil over moderately high heat. Add the chicken, and cook for 4 minutes on each side or until browned; using a slotted spoon, transfer to a plate.

2 Add the vegetables, marjoram, and thyme to the skillet and sauté for 5 minutes. Stir in the flour and cook until bubbly, then stir in the stock and milk. Add the chicken and bring to a boil. Lower the heat, cover, and simmer for 20 minutes. Stir in the lemon juice.

3 To make the dumplings: In a medium-size bowl, combine the flour, baking soda, and salt. Using 2 knives, cut in the shortening, then stir in enough buttermilk to form a soft dough. On a floured surface, roll out the dough into an 8" x 8" x ½" square; cut into sixteen 2-inch squares.

4 Slide the dumplings into the skillet. Cover and simmer for 10 minutes or until cooked through (page 363). Top with the parsley; serve with Tomato Aspic (page 258). Makes 4 servings.

1 serving: Calories 687; Saturated Fat 5 g;
Total Fat 22 g; Protein 51 g; Carbohydrate 71 g; Fiber 6 g;
Sodium 688 mg; Cholesterol 125 mg

CAROLINA CHICKEN

◆◆◆

From the Carolina Low Country comes this popular way of coating chicken with benne seeds, which is the locals' name for sesame seeds.

⅓ cup all-purpose flour	1 tablespoon bacon drippings or vegetable oil
¼ cup benne seeds (sesame seeds)	1 tablespoon unsalted butter or margarine
1 tablespoon grated orange rind	½ cup orange juice
½ teaspoon salt	1½ cups Chicken Stock (page 74) or low-sodium chicken broth
¼ teaspoon ground red pepper (cayenne)	½ cup low-fat (1% milkfat) milk
1 broiler-fryer chicken (2½ to 3 pounds), skinned and cut into 8 pieces	

PREP TIME: 20 MIN. / COOKING TIME: 1¼ HR.

1 Preheat the oven to 350°F and grease a 2-quart casserole. In a brown paper bag, shake the flour, benne seeds, orange rind, salt, and ground red pepper. Shake the chicken in the bag to coat well, reserving the remaining flour.

2 In a 12-inch nonstick skillet, heat the bacon drippings over moderate heat. Add the chicken and cook for about 4 minutes on each side or until browned, then transfer to the casserole.

3 In the same skillet, melt the butter. Whisk in 2 tablespoons of the flour mixture and cook until bubbly. Whisk in the orange juice and cook 2 minutes longer. Add the stock and milk (the mixture will look slightly curdled); bring to a boil.

4 Lower the heat and simmer, stirring, for 2 minutes or until slightly thickened. Pour the sauce over the chicken, cover, and bake for 45 minutes, then uncover and bake 10 minutes more or until browned. Serve with Green Rice (page 207). Makes 4 servings.

1 serving: Calories 379; Saturated Fat 5 g;
Total Fat 17 g; Protein 41 g; Carbohydrate 15 g; Fiber 2 g;
Sodium 412 mg; Cholesterol 128 mg

Richmond Fried Chicken: Packed for a picnic without its gravy, but with Picnic Potato Salad (page 255) and fruit

RICHMOND FRIED CHICKEN

◆◆◆

*This recipe for fried chicken
combines the down-home flavors of yesteryear
with the nutrition know-how of today.*

½ cup all-purpose flour

½ teaspoon each
salt and paprika

¼ teaspoon each
ground allspice and
crushed red pepper
flakes

⅛ teaspoon each
ground cloves and
nutmeg

1 broiler-fryer
(3 pounds), skin
and wing tips
removed, cut into
8 pieces

2 tablespoons
vegetable oil

1⅔ cups low-fat
(1% milkfat) milk

PREP TIME: 20 MIN. / COOKING TIME: 26 MIN.

1 Preheat the oven to 400°F. Line a 13"x 9"x 2"
baking pan with foil and grease it lightly. On
a piece of wax paper, combine the flour, salt,
paprika, allspice, red pepper flakes, cloves, and
nutmeg. Set aside 2 tablespoons of the mixture.

2 Dredge the chicken in the remaining flour
mixture. In a 12-inch nonstick skillet, heat the
oil over moderately high heat. Brown the chicken,
turning occasionally, for about 6 minutes or until
golden-brown. Using a slotted spoon, transfer to
the baking pan, reserving 2 tablespoons of the
drippings in the skillet. Bake the chicken, uncovered, for 10 minutes on each side or until crispy.

3 Meanwhile, prepare the gravy: Whisk the
reserved flour mixture into the drippings in
the skillet. Cook over moderate heat for 2 minutes
or until cinnamony brown. Gradually whisk in
the milk, lower the heat, and whisk constantly
5 minutes more or until the gravy is slightly thickened. Serve hot with mashed sweet potatoes,
steamed green beans and wax beans, and Beth's
Buttermilk Biscuits (page 306). Or serve cold,
without the gravy, with Picnic Potato Salad (page
255) and fresh fruits instead. Makes 4 servings.

*1 serving: Calories 408; Saturated Fat 4 g;
Total Fat 14 g; Protein 49 g; Carbohydrate 16 g; Fiber 0 g;
Sodium 477 mg; Cholesterol 147 mg*

BUFFALO CHICKEN FINGERS

◆◆◆

Try this healthier version of a famous chicken favorite, which keeps the flavor yet lowers the fat.

2 large egg whites	¼ cup Neufchâtel cream cheese at room temperature (2 ounces)
2 tablespoons water	
¾ cup dry unseasoned bread crumbs	1 tablespoon red wine vinegar
¼ teaspoon ground red pepper (cayenne)	2 tablespoons dry sherry
1 pound skinned and boned chicken breasts, cut into 4- x 1-inch strips	1 teaspoon Worcestershire sauce
2 tablespoons vegetable oil	¼ teaspoon garlic powder
For the dipping sauce:	⅛ teaspoon black pepper
½ cup plain low-fat yogurt	
⅓ cup blue cheese, crumbled (2 ounces)	

PREP TIME: 15 MIN. / COOKING TIME: 10 MIN.

1 Preheat the oven to 450° F. Line a 13"x 9"x 2" baking pan with foil and oil lightly. In a pie plate or shallow dish, whisk the egg whites with the water for 1 minute or just until frothy. On a piece of wax paper, mix the bread crumbs with the ground red pepper.

2 Dip the chicken strips into the egg white mixture, coat with the seasoned bread crumbs, and place in the baking pan. Drizzle with the oil and bake, uncovered, for 5 minutes on each side or until crispy and golden-brown.

3 To prepare the dipping sauce: While the chicken is baking, blend all of the sauce ingredients in a medium-size bowl and spoon into a small serving bowl. Arrange the chicken fingers on a warm platter and serve with the sauce for dipping. Makes 4 servings.

1 serving: Calories 387; Saturated Fat 7 g; Total Fat 17 g; Protein 38 g; Carbohydrate 18 g; Fiber 0 g; Sodium 528 mg; Cholesterol 91 mg

---

DOWN HOME TRADITION

One day in 1964, at the Anchor Bar in Buffalo, New York, owner Theresa Bellissimo accidentally received a very large number of chicken wings from one of her suppliers. She spiced them very hot, served them with a cooling cheese dip, and created an overnight sensation.

◆ Buffalo Chicken Wings ◆

1½ pounds chicken wings (about 8), wing tips removed

1 cup vegetable oil

3 tablespoons melted butter

2 tablespoons red wine vinegar

½ teaspoon ground red pepper (cayenne)

⅓ cup blue cheese, crumbled (2 ounces)

¼ cup cream cheese (2 ounces)

2 tablespoons mayonnaise

2 tablespoons dry sherry

1 teaspoon Worcestershire sauce

¼ teaspoon each celery salt and garlic powder

PREP TIME: 15 MIN. / COOKING TIME: 8 MIN.

1 Using kitchen shears, cut each wing into 2 pieces. In a large deep skillet, heat the oil over moderate heat to 365° F or until a 1-inch cube of bread turns golden in 1 minute. Fry the wings for about 5 minutes or until cooked through, then transfer to paper towels.

2 In a pie plate or shallow dish, combine the butter, vinegar, and ground red pepper. Add the chicken wings, toss to coat, then arrange on a warm platter. In a small bowl, blend the remaining ingredients and serve with the chicken wings. Makes 4 servings.

1 serving: Calories 467; Saturated Fat 17 g; Total Fat 40 g; Protein 23 g; Carbohydrate 3 g; Fiber 0 g; Sodium 566 mg; Cholesterol 109 mg

HILLARY'S CHICKEN

◆◆◆

Many Arkansas hostesses are experts at cooking chicken. This favorite recipe for entertaining comes from First Lady Hillary Rodham Clinton.

2 tablespoons unsalted butter or margarine, melted	¼ teaspoon ground dried sage
1 tablespoon finely grated onion	⅛ teaspoon dried marjoram leaves
1 clove garlic, crushed	Dash hot red pepper sauce
1 teaspoon dried thyme leaves	4 skinned and boned chicken breast halves (about 5 ounces each)
½ teaspoon each salt and black pepper	
½ teaspoon dried rosemary leaves	2 tablespoons minced parsley

PREP TIME: 15 MIN. / COOKING TIME: 14 MIN.

1 Heat the oven to 425°F. In a shallow baking dish, combine the butter, onion, garlic, thyme, salt, pepper, rosemary, sage, marjoram, and red pepper sauce. Add the chicken and turn to coat. Tuck the edges of each breast under, forming a rectangular shape about 1½ inches thick.

2 Bake, uncovered, basting frequently with the pan juices, for 14 minutes or just until the juices run clear when the chicken is pricked with a fork. Transfer to a warm serving platter, spoon over the pan juices, and sprinkle with the parsley. Serve with Wild Rice with Pecans (page 207). Makes 4 servings.

1 serving: Calories 219; Saturated Fat 4 g; Total Fat 8 g; Protein 35 g; Carbohydrate 1 g; Fiber 0 g; Sodium 366 mg; Cholesterol 101 mg

A chicken in every pot.

—Republican campaign slogan, 1928

CHICKEN PAPRIKASH

◆◆◆

This Austro-Hungarian dish is a favorite in Hungarian communities in the Midwest. It's more authentic when made with sweet Hungarian paprika, often found in food specialty shops.

1 tablespoon vegetable oil	¾ teaspoon salt
6 skinned and boned chicken breast halves (about 5 ounces each)	¼ teaspoon black pepper
	6 cups hot, cooked egg noodles (12 ounces uncooked)
1 cup chopped onion	
1 cup chopped sweet green pepper	1 tablespoon poppy seeds (optional)
1 clove garlic, minced	¼ cup all-purpose flour
2 tablespoons paprika	¼ cup cold water
1 cup Chicken Stock (page 74) or low-sodium chicken broth	½ cup reduced-fat sour cream
	2 tablespoons minced parsley
½ cup diced tomato	

PREP TIME: 20 MIN. / COOKING TIME: 30 MIN.

1 In a 12-inch nonstick skillet, heat the oil over moderately high heat. Cook the chicken breasts for about 3 minutes on each side or until well browned, then transfer to a plate.

2 Add the onion, green pepper, and garlic to the skillet and sauté for 5 minutes or until tender. Add the paprika and cook 2 minutes longer. Stir in the stock, tomato, salt, black pepper, and chicken; bring to a boil. Lower the heat, cover, and simmer, stirring often, for 15 minutes. On a warm platter, toss the noodles with the poppy seeds if you wish and top with the chicken.

3 In a cup, whisk the flour and water; slowly stir into the stock mixture in the skillet. Simmer for 3 minutes, then stir in the sour cream and parsley and heat just until hot (do not boil). Pour over the chicken. Serve with braised cabbage and fresh tomato wedges. Makes 6 servings.

1 serving: Calories 453 ; Saturated Fat 2 g; Total Fat 8 g; Protein 45 g; Carbohydrate 50 g; Fiber 1 g; Sodium 448 mg; Cholesterol 140 mg

Chicken Paprikash: Served atop noodles with poppy seeds

CHICKEN DIVAN
◆◆◆

The chef at the Divan Parisian Restaurant in New York created this dish, using slices of turkey, then served it on rich, buttery pastry. This version contains chicken and forgets the pastry.

1½	pounds skinned, boned, cooked, and sliced chicken breasts, or slices of roast chicken
1	pound broccoli, trimmed and cut into individual spears

For the sauce:

2	cups low-fat (1% milkfat) milk
1	cup Chicken Stock (page 74) or low-sodium chicken broth
2	tablespoons reduced-fat sour cream
3	tablespoons cornstarch
2	tablespoons grated Parmesan cheese
2	tablespoons dry sherry or Chicken Stock
1	teaspoon Dijon mustard
½	teaspoon salt
⅛	teaspoon each nutmeg and ground red pepper (cayenne)
½	cup shredded Cheddar cheese (2 ounces)
2	tablespoons plain dry bread crumbs

⏱ PREP TIME: 15 MIN. / COOKING TIME: 45 MIN.

1 Preheat the oven to 375°F. Lightly grease a 2-quart au gratin or other shallow baking dish. Arrange the chicken slices in the dish.

2 Half-fill a large saucepan with cold water and bring to a boil over high heat. Add the broccoli, return to a boil, and cook, uncovered, for 2 minutes or until crisp-tender. Drain, rinse with cold water, and drain again. Arrange in a single layer on top of the chicken.

3 In a medium-size saucepan, bring the milk and stock to a simmer over moderate heat. In a small bowl, whisk together the sour cream, cornstarch, Parmesan cheese, sherry, mustard, salt, nutmeg, and ground red pepper. Whisk into the broth mixture and simmer, uncovered, for 5 minutes or until slightly thickened, stirring frequently. Pour the sauce over the chicken and broccoli. Sprinkle the Cheddar cheese and bread crumbs over the top.

4 Bake, uncovered, for 20 to 25 minutes or until hot and bubbly. Preheat the broiler and broil 4 inches from the heat for 2 minutes or until golden. Serve with freshly baked Portland Popovers (page 310). Makes 6 servings.

1 serving: Calories 318 ; Saturated Fat 4 g; Total Fat 8 g; Protein 44 g; Carbohydrate 16 g; Fiber 1 g; Sodium 567 mg; Cholesterol 102 mg

◆

Turkey Divan

Prepare as for Chicken Divan, substituting **1½ pounds of skinned, boned, cooked, and sliced turkey breast or slices of roast turkey** for the chicken. Makes 6 servings. 1 serving: *Calories 348; Saturated Fat 4 g; Total Fat 8 g; Protein 52 g; Carbohydrate 16 g; Fiber 1 g; Sodium 546 mg; Cholesterol 134 mg*

Chicken shortcake, Dixieland-style — sandwiched between slabs of homemade corn bread

DIXIELAND SHORTCAKE

◆◆◆

In the deep South, this main-dish version of shortcake is popular with corn bread for the "cake" and a chicken sauce for the filling.

½ recipe Corn Pone (page 301)

2 large sweet red or green peppers

1 tablespoon unsalted butter or margarine

4 ounces fresh mushrooms, sliced (1½ cups)

4 green onions, with tops, sliced (½ cup)

¼ cup all-purpose flour

2 cups Chicken Stock (page 74) or low-sodium chicken broth

3 cups bite-size pieces cooked chicken (1 pound, 2 ounces)

¼ teaspoon black pepper

PREP TIME: 30 MIN. / COOKING TIME: 30 MIN.

1 Preheat the oven to 400°F and grease an 8" x 8" x 2" baking pan. Prepare the Corn Pone batter as the recipe directs; bake for 20 minutes.

2 Meanwhile, core and seed the sweet peppers. Using a small star cutter, cut 1 pepper into stars; chop the remaining one, making 1½ cups.

3 In a large nonstick saucepan, melt the butter over moderate heat. Add the mushrooms, chopped sweet pepper, and green onions; sauté for 5 minutes or until crisp-tender. Using a slotted spoon, transfer the vegetables to a bowl.

4 Stir the flour into the saucepan and cook until bubbly. Whisk in the stock and bring to a boil. Lower the heat and simmer, uncovered, stirring for 5 minutes. Stir in the chicken, black pepper, and vegetables and heat through.

5 Cut the Corn Pone into 4 squares, split them and fill with the chicken. Garnish with the red pepper stars. Serve with heaping portions of Fried Greens (page 222). Makes 4 servings.

1 serving: Calories 617; Saturated Fat 7 g;
Total Fat 22 g; Protein 30 g; Carbohydrate 73 g; Fiber 1 g;
Sodium 449 mg; Cholesterol 117 mg

CAPITOLADE OF CHICKEN

◆◆◆

One of Thomas Jefferson's favorite breakfasts at Monticello featured this chicken hash, served over hot buttermilk biscuits.

1 recipe Beth's Buttermilk Biscuits (page 306)	1½ cups Chicken Stock (page 74) or low-sodium chicken broth
2 tablespoons unsalted butter or margarine	⅓ cup dry white wine or Chicken Stock
4 ounces fresh mushrooms, sliced (1½ cups)	1½ teaspoons chopped fresh thyme or ½ teaspoon dried thyme leaves
4 green onions, with tops, sliced (½ cup)	2 cups bite-size pieces cooked chicken (12 ounces)
1 large carrot, peeled and sliced (½ cup)	¼ teaspoon each salt and black pepper
¼ cup finely chopped celery	2 tablespoons minced parsley
1 clove garlic, minced	
2 tablespoons all-purpose flour	

PREP TIME: 35 MIN. / COOKING TIME: 30 MIN.

1 Preheat the oven to 425°F. Prepare and bake the biscuits. Meanwhile, in a large saucepan, melt the butter over moderate heat. Stir in the mushrooms, green onions, carrot, celery, and garlic. Sauté for 6 minutes or until tender.

2 Stir in the flour and cook until bubbly. Whisk in the stock, wine, and thyme and bring to a boil. Lower the heat and simmer, uncovered, stirring, for 10 minutes or until slightly thickened.

3 Stir in the chicken, salt, and pepper and heat through. Stir in the parsley and spoon over the hot biscuits. Serve with Spicy Pickled Peaches (page 271). Makes 4 servings.

1 serving: Calories 417; Saturated Fat 8 g; Total Fat 19 g; Protein 27 g; Carbohydrate 31 g; Fiber 1 g; Sodium 571 mg; Cholesterol 77 mg

CHICKEN IN THE SHELL

◆◆◆

This popular Pennsylvania-Dutch dish is usually reserved for very special guests.

1 package (1 pound, 1¼ ounces) frozen puff pastry sheets, thawed 20 minutes	½ cup Chicken Stock (page 74) or low-sodium chicken broth
2 teaspoons chopped fresh thyme or ½ teaspoon dried thyme leaves	4 cups bite-size pieces cooked chicken (1½ pounds)
For the filling:	½ cup cooked fresh or uncooked frozen peas
1 tablespoon unsalted butter or margarine	¼ cup minced parsley
2 tablespoons all-purpose flour	¾ teaspoon salt
1 cup low-fat (1% milkfat) milk	½ teaspoon paprika
	¼ teaspoon white pepper

PREP TIME: 40 MIN. / COOKING TIME: 30 MIN.

1 Preheat the oven to 375°F and set out a jumbo muffin pan. On a lightly floured surface, roll out the dough. Cut into six 6-inch rounds and press each round into a muffin cup. Prick all over with a fork and spinkle with the thyme. Bake for 16 minutes or until crisp, then transfer to a rack.

2 Meanwhile, prepare the filling: In a large saucepan, melt the butter over moderate heat. Stir in the flour and cook until bubbly. Gradually whisk in the milk and stock and bring to a boil.

3 Lower the heat and simmer, whisking frequently, for 5 minutes, or until the sauce is slightly thickened. Stir in all the remaining ingredients and cook until heated through. Spoon into the patty shells and serve with Green Beans Amandine (page 220). Makes 6 servings.

1 serving: Calories 465; Saturated Fat 5 g; Total Fat 23 g; Protein 35 g; Carbohydrate 28 g; Fiber 0 g; Sodium 574 mg; Cholesterol 81 mg

DOWN HOME TRADITION

Stories of the origins of Chicken à la King abound, all dating back to the late 19th century. One tale credits its creation to the chef at New York's Brighton Beach Hotel, who may have prepared it for the proprietors, Mr. and Mrs. E. Clark King III. Another story traces the dish to Foxhall P. Keene, son of financier James R. Keene. He supposedly originated the dish at Delmonico's in the 1880's. And still another tale credits Claridge's restaurant in London for first serving the dish to James R. Keene himself, after his horse won the Grand Prix in 1881. Whatever its namesake, Chicken à la King was usually served in grand style by being ladled from an elegant chafing dish over rich pastry shells.

◆ Chicken à la King ◆

4 frozen prepared puff pastry shells
¼ cup (½ stick) unsalted butter or margarine
4 ounces fresh mushrooms, sliced (1½ cups)
1 small sweet green pepper, cored, seeded, and diced (¾ cup)
5 tablespoons all-purpose flour
2 cups half-and-half
4 cups bite-size pieces cooked chicken (1½ pounds)
½ cup finely chopped pimientos, well drained
1 teaspoon salt
¼ teaspoon white pepper, or to taste
1 large egg yolk
1 tablespoon dry sherry (optional)
2 tablespoons minced parsley

PREP TIME: 30 MIN. / COOKING TIME: 25 MIN.

1 Prepare and bake the patty shells as the package directs. Meanwhile, in a deep 12-inch skillet, melt the butter over moderate heat. Add the mushrooms and green pepper and sauté for 5 minutes or until tender. Whisk in the flour and cook until bubbly.

2 Gradually whisk in the half-and-half; cook, stirring frequently, for 5 minutes or just until thickened (do not boil). Stir in the chicken, pimientos, salt, and white pepper and cook until heated through. In a small bowl, beat the egg yolk with about ¼ cup of the sauce, then whisk the mixture into the skillet.

3 Simmer gently, stirring constantly, for 2 minutes or until thickened. Stir in the sherry if you wish. To serve, place 1 patty shell on each plate, spoon in the Chicken à la King, and garnish with the parsley. Serve with a tossed green salad. Makes 4 servings.

1 serving: Calories 736; Saturated Fat 17 g; Total Fat 45 g; Protein 51 g; Carbohydrate 33 g; Fiber 1 g; Sodium 806 mg; Cholesterol 233 mg

Creamed Chicken with Mushrooms and Peppers: A slimmed-down version of Chicken à la King

CREAMED CHICKEN WITH MUSHROOMS AND PEPPERS

◆◆◆

This updated version has less fat than the original, plus it's served over toast points instead of rich pastry.

2 tablespoons unsalted butter or margarine

4 ounces mushrooms, sliced (1½ cups)

1 small sweet green pepper, cored, seeded, and diced (¾ cup)

¼ cup all-purpose flour

2 cups low-fat (1% milkfat) milk

2½ to 3 cups bite-size pieces cooked chicken (15 ounces)

½ cup finely chopped pimientos, well drained

¼ teaspoon salt, or to taste

⅛ teaspoon white pepper, or to taste

1 tablespoon dry sherry (optional)

4 slices white or whole-wheat bread

2 tablespoons minced parsley

PREP TIME: 20 MIN. / COOKING TIME: 15 MIN.

1 In a deep 12-inch nonstick skillet, melt the butter over moderate heat. Add the mushrooms and green pepper and sauté for 5 minutes or until tender. Whisk in the flour and cook until bubbly.

2 Gradually whisk in the milk and cook, stirring frequently, for 5 minutes or just until thickened (do not boil). Stir in the chicken, pimientos, salt, and white pepper and cook until heated through. Stir in the sherry if you wish.

3 Toast the bread and cut each slice diagonally into 4 triangles. Place 4 triangles on each plate, ladle over 1 cup of the chicken mixture, and garnish with the parsley. Serve with Minted Green Peas (page 226). Makes 4 servings.

1 serving: Calories 339; Saturated Fat 5 g; Total Fat 10 g; Protein 34 g; Carbohydrate 28 g; Fiber 1 g; Sodium 402 mg; Cholesterol 85 mg

The traditional
Thanksgiving feast:
Roast Turkey and all
its trimmings

Roast Turkey
with Corn Bread Stuffing

◆◆◆

1 pound bulk pork sausage, crumbled	3 teaspoons dried thyme leaves
2 tablespoons unsalted butter or margarine	1 teaspoon rubbed sage
1½ cups chopped celery	¾ teaspoon each salt and black pepper
1 cup chopped onion	2 cups chopped pecans toasted (optional)
1 recipe Corn Pone 8 inches square (page 301), crumbled	1 16-pound fresh or thawed frozen turkey
3 cups Chicken Stock (page 74) or low-sodium chicken broth	⅓ cup all-purpose flour
1½ cups cored, chopped, unpeeled apples	3 cups low-fat (1% milkfat) milk
½ cup minced parsley	

⏱ PREP TIME: 1 HR. / COOKING TIME: 5¼ HR.
STANDING TIME: 10 MIN.

1 In a 12-inch nonstick skillet, brown the sausage over moderate heat for 5 minutes and transfer to a large bowl. Melt the butter in the skillet, add the celery and onion and sauté for 5 minutes or until tender. Transfer to the bowl; toss with the corn pone, stock, apples, parsley, 2 teaspoons of the thyme, the sage, ½ teaspoon each of the salt and pepper, and the pecans if you wish.

2 Preheat the oven to 325°F. Stuff the body and neck cavities of the turkey, then truss (page 363). Insert a roasting thermometer in its thigh. Transfer the rest of the stuffing to a buttered baking dish, cover tightly with foil, and refrigerate.

3 Roast the turkey on a rack in a large open roasting pan, basting often, for 4½ hours or until the thermometer registers 180°F. Bake the extra stuffing, covered, during the last 30 minutes. Let the turkey stand for 10 minutes; carve it, discarding the skin. Reserve the pan drippings.

4 To prepare the gravy: In a 12-inch skillet, heat ¼ cup of the drippings over moderate heat. Whisk in the flour, the remaining thyme, salt, and pepper and cook until bubbly. Whisk in the milk; cook, stirring, for 5 minutes or until thickened. Serve with the turkey and Roasted Vegetables (page 237). Makes 16 servings.

*1 serving: Calories 483; Saturated Fat 6 g;
Total Fat 19 g; Protein 44 g; Carbohydrate 31 g; Fiber 0 g;
Sodium 501 mg; Cholesterol 135 mg*

CRANBERRY-ORANGE CORNISH HENS

◆ ◆ ◆

Poultry breeding in mid-19th-century America gave birth to this small tender bird, a cross between a Plymouth Rock Chicken and Cornish Game Hen.

1	5-ounce package brown and wild rice mix	1¾	cups Chicken Stock (page 74) or low-sodium chicken broth
2	Cornish hens with livers (1½ pounds each)	¾	cup fresh or frozen cranberries
1	tablespoon unsalted butter or margarine	1	tablespoon grated orange rind
8	ounces white button mushrooms, thinly sliced (3 cups)	1	teaspoon black pepper
1	cup chopped onion	½	teaspoon salt
½	cup chopped celery	2	tablespoons honey
		2	tablespoons fresh orange juice

PREP TIME: 40 MIN. / COOKING TIME: 1½ HR.
STANDING TIME: 10 MIN.

1 Preheat the oven to 450°F. Cook the rice mix according to the package directions and drain. Meanwhile, coarsely chop the livers. In a 12-inch nonstick skillet, melt the butter over moderately high heat. Add the mushrooms, onion, and celery and sauté for 8 minutes or until tender. Add the livers and sauté 2 minutes more or until no longer pink. Transfer to a large bowl.

2 To the bowl, add the rice, 1 cup of the stock, the cranberries, orange rind, ½ teaspoon of the pepper, and ¼ teaspoon of the salt; toss to mix well. Stuff the hens and truss (page 363). Wrap extra stuffing in foil. In a cup, prepare a basting sauce by whisking the honey and orange juice.

3 Roast the hens on a rack in a large open roasting pan for 15 minutes. Lower the oven temperature to 350°F; roast, basting frequently with the sauce, for 45 minutes or until the juices run clear when a thigh is pricked with a fork. Bake extra stuffing during the last 30 minutes.

Transfer the hens to a warm platter, sprinkle with the remaining ½ teaspoon of pepper and ¼ teaspoon of salt, and surround with extra stuffing. Cover loosely with foil; let stand for 10 minutes.

4 Meanwhile, whisk the remaining ¾ cup of stock into the roasting pan; bring to a boil over moderate heat. Boil, uncovered, for 3 minutes; strain into a gravy boat. Remove the strings, cut the hens in half, and serve with the stuffing, gravy, and steamed asparagus. Makes 4 servings.

1 serving (½ hen): Calories 457; Saturated Fat 7 g; Total Fat 19 g; Protein 25 g; Carbohydrate 48 g; Fiber 2 g; Sodium 379 mg; Cholesterol 127 mg

◆ Giving Thanks on Thanksgiving ◆

The year was 1621 in the colonial settlement at Plymouth, Massachusetts. Having survived a year of hardship, the colonists invited the local Wampanoag Indians to a harvest feast to give "Thanks to God." They dined on venison, roast goose and duck, oysters and clams, eels, watercress, leeks, corn bread, popcorn, wild plums, and homemade wine—and possibly wild turkey, though sources differ as to the authenticity of this fact.

The event became a tradition that grew gradually until George Washington proclaimed the first national Thanksgiving observance on November 26, 1789.

In 1827, Sarah Joseph Hale, the editor of *Godie's Lady's Book*, began a relentless campaign to set aside an annual family holiday of thanksgiving "to celebrate the bounty of peace and plenty." Her magazine showed pictures of feasts that featured roast turkey and all the trimmings.

In 1863, President Lincoln declared the last Thursday in November (later changed to the fourth Thursday) an official Thanksgiving Day, the tradition we know so well today.

ROAST GOOSE WITH DRIED APPLE STUFFING

◆◆◆

This bird, with its sumptuous stuffing and flavorful gravy could be the star of your next holiday feast. Look for goose in your super-market's freezer at holiday time.

For the stuffing:

- 2 tablespoons unsalted butter or margarine
- 2 cups chopped onions
- 1 cup chopped celery
- 3 cloves garlic, minced
- 1 teaspoon each dried marjoram, sage, and thyme
- 8 ounces dried apples, soaked, drained, and chopped
- 6 cups toasted white or whole wheat bread cubes (12 slices)
- ½ cup minced parsley
- ½ teaspoon each salt and black pepper
- ½ cup Chicken Stock (page 74) or low-sodium chicken broth

For the goose:

- 1 goose with giblets (10 to 12 pounds)
- ½ teaspoon each salt and black pepper

- 1 large yellow onion, quartered
- 2 stalks celery, quartered
- 1 carrot, scrubbed and quartered
- 4 cloves garlic, peeled

For the gravy:

- 4 cups Chicken Stock (page 74) or low-sodium chicken broth
- 1 tablespoon tomato paste
- 12 sprigs parsley
- 1 teaspoon each dried marjoram, sage, and thyme
- ¼ teaspoon salt
- 6 each whole cloves, juniper berries, and black peppercorns (optional)
- 2 tablespoons cornstarch
- ¼ cup Madeira, port, or water

PREP TIME: 1 HR. / COOKING TIME: 3¼ HR. STANDING TIME: 15 MIN.

1 To prepare the stuffing: In a 12-inch nonstick skillet, melt the butter over moderately high heat. Add the onions, celery, garlic, marjoram, sage, and thyme and sauté for 5 minutes or until tender. Transfer to a large bowl, and toss with the remaining stuffing ingredients.

2 To prepare the goose: Preheat the oven to 425°F. Wash the goose and pat it dry, reserving the giblets and discarding the fat and liver.

Loosely stuff the body and neck cavities and prick the skin on the lower breast, legs, and around the wings with a skewer. Truss (page 363), then sprinkle with the salt and pepper. Transfer the rest of the stuffing to a buttered au gratin dish, cover tightly with foil, and refrigerate.

3 Place the goose, breast-side-up, on a rack in a large shallow roasting pan, insert a roasting thermometer in its thigh, and surround with the onion, celery, carrot, garlic, and reserved giblets. Roast the goose, uncovered, for 30 minutes. Lower the heat to 325°F and pour over 1 cup of boiling water. Continue to roast, basting with the pan juices and skimming off the fat, for 2 to 2½ hours more or until the thermometer registers 175°F. Bake the extra stuffing, covered, during the last 30 minutes. Let the goose stand for 15 minutes, then carve it, and discard the skin.

4 Meanwhile, prepare the gravy: After the vegetables and giblets have cooked with the goose for 1 hour and are well browned, transfer them to a medium-size saucepan. Add the stock, tomato paste, parsley, marjoram, sage, thyme, and salt, plus the cloves, juniper berries, and pepper-corns if you wish; bring to a boil over high heat. Lower the heat and simmer, uncovered, for 1 hour, skimming occasionally, then strain.

5 In a cup, whisk the cornstarch and Madeira until smooth; whisk into the gravy. Return to a boil and cook for 3 minutes, whisking, until the gravy thickens slightly. Serve with the goose and your favorite accompaniments. Makes 6 servings.

1 serving: Calories 571; Saturated Fat 8 g; Total Fat 20 g; Protein 38 g; Carbohydrate 56 g; Fiber 2 g; Sodium 660 mg; Cholesterol 122 mg

What is sauce for the goose may be sauce for the gander.

—Alice B. Toklas

DUCK IN ORANGE SAUCE

◆◆◆

Domestication of ducks began here in 1873, when a Yankee clipper ship docked in New York carrying a flock from Peking. Since that time, Americans have enjoyed eating duck with orange sauce, this one enhanced with roasted vegetables and giblets.

Fancy Fare: Duck in a tangy orange sauce

1 **duck with giblets (5 pounds)**	6 **whole white or black peppercorns (optional)**
2 **teaspoons dried rosemary leaves**	4 **whole cloves**
½ **teaspoon each salt and black pepper**	¼ **cup white wine vinegar**
2 **strips orange zest (colored part of the rind)**	3 **tablespoons sugar**
1 **large yellow onion, quartered**	⅓ **cup blanched julienned orange zest (page 364)**
1 **large carrot, thickly sliced (½ cup)**	1 **tablespoon cornstarch dissolved in 2 tablespoons water**
2 **large cloves garlic**	
1½ **cups Chicken Stock (page 74) or low-sodium chicken broth**	1 **teaspoon fresh lemon juice, or to taste**
2 **tablespoons tomato paste**	1 **small orange, peeled, and sectioned**

PREP TIME: 30 MIN. / COOKING TIME: 1½ HR.

1 Preheat the oven to 475°F. Rinse the duck and pat it dry. Reserve the giblets; discard the liver. Season the cavity with 1 teaspoon of the rosemary, ¼ teaspoon each of the salt and pepper, and the 2 strips of orange zest. Using a skewer, prick the skin on the lower breast, legs, and around the wings. Truss (page 363) and place breast-side-up on a rack in a shallow roasting pan. Surround it with the onion, carrot, garlic, and reserved giblets. Roast, uncovered, for 30 minutes.

2 Lower the temperature to 350°F. Remove the pan from the oven, discard the fat, and transfer the vegetables and giblets to a medium-size saucepan. Roast the duck for 1 hour or until the juices run clear when the thigh is pierced with a fork. Transfer the duck to a serving platter and cover loosely with foil.

3 To the vegetable mixture, add the stock, tomato paste, peppercorns if you wish, cloves, the remaining 1 teaspoon of rosemary, and the remaining ¼ teaspoon each of salt and pepper. Bring to a boil, lower the heat, and simmer, uncovered, for 45 minutes, skimming the surface.

4 In another medium-size saucepan, stir the vinegar and sugar. Cook over moderate heat for 5 minutes, swirling the pan, until golden. Strain the stock mixture into this pan, stir in the blanched orange zest, and simmer for 5 minutes. Whisk in the cornstarch mixture, boil for 2 minutes, then stir in the lemon juice and orange sections. Serve the duck with the orange sauce, Duchesse Potatoes (page 233), and Honey-Spiced Carrots (page 216). Makes 4 servings.

1 serving: Calories 217; Saturated Fat 3 g; Total Fat 7 g; Protein 16 g; Carbohydrate 24 g; Fiber 1 g; Sodium 411 mg; Cholesterol 54 mg

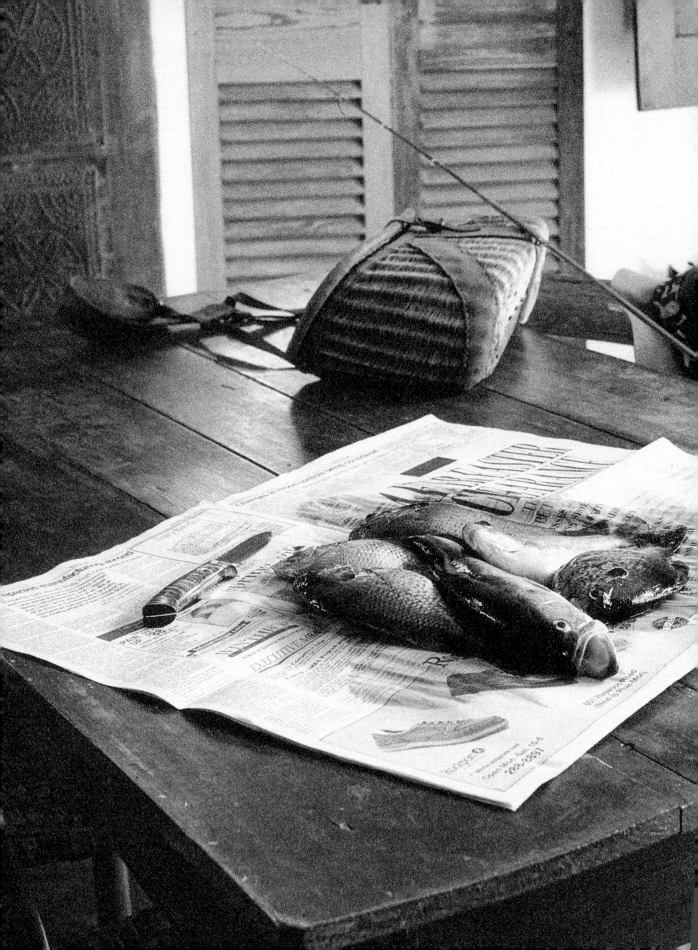

CATCH OF THE DAY

♦♦♦

From America's salt-water bays and oceans to her freshwater streams and lakes, fish and shellfish have long been mainstays in local cuisines. The catch of the day might be cod in New England, pompano in Florida, crawfish in the Cajun country around New Orleans, and salmon in the Pacific Northwest. Nowadays, even those Americans who live far from water can enjoy a large selection of fresh fish and shellfish, thanks to modern transportation and refrigeration methods and the growth of fish farming. The choices nationwide are broad and varied.

With the fish bounty they encountered, our forefathers created many wonderful dishes. A goodly number of them are included in this chapter, but they've been lightened a bit. Croquettes and crab cakes and the traditional Friday-night fish fry are made with much less fat. Scalloped Seafood, Shrimp Wiggle, and Lobster Newburg contain nary a drop of cream but retain their characteristic flavors and textures. It's our way of helping you to take advantage of the healthful qualities of fish—high protein and relatively low fat—and still enjoy the old-time ways of preparing it.

FRIED CATFISH

◆◆◆

*Catfish, so named because of its whiskers
(barbels), is often soaked in buttermilk to make
it moister, then dredged in cornmeal before
pan-frying. In the South, white cornmeal
is generally used; in the Midwest, yellow.*

1½ cups low-fat buttermilk	1¼ cups yellow or white cornmeal
¼ teaspoon each salt and ground red pepper (cayenne), or to taste	¼ cup vegetable oil
4 catfish (10 to 12 ounces each), pan dressed, with heads and tails left on	**Garnish:** 2 large unpeeled lemons, thinly sliced

🕐 PREP TIME: 10 MIN. / MARINATING TIME: 1 HR.
COOKING TIME: 9 MIN.

1 In a shallow pan large enough to hold the fish in a single layer, combine the buttermilk, salt, and ground red pepper. Add the fish, cover, and refrigerate for 1 hour, turning once.

2 Dredge the fish in the cornmeal. In a 12-inch nonstick skillet, heat the oil over moderately high heat. Add the fish and fry for 4 minutes on each side or until golden and crisp. Garnish with the lemon slices and serve with Hush Puppies (page 299) and Prayer Meeting Coleslaw (page 253). Makes 4 servings.

*1 serving: Calories 429; Saturated Fat 2 g;
Total Fat 11 g; Protein 45 g; Carbohydrate 40 g; Fiber 1 g;
Sodium 416 mg; Cholesterol 144 mg*

*Like most Southerners,
I adore catfish.*

—Craig Claiborne

BASS BARBECUED IN CORN HUSKS

◆◆◆

*In 19th-century America, deep-sea fishing
parties were so popular that posters showing men
on docks with long strings of sea bass were common,
especially on the East coast. Here, the fish
is cooked in corn husks, which give
it a special flavor.*

4 ears fresh corn	¼ teaspoon each salt and black pepper, or to taste
1 sea bass (3½ to 4 pounds) or 2 striped bass (1½ pounds each), pan dressed, with head and tail left on	2 tablespoons olive oil
2 tablespoons fresh lemon juice	**Garnish:** 2 large unpeeled lemons, cut into wedges

🕐 PREP TIME: 15 MIN. / COOKING TIME: 20 MIN.

1 Preheat the grill and place the rack 8 inches from the coals. Remove the husks from the corn, soak them for 5 minutes in cold water, and drain. Discard the silks.

2 Sprinkle the cavity of the bass with the lemon juice, salt, and pepper, then brush the outside with the oil. On a piece of heavy-duty foil large enough to enclose the fish, arrange some of the corn husks. Place the fish in the center, cover with more husks, and seal the packet tightly.

3 Place the packet on the grill over medium hot coals for 20 minutes or until the fish flakes when tested with a fork. Meanwhile, in a large saucepan, steam the corn in a small amount of boiling water over high heat for 5 to 7 minutes or until tender. Unwrap the fish, transfer to a warm platter, surround with the corn, and garnish with the lemon wedges. Serve with Warm Spinach-Bacon Salad (page 257). Makes 4 servings.

*1 serving: Calories 375; Saturated Fat 2 g;
Total Fat 12 g; Protein 45 g; Carbohydrate 26 g; Fiber 1 g;
Sodium 303 mg; Cholesterol 93 mg*

Cajun Red Snapper: Stuffed with shrimp and spices and other things nice

CAJUN STUFFED SNAPPER

◆◆◆

2 tablespoons unsalted butter or margarine	1 cup chopped cooked shrimp
¼ cup chopped yellow onion	2 cups ½-inch cubes white bread (4 slices)
3 tablespoons chopped celery	⅓ cup crab meat, picked through
3 tablespoons chopped sweet green pepper	¼ teaspoon each salt, paprika, and dried thyme leaves
2 tablespoons minced shallots	⅛ teaspoon each black pepper and ground red pepper (cayenne)
1 clove garlic, minced	
¼ cup sliced green onions	1 red snapper (about 4 pounds), pan dressed and boned, with head and tail left on
2 tablespoons minced parsley	

PREP TIME: 30 MIN. / COOKING TIME: 30 MIN.

1 Preheat the oven to 450°F. Lightly oil a large shallow roasting pan. In a 12-inch nonstick skillet, melt 1 tablespoon of the butter over moderately high heat. Add the onion, celery, green pepper, shallots, and garlic and cook for 5 minutes. Stir in the green onions and parsley and cook 1 minute longer. Transfer to a large bowl.

2 In the same skillet, melt the remaining tablespoon of butter. Add the shrimp and sauté for 3 minutes or just until heated through. Add to the onion mixture along with the bread cubes, crab meat, salt, paprika, thyme, and the black and ground red peppers. Mix well, then spoon into the cavity of the snapper. Close with toothpicks.

3 Place the fish in the pan. Using a sharp knife, make several diagonal slits in the body. Bake for 20 minutes or until the fish flakes when tested with a fork. Serve with generous helpings of Spider Spoon Bread (page 300). Makes 4 servings.

1 serving: Calories 385; Saturated Fat 5 g; Total Fat 10 g; Protein 59 g; Carbohydrate 10 g; Fiber 0 g; Sodium 433 mg; Cholesterol 161 mg

◆

Gulf Coast Flounder

Prepare as for Cajun Stuffed Snapper, substituting **one 3- to 4-pound flounder or four 12-ounce flounders** for the red snapper. Bake the large flounder for 20 minutes and the smaller ones for 15 minutes or until the fish flakes when tested with a fork. *1 serving: Calories 343; Saturated Fat 4 g; Total Fat 9 g; Protein 49 g; Carbohydrate 15 g; Fiber 1 g; Sodium 348 mg; Cholesterol 261 mg*

STUFFED BROOK TROUT ON A PLANK

◆◆◆

Abundant throughout the mountain lakes and streams of the American West, brook trout is a prized catch. Stuff it, then bake it on a board, ovenproof platter, or baking dish for a true Western supper.

1 tablespoon unsalted butter or margarine	1 tablespoon fresh thyme or 1 teaspoon dried thyme leaves
1 medium-size onion, finely chopped (1 cup)	¼ teaspoon salt
4 ounces fresh mushrooms, sliced (1½ cups)	4 brook trout (about 10 ounces each), pan dressed and boned with head and tail left on (page 362)
1 cup fresh white bread crumbs (2 slices)	4 teaspoons olive oil

PREP TIME: 15 MIN. / COOKING TIME: 36 MIN.

1 Preheat the oven to 350°F. Pre-soak and oil a large hardwood board about 1-inch thick, for planking (page 363), or set out an ovenproof platter or baking dish.

2 In a 12-inch nonstick skillet, melt the butter over moderate heat. Add the onion and sauté for 5 minutes. Stir in the mushrooms and sauté 5 minutes more. Add the bread crumbs, thyme, and salt and mix well.

3 Spoon some of the stuffing into the cavity of each trout and brush both sides with the oil, then arrange on the plank. Place the plank in the oven on a piece of foil. Bake for 25 minutes or until the fish flakes when tested with a fork. Serve with Corn Roasted on the Grill (page 219). Makes 4 servings.

1 serving: Calories 282; Saturated Fat 5 g; Total Fat 14 g; Protein 13 g; Carbohydrate 24 g; Fiber 1 g; Sodium 348 mg; Cholesterol 17 mg

TUNA ON THE GRILL

◆◆◆

Tuna is the name given to the English tunny by the Californians. Even today, most tuna caught in the United States is from Pacific waters, centering around California. This classic way of grilling tuna works well with swordfish, too.

2 tablespoons olive oil	¼ cup fresh orange juice
2 cloves garlic, crushed	¼ teaspoon each salt and black pepper
3 strips orange zest (colored part of the rind)	⅛ teaspoon ground red pepper (cayenne)
2 tablespoons chopped fresh basil or 2 teaspoons dried basil leaves	4 tuna or swordfish steaks, ¾ inch thick (6 ounces each)

PREP TIME: 15 MIN. / MARINATING TIME: 1 HR. COOKING TIME: 8 MIN.

1 In a small skillet, heat the oil, garlic, and orange zest for 4 minutes over low heat or until the garlic is golden and the oil is fragrant. Stir in the basil and set aside for 30 minutes or up to 3 hours. Strain through a sieve, mashing the solids with a wooden spoon, pushing through as much of the oil as possible. Stir in the orange juice, salt, and the black and ground red peppers.

2 Meanwhile, in a shallow glass dish, arrange the tuna in a single layer. Pour over the oil mixture, cover with plastic wrap, and refrigerate for 1 hour, turning the tuna once.

3 Preheat the grill or broiler. Grill the fish over medium-hot coals or broil 4 inches from the heat, brushing frequently with the marinade, for 4 minutes on each side or until the fish flakes when tested with a fork. Serve with Potatoes au Gratin (page 228). Makes 4 servings.

1 serving: Calories 248; Saturated Fat 3 g; Total Fat 13 g; Protein 29 g; Carbohydrate 3 g; Fiber 0 g; Sodium 182 mg; Cholesterol 47 mg

POACHED SALMON WITH CUCUMBER-DILL SAUCE

Throughout New England, the traditional Fourth of July menu calls for gently simmered (poached) salmon and freshly picked peas.

1½ cups cold water

1 cup dry white wine (with or without alcohol)

2 green onions, with tops, thinly sliced (¼ cup)

8 black peppercorns

4 salmon steaks, ¾ inch thick (6 ounces each)

For the sauce:

1 cup reduced-fat sour cream

½ cup diced peeled cucumber

3 tablespoons snipped dill or 2 teaspoons dried dill weed

2 tablespoons prepared horseradish

2 teaspoons fresh lemon juice

¼ teaspoon salt

⅛ teaspoon black pepper

Garnishes:

1 small unpeeled cucumber, thinly sliced

Sprigs of fresh dill

PREP TIME: 15 MIN. / COOKING TIME: 10 MIN.
CHILLING TIME: 1 HR.

1 In a deep 12-inch skillet, combine the water, wine, green onions, and peppercorns. Arrange the salmon steaks in a single layer in the skillet and bring just to a boil over high heat.

2 Lower the heat, cover, and simmer for 5 to 8 minutes or until the fish flakes when tested with a fork. Using a slotted spatula, carefully remove the salmon steaks to a large platter. Cover and refrigerate for 1 hour or until well chilled.

3 Meanwhile, make the sauce: In a small bowl, mix all of the sauce ingredients until well blended. Cover and refrigerate until chilled. Serve each salmon steak with a little Cucumber-Dill Sauce, garnished with cucumber slices and dill sprigs, and accompanied by steamed sugarsnap peas. Makes 4 servings.

1 serving: Calories 222; Saturated Fat 3 g; Total Fat 8 g; Protein 19 g; Carbohydrate 11 g; Fiber 0 g; Sodium 362 mg; Cholesterol 32 mg

A superb summertime supper: Cold poached salmon and steamed sugarsnap peas

◆ Salmon Fest ◆

Fresh salmon, hot off the grill, with all the fixings—it's a treat you won't soon forget! Just ask Warren Aakervik of Ballard, Washington near Seattle on Puget Sound. Every year, with the help of others, Warren serves more than 10,000 people this wonderful specialty, grilled on large covered cookers at various outdoor salmon fests.

One such event, sponsored by the commercial fishing industry, is free to all, while others have a nominal fee, with the proceeds going to special community efforts.

Warren is owner of the Ballard Oil Company, yet he finds the time not only to organize, but actually do a lot of the grilling at these fests. According to Warren, "the best barbecued salmon comes from cooking with a low smoky heat, flavored with a pungent wood." He follows a few simple steps:

1. Use a covered grill that has adjustable vents on the top and bottom. You need very few briquettes: 9 to 12 for up to 10 pounds of salmon. After the briquettes turn ashen white, add a few sticks of alder, cherry, or hickory, preferably fresh, to add extra flavor to the fish.

2. Season the salmon lightly. A little salt and pepper and fresh lemon juice will do, or use the recipe given at the right.

3. Make a grilling pan from a double thickness of aluminum foil, folding up the edges to form sides. Lay the salmon in the center, then place on the grill rack, as far above the coals as possible.

4. Cover the grill and smoke the fish—about 45 minutes for fillets, longer for a whole one—keeping the vents open slightly. Tip: The grill cover should be barely hot to the touch. To lower the heat, close the vents a little bit more.

"Avoid overcooking fish. It's ready when the cooked flesh flakes easily when touched with a fork."

SALMON ON THE GRILL
◆◆◆

Here is Warren Aakervik's own special recipe for perfectly grilled smoked salmon.

2 fresh salmon fillets (2¼ to 2½ pounds each), skinned	2 tablespoons minced parsley
¼ cup (½ stick) unsalted butter or margarine, melted	6 to 8 fresh sticks hickory, cedar, or cherry wood, soaked in water if dried
1 tablespoon fresh lemon juice	4 sprigs each fresh rosemary and thyme, about 5 inches long (optional)
½ teaspoon each garlic salt, black pepper, and paprika	
¼ teaspoon salt	

PREP TIME: 30 MIN. / COOKING TIME: 45 MIN.

1 In a covered grill, light 10 charcoal briquettes and wait for 30 minutes or until they turn ashen white. Spread out the coals to form a single layer.

2 Meanwhile, lay the salmon fillets on double sheets of heavy-duty aluminum foil, leaving a 6-inch border, then fold up the edges to make a rim. Brush both sides of the fillets with the butter and sprinkle with the lemon juice, garlic salt, pepper, paprika, salt, and parsley.

3 Lay the wood sticks directly on the coals with the rosemary and thyme, if using. Place the foil tray of salmon on the grill rack. Cover the grill, opening the top and bottom vents slightly. (The cover of the grill should be barely hot to the touch.) Smoke the fish for about 45 minutes or until it flakes easily when touched with a fork. Serve with Green Rice (page 207) and a tomato and avocado salad. Makes 12 servings.

1 serving: Calories 236; Saturated Fat 4 g;
Total Fat 10 g; Protein 34 g; Carbohydrate 1 g; Fiber 0 g;
Sodium 245 mg; Cholesterol 99 mg

Fish of the Day: Fillets of fresh-caught trout with a crunchy almond crust

TROUT AMANDINE

◆◆◆

Teaming up trout with almonds began with the Parisians, who prepare the dish with whole trout and sautéed almonds. The American version usually calls for fillets.

½ cup sliced almonds

¼ cup all-purpose flour

¼ teaspoon ground cumin (optional)

¼ teaspoon each salt and black pepper, or to taste

4 fresh trout fillets (4 ounces each), skinned, or frozen and thawed fillets

¼ cup low-fat buttermilk

2 tablespoons unsalted butter or margarine

¼ cup water

¼ cup white wine or Fish Stock (page 75)

1 tablespoon fresh lemon juice

1 large unpeeled lemon, thinly sliced

¼ cup minced parsley

PREP TIME: 10 MIN. / COOKING TIME: 10 MIN.

1 In a self-sealing plastic bag, toss ¼ cup of the almonds, the flour, the cumin if you wish, and ⅛ teaspoon each of the salt and pepper. Using a rolling pin, carefully crush the mixture, then spread on a plate. Dip the fillets in the buttermilk, then dredge in the seasoned flour.

2 In a 12-inch nonstick skillet, melt 1 tablespoon of the butter over moderately high heat. Add the fillets and sauté for 3 to 4 minutes on each side or until the fish flakes when touched with a fork. Transfer to a warm platter.

3 Stir the remaining 1 tablespoon of butter into the pan and lower the heat. Add the remaining ¼ cup of almonds and sauté until golden. Stir in the water, wine, lemon juice, the remaining ⅛ teaspoon each of salt and pepper, the lemon slices, and parsley. Bring just to a boil and quickly pour over the fillets. Makes 4 servings.

1 serving: Calories 304; Saturated Fat 5 g; Total Fat 17 g; Protein 25 g; Carbohydrate 11 g; Fiber 1 g; Sodium 315 mg; Cholesterol 74 mg

NEW ORLEANS POMPANO

◆◆◆

*This grand recipe was created in the early
1900's by Jules Alciatore, owner of Antoine's
restaurant in New Orleans. When movie director
Cecil B. De Mille was there filming
The Pirate's Lady, he enjoyed the dish so
much that he wrote it into the script.*

4 teaspoons unsalted butter or margarine	⅛ teaspoon each salt and black pepper, or to taste
2 shallots or green onions, minced (¼ cup)	⅛ teaspoon hot pepper sauce
8 ounces fresh mushrooms, sliced (3 cups)	8 ounces large shrimp (about 10), thawed if frozen, peeled and deveined with tails left on (page 362)
⅓ cup white wine or Fish Stock (page 75)	
3 tablespoons all-purpose flour	2 pompano or other white fish fillets (6 ounces each), skinned
1 cup plus 2 table-spoons low-fat (1% milkfat) milk	
¼ teaspoon paprika	8 sprigs chives, about 6 inches long

🕐 PREP TIME: 20 MIN. / COOKING TIME: 30 MIN.

1 In a 12-inch nonstick skillet, melt 2 teaspoons of the butter over moderate heat. Add the shallots and sauté for 5 minutes or until tender. Stir in the mushrooms and wine; sauté 4 minutes more or until only 3 tablespoons of liquid remain.

2 Add the flour and cook until bubbly, then whisk in 1 cup of the milk, paprika, salt, and pepper. Cook, stirring occasionally, for 3 minutes or until thickened. Stir in the remaining 2 table-spoons of milk, the hot pepper sauce, and shrimp and cook, uncovered, 3 minutes more or just until the shrimp turns opaque; remove from the heat.

3 Preheat the oven to 450°F. Grease two 12-x 18-inch pieces of parchment paper or aluminum foil with the remaining 2 teaspoons of butter. Place one fillet parallel to the narrow edge of each piece of foil about 3 inches from the edge; top with ½ of the sauce and the shrimp, and 4 chives.

**Dining in New Orleans style: Pompano and
shrimp for two, elegant yet so simple to prepare**

4 Bring the foil over each fillet, then seal the edges tightly and place on a baking sheet. Bake for 12 to 15 minutes or until puffed. Place a packet on each plate, cut a "X" slit, and carefully open, standing away from the steam. Serve with Long Island Potatoes (page 232). Makes 2 servings.

*1 serving: Calories 411; Saturated Fat 6 g;
Total Fat 14 g; Protein 41 g; Carbohydrate 23 g; Fiber 1 g;
Sodium 407 mg; Cholesterol 174 mg*

RED SNAPPER VERA CRUZ

◆◆◆

The Spanish settlers in California were known for creating dishes that combined hot peppers with local fish.

2 tablespoons olive oil

1 large red onion, chopped (1½ cups)

3 cloves garlic, minced

2 large fresh jalapeño peppers without seeds, minced, or 1 can (4 ounces) chopped mild green chilies, drained

1 can (14½ ounces) low-sodium whole, peeled tomatoes, undrained

1 can (8 ounces) no-salt-added tomato sauce

½ teaspoon dried oregano leaves

¼ teaspoon black pepper

¼ teaspoon grated lime rind

1 tablespoon fresh lime juice

4 red snapper or cod fillets (6 ounces each), skinned

Optional garnish:

2 tablespoons chopped, pitted black olives, preferably oil-cured

PREP TIME: 15 MIN. / COOKING TIME: 30 MIN.

1 Preheat the oven to 350°F. In a 12-inch oven-proof skillet, heat the oil over moderately high heat. Add the onion, garlic, and jalapeño peppers and sauté for 8 minutes or until tender.

2 Add the tomatoes with their juices, the tomato sauce, oregano, and black pepper and simmer, uncovered, for 5 minutes. Stir in the lime rind and juice and remove the skillet from the heat.

3 Place the fillets in a single layer in the skillet, spooning some of the sauce on top. Cover the skillet handle with foil. Bake, uncovered, for 15 minutes or until the fish flakes when touched with a fork. Garnish with the olives if you wish and serve with Wild Rice with Pecans (page 207). Makes 4 servings.

1 serving: Calories 280; Saturated Fat 1 g; Total Fat 9 g; Protein 32 g; Carbohydrate 18 g; Fiber 1 g; Sodium 437 mg; Cholesterol 53 mg

BLACKENED REDFISH

◆◆◆

This blackening technique, popular in Cajun cooking, involves seasoning fish or meats with hot spices, then searing and cooking them in a heavy skillet, preferably one of cast iron.

1 teaspoon dried thyme leaves

1 teaspoon each garlic powder, onion powder, and paprika

¾ teaspoon salt, or to taste

½ teaspoon each black pepper and ground red pepper (cayenne)

4 redfish fillets (6 ounces each), skinned

3 tablespoons unsalted butter or margarine, melted

Garnish:

4 lemon wedges

PREP TIME: 10 MIN. / COOKING TIME: 10 MIN.

1 In a small bowl, mix the thyme, the garlic and onion powders, paprika, salt, and the black and red peppers. Sprinkle this mixture on both sides of the fillets. Pour the butter in a pie plate.

2 Heat a heavy 12-inch skillet (preferably cast iron) over high heat until very hot. Dip the fish fillets in the melted butter, turning to coat and place in a single layer in the hot pan.

3 Cook for about 4 minutes on each side until blackened and the fish flakes when touched with a fork. Transfer to a warm platter and garnish with the lemon wedges. Serve with Carolina Red Rice (page 202) and Creole Okra and Tomatoes (page 223). Makes 4 servings.

1 serving: Calories 198; Saturated Fat 5 g; Total Fat 9 g; Protein 26 g; Carbohydrate 2 g; Fiber 0 g; Sodium 529 mg; Cholesterol 126 mg

◆

Cajun Catfish

Prepare as for Blackened Redfish substituting **4 skinned and boned catfish fillets** for the red-fish. Makes 4 servings. *1 serving: Calories 198; Saturated Fat 5 g; Total Fat 9 g; Protein 26 g; Carbohydrate 2 g; Fiber 0 g; Sodium 529 mg; Cholesterol 126 mg*

Fish to
be fried
should be
well dried
after washing,
and it is
usually cut
into pieces
convenient for
serving.

*—Mrs. Beeton's
Cookery Book, 1911*

DOWN HOME TRADITION

The meatless Fridays advocated by certain religious groups inspired the tradition of hometown fish fries on Friday night. Restaurants often featured a special menu: all you can eat for one fixed price. The type of fish varied with the season and what was available that day. Usually the catch included fillets of white fish, such as flounder, trout, halibut, or perch, plus shrimp, oysters, or scallops. Whatever fish was served, it always arrived with a heaping serving of golden French fries.

◆ Friday Fish Fry ◆

3½ cups all-purpose flour

2 tablespoons baking powder

2 teaspoons salt

4 large eggs

1¾ cups milk

1 teaspoon hot red pepper sauce, or to taste

3½ cups vegetable shortening or lard

2 large flounder or other white fish fillets (2 pounds), quartered

1 pound large shrimp (about 20), peeled and deveined with tails left on (Page 362)

8 ounces sea scallops or shucked oysters

Garnish:

2 large lemons, thinly sliced

PREP TIME: 25 MIN. / COOKING TIME: 12 MIN.

---

1 In a large bowl, combine 2½ cups of the flour, the baking powder, and salt. In a medium-size bowl, whisk the eggs, milk, and red pepper sauce. Add to the flour mixture all at once, and stir until smooth.

2 Heat the oven to 200°F and line a large, shallow pan with paper towels. In a deep-fat fryer or deep, heavy skillet, heat the shortening to 375°F. Meanwhile, on a piece of wax paper, spread the remaining 1 cup of flour and coat the fillets, shrimp, and scallops with it.

3 Using tongs, dip the flounder pieces into the batter, then slip into the fryer. Cook for 3 minutes or until puffy and golden brown, then transfer to the pan and place in the oven to keep warm. Repeat with the shrimp, then the scallops, cooking each for 2 to 3 minutes and transferring to the pan as you go. Garnish with the lemon slices and serve with Tartar Sauce (page 277), Steak Fries (page 230), and a tossed green salad. Makes 8 servings.

---

1 serving: Calories 500; Saturated Fat 4 g; Total Fat 14 g; Protein 49 g; Carbohydrate 41 g; Fiber 0 g; Sodium 1089 mg; Cholesterol 292 mg

A real crowd pleaser: A double recipe of Beer-Batter Fish Fry

BEER-BATTER FISH FRY

◆◆◆

*Try this light way of frying fish by replacing
the rich old-fashioned coating with a light beer
batter. Instead of deep-fat frying, use a
nonstick skillet with just a little oil.*

2 cups all-purpose flour	⅓ to ½ cup vegetable oil
½ teaspoon salt, or to taste	2 large flounder or other white fish fillets (2 pounds), quartered
¼ teaspoon ground red pepper (cayenne)	1 pound large shrimp (about 20), thawed if frozen, peeled and deveined with tails left on (page 362)
12 ounces beer (with or without alcohol)	
2 green onions, with tops, finely chopped (¼ cup)	8 ounces sea scallops
2 tablespoons minced parsley	Garnish:
3 large egg whites	2 large lemons, thinly sliced

PREP TIME: 25 MIN. / COOKING TIME: 15 MIN.

1 In a large bowl, combine the flour, salt, and ground red pepper. Gradually whisk in the beer until smooth, then add the green onions and parsley. In a clean medium-size bowl, beat the egg whites with an electric mixer set on high until soft peaks form and fold into the beer mixture.

2 Heat the oven to 200°F and line a large shallow pan with paper towels. In a deep, 12-inch nonstick skillet, heat ¼ cup of the oil over moderately high heat until a haze forms on top.

3 Using tongs, dip the flounder pieces into the batter, then slip into the skillet. Cook for 2 minutes on each side or until puffy and golden-brown, then transfer to the pan and place in the oven to keep warm.

4 Add 1 or 2 tablespoons of oil to the skillet, if necessary. Repeat the battering and cooking processes with the shrimp, then the scallops, cooking each for 1 to 2 minutes on each side and transferring to the pan as you go. Garnish with the lemon slices and serve with Shrimper's Sauce (page 276) and ears of Corn Roasted on the Grill (page 219). Makes 8 servings.

*1 serving: Calories 383; Saturated Fat 2 g;
Total Fat 8 g; Protein 46 g; Carbohydrate 27 g; Fiber 0 g;
Sodium 421 mg; Cholesterol 173 mg*

Grilled Scallops:
Inspired by Native
Americans, who
cooked their fish
over an open fire

GRILLED SCALLOPS

◆◆◆

2 teaspoons vegetable oil	¾ teaspoon ground ginger
2 cloves garlic, minced	⅛ teaspoon crushed red pepper
¼ cup finely chopped sweet green pepper	1 pound sea scallops
3 tablespoons finely chopped green onions	1 cup sweet red pepper chunks (1½ -inch squares)
½ cup ketchup	4 strips lean bacon, cut into 1-inch pieces
¼ cup cider vinegar	2 cups fresh pineapple wedges (1-inch thick)
2 tablespoons pineapple juice	Sprigs of fresh basil
¼ cup firmly packed light brown sugar	

PREP TIME: 30 MIN. / MARINATING TIME: 2 HR.
COOKING TIME: 30 MIN.

1 In a small saucepan, heat the oil over low heat. Add the garlic, green pepper, and green onions and cook for 5 minutes or until tender. Stir in the ketchup, vinegar, pineapple juice, sugar, ginger, and crushed red pepper and simmer gently for 10 minutes. Strain into a medium-size bowl, pushing gently with a spoon to release all of the liquid. Discard the solids and let the liquid cool.

2 Stir the scallops into the marinade, cover, and refrigerate for 2 hours, turning once. Using a slotted spoon, transfer the scallops to a plate.

3 Preheat a grill or broiler. In a small saucepan of boiling water, blanch the sweet red pepper for 2 minutes, add the bacon and blanch 1 minute longer, then drain on paper towels. On four 12-inch metal skewers, alternately thread the scallops, bacon, sweet red pepper, and pineapple.

4 Grill or broil 8 inches from the heat, turning and basting frequently with the marinade, for 12 minutes or until cooked through. Serve on a bed of wild and white rice and garnish with the basil. Makes 4 servings.

1 serving: Calories 294; Saturated Fat 2 g;
Total Fat 7 g; Protein 22 g; Carbohydrate 38 g; Fiber 1 g;
Sodium 603 mg; Cholesterol 43 mg

SCALLOPED SEAFOOD

◆◆◆

Although the word "scalloped" now refers to any food baked in a cream sauce, it once meant creamed seafood served in large scallop shells. We present a traditional version of the dish here.

½ cup cold water
½ cup white wine or Fish Stock (page 75)
2 shallots or green onions, minced (¼ cup)
1 clove garlic, minced
½ teaspoon dried thyme leaves
¼ teaspoon salt
1 bay leaf
12 ounces sea scallops, halved and rinsed
12 ounces large shrimp, thawed if frozen, peeled and deveined with tails removed (page 362)
8 ounces fresh mushrooms, sliced (3 cups)
¾ cup low-fat (1% milkfat) milk
4 teaspoons cornstarch
1 teaspoon Dijon mustard
¼ teaspoon ground red pepper (cayenne)
1 teaspoon fresh lemon juice
2 tablespoons minced parsley
½ cup shredded Swiss cheese (2 ounces)

PREP TIME: 25 MIN. / COOKING TIME: 23 MIN.

1 In a medium-size saucepan, bring the water, wine, shallots, garlic, thyme, salt, and bay leaf to a boil over high heat. Lower the heat; simmer, uncovered, for 5 minutes. Add the scallops and shrimp; simmer for 3 minutes or until opaque, then transfer to a platter with a slotted spoon.

2 Add the mushrooms. Simmer for 3 minutes or until soft, then transfer the mushrooms to the same platter with the seafood. Increase the heat to high and boil, uncovered, for 5 minutes or until only about 1 cup of liquid remains.

3 In a small bowl, stir the milk and cornstarch, then whisk into the simmering wine mixture. Season with the mustard, ground red pepper, lemon juice, parsley, and ¼ cup of the cheese. Remove from the heat and discard the bay leaf. Stir in the seafood, mushrooms, and any juices that have collected on the platter.

4 Preheat the broiler; butter four scallop shells or 1½-cup gratin or other flame-proof dishes. Spoon in the seafood mixture and sprinkle with the remaining ¼ cup of cheese. Broil, 4 inches from the heat, for 3 minutes or until golden. Serve with Rice Ring (page 206). Makes 4 servings.

1 serving: Calories 290; Saturated Fat 3 g; Total Fat 7 g; Protein 39 g; Carbohydrate 12 g; Fiber 1 g; Sodium 497 mg; Cholesterol 175 mg

LONG ISLAND SCALLOP SAUTÉ

◆◆◆

Residents of Long Island, New York, claim that the small bay scallops found in their inlets and bays are much sweeter and tenderer than the larger sea scallops. This simple method of cooking them is one of the most popular.

2 tablespoons unsalted butter or margarine
1 pound bay scallops
1 clove garlic, minced
2 tablespoons white wine or fresh lemon juice
⅛ teaspoon salt
Dash ground red pepper (cayenne)
1 tablespoon minced parsley
Garnish:
2 large unpeeled lemons, sliced

PREP TIME: 10 MIN. / COOKING TIME: 6 MIN.

1 In a 10-inch skillet, melt the butter over moderately high heat. Add the scallops and garlic and cook, uncovered, stirring occasionally, for 4 minutes or until the scallops are opaque.

2 Add the wine, salt, and ground red pepper; simmer 1 minute longer to blend the flavors. Sprinkle with the parsley and garnish with the lemon. Serve with Green Beans Amandine (page 220) and steamed brown rice. Makes 4 servings.

1 serving: Calories 160; Saturated Fat 4 g; Total Fat 7 g; Protein 19 g; Carbohydrate 3 g; Fiber 0 g; Sodium 251 mg; Cholesterol 54 mg

HANGTOWN FRY

◆◆◆

During the California Gold Rush, oysters and eggs were expensive. This dish was created for one lucky miner who struck it rich and demanded the best meal that gold could buy at a café in Placerville, California, a town known for public hangings.

2 tablespoons all-purpose flour	3 large eggs
10 unsalted saltine crackers, crumbled (⅓ cup)	¼ cup low-fat (1% milkfat) milk
2 large egg whites	1 tablespoon minced parsley
1 dozen oysters or cherrystone clams, shucked, rinsed, and drained (page 362)	¼ teaspoon each salt and black pepper
	2 strips lean bacon, diced

PREP TIME: 15 MIN. / COOKING TIME: 15 MIN.

1 Spread the flour on a piece of wax paper and the cracker crumbs on a plate. Lightly beat 1 of the egg whites in a pie plate. Dip the oysters in the flour, then the egg white, then the crumbs.

2 In a medium-size bowl, beat the whole eggs and the remaining 1 egg white with the milk, parsley, salt, and pepper.

3 In a 12-inch nonstick skillet, cook the bacon over moderate heat for 5 minutes or until crisp, then transfer to paper towels. Pour off all but 1 tablespoon of the drippings.

4 Preheat the broiler. Add the oysters to the skillet and cook for 3 minutes on each side or just until golden. Pour the egg mixture over the oysters and cook 3 minutes longer, constantly lifting the eggs with a spatula to allow the uncooked eggs to flow to the bottom. When set, wrap the skillet handle with foil and broil for 1 minute. Top with the bacon and serve with San Francisco Sourdough (page 290). Makes 4 servings.

1 serving: Calories 214; Saturated Fat 2 g; Total Fat 6 g; Protein 15 g; Carbohydrate 24 g; Fiber 0 g; Sodium 389 mg; Cholesterol 185 mg

LOBSTER NEWBURG

◆◆◆

In 1876, Charles Delmonico, of New York restaurant fame, named this dish for his friend Ben Wenberg, a sea captain from the West Indies. Later, when the men quarreled, Charles reversed the first three letters of the name to make it Newberg; eventually it became Newburg.

2 lobsters (1½-pounds each) or 2 pounds monkfish fillets, skinned	Pinch ground red pepper (cayenne)
¾ cup half-and-half or whole milk	¼ cup dry sherry or fish stock
¼ cup Fish Stock (page 75) or low-sodium chicken broth	1 teaspoon fresh lemon juice
1 tablespoon unsalted butter or margarine	2 large egg yolks, slightly beaten
¼ teaspoon salt, or to taste	2 tablespoons minced parsley
	1 large unpeeled lemon, thinly sliced, for garnish

PREP TIME: 20 MIN. / COOKING TIME: 20 MIN.

1 Half-fill a lobster pot or 8-quart stockpot with water and bring to a boil. Add the lobsters, cover, and cook for 9 minutes or until a leg removes easily. Transfer to a cutting board. When cool enough to handle, crack the shells, and remove the meat. Cut into bite-size pieces and arrange in 4 scallop shells or 1½-cup gratin dishes.

2 Meanwhile, in a medium-size double boiler or heavy saucepan placed over a pan of simmering water, bring the half-and-half, stock, butter, salt, and pepper to a boil, whisking occasionally.

3 Whisk in the sherry and lemon juice, then the egg yolks. Cook, whisking, for 3 minutes or just until thick. (Do not boil.) Remove from the heat, stir in the parsley, and ladle over the lobster. Garnish with the lemon slices and serve with steamed asparagus. Makes 4 servings.

1 serving: Calories 194; Saturated Fat 6 g; Total Fat 11 g; Protein 15 g; Carbohydrate 4 g; Fiber 0 g; Sodium 378 mg; Cholesterol 173 mg

Mussels fresh from the sea, served in a spicy marinara sauce over linguine

MUSSELS MARINARA

❖❖❖

*Immigrants from the Mediterranean introduced
Americans to this favorite way with mussels.*

4 dozen mussels in their shells	¼ teaspoon crushed red pepper
¼ cup cornmeal	2 cups crushed canned tomatoes, undrained
1 tablespoon olive oil	1 pound cooked and drained hot linguine
1 medium-size yellow onion, chopped (1 cup)	¼ cup minced parsley
3 cloves garlic, minced	

PREP TIME: 20 MIN. / STANDING TIME: 15 MIN.
COOKING TIME: 15 MIN.

1 Using a stiff brush, scrub the mussels under cold running water, removing their beards and discarding any mussels that have opened. Half-fill a large bowl with water, stir in the cornmeal, and add the mussels. Let them stand for 15 minutes, to disgorge their sand, then rinse them well.

2 Meanwhile, in a large saucepan, heat the oil over moderately high heat. Add the onion and sauté for 5 minutes. Add the garlic and pepper and cook 2 minutes longer or until tender.

3 Stir in the tomatoes with their juices and bring to a boil. Add the mussels, lower the heat, cover, and simmer for 5 minutes or until the mussels open. (Discard any mussels that have not opened.) Fill a large serving bowl with the linguine and ladle the mussels with the sauce over the top. Sprinkle with the parsley and serve with slices of garlic bread. Makes 4 servings.

*1 serving: Calories 363; Saturated Fat 1 g;
Total Fat 8 g; Protein 25 g; Carbohydrate 45 g; Fiber 1 g;
Sodium 700 mg; Cholesterol 80 mg*

A spicy taste of down-home Cajun cookin': Shrimp Jambalaya served straight from the old iron skillet

STUFFED JUMBO SHRIMP

◆◆◆

More shrimp is harvested in America than any other country. Look for the jumbo ones for stuffing.

16 **jumbo shrimp (about 1½ pounds), thawed if frozen, peeled and deveined with tails left on**	½ **cup plain dry bread crumbs**
	¼ **cup each chopped onion and parsley**
6 **tablespoons fresh lemon juice**	3 **tablespoons unsalted butter, melted**
8 **ounces fresh, frozen, or canned crab meat, picked through and flaked (1 cup)**	1 **clove garlic, minced**
	¼ **teaspoon salt**
	⅛ **teaspoon ground red pepper (cayenne)**

PREP TIME: 30 MIN. / COOKING TIME: 15 MIN.

1 Preheat the oven to 400°F and grease a large baking sheet. Butterfly the shrimp by cutting along the outer curved edge almost all the way through. Open each shrimp up like a book and remove any dark outer veins. In a medium-size bowl, toss the shrimp with 4 tablespoons of the lemon juice. Let stand for 15 minutes at room temperature, stirring occasionally.

2 Meanwhile, in a large bowl, mix the crab meat with the remaining ingredients, including the 2 tablespoons of lemon juice. Place the shrimp on the baking sheet with the cut-sides-down and tails sticking up. Mound a heaping tablespoon of the crab mixture on top of each shrimp.

3 Bake, basting with the pan juices, for 15 minutes or just until the shrimp turn opaque. Serve with Shrimper's Sauce (page 276) and Spanish Rice (page 203). Makes 4 servings.

1 serving: Calories 145; Saturated Fat 2 g; Total Fat 5 g; Protein 12 g; Carbohydrate 12 g; Fiber 0 g; Sodium 414 mg; Cholesterol 69 mg

SHRIMP JAMBALAYA

- 1 tablespoon vegetable oil
- 8 ounces andouille, chorizo, or kielbasa sausage, cut into ½-inch pieces (about 2 cups)
- 6 ounces smoked ham, diced (1 cup) (optional)
- 2 stalks celery, chopped (1 cup)
- 1 medium-size yellow onion, chopped (1 cup)
- 1 large sweet green pepper, cored, seeded, and chopped (1 cup)
- 2 cloves garlic, minced
- 3 tablespoons all-purpose flour
- 2 bay leaves
- 1 teaspoon each dried oregano and thyme leaves
- ½ teaspoon black pepper
- ¼ teaspoon ground red pepper (cayenne)
- 4 cups Chicken Stock (page 74) or low-sodium chicken broth
- 1 cup uncooked long-grain white rice
- 1½ pounds medium-size shrimp (about 40), thawed if frozen, peeled and deveined with tails left on (page 362)
- 2 large tomatoes, chopped (2 cups)

PREP TIME: 35 MIN. / COOKING TIME: 38 MIN.

1 In a 6-quart Dutch oven or stockpot, heat the oil over moderately high heat. Add the sausage plus the ham, if you wish, and sauté for 5 minutes. Add the celery, onion, green pepper, and garlic and sauté for 5 minutes or until soft.

2 Stir in the flour, bay leaves, oregano, thyme, and the black and red peppers. Cook, stirring constantly, for 5 minutes or until the flour has browned. Stir in the stock, then the rice, and bring to a boil. Lower the heat, cover, and simmer for 15 minutes or until the rice is nearly tender. Discard the bay leaves.

3 Stir in the shrimp and tomatoes, cover, and cook 5 minutes longer or just until the shrimp turn opaque. Serve with Fried Greens (page 222). Makes 6 servings.

1 serving: Calories 452; Saturated Fat 7 g; Total Fat 19 g; Protein 30 g; Carbohydrate 37 g; Fiber 1 g; Sodium 843 mg; Cholesterol 155 mg

◆ Cajun Jambalaya ◆

In Cajun country, down Louisiana way, many locals have their own recipes for jambalaya. The recipes may differ, but all are authentic.

Stories abound about how the dish got its name. One is about a gentleman, visiting a New Orleans inn late one evening, who found little left to eat. The owner asked his cook, Jean, to *balayez*, which means to "mix some things together" in the Louisiana (Acadian) dialect. The guest, delighted with Jean's concoction, named it Jean Balayez, known as jambalaya today.

Some people believe that the Spaniards introduced the dish in Louisiana, and that the name is partly derived from the Spanish word for ham, *jamon*. Whatever its origin, jambalaya usually contains ham, rice, spice, and other good things. It all depends on the cook.

Typically, jambalaya is made from leftovers… once you get the idea, you can take it from there.

—from Patout's Cajun Home Cooking by Alex Patout

CAPE COD CLAM PIE

◆◆◆

The tradition of fish pies was brought here by the British in colonial days. On Cape Cod, the pies are often made with fresh cherrystone clams from saltwater farms along the New England coast.

Pastry for double-crust pie (page 368)	1 cup chopped onion
4 dozen shucked cherrystone clams, chopped, with liquor reserved (page 362), or 1½ cups chopped canned clams with liquor reserved	3 tablespoons all-purpose flour
	1 cup plus 2 tablespoons low-fat (1% milkfat) milk or half-and-half
	1½ cups peeled, cooked, diced potatoes
1 tablespoon unsalted butter or margarine	¼ cup minced parsley
	½ teaspoon black pepper

PREP TIME: 45 MIN. / CHILLING TIME: 30 MIN.
COOKING TIME: 55 MIN.

1 Prepare the pastry dough and refrigerate. Measure out ½ cup of the clam liquor, adding water if necessary. In a 12-inch nonstick skillet, melt the butter over moderate heat. Add the onion and sauté for 5 minutes or until soft.

2 Whisk in the flour and cook until bubbly, then whisk in 1 cup of the milk and the clam liquor. Cook, stirring constantly, for 3 minutes or until thickened. Remove from the heat and stir in the clams, potatoes, parsley, and pepper.

3 Preheat the oven to 400°F. On a lightly floured surface, roll out the pastry into two 12-inch circles. Line a 9-inch pie plate with 1 dough circle; spoon in the clam mixture and top with the second. Crimp, seal, and trim the edges.

4 Make six 3-inch slashes in the top to vent the steam. Brush with the remaining 2 tablespoons of milk; bake for 45 minutes or until golden. Serve with steamed carrots. Makes 6 servings.

1 serving: Calories 732; Saturated Fat 19 g; Total Fat 41 g; Protein 16 g; Carbohydrate 77 g; Fiber 1 g; Sodium 144 mg; Cholesterol 99 mg

SHRIMPER'S PIE

◆◆◆

Fish pies from Dixie are often filled with shrimp and both sweet and hot peppers. Use fresh shrimp if handy, but frozen ones work well too.

Pastry for double-crust pie (page 368)	¼ teaspoon each paprika and black pepper
1 tablespoon unsalted butter or margarine	⅛ teaspoon ground red pepper (cayenne)
1 cup chopped onion	1 cup low-fat (1% milkfat) milk
¾ cup chopped sweet green pepper	2 pounds large shrimp (about 40), thawed if frozen, peeled, tails removed, deveined, halved horizontally (page 362)
1 clove garlic, minced	
¼ cup all-purpose flour	
½ teaspoon each dried oregano and thyme leaves	
¼ teaspoon salt	1 large egg white, lightly beaten

PREP TIME: 45 MIN. / CHILLING TIME: 30 MIN.
COOKING TIME: 40 MIN.

1 Prepare the pastry dough and refrigerate. In a large saucepan, melt the butter over moderately high heat. Add the onion, green pepper, and garlic; sauté for 5 minutes or until soft.

2 Whisk in the flour, oregano, thyme, salt, paprika, and the black and red peppers; cook until bubbly, then whisk in the milk. Cook, stirring constantly, for 3 minutes or until thickened. Remove from the heat and stir in the shrimp.

3 Preheat the oven to 400°F. On a lightly floured surface, roll out the pastry into two 12-inch circles. Line a 9-inch pie plate with 1 dough circle; spoon in the shrimp mixture and top with the second. Crimp, seal, and trim the edges.

4 Make six 3-inch slashes in the top to vent the steam. Brush with the egg white and bake for 30 minutes or until golden. Serve with Chopped Tomato Salad (page 256). Makes 6 servings.

1 serving: Calories 820; Saturated Fat 17 g; Total Fat 40 g; Protein 42 g; Carbohydrate 70 g; Fiber 1 g; Sodium 440 mg; Cholesterol 288 mg

Supper in a hurry: Fresh Shrimp Wiggle served on golden toast points

SHRIMP WIGGLE

◆◆◆

Wiggle, which refers to anything done in a hurry, is the ideal name for this quick-and-easy New England dish. According to James Beard, it was once "in the repertoire of every co-ed with a chafing dish and every girl who had a beau to cook for."

2 tablespoons unsalted butter or margarine	1 teaspoon paprika
1½ cups finely chopped sweet red pepper	1¼ cups low-fat (1% milkfat) milk
4 ounces fresh mushrooms, sliced (1½ cups)	1 cup frozen peas, thawed and drained
1 pound large shrimp (about 20), thawed if frozen, peeled and deveined with tails removed (page 362)	½ teaspoon salt, or to taste
	¼ teaspoon black pepper
2 tablespoons all-purpose flour	4 slices whole wheat or white toast, each cut diagonally into 2 triangles

PREP TIME: 20 MIN. / COOKING TIME: 15 MIN.

1 In a 12-inch nonstick skillet, melt 1 tablespoon of the butter over moderately high heat. Add the red pepper and mushrooms and sauté for 5 minutes. Using a slotted spoon, transfer to a plate. Add the shrimp to the skillet and cook, stirring, for 3 minutes or just until pink and opaque. Transfer to the plate with the vegetables.

2 Melt the remaining 1 tablespoon of butter in the skillet. Stir in the flour and paprika and cook until bubbly. Whisk in the milk and cook, stirring constantly, 3 minutes longer or until the sauce thickens. Stir in the peas, salt, black pepper, vegetables, and shrimp and heat through. Ladle over the toast points and serve with Caesar Salad (page 257). Makes 4 servings.

*1 serving: Calories 334; Saturated Fat 5 g;
Total Fat 11 g; Protein 31 g; Carbohydrate 28 g; Fiber 1 g;
Sodium 608 mg; Cholesterol 195 mg*

NANTUCKET BOUNTY

◆◆◆

*You don't have to hail from Nantucket,
an island off of Cape Cod, to love fresh seafood
cooked the New England way.*

1 dozen mussels	⅓ cup slivered fresh basil or 1 tablespoon dried basil leaves
1 dozen littleneck clams	1 tablespoon chopped fresh rosemary or 1 teaspoon dried rosemary leaves
2 tablespoons cornmeal	
2 tablespoons vegetable oil	¼ teaspoon each salt and black pepper, or to taste
1 medium-size yellow onion, chopped (1 cup)	12 ounces large shrimp (about 16), thawed if frozen, peeled and deveined with tails left on (page 362)
1 large sweet green pepper, coarsely chopped (1½ cups)	
2 cloves garlic, minced	1 lobster (1½ pounds), cooked, removed from shell, and cut into chunks, or 1 pound cooked monkfish chunks
4 medium-size tomatoes, chopped (4 cups)	
1 cup dry white wine or Fish Stock (page 75)	

PREP TIME: 45 MIN. / STANDING TIME: 30 MIN.
COOKING TIME: 23 MIN.

1 Using a stiff brush, scrub the mussels and clams well under cold running water, removing the beards from the mussels and discarding any shells that have opened. Half-fill a large bowl with cold water, stir in the cornmeal, and add the mussels and clams. Let them stand for 15 minutes, to disgorge their sand, then rinse them well.

2 Meanwhile, in an 8-quart saucepot or Dutch oven, heat the oil over moderately high heat. Add the onion, green pepper, and garlic and sauté for 5 minutes or until soft. Stir in 3 cups of the tomatoes, the wine, basil, rosemary, salt, and black pepper and bring to a boil. Lower the heat, cover, and simmer for 5 minutes.

**A Real Down East Clambake from the heart
of Maine—steamed easily indoors in a pot on the range**

3 Add the mussels and clams, cover, and steam 5 minutes longer, then add the shrimp and cook 5 minutes more. Stir in the lobster with the remaining 1 cup of tomatoes and cook for 2 minutes or just until heated through. (Discard any mussels and clams that have not opened.) Serve with steamed brown rice. Makes 4 servings.

*1 serving: Calories 328; Saturated Fat 2 g;
Total Fat 11 g; Protein 30 g; Carbohydrate 17 g; Fiber 2 g;
Sodium 528 mg; Cholesterol 157 mg*

DOWN EAST CLAMBAKE
◆◆◆

From the Indians, the Pilgrims learned about clambakes — a way of steaming fresh seafood and corn in a large pit, layered with hot stones and seaweed. Here's a much quicker way, using a kettle instead of a pit, corn husks instead of seaweed.

3 tablespoons sea salt or Kosher salt	2 tablespoons cornmeal
4 ears corn on the cob	6 cups cold water
2 dozen mussels	4 live lobsters (1¼ to 1½ pounds each)
2 dozen littleneck clams	1½ pounds small red new potatoes

PREP TIME: 20 MIN. / STANDING TIME: 1 HR.
COOKING TIME: 35 MIN.

1 Half-fill a stockpot or large bowl with cold water; stir in 1 tablespoon of the salt. Remove the husks from the corn; soak both corn and husks in the salt water for 1 hour. Discard the silks.

2 Using a stiff brush, scrub the mussels and clams under cold running water, removing the beards from the mussels and discarding any shells that have opened. Half-fill another stockpot or large bowl with cold water, stir in the cornmeal, and add the mussels and clams. Let them stand for 15 minutes to disgorge their sand; rinse well.

3 Place a rack in a 20-quart kettle or lobster pot, add the 6 cups of water and the remaining 2 tablespoons of salt, and bring to a boil over high heat. Add the lobsters, cover, and cook for 5 minutes. Cover the lobsters with ½ of the corn husks, then layers of the corn and potatoes, then the remaining husks. Cover, return to a boil, then lower the heat and simmer for 20 minutes. Add the mussels and clams, cover and steam 5 to 10 minutes longer or until they open. Serve with hot Portland Popovers (page 310). Makes 4 servings.

*1 serving: Calories 440; Saturated Fat 1 g;
Total Fat 5 g; Protein 42 g; Carbohydrate 60 g; Fiber 1 g;
Sodium 813 mg; Cholesterol 131 mg*

CIOPPINO
◆◆◆

Italian immigrants around San Francisco Bay invented Cioppino, which means "fish stew." Judy Infelise, a terrific hostess in Minnesota, created this version to cook for a crowd. You can also halve the recipe for a smaller group.

2 tablespoons olive oil	3 cups white wine or Fish Stock (page 75)
1 cup chopped onion	4 pounds small live lobsters or live crabs
1 cup chopped sweet green pepper	2 pounds white fish fillets (cod, snapper, or halibut), skinned, cut into 2-inch pieces
3 cloves garlic, minced	
1 teaspoon each dried basil and oregano leaves	24 littleneck clams in their shells, scrubbed
2 teaspoons black pepper	12 ounces scallops
4 cups chopped, seeded, peeled, ripe plum tomatoes (2 pounds)	12 ounces large shrimp (about 16), thawed if frozen, peeled and deveined with tails left on (page 362)
3 tablespoons tomato paste	¼ cup minced parsley
2 bay leaves	

PREP TIME: 35 MIN. / COOKING TIME: 25 MIN.

1 In a 20-quart kettle, Dutch oven, or lobster pot, heat the oil over moderately high heat. Stir in the onion, green pepper, garlic, basil, oregano, and black pepper; cook for 5 minutes. Add the tomatoes, tomato paste, bay leaves, and wine and simmer, uncovered, for 5 minutes.

2 Meanwhile, in another large, covered pot of boiling water, cook the lobsters or crabs for 5 minutes. Add to the kettle with the fish and clams. Lower the heat, cover, and simmer for 6 minutes. Add the scallops and shrimp and cook 3 minutes more or just until the shrimp turn opaque. Discard the bay leaves, sprinkle with the parsley, and serve with San Francisco Sourdough (page 290). Makes 8 servings.

*1 serving: Calories 468; Saturated Fat 1 g;
Total Fat 8 g; Protein 67 g; Carbohydrate 15 g; Fiber 1 g;
Sodium 1471 mg; Cholesterol 209 mg*

NEW ENGLAND CODFISH BALLS

Some have said that eating codfish balls (actually patties or cakes) on Sunday morning in New England is as important as reading the Scriptures.

2	cups Mashed Potatoes (page 361)	½	teaspoon each dry mustard and black pepper
8	ounces cod or any white fish fillets (such as flounder, sole, halibut, or perch), poached (page 362), drained, and flaked (1 cup)	½	teaspoon Worcestershire sauce
		¼	teaspoon salt, or to taste
1	large egg, lightly beaten	1	tablespoon unsalted butter or margarine
2	tablespoons minced parsley		

Garnish:

2 large unpeeled lemons, thinly sliced

PREP TIME: 30 MIN. / COOKING TIME: 10 MIN.

1 In a medium-size bowl, mix the potatoes, cod, egg, parsley, mustard, pepper, Worcestershire, and salt until well blended. Form into four 4-inch round patties, about 1 inch thick.

2 In a 10-inch nonstick skillet, melt the butter over moderately high heat. Cook the fish cakes for 4 minutes on each side or until well browned. Garnish with the lemon slices and serve with Corn Relish (page 274). Makes 4 servings.

1 serving: Calories 179; Saturated Fat 3 g; Total Fat 6 g; Protein 14 g; Carbohydrate 19 g; Fiber 0 g; Sodium 406 mg; Cholesterol 89 mg

Nice oyster sauce
gives zest to cod—a fish,
when fresh, to feast a god!

—*Anonymous*

SALMON CROQUETTES

While croquettes are usually deep-fat fried, ours are cooked with just a little oil in a nonstick skillet. They're not quite as crispy as the traditional types, but the wonderful flavor is still there.

2	cups Mashed Potatoes (page 361)		Pinch ground red pepper (cayenne)
1	can (14 ¾ ounces) pink salmon, picked through, rinsed, drained, and flaked	1	large egg
		2	tablespoons cold water
4	green onions, with tops, finely chopped (½ cup)	½	cup plain dry bread crumbs
1	tablespoon fresh lemon juice	1	tablespoon vegetable oil
½	teaspoon black pepper, or to taste		
¼	teaspoon salt, or to taste		

Garnish:

2 unpeeled lemons, thinly sliced

PREP TIME: 30 MIN. / COOKING TIME: 7 MIN.

1 In a large bowl, mix the potatoes, salmon, green onions, lemon juice, black pepper, salt, and ground red pepper until well blended. Form into eight 3- x 1-inch logs (or 2½-inch round patties, 1 inch thick).

2 In a pie plate, whisk the egg and water; spread the bread crumbs on a plate. Dip the patties in the egg mixture, then the bread crumbs, pressing lightly to coat.

3 In a 10-inch nonstick skillet, heat the oil over moderately high heat. Cook the croquettes, turning frequently, for 6 minutes or until golden. Garnish with the lemon slices and serve with Green Bean Casserole (page 221) and hot Portland Popovers (page 310). Makes 4 servings.

1 serving: Calories 324; Saturated Fat 3 g; Total Fat 11 g; Protein 27 g; Carbohydrate 29 g; Fiber 1 g; Sodium 523 mg; Cholesterol 94 mg

Supper in Maryland, with fresh-made Crab Cakes and Oven Fries (page 231)

MARYLAND CRAB CAKES

◆◆◆

Since Colonial days, Maryland has prided itself on serving some of the finest crab cakes in the land, often made from the blue crabs of Chesapeake Bay.

1½ pounds lump crab meat, picked over and flaked

3 green onions, with tops, finely chopped (6 tablespoons)

¼ cup minced parsley

3 tablespoons plain low-fat yogurt

3 tablespoons fresh lemon juice

2 cloves garlic, minced

1½ teaspoons dry mustard

1½ teaspoons Old Bay or Creole seasoning (optional)

1½ teaspoons Worcestershire sauce

¼ teaspoon salt, or to taste

½ teaspoon hot red pepper sauce

1 cup plain dry bread crumbs

3 large egg whites

4 tablespoons vegetable oil

Garnish:

3 large unpeeled lemons, thinly sliced

PREP TIME: 30 MIN. / CHILLING TIME: 1 HR.
COOKING TIME: 17 MIN.

1 In a large bowl, lightly toss the crab with the green onions, parsley, yogurt, lemon juice, garlic, mustard, Old Bay seasoning if you wish, Worcestershire, salt, and red pepper sauce. Stir in ¼ cup of the bread crumbs.

2 In a small clean bowl, beat the egg whites with an electric mixer on high until soft peaks form, then fold into the crab mixture. Form the mixture into twelve 4-inch round patties, about 1 inch thick. On a piece of wax paper, spread the remaining ¾ cup of bread crumbs and use to coat each patty. Refrigerate for 1 hour.

3 In a 12-inch nonstick skillet, heat 1 tablespoon of the oil over moderately high heat. Cook the crab cakes for 3 minutes on each side or until brown, adding the remaining 3 tablespoons of oil as needed. Serve with the lemon slices and Tartar Sauce (page 277). Makes 6 servings.

*1 serving: Calories 293; Saturated Fat 2 g;
Total Fat 13 g; Protein 25 g; Carbohydrate 18 g; Fiber 0 g;
Sodium 549 mg; Cholesterol 114 mg*

EGG & CHEESE SPECIALS

◆◆◆

Egg and cheese dishes have always been part of our country's traditions, arriving with the first colonists, added to by later immigrants, and handed down through many generations. We've gathered some of the best recipes from this heritage and updated them to lower the fat, cholesterol, and sodium. Try Cheese Strata, a wonderful make-ahead, for your next brunch; Vermont Cheddar-Apple Bake or Wisconsin Cheese Puff when you want a great luncheon dish; Old Country Quiche or Plantation Skillet Cake for a light Sunday supper.

You can use our techniques to adapt your own favorite recipes. For example, when making omelets or scrambled eggs, use one whole egg plus one or two egg whites per serving (the fat is in the yolk). When cream cheese is an ingredient, use Neufchâtel, which contains 1/3 less fat than the regular variety; buy mozzarella and ricotta made with skim milk; and when a recipe calls for Cheddar, substitute up to half of the amount indicated with a reduced-fat type. Remember too that shredding cheese makes a little go much further, especially when sprinkled on top of a dish, where it reaches the taste buds first.

STEAK AND EGGS

◆◆◆

In these health-conscious days, this all-American favorite is designated for special occasions.

3 tablespoons minced parsley	4 large eggs
1 tablespoon chopped fresh thyme or 1 teaspoon dried thyme leaves	4 large egg whites
	¼ cup finely chopped yellow onion
½ teaspoon each salt and black pepper	2 tablespoons low-fat (1% milkfat) milk
1 pound boneless beef sirloin steak, about ¾ inch thick, trimmed	2 drops hot red pepper sauce
	1 tablespoon unsalted butter or margarine

PREP TIME: 15 MIN. / COOKING TIME: 10 MIN.

1 Preheat the grill or broiler. In a small cup, mix 1 tablespoon of the parsley, the thyme, ¼ teaspoon of the salt, and all of the pepper and rub this mixture into both sides of the steak. Grill the steak over medium-hot coals or broil, 4 inches from the heat, for 3 minutes on each side for medium-rare or until the steak is the way you like it. Transfer to a cutting board, cover with foil, and keep warm.

2 In a medium-size bowl, whisk the eggs, egg whites, onion, milk, the remaining 2 tablespoons of parsley, the remaining ¼ teaspoon of salt, and the red pepper sauce.

3 In a 10-inch nonstick skillet, melt the butter over moderately high heat. Pour in the egg mixture and cook, gently scrambling the eggs with a wooden spoon, for 3 minutes or just until firm yet moist.

4 Diagonally slice the steak, across the grain, ½ inch thick. Serve the steak with heaping spoonfuls of scrambled eggs and slices of toasted whole-grain bread. Makes 4 servings.

1 serving: Calories 327; Saturated Fat 9 g; Total Fat 21 g; Protein 30 g; Carbohydrate 3 g; Fiber 0 g; Sodium 446 mg; Cholesterol 285 mg

WESTERN OMELET

◆◆◆

Out West in Rocky Mountain territory, ranch hands eat hefty mid-morning breakfasts after their morning chores. Hearty foods like this Western Omelet, also called a Denver Omelet, are popular.

4 slices lean bacon	2 large egg whites
1 cup chopped onion	1 tablespoon cold water
1 cup chopped sweet green pepper	½ teaspoon hot red pepper sauce
2 cloves garlic, minced	2 tablespoons minced parsley
¼ teaspoon black pepper, or to taste	
3 large eggs	

PREP TIME: 18 MIN. / COOKING TIME: 15 MIN.

1 In a 10-inch nonstick skillet, cook the bacon over moderate heat for 5 minutes or until crisp; drain on paper towels and crumble. Discard the drippings.

2 Preheat the broiler. In the skillet, sauté the onion, green pepper, garlic, and ⅛ teaspoon of the black pepper, stirring occasionally, for 5 minutes or until tender. Stir in the bacon.

3 Meanwhile, in a medium-size bowl, whisk together the eggs, egg whites, water, red pepper sauce, and the remaining ⅛ teaspoon of black pepper. Pour this mixture over the vegetables, lower the heat and cook, without stirring, for 2 minutes or until the eggs are set on the bottom.

4 Wrap the skillet handle with foil and broil the eggs, 4 inches from the heat, for 3 minutes or until set. Sprinkle with the parsley; serve immediately with generous helpings of Hash Browns (page 226). Makes 2 servings.

1 serving: Calories 252; Saturated Fat 5 g; Total Fat 15 g; Protein 18 g; Carbohydrate 12 g; Fiber 1 g; Sodium 369 mg; Cholesterol 361 mg

Breakfast
on the range:
Huevos Rancheros
served on a tortilla

HUEVOS RANCHEROS
◆◆◆

Huevos Rancheros, *which means*
"ranch eggs" in Spanish, is a Southwest staple
of fried eggs, served on tortillas and surrounded
by salsa. If you prefer, substitute
parsley for the cilantro.

1	tablespoon olive oil
1	small yellow onion, chopped (½ cup)
1	small sweet green pepper, chopped (½ cup)
2	cloves garlic, minced
1½	cups canned low-sodium crushed tomatoes in purée
1	large fresh or pickled jalapeño pepper, seeded and minced

1	teaspoon each dried oregano and thyme leaves
¼	teaspoon each salt and black pepper
3	tablespoons minced fresh cilantro, or 3 teaspoons dried cilantro
2	slices lean bacon, diced
4	large eggs
4	corn tortillas, thawed if frozen, then wrapped in aluminum foil

PREP TIME: 25 MIN. / COOKING TIME: 27 MIN.

1 In a medium-size saucepan, heat the oil over moderately high heat. Add the onion, green pepper, and garlic and sauté for 5 minutes or until soft. Add the tomatoes in their purée, the jalapeño pepper, oregano, thyme, salt, and black pepper and bring to a boil. Lower the heat; simmer, uncovered for 10 minutes or until the flavors blend. Stir in 2 tablespoons of the cilantro; keep warm.

2 Preheat the oven to 350°F. In an 8-inch non-stick skillet, cook the bacon over moderate heat for 5 minutes or until crisp, then drain on paper towels and crumble. Discard the drippings. Add the eggs to the skillet, lower the heat, cover, and cook over low heat for 4 minutes or until set.

3 Meanwhile, on a baking sheet, bake the tortillas for 5 minutes or until soft; arrange on a platter. Top with the eggs, surround with the salsa, and sprinkle with the bacon and remaining 1 tablespoon of cilantro. Makes 4 servings.

1 serving: Calories 226; Saturated Fat 3 g;
Total Fat 12 g; Protein 11 g; Carbohydrate 21 g; Fiber 1 g;
Sodium 439 mg; Cholesterol 216 mg

EGG SALAD

◆◆◆

After Easter, make a bowl of down-home egg salad. Our version still has the flavor of yesteryear, with less fat and fewer calories.

- 3 tablespoons reduced-calorie mayonnaise
- 3 tablespoons reduced-fat sour cream
- ¾ teaspoon curry powder
- ¼ teaspoon each salt and black pepper
- 3 large hard-cooked eggs (page 363), coarsely chopped
- 5 large hard-cooked egg whites, (page 363) coarsely chopped (reserve the yolks for another use)
- ¼ cup finely chopped celery
- ¼ cup finely chopped green onions, with tops
- 3 tablespoons minced dill pickles

PREP TIME: 20 MIN.

1 In a medium-size bowl, whisk the mayonnaise, sour cream, curry powder, salt, and pepper. Fold in the remaining ingredients. Serve on curly lettuce leaves. Makes 2 cups salad or 4 servings.

½ cup: Calories 124; Saturated Fat 2 g; Total Fat 8 g; Protein 10 g; Carbohydrate 4 g; Fiber 0 g; Sodium 352 mg; Cholesterol 166 mg

◆

Egg Salad Sandwich

Spread **2 slices of whole grain bread** with **2 teaspoons of butter** and sprinkle with **black pepper**. Fill the sandwich with **½ cup Egg Salad**, **1 slice of tomato**, and **1 lettuce leaf**. *1 sandwich: Calories 312; Saturated Fat 6 g; Total Fat 16 g; Protein 15 g; Carbohydrate 28 g; Fiber 1 g; Sodium 675 mg; Cholesterol 183 mg*

◆ Egg Rolling at the White House ◆

"The tradition of egg rolling at the White House dates back to the early 1800's, when Dolly Madison visited Egypt," explains Robin Dickey of the White House Visitors' Staff. "Mrs. Madison was so delighted to see children rolling colored eggs at the base of the pyramids that she decided to organize the first national Easter egg roll on the long sloping lawn of the Capitol in 1816.

"The event gradually grew in popularity. By the 1880's, thousands of children were attending and leaving many broken eggs on the grounds. The sight was so disturbing to many people that Congress passed a law prohibiting future egg rolls at the Capitol. The following year, First Lady

Mrs. Rutherford B. Hayes invited the country's children to an Easter Egg Roll at the White House on the Monday after Easter. The event continued, over the years, at various places in Washington (even the zoo). Finally, in the mid-1940's, it returned to the White House and became an official First Lady event.

"The custom still continues today. A few days before

Easter, the National Egg Association donates eggs (7,500 for a recent roll). In enormous vats in the White House kitchen, chefs cook and dye them in pretty pastels, while outside on the South Lawn, egg rolling lanes are marked off. Each year a few more lanes are added to accommodate the increasing number of eager participants. Everyone is invited!

"Children line up very early on the Monday after Easter. Officially, the races begin at 10:00 A.M., with the sound of a whistle, and last all day. Only a few children race at one time; each child has his own lane, one colored egg, and a spoon for rolling the egg to the finish line.

"After completing the egg roll, the children then hunt for souvenir wooden eggs in another area. Every year these mementos are designed differently, often carrying the President's and First Lady's signatures. A few are signed by visiting celebrities during the year. In 1993, Socks, the White House cat, signed 100 with his own paw-print; they are now a prized possession of each child who found one!"

After the egg hunt: Egg Salad on whole grain bread

An egg is dear on Easter day.

—*An old Russian Proverb*

PICKLED BEETS AND EGGS
◆◆◆

The Pennsylvania Dutch combine their leftover Easter eggs with pickled beets in this traditional sweet and sour specialty. The dish will keep for up to 2 days in the refrigerator.

2 **pounds medium-size beets, without tops**	1 **teaspoon black peppercorns**
1 **cup sugar**	¾ **teaspoon salt**
1 **cup cider vinegar**	½ **teaspoon whole allspice**
1 **cup cold water**	
1 **tablespoon pickling spices**	3 **large hard-cooked eggs (page 363), peeled**

PREP TIME: 20 MIN. / COOKING TIME: 45 MIN.
CHILLING TIME: 2½ HR.

1 Place the beets in a large saucepan and add enough cold water to cover. Over high heat, bring to a boil. Lower the heat and simmer, uncovered, for 40 minutes or until tender. Drain the beets and cool. Peel and slice the beets ½ inch thick, then place in a medium-size bowl.

2 In a medium-size enamel or stainless steel saucepan, bring the sugar, vinegar, water, pickling spices, peppercorns, salt, and allspice to a boil over high heat. Lower the heat and simmer, uncovered, for 5 minutes. Pour over the beets, cover, and refrigerate for 30 minutes.

3 Add the eggs to the beets, gently turning them until completely coated with the liquid. Cover and refrigerate, turning occasionally, for 2 more hours or until cold, or marinate overnight.

4 To serve, transfer the beets with a slotted spoon to a shallow dish and spoon over about 1 cup of the marinating liquid. Slice the eggs crosswise ½ inch thick and arrange on top of the beets. Serve with Mom's Mac and Cheese (page 190). Makes 6 servings.

1 serving: Calories 205; Saturated Fat 1 g;
Total Fat 3 g; Protein 5 g; Carbohydrate 45 g; Fiber 1 g;
Sodium 374 mg; Cholesterol 107 mg

Breakfast time down South, with a Plantation Skillet Cake and fresh-picked berries

PLANTATION SKILLET CAKE

◆◆◆

*Southerners have long been known
for inviting the neighbors in for large country
breakfasts. This skillet cake, which
originated in South Carolina in the 18th century,
resembles a giant puffy pancake.*

2 tablespoons unsalted butter or margarine

3 large eggs

1 large egg white

1 cup low-fat (1% milkfat) milk

⅔ cup all-purpose flour

2 tablespoons granulated sugar

1½ teaspoons grated orange rind

3 tablespoons fresh orange juice

1¼ teaspoons ground cinnamon

¼ teaspoon ground nutmeg

2 tablespoons confectioners' sugar

Assorted fresh berries, such as strawberries, blueberries, or raspberries (optional)

Maple syrup (optional)

PREP TIME: 18 MIN. / COOKING TIME: 20 MIN.

1 Preheat the oven to 425°F. In a heavy 12-inch ovenproof skillet, melt the butter in the oven. Meanwhile, in a large bowl, with an electric mixer on medium, beat the eggs, egg white, milk, flour, granulated sugar, orange rind and juice, ¼ teaspoon of the cinnamon, and the nutmeg for 2 minutes or just until smooth.

2 Remove the skillet from the oven; tilt to coat the sides with the butter. Pour in the batter; bake for 20 minutes or until puffed and golden.

3 In a small bowl, mix the confectioners' sugar with the remaining 1 teaspoon of cinnamon and sprinkle over the cake. Serve with fresh berries or syrup if you wish. Makes 4 servings.

*1 serving: Calories 256; Saturated Fat 6 g;
Total Fat 11 g; Protein 10 g; Carbohydrate 31 g; Fiber 0 g;
Sodium 95 mg; Cholesterol 179 mg*

WISCONSIN CHEESE PUFF

❖❖❖

*In the Midwest, an omelet is
often filled with melted Cheddar.*

4 large eggs	¾ cup shredded sharp Cheddar cheese (3 ounces)
2 large egg whites	
¼ teaspoon black pepper	**Garnishes:**
1 tablespoon unsalted butter or margarine	4 tomato wedges
	4 sprigs parsley

PREP TIME: 15 MIN. / COOKING TIME: 8 MIN.

1 Preheat the broiler. In a large bowl, with an electric mixer on high, beat the whole eggs, egg whites, and pepper for 5 minutes or until very thick and tripled in volume.

2 In a 10-inch nonstick skillet, melt the butter over moderate heat. Pour in the eggs, spreading evenly. Cook gently for 4 minutes or just until the omelet begins to set. While cooking, constantly lift the cooked edges with a spatula, allowing uncooked egg to flow to the bottom.

3 Sprinkle with the cheese. Cover the skillet handle with foil and broil, 4 inches from the heat, for 2 minutes or until the cheese melts and the omelet is puffy and firm to the touch.

4 Using a spatula, gently fold the omelet in half and slide onto a warm serving platter. Garnish with the tomato wedges and parsley sprigs and serve immediately with slices of hot Sally Lunn Bread (page 289). Makes 4 servings.

*1 serving: Calories 196; Saturated Fat 8 g;
Total Fat 15 g; Protein 13 g; Carbohydrate 1 g; Fiber 0 g;
Sodium 223 mg; Cholesterol 244 mg*

EGGS WITH MUSHROOM SAUCE

❖❖❖

*The colonists found edible mushrooms in the
forests when they arrived. It's no wonder that dishes
containing mushrooms are American favorites.*

1 tablespoon unsalted butter or margarine	3 tablespoons minced parsley
8 ounces mushrooms, thinly sliced (3 cups)	⅛ teaspoon black pepper
⅓ cup Beef Stock (page 74) or low-sodium beef broth	3 large eggs
	2 large egg whites
½ cup dry white wine or Beef Stock	2 tablespoons low-fat (1% milkfat) milk
¼ cup tomato purée	½ teaspoon salt
3 tablespoons brandy or Beef Stock	1 tablespoon olive oil

PREP TIME: 15 MIN. / COOKING TIME: 18 MIN.

1 In a 10-inch nonstick skillet, melt the butter over low heat. Add the mushrooms and cook, stirring occasionally, for 3 minutes. Pour in the stock; cook 4 minutes longer or until tender.

2 Raise the heat to moderate, add the wine, tomato purée, and brandy. Cook, uncovered, 5 minutes more or until well blended. Stir in the parsley and pepper and keep the sauce warm.

3 Preheat the broiler. In a medium-size bowl, whisk the eggs, egg whites, milk, and salt. In an 8-inch nonstick skillet, heat the oil over moderate heat. Pour in the egg mixture; cook for 4 minutes or just until the eggs are set. While cooking, constantly lift the cooked edges with a spatula, allowing uncooked egg to flow to the bottom.

4 Cover the skillet handle with foil; broil, 4 inches from the heat, for 1 minute or just until set. Serve the eggs with the sauce and Monkey Bread (page 293). Makes 4 servings.

*1 serving: 198 Calories; Saturated Fat 4 g;
Total Fat 11 g; Protein 9 g; Carbohydrate 7 g; Fiber 1 g;
Sodium 421 mg; Cholesterol 169 mg*

Hollandaise
sauce enrobes
dozens of
famous dishes...
the most
famous to be
laved lavishly
is Eggs Benedict.

—*from The Cook's Tales
by Lee Edwards Benning*

DOWN HOME TRADITION

Several legends describe the origin of this popular American brunch dish. One traces its beginning to the famous Delmonico's Restaurant in New York City. Mr. Delmonico himself created it for one of his regular wealthy customers, Mrs. LeGand Benedict, when she complained one day that there was nothing new on the menu. Another legend connects the dish's inspiration to Wall Street broker Lemuel Benedict. Whatever the authentic origin, the dish is so rich and special, it's usually reserved for company.

◆ Eggs Benedict ◆

6 large egg yolks
1½ cups (3 sticks) unsalted butter (not margarine), melted
2 tablespoons fresh lemon juice
¼ teaspoon salt
Dash ground red pepper (cayenne)
3 English muffins, split
6 thick slices Canadian bacon
1 teaspoon white vinegar
6 large eggs

PREP TIME: 15 MIN. / COOKING TIME: 15 MIN.

---

1 In a double boiler or a saucepan placed over hot water, whisk the egg yolks over moderate heat for 1 minute or until smooth. Slowly whisk in the melted butter, then the lemon juice, salt, and ground red pepper. Cook, whisking constantly, 3 minutes more or until smooth and thickened. Remove from the heat, cover, and keep the sauce warm over the hot water.

2 Preheat the broiler. On a baking sheet, arrange the 6 muffin halves, light-sides-up. Toast for 1 minute or until golden and keep warm. In a 12-inch skillet, cook the bacon over moderate heat for 2 minutes or until lightly browned. Place one slice of bacon on each muffin half.

3 Fill the same skillet two-thirds-full with water. Add the vinegar; bring to a simmer over moderate heat. Break each egg into a saucer, then slide the egg into the water. Cook the eggs, spooning the water over them, for 3 minutes or until cooked the way you like them. Using a slotted spoon, top each muffin half with 1 egg. Ladle over some sauce. Serve immediately with fresh steamed asparagus and lemon wedges. Makes 3 servings, 2 eggs each.

---

*1 serving: Calories 1308; Saturated Fat 65 g; Total Fat 117 g; Protein 36 g;
Carbohydrate 32 g; Fiber 0 g; Sodium 1488 mg; Cholesterol 1129 mg*

LIGHT EGGS BENEDICT

◆◆◆

This version, with much less butter and fewer egg yolks than the original, is still luscious.

1 large egg yolk	1 tablespoon cornstarch
2 tablespoons fresh lemon juice	½ cup low-fat (1% milkfat) milk
2 tablespoons unsalted butter (not margarine), melted	3 English muffins, split
¼ cup hot water	6 thin slices Canadian bacon
⅛ teaspoon salt	1 teaspoon white vinegar
Dash ground red pepper (cayenne)	6 large eggs

PREP TIME: 15 MIN. / COOKING TIME: 12 MIN.

1 In a double boiler or a saucepan placed over hot water, whisk the egg yolk over moderate heat for 1 minute or until smooth. Whisk in the lemon juice, then the melted butter, water, salt, and ground red pepper.

2 In a small cup, dissolve the cornstarch in the milk, then whisk into the sauce. Cook for 4 minutes, whisking constantly, until the sauce thickens slightly. Remove from the heat, cover, and keep the sauce warm over the hot water.

3 Preheat the broiler. On a baking sheet, arrange the 6 muffin halves, light-sides-up. Toast for 1 minute or until golden and keep warm. In a 12-inch nonstick skillet, cook the bacon over moderate heat for 2 minutes or until lightly browned. Place one slice of bacon on each muffin half.

4 Fill the same skillet two-thirds-full with water. Add the vinegar and bring to a simmer over moderate heat. Break each egg into a saucer, then slide the egg into the water. Cook the eggs, spooning the water over them, for 3 minutes or until cooked the way you like them. Using a slotted spoon, top each muffin half with 1 egg. Ladle over some sauce. Serve with fresh berries tossed with mint. Makes 6 servings, 1 egg each.

1 serving: Calories 247; Saturated Fat 5 g; Total Fat 13 g; Protein 16 g; Carbohydrate 17 g; Fiber 0 g; Sodium 698 mg; Cholesterol 274 mg

Brunch for company: Light Eggs Benedict served with a fresh fruit salad

Apples and Cheddar cheese from Vermont in a puffy brunch bake

CHEESE STRATA

◆◆◆

Americans created this fool-proof version of a soufflé. It's wonderful for brunch, or you can halve the recipe to serve as a light supper dish for four.

8 ounces bulk pork sausage, thawed if frozen	6 slices home-style, day-old white bread, crusts removed, cut into 2-inch squares
1 cup chopped onion	1½ cups shredded sharp Cheddar cheese (6 ounces)
2 cloves garlic, minced	
¼ teaspoon salt, or to taste	1½ cups low-fat (1% milkfat) milk
1 can (16 ounces) low-sodium whole tomatoes, drained and chopped	3 large eggs
	1 large egg white
½ teaspoon each dried basil leaves and rubbed sage	2 teaspoons Dijon mustard
	¼ teaspoon ground red pepper (cayenne)

PREP TIME: 25 MIN. / COOKING TIME: 1¼ HR.
STANDING TIME: OVERNIGHT (12 HR.)

1 In a 12-inch nonstick skillet, brown the sausage over moderate heat, stirring to break up, then transfer to paper towels. Discard all but 1 tablespoon of drippings from the skillet. Add the onion, garlic, and ⅛ teaspoon of the salt; sauté for 5 minutes. Stir in the tomatoes, basil, and sage; cook, uncovered 5 minutes longer or until most of the liquid has evaporated. Remove from the heat, stir in the sausage, and let cool.

2 Grease a shallow 2-quart ovenproof dish and line the bottom with ½ of the bread. Layer with ½ of the sausage and ½ of the cheese, then repeat with the remaining sausage and cheese. Top with the remaining bread.

3 In a medium-size bowl, whisk the milk, eggs, egg white, mustard, and ground red pepper. Pour over the strata and cover tightly with foil. Refrigerate overnight.

4 Preheat the oven to 350°F. Remove the strata from the refrigerator 30 minutes before baking. Bake, covered, for 1 hour or until puffy; remove the cover. Turn the oven to broil and broil, 4 inches from the heat, for 2 minutes or until golden. Serves 8.

1 serving: Calories 264; Saturated Fat 7 g;
Total Fat 16 g; Protein 15 g; Carbohydrate 15 g; Fiber 0 g;
Sodium 601 mg; Cholesterol 119 mg

VERMONT CHEDDAR-APPLE BAKE
◆◆◆

4 tablespoons unsalted butter or margarine, softened

8 slices whole wheat bread, crusts removed

⅓ cup all-purpose flour

2 cups low-fat (1% milkfat) milk

½ teaspoon each salt and black pepper

¼ teaspoon ground nutmeg

1 large egg, beaten

5 large baking apples, such as McIntosh or Rome Beauty, peeled, cored, and thinly sliced (5 cups)

1 large yellow onion, peeled and thinly sliced (1½ cups)

2 cups shredded extra sharp Cheddar cheese (8 ounces)

Optional garnish:
Fresh apple slices

PREP TIME: 20 MIN. / STANDING TIME: 1 HR.
COOKING TIME: 50 MIN.

1 Preheat the oven to 350°F; butter a 13" x 9" x 3" ovenproof dish. Using 2 tablespoons of the butter, thinly coat one side of each bread slice. Cut each slice into 4 triangles, making 32; line the dish with 16 triangles, buttered-side-up.

2 In a medium-size saucepan, melt the remaining 2 tablespoons of butter over moderate heat. Stir in the flour and cook until bubbly. Whisk in the milk, salt, pepper, and nutmeg; bring to a boil and cook until thickened. Remove from the heat, cool, then whisk in the egg.

3 Top the bread in the dish with ½ of the apples, ½ of the onion, ½ of the cheese, and ½ of the sauce; repeat. Arrange the remaining 16 bread triangles, buttered-side-up, around the edge of the dish, overlapping them slightly. Cover and refrigerate for 1 hour. Uncover and bake for 50 minutes or until puffy and golden. Let stand for 10 minutes; garnish with the apple slices if you wish. Serve with spinach salad. Makes 8 servings.

1 serving: Calories 335; Saturated Fat 10 g; Total Fat 18 g; Protein 13 g; Carbohydrate 32 g; Fiber 1 g; Sodium 483 mg; Cholesterol 76 mg

HUNT BREAKFAST GRITS
◆◆◆

Since 1776, the Griswold Inn in Essex, Connecticut has been welcoming guests to its country quarters. People come for miles around for the Hunt Breakfasts —many returning again and again for these grits, made from a recipe of the innkeeper's mother.

5 cups water

1 tablespoon unsalted butter or margarine

½ teaspoon black pepper

¼ teaspoon dry mustard

¼ teaspoon salt or to taste

¼ teaspoon Worcestershire sauce

1 cup regular grits

2 cups shredded sharp Cheddar cheese (8 ounces)

1 large egg

2 large egg whites

PREP TIME: 15 MIN. / COOKING TIME: 1 HR.

1 Preheat the oven to 350°F. Butter a 1-quart casserole. In a medium-size saucepan, bring the water, butter, pepper, mustard, salt, and Worcestershire to a boil over moderately high heat, then slowly stir in the grits.

2 Lower the heat; cook, uncovered, for 15 minutes or until thickened. Remove from the heat, add 1½ cups of cheese, and stir until melted.

3 In a medium-size bowl, with an electric mixer on high, beat the egg and egg whites for 3 minutes or until light yellow and thickened. Whisk into the grits, then let cool slightly.

4 Spoon into the casserole, sprinkle with the remaining ½ cup of cheese, cover loosely with foil, and bake for 30 minutes. Uncover and cook 15 minutes more or until puffy. Reset the oven to broil and broil, 4 inches from the heat, for 2 minutes or until golden brown. Serve with Ham and Red-Eye Gravy (page 109). Makes 6 servings.

1 serving: Calories 286; Saturated Fat 10 g; Total Fat 16 g; Protein 14 g; Carbohydrate 22 g; Fiber 0 g; Sodium 361 mg; Cholesterol 81 mg

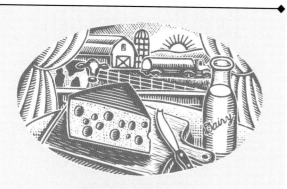

◆ Cheese Making ◆

Welcome to the Welcome Dairy, in the rolling farmlands of Colby in central Wisconsin. Giant tanker trucks of fresh milk are just arriving from nearby dairy farms. Our host is Terry Eggebrecht, president of this fine, family-owned cheese-making business, known for its many award-winning specialty cheeses.

"The milk being delivered today will be turned into cheese tomorrow. The process takes about five hours from start to finish," explains Terry.

"First it's pasteurized, that is, heated to 162°F to get rid of any harmful bacteria that might be present. Next, it's subjected to various temperature changes. The actual cheese making begins when the milk is inoculated with a culture related to the type of cheese being made. Then rennet, an enzyme, coagulates (thickens) the milk and wire knives cut through the soft curd to separate the whey (watery part) from the curd.

"Next, the curd is subjected to various temperatures for different amounts of time.

One batch becomes a mild Colby, another is made into Monterey Jack, and yet another becomes Cheddar.

"A salting procedure slows down bacterial growth, stopping the cheese making process. Then it's only a short time before the curd is molded and pressed into shapes, such as a 40-pound block of Muenster, or a 500-pound barrel of Cheddar.

"About half of the cheese we produce is natural. The other half is processed, which is begun by grinding together a blend of cheeses, such as younger mild Cheddars with stronger aged ones. The blend is next steamed in large cookers to a molten state, then combined with emulsifying salts to make the product less perishable.

"At this point, the cheese is poured into forms, such as rounds or bricks, or it's poured into thin sheets on conveyor belts, then cooled and cut into slices. Finally the cheeses are packaged and shipped to markets, far from the farmlands of the Midwest."

COLBY SOUFFLÉ
◆◆◆

For several generations, the Eggebrechts of Colby, Wisconsin, have run the family's cheese business. They use Colby cheese, a mild type of Cheddar which melts perfectly, to make this smooth soufflé.

¼ **cup unsalted butter or margarine**	2 **cups shredded Colby or other mild cheese (8 ounces)**
¼ **cup all-purpose flour**	6 **large eggs at room temperature, separated**
1½ **cups low-fat (1% milkfat) milk**	
¼ **teaspoon salt**	2 **tablespoons finely chopped parsley**
⅛ **teaspoon ground red pepper (cayenne)**	¼ **teaspoon dried thyme leaves**

PREP TIME: 15 MIN. / COOKING TIME: 55 MIN.

1 Preheat the oven to 325°F. Grease a 2-quart soufflé dish. In a medium-size saucepan, melt the butter over moderate heat. Stir in the flour and cook until bubbly. Whisk in the milk, salt, and ground red pepper, then cook, whisking constantly, for 5 minutes or until thickened. Add the cheese and stir until melted. Remove from heat.

2 In a small bowl, whisk the egg yolks until light. Add a little of the hot cheese mixture, then slowly whisk it all into the sauce. Add the parsley and thyme and transfer to a large bowl.

3 In a clean medium-size bowl, beat the egg whites with an electric mixer on high until soft peaks form. Stir ¼ of the whites into the cheese mixture, then quickly fold in the remaining whites. Spoon into the soufflé dish; bake for 45 minutes or until puffy and golden. Serve immediately with Fresh Fruit Salad with Poppy Seed Dressing (page 250). Serves 8.

1 serving: Calories 256; Saturated Fat 11 g; Total Fat 19 g; Protein 13 g; Carbohydrate 7 g; Fiber 0 g; Sodium 309 mg; Cholesterol 205 mg

Brunch break: Time for a slice of cheesy Old Country Quiche

OLD COUNTRY QUICHE

In 1936, Werner Zimmerman, Sr. immigrated from Switzerland to the Swiss-German community of Green County, Wisconsin, and began a family tradition of making cheese. Here is the Zimmermans' favorite recipe for a holiday brunch.

Pastry for single-crust pie (page 368)

1 teaspoon unsalted butter or margarine

1 small yellow onion, chopped (½ cup)

2 cups shredded Swiss cheese (8 ounces)

6 slices lean bacon, cooked and crumbled

2 tablespoons all-purpose flour

3 large eggs

1 cup low-fat (1% milkfat) milk

¼ teaspoon salt, or to taste

⅛ teaspoon ground nutmeg

PREP TIME: 30 MIN. / COOKING TIME: 1 HR.

1 Preheat the oven to 400°F. Line a 9-inch quiche dish with the pastry, flute the edges, fill with dried beans, and bake for 15 minutes or until light brown. Discard the beans and cool on a rack.

2 Meanwhile, in a 6-inch nonstick skillet, melt the butter over moderately high heat. Add the onion and sauté for 5 minutes or until soft, then transfer to a medium-size bowl. Toss with the cheese, bacon, and flour. Spread in the pie crust.

3 In the same bowl, whisk the eggs with the milk, salt, and nutmeg. Pour over the pie mixture and bake, uncovered, for 35 minutes or until the center is set. Serve with a Chopped Tomato Salad (page 256). Makes 6 servings.

1 serving: Calories 537; Saturated Fat 16 g; Total Fat 34 g; Protein 22 g; Carbohydrate 36 g; Fiber 0 g; Sodium 387 mg; Cholesterol 171 mg

FOUR-CHEESE FONDUE

◆◆◆

This Swiss dish was introduced to the United States in the 1950's and became popular as a party food during ski weekends. It's usually served in a pot set over a candle or liquid fuel to keep it warm; long handled forks are used for dipping.

2 teaspoons cornstarch	½ cup shredded sharp Cheddar cheese (2 ounces)
⅔ cup cold water	½ teaspoon ground coriander (optional)
½ cup dry white wine, (with or without alcohol)	½ teaspoon garlic powder
4 ounces Neufchâtel cream cheese	½ teaspoon paprika
½ cup shredded Gruyère cheese (2 ounces)	¼ teaspoon dry mustard
½ cup shredded Gouda cheese (2 ounces)	¼ teaspoon black pepper

PREP TIME: 15 MIN. / COOKING TIME: 10 MIN.

1 In a large saucepan, dissolve the cornstarch in the water, then add the wine and cream cheese. Stirring constantly, bring to a boil over medium heat and cook for 3 minutes or until thickened.

2 Gradually add the Gruyère, Gouda, and Cheddar cheeses and stir until melted, then add the remaining ingredients. Cook 2 minutes longer or until blended. Pour into a fondue pot and serve with bite-size pieces of assorted breads and fresh vegetables. Offer long handled forks for dipping. Makes 4 servings.

1 serving: Calories 267; Saturated Fat 12 g; Total Fat 20 g; Protein 14 g; Carbohydrate 3 g; Fiber 0 g; Sodium 367 mg; Cholesterol 68 mg

Fun around the fondue pot: Four-Cheese Fondue and plenty of fresh vegetables and bites of bread for dunking

BAKED CHEESE TOAST
◆◆◆

Swiss-born René Weber, now one of Wisconsin's paramount cheesemakers, continues the Swiss tradition of cooking with Gruyère cheese. This is one of his favorite recipes for entertaining at brunch; it can easily be doubled to serve 8.

8 slices home-style white or whole-wheat bread

2 tablespoons unsalted butter or margarine, melted

½ cup low-fat (1% milkfat) milk

2 cups shredded Wisconsin Gruyère cheese (8 ounces)

2 large eggs, separated

1 tablespoon Kirsch or cherry brandy (optional)

¼ teaspoon each ground nutmeg, salt, and black pepper

PREP. TIME: 15 MIN. / COOKING TIME: 25 MIN.

1 Preheat the oven to 350°F and lightly grease an 8-inch square baking dish (single recipe) or a 12" x 8" x 2" baking dish (double recipe). Arrange ½ of the bread slices in the bottom and brush with the melted butter.

2 In a medium-size bowl, whisk together the milk, cheese, egg yolks, Kirsch if you wish, nutmeg, salt, and pepper for 2 minutes or until foamy. In a clean small bowl, beat the egg whites with an electric mixer on high for 3 minutes or until stiff peaks form.

3 Gently fold the whites into the cheese mixture and pour ½ of this mixture over the bread slices. Top with the remaining bread, then drizzle with the remaining cheese mixture. Bake for 25 minutes (single recipe) or 35 minutes (double recipe) or until puffy and golden brown. Serve immediately with Fresh Fruit Salad with Poppy Seed Dressing (page 250). Makes 4 servings.

1 serving: Calories 378; Saturated Fat 14 g; Total Fat 24 g; Protein 21 g; Carbohydrate 21 g; Fiber 1 g; Sodium 502 mg; Cholesterol 149 mg

CHEESE ENCHILADAS
◆◆◆

The name enchilada comes from the Spanish-American term meaning "filled with chilies." But in this recipe, the tortillas are filled with hot-pepper cheese instead.

¼ cup all-purpose flour

1⅓ cup low-fat (1% milkfat) milk

½ cup shredded Monterey Jack cheese with jalapeño peppers (2 ounces)

1 green onion, with tops, chopped (2 tablespoons)

4 7-inch corn tortillas, thawed if frozen

½ cup medium-hot salsa

PREP TIME: 20 MIN. / COOKING TIME: 30 MIN.

1 In a medium-size saucepan, whisk the flour and milk over moderate heat. Cook, stirring frequently, for 7 minutes or until thickened. Stir in ¼ cup of the cheese and the green onion; cook the sauce 2 minutes longer or until the cheese is melted and the flavors are well blended.

2 Preheat the oven to 350°F and grease an 8-inch square baking dish. Half-fill an 8-inch skillet with water and bring to a simmer over low heat. Quickly dip a corn tortilla in the skillet to soften it slightly and place on a plate. Spoon 1 tablespoon of the cheese sauce in a strip down the center and top with 1 tablespoon of salsa. Roll up and place seam-side-down in the baking dish. Repeat with the remaining tortillas.

3 Pour the remaining sauce over all and bake for 20 minutes or until bubbly and lightly browned. Top with the remaining salsa and shredded cheese. Serve immediately with tomato and avocado slices. Makes 4 servings.

1 serving: Calories 179; Saturated Fat 1 g; Total Fat 4 g; Protein 8 g; Carbohydrate 29 g; Fiber 1 g; Sodium 454 mg; Cholesterol 9 mg

EGG FOO YUNG

These oriental pancakes were brought to America by the first Chinese immigrants, who settled in San Francisco in the mid-19th century. Serve them for brunch or a Sunday supper.

2 tablespoons vegetable oil	2 tablespoons chopped fresh or canned mushrooms
½ cup diced uncooked boneless chicken breast (3 ounces)	½ cup fresh or canned bean sprouts, well drained
2 tablespoons chopped celery	1 tablespoon all-purpose flour
2 tablespoons chopped green onions, with tops	1 tablespoon reduced-sodium soy sauce
2 tablespoons chopped water chestnuts	4 large eggs
	3 large egg whites

PREP TIME: 20 MIN. / COOKING TIME: 32 MIN.

1 In a 12-inch nonstick skillet, heat 1 tablespoon of the oil over moderate heat. Add the chicken and stir-fry for 3 minutes or until opaque. Add the celery, green onions, water chestnuts, mushrooms, and bean sprouts and sauté for 3 minutes or until crisp-tender. (Tip: Refrigerate the remaining water chestnuts and use later in salads.)

2 Remove from the heat and stir in the flour and soy sauce. In a medium-size bowl, whisk the eggs with the egg whites until frothy, then stir in the chicken mixture until coated.

3 Wipe out the skillet and heat the remaining 1 tablespoon of oil over moderately high heat. Drop in the egg mixture by heaping tablespoonfuls, forming 3-inch pancakes, and cook for 2 minutes on each side or until golden brown. Serve with wedges of fresh pineapple. Makes 24 pancakes.

1 pancake: Calories 30; Saturated Fat 1 g; Total Fat 2 g; Protein 2 g; Carbohydrate 1 g; Fiber 0 g; Sodium 44 mg; Cholesterol 28 mg

DUTCH BABIES

Pancake houses often feature these individual egg puffs, which are not Dutch at all but really American versions of the German pancake.

4 teaspoons unsalted butter, melted	½ teaspoon grated lemon rind
3 large eggs	⅛ teaspoon salt
2 large egg whites	½ cup all-purpose flour
½ cup low-fat (1% milkfat) milk	2 tablespoons fresh lemon juice
1 tablespoon granulated sugar	2 tablespoons confectioners' sugar

PREP TIME: 15 MIN. / COOKING TIME: 10 MIN.

1 Preheat the oven to 425°F and butter four 6-inch gratin ovenproof dishes with 1 teaspoon of the butter. In a medium-size bowl, whisk the eggs, egg whites, milk, granulated sugar, lemon rind, and salt until well combined. Sift in the flour, whisking until the batter is smooth.

2 Place the gratin dishes in the oven to heat. Whisk the remaining 3 teaspoons of butter into the batter, then divide the batter evenly among the 4 dishes.

3 Bake for 8 minutes or until puffed and set. Sprinkle with the lemon juice and confectioners' sugar. Serve immediately. Makes 4 servings.

1 serving: Calories 192; Saturated Fat 4 g; Total Fat 8 g; Protein 9 g; Carbohydrate 20 g; Fiber 0 g; Sodium 158 mg; Cholesterol 172 mg

◆

Dutch Mama

Grease **a 12-inch ovenproof, nonstick skillet** with all of the butter. Prepare the batter as for Dutch Babies, pour into the skillet, and bake for 15 minutes or until puffed and set, then sprinkle with the lemon juice and confectioners' sugar. Makes 3 servings. *1 serving: Calories 256; Saturated Fat 5 g; Total Fat 11 g; Protein 12 g; Carbohydrate 26 g; Fiber 0 g; Sodium 210 mg; Cholesterol 229 mg*

Great for a weekend brunch: Cheese Blintzes topped with fresh berries

CHEESE BLINTZES

◆◆◆

*An American-Jewish specialty, these
cheese-filled pancakes are one of the dairy dishes
traditionally served for Shabuoth or Pentecost —
but they're popular the year around.*

For the blintz batter:

- ½ cup all-purpose flour
- 1 large egg
- 2 large egg whites
- ¾ cup low-fat (1% milkfat) milk
- 1 tablespoon unsalted butter, melted
- ½ teaspoon sugar
- 1 tablespoon vegetable oil

For the cheese filling:

- 1 pound low-fat (1% milkfat) cottage cheese
- ¼ cup sugar
- 3 tablespoons all-purpose flour
- 1 large egg
- ½ teaspoon vanilla
- Assorted fresh berries (optional)

PREP TIME: 15 MIN. / COOKING TIME: 27 MIN.

1 To prepare the blintzes: In a large bowl, with an electric mixer set on high, beat the flour, egg, egg whites, milk, melted butter, and sugar for 1 minute or until smooth.

2 Brush the inside of a crepe pan or a heavy 6-inch skillet with a little of the oil and heat over moderately high heat. Spoon 2 tablespoons of the batter into the skillet, tilting it quickly so the batter spreads evenly and thinly coats the bottom. Cook on one side for 1 minute or only until the top is dry and blistered, then transfer with a spatula to a flat surface, browned-side-down. Repeat the process, making 12 blintzes.

3 Preheat the oven to 375°F. Set out an un-greased baking sheet. To prepare the filling: In a medium-size bowl, stir all of the ingredients until blended. Spoon about 3 tablespoons of filling in the center of each blintz, fold in 2 sides about 1 inch, then the other 2 sides, overlapping them slightly to resemble an envelope. Place seam-side-down on an ungreased baking sheet. Bake for 12 minutes or until the filling is set, then re-set the oven to broil. Broil the blintzes for 2 minutes or until lightly browned. Top with the fresh berries and serve hot. Makes 6 servings of 2 blintzes each.

*1 serving (2 blintzes): Calories 216; Saturated Fat 3 g;
Total Fat 7 g; Protein 15 g; Carbohydrate 23 g; Fiber 0 g;
Sodium 362 mg; Cholesterol 81 mg*

VEGETABLE-HAM FRITTATA

◆◆◆

*From Italian immigrants comes this
egg dish that resembles an omelet. You can eat
it hot, or cook it ahead of time and serve
it at room temperature.*

1 tablespoon unsalted butter or margarine	½ cup diced cooked ham (3 ounces)
1 cup diced red-skinned potatoes (about 4 ounces)	4 large whole eggs
	4 large egg whites
½ cup chopped yellow onion	¼ cup grated Parmesan cheese
1 clove garlic, minced	2 tablespoons slivered fresh basil, or 2 teaspoons dried basil
1 cup chopped fresh asparagus or zucchini	
½ cup chopped sweet red pepper	¼ teaspoon salt, or to taste
	⅛ teaspoon black pepper

PREP TIME: 25 MIN. / COOKING TIME: 22 MIN.

1 Preheat the broiler. In a 12-inch nonstick skillet, melt the butter over moderate heat. Add the potatoes, onion, and garlic and cook, stirring occasionally, for 7 minutes or until the potatoes are almost cooked. Stir in the asparagus, sweet red pepper, and ham. Cook 3 minutes more or until the vegetables are crisp-tender.

2 In a medium-size bowl, whisk together the eggs, egg whites, cheese, basil, salt, and black pepper, then pour over the vegetables. Lower the heat and cook, uncovered, for 10 minutes, or just until the egg mixture is almost set.

3 Wrap the skillet handle with foil. Slide the skillet under the broiler for 1 minute or just until the eggs are set on top. Serve with warm Italian bread. Makes 4 servings.

---

*1 serving: Calories 205; Saturated Fat 4 g;
Total Fat 10 g; Protein 16 g; Carbohydrate 12 g; Fiber 1 g;
Sodium 475 mg; Cholesterol 228 mg*

Frittata: A terrific one-dish meal, morning, noon, or night

Unlike the French omelet,
the frittata is cooked slowly over
very low heat... is firm and set...
is flat and perfectly round.

—*from The Classic Italian Cook Book
by Marcella Hazan*

ALL-AMERICAN PIZZA

American innovations on the Italian pizza have become so numerous that the dish now seems a part of our own heritage. This version, topped with broiled vegetables, is a case in point.

3 tablespoons olive oil	1 recipe Pizza Crust (page 298) or 1 package (10 ounces) refrigerated pizza dough
1 large clove garlic, minced	
⅛ teaspoon black pepper	
1 large zucchini, trimmed (12 ounces)	1½ cups shredded part-skim mozzarella cheese (6 ounces)
1 large yellow squash, trimmed (8 ounces)	1 large tomato, diced (1½ cups)
1 cup bite-size sweet red pepper squares	2 tablespoons grated Parmesan cheese
1½ cups sliced fresh mushrooms	1 tablespoon minced fresh thyme or 1 teaspoon dried thyme leaves
2 tablespoons yellow cornmeal	

PREP TIME: 45 MIN. / COOKING TIME: 20 MIN.

1 Preheat the broiler. In a small cup combine the oil, garlic, and black pepper. Cut the zucchini and yellow squash lengthwise into thin slices and arrange with the red pepper and mushrooms on a broiler pan. Brush both sides with the oil mixture and broil, 4 inches from the heat, for 2 minutes on each side or until tender.

2 Preheat the oven to 425°F. Grease a 15½" x 10½" x 2" baking pan and sprinkle with the cornmeal. Gently press the dough onto the bottom and up the sides of the pan. Sprinkle with 1 cup of the mozzarella.

3 Arrange the broiled vegetables and tomatoes on top, and bake for 10 minutes. Sprinkle with the remaining ½ cup mozzarella cheese, the Parmesan, and thyme; bake for 5 to 10 minutes longer or until bubbly. Makes 6 servings.

1 serving: Calories 450; Saturated Fat 5 g; Total Fat 18 g; Protein 17 g; Carbohydrate 57 g; Fiber 1 g; Sodium 357 mg; Cholesterol 18 mg

---

◆

Sausage and Vegetable Pizza

In a 10-inch nonstick skillet, brown **8 ounces Italian or country sausage** over moderately high heat for 5 minutes, stirring to break up the meat. Prepare All-American Pizza, spreading the sausage over the dough before adding the mozzarella and vegetables. Makes 6 servings *1 serving: Calories 550; Saturated Fat 5 g; Total Fat 25 g; Protein 19 g; Carbohydrate 58 g; Fiber 1 g; Sodium 609 mg; Cholesterol 45 mg*

CRUSTLESS TOMATO PIE

The Italians were among the first to accept the tomato as an edible food. In early recipes it was usually cooked before eating, as in this open-face pie.

1 cup coarsely torn Italian bread (2 ounces)	1 clove garlic, minced
1 cup shredded mozzarella cheese (4 ounces)	3 large ripe tomatoes, sliced crosswise
1 tablespoon olive oil	¼ cup slivered fresh basil leaves or chopped parsley
1 tablespoon grated Parmesan cheese	⅛ teaspoon freshly ground pepper
1 tablespoon minced fresh parsley	

PREP TIME: 20 MIN. / COOKING TIME: 10 MIN.

1 Preheat the oven to 400°F. Set out a 12-inch round quiche or baking dish. In a small bowl, toss the bread with the mozzarella, oil, Parmesan, parsley, and garlic.

2 Line the baking dish with the tomato slices, overlapping them slightly. Sprinkle with the basil and pepper, then top with the bread mixture. Bake, uncovered, for 10 minutes or until melted and golden brown. Serve hot with slices of Country Loaf (page 288). Makes 4 servings.

1 serving: Calories 201; Saturated Fat 5 g; Total Fat 11 g; Protein 9 g; Carbohydrate 17 g; Fiber 1 g; Sodium 256 mg; Cholesterol 23 mg

PASTA & RICE FAVORITES

◆◆◆

The pasta and rice dishes served on this country's tables are a wonderful eclectic mix of Old World traditions and New World inventiveness. Two typical examples are Rice Croquettes, inspired by the French but re-created with local ingredients by cooks on Southern plantations, and Mexicalli Rice Bake, a Southwestern dish with flavors from south of the Texas border. Similarly, pasta, introduced to us by Italians, has been adapted in such favorites as macaroni and cheese and tuna-noodle casserole.

These pasta and rice dishes fit in well with today's emphasis on foods that are high in complex carbohydrates. But often they are high too in fat, cholesterol, and sodium. We've made them healthier by trimming back the quantity of such high-fat ingredients as bacon and cheese. We've lightened the sauces with the use of low-fat milk instead of cream. And we've cut down on sodium by using no-salt-added tomato products and homemade soup stocks. Rest assured that none of the flavor has been lost. Spices, peppers, garlic, and herbs all contribute to the sense that good down-home cooking is here to stay.

DOWN HOME TRADITION

After one of Thomas Jefferson's trips to Europe, he returned home with a recipe for macaroni: "Two eggs beaten with a wine glass of milk, a teaspoon of salt, and enough flour to make a smooth, firm dough." His papers even included drawings of a gadget to form the dough into tubular shapes, not unlike the machines used today. Jefferson gradually introduced macaroni and cheese to his countrymen, long before the great influx of Italian immigrants. The White House menu for February 6, 1802, in fact, featured a macaroni pie. (The word *macaroni* appears in a line from the famous 18th-century song, Yankee Doodle Dandy: "Stuck a feather in his cap and called it macaroni." Macaroni in this case refers not to pasta but to the slang word for a fashionably dressed gentleman, of the type who might belong to the exclusive London Macaroni Club.) Over the years, macaroni and cheese has become an American tradition. From Mary Sonnier, a pastry chef in New Orleans, Louisiana, comes this rich version. She writes: "My daughter's favorite is Mom's Mac and Cheese."

◆ Mom's Mac and Cheese ◆

8 ounces elbow macaroni or rigatoni
2 tablespoons unsalted butter
1 clove garlic, minced
2 tablespoons all-purpose flour
2 cups whole milk
¼ teaspoon hot red pepper sauce
3 cups shredded extra-sharp Cheddar cheese (12 ounces)
¼ cup seasoned dry bread crumbs
¼ cup grated Parmesan Cheese

PREP TIME: 15 MIN. / COOKING TIME: 47 MIN.

1 Preheat the oven to 350°F and lightly butter a 2½-quart casserole or baking dish. Bring a stockpot of salted water to a boil over high heat, add the macaroni, and cook for 6 minutes or just until tender but still firm. Drain, rinse, drain again, and keep warm.

2 Meanwhile, in a large saucepan, melt the butter over moderately high heat Add the garlic and sauté for 1 minute or until softened. Stir in the flour and cook for 1 minute or until bubbly. Gradually whisk in the milk and red pepper sauce and cook, stirring occasionally, for 5 minutes or until thickened.

3 Add the Cheddar cheese and cook, stirring constantly, 5 minutes more or until melted and smooth. Remove from the heat, add the macaroni, and toss to coat well. Spoon into the casserole. In a small bowl, toss the bread crumbs with the Parmesan cheese and sprinkle on top of the macaroni mixture. Bake, uncovered, for 25 minutes or until bubbling and golden brown. Serve with tomato slices drizzled with Old Fashioned French Dressing (page 263). Makes 6 side-dish or 3 to 4 main-dish servings.

1 side-dish serving: Calories 499; Saturated Fat 17 g; Total Fat 28 g; Protein 24 g; Carbohydrate 38 g; Fiber 0 g; Sodium 503 mg; Cholesterol 85 mg

A down-home dinner: Macaroni and Cheese, hot and bubbling, right out of the oven

MACARONI AND CHEESE

♦♦♦

8 ounces elbow macaroni or rigatoni	2 cups low-fat (1% milkfat) milk
1 tablespoon unsalted butter or margarine	1 cup shredded extra-sharp Cheddar cheese (4 ounces)
1 small yellow onion, chopped (½ cup)	1 cup shredded Swiss cheese (4 ounces)
2 tablespoons all-purpose flour	**For the topping:**
½ teaspoon dry mustard	3 tablespoons plain dry bread crumbs
Pinch ground red pepper (cayenne)	2 tablespoons minced parsley

PREP TIME: 20 MIN. / COOKING TIME: 39 MIN.

1 Preheat the oven to 350°F and lightly butter a 14-inch oval baking dish or 2½-quart casserole. Bring a stockpot of unsalted water to a boil, add the macaroni, and cook for 6 minutes or just until tender but still firm. Drain, rinse, drain again, and keep warm.

2 Meanwhile, in a large saucepan, melt the butter over moderately high heat. Add the onion and sauté for 3 minutes or until softened. Stir in the flour, mustard, and ground red pepper and cook for 1 minute or until bubbly. Gradually whisk in the milk and cook, stirring occasionally, for 5 minutes or until thickened.

3 Add the two cheeses and cook, stirring constantly, 5 minutes more or until melted and smooth. Remove from the heat, add the macaroni, and toss to coat well. Spoon into the baking dish. In a small bowl, toss the bread crumbs with the parsley and sprinkle on top of the macaroni. Bake, uncovered, for 25 minutes or until bubbling. Serve with Ceasar Salad (page 257). Makes 6 side-dish or 3 to 4 main-dish servings.

1 side-dish serving: Calories 368; Saturated Fat 9 g; Total Fat 15 g; Protein 19 g; Carbohydrate 39 g; Fiber 0 g; Sodium 255 mg; Cholesterol 46 mg

♦

Tex-Mex Macaroni & Cheese

Prepare Macaroni and Cheese as directed, stirring in **2 teaspoons ground cumin** with the flour. Substitute **1 cup shredded Monterey Jack cheese with jalapeño peppers** for the Swiss cheese. With the cooked macaroni, toss 1 cup seeded and diced plum tomatoes. Makes 6 side-dish or 3 to 4 main-dish servings. *1 side-dish serving: Calories 381; Saturated Fat 9 g; Total Fat 15 g; Protein 18 g; Carbohydrate 41 g; Fiber 1 g; Sodium 290 mg; Cholesterol 42 mg*

◆ Macaroni Tales ◆

Meet Luke Marano, Pasta Man of the Year for 1992. He was awarded this honor by the National Pasta Association in recognition of his outstanding contributions to the pasta industry. Luke is president of his family's macaroni company in Philadelphia, which was founded by his grandfather, Antonio Marano, in 1914.

At that time, World War I was just beginning. But this didn't hinder Antonio from starting a small grocery business with products, especially pasta, imported from Italy. As the war grew closer, however, ships carrying many of his goods were sunk by Germans. So Antonio decided to produce his own pastas.

In just one of the company's plants, over 75,000 pounds of pasta are produced every day. One batch alone is about 300 pounds!

"The best pasta starts with a good durum semolina flour," explains Luke. "Durum is an amber-colored wheat, with a nutty flavor. It yields a high-gluten flour that is ideal for pastas. To make 300 pounds of macaroni, we mix 290 pounds of durum flour with 60 pounds of fresh eggs, or about 15 pounds of dried ones, then add water until the dough is the right consistency for shaping.

"The dough travels next to the extruder, which forces it through a metal plate, or die, with holes that vary in size and shape to make elbows, for example, or spaghetti, twists, or shells. A sharp knife then cuts each piece into the right length. The pasta moves on to a drying area, where it stays for about four hours before being packaged and labeled for shipping.

"Dough for noodles, such as fettuccine or lasagna, takes a different path. First, it is flattened by a series of rollers, next, cut for the type of pasta, then hung on rollers to dry. Later it is cut to the appropriate length."

All of this concern, care, and know-how ensure that only the finest pastas leave Luke's plants for market.

YANKEE-DOODLE MACARONI
◆◆◆

1	tablespoon vegetable oil	½	teaspoon black pepper
2	large carrots, peeled and chopped (1 cup)	2	cans (28 ounces each) whole tomatoes in thick purée
1	medium-size yellow onion, chopped (1 cup)	1½	teaspoons dried oregano leaves
1	medium-size sweet green pepper, chopped (1 cup)	½	teaspoon sugar
1	clove garlic, minced	8	ounces elbow macaroni
1	pound lean ground beef or 1 pound boned and skinned chicken breasts, cut into thin strips	¼	cup minced parsley
		1	cup shredded sharp Cheddar cheese (4 ounces)

PREP TIME: 25 MIN. / COOKING TIME: 53 MIN.

1 Preheat the oven to 400°F. Set out a 13" x 9" x 3" baking dish. In a 12-inch nonstick skillet, heat the oil over moderate heat. Stir in the carrots, onion, green pepper, and garlic and sauté for 5 minutes or until almost tender.

2 Stir in the beef and black pepper. Cook, stirring to break up the meat, for 5 minutes or until the meat is no longer pink. Add the tomatoes and their purée, the oregano, and sugar; raise the heat to high and bring to a boil. Reduce the heat. Simmer, partially covered, for 25 minutes, stirring occasionally to break up the tomatoes.

3 Meanwhile, bring a stockpot of unsalted water to a boil, add the macaroni, and cook for 6 minutes or just until tender but still firm to the bite. Drain, rinse, and drain again, then combine with the beef mixture and put in the baking dish. Sprinkle with the parsley and cheese and bake, uncovered, for 15 minutes or until the cheese melts and the mixture is bubbling hot. Makes 4 to 6 main-dish servings.

1 serving (for 4): Calories 632; Saturated Fat 10 g;
Total Fat 23 g; Protein 32 g; Carbohydrate 73 g; Fiber 1 g;
Sodium 772 mg; Cholesterol 74 mg

A spur-of-the-moment supper of Potluck Pasta...Westward Ho!

POTLUCK PASTA

❖❖❖

Originating out West, potluck was a shared spread for which each guest brought a dish. Today, it also means a meal made from whatever is on hand.

8 ounces pasta wheels, bows, twists, or elbow macaroni

2 medium-size sweet green, red, or yellow peppers

1 cup fresh or frozen lima beans or green peas, cooked and drained

½ cup chopped green onions, with tops

½ cup slivered fresh basil, or ½ cup minced parsley tossed with 2 teaspoons dried basil leaves

¼ cup grated Parmesan cheese

½ cup chopped walnuts, toasted (optional)

Curly lettuce leaves

For the dressing

¼ cup each olive oil and white wine vinegar

3 tablespoons reduced-calorie mayonnaise

1 tablespoon evaporated skim milk or heavy cream

1 teaspoon minced garlic

1 teaspoon Dijon mustard

½ teaspoon salt, or to taste

½ teaspoon black pepper

PREP TIME: 25 MIN. / COOKING TIME: 15 MIN.

1 Preheat the broiler. Bring a stockpot of water to a boil, add the pasta, and cook for 8 to 10 minutes or just until tender but still firm to the bite. Drain, rinse, and drain again; transfer to a large bowl and keep warm.

2 While the pasta is cooking, broil the peppers, 4 inches from the heat, turning, for 5 minutes or until soft and charred all over. When cool enough to handle, peel, seed, and cut them into thin strips. Add to the pasta with the lima beans, green onions, basil, cheese, and walnuts if you wish. Toss to mix well.

3 In a measuring cup, whisk all of the dressing ingredients together. Pour over the pasta mixture and toss to coat. Line a serving platter with the lettuce, spoon the pasta in the center, and serve at room temperature or cold. Makes 6 first-course or 3 to 4 main-dish servings.

1 first-course serving: Calories 310; Saturated Fat 2 g; Total Fat 15 g; Protein 9 g; Carbohydrate 39 g; Fiber 1 g; Sodium 276 mg; Cholesterol 6 mg

SPÄTZLE

◆◆◆

*The name means little sparrow,
referring to the tiny size of these noodles. German-
Americans often serve them instead of potatoes.
In the old country, the dough is soft enough to push
through a sieve, but we have made it firmer so
that it can be rolled and cut easily.*

2½ cups all-purpose flour	¼ cup yellow cornmeal
½ teaspoon salt	2 tablespoons unsalted butter or margarine
2 large eggs	½ teaspoon black pepper
½ cup low-fat (2% milkfat) milk	

PREP TIME: 30 MIN. / COOKING TIME: 5 MIN.

1 Stir together the flour and salt in a medium-size bowl. Make a well in the center and drop in the eggs and milk. Stir until a soft (but not sticky) dough forms.

2 Sprinkle a pastry cloth, board, or marble surface with the cornmeal. Divide the dough into 2 equal pieces, then roll out each piece into a 12- x 6-inch rectangle, ¼ inch thick. Cut into 3- x 1-inch pieces, making about 4 dozen spätzle.

3 Meanwhile, half-fill a large stockpot with cold water and bring to a boil. Drop half the spätzle into the water and cook for 1 minute or until they float to the top. Using a slotted spoon, remove to a warm plate. Repeat with the second half, then toss all the spätzle with the butter and pepper and serve immediately with Veal Cordon Bleu (page 114). Makes 6 side-dish servings.

*1 serving: Calories 280; Saturated Fat 3 g;
Total Fat 7 g; Protein 9 g; Carbohydrate 45 g; Fiber 0 g;
Sodium 212 mg; Cholesterol 84 mg*

**Reminiscent of many down-home suppers
around the kitchen table: Tuna-Noodle Casserole**

◆

Cheesy-Spätzle Supper Bake

Preheat the oven to 350°F. Prepare and cook the spätzle, omitting the salt, then transfer to an oiled 2-quart shallow baking dish. Toss with **6 slices crumbled cooked bacon, 1 cup shredded Swiss cheese (4 ounces), 1 cup finely chopped onion, and ¼ cup dry white wine or low-sodium chicken broth.** Sprinkle with **3 tablespoons minced parsley.** Bake, uncovered, for 20 minutes or until golden brown and bubbly. Makes 4 main-dish servings. *1 serving: Calories 607; Saturated Fat 12 g; Total Fat 25 g; Protein 24 g; Carbohydrate 72 g; Fiber 0 g; Sodium 280 mg; Cholesterol 159 mg*

TUNA-NOODLE CASSEROLE
◆◆◆

Anyone who lived in America in the 1950's has to remember tuna-noodle casserole. Here is a revived version from Gilly Sullivan of Grass Valley, California.

1 tablespoon unsalted butter or margarine

1 cup sliced fresh mushrooms

1 can (10¾ ounces) reduced-sodium condensed mushroom soup, undiluted

1 cup shredded Jarlsburg or sharp Cheddar cheese (4 ounces)

1 cup plain nonfat yogurt

½ cup sliced green onions, with tops

½ teaspoon black pepper

¼ teaspoon each celery seeds and crushed red pepper

8 ounces macaroni shells, corkscrews, or wheels, cooked, rinsed, and drained

1 can (12¼ ounces) water-packed, chunk light tuna, rinsed, drained, and flaked

2 cups blanched fresh or frozen vegetables

For the topping:

½ cup crushed Ritz crackers or toasted fresh bread crumbs

¼ cup grated Parmesan cheese

PREP TIME: 30 MIN. / COOKING TIME: 36 MIN.

1 Preheat the oven to 350°F and oil a 2½-quart shallow casserole. In a 12-inch nonstick skillet, melt the butter over moderately high heat. Add the mushrooms and sauté for 5 minutes or until soft, then transfer to the casserole.

2 Stir in the soup, Jarlsberg cheese, yogurt, onions, black pepper, celery seeds, and red pepper and toss until well blended. Fold in the cooked macaroni, tuna, and vegetables.

3 Combine the topping ingredients and sprinkle on top. Bake, uncovered, for 30 minutes or until bubbly. Serve with slices of ripe tomatoes. Makes 4 to 6 main-dish servings.

1 serving (for 4): Calories 633; Saturated Fat 11 g; Total Fat 23 g; Protein 40 g; Carbohydrate 68 g; Fiber 2 g; Sodium 967 mg; Cholesterol 55 mg

CHICKEN-NOODLE CASSEROLE
◆◆◆

2 tablespoons unsalted butter or margarine

4 ounces sliced fresh mushrooms (1½ cups)

1 cup chopped sweet red peppers

½ cup each chopped carrot, celery, and onion

3 tablespoons all-purpose flour

2 cups low-fat (1% milkfat) milk

1½ cups Chicken Stock (page 74) or low-sodium chicken broth

½ teaspoon each poultry seasoning, salt, and black pepper

2 cups bite-size pieces cooked chicken (about 10 ounces)

½ cup frozen peas, thawed

8 ounces curly or plain egg noodles, cooked, rinsed, and drained

For the topping:

1 tablespoon unsalted butter or margarine

¾ cup fresh breadcrumbs

¼ cup minced parsley

PREP TIME: 30 MIN. / COOKING TIME: 55 MIN.

1 Preheat the oven to 350°F and oil a 2½-quart shallow casserole. In a 4-quart nonstick Dutch oven or large saucepan, melt the butter over moderate heat. Add the mushrooms, red peppers, carrot, celery, and onion and sauté for 5 minutes or until soft.

2 Stir in the flour and cook for 1 minute or until bubbly. Gradually whisk in the milk and stock and bring to a boil, then stir in the poultry seasoning, salt, and black pepper.

3 Lower the heat and simmer, stirring, for 5 minutes or until thickened. Stir in the chicken, peas, and noodles; spoon into the casserole.

4 To make the topping: In a small saucepan, melt the butter over moderate heat. Remove from the heat, stir in the bread crumbs and parsley, and sprinkle on top of the casserole. Cover and bake for 35 minutes or until bubbly. Uncover and bake 5 minutes longer or until golden brown. Makes 4 to 6 main-dish servings.

1 serving (for 4): Calories 476; Saturated Fat 6 g; Total Fat 11 g; Protein 19 g; Carbohydrate 74 g; Fiber 1 g; Sodium 459 mg; Cholesterol 54 mg

FETTUCCINE ALFREDO

◆◆◆

This dish, invented in 1920 at Alfredo's restaurant in Rome, has been an American favorite since the 1960's. The original called for 1 pint of heavy cream, ½ pound each of triple rich butter and Parmesan cheese, tossed with a pound of pasta.

8 ounces fettuccine (preferably fresh)	1 tablespoon unsalted butter or margarine
1 cup low-fat (1% milkfat) milk	½ cup grated Parmesan cheese
¼ cup evaporated skim milk or heavy cream	2 tablespoons minced parsley
2 teaspoons cornstarch	¼ teaspoon black pepper
Pinch ground nutmeg	

PREP TIME: 10 MIN. / COOKING TIME: 15 MIN.

1 Bring a stockpot of unsalted water to a boil, add the fettuccine, and cook for 10 minutes or just until tender but still firm to the bite. Drain.

2 Meanwhile, in a medium-size bowl, whisk together the milks, cornstarch, and nutmeg. In a deep 12-inch nonstick skillet, melt the butter over moderately high heat. Whisk in the milk mixture and bring to a boil, then simmer for 2 minutes or until slightly thickened.

3 Add the fettuccine to the skillet with the Parmesan, parsley, and pepper and toss well for 1 minute or until heated through. Makes 4 to 6 first-course or 2 to 3 main-dish servings.

1 first-course serving (for 4): Calories 332; Saturated Fat 5 g; Total Fat 8 g; Protein 9 g; Carbohydrate 55 g; Fiber 0 g; Sodium 320 mg; Cholesterol 23 mg

◆

Spaghetti Carbonara

Prepare as for Fettuccine Alfredo, substituting **spaghetti** for the fettuccine and adding **3 strips diced, cooked bacon** to the sauce along with the cooked spaghetti. *1 first-course serving (for 4): Calories 386; Saturated Fat 6 g; Total Fat 11 g; Protein 18 g; Carbohydrate 52 g; Fiber 0 g; Sodium 392 mg; Cholesterol 27 mg*

BAKED ZITI WITH SAUSAGE

◆◆◆

The long tubes of macaroni called ziti are frequently layered with sausage and tomato sauce to create this Americanized version of an Italian classic.

4 cups Marinara Sauce (page 277)	5 tablespoons grated Parmesan cheese
8 ounces sweet Italian sausage, pricked	1 large egg white
8 ounces ziti	1 clove garlic, minced
1 cup part-skim ricotta cheese	¾ cup shredded part-skim mozzarella cheese (3 ounces)

PREP TIME: 25 MIN. / COOKING TIME: 1½ HR.

1 Preheat the broiler. While the Marinara Sauce is cooking, arrange the sausage on a broiler pan and broil, turning frequently, 4 inches from the heat for 10 minutes or until browned. Transfer to a cutting board and cut into thin slices.

2 Meanwhile, bring a stockpot of unsalted water to a boil, add the ziti, and cook for 12 minutes or until almost tender but still firm to the bite. Drain, rinse, and drain again.

3 Preheat the oven to 375°F and oil an 13" x 9" x 3" baking dish. In a medium-size bowl, combine the ricotta cheese, 3 tablespoons of the Parmesan cheese, the egg white, and garlic.

4 Spread ½ of the ziti on the bottom of the baking dish. Layer with ½ of the sauce, all of the ricotta mixture, ½ of the sausage, then the remaining ziti, sausage, and sauce. Sprinkle with the mozzarella and the remaining 2 tablespoons of Parmesan. Cover loosely and bake for 45 minutes or until bubbly and hot. Serve with slices of Rustic Whole-Wheat Round (page 289). Makes 4 to 6 first-course or 2 to 3 main-dish servings.

1 first-course serving (for 4): Calories 633; Saturated Fat 7 g; Total Fat 24 g; Protein 37 g; Carbohydrate 70 g; Fiber 3 g; Sodium 653 mg; Cholesterol 38 mg

SPAGHETTI & MEATBALLS

◆◆◆

4 cups Marinara Sauce (page 277)	½ teaspoon salt
1½ pounds lean ground beef	¼ teaspoon black pepper
1 cup fresh bread crumbs (2 slices)	1 large egg, lightly beaten
1 small yellow onion, grated (½ cup)	1 tablespoon olive oil
½ cup minced parsley	1 pound regular or thin spaghetti
¼ cup cold water	

PREP TIME: 45 MIN. / COOKING TIME: 25 MIN.

1 While the Marinara Sauce cooks, make the meatballs: In a large bowl mix the beef, bread, onion, ¼ cup of the parsley, the water, salt, pepper, and egg. Shape into twenty-four 2-inch balls.

2 In a 12-inch nonstick skillet, heat the oil over moderately high heat. Sauté the meatballs, turning frequently, for 5 minutes or until browned. Add the meatballs to the sauce, cover, and simmer for 20 minutes, stirring occasionally.

3 Meanwhile, bring a stockpot of unsalted water to a boil; add the spaghetti and cook for 8 to 10 minutes or just until tender but still firm to the bite. Drain, transfer to a pasta bowl or other large bowl, and top with the meatballs and sauce. Sprinkle with the remaining ¼ cup of parsley. Serve with Caesar Salad (page 257). Makes 6 main-dish servings.

1 serving: Calories 629; Saturated Fat 6 g; Total Fat 20 g; Protein 36 g; Carbohydrate 76 g; Fiber 2 g; Sodium 404 mg; Cholesterol 106 mg

Fresh-cooked spaghetti with meatballs in a homemade marinara sauce ... Buon Appetito!

CHEESE-STUFFED CANNELLONI

◆◆◆

Although the Italian version of this dish calls for squares of homemade pasta, Americans often make it an easier way, with light pancakes instead.

For the topping:
2 cups Marinara Sauce (page 277)

For the pancakes:
¾ cup low-fat (1% milkfat) milk
1 large egg
1 large egg white
¼ teaspoon salt, or to taste
¾ cup all-purpose flour
1 tablespoon olive oil

For the filling:
1 pound part-skim ricotta cheese
3 tablespoons minced parsley
2 tablespoons grated Parmesan cheese
¼ teaspoon each salt and black pepper
1 large egg

PREP TIME: 30 MIN. / COOKING TIME: 1½ HR.

1 Preheat the oven to 350°F and lightly grease a 13" x 9" x 2" baking dish. While the Marinara sauce is cooking, prepare the pancakes: In a large bowl, whisk together the milk, egg, egg white, salt, and flour until smooth. Pour the oil into a cup or small bowl.

2 Heat a 6-inch skillet or crepe pan over moderately high heat for 3 minutes or until hot. Brush with a little of the oil and add ¼ cup batter to the heated pan, tilting quickly to coat the bottom. Cook for 1 minute or until lightly browned, turn and cook 30 seconds more or just until cooked through. Invert the skillet over a plate to remove the pancake. Repeat, making 6 pancakes.

3 To make the filling: In a large bowl, mix all the filling ingredients. Spoon ⅓ cup of filling down the center of a pancake; roll up and place seam-side-down in the baking dish. Repeat, making 6 cannelloni. Top with the sauce, cover, and bake for 30 minutes. Uncover and bake 10 minutes longer or until bubbly. Makes 6 cannelloni.

1 cannelloni: Calories 270; Saturated Fat 5 g; Total Fat 12 g; Protein 16 g; Carbohydrate 25 g; Fiber 1 g; Sodium 373 mg; Cholesterol 97 mg

BEEF-STUFFED MANICOTTI

◆◆◆

In Italy, this pasta dish is usually served as a first course. But in America, manicotti are popular main-dish fare.

8 ounces ground beef
1½ cups yellow onion, finely chopped
1 package (10 ounces) chopped frozen spinach, thawed and squeezed dry
2 cloves garlic, minced
½ teaspoon salt
¼ teaspoon black pepper
½ teaspoon each dried oregano and basil leaves
1 large egg, lightly beaten
⅔ cup grated Parmesan cheese
8 ounces manicotti
4 cups Medium White Sauce (page 363)

PREP TIME: 35 MIN. / STANDING TIME: 10 MIN.
COOKING TIME: 55 MIN.

1 Heat a 12-inch nonstick skillet over moderately high heat. Add the beef and onion and sauté for 5 minutes or until browned. Stir in the spinach, garlic, salt, pepper, oregano, and basil and cook, stirring frequently, for 3 minutes or until the liquid has evaporated. Remove from the heat, let stand for 10 minutes, then stir in the egg and 3 tablespoons of the Parmesan.

2 Meanwhile, cook the manicotti according to package directions and make the White Sauce. Stir into the sauce all but 1 tablespoon of the remaining Parmesan. Stir 1 cup of the sauce into the meat mixture. Preheat the oven to 375°F. Lightly grease a 13" x 9" x 2" baking pan.

3 Using a small spoon, stuff the manicotti with the meat mixture and arrange in a single layer in the pan. Pour on the remaining sauce; sprinkle with the reserved Parmesan. Cover with foil; bake for 30 minutes or until bubbly. Uncover, turn the oven to broil, and broil 4 inches from the heat for 5 minutes or until browned. Makes 6 servings.

1 serving: Calories 471; Saturated Fat 10 g; Total Fat 19 g; Protein 26 g; Carbohydrate 49 g; Fiber 1 g; Sodium 533 mg; Cholesterol 96 mg

A plate of Peppered Pasta... beautiful to behold!

PEPPERED PASTA

This healthful dish will taste just as good if you make it with one type of sweet pepper instead of three.

2	**tablespoons olive oil**
3	**small sweet peppers (1 green, 1 red, 1 yellow), cored, seeded, and thinly sliced (2¼ cups)**
2	**plum tomatoes, sliced ¼ inch thick (1 cup)**
8	**ounces ziti**
½	**cup Chicken Stock (page 74) or low-sodium chicken broth**
½	**teaspoon each salt and black pepper**
8	**oil cured black olives, pitted and halved (optional)**
⅓	**cup slivered fresh basil or ⅓ cup minced parsley mixed with 2 teaspoons dried basil leaves**
2	**tablespoons grated Parmesan cheese**

PREP TIME: 20 MIN. / COOKING TIME: 15 MIN.

1 In a deep 12-inch nonstick skillet, heat the oil over low heat; add the sweet peppers and cook, stirring, for 5 minutes or until soft. Add the tomatoes and cook 3 minutes longer.

2 Meanwhile, bring a stockpot of unsalted water to a boil; add the ziti; cook for 12 minutes or just until tender but still firm to the bite. Drain.

3 While the pasta is cooking, stir into the skillet the stock, salt, black pepper, and olives if you wish. Raise the heat to high and cook, uncovered, for 3 minutes, then stir in the basil.

4 Add the pasta to the skillet, toss well, and sprinkle with the Parmesan. Makes 4 to 6 first-course or 2 to 3 main-dish servings.

1 first-course serving (for 4): Calories 313; Saturated Fat 2 g; Total Fat 9 g; Protein 10 g; Carbohydrate 48 g; Fiber 1 g; Sodium 347 mg; Cholesterol 3 mg

LASAGNA BOLOGNESE

Following World War II, pastas became popular party fare. Lasagna, a many-splendored dish, was a favorite then and remains one today.

1 recipe (10 cups) Bolognese Sauce (page 277)
1 pound lasagna noodles
1 pint part-skim ricotta cheese
½ cup grated Parmesan cheese
2 cups shredded part-skim mozzarella cheese (8 ounces)

PREP TIME: 1 HR. / COOKING TIME: 1¾ HR.
STANDING TIME: 10 MIN.

1 Preheat the oven to 350°F and lightly oil a 13" x 9" x 3" baking dish. While the Bolognese Sauce is cooking, bring a stockpot of unsalted water to a boil, add the noodles, and cook for 10 minutes or until almost tender. Drain, rinse, and drain again.

2 Cover the bottom of the baking dish with ¼ of the Bolognese Sauce. Layer ⅓ of the noodles over the sauce with edges overlapping; spread ⅓ of the ricotta cheese over the noodles, then ¼ of the sauce; sprinkle on 2 tablespoons of the Parmesan cheese. Repeat this layering process 2 more times.

3 Sprinkle with the mozzarella cheese and the remaining 2 tablespoons of Parmesan. (If making ahead, cover and refrigerate for up to 24 hours, then let stand at room temperature for 1 hour before baking.) Cover with foil and bake for 30 minutes. Uncover and bake 10 minutes longer or until golden brown and heated through. Let stand for 10 minutes before cutting into squares for serving. Serve with a crisp green salad. Makes 9 main-dish servings.

1 serving: Calories 612; Saturated Fat 11 g; Total Fat 24 g; Protein 39 g; Carbohydrate 62 g; Fiber 3 g; Sodium 701 mg; Cholesterol 85 mg

SPINACH LASAGNA

In 18th-century Italy, summertime was noodle-making time, as the summer sun was needed to dry them. The introduction of gas-fired machines during the 19th century made it possible to dry pasta the year around. Production increased and so did exports to the United States and other countries.

5 cups Marinara Sauce (page 277)
8 ounces lasagna noodles
2 packages (10 ounces each) chopped frozen spinach, thawed and squeezed dry
1 pint part-skim ricotta cheese
4 tablespoons Parmesan cheese
1 teaspoon garlic powder
½ teaspoon each ground nutmeg and black pepper
1 cup shredded part-skim mozzarella cheese (4 ounces)

PREP TIME: 1 HR. / COOKING TIME: 1½ HR.
STANDING TIME: 10 MIN.

1 Preheat the oven to 350°F. Lightly oil a 13" x 9" x 3" baking dish. While the Marinara Sauce is cooking, bring a stockpot of unsalted water to a boil, add the noodles, and cook for 10 minutes or until almost tender. Drain, rinse, and drain again.

2 Meanwhile, in a large bowl mix the spinach, ricotta cheese, 2 tablespoons of the Parmesan cheese, the garlic powder, nutmeg, and pepper. Cover the bottom of the baking dish with 1 cup of the Marinara Sauce. Layer ⅓ of the noodles over the sauce with edges overlapping, then spread on ⅓ of the spinach mixture, and 1⅓ cups of the sauce. Repeat this layering process 2 more times.

3 Sprinkle with the mozzarella cheese and the remaining 2 tablespoons of Parmesan. Cover and bake for 30 minutes or until golden brown and heated through. Let stand for 10 minutes before serving. Makes 4 to 6 main-dish servings.

1 serving (for 4): Calories 653; Saturated Fat 11 g; Total Fat 21 g; Protein 39 g; Carbohydrate 83 g; Fiber 4 g; Sodium 880 mg; Cholesterol 60 mg

STRAW AND HAY

◆◆◆

If your grandmother was Italian, she probably prepared paglia e fieno, *a toss of yellow and green pastas affectionately known as straw and hay.*

2	tablespoons unsalted butter or margarine	2¾	cups low-fat (1% milkfat) milk
1	small yellow onion, chopped (½ cup)	1	tablespoon cornstarch
8	ounces fresh mushrooms, sliced (2½ cups)	½	cup frozen peas, thawed
8	ounces egg fettuccine or linguine (preferably fresh)	4	ounces thinly sliced prosciutto, cut into thin strips
8	ounces spinach fettuccine (preferably fresh)	¼	teaspoon black pepper
		½	cup grated Parmesan cheese

PREP TIME: 15 MIN. / COOKING TIME: 15 MIN.

1 In a 12-inch nonstick skillet, melt the butter over moderate heat. Stir in the onion and sauté for 2 minutes. Add the mushrooms and sauté, stirring occasionally, 5 minutes longer or until the mushrooms are soft.

2 Meanwhile, bring a stockpot of unsalted water to a boil, add both the egg and spinach fettuccine and cook according to package directions or just until tender but still firm to the bite. Drain.

3 While the pasta is cooking, whisk together the milk and cornstarch, in a medium-size bowl, then add to the skillet with the peas, prosciutto, and pepper. Raise the heat to high and bring to a boil. Lower the heat and simmer, stirring, for 2 minutes or until thickened.

4 Fold in both of the fettuccine and the cheese and heat 1 minute more or until heated through. Serve with Love Knots (page 296). Makes 6 to 8 first-course or 4 to 6 main-dish servings.

1 first-course serving (for 6): Calories 340; Saturated Fat 6 g; Total Fat 11 g; Protein 19 g; Carbohydrate 43 g; Fiber 1 g; Sodium 441 mg; Cholesterol 70 mg

The 30-minute pasta dinner featuring Straw and Hay

Cooked pasta should be tender, but quite firm, with no hard core.

—Fannie Farmer

SHRIMP BOATERS' RICE

◆◆◆

This dish grew up with Charleston where rice was once called Charleston Gold. Dating back to the days of slavery, it blends ingredients of a popular African dish with local ones.

3 slices lean bacon, cut into ½-inch pieces	2 tablespoons minced fresh thyme or 1 teaspoon dried thyme leaves
½ cup chopped green onions, with tops	½ teaspoon salt, or to taste
1 cup chopped sweet green pepper	2 cups uncooked long-grain white rice
2 tablespoons minced jalapeño pepper with seeds	1½ to 2 pounds medium-size shrimp, shelled, deveined, with tails removed (page 362)
2 cups tomato purée	
3 cups cold water	2 tablespoons minced parsley

PREP TIME: 30 MIN. / COOKING TIME: 1 HR.

1 Preheat the oven to 350°F and lightly oil a 3-quart casserole. In a 12-inch nonstick skillet, cook the bacon over moderately high heat for 6 minutes or until crisp, then transfer to paper towels with a slotted spoon. Pour off all but 1 tablespoon of the fat.

2 Add the green onions and the sweet green and jalapeño peppers and sauté for 3 minutes. Stir in the tomato purée, water, thyme, and salt. Bring to a boil, then stir in the rice.

3 Transfer to the casserole, cover tightly, and bake for 30 minutes. Stir in the shrimp, then bake, covered, 15 minutes longer or until the rice is tender. Sprinkle with the bacon and parsley. Serve with Beaten Biscuits (page 307). Makes 6 side-dish or 4 main-dish servings.

1 side-dish serving: Calories 331; Saturated Fat 1 g; Total Fat 3 g; Protein 16 g; Carbohydrate 60 g; Fiber 1 g; Sodium 710 mg; Cholesterol 90 mg

◆

Carolina Red Rice

Prepare as for Shrimp Boaters' Rice, substituting **2 cups chopped cooked ham** for the shrimp.
1 side-dish serving: Calories 360; Saturated Fat 2 g; Total Fat 5 g; Protein 19 g; Carbohydrate 60 g; Fiber 1 g; Sodium 1230 mg; Cholesterol 28 mg

Supper from the North Carolinian Coast: A plate of steaming Shrimp Boaters' Rice

SPANISH RICE

*The Spaniards contributed their love
for tomatoes and spices to many favorite dishes
in the Creole country of Louisiana.*

2 tablespoons olive oil	3 cups tomato juice
2 cups each chopped onion and sweet green pepper	2 cups Chicken Stock (page 74) or low-sodium chicken broth
1 cup chopped celery	1 teaspoon paprika
3 cloves garlic, minced	½ teaspoon each salt and black pepper
8 ounces fresh mushrooms, sliced (3 cups)	2 bay leaves
2 cups uncooked long-grain white rice	6 cups seeded and chopped plum tomatoes (about 15)

PREP TIME: 25 MIN. / COOKING TIME: 40 MIN.

1 In a deep, 12-inch nonstick skillet, heat the oil over moderately high heat. Stir in the onion, green pepper, celery, and garlic and sauté for 3 minutes. Stir in the mushrooms and rice and sauté 5 minutes longer.

2 Add the tomato juice, stock, paprika, salt, black pepper, and bay leaves and bring to a boil; lower the heat, cover tightly, and simmer for 15 minutes. Stir in the tomatoes, cover, and cook 15 minutes longer or until the rice is tender and all of the liquid is absorbed. Discard the bay leaves. Serve with Fried Catfish (page 146). Makes 8 side-dish or 4 main-dish servings.

*1 side-dish serving: Calories 306; Saturated Fat 1 g;
Total Fat 5 g; Protein 8 g; Carbohydrate 59 g; Fiber 5 g;
Sodium 524 mg; Cholesterol 2 mg*

◆

Shrimp Creole

Prepare as for Spanish rice, adding 1 **teaspoon hot red pepper sauce** with the seasonings. While the rice simmers, peel and devein 1½ **to 2 pounds medium-size shrimp**. In a 12-inch nonstick skillet, heat **1 tablespoon vegetable oil** over moderately high heat, add the shrimp, and sauté for

3 minutes or until cooked through. Toss with the rice during the last 2 minutes of cooking time. Sprinkle with ½ **cup minced parsley** just before serving. Makes 8 side-dish or 4 main-dish servings. *1 side-dish serving: Calories 353; Saturated Fat 1 g; Total Fat 7 g; Protein 15 g; Carbohydrate 59 g; Fiber 5 g; Sodium 603 mg; Cholesterol 67 mg*

RICE PILAU

*Whether you call it by the Mideastern names
of pilau, pilav or pilaf, or the Southern names of
perlew or purlow, this dish refers to rice, simmered
in stock, often with fruits and/or nuts added.*

2 tablespoons unsalted butter or margarine	¼ teaspoon each ground mace and cloves
1 medium-size onion, chopped (1 cup)	2½ cups Chicken Stock (page 74) or low-sodium chicken broth
1 cup uncooked long-grain white or brown rice	1 cup chopped dried apricots
½ teaspoon each ground allspice, cinnamon, salt, and black pepper	½ cup golden raisins
	½ cup slivered almonds, toasted (page 365)

PREP TIME: 15 MIN. / COOKING TIME: 25 MIN.

1 In a large saucepan, melt 1 tablespoon of the butter over moderately high heat. Stir in the onion and rice and sauté for 5 minutes or until the onion is browned, then add the seasonings and stock. Lower the heat, cover tightly, and simmer for 20 minutes or until the stock is absorbed.

2 Meanwhile, in a small skillet, melt the remaining 1 tablespoon of butter. Add the apricots, raisins, and almonds and sauté for 5 minutes or until sizzling. Toss with the rice. Serve with Hillary's Chicken (page 134). (Tip: This recipe can be doubled.) Makes 4 side-dish servings.

*1 serving: Calories 505; Saturated Fat 5 g;
Total Fat 15 g; Protein 10 g; Carbohydrate 87 g; Fiber 2 g;
Sodium 336 mg; Cholesterol 21 mg*

MEXICALLI RICE BAKE

◆◆◆

Throughout the Rio Grande Valley in south Texas, the abundance of chilies in dishes like this one has been traditional since the days when the area was part of Mexico.

3 cups cold water	1 can (4 ounces) chopped mild green chilies, drained
1½ cups uncooked long-grain white rice	¼ cup minced cilantro or parsley
1 tablespoon unsalted butter or margarine	1½ cups reduced-fat sour cream
1 cup chopped onion	½ cup low-fat (1% milkfat) milk
1 medium-size avocado, peeled, pitted, and diced (1 cup)	¼ cup shredded Monterey Jack cheese (1 ounce)
4 ounces Monterey Jack cheese, cut into ½-inch cubes	

PREP TIME: 15 MIN. / COOKING TIME: 55 MIN.

1 Preheat the oven to 350°F and grease a shallow 2-quart baking dish. In a large saucepan, bring the water to a boil over high heat. Stir in the rice, lower the heat, cover tightly, and simmer for 20 minutes or until the water is absorbed. Transfer to a large bowl.

2 Meanwhile, in a 12-inch nonstick skillet, melt the butter over moderately high heat. Add the onion and sauté for 5 minutes or until soft. Toss with the rice, then gently stir in the avocado, cubed cheese, chilies, and cilantro.

3 In a small bowl, whisk the sour cream with the milk, stir into the rice mixture in the skillet, then spoon into the baking dish. Sprinkle with the shredded cheese and bake, uncovered, for 30 minutes or until golden and bubbly. Serve immediately with slices of red tomatoes. Makes 6 side-dish or 4 main-dish servings.

1 side-dish serving: Calories 421; Saturated Fat 9 g; Total Fat 18 g; Protein 13 g; Carbohydrate 54 g; Fiber 2 g; Sodium 469 mg; Cholesterol 39 mg

FRIED RICE

◆◆◆

Fried rice was one of the Chinese dishes eagerly accepted by Americans during the early 20th century. Typically, it's made with short-grain rice, but long-grain works fine too.

1 tablespoon vegetable oil	½ cup cooked fresh peas or frozen peas
½ cup chopped green onions, with tops	2 large eggs, lightly beaten
2 teaspoons peeled and minced fresh ginger	4 cups cooked short- or long-grain white rice
8 ounces frozen baby shrimp, thawed and drained	2 tablespoons reduced-sodium soy sauce
½ cup diced cooked lean ham (3 ounces)	2 teaspoons sesame oil

PREP TIME: 30 MIN. / COOKING TIME: 11 MIN.

1 In a large wok or 12-inch nonstick skillet, heat the vegetable oil over moderately high heat. Add the onions and ginger and sauté for 2 minutes. Add the shrimp, ham, and peas and stir-fry for 2 minutes or until heated through. Push the shrimp mixture up the sides of the wok.

2 Pour the beaten eggs into the center of the wok and cook for 3 minutes or until set. As the eggs set, cut them into strips with a spatula.

3 Add the rice, soy sauce, and sesame oil to the skillet and stir-fry with the shrimp mixture and the egg strips for 3 minutes or until heated through. Serve with fresh orange slices and fortune cookies for dessert. Makes 6 side-dish or 3 main-dish servings.

1 side-dish serving: Calories 292; Saturated Fat 2 g; Total Fat 7 g; Protein 15 g; Carbohydrate 41 g; Fiber 1 g; Sodium 398 mg; Cholesterol 132 mg

Down-home supper of Rice Croquettes plus Ham and Red-Eye Gravy (page 109)

RICE CROQUETTES

◆◆◆

*Croquettes in America date back at least
to plantation days in the deep South, where slaves in
the South Carolina Low Country made croquettes
out of many different foods.*

1 tablespoon unsalted butter or margarine	¼ teaspoon black pepper
6 tablespoons flour	Pinch ground red pepper (cayenne)
½ cup low-fat (1% milkfat) milk	1 cup fresh white bread crumbs (2 slices)
4 cups cooked long-grain white rice	¼ cup vegetable oil
2 large eggs	
½ teaspoon salt	

PREP TIME: 45 MIN. / CHILLING TIME: 1 HR.
COOKING TIME: 40 MIN.

1 In an 8-inch nonstick skillet, melt the butter over moderate heat. Stir in 2 tablespoons of the flour and cook until bubbly. Whisk in the milk and bring to a boil. Lower the heat and simmer, stirring frequently, for 5 minutes. Pour into a large mixing bowl and stir in the rice, 1 of the eggs, the salt, and the black and ground red peppers. Shaping with your hands, form into eighteen 3- x 1-inch logs. Cover and refrigerate for 1 hour or up to 24 hours.

2 On a piece of wax paper, spread the remaining 4 tablespoons of flour and on a second piece, spread the bread crumbs. In a pie plate, whisk the remaining egg. Dredge each croquette in the flour, dip into the egg, then roll in the bread crumbs, coating well.

3 In a 12-inch nonstick skillet, heat the oil over moderately high heat until very hot but not smoking. Add the croquettes and fry, turning frequently, for 6 minutes or until golden-brown. Using a slotted spoon, transfer to paper towels. Serve with Ham and Red-Eye Gravy (page 109). Makes 6 side-dish servings.

*1 serving: Calories 374; Saturated Fat 5 g;
Total Fat 16 g; Protein 8 g; Carbohydrate 49 g; Fiber 0 g;
Sodium 251 mg; Cholesterol 83 mg*

Rice Ring, decorated in an easy and elegant way, and served with Harvard Beets (page 213)

RICE RING

◆◆◆

*Church suppers in America have fostered
not only fellowship but often fund-raising as well.
Rice dishes, especially attractive ones like this Rice
Ring, have always been favorites at such events.*

5 cups cooked long-grain white rice	¼ cup diced sweet yellow pepper
1 cup cooked fresh or frozen green peas, thawed	⅓ cup reduced-calorie mayonnaise
¼ cup chopped green onions, with tops	½ teaspoon each salt and black pepper
¼ cup dry roasted peanuts, chopped	Nonstick cooking spray
¼ cup diced sweet red pepper	1 large bunch watercress, large stems removed

PREP TIME: 40 MIN. / CHILLING TIME: 2 HR.

1 In a large bowl, toss the rice, peas, onions, peanuts, and the red and yellow peppers. In a cup, blend the mayonnaise with the salt and black pepper, then stir into the rice mixture.

2 Coat an 8-cup ring mold with the cooking spray. Spoon the rice mixture into the mold, pressing it down. Refrigerate for at least 2 hours. Invert onto a platter, fill with the watercress, and decorate with vegetable flowers (page 366) if you wish. Makes 8 to 10 side-dish servings.

*1 serving (for 8): Calories 229; Saturated Fat 0 g;
Total Fat 5 g; Protein 5 g; Carbohydrate 40 g; Fiber 1 g;
Sodium 167 mg; Cholesterol 5 mg*

◆

Chicken 'n Rice Ring

Prepare as for Rice Ring, stirring **2 cups chopped cooked chicken** into the rice mixture. Add **1 teaspoon curry powder** to the mayonnaise mixture. Makes 6 main-dish servings. *1 serving: Calories 348; Saturated Fat 1 g; Total Fat 8 g; Protein 13 g; Carbohydrate 54 g; Fiber 1 g; Sodium 237 mg; Cholesterol 22 mg*

Pacific Rim Rice Ring

Prepare as for Rice Ring, adding **1 can (12¼ ounces) drained and flaked water-packed tuna,** to the rice mixture. Makes 6 servings. *1 serving: Calories 379; Saturated Fat 1 g; Total Fat 7 g; Protein 24 g; Carbohydrate 54 g; Fiber 1 g; Sodium 420 mg; Cholesterol 14 mg*

GREEN RICE
◆◆◆

The first documented rice harvest in New England colonies was in 1622. Simple recipes, such as this Green Rice, quickly became popular.

2 cups cold water	½ cup minced green onions, with tops
1½ teaspoons unsalted butter or margarine	⅓ cup minced parsley
1½ teaspoons olive oil	⅓ cup finely chopped fresh spinach or watercress
½ teaspoon each salt and black pepper	
1 cup uncooked long-grain white rice	2 teaspoons chopped fresh tarragon or ½ teaspoon dried tarragon leaves
½ cup finely chopped fresh broccoli florets, thawed if frozen	½ cup shredded Cheddar cheese (2 ounces)

PREP TIME: 20 MIN. / COOKING TIME: 25 MIN.

1 In a medium-size saucepan, bring the water, butter, oil, salt, and pepper to a boil over moderately high heat. Stir in the rice, lower the heat, cover tightly, and simmer for 20 minutes or until the water is absorbed.

2 Meanwhile, in a medium-size bowl, combine all the remaining ingredients. Stir the mixture into the hot rice and serve immediately with Louisiana Chicken (page 121). Makes 4 side-dish servings.

1 serving: Calories 266 g; Saturated Fat 4 g; Total Fat 8 g; Protein 8 g; Carbohydrate 40 g; Fiber 1 g; Sodium 372 mg; Cholesterol 19 mg

WILD RICE WITH PECANS
◆◆◆

Wild rice is native to the area around Lake Superior. The Native Americans named it manomin *(the good berry); local settlers called it Indian rice or water oats. Tossed with pecans, as in this recipe, it makes a perfect company dish that can easily be doubled.*

1 tablespoon unsalted butter or margarine	¾ cup uncooked long-grain white rice
¾ cup sliced green onions, with tops	⅓ cup chopped pecans, toasted (page 365)
½ cup wild rice	2 tablespoons shredded fresh basil or chopped parsley
2 cups Chicken Stock (page 74) or low-sodium chicken broth	
1½ cups boiling water	

PREP TIME: 20 MIN. / COOKING TIME: 1½ HR.

1 In a large saucepan, melt the butter over moderate heat. Add the onions and sauté for 5 minutes or until soft. Stir in the wild rice, coating it with the butter. Pour in the stock, bring to a boil, and stir. Lower the heat, cover tightly, and simmer, stirring occasionally, for 1 hour.

2 Add the water, stir in the white rice, cover, and steam 20 minutes longer or until both rices are tender. Stir in the chopped pecans and basil. Serve with Carolina Chicken (page 131). Makes 4 side-dish servings. For 8 servings, just double the recipe.

1 serving: Calories 308; Saturated Fat 3 g; Total Fat 10 g; Protein 7 g; Carbohydrate 46 g; Fiber 1 g; Sodium 53 mg; Cholesterol 12 mg

Same old slippers, same old rice, same old glimpse of Paradise.

— William James Lampton

FROM THE VEGETABLE PATCH

◆◆◆

American ways with vegetables have certainly changed over the years. Mary Randolph, in her 1824 cookbook, *The Virginia House-Wife*, suggests boiling carrots for up to 2½ hours, roasting potatoes for up to 2 hours, and steaming broccoli for as long as 30 minutes. Now, of course, we know that many of the vitamins that make vegetables so good for us are better preserved by cooking vegetables just until they are almost tender. And we've discovered that minimal cooking also brings out their best flavor.

This chapter features a collection of fabulous recipes that are now part of our tradition: Asparagus "ambushed" with a bacon-flavored sauce, for example; beans baked the long, slow Boston way; greens prepared as only those in the South know how; and cauliflower smothered with a light cheese sauce. Corn appears in fritters, in a pudding, and roasted on a grill. And onions are "fried" in the oven, instead of in deep fat. As for the potato, this all-American favorite shows up cottage-fried, twice-baked and overstuffed, scalloped, mashed, and parsleyed, but always with the calories kept in check. So have all you want, the new down-home, healthier way.

ASPARAGUS IN AMBUSH

The original of this recipe, which came from England with the colonists, called for baking asparagus with a rich egg mixture in hollowed-out rolls. Our version uses a light cream sauce and English muffins instead.

2 strips lean bacon, diced	¼ teaspoon each salt and black pepper
1 pound thin fresh asparagus spears, trimmed and cut into 1-inch lengths (2½ cups)	⅛ teaspoon each ground nutmeg and ground red pepper (cayenne)
1 tablespoon unsalted butter or margarine	1 tablespoon heavy cream or low-fat milk
3 tablespoons all-purpose flour	4 whole-wheat English muffins, split and toasted
1 cup low-fat (1% milkfat) milk	2 tablespoons minced parsley

PREP TIME: 15 MIN. / COOKING TIME: 20 MIN.

1 In a 10-inch nonstick skillet, cook the bacon over moderate heat for 5 minutes or until crisp; transfer to paper towels to drain.

2 Meanwhile, half-fill a medium-size saucepan with cold water and bring to a boil over high heat. Add the asparagus, lower the heat, and simmer for 3 minutes or until just crisp-tender. Drain, rinse with cold water, and drain again.

3 In the same saucepan, melt the butter over moderately high heat. Whisk in the flour and cook until bubbly. Whisk in the milk and bring to a boil. Lower the heat; cook, stirring constantly, for 3 minutes or until thickened.

4 Stir in the asparagus with the seasonings and cream; cook for 2 minutes or until heated through. Ladle over the muffin halves; sprinkle with the bacon and parsley. Makes 4 servings.

1 serving: Calories 267; Saturated Fat 4 g; Total Fat 8 g; Protein 11 g; Carbohydrate 39 g; Fiber 1 g; Sodium 576 mg; Cholesterol 19 mg

Ambushed for brunch: Fresh asparagus in a light cream sauce

With fresh asparagus, the higher your income the higher up the stalk you cut off the tip.

—Bill Rathje

RANCH HAND BEANS

◆◆◆

"In the Southwest, beans eaten around the campfire often have that characteristic barbecue taste," explains Stella Hughes in her Bacon and Beans *(ranch cookbook). "Some like to add a generous helping of hot pepper sauce,"* as *in this recipe adapted from her book.*

2 pounds dried navy or pinto beans, soaked (page 361)	½ cup brown sugar
	2 tablespoons chili powder
6 slices bacon, diced	2 tablespoons prepared mustard
2 medium-size yellow onions, chopped (2 cups)	¼ teaspoon hot red pepper sauce, or to taste
1 cup ketchup	
1 cup barbecue sauce	

PREP TIME: 15 MIN. / SOAKING TIME: 1 HR. OR 8 HR. / COOKING TIME: 2 HR.

1 Cook the beans according to the package directions. Drain, rinse, and drain again; place in a 4-quart bean pot, baking dish, or casserole.

2 Preheat the oven to 350°F. While the beans are cooking, in a 10-inch nonstick skillet, cook the bacon and onions over moderate heat for 10 minutes or until the onions are browned.

3 Stir the bacon, onions, and all the remaining ingredients into the cooked beans. Cover and bake for 1 hour or until bubbly. Makes 12 side-dish or 7 to 8 main-dish servings.

1 side-dish serving: Calories 209; Saturated Fat 1 g; Total Fat 3 g; Protein 8 g; Carbohydrate 39 g; Fiber 5 g; Sodium 479 mg; Cholesterol 3 mg

◆ Chuck-Wagon Cookin' ◆

"When I first started using a Dutch oven over a campfire, I burned everything," confesses Stella Hughes, a recognized chuck wagon cook extraordinaire and member of the National Cowgirl Hall of Fame. But since cooking her first campfire meal, things have changed. For the past 30 years, she and her husband Mack have lived on the Apache Indian Reservation in San Carlos, Arizona, where Mack is the herd manager. Today, Stella is read and quoted on the many aspects of campfire cooking—from creating the best batch of biscuits in a dutch oven to running deep-pit barbecues for 2,000.

In 1976, Stella hauled her chuck wagon (a "kitchen on wheels", equipped with a stove and other essentials for cooking) to the Bicentennial Festival of American Folklore in Washington, D.C. There she demonstrated cooking on the trail, especially the technique of using a Dutch oven.

"First, build the fire only with hardwood, such as oak, mesquite, or hickory. This will make coals that hold the heat well. The fire's ready when the coals are red—no flames allowed. Prewarm the Dutch oven and heat the lid until it's hot (but not too hot!), then set the oven on the coals, piling some around the sides.

Add a food that cooks best in a Dutch oven, such as chili, stews, biscuits, or a cobbler. Put the lid on, shovel some hot coals on top, and let it cook, rotating the oven a quarter-turn every 10 minutes, to keep everything cooking evenly.

"When cooking beans over a campfire, use a pot made of heavy aluminum or stainless steel. Start with the freshest beans you can find (old ones take longer to cook), then soak them overnight. Out West, we use pinto beans, but navy beans are fine too. I often bury some salt pork or diced bacon in the pot, then add a big juicy onion, a rib of celery, some fresh garlic, a spoonful of sugar, and a few spices, such as chili and cracked pepper. To keep the beans tender, hold off adding the salt until about 10 minutes before serving.

"Simmer the beans slowly; cooking too quickly can also toughen them. Watch them carefully, adding *hot* (never cold) water, if needed, to keep them moist. The cooking time depends on the altitude: about 3 hours at sea level, as many as 8 hours in the mountains."

When tender, the beans are ready for eating, down to the last delicious spoonful.

Supper in the old
Yankee tradition:
Boston Baked Beans
and Boston Brown
Bread (page 302)

BOSTON BAKED BEANS

◆◆◆

*Following a New England tradition,
these beans are often baked for about seven hours
every Saturday night. You can do them this slow
way or use our fast-bake method instead.*

2 pounds dried yellow-eye, navy, or pea beans, soaked (page 361)	2 cups cold water
	½ cup molasses
8 ounces salt pork, cut into 12 pieces, with the rind slashed	1 large onion, coarsely chopped (1½ cups)
	2 teaspoons salt, or to taste

PREP TIME: 30 MIN. / SOAKING TIME: 1 HR. OR 8 HR.
SLOW-BAKE: 7 HR. / FAST-BAKE: 1 HR.

1 In a 6-quart Dutch oven, precook the soaked beans, allowing 10 minutes for the slow-bake method (30 minutes for the fast-bake). Rinse the beans and drain them well.

2 Preheat the oven to 300°F for slow-bake (350°F for fast-bake). Place ½ the salt pork in a 4-quart bean pot or casserole. Ladle in the beans and bury the remaining salt pork.

3 In a small saucepan, bring the water, and molasses to a boil over high heat, then pour over the beans. Top with the onion. Cover and bake for 7 hours for slow-bake (1 hour for fast-bake) or until tender, adding more boiling water if needed to keep the beans moist. Stir in the salt during the last 10 minutes of baking. Makes 12 side-dish or 7 to 8 main-dish servings.

*1 side-dish serving: Calories 303; Saturated Fat 1 g;
Total Fat 3 g; Protein 15 g; Carbohydrate 55 g; Fiber 6 g;
Sodium 405 mg; Cholesterol 3 mg*

◆

Tipsy Beans

Prepare as for Boston Baked Beans, substituting **1 cup beer, with or without alcohol,** for half of the water in the molasses mixture. *1 side-dish serving: Calories 312; Saturated Fat 1 g; Total Fat 3 g; Protein 15 g; Carbohydrate 56 g; Fiber 6 g; Sodium 405 mg; Cholesterol 3 mg*

BUTTER BEANS AND HAM
◆◆◆

*Down South, lima beans are known as
butter beans. In Louisiana, the natives have been
cooking butter beans with ham hocks for
well over a 100 years.*

1 pound large butter beans or baby lima beans, soaked (page 361)	3 cloves garlic, peeled
	2 bay leaves
1 ham hock or ham shank (14 ounces)	1 tablespoon unsalted butter or margarine
2 medium-size yellow onions, 1 quartered, 1 finely chopped	1½ teaspoons hot red pepper sauce
	½ teaspoon each salt and black pepper

PREP TIME: 15 MIN. / SOAKING TIME: 1 HR. OR 8 HR.
COOKING TIME: 1¼ HR.

1 Half-fill a large saucepan with water and stir in the beans, ham hock, the quartered onion, garlic, and bay leaves. Bring to a boil, then lower the heat and simmer, uncovered, for 1 hour or until the beans are tender.

2 Drain the beans, reserving all of the liquid and discarding the onion, garlic, and bay leaves. Transfer the beans to a bowl and the ham hock to a cutting board. Cut the meat into small pieces (you should have about 1 cup). Discard the bone.

3 In the same saucepan, melt the butter over moderate heat. Add the chopped onion and sauté for 5 minutes or until tender. Stir in the ham and enough reserved bean liquid to make the beans soupy (about 2 cups); bring to a boil.

4 Lower the heat and simmer, uncovered, for 5 minutes. Stir in the beans, red pepper sauce, salt, and black pepper; heat for 3 minutes or until hot. Serve with Spider Spoon Bread (page 300). Makes 6 side-dish or 4 main-dish servings.

*1 side-dish serving: Calories 264; Saturated Fat 2 g;
Total Fat 4 g; Protein 18 g; Carbohydrate 42 g; Fiber 6 g;
Sodium 199 mg; Cholesterol 14 mg*

HARVARD BEETS
◆◆◆

*Various tales exist concerning how
these beets were named. The most obvious story
relates their deep crimson color to the hue of
Harvard's football-team jerseys.*

2 pounds medium-size beets (about 12)	¼ cup honey
1 bay leaf	1 tablespoon mustard seeds
4 allspice berries (optional)	½ teaspoon salt
6 whole cloves	¼ teaspoon black pepper
½ cup raspberry or cider vinegar	1 tablespoon unsalted butter or margarine
2 teaspoons cornstarch	

PREP TIME: 15 MIN. / COOKING TIME: 45 MIN.

1 Trim the beets ½-inch above the stems and place in a large saucepan. Cover with water and add the bay leaf, allspice berries, if using, and the cloves. Bring to a boil, cover, and simmer for 35 minutes or until tender. Drain the beets and peel while still warm; cut into 1-inch chunks. Discard the allspice berries, if using, and the cloves.

2 In the same saucepan, whisk the vinegar and cornstarch until smooth. Add the honey, mustard seeds, salt, and pepper. Bring to a boil over moderate heat and whisk for 2 minutes or until thickened. Stir in the beets and butter; heat through, stirring occasionally. Makes 6 servings.

*1 serving: Calories 119; Saturated Fat 1 g;
Total Fat 3 g; Protein 2 g; Carbohydrate 24 g; Fiber 1 g;
Sodium 253 mg; Cholesterol 6 mg*

◆

Yale Beets

Prepare as for Harvard Beets, substituting ½ **cup fresh orange juice** and 1 tablespoon **fresh lemon juice** for the vinegar. *1 serving: Calories 129; Saturated Fat 1 g; Total Fat 3 g; Protein 2 g; Carbohydrate 25 g; Fiber 1 g; Sodium 253 mg; Cholesterol 6 mg*

Harvest season—time for Brussels Sprouts with Chestnuts

BRUSSELS SPROUTS WITH CHESTNUTS

◆◆◆

These tiny cabbage-like vegetables were first known in 14th-century Belgium but did not arrive in America until the late 19th century. This dish is traditionally served on Thanksgiving Day.

1 **pound Brussels sprouts, trimmed and washed, or 2 packages (10 ounces each) frozen Brussels sprouts**	1 **tablespoon unsalted butter or margarine**
	2 **tablespoons minced parsley**
	½ **teaspoon black pepper**
1 **can (16 ounces) chestnuts in brine, drained (1⅔ cups)**	¼ **teaspoon ground nutmeg**

PREP TIME: 10 MIN. / COOKING TIME: 10 MIN.

1 Using a sharp pointed knife, cut an X in the end of the stem of each sprout (to allow the stem to cook as quickly as the leaves).

2 In a large saucepan half-filled with boiling salted water, cook the sprouts for 7 minutes or just until tender. Add the chestnuts and cook for 30 seconds or until heated through and drain.

3 Add the butter, parsley, pepper, and nutmeg to the saucepan; toss until the sprouts are coated. Transfer to a serving dish and serve with Roast Turkey (page 140). Makes 4 servings.

1 serving: Calories 327; Saturated Fat 2 g; Total Fat 5 g; Protein 8 g; Carbohydrate 66 g; Fiber 4 g; Sodium 29 mg; Cholesterol 8 mg

HOT SLAW

◆◆◆

The Amish and Mennonites brought to America hearty recipes, such as this dish of bacon- and onion-flavored cabbage. The "hot" refers not to spice, but to the warm dressing.

1 small green or red cabbage (1 pound), thinly shredded (4 cups)	2 tablespoons sugar
	⅓ cup cider vinegar
2 slices lean bacon, diced	2 teaspoons cornstarch
	⅓ cup water
1 small red onion, thinly sliced	¼ teaspoon each salt and black pepper

PREP TIME: 15 MIN. / COOKING TIME: 14 MIN.

1 Place the cabbage in a heatproof serving bowl. In a 10-inch nonstick skillet, cook the bacon over moderate heat for 5 minutes or until crisp. Using a slotted spoon, transfer the bacon to paper towels to drain, then toss with the cabbage.

2 Discard all but 1 tablespoon of the fat from the skillet. Add the onion and sauté for 5 minutes or until soft. Sprinkle the sugar over the top and cook 2 minutes longer or until the sugar dissolves. Stir in the vinegar and bring to a boil.

3 In a small bowl, whisk the cornstarch with the water until smooth. Stir this mixture into the skillet along with the salt and pepper. Return to a boil and cook 1 minute longer. Pour the mixture over the cabbage, toss well, and serve with Cider-Baked Pork Chops (page 104). Makes 4 servings.

1 serving: Calories 89; Saturated Fat 1 g; Total Fat 3 g; Protein 3 g; Carbohydrate 16 g; Fiber 1 g; Sodium 219 mg; Cholesterol 4 mg

SWEET AND SOUR RED CABBAGE

◆◆◆

In this recipe, cabbage is simmered in the German, or Pennsylvania Dutch, tradition, with a blend of sweet and sour flavors.

1 tablespoon unsalted butter or margarine	½ cup cider vinegar
	¼ cup dark raisins
1 medium-size red onion, slivered	3 tablespoons light brown sugar
2 large unpeeled red cooking apples, cored and coarsely chopped (2 cups)	½ teaspoon ground nutmeg
	½ teaspoon salt, or to taste
1 large red cabbage (2 pounds), thinly shredded (8 cups)	¼ teaspoon each ground cloves and black pepper

PREP TIME: 15 MIN. / COOKING TIME: 45 MIN.

1 In a large heavy saucepan, melt the butter over moderately high heat. Add the onion and apples and sauté for 5 minutes or until soft.

2 Stir in the remaining ingredients and toss to coat. Lower the heat, cover, and simmer, stirring occasionally, for 40 minutes or until tender. Serve with Schnitz-Un-Gnepp (page 109). Makes 4 to 6 servings.

1 serving (for 4): Calories 184; Saturated Fat 2 g; Total Fat 4 g; Protein 3 g; Carbohydrate 41 g; Fiber 2 g; Sodium 289 mg; Cholesterol 8 mg

Pick cabbages very clean, and wash them thoroughly, then look them carefully over again.

—The Virginia Housewife (1824) by Mary Randolph

CAULIFLOWER WITH CHEESE SAUCE

◆◆◆

As the legend goes, only one family among the early Dutch settlers was given cauliflower seeds to bring to the New World. They planted them on Long Island, New York, where, coincidentally, some of the finest cauliflower is still grown.

1 small cauliflower (1½ pounds), cored and cut into florets (4 cups)	1 cup shredded Cheddar cheese (4 ounces)
2 tablespoons unsalted butter or margarine	1 teaspoon dry mustard
¼ cup all-purpose flour	½ teaspoon black pepper
2 cups low-fat (1% milkfat) milk	1 large tomato, sliced then halved
	2 tablespoons fresh bread crumbs

PREP TIME: 20 MIN. / COOKING TIME: 45 MIN.

1 Lightly grease a shallow 2-quart baking dish. In a steamer or colander placed over a large saucepan of boiling water, cover and steam the cauliflower for 10 minutes or just until crisp-tender. Transfer to the baking dish.

2 Preheat the oven to 400°F. Meanwhile, in a small saucepan, melt the butter over moderately high heat. Add the flour and cook until bubbly. Whisk in the milk and cook, whisking constantly, for 5 minutes or until thickened. Stir in ¾ cup of the cheese, the mustard, and pepper, then pour the sauce over the cauliflower.

3 Arrange the tomato slices around the edge of the dish. Sprinkle with the bread crumbs and the remaining ¼ cup of cheese. Bake, uncovered, for 30 minutes. Serve with Kansas City Strips, hot off the grill (page 82). Makes 4 servings.

1 serving: Calories 286; Saturated Fat 11 g; Total Fat 17 g; Protein 15 g; Carbohydrate 20 g; Fiber 1 g; Sodium 263 mg; Cholesterol 51 mg

---

◆

Broccoli au Gratin

Prepare as for Cauliflower with Cheese Sauce, substituting **4 cups broccoli florets** for the cauliflower. Makes 4 servings. *1 serving: Calories 286; Saturated Fat 11 g; Total Fat 18 g; Protein 15 g; Carbohydrate 20 g; Fiber 1 g; Sodium 272 mg; Cholesterol 51 mg*

HONEY-SPICED CARROTS

◆◆◆

Carrots have long been an American staple and this way of preparing them, a favorite.

4 cups cold water	1 teaspoon sugar
¼ teaspoon salt	½ teaspoon ground allspice
1½ pounds carrots, peeled and cut into 1½- x ½-inch sticks	¼ teaspoon black pepper
1 tablespoon unsalted butter or margarine	⅛ teaspoon ground cinnamon
¼ cup honey	

PREP TIME: 10 MIN. / COOKING TIME: 10 MIN.

1 In a medium-size saucepan, bring the water and salt to a boil over high heat. Add the carrots; cook for 3 minutes or until crisp-tender. Transfer to a colander and rinse with cold water.

2 In the same saucepan, melt the butter over moderate heat. Add the honey, sugar, allspice, pepper, and cinnamon and stir until bubbly. Add the carrots and heat, tossing, for 3 minutes or until well coated and hot. Makes 4 servings.

1 serving: Calories 170; Saturated Fat 2 g; Total Fat 3 g; Protein 2 g; Carbohydrate 36 g; Fiber 2 g; Sodium 202 mg; Cholesterol 8 mg

◆

Glazed Carrots and Parsnips

Prepare as for Honey-Spiced Carrots, adding **½ pound peeled parsnips, cut into thin sticks,** with the carrots. Makes 4 servings. *1 serving: Calories 216; Saturated Fat 2 g; Total Fat 4 g; Protein 3 g; Carbohydrate 47 g; Fiber 3 g; Sodium 207 mg; Cholesterol 8 mg*

Corn Pudding, made
the wholesome way,
in true Amish style

AMISH CORN PUDDING
◆◆◆

*The Amish migrated from Alsace-Lorraine to
Pennsylvania in the 18th century. Many of their
descendants still live a simple farming life, travel
by horse and buggy, and eat plain wholesome
foods such as this corn pudding.*

3 large eggs	1 can (16½ ounces) no-salt-added cream-style corn
2 tablespoons all-purpose flour	
2 tablespoons sugar	1 cup corn kernels
½ teaspoon black pepper	1 tablespoon unsalted butter or margarine
⅓ cup low-fat (1% milkfat) milk	¼ teaspoon paprika
	2 tablespoons minced parsley

PREP TIME: 10 MIN. / COOKING TIME: 40 MIN.
STANDING TIME: 10 MIN.

1 Preheat the oven to 350°F. Butter a 1½-quart
soufflé or round baking dish; place in the oven.
(If doubling the recipe, use a 2½-quart dish.)

2 Meanwhile, in a large bowl, with an electric
mixer on high, beat the eggs, flour, sugar, and
pepper until smooth. Stir in the milk, creamed
corn, and corn kernels and pour into the hot dish.

3 Dot with the butter and sprinkle with the
paprika. Bake, uncovered, for 40 minutes or
until set. Let stand for 10 minutes, then sprinkle
with the chopped parsley. Makes 4 servings.

*1 serving: Calories 254; Saturated Fat 3 g;
Total Fat 8 g; Protein 9 g; Carbohydrate 40 g; Fiber 0 g;
Sodium 94 mg; Cholesterol 162 mg*

◆

Tex-Mex Corn Pudding

Prepare as for Amish Corn Pudding, adding with
the corn: **⅓ cup chopped sweet red pepper,
¼ cup sliced green onions** and **2 tablespoons
minced fresh cilantro.** Substitute **¼ cup shredded Monterey Jack cheese with jalapeño peppers** for the butter. Makes 4 servings. *1 serving:
Calories 263; Saturated Fat 3 g; Total Fat 9 g; Protein 11 g;
Carbohydrate 43 g; Fiber 0 g; Sodium 133 mg; Cholesterol 166 mg*

Corn Fritters: Served hot off the griddle

CORN FRITTERS
◆◆◆

*Fritters traditionally have been deep fried.
Ours are cooked like pancakes on a lightly oiled
nonstick griddle, resulting in a great-tasting,
light fritter that's much lower in fat.*

1 **large egg, lightly beaten**	1 **tablespoon low-fat (1% milkfat) milk**
2 **tablespoons all-purpose flour**	2 **cups fresh corn kernels, thawed if frozen**
2 **teaspoons sugar**	
¼ **teaspoon salt, or to taste**	2 **tablespoons minced green onions**
¼ **teaspoon baking powder**	2 **large egg whites**
⅛ **teaspoon black pepper**	1 **teaspoon vegetable oil**
	1 **teaspoon unsalted butter or margarine**

PREP TIME: 10 MIN. / COOKING TIME: 18 MIN.

1 In a medium-size bowl, whisk the egg, flour, sugar, salt, baking powder, and pepper until well combined. Stir in the milk, corn, and onion.

2 In a clean small bowl, with an electric mixer on high, beat the egg whites until stiff peaks form. Fold into the corn mixture.

3 On a nonstick griddle or in a 12-inch nonstick skillet, heat the oil and butter over moderate heat. For each fritter, spoon a scant ¼ cup of batter onto the griddle and cook for 3 minutes on each side or until golden and set. Serve with warmed maple syrup and a fresh spinach salad. Makes twelve 3-inch fritters or 4 servings.

*1 serving: Calories 373; Saturated Fat 2 g;
Total Fat 7 g; Protein 12 g; Carbohydrate 67 g; Fiber 2 g;
Sodium 229 mg; Cholesterol 56 mg*

CAJUN CORN

◆◆◆

In Louisiana, this dish is almost always found on the Thanksgiving table.

4	large ears corn on the cob	2	cups chopped ripe tomatoes
½	cup low-fat (1% milkfat) milk	½	teaspoon dried thyme leaves
2	slices lean bacon, diced	½	teaspoon salt
1	cup chopped onion	⅛	to ¼ teaspoon black pepper
½	cup chopped sweet green pepper		

PREP TIME: 20 MIN. / COOKING TIME: 25 MIN.

1 Cut the corn niblets off of the cobs (you should have about 3 cups). Break the cobs into thirds, place in a medium-size saucepan, and add the milk. Cover and bring to a boil over high heat and simmer for 10 minutes, then discard the cobs.

2 Meanwhile, in a 12-inch nonstick skillet over moderate heat, cook the bacon for 5 minutes or until crisp, then transfer to paper towels. Discard all but 1 tablespoon of the bacon fat.

3 In the same skillet, sauté the onion and green pepper, for 5 minutes or until soft. Add the corn niblets, tomatoes, thyme, salt, and pepper and simmer gently for 10 minutes. Stir in the milk and cook 5 minutes longer. Serve with Blackened Redfish (page 153). Makes 4 servings.

1 serving: Calories 161; Saturated Fat 1 g; Total Fat 3 g; Protein 6 g; Carbohydrate 32 g; Fiber 2 g; Sodium 358 mg; Cholesterol 4 mg

◆

Cajun Chicken and Corn

Prepare as for Cajun Corn, adding with the onion, **1 pound skinned and boned chicken breasts, cut into 1-inch-wide strips.** Makes 4 servings. *1 serving: Calories 289; Saturated Fat 1 g; Total Fat 5 g; Protein 34 g; Carbohydrate 32 g; Fiber 2 g; Sodium 455 mg; Cholesterol 72 mg*

CORN ROASTED ON THE GRILL

◆◆◆

The colonists learned about corn from Native Americans, who referred to this vegetable as "Sacred Mother" and "Giver of Life." They often roasted it right in the husks, over an open fire.

4	whole ears of corn in husks		Pinch ground red pepper (cayenne)
2	tablespoons fresh lime juice	2	tablespoons minced parsley for garnish (optional)
2	tablespoons unsalted butter or margarine, melted		

PREP TIME: 10 MIN. / SOAKING TIME: 30 MIN.
COOKING TIME: 20 MIN.

1 Peel back the outer leaves of the corn; remove all the silk. Soak the corn with their husks in cold water for at least 30 minutes. Meanwhile, make the basting sauce by whisking together the lime juice, butter, and red pepper.

2 Preheat the grill. Remove the corn from the water (do not let dry). Pull back the husks, brush each ear with ¼ of the lime mixture and replace the husks. Place on a rack over medium-hot coals, cover the grill, and cook for 20 minutes or until the husks are dark and the kernels are tender, turning often. Makes 4 servings.

1 serving: Calories 137; Saturated Fat 4 g; Total Fat 7 g; Protein 3 g; Carbohydrate 20 g; Fiber 0 g; Sodium 14 mg; Cholesterol 16 mg

◆

Winter Roasted Corn

Preheat the oven to 375°F. Prepare as for Corn Roasted on the Grill, tightly wrapping each ear of corn with its husks in a foil packet. Bake in the oven for 45 minutes or until tender, turning occasionally. Makes 4 servings. *1 serving: Calories 137; Saturated Fat 4 g; Total Fat 7 g; Protein 3 g; Carbohydrate 20 g; Fiber 1 g; Sodium 14 mg; Cholesterol 16 mg*

EGGPLANT PARMESAN
◆◆◆

*Over the years, this way with
eggplant has become an American favorite.*

2 medium-size egg-plants, unpeeled and sliced ½-inch thick	1 cup shredded mozzarella cheese (4 ounces)
½ teaspoon black pepper	½ cup fresh bread crumbs (1 slice)
¼ teaspoon salt, or to taste	¼ cup grated Parmesan cheese
2 tablespoons olive oil	1 tablespoon minced parsley
2 cloves garlic, minced	
2 cups Marinara Sauce (page 277) or canned tomato sauce	

PREP TIME: 30 MIN. / COOKING TIME: 1¼ HR.

1 Preheat the broiler. Sprinkle the eggplant with the pepper and salt and arrange in a single layer on a baking sheet.

2 In a small cup, stir together the oil and garlic. Using a pastry brush, coat the eggplant slices with the oil-garlic mixture. Broil, 4 inches from the heat, for 5 minutes on each side or until soft.

3 Turn the oven to 375°F. In a shallow 13" x 9" x 3" baking dish, layer ⅓ of the eggplant slices, ⅓ of the Marinara Sauce, and ⅓ of the mozzarella cheese; repeat 2 times. Sprinkle with the bread crumbs and Parmesan cheese and bake for 30 minutes or until bubbly. Sprinkle with the parsley and serve immediately with a tossed salad and garlic bread. Makes 4 servings.

*1 serving: Calories 273; Saturated Fat 5 g;
Total Fat 15 g; Protein 13 g; Carbohydrate 24 g; Fiber 5 g;
Sodium 506 mg; Cholesterol 21 mg*

GREEN BEANS AMANDINE
◆◆◆

*This has long been a popular dish
to serve for company. Try the version with
tiny red-skinned potatoes too.*

1 pound fresh green beans, trimmed	2 tablespoons fresh lemon juice
¼ cup sliced almonds, toasted (page 365)	½ teaspoon black pepper
2 tablespoons unsalted butter, melted	¼ teaspoon salt

PREP TIME: 15 MIN. / COOKING TIME: 10 MIN.

1 Half-fill a medium-size saucepan with cold water; bring to a boil over medium heat. Stir in the beans and simmer, uncovered, for 6 minutes or just until tender. Drain in a colander, transfer to a shallow dish, and toss with the remaining ingredients. Serve with Salmon on the Grill (page 150). Makes 4 servings.

*1 serving: Calories 140; Saturated Fat 4 g;
Total Fat 10 g; Protein 4 g; Carbohydrate 12 g; Fiber 2 g;
Sodium 139 mg; Cholesterol 25 mg*

◆

Green Bean and Potato Amandine

Cook the beans as for Green Beans Amandine. With a slotted spoon, transfer to a large bowl. Add **1 pound small red-skinned potatoes** to the water and simmer for 10 minutes or until tender. Add to the beans and toss with the remaining ingredients, increasing the **butter and lemon juice** to ¼ cup each and adding **1 teaspoon dried thyme leaves**. Garnish with **2 tablespoons minced red onion**. Makes 6 servings. *1 serving: Calories 196; Saturated Fat 5 g; Total Fat 11 g; Protein 4 g; Carbohydrate 24 g; Fiber 2 g; Sodium 96 mg; Cholesterol 22 mg*

Newly sprouted eggplants with fewer seeds produce sweeter
marriages with other ingredients in the pot.

—*Old Wives Tale, Provence, France*

Pick of the summer vegetable garden: Green Bean and Potato Amandine

GREEN BEAN CASSEROLE

◆◆◆

In America in the 1940's and '50's, this dish, made with canned vegetables, appeared at family reunions, church suppers, and backyard barbecues. We've made it with fresh green beans instead, but you could also use frozen.

1 pound fresh green beans, trimmed and cut into bite-size pieces (5 cups)

1 tablespoon unsalted butter or margarine

2 tablespoons finely chopped onion

6 ounces fresh mushrooms, thinly sliced (2¼ cups)

1 can (10¾ ounces) low-sodium condensed cream of mushroom soup, undiluted

¼ cup slivered almonds, toasted (page 365)

3 tablespoons low-fat (1% milk fat) milk

½ teaspoon Worcestershire sauce

⅛ teaspoon ground red pepper (cayenne)

½ cup shredded sharp Cheddar cheese (2 ounces)

¾ cup canned or frozen and thawed fried onions (optional)

PREP TIME: 30 MIN. / COOKING TIME: 40 MIN.

1 Preheat the oven to 350°F and grease a 1½ quart shallow baking dish. Half-fill a large saucepan with water and bring to a boil over moderately high heat. Add the green beans, cook for 5 minutes or just until crisp-tender. Rinse with cold water, drain well, and place in a large bowl.

2 In a 12-inch nonstick skillet, melt the butter over moderately high heat. Add the onion and sauté for 5 minutes or until tender. Add the mushrooms and cook 5 minutes longer or until soft. Add to the green beans with the soup, almonds, milk, Worcestershire, and ground red pepper.

3 Spoon into the baking dish and sprinkle with the cheese. Bake, uncovered, for 20 minutes. Top with the onions if you wish; bake 5 minutes more or until the onions are crispy. Serve with Auto-Train Special (page 124). Makes 6 servings.

1 serving: Calories 144; Saturated Fat 4 g; Total Fat 10 g; Protein 6 g; Carbohydrate 11 g; Fiber 2 g; Sodium 243 mg; Cholesterol 16 mg

Southern vittles
for supper: Fried
Greens, smoked
pork chops,
and wedges of
Tex-Mex Corn
Bread (page 301)

FRIED GREENS

◆◆◆

*Southerners have long been cooking fresh
greens in bacon fat. We've cut down the amount
of fat but kept the down-home flavor.*

2 **pounds fresh greens, such as collard, mustard or turnip (about 3 bunches)**	⅓ **cup diced sweet red pepper**
2 **slices lean bacon, diced**	3 **tablespoons chopped yellow onion**
	¼ **teaspoon black pepper**

PREP TIME: 15 MIN. / COOKING TIME: 20 MIN.

1 Wash the greens, leaving droplets of water
on the leaves. Remove any tough stems and
tear leaves into bite-size pieces. In a 12-inch nonstick skillet, cook the bacon over moderate heat
for 5 minutes or until crisp; transfer to paper towels. Pour off all but 1 tablespoon of the drippings.

2 Add the red pepper and onion to the drippings in the skillet and sauté for 5 minutes or
until soft. Stir in the greens and black pepper.
Sauté 10 minutes longer or until the greens are
tender. Top with the bacon and serve with Tex-
Mex Corn Bread (page 301). Makes 4 servings.

*1 serving: Calories 95; Saturated Fat 1 g;
Total Fat 2 g; Protein 5 g; Carbohydrate 18 g; Fiber 1 g;
Sodium 93 mg; Cholesterol 3 mg*

◆

Tennessee Fried Corn

Prepare as for Fried Greens, substituting **3 cups
fresh or frozen corn kernels** for the greens.
Sauté for 4 minutes or until tender. Makes
4 Servings. *1 serving: Calories 124; Saturated Fat 1 g; Total
Fat 2 g; Protein 5 g; Carbohydrate 27 g; Fiber 1 g; Sodium 57 mg;
Cholesterol 3 mg*

DEVILED MUSHROOMS
◆◆◆

In the 1940's, when Americans were beginning to cultivate edible mushrooms, this dish was served for a special breakfast or brunch.

1 tablespoon unsalted butter or margarine	1 tablespoon Worcestershire sauce
1 tablespoon vegetable oil	¼ to ½ teaspoon hot red pepper sauce, or to taste
1 pound button mushrooms, washed and ends trimmed	1 tablespoon dry sherry (optional)
½ teaspoon each salt and black pepper	4 slices white or whole-wheat bread, toasted
¼ cup Chicken Stock (page 74) or low-sodium chicken broth	2 tablespoons minced fresh parsley
1 tablespoon fresh lemon juice	

PREP TIME: 15 MIN. / COOKING TIME: 7 MIN.

1 In a 12-inch nonstick skillet, heat the butter and oil over moderately high heat. Add the mushrooms, salt, and pepper; sauté for 1 minute.

2 Lower the heat and stir in the stock, lemon juice, Worcestershire, the red pepper sauce, and the sherry if you wish. Boil, uncovered, for 5 minutes or until the liquid is reduced to ½ cup.

3 For each serving, cut a piece of toast diagonally into 4 triangles, ladle ¼ of the mushroom mixture on top, and sprinkle with the parsley. Serve with Fresh Fruit Salad with Poppy Seed Dressing (page 250). Makes 4 servings.

1 serving: Calories 160; Saturated Fat 3 g; Total Fat 8 g; Protein 5 g; Carbohydrate 19 g; Fiber 1 g; Sodium 445 mg; Cholesterol 9 mg

CREOLE OKRA AND TOMATOES
◆◆◆

1 pound fresh okra, trimmed and sliced 1-inch thick (4 cups) or 2 packages (10 ounces each) sliced frozen okra	1 can (16 ounces) peeled tomatoes, drained and chopped, with liquid reserved
2 slices lean bacon	1 clove garlic, minced
1 medium-size yellow onion, thinly sliced	½ teaspoon dried thyme leaves
1 medium-size sweet green pepper, cored, seeded, and chopped (1 cup)	¼ teaspoon each salt, black pepper, and sugar
	Dash hot red pepper sauce

PREP TIME: 20 MIN. / COOKING TIME: 30 MIN.

1 Half-fill a large saucepan with cold water; bring to a boil over high heat. Stir in the okra, cook for 3 minutes, and drain well.

2 In a 12-inch nonstick skillet, cook the bacon over moderate heat for 5 minutes or until crisp, then transfer to paper towels and crumble. Pour off all but 2 teaspoons of the drippings. Lower the heat, add the onion and green pepper, and sauté for 5 minutes or until tender.

3 Stir in the tomatoes and their liquid with the remaining ingredients. Cover and simmer, stirring occasionally, for 10 minutes. Return the okra to the skillet, cover, and simmer 5 minutes longer or until tender. Sprinkle the bacon on top. Serve with Southern-Fried Steak (page 88). Makes 4 side-dish servings.

1 serving: Calories 96; Saturated Fat 1 g; Total Fat 2 g; Protein 5 g; Carbohydrate 18 g; Fiber 1 g; Sodium 376 mg; Cholesterol 3 mg

◆

Okra and Shrimp Supper

Prepare as for Okra and Tomatoes, adding **1 pound shelled and deveined medium-size shrimp** with the okra during the last 5 minutes of cooking. Makes 4 main-dish servings. *1 serving: Calories 188; Saturated Fat 1 g; Total Fat 4 g; Protein 22 g; Carbohydrate 18 g; Fiber 1 g; Sodium 503 mg; Cholesterol 134 mg*

ONION PIE

◆◆◆

"Learning to make quiche (a custard cooked in a tart shell) is a good way to add variety to a cook's repertoire," wrote Fannie Farmer in the mid-1900's. This pie is an American version, updated to reduce the fat.

Pastry for a single crust pie shell (page 368)	½ cup slivered fresh basil or minced parsley
2 tablespoons unsalted butter or margarine	1½ cups reduced-fat sour cream
4 large yellow onions (2 pounds), thinly sliced (4 cups)	2 large eggs
	2 large egg whites
	½ teaspoon each salt and black pepper

PREP TIME: 30 MIN. / COOKING TIME: 45 MIN.
STANDING TIME: 5 MIN.

1 Preheat the oven to 375°F. Spread the pastry in a 10-inch flan dish or a 9-inch deep-dish pie plate. Prick with a fork, fill with dried beans, and bake for 5 minutes. Remove the beans and bake 3 minutes more or just until set but not brown.

2 Meanwhile, in a 12-inch nonstick skillet, melt the butter over moderate heat. Stir in the onions and cook, stirring occasionally, for 15 minutes or until they turn a rich golden brown. Spread in the pie shell and sprinkle with the basil.

3 In a medium-size bowl, whisk together the sour cream, eggs, egg whites, salt, and pepper. Pour over the onion mixture and bake, uncovered, for 30 minutes or until set. Let stand for 5 minutes before serving. Serve with Three Bean Salad (page 252). Makes 8 servings.

*1 serving: Calories 362; Saturated Fat 9 g;
Total Fat 20 g; Protein 9 g; Carbohydrate 40 g; Fiber 1 g;
Sodium 278 mg; Cholesterol 86 mg*

CREAMED ONIONS

◆◆◆

Pearl onions are traditionally served at Thanksgiving in a cream sauce. We've lowered the fat by making the sauce with half-and-half and some of the cooking liquid instead of heavy cream.

1 pound pearl onions (4 cups), root ends cut off, or 2 packages (8 ounces each) frozen pearl onions	½ cup half-and-half or evaporated skim milk
1½ tablespoons unsalted butter or margarine	½ teaspoon each salt and black pepper
3 tablespoons all-purpose flour	⅛ teaspoon ground red pepper (cayenne)
½ cup low-fat (1% milkfat) milk	1 cup shredded Gruyère or other Swiss cheese (4 ounces) (optional)

PREP TIME: 20 MIN. / COOKING TIME: 35 MIN.

1 Preheat the oven to 350°F. Half-fill a large saucepan with cold water and bring to a boil over high heat. Add the fresh onions and cook for 1 minute. Using a slotted spoon, remove the onions, peel them, and return to the boiling water. Simmer for 10 minutes or until tender. (If using frozen onions, cook according to the package directions.) Transfer to a shallow 2-quart baking dish, reserving ⅓ cup of the cooking liquid.

2 In a small saucepan, melt the butter over moderate heat. Whisk in the flour and cook until bubbly. Add the milk, half-and-half, reserved cooking liquid, salt, and the black and ground red peppers. Cook, whisking constantly, for 3 minutes or until thickened.

3 Pour over the onions and sprinkle with the cheese if you wish. Bake for 15 minutes or until bubbly. Serve with Roast Turkey with Corn Bread Stuffing (page 140). Makes 6 servings.

*1 serving: Calories 105; Saturated Fat 4 g;
Total Fat 6 g; Protein 3 g; Carbohydrate 12 g; Fiber 1 g;
Sodium 199 mg; Cholesterol 17 mg*

OVEN-FRIED ONION RINGS

◆◆◆

At the turn of the 20th century, fried onion rings were almost always a daily offering at roadside eateries. Though baked, these still have all the flavor of, but much less fat than, the deep-fried kind.

Nonstick cooking spray

2 large Spanish onions (4 pounds)

2 cups fresh white or whole-wheat bread crumbs (4 slices)

2 tablespoons minced parsley

½ teaspoon black pepper

¼ teaspoon salt

2 large eggs

PREP TIME: 20 MIN. / COOKING TIME: 25 MIN.

1 Preheat the oven to 375°F. Coat 2 large baking sheets with the cooking spray. Peel and slice the onions ½ inch thick.

2 In a pie plate, toss the bread crumbs, parsley, pepper, and salt. In a shallow dish whisk the eggs until foamy. Dip each onion ring first into the eggs, then into the bread crumbs. Arrange in a single layer on the baking sheets.

3 Coat the onion rings lightly with the cooking spray. Bake, turning 2 or 3 times, for 25 minutes or until crispy. Serve with Blue Ribbon Burgers (page 316). Makes 4 servings.

1 serving: Calories 272; Saturated Fat 1 g; Total Fat 4 g; Protein 10 g; Carbohydrate 51 g; Fiber 3 g; Sodium 295 mg; Cholesterol 107 mg

From the roadhouse to your house: Oven-Fried Onion Rings

MINTED GREEN PEAS

◆◆◆

In the first American cookbook, American Cookery (1796), *Amelia Simmons advised: "Peas should be picked carefully from the vines as soon as the dew is off, shelled and cleaned without water, and boiled immediately; they are thus the richest flavored."*

4 pounds fresh green peas, shelled, or 2 packages (10 ounces each) frozen peas	½ teaspoon salt
	¼ teaspoon black pepper
1 tablespoon unsalted butter or margarine	2 tablespoons chopped fresh mint or 2 teaspoons dried mint leaves
1 teaspoon sugar	

PREP TIME: 20 MIN. / COOKING TIME: 8 MIN.

1 Half-fill a large saucepan with cold water and bring to a boil over high heat. Add the peas, lower the heat, and cook for 8 minutes or just until tender. Drain well and place in a medium-size serving bowl, then stir in all of the remaining ingredients. Serve with Michael's Veal Surprise (page 115). Makes 4 servings.

1 serving: Calories 215; Saturated Fat 2 g; Total Fat 4 g; Protein 12 g; Carbohydrate 34 g; Fiber 5 g; Sodium 279 mg; Cholesterol 8 mg

◆

Minted Peas and Carrots

Peel and thinly slice **4 large carrots** (2 cups). Prepare Minted Green Peas, cooking the carrots with the peas and increasing the butter to **2 tablespoons**. Makes 6 servings. *1 serving: Calories 182; Saturated Fat 3 g; Total Fat 5 g; Protein 9 g; Carbohydrate 28 g; Fiber 4 g; Sodium 203 mg; Cholesterol 11 mg*

No vegetable exists which is not better slightly undercooked.

—James Beard

COTTAGE FRIES

◆◆◆

3 slices lean bacon, diced	1 tablespoon minced fresh rosemary or 1 teaspoon dried rosemary leaves (optional)
⅓ cup chopped sweet green pepper	
⅓ cup chopped sweet red pepper	½ teaspoon salt, or to taste
¼ cup chopped yellow onion	¼ teaspoon black pepper
4 large all-purpose potatoes, peeled, cooked, and diced (2 pounds)	

PREP TIME: 20 MIN. / COOKING TIME: 35 MIN.

1 In a heavy 12-inch skillet (preferably a cast iron one), cook the bacon over moderately high heat for 5 minutes or until crisp. Using a slotted spoon, transfer to paper towels to drain.

2 Pour off all but 2 tablespoons of the bacon drippings from the skillet. Add the green and red pepper and onion and sauté for 5 minutes or until tender. Stir in the potatoes with the bacon, rosemary, salt, and black pepper.

3 Lower the heat to moderately-low. Using a metal spatula, press the potatoes into an even layer. Cook, turning and pressing down several times, for 10 minutes or until the potatoes are nicely browned and crisp. Serve with This Is It! Meat Loaf (page 101). Makes 4 servings.

1 serving: Calories 268; Saturated Fat 4 g; Total Fat 9 g; Protein 5 g; Carbohydrate 43 g; Fiber 1 g; Sodium 353 mg; Cholesterol 11 mg

◆

Hash Browns

Prepare as for Cottage Fries, omitting the bacon and substituting **1 tablespoon vegetable oil** and **1 tablespoon unsalted butter or margarine** for the bacon drippings. Omit the sweet green and red peppers. Makes 4 servings. *1 serving: Calories 240; Saturated Fat 3 g; Total Fat 7 g; Protein 4 g; Carbohydrate 43 g; Fiber 1 g; Sodium 278 mg; Cholesterol 8 mg*

Summer harvest specialties to enjoy any time of year: O'Brien Potatoes and Minted Peas and Carrots

O'BRIEN POTATOES

◆◆◆

*This recipe turns leftover potatoes
(or freshly cooked ones) into a wonderful
supper dish. Accompany it with a steamed
vegetable or a favorite salad and
crusty whole-grain bread.*

2	tablespoons unsalted butter or margarine
1	medium-size yellow onion, thinly sliced
4	large all-purpose potatoes, peeled, cooked, and diced (2 pounds)
1½	teaspoons minced fresh thyme or ½ teaspoon dried thyme leaves
¼	teaspoon black pepper, or to taste
6	to 12 ounces baked ham, diced (1 to 2 cups)
½	cup finely chopped sweet green or red pepper
⅓	cup evaporated skim milk or half-and-half
¼	cup minced parsley

PREP TIME: 20 MIN. / COOKING TIME: 37 MIN.

1 In a heavy 12-inch skillet (preferably a cast iron one), melt 1 tablespoon of the butter over moderately high heat. Add the onion and sauté for 5 minutes or until soft. Using a slotted spoon, remove the onion to a small bowl.

2 Add the remaining 1 tablespoon of butter to the skillet and stir in the potatoes, thyme, and black pepper. Cook, without stirring, for 5 minutes or until the potatoes begin to brown. Stir and continue cooking the potatoes 5 minutes more or until browned throughout.

3 Return the onion to the skillet, add the ham and sweet pepper, and cook 5 minutes longer or until the vegetables are tender. Stir in the milk, cook 1 minute more, then sprinkle with the parsley. Serve with Gazpacho Salad (page 259). Makes 4 main-dish servings.

*1 serving: Calories 265; Saturated Fat 5 g;
Total Fat 9 g; Protein 13 g; Carbohydrate 34 g; Fiber 1 g;
Sodium 546 mg; Cholesterol 40 mg*

CHURCH SUPPER POTATOES

◆◆◆

This scalloped-potato dish was once a standby at church suppers and reunions across America.

1 clove garlic, peeled and halved	1 cup thin strips yellow onion
4 medium-size russet (baking) potatoes, peeled (2 pounds)	2 strips bacon, diced and cooked (optional)
3 tablespoons all-purpose flour	2 tablespoons unsalted butter, melted
½ teaspoon each salt and black pepper	1½ cups low-fat (1% milkfat) milk, heated

PREP TIME: 30 MIN. / COOKING TIME: 1 HR.

1 Preheat the oven to 375°F. Grease the bottom and sides of a 13" x 9" x 3" baking dish and rub with the garlic clove. Thinly slice the potatoes and quickly place in a large bowl of ice water.

2 In a cup, mix the flour, salt, and pepper. Drain the potatoes and arrange ½ of them in the dish. Top with the onions, flour mixture, bacon if using, and the remaining potatoes. Brush with the butter, then pour the milk over all.

3 Cover and bake for 45 minutes. Uncover and bake 15 minutes more or until tender. Serve with Richmond Fried Chicken (page 132). Makes 4 servings.

1 serving: Calories 246; Saturated Fat 5 g; Total Fat 7 g; Protein 7 g; Carbohydrate 40 g; Fiber 1 g; Sodium 322 mg; Cholesterol 20 mg

◆

Potatoes au Gratin

Prepare Church Supper Potatoes, sprinkling **1½ cups shredded Gruyère cheese** over the flour mixture in Step 2 and omitting the butter. Makes 4 servings. *1 serving: Calories 368; Saturated Fat 9 g; Total Fat 15 g; Protein 19 g; Carbohydrate 40 g; Fiber 1 g; Sodium 463 mg; Cholesterol 50 mg*

Church Supper Potatoes: A good choice for any sort of gathering

'TATER BOATS

Probably first created as a way to use leftover baked potatoes, these twice-baked versions are very popular, especially in the Northwest potato country.

4	large russet (baking) potatoes (2½ pounds)
1	tablespoon unsalted butter or margarine
¾	cup low-fat (1% milkfat) milk, heated
¾	cup shredded extra-sharp Cheddar cheese (3 ounces)
¼	cup reduced-fat sour cream
3	tablespoons finely chopped green onion
½	teaspoon black pepper
¼	teaspoon salt, or to taste

PREP TIME: 20 MIN. / COOKING TIME: 1¼ HR.

1 Preheat the oven to 400°F. Scrub the potatoes and prick with a fork. Bake for 1 hour or until tender. While the potatoes are still hot, carefully cut off a ½-inch lengthwise slice from each one; scoop the contents of the slices into a large bowl.

2 Into the same bowl, scoop out the remaining potatoes, leaving ¼-inch shells. Add the butter and ¼ cup of the hot milk. Mash the potatoes with a potato masher or beat with an electric mixer set on medium for 3 minutes or until almost smooth. Gradually add the remaining ½ cup of milk, beating until the potatoes are fluffy.

3 Fold in ½ cup of the cheese, plus the sour cream, green onions, pepper, and salt. Spoon the mixture into the shells, mounding the top, then sprinkle with the remaining ¼ cup of cheese. Bake for 15 to 20 minutes or until hot. Serve with Swiss Steak (page 86). Makes 4 servings.

1 serving: Calories 265; Saturated Fat 7 g; Total Fat 12 g; Protein 10 g; Carbohydrate 52 g; Fiber 1 g; Sodium 520 mg; Cholesterol 36 mg

◆ The Great American Spud ◆

White potatoes, native to the Andes, were introduced in Europe by the Spaniards in the late 16th century. By 1719 potatoes had circled back to the New World with Irish settlers in New England. At the end of the 19th century, they were growing in almost every American state, with Maine, Idaho, New York, Washington, and California leaders in their production.

Today, the potato—also known as the spud after an English digging tool of the same name—is the most popular vegetable in America; each person eats at least 126 pounds per year! Some 5 billion of those pounds are consumed in the form of French fries alone. There is ample basis for favoring the potato. It is rich in vitamins and minerals, particularly potassium, the B complex, and vitamin C, with the greatest concentration of these nutrients in the skin (good reason for eating the skin whenever possible).

Potatoes were once kept in root cellars, the perfect sort of place—cool, dry, and dark— for storing them. Unless you can provide such conditions at home (a refrigerator is too cold), it is best to buy these vegetables in limited quantities; select potatoes that are smooth, with no signs of sprouting or green tinge (the green indicates development of a toxin that must be peeled away).

Enjoy this favorite as often as you like; it's an ideal food.

◆

Over-Stuffed Potatoes

Prepare the potatoes as for 'Tater Boats and spoon into the shells. Top each potato with ¼ **cup cooked small broccoli florets** before sprinkling with the cheese; bake. Makes 4 servings. *1 serving: Calories 271; Saturated Fat 7 g; Total Fat 12 g; Protein 10 g; Carbohydrate 53 g; Fiber 1 g; Sodium 526 mg; Cholesterol 36 mg*

POTATO PANCAKES

2 medium-size russet (baking) potatoes, peeled (1 pound)

½ small yellow onion, peeled

1 large egg, beaten

1 tablespoon plain dry bread crumbs

2 tablespoons minced parsley

1½ teaspoons chopped fresh thyme, or ½ teaspoon dried thyme leaves

½ teaspoon salt

¼ teaspoon black pepper

2 tablespoons unsalted butter or margarine

PREP TIME: 20 MIN. / COOKING TIME: 15 MIN.

1 Preheat the oven to 200°F and place a large baking sheet in the oven to warm. Using the shredding disc of a food processor or the coarse side of a hand grater, grate the potatoes and place in a bowl of ice water. Grate the onion.

2 In a large bowl, combine the egg, bread crumbs, parsley, thyme, salt, and pepper. Transfer the potatoes and the onion to a strainer, press them gently with your hand to squeeze out any excess liquid, and discard the liquid. Add the potatoes and onion to the egg mixture and toss until thoroughly coated.

3 In a 12-inch nonstick skillet, melt 1 tablespoon of the butter over moderate heat. Using a scant ¼ cup of batter for each pancake, drop the potato mixture into the skillet, flattening each cake with a spatula to form 4-inch rounds.

4 Cook the pancakes for 3 to 4 minutes on each side or until golden brown, then transfer to the baking sheet in the oven while you bake the remaining cakes. Add the remaining tablespoon of butter to the skillet when needed. Serve piping hot with Chunky Cinnamon Applesauce (page 279). This recipe may easily be doubled. Makes eight 4-inch pancakes.

1 pancake: Calories 94; Saturated Fat 2 g; Total Fat 4 g; Protein 2 g; Carbohydrate 13 g; Fiber 0 g; Sodium 151 mg; Cholesterol 35 mg

---

DOWN HOME TRADITION

Traditionally, these thick potato sticks have been piled high on a plate beside a beefsteak; it's for this reason that they are usually referred to as Steak Fries. They are best when made with high-starch russets, commonly called baking potatoes. Although Idaho is known for its baking potato, excellent ones also come from Maine, Washington State, and New York. We've made these fries the authentic down-home way by leaving their skins on.

◆ Steak Fries ◆

4 cups vegetable oil

4 large russet (baking) potatoes, unpeeled (2½ pounds)

1 teaspoon salt

PREP TIME: 10 MIN. / STANDING TIME: 15 MIN.
COOKING TIME: 12 MIN.

1 Preheat the oven to 200°F and place a large baking sheet in the oven to warm. In a deep-fat fryer or deep heavy skillet, preheat the oil to 375°F or until a 1-inch cube of bread browns in 1 minute.

2 Scrub the potatoes well and cut lengthwise into sticks, 1 inch thick. Place in a bowl of ice water for 15 minutes to rinse out the starch (do not leave them longer, for they will become water-logged). Drain them well, then dry thoroughly with paper towels.

3 Deep-fry, in 3 to 4 batches, for 4 to 5 minutes or until dark golden brown and crispy. As you complete each batch, transfer it to the baking sheet in the oven. Sprinkle with the salt and toss. Serve with Sharon's Best Rib Eye Steaks (page 81). Makes 4 servings.

1 serving: Calories 384; Saturated Fat 3 g; Total Fat 14 g; Protein 6 g; Carbohydrate 61 g; Fiber 1 g; Sodium 547 mg; Cholesterol 0 mg

OVEN FRIES

◆◆◆

Here's the way to have great
Steak Fries without deep-frying them.

	Nonstick cooking spray	3	tablespoons vegetable oil
4	large russet (baking) potatoes, unpeeled (2½ pounds)	½	teaspoon salt, or to taste

PREP TIME: 10 MIN. / STANDING TIME: 15 MIN.
COOKING TIME: 1 HR.

1 Preheat the oven to 375°F. Coat 2 baking sheets with the cooking spray. Scrub the potatoes well; cut lengthwise into sticks, 1 inch thick.

2 Place in a bowl of ice water for 15 minutes to rinse out the starch (do not leave them longer in the water, for they will become water-logged). Drain well, then dry thoroughly with paper towels.

3 Using a pastry brush, lightly brush all sides of the potato sticks with the oil. Arrange them in a single layer on the baking sheets.

4 Bake, turning 2 or 3 times, for 1 hour or until crisp and golden brown. Sprinkle immediately with the salt and toss. Serve with London Broil (page 81). Makes 4 servings.

1 serving: Calories 354; Saturated Fat 2 g;
Total Fat 11 g; Protein 6 g; Carbohydrate 61 g; Fiber 1 g;
Sodium 281 mg; Cholesterol 0 mg

◆

Sweet Potato Fries

Prepare as for Oven Fries, substituting **4 large unpeeled sweet potatoes** (2½ pounds) for the russets. Makes 4 servings. *1 serving: Calories 382; Saturated Fat 2 g; Total Fat 11 g; Protein 5 g; Carbohydrate 69 g; Fiber 2 g; Sodium 295 mg; Cholesterol 0 mg*

Seventh Inning Stretch: Time out for
Ballpark Franks (page 323) and Saratoga Chips

◆

Saratoga Chips

Preheat the oven to 400°F. Follow Step 1 for Oven Fries, but **cut the potatoes crosswise into thin slices** instead of sticks. Continue as directed, baking and turning frequently, for 45 minutes. Makes 4 servings. *1 serving: Calories 354; Saturated Fat 2 g; Total Fat 11 g; Protein 6 g; Carbohydrate 61 g; Fiber 1 g; Sodium 281 mg; Cholesterol 0 mg*

From the farms and the shores of Long Island: Parsleyed Potatoes and Tuna on the Grill (page 148)

LONG ISLAND PARSLEYED POTATOES

◆◆◆

On Long Island, New York, spring revives memories of fresh crops of tiny red-skinned potatoes. Tossing them with parsley, fresh from the garden, is now a down-home tradition.

2	pounds small new red-skinned potatoes, scrubbed and quartered
1	tablespoon unsalted butter or margarine

1	tablespoon olive oil
½	teaspoon each salt and black pepper
1	teaspoon grated lemon rind
⅓	cup minced parsley

PREP TIME: 15 MIN. / COOKING TIME: 10 MIN.

1 Half-fill a large saucepan with water and bring to a boil over high heat. Add the potatoes and simmer for 6 minutes or until tender, then drain.

2 In the same saucepan, whisk the butter, oil, salt, and pepper over moderate heat for 3 minutes or until combined. Return the potatoes to the saucepan with the lemon rind and parsley. Using a spatula, toss them gently until well coated and steaming hot. Serve with Tuna on the Grill (page 148). Makes 4 servings.

1 serving: Calories 281; Saturated Fat 4 g;
Total Fat 10 g; Protein 4 g; Carbohydrate 46 g; Fiber 1 g;
Sodium 281 mg; Cholesterol 17 mg

DUCHESSE MASHED POTATOES

❖❖❖

These potato rosettes are a glorious rendition of good old-fashioned mashed potatoes. If you do not have a pastry tube, just spoon them into mounds.

4 large russet (baking) potatoes, peeled (2½ pounds)	⅛ teaspoon grated nutmeg
1 tablespoon unsalted butter or margarine, softened	¼ cup low fat (1% milkfat) milk
	1 large egg
½ teaspoon salt, or to taste	1 large egg yolk
	For the glaze:
⅛ teaspoon white pepper, or to taste	1 large egg white
	2 teaspoons cold water

PREP TIME: 20 MIN. / COOKING TIME: 45 MIN.

1 Half-fill a large saucepan with water and bring to a boil over high heat. Add the potatoes and cook for 25 minutes or until tender, then transfer with a slotted spoon to a large bowl.

2 Preheat the oven to 400°F and grease a baking sheet. With an electric mixer set on low, whip the potatoes for 3 minutes or until coarsely mashed. Add the remaining ingredients, increase the speed to medium, and beat until fluffy.

3 Fit a pastry bag with a large rosette tip, spoon the potato mixture into it, and pipe the potatoes onto the baking sheet. You should have 12 rosettes, each about 2 inches in diameter. (If making ahead, loosely cover with plastic wrap and refrigerate for up to 4 hours.)

4 To make the glaze, whisk the egg white and water in a cup. Gently brush on the potatoes. Bake for 15 minutes or until golden. Serve with Pepper-Crusted Tenderloin Roast (page 78). Makes 4 servings of 3 rosettes each.

1 serving: Calories 351; Saturated Fat 3 g; Total Fat 6 g; Protein 9 g; Carbohydrate 58 g; Fiber 1 g; Sodium 320 mg; Cholesterol 115 mg

CREAMED SPINACH

❖❖❖

In 1919, Elzie Crisler Segar created Popeye, the cartoon character who still reminds children of all ages to eat their spinach so they will grow up big and strong like him.

2 teaspoons unsalted butter or margarine	½ teaspoon each ground nutmeg and black pepper
2 pounds fresh spinach, washed, dried, and coarsely chopped or 2 packages (10 ounces each) frozen chopped spinach, thawed and squeezed dry	¼ teaspoon salt, or to taste
	¾ cup low-fat (1% milkfat) milk
	¾ cup Neufchâtel cream cheese (6 ounces)
	2 large egg whites
2 green onions, with tops, chopped (¼ cup)	Garnish:
	1 large ripe tomato, cut into wedges

PREP TIME: 20 MIN. / COOKING TIME: 30 MIN.

1 Preheat the oven to 350°F and grease a 1½-quart shallow baking dish. In a medium-size saucepan, melt the butter over moderate heat.

2 To the saucepan, add the spinach, green onions, nutmeg, pepper, and salt and cook for 2 minutes or until heated through. Add the milk and cream cheese and stir for 5 minutes or until the cheese melts. Remove from the heat.

3 In a clean medium-size bowl, with an electric mixer set on high, beat the egg whites until stiff peaks form. Gently fold into the spinach mixture and spoon into the baking dish. Bake, uncovered, for 20 minutes or until puffy and lightly browned. Garnish with the tomato wedges and serve immediately with City Chicken (page 110). Makes 4 servings.

1 serving: Calories 197; Saturated Fat 8 g; Total Fat 15 g; Protein 12 g; Carbohydrate 11 g; Fiber 2 g; Sodium 468 mg; Cholesterol 40 mg

TEXAS SQUASH PUDDING
◆◆◆

1¾ pounds yellow summer squash or zucchini, sliced ¼ inch thick (6 cups)	1 cup grated Monterey Jack cheese with jalapeño peppers (4 ounces)
2 tablespoons unsalted butter or margarine	½ cup Neufchâtel cream cheese (4 ounces)
1 medium-size yellow onion, chopped (1 cup)	1 cup low-fat (1% milkfat) milk
3 tablespoons all-purpose flour	⅓ cup Ritz cracker crumbs

PREP TIME: 20 MIN. / COOKING TIME: 45 MIN.

1 Preheat the oven to 350°F and grease a 2-quart casserole. Half-fill a 12-inch nonstick skillet with water and bring to a boil over high heat. Add the squash, lower the heat, and simmer for 5 minutes or just until tender, then transfer to a colander and drain well.

2 In the same skillet, melt 1 tablespoon of the butter over moderate heat. Add the onion and sauté for 5 minutes or until soft. Whisk in the flour and cook until bubbly.

3 Lower the heat and stir in ½ cup of the Monterey Jack cheese, plus all of the cream cheese and the milk. Cook, stirring constantly, for 5 minutes or until smooth. Gently fold in the squash and spoon the mixture into the casserole.

4 Wipe out the skillet and melt the remaining tablespoon of butter over moderate heat. Toss with the cracker crumbs and the remaining ½ cup of shredded cheese; sprinkle over the top of the casserole. Bake, uncovered, for 25 minutes or until golden brown and heated through. Serve with Southern-Fried Steak (page 88). Makes 6 servings.

1 serving: Calories 228; Saturated Fat 9 g; Total Fat 15 g; Protein 10 g; Carbohydrate 14 g; Fiber 1 g; Sodium 220 mg; Cholesterol 41 mg

GLAZED ACORN SQUASH
◆◆◆

One of the new vegetables that colonists discovered in America was the sweet acorn squash, which remains a fall favorite today.

2 acorn squash (1½ pounds each), halved lengthwise and seeded	1 teaspoon ground cinnamon
⅓ cup firmly packed dark brown sugar	½ teaspoon ground nutmeg
¼ cup fresh orange juice	2 tablespoons unsalted butter or margarine
	½ teaspoon salt
	¼ teaspoon black pepper

PREP TIME: 10 MIN. / COOKING TIME: 50 MIN.

1 Preheat the oven to 425°F. In a baking pan large enough to hold the squash in a single layer, place the squash cut-side-down. Pour in enough boiling water to come about 1 inch up the sides of the squash. Bake, uncovered, for 30 minutes or just until tender, then drain.

2 Meanwhile, in a small saucepan, bring the sugar, orange juice, cinnamon, and nutmeg to a boil over moderately high heat. Boil for 4 minutes, then stir in the butter and cook for 1 minute more or until melted.

3 Using a spatula, carefully turn the squash cut-side-up in the baking pan and sprinkle with the salt and pepper. Spoon 1 tablespoon of the butter mixture into each squash half and bake for 20 minutes more, basting with the remaining butter mixture every 5 minutes. Serve with Kansas City Strips (page 82). Makes 4 servings. For 8 servings, simply double the recipe.

1 serving: Calories 323; Saturated Fat 4 g; Total Fat 7 g; Protein 4 g; Carbohydrate 70 g; Fiber 7 g; Sodium 287 mg; Cholesterol 17 mg

Ushering in the first cool days of fall with Stuffed Acorn Squash

STUFFED ACORN SQUASH

❖❖❖

2	acorn squash (1½ pounds each), halved lengthwise and seeded	1	tablespoon chopped fresh rosemary or 1 teaspoon dried rosemary leaves
2	teaspoons olive oil	¼	teaspoon black pepper
1	large yellow onion, chopped (1 cup)	¼	cup minced parsley
1	large Granny Smith apple, peeled, cored, and diced (1 cup)	1½	cups fresh whole-wheat bread crumbs (3 slices)
¼	cup cold water	¼	cup low-fat (1% milkfat) milk
6	ounces bulk pork sausage, crumbled		

PREP TIME: 15 MIN. / COOKING TIME: 50 MIN.

1 Preheat the oven to 425°F. In a baking pan large enough to hold the squash in a single layer, place the squash cut-side-down. Pour in enough boiling water to come about 1 inch up the sides of the squash. Bake, uncovered, for 30 minutes or just until tender, then drain.

2 Meanwhile, in a 12-inch nonstick skillet, heat the oil over moderately high heat and sauté the onion for 5 minutes. Add the apple and water; cook, uncovered, 5 minutes longer or until tender.

3 Stir in the sausage, rosemary, and pepper and sauté for 5 minutes or until the sausage is no longer pink. Remove from the heat and stir in the parsley, bread crumbs, and milk.

4 Using a spatula, carefully turn the squash cut-side-up in the baking pan and fill each half with ¼ of the sausage mixture. Bake for 20 minutes or until heated through. Serve with a green salad tossed with Buttermilk Dressing (page 260). Makes 4 main-dish servings.

1 serving: Calories 401; Saturated Fat 4 g; Total Fat 15 g; Protein 13 g; Carbohydrate 60 g; Fiber 7 g; Sodium 600 mg; Cholesterol 30 mg

◆

Stuffed Zucchini

Prepare as for Stuffed Acorn Squash, substituting for the squash **4 medium-size zucchini,** halved, with pulp scooped out, leaving a ¼-inch shell. Bake the shells, (cut-side-down as in Step 1) at 375°F for 20 minutes or just until tender. Meanwhile, chop the pulp and cook with the other ingredients in Step 3. Stuff the zucchini and continue baking 15 minutes more. Makes 4 main-dish servings. *1 serving: Calories 257; Saturated Fat 4 g; Total Fat 15 g; Protein 11 g; Carbohydrate 22 g; Fiber 1 g; Sodium 592 mg; Cholesterol 30 mg*

Fresh green tomatoes, picked off the vine, then fried until crisp, golden, and fine

SUCCOTASH

◆◆◆

1 **tablespoon unsalted butter or margarine**	1 **teaspoon sugar**
1 **small onion, finely chopped (½ cup)**	½ **teaspoon salt** **Pinch white pepper**
2 **cups shelled fresh baby lima beans, or 1 package (10 ounces) frozen lima beans**	2 **cups fresh corn kernels or 1 package (10 ounces) frozen corn kernels**
1 **cup Chicken Stock (page 74) or low-sodium chicken broth**	¼ **cup evaporated skim milk or half-and-half**
	1 **teaspoon cornstarch**

 PREP TIME: 20 MIN. / COOKING TIME: 25 MIN.

1 In a large saucepan, melt the butter over moderate heat. Stir in the onion and sauté for 5 minutes or until tender. Add the lima beans, stock, sugar, salt, and pepper; bring to a boil.

2 Lower the heat and simmer uncovered for 10 minutes. Stir in the corn and simmer 5 minutes longer (only 3 minutes for frozen corn) or until tender.

3 In a cup, whisk the milk with the cornstarch and add to the saucepan. Return to a boil and cook for 2 minutes or until slightly thickened. Serve hot with Country Style Ribs (page 85). Makes 6 servings.

1 serving: Calories 210; Saturated Fat 2 g; Total Fat 5 g; Protein 12 g; Carbohydrate 37 g; Fiber 4 g; Sodium 210 mg; Cholesterol 7 mg

◆

Succotash Stew

Prepare as for Succotash, adding **2 cups (12 ounces) bite-size pieces cooked chicken, turkey, or ham** to the saucepan with the corn. Makes 4 main-dish servings. *1 serving: Calories 274; Saturated Fat 2 g; Total Fat 5 g; Protein 26 g; Carbohydrate 37 g; Fiber 4 g; Sodium 248 mg; Cholesterol 41 mg*

FRIED GREEN TOMATOES

◆◆◆

Frying green tomatoes is an old Southern custom, perhaps started by a landowner who could not wait until the spring tomatoes ripened before picking them. Whatever the beginning, the treat is a taste worth discovering. Try this same recipe with firm red tomatoes too.

1 large egg	¼ teaspoon black pepper
¼ cup low-fat (1% milkfat) milk	½ cup yellow cornmeal
½ to 1 teaspoon hot red pepper sauce, or to taste	3 medium-size green tomatoes, sliced ¼ inch thick (1 pound)
1 teaspoon sugar	2 tablespoons corn oil or bacon drippings
½ teaspoon salt	

PREP TIME: 15 MIN. / COOKING TIME: 10 MIN.

1 In a pie plate, whisk the egg, milk, and hot pepper sauce. In a cup, mix the sugar, salt, and pepper. Spread the cornmeal on a plate. Dip the tomato slices into the egg mixture, sprinkle with the sugar mixture, then coat with the cornmeal.

2 In a 12-inch nonstick skillet, heat 1 tablespoon of the oil over moderate heat. Slide in about half of the tomato slices, without crowding, and cook for 2 minutes on each side or until golden-brown; transfer to paper towels to drain.

3 Repeat with the remaining oil and tomatoes. Serve immediately, as they lose their crispy texture upon standing. These are the perfect accompaniment for Carolina Chicken (page 131). Makes 4 servings.

1 serving: Calories 167; Saturated Fat 2 g; Total Fat 9 g; Protein 4 g; Carbohydrate 18; Fiber 1 g; Sodium 307 mg; Cholesterol 54 mg

ROASTED VEGETABLES

◆◆◆

Roasted vegetables have a more intense flavor than boiled or steamed versions. They make perfect go-alongs for the holiday turkey.

2 tablespoons unsalted butter or margarine	3 tablespoons chopped fresh thyme or 1 tablespoon dried thyme leaves
2 tablespoons olive oil	1 teaspoon salt
2 pounds small red-skinned potatoes, scrubbed and halved	½ teaspoon coarsely ground black pepper
2 cups small white onions, peeled and halved	1 pint (10 ounces) Brussels sprouts, trimmed or 1 package (10 ounces) frozen Brussels sprouts, thawed
1 pound carrots, peeled and cut into bite-size chunks	
1 pound parsnips, peeled and cut into bite-size chunks	1 medium-size red onion, peeled and cut into thin strips
1 pound turnips, peeled and cut into bite-size chunks	2 large cloves garlic, minced

PREP TIME: 35 MIN. / COOKING TIME: 1 HR.

1 Preheat the oven to 425°F. In a large roasting pan, combine the butter and oil. Place in the oven for 2 minutes to melt the butter. Add the potatoes, onions, carrots, parsnips, turnips, thyme, salt, and pepper. Toss until coated, cover with foil, and bake for 30 minutes. Increase the oven temperature to 450°F.

2 Stir in the sprouts, red onion, and garlic. Bake, uncovered, for 30 to 45 minutes or until the vegetables are lightly browned and tender, stirring frequently. (If roasting alongside a turkey, bake the vegetables, covered, at 325°F during the last 1½ hours of roasting time. Remove the turkey, increase the oven temperature to 450°F, uncover the vegetables, and roast 15 to 30 minutes longer or until browned.) Makes 8 servings.

1 serving: Calories 289; Saturated Fat 3 g; Total Fat 7 g; Protein 6 g; Carbohydrate 55 g; Fiber 4 g; Sodium 336 mg; Cholesterol 8 mg

IN THE SALAD BOWL

◆◆◆

Many American dishes were influenced mainly by traditions from other countries, but salads seem to reflect the special bounty of this land and the inventiveness of its cooks as well. Where else would you find such variety as Iowa Corn Salad, Texas Steak Salad, and Jambalaya Salad? A few selections here, such as Prayer Meeting Coleslaw and Waldorf Salad, are at least a century old. Others, such as Chef's Salad, Brown Derby Cobb Salad, and Three Bean Salad, hark back to the 1940's and 1950's.

Now you can prepare these popular dishes in healthier ways than before, thanks to our slimmed-down, low-fat dressings. (One secret to reducing fat is to replace part of the oil with fruit or vegetable purées. Another is to use low-fat types of mayonnaise, buttermilk, or sour cream.) We've also re-created a creamy seafood mousse in a calorie-conscious way and tossed the ingredients from the club sandwich into the salad bowl. And we tell you how to select greens and store them to keep their peak of flavor and freshness. So whether you want a salad that's a supporting player on the menu or one that makes the whole meal, try these delightful new versions of old favorites.

CHEF'S SALAD

◆◆◆

During the 1950's, many restaurant chefs began featuring their own salad creations, which were substantial enough to make a meal. These chef's salads, as they are still called, differ from day to day, but usually contain at least two meats, one cheese, and hard-cooked eggs.

10	cups bite-size mixed salad greens (such as iceberg, Bibb, Boston, curly leaf, endive, romaine)
1	large bunch watercress, rinsed and large stems removed (3 cups)
½	cup radish slices
½	medium-size cucumber, halved lengthwise and thinly sliced crosswise
2	green onions, with tops, finely chopped (4 tablespoons)
1	cup cooked corn kernels, drained
3	large carrots, peeled and grated (3 cups)
12	cherry tomatoes, halved
4	ounces Swiss cheese slices, cut into thin strips
4	ounces baked ham slices, cut into thin strips
8	ounces roasted turkey slices, cut into thin strips
2	large eggs, hard-cooked (page 363), peeled and thinly sliced
¾	cup Thousand Island Dressing (page 260)

PREP TIME: 45 MIN. / COOKING TIME: 15 MIN.

1 In a large salad bowl, toss together the salad greens, watercress, radishes, cucumber, and 2 tablespoons of the green onions. Sprinkle with the corn, then mound the carrots in the center and circle with the tomatoes.

2 Alternately arrange the cheese, ham, and turkey slices in a spoke design on top of the salad. Arrange the egg slices around the edge. Sprinkle with the remaining 2 tablespoons of green onions and serve with the Thousand Island Dressing. Makes 4 servings.

1 serving: Calories 437; Saturated Fat 8 g; Total Fat 16 g; Protein 39 g; Carbohydrate 42 g; Fiber 5 g; Sodium 850 mg; Cholesterol 196 mg

BAKED HAM SALAD

◆◆◆

Here's a great use for that leftover baked ham.

⅓	cup reduced-fat mayonnaise
3	tablespoons minced parsley
2	tablespoons minced yellow onion
2	tablespoons diced dill pickle
1	tablespoon sweet pickle relish
1	teaspoon yellow prepared mustard
¾	teaspoon fresh lemon juice
12	ounces cooked ham, diced (2 cups)

PREP TIME: 20 MIN.

1 In a large bowl, stir together the mayonnaise, parsley, onion, dill pickle, relish, mustard, and lemon juice. Stir in the ham. Serve with Beth's Buttermilk Biscuits (page 306). Makes 4 servings.

1 serving: Calories 153; Saturated Fat 2 g; Total Fat 6 g; Protein 18 g; Carbohydrate 6 g; Fiber 0 g; Sodium 1269 mg; Cholesterol 54 mg

◆

Rest-of-the-Roast Salad

Prepare as for Baked Ham Salad substituting **12 ounces cooked roast beef** for the ham and adding **1 tablespoon chili sauce** and **2 teaspoons prepared horseradish**. Makes 4 servings. *1 serving: Calories 169; Saturated Fat 3 g; Total Fat 7 g; Protein 20 g; Carbohydrate 6 g; Fiber 0 g; Sodium 354 mg; Cholesterol 67 mg*

Though it seems a simple thing to prepare, a fine salad is an art.

—from American Cookery
by James Beard

TEXAS STEAK SALAD

Texans like beefsteak. Often, they throw an extra one on the grill to make this salad the next day. It's perfect to tote to a picnic or potluck supper.

1½ teaspoons chili powder	Chicory leaves
1 teaspoon salt	½ teaspoon black pepper
¾ teaspoon dried thyme leaves	1 medium-size red onion, halved and thinly sliced (¾ cup)
½ teaspoon sugar	**For the dressing:**
2 pounds boneless beef sirloin steak, 1 inch thick, trimmed	½ cup red wine
	2 cloves garlic, minced
1 pound small new potatoes, cooked and halved	¼ cup plus 2 table-spoons balsamic or red wine vinegar
1 pound ripe tomatoes, cut into wedges (3 cups)	2 tablespoons olive oil
	1½ teaspoons dry mustard
8 ounces green beans, trimmed, cut into bite-size pieces and blanched (page 360) (about 2 cups)	½ teaspoon cornstarch
	1½ teaspoons cold water

PREP TIME: 30 MIN. / MARINATING TIME: 1 HR.
COOKING TIME: 30 MIN.

1 In a small bowl combine the chili powder, ½ teaspoon of the salt, the thyme, and sugar; rub into the steak, cover, and refrigerate for 1 hour. On a large platter, attractively arrange the potatoes, tomatoes, and green beans.

2 Preheat the grill or broiler. Grill the steak over medium-hot coals, or broil 4 inches from the heat, for about 5 minutes on each side for medium-rare, or until the steak is the way you like it. Let stand for 5 minutes, then slice diagonally across the grain, ¼ inch thick. Arrange the steak and chicory on the platter with the vegetables. Sprinkle with the remaining ½ teaspoon of salt and the pepper, then top with the onion.

3 While the steak is standing, prepare the dressing: In a medium-size saucepan, bring the wine and garlic to a boil over moderately high

Down-home vittles in the Lone Star State, featuring Texas Steak Salad

heat and boil for 3 minutes. Whisk in ¼ cup of the vinegar, the oil, and mustard; return to a boil. In a cup, dissolve the cornstarch in the cold water, add to the wine mixture, and boil for 2 minutes or until slightly thickened. Whisk in the remaining 2 tablespoons of vinegar and drizzle over the salad. Serve immediately or let stand at room teperature for 1 hour. This dish can be prepared ahead. Refrigerate, then let stand at room temperature for 1 hour before serving. Serve with Sally Lunn Bread (page 289). Makes 8 servings.

1 serving: Calories 295; Saturated Fat 3 g;
Total Fat 11 g; Protein 24 g; Carbohydrate 25 g; Fiber 1 g;
Sodium 332 mg; Cholesterol 64 mg

All-American Lunch: Club Salad, created from the makings of the club sandwich

Taco Salad

◆◆◆

This salad, based upon ingredients for the Mexican-American taco, is now a tradition throughout the Southwest.

1½ teaspoons olive oil

1 small yellow onion, finely chopped (½ cup)

1 pound lean ground beef round

1 package (1¼ ounces) taco seasoning mix

1½ cups chunky salsa

¾ cup cold water

1 can (10½ ounces) kidney beans, rinsed well and drained

4 green onions, chopped (½ cup)

6 cups shredded curly leaf or iceberg lettuce or romaine

2 large ripe tomatoes, cut into wedges (1 pound)

½ ripe avocado, peeled, seeded, and thinly sliced

2 cups unsalted baked taco chips (3 ounces)

½ to 1 cup shredded Monterey Jack cheese (2 to 4 ounces)

¼ cup sliced, pitted black olives

PREP TIME: 30 MIN. / COOKING TIME: 20 MIN.

1 In a 12-inch nonstick skillet, heat the oil over moderate heat. Add the onion and sauté for 5 minutes or until soft. Add the beef and cook, stirring, for 3 minutes or until no longer pink. Blend in the taco seasoning and cook 1 minute longer.

2 Add ½ cup of the salsa, the water, kidney beans, and ¼ cup of the green onions. Lower the heat and simmer, uncovered, for 10 minutes or until the mixture has thickened slightly and the flavors have blended.

3 Line 4 plates with the lettuce and arrange the tomatoes, avocado, and chips around the edges. Spoon the meat mixture in the center and top with the remaining salsa and green onions. Sprinkle with the cheese and garnish with the black olives if you wish. Makes 4 servings.

1 serving: Calories 519; Saturated Fat 9 g;
Total Fat 21 g; Protein 30 g; Carbohydrate 55 g; Fiber 4 g;
Sodium 774 mg; Cholesterol 68 mg

CLUB SALAD

◆◆◆

Take the ingredients of the All-American club sandwich, turn them into a salad, and you have a dish that's ideal for a summer's eve.

4	slices whole wheat or white bread, crusts cut off, quartered	2	slices lean bacon, cooked and coarsely crumbled
1¼	pounds boned and skinned chicken breasts, poached (page 363) and thinly sliced, or 2¾ cups sliced roast chicken	¼	teaspoon each salt and black pepper
		¾	cup Russian Dressing (page 260)
2	large ripe tomatoes, cut into wedges (1 pound)	6	cups bite-size mixed salad greens (such as iceberg, Bibb, Boston, curly leaf, romaine, watercress)

COOKING TIME: 20 MIN. / PREP TIME: 30 MIN.

1 Preheat the oven to 400°F. Place the bread on a baking sheet and bake, turning once, for 7 minutes or until crisp and lightly browned.

2 In a large bowl, combine the chicken, tomatoes, and bacon. Sprinkle with the salt and pepper. Spoon the dressing over all and toss. Place the greens on four dinner plates, spoon the salad mixture on top, and arrange 4 croutons along the edge of each plate. Makes 4 servings.

1 serving: Calories 376; Saturated Fat 2 g; Total Fat 12 g; Protein 37 g; Carbohydrate 34 g; Fiber 3 g; Sodium 807 mg; Cholesterol 85 mg

To make a good salad is to be a brilliant diplomat... the problem is how much oil one must mix with one's vinegar.

—*Oscar Wilde*

BROWN DERBY COBB SALAD

◆◆◆

In 1936, so the story goes, owner Robert Cobb of Hollywood's Brown Derby Restaurant prepared a salad for a late-night supper guest, long after the kitchen had closed. He began with a little of this and a little of that and ended up creating a tradition. We've updated the original dressing by lowering the fat.

½	large head iceberg lettuce	2	medium-sized ripe tomatoes, chopped (2 cups)
½	bunch watercress, large stems removed	1	large avocado, peeled, seeded, and diced
1	small bunch chicory	3	large hard-cooked eggs (page 363), peeled and chopped
½	large head romaine		
2	pounds boned and skinned chicken breasts, poached (page 363) and cut into bite-size pieces (5 cups)	2	tablespoons chopped chives or green onions, with tops
		½	cup finely crumbled Roquefort cheese
6	strips lean bacon, cooked and crumbled	1	cup Cobb Salad Dressing (page 262)

PREP TIME: 45 MIN. / COOKING TIME: 20 MIN.

1 Tear the lettuce, watercress, chicory, and romaine into bite-size pieces, place in a large salad bowl, and toss. Arrange the chicken, bacon, tomatoes, and avocado on top of the salad.

2 Sprinkle with the eggs, chives, and cheese. Refrigerate until serving time. Just before serving, drizzle the salad with the dressing. Makes 6 servings.

1 serving (for 6): Calories 456; Saturated Fat 9 g; Total Fat 34 g; Protein 27 g; Carbohydrate 11 g; Fiber 2 g; Sodium 455 mg; Cholesterol 172 mg

LADIES' LUNCHEON CHICKEN SALAD

◆◆◆

*Where women have gathered for fun,
fellowship or good causes, chicken salad has often
been on the menu. This one calls for poached
chicken breasts, but you can easily
substitute leftover baked chicken.*

2 pounds boned and skinned chicken breasts, trimmed	⅓ cup slivered almonds, toasted (page 365)
⅓ cup raspberry or white wine vinegar	½ pound red seedless grapes, cut in half (1½ cups)
½ cup reduced-calorie mayonnaise	2 stalks celery, thinly sliced on the diagonal (1 cup)
¼ cup reduced-fat sour cream	⅓ cup finely chopped red onion
½ teaspoon each salt and black pepper	

PREP TIME: 20 MIN. / COOKING TIME: 10 MIN.
CHILLING TIME: 3 HR.

1 Half-fill a deep 12-inch skillet with cold water and bring to a boil over high heat. Add the chicken, lower the heat, and simmer for 8 minutes or just until the chicken is cooked through; drain.

2 When cool enough to handle, cut into bite-size pieces and transfer to a medium-size bowl. Toss with the vinegar, cover, and refrigerate for 1 hour or until cold, stirring occasionally.

3 In a large bowl, stir together the mayonnaise, sour cream, salt, and pepper. Add the chicken with the remaining ingredients and toss. Chill for at least 2 hours. Serve with Vermont Cheddar Straws (page 23). Makes 6 servings.

*1 serving: Calories 287; Saturated Fat 2 g;
Total Fat 9 g; Protein 38 g; Carbohydrate 13 g; Fiber 1 g;
Sodium 392 mg; Cholesterol 107 mg*

◆ From the Farmers' Market ◆

It's 4 o'clock in the morning in Long Beach, California. Kachi Takahashi, her daughter, and their 22 farm workers are picking and packing wooden crates of lettuce and other produce for market. By 5 A.M., they're on their way to the famous Santa Monica Farmers' Market in their 10-ton truck with the Top Veg Farm sign on the door. Six days a week they travel, doing more than 15,000 miles a year, reaching thousands of customers.

"My mother and father began farming in Southern California in the 1930's," explains Kachi. "Today we are

best known for our lettuces, but also for a few other specialties, such as bitter melons and baby eggplants."

Kachi often advises her customers about ways to make great salads. "First, buy the freshest ingredients you can find; nothing should look wilted or bruised. Wash the

greens, spin or towel dry them thoroughly, then wrap them in a cotton or paper towel and store in the refrigerator, either in the vegetable bin or a plastic bag. They will keep this way for up to one week and will be crisp and ready to eat any time. Try to use a mixture of greens: a

basic like iceberg, green leaf lettuce, or romaine, plus perhaps a sweet butter lettuce, such as Boston or Bibb. The darker and more bitter the green is, the richer it is in vitamins and minerals and the better it is for you.

"Next, add a little of the unusual, such as the nutty flavor of red or green oak leaf lettuce, the bitter taste of endive or escarole, the spicy bite of arugula. Top with a few extras: radishes, purple or green cabbage, watercress, chives, onions, or sweet basil.

"And always dress greens lightly; too much dressing drowns out their flavor."

Salad Niçoise from southern France....bon appétit!

SALAD NIÇOISE

◆◆◆

From Nice comes a salad featuring tuna and other ingredients of the region. This Americanized version contains potatoes instead of the original fava beans.

1 pound red-skinned potatoes, scrubbed, cooked, and cut into bite-size pieces (2 cups)

8 ounces green beans, trimmed, cut into bite-size pieces, and blanched (page 360) (2 cups)

2 cups cherry tomato halves

1 can (12 ¼ ounces) albacore white-meat tuna packed in water, drained and flaked (2 cups)

1 cup sweet yellow pepper strips

8 cups packed bite-size romaine lettuce leaves

¾ cup Roasted Tomato Vinaigrette (page 263)

2 large eggs, hard-cooked (page 363), peeled, and quartered

12 black olives, preferably salt-cured
Fresh basil leaves (optional)

PREP TIME: 30 MIN. / COOKING TIME: 25 MIN.

1 In a large bowl, gently toss together the pota-toes, green beans, tomatoes, tuna, and yellow pepper. Line a serving platter with the lettuce leaves and mound the potato-tuna mixture in the center. Drizzle with the dressing and garnish with the eggs, olives, and basil if you wish. Serve with slices of Country Loaf (page 288). Makes 4 servings.

*1 serving: Calories 364; Saturated Fat 2 g;
Total Fat 8 g; Protein 33 g; Carbohydrate 44 g; Fiber 3 g;
Sodium 604 mg; Cholesterol 143 mg*

TUNA SALAD

◆◆◆

Versatile canned tuna is a favorite in all corners of this country and nearly everyone has a favorite recipe for tuna salad. We like this one especially. Try it on a bun, pita bread, or mound of lettuce.

⅓ cup reduced-calorie mayonnaise

1½ tablespoons fresh lemon juice

3 tablespoons diced, peeled, and seeded cucumber

3 tablespoons chopped red onion

2 tablespoons each thinly sliced green onion, chopped celery, and chopped fresh dill

¼ teaspoon each salt and black pepper

1 can (12¼ ounces) light-meat tuna packed in water, drained and flaked

PREP TIME: 25 MIN.

1 In a large bowl, stir together the mayonnaise, lemon juice, cucumber, red and green onions, celery, dill, salt, and pepper. Add the tuna and toss to coat. Serve with slices of Rustic Whole-Wheat Round (page 289). Makes 4 servings.

*1 serving: Calories 147; Saturated Fat 1 g;
Total Fat 3 g; Protein 24 g; Carbohydrate 5 g; Fiber 0 g;
Sodium 579 mg; Cholesterol 45 mg*

Dressed up for company: A spectacular Seafood Mousse that's simple to prepare

SEAFOOD MOUSSE

◆◆◆

Add cream to a gelatin-based salad and you have a light yet richly flavored mousse. The one here is filled with delectable crab meat and shrimp.

2 tablespoons cold water

1 envelope unflavored gelatin (2 teaspoons)

1½ cups cooked fresh or canned lump crab meat

1 can (10¾ ounces) condensed cream of mushroom soup, undiluted

1 cup Neufchâtel cream cheese (8 ounces)

1 cup cooked shrimp, coarsely chopped

½ cup each finely chopped celery and sweet green pepper

3 tablespoons chopped fresh dill or 2 teaspoons dried dill weed

½ cup reduced-calorie mayonnaise

¼ cup reduced-fat sour cream

¼ cup chopped green onions, with tops

1 tablespoon fresh lemon juice

¼ teaspoon black pepper

Garnishes:

Very thin cucumber slices

Tiny cherry tomatoes, stemmed

🕙 PREP TIME: 35 MIN. / COOKING TIME: 10 MIN.
CHILLING TIME: 3 HR.

1 Lightly oil a 1½-quart fish-shaped or other decorative mold. Into a small cup, pour the cold water and stir in the gelatin. Pick through the crab meat, rinse, drain, and flake.

2 In a large saucepan, heat the soup over low heat until hot. Remove from the heat, add the gelatin mixture, and stir until dissolved.

3 Fold in the remaining ingredients and spoon into the mold. Cover with plastic wrap and refrigerate for 3 hours or until set. Unmold (page 365) onto a platter. Surround with the cucumber slices and cherry tomatoes and garnish the seafood mold in any way you wish. Serve with an assortment of crackers. Makes 6 main-dish servings or 12 appetizer servings.

1 appetizer serving: Calories 115; Saturated Fat 4 g; Total Fat 7 g; Protein 9 g; Carbohydrate 4 g; Fiber 0 g; Sodium 355 mg; Cholesterol 59 mg

PALACE COURT SALAD

Originally, this salad was made in the Garden Court of the Palace Hotel in San Francisco with fresh crab meat. But any freshly cooked seafood works well; choose the best catch of the day.

1 package (10 ounces) frozen artichoke hearts	4 cups shredded iceberg lettuce
1½ pounds mixed cooked seafood (crab, lobster, scallops, shrimp)	2 large hard-cooked eggs (page 363), peeled and finely chopped
2 stalks celery, finely chopped (1 cup)	½ teaspoon black pepper
1 tablespoon minced red onion	2 tablespoons chopped chives
⅓ cup thin radish slices	2 large tomatoes, sliced
⅓ cup reduced-calorie mayonnaise	½ cup Green Goddess Dressing (page 261)

PREP TIME: 30 MIN. / COOKING TIME: 20 MIN.

1 Cook the artichoke hearts according to the package directions. Rinse with cold water and drain. In a large bowl, mix the seafood with the celery, onion, and radishes. Stir in the mayonnaise until the mixture is lightly coated.

2 Line a serving platter with the shredded lettuce and mound the seafood mixture in the center. Sprinkle with the chopped egg, then the pepper and chives.

3 Surround the seafood with the tomato slices and arrange the artichoke hearts on top of the tomatoes. Serve immediately with the dressing and thick slices of freshly baked San Francisco Sourdough (page 290). Makes 4 servings.

1 serving: Calories 267; Saturated Fat 3 g; Total Fat 8 g; Protein 30 g; Carbohydrate 22 g; Fiber 2 g; Sodium 752 mg; Cholesterol 236 mg

SEAFOOD LOUIS

This recipe is based on the popular West Coast salad of Crab Louis. We've made ours with less fat, but it has just as much great flavor.

For the dressing:	1½ pounds mixed cooked seafood (crab, lobster, scallops, shrimp)
¾ cup reduced-calorie mayonnaise	
⅓ cup reduced-fat sour cream	2 stalks celery, finely chopped (1 cup)
¼ cup bottled chili sauce	1 small sweet red pepper, roasted (page 360), cored, seeded, and cut into thin strips
¼ cup chopped green onions, with tops	
1 tablespoon fresh lemon juice	2 large hard-cooked eggs (page 363), peeled, 1 chopped and 1 quartered
¼ teaspoon each salt and black pepper	
For the salad:	6 large pimiento stuffed olives, sliced (optional)
10 cups bite-size mixed greens (such as iceberg, Bibb, Boston, curly leaf, endive, romaine, watercress)	¼ cup minced parsley

PREP TIME: 30 MIN. / COOKING TIME: 15 MIN.

1 To prepare the dressing: In the bowl of a food processor or blender, place all of the ingredients. Process until smooth.

2 To prepare the salad: Line a large serving plate with the greens. In a medium-size bowl, toss the seafood, celery, red pepper, and chopped egg. Add the dressing and coat well, then mound on top of the greens. Garnish with the olives if you wish, plus the egg quarters and the parsley. Serve with Cheesy Penny Wafers (page 23). Makes 4 servings.

1 serving: Calories 336; Saturated Fat 3 g; Total Fat 9 g; Protein 36 g; Carbohydrate 33 g; Fiber 4 g; Sodium 1187 mg; Cholesterol 246 mg

JAMBALAYA SALAD
◆◆◆

All the fixings for the Cajun dish of Jambalaya go into making this cold rice salad. It's an ideal supper dish for summer entertaining.

2 tablespoons olive oil	4 cups cooked long-grain white rice, drained
12 ounces baked ham, cut into bite-size pieces (2 cups)	2 stalks celery, thinly sliced (1 cup)
⅓ cup chopped yellow onion	½ cup each sweet red and green peppers strips
2 cloves garlic, minced	1½ pounds medium-size shrimp (about 40), peeled, deveined, tails removed (page 362), and cooked
1 teaspoon each dried oregano and thyme leaves	
½ teaspoon ground red pepper (cayenne)	
¼ teaspoon black pepper	2 green onions, with tops, sliced (¼ cup)
⅓ cup red wine vinegar	1 pint cherry tomatoes, stemmed and halved

PREP TIME: 35 MIN. / COOKING TIME: 25 MIN.
CHILLING TIME: 2 HR.

1 In a 12-inch nonstick skillet, heat the oil over moderate heat. Stir in the ham, onion, garlic, oregano, thyme, and the ground red and black peppers; sauté for 5 minutes or until the onion is tender. Stir in the vinegar, remove from the heat, and cool for 5 minutes.

2 In a large bowl, toss the rice with the celery, sweet peppers, and vinegar mixture. Stir in the shrimp, cover with plastic wrap, and refrigerate for at least 2 hours.

3 To serve, mound the salad in the center of a platter and sprinkle with the green onions. Surround with the cherry tomatoes. Serve with Corn Pone (page 301). Makes 6 servings.

1 serving: Calories 417; Saturated Fat 2 g; Total Fat 10 g; Protein 34 g; Carbohydrate 46 g; Fiber 1 g; Sodium 955 mg; Cholesterol 161 mg

GARDEN MACARONI SALAD
◆◆◆

8 ounces uncooked elbow macaroni	¾ cup grated carrots
¾ cup reduced-calorie mayonnaise	½ cup each chopped celery, sweet red pepper, sweet green pepper, and red onion
¼ cup plain low-fat yogurt	
¼ cup minced parsley	3 tablespoons pickle relish
3 tablespoons fresh lemon juice	6 slices lean bacon, cooked and crumbled or 1 cup chopped baked ham (optional)
1 tablespoon Dijon mustard	
¾ teaspoon each salt and black pepper, or to taste	

PREP TIME: 30 MIN. / COOKING TIME: 10 MIN.
CHILLING TIME: 2 HR.

1 Bring a large saucepan of unsalted water to a boil, add the macaroni, and cook for 8 minutes or just until tender. Drain, rinse with cold water, and drain again.

2 Meanwhile, in a large bowl, whisk together the mayonnaise, yogurt, parsley, lemon juice, mustard, salt, and pepper. Fold in the macaroni and the remaining ingredients until well coated. Cover and refrigerate for at least 2 hours. Serve with Denver Barbecued Chicken (page 119). Makes 8 servings.

1 serving: Calories 196; Saturated Fat 0 g; Total Fat 7 g; Protein 5 g; Carbohydrate 29 g; Fiber 1 g; Sodium 312 mg; Cholesterol 8 mg

He that sups upon salad, goes not to be fasting.

— *Thomas Fuller*

WILTED CUKES

◆◆◆

In the Midwest, especially in Dutch and German communities, this way of smothering cucumbers in vinegar and sour cream has been handed down for generations. We've added the crunch of fresh radishes.

4 large cucumbers (2 pounds)
1 cup thinly sliced red onion
¾ cup cider vinegar
1 teaspoon salt
½ cup reduced-fat sour cream

2 tablespoons chopped fresh dill or 2 teaspoons dried dill weed
2 tablespoons sugar
¼ teaspoon black pepper
8 thinly sliced radishes

PREP TIME: 20 MIN. / STANDING TIME: 2½ HR.

1 Peel the cucumbers lengthwise, leaving thin strips of the skin. Halve the cucumbers lengthwise and remove the seeds with a spoon. Cut the cucumbers crosswise into thin slices. In a large bowl, mix the cucumber slices, onion, vinegar, and ¾ teaspoon of the salt. Cover and let stand at room temperature for 30 minutes, then drain.

2 Fold in the sour cream, dill, sugar, the remaining ¼ teaspoon of salt, and the pepper. Cover and refrigerate for 2 hours, preferably overnight. Stir in the radishes and serve with Smorgasbord Meatballs (page 103). Makes 6 servings.

1 serving: Calories 60; Saturated Fat 1 g; Total Fat 2 g; Protein 2 g; Carbohydrate 13 g; Fiber 1 g; Sodium 396 mg; Cholesterol 4 mg

A traditional treat from our European ancestors: Cucumbers, plus radishes too, in peppery sour cream

FRESH FRUIT SALAD WITH POPPY SEED DRESSING

Throughout the South, a favorite way to serve fresh fruits of the season is with a lacing of poppy seed dressing. This dish makes a spectacular presentation on a buffet.

1   each large grapefruit and orange, peeled and sectioned

1   Red Delicious or Granny Smith apple, unpeeled, cored and thinly sliced

1   small cantaloupe or honeydew melon, seeded and scooped into balls

2   medium-size peaches, nectarines, or plums, pitted and sliced

2   cups mixed fresh berries such as raspberries, strawberries, and blueberries, washed and hulled

1   cup seedless red or green grapes

1   small pineapple, peeled, cored, and cut into wedges

1   kiwi, peeled and sliced crosswise

1   cup Poppy Seed Dressing (page 263)

PREP TIME: 45 MIN.

1 In a large bowl or on a large platter (preferably a glass one), arrange all of the fruits in an attractive design. Drizzle the dressing over the top. Serve with hot Portland Popovers (page 310). Makes 8 side-dish or 4 main-dish servings.

1 serving (for 8): Calories 151; Saturated Fat 0 g; Total Fat 3 g; Protein 2 g; Carbohydrate 34 g; Fiber 2 g; Sodium 73 mg; Cholesterol 0 mg

Treasures from the fresh fruit stand—ready for tossing with Poppy Seed Dressing (page 263)

Four persons are wanted to make a
good salad: a spendthrift for oil, a miser for vinegar, a counsellor
for salt, and a madman to stir it all up.

—Old Spanish Proverb

FROZEN FRUIT SALAD

❖❖❖

In the 1940's and 1950's, rich frozen fruit salads made with whipped cream and cream cheese were frequently served with dinner or even for dessert. We have recreated this old favorite, but with less fat.

3 medium-size peaches, peeled, pitted, and coarsely chopped (1½ cups)	⅔ cup low-fat plain yogurt (not nonfat)
4 large plums, peeled, pitted, and coarsely chopped (1⅓ cups)	¼ cup reduced-fat sour cream
	3 tablespoons Neufchâtel cream cheese
⅔ cup pitted Bing cherry halves	1 tablespoon superfine sugar
⅔ cup drained canned unsweetened pineapple chunks	Curly leaf lettuce

PREP TIME: 20 MIN. / FREEZING TIME: 3 HR.
STANDING TIME: 15 MIN.

1 Set out an 8-inch square baking pan or freezer-safe dish. In a large bowl, toss together the peaches, plums, cherries, and pineapple.

2 In a small bowl, whisk the yogurt, sour cream, cream cheese, and sugar until smooth. Gently fold into the fruit mixture, then spoon into the pan. Cover with plastic wrap and freeze for about 3 hours or until set.

3 Remove from the freezer 15 minutes before serving. Cut into six equal portions, lift out with a spatula, and arrange on lettuce leaves. Serve with Chicken with Sage-Onion Stuffing (page 119). Makes 6 servings.

*1 serving: Calories 102; Saturated Fat 2 g;
Total Fat 3 g; Protein 3 g; Carbohydrate 17 g; Fiber 1 g;
Sodium 64 mg; Cholesterol 9 mg*

WALDORF SALAD

❖❖❖

Maitre d' Hotel Oscar Tschirky of the Waldorf Astoria Hotel in New York City created this salad in 1896. Nearly three decades later, in February 1924, it was featured at a dinner held there for President Coolidge. The original version had no walnuts, but they are a standard ingredient today.

¼ cup reduced-calorie mayonnaise	4 cups bite-size mixed salad greens (bibb, Boston, curly leaf lettuce, romaine)
¼ cup reduced-fat sour cream	
¼ cup low-fat (1% milkfat) milk	4 stalks celery, chopped (2 cups)
6 tablespoons fresh lemon juice	½ cup chopped walnuts, lightly toasted
½ teaspoon black pepper	
3 large Red Delicious apples, unpeeled	

PREP TIME: 25 MIN.

1 In a small bowl, whisk together the mayonnaise, sour cream, milk, 3 tablespoons of the lemon juice, and the pepper until combined.

2 Cut the apples into quarters, then core and slice them lengthwise ⅛ inch thick. Place in a medium-size bowl and toss with the remaining 3 tablespoons of lemon juice.

3 Line a platter with the salad greens. Arrange the apples, celery, and walnuts on top, drizzling the dressing over them as you go. Serve as a first course. Makes 4 servings.

*1 serving: Calories 325; Saturated Fat 3 g;
Total Fat 20 g; Protein 9 g; Carbohydrate 36 g; Fiber 4 g;
Sodium 200 mg; Cholesterol 10 mg*

THREE BEAN SALAD

◆◆◆

In the 1940's and 1950's, this salad was a favorite at picnics and church suppers. It not only travels well but also becomes more flavorful as it stands.

- 8 ounces green beans, trimmed and cut into 2-inch lengths
- 8 ounces wax beans, trimmed and cut into 2-inch lengths
- 3 tablespoons cider vinegar
- 1 tablespoon olive oil
- 1 tablespoon Dijon mustard
- 1 clove garlic, minced

- ½ teaspoon sugar
- ½ teaspoon dried oregano leaves
- ¼ teaspoon each salt and black pepper
- 1 can (16 ounces) red kidney beans, rinsed and drained
- 1 small sweet red pepper, chopped (½ cup)
- ¼ cup each diced celery and red onion

PREP TIME: 30 MIN. / COOKING TIME: 10 MIN.
CHILLING TIME: 1 HR.

1 Half-fill a large saucepan with water and bring to a boil over high heat. Add the green and wax beans and cook for 7 to 10 minutes or until tender. Drain and rinse with cold water until cooled, then pat dry with paper towels.

2 In a large bowl, whisk the vinegar, oil, mustard, garlic, sugar, oregano, salt, and black pepper. Add all 3 kinds of beans and remaining ingredients and mix well. Cover and refrigerate for at least 1 hour or until chilled and the flavors have blended. To tote, place in self sealing plastic containers or bags. Makes 8 servings.

1 serving: Calories 95; Saturated Fat 0 g;
Total Fat 2 g; Protein 5 g; Carbohydrate 16 g; Fiber 1 g;
Sodium 301 mg; Cholesterol 0 mg

Picnic Perfect: Three Bean Salad and Iowa Corn Salad, plus a loaf of French bread and assorted cheeses

PRAYER MEETING COLESLAW

◆◆◆

Cabbage salads were probably brought to America by Pennsylvania Dutch settlers in the late 18th-century.

1 cup low-fat buttermilk	1½ teaspoons celery seeds
⅓ cup reduced-fat sour cream	½ teaspoon salt
¼ cup reduced-calorie mayonnaise	⅛ teaspoon hot red pepper sauce
3 tablespoons cider vinegar	1 small green cabbage, shredded (4 cups)
2 teaspoons sugar	3 large carrots, peeled and shredded (1½ cups)
2 teaspoons whole grain mustard	1 small yellow onion, chopped (½ cup)

PREP TIME: 20 MIN. / CHILLING TIME: 2 HR.

1 In a large bowl, whisk together the buttermilk, sour cream, mayonnaise, vinegar, sugar, mustard, celery seeds, salt, and red pepper sauce. Add the cabbage, carrots and onion; toss to combine. Cover and refrigerate for 2 hours or overnight, to allow the flavors to blend. Serve with Country Style Ribs (page 85). Makes 6 servings.

1 side-dish serving: Calories 83; Saturated Fat 1 g; Total Fat 2 g; Protein 4 g; Carbohydrate 14 g; Fiber 1 g; Sodium 314 mg; Cholesterol 8 mg

IOWA CORN SALAD

◆◆◆

3 tablespoons reduced-calorie mayonnaise	3 cups fresh or frozen corn kernels
1½ tablespoons cider vinegar	1 medium-size tomato, coarsely chopped (1 cup)
1½ tablespoons cold water	⅔ cup thinly sliced green onions
1 teaspoon sugar	¾ cup chopped sweet green pepper
½ teaspoon each salt and black pepper	½ cup chopped sweet red pepper

PREP TIME: 25 MIN. / COOKING TIME: 5 MIN.

1 In a large bowl, whisk together the mayonnaise, vinegar, water, sugar, salt, and pepper. Half-fill a large saucepan with water and bring to a boil over high heat. Add the corn and cook for 2 minutes or just until crisp-tender. Drain, rinse with cold water, and drain again, then add to the mayonnaise mixture.

2 Stir in the remaining ingredients and mix well. Serve at room temperature or cold. Keeps refrigerated for up to 3 days. Serve with Honey Baked Ham (page 108). Makes 4 servings.

1 serving: Calories 129; Saturated Fat 0 g; Total Fat 1 g; Protein 5 g; Carbohydrate 31 g; Fiber 1 g; Sodium 333 mg; Cholesterol 5 mg

CARROT RAISIN SLAW

◆◆◆

Slaws usually begin with cabbage, but not this one. It starts with grated carrots instead. Traditionally, this salad contained only carrots and raisins, but we've added fresh apples, too.

3 tablespoons fresh lemon juice	⅛ teaspoon black pepper
3 tablespoons reduced-calorie mayonnaise	6 large carrots, peeled and shredded (3 cups)
3 tablespoons reduced-fat sour cream	1 large Granny Smith apple, peeled, cored, and diced (1 cup)
¼ teaspoon each sugar and salt	⅓ cup dark raisins

PREP TIME: 20 MIN.

1 In a large bowl, whisk together the lemon juice, mayonnaise, sour cream, sugar, salt, and pepper. Add the carrots, apple, and raisins and toss well to combine. Makes 4 servings.

1 serving: Calories 118; Saturated Fat 1 g; Total Fat 2 g; Protein 2 g; Carbohydrate 27 g; Fiber 1 g; Sodium 240 mg; Cholesterol 7 mg

COPPER PENNY SALAD

◆◆◆

In the 1950's, this carrot salad appeared at many church suppers and picnics. Our recipe comes from fashion consultant Renée Nahas of Culver City, California. "Because it's made the day before, this salad is one of my favorites for entertaining."

10	large carrots, peeled and sliced crosswise ½ inch thick (5 cups)
1	can (10¾ ounces) condensed tomato soup, undiluted
1	cup sugar
¾	cup red wine vinegar
¼	cup olive oil or vegetable oil
1	large sweet green pepper, chopped (1 cup)
1	medium-size yellow onion, chopped (1 cup)
1	teaspoon Worcestershire sauce
1	teaspoon Dijon mustard

PREP TIME: 20 MIN. / COOKING TIME: 8 MIN.
MARINATING TIME: OVERNIGHT

1 Half-fill a medium-size saucepan with water and bring to a boil over high heat. Add the carrots, lower the heat, and simmer for 5 minutes or just until crisp-tender.

2 Drain, rinse with cold water, and drain again. Transfer to a large bowl and stir in the remaining ingredients. Cover and refrigerate overnight, stirring 2 or 3 times. (This salad keeps for up to 7 days in the refrigerator.) Serve with Lamb Chops with Mint (page 112). Makes 8 servings.

1 serving: Calories 228; Saturated Fat 1 g; Total Fat 8 g; Protein 2 g; Carbohydrate 42 g; Fiber 1 g; Sodium 319 mg; Cholesterol 0 mg

---

DOWN HOME TRADITION

Our country's birthday on the 4th of July is traditionally celebrated with parades, American flags waving in the breeze, fireworks exploding in summery skies, and picnics under cool shade trees. Of course, the picnic has almost always included potato salad, often this creamy old-time version.

◆ Fourth of July Potato Salad ◆

3 pounds all-purpose potatoes, peeled, cooked, and cut into bite-size pieces (9 cups)

⅓ cup apple cider vinegar

2 teaspoons sugar

1½ teaspoons each dry mustard and salt

¾ teaspoon black pepper

½ cup each mayonnaise and sour cream

¼ cup heavy cream

¾ cup chopped yellow onion

½ cup chopped celery

¼ cup minced parsley

3 hard-cooked eggs (page 363), peeled and coarsely chopped

8 slices bacon, cooked and crumbled

PREP TIME: 30 MIN. / COOKING TIME: 20 MIN.
MARINATING TIME: 30 MIN.

1 While the potatoes cook, in a large bowl, whisk together the vinegar, sugar, mustard, salt, and pepper. Stir in the potatoes, and let marinate for 30 minutes to absorb the flavors.

2 In a small bowl, whisk the mayonnaise, sour cream, and heavy cream. Fold into the potato mixture along with the remaining ingredients. Cover and chill before serving if you wish. (This salad keeps for up to 3 days in the refrigerator.) Serve with Arkansas Slabs of Ribs (page 83). Makes 8 servings.

1 serving: Calories 403; Saturated Fat 7 g; Total Fat 22 g; Protein 9 g; Carbohydrate 45 g; Fiber 1 g; Sodium 633 mg; Cholesterol 110 mg

Lunchtime on the bike trail on the Fourth of July: Time for Picnic Potato Salad

PICNIC POTATO SALAD

◆◆◆

Here is a perfect potato salad to pack for a picnic today. It's light in calories and can be toted in the picnic basket without chilling.

1½ pounds small red-skinned new potatoes, halved, cooked, and cooled (4½ cups)

3 slices lean bacon

1 teaspoon olive oil

¼ cup Chicken Stock (page 74) or low-sodium chicken broth

3 tablespoons white wine vinegar or apple cider vinegar

2 teaspoons whole-grain Dijon mustard

½ teaspoon salt

¼ teaspoon black pepper

⅓ cup thinly sliced green onions

¼ cup finely chopped sweet green pepper

¼ cup finely chopped sweet red pepper

¼ cup minced parsley

PREP TIME: 30 MIN. / COOKING TIME: 15 MIN.

1 While the potatoes cook, in an 8-inch skillet, cook the bacon over moderately high heat for 5 minutes or until crisp. Using a slotted spoon, transfer to paper towels to drain, then crumble.

2 Measure 2 teaspoons of the bacon drippings into a small bowl; discard any remaining drippings. Whisk in the oil until combined, then the stock, vinegar, mustard, salt, and black pepper. Add the potatoes, onions and the sweet green and red peppers; toss gently to coat. Garnish with the bacon and parsley. Serve at room temperature with fresh fruit and sandwiches stuffed with Honey Baked Ham (page 108). Makes 4 servings.

1 serving: Calories 199; Saturated Fat 1 g; Total Fat 2 g; Protein 5 g; Carbohydrate 41 g; Fiber 1 g; Sodium 374 mg; Cholesterol 2 mg

CHOPPED TOMATO SALAD

◆◆◆

- 4 large vine-ripened tomatoes (2 pounds), cut into 1-inch cubes (6 cups)
- 1 large, unpeeled cucumber, chopped (1½ cups)
- 1 cup each chopped red onion and sweet green pepper
- ⅓ cup minced fresh basil or parsley

For the dressing:
- ⅓ cup apple cider vinegar
- 1 tablespoon olive oil
- 2 cloves garlic, minced
- ½ teaspoon each salt, black pepper, and sugar

PREP TIME: 25 MIN. / CHILLING TIME: 1 HR.

1 In a large salad bowl, toss the tomatoes with the cucumber, onion, green pepper, and basil. In a small cup, whisk together all of the dressing ingredients, pour over the salad, and toss to combine. Cover with plastic wrap and refrigerate for at least 1 hour. (This salad keeps for up to 3 days in the refrigerator.) Makes 6 servings.

1 serving: Calories 58; Saturated Fat 0 g; Total Fat 3 g; Protein 1 g; Carbohydrate 9 g; Fiber 1 g; Sodium 188 mg; Cholesterol 0 mg

SUNSHINE SALAD

◆◆◆

In the 1940's and 1950's, molded gelatin salads made their grand appearances on buffet party tables throughout America. This bright one gets its name from the yellow- and orange-colored ingredients.

- 3 packages (3 ounces each) lemon-flavored gelatin mix
- 1½ cups boiling water
- 4½ cups iced cold water
- ½ teaspoon salt
  Nonstick cooking spray
- 3 large carrots, peeled and grated (1½ cups)
- 1 cup finely shredded green cabbage
- ⅓ cup each chopped sweet green, red, and yellow pepper
- 1 can (8¼ ounces) crushed pineapple, drained
- 2 tablespoons finely chopped fresh mint, or 2 teaspoons dried mint leaves
  Sprigs of chicory and fresh mint for garnish

Spectacular to look at, yet simple to make—a glorious Sunshine Salad

PREP TIME: 25 MIN. / CHILLING TIME: 5½ HR.

1 In a large bowl, dissolve the gelatin in the boiling water. Stir in the cold water and salt. Cover with plastic wrap and refrigerate for 2½ hours or until thickened but not solid, or until a spoon leaves an impression when drawn through it.

2 Spray a 3-quart mold with the cooking spray. Fold the remaining ingredients into the gelatin; spoon into the mold. Cover and chill about 2½ hours longer or until firm. About 30 minutes before serving time, unmold onto a serving platter (page 365) and garnish with chicory and fresh mint sprigs. Refrigerate until serving time. Makes 8 servings.

1 serving: Calories 141; Saturated Fat 0 g; Total Fat 0 g; Protein 28 g; Carbohydrate 7 g; Fiber 1 g; Sodium 185 mg; Cholesterol 0 mg

CAESAR SALAD

Created in 1924 at Caesar's Place in Tijuana, Mexico, this salad soon became a favorite. Today, it's popular in every corner of America. Because of salmonella concerns, our version has cooked egg instead of the traditional raw.

2 cups Oven-baked Garlic Croutons (page 361)	2 cloves garlic, roasted (page 360)
1 large egg	½ teaspoon each salt and black pepper
2 tablespoons each fresh lemon juice and olive oil	¼ teaspoon dry mustard
1 teaspoon Worcestershire sauce	16 cups washed and coarsely chopped romaine lettuce
	½ cup freshly grated Parmesan cheese

PREP TIME: 30 MIN. / COOKING TIME: 8 MIN.

1 Prepare the croutons. While they are baking, half-fill a small saucepan with water and bring to a simmer over moderate heat. Slide in the egg and cook for 5 minutes. Using a slotted spoon, plunge the egg into cold water; when cool enough to handle, peel it.

2 In a food processor or blender, purée the egg, lemon juice, oil, Worcestershire, garlic, salt, pepper, and mustard for 1 minute or until smooth.

3 In a large salad bowl, toss together the lettuce, croutons, and Parmesan. Pour over the dressing and toss to coat thoroughly. Serve immediately, while still crisp. Makes 4 servings.

1 serving: Calories 301; Saturated Fat 6 g; Total Fat 20 g; Protein 13 g; Carbohydrate 19 g; Fiber 2 g; Sodium 665 mg; Cholesterol 63 mg

WARM SPINACH-BACON SALAD

1 cup Oven-baked Pepper Croutons (page 361)	1 clove garlic, minced
1½ pounds fresh spinach	⅓ cup apple cider vinegar
6 ounces mushrooms, sliced (2¼ cups)	¼ cup dry white wine or fresh lemon juice
For the dressing:	2 teaspoons whole-grain Dijon mustard
4 slices lean bacon	1 teaspoon honey
1 cup chopped red onion	½ teaspoon black pepper

PREP TIME: 30 MIN. / COOKING TIME: 13 MIN.

1 Prepare the croutons. While they are baking, wash the spinach well, spin it dry, and discard the stems. Tear the spinach into bite-size pieces (you should have about 9 cups); toss with the mushrooms in a large salad bowl.

2 To make the dressing: In an 8-inch skillet, cook the bacon over moderately high heat for 5 minutes or until crisp. Using a slotted spoon, transfer to paper towels to drain, then crumble. Discard all but 2 tablespoons of the bacon drippings from the skillet.

3 Add the onion and garlic to the skillet and sauté for 5 minutes or until tender. Stir in the remaining dressing ingredients, bring just to a simmer, and cook for 1 minute.

4 Pour the dressing over the spinach, sprinkle in the croutons and toss thoroughly, just until the salad begins to wilt. Top with the bacon and serve immediately. Makes 4 servings.

1 serving: Calories 171; Saturated Fat 2 g; Total Fat 7 g; Protein 9 g; Carbohydrate 21 g; Fiber 2 g; Sodium 335 mg; Cholesterol 4 mg

To make a salad, one must have a spark of genius.

—*Author Unknown*

Ten layers of vegetables, all dressed up for a party

TOMATO ASPIC

◆◆◆

Because it complements many dishes, this gelled salad has been an American favorite throughout the 20th century. When preparing it for guests, use your prettiest mold.

2 tablespoons cold water

2 envelopes (¼ ounce each) unflavored gelatin

2½ cups tomato juice

1 can (14 ounces) plum tomatoes, seeded and finely chopped, juice reserved

½ cup finely chopped celery

½ cup finely chopped sweet green pepper

¼ cup finely chopped red onion

¼ cup apple cider vinegar

2 tablespoons finely chopped fresh basil or 2 teaspoons dried basil leaves

2 tablespoons sugar

½ teaspoon each salt and black pepper

1 recipe Farmhouse Horseradish Cream (page 261)

PREP TIME: 30 MIN. / COOKING TIME: 5 MIN.
CHILLING TIME: 4 HR.

1 Oil a 2-quart ring or other decorative mold. Put the water in a medium-size saucepan, sprinkle the gelatin on top, and stir in ½ cup of the tomato juice. Cook over moderate heat for about 5 minutes, or until the gelatin is thoroughly dissolved and remove from the heat.

2 Stir in the remaining 2 cups of tomato juice, the tomatoes and their juices, celery, green pepper, onion, vinegar, basil, sugar, salt, and black pepper. Pour into the mold.

3 Cover the mold and refrigerate for 4 hours or until set. Unmold onto a serving platter (page 365) and serve with Farmhouse Horseradish Cream (page 261). Makes 8 servings.

1 serving: Calories 50; Saturated Fat 0 g; Total Fat 1 g; Protein 3 g; Carbohydrate 10 g; Fiber 1 g; Sodium 510 mg; Cholesterol 1 mg

10-LAYER VEGETABLE SALAD

◆◆◆

1 pound, unpeeled red-skinned potatoes, cut into ¾-inch cubes (3 cups)

10 ounces green beans, trimmed and cut into 1½-inch pieces (2 cups)

1 package (10 ounces) frozen corn kernels (2 cups)

1 package (10 ounces) frozen peas (2 cups)

4 large carrots, peeled and thinly sliced (2 cups)

6 cups shredded Romaine lettuce

1 large sweet red pepper, cored, seeded, and thinly sliced (1 cup)

3 stalks celery, thinly sliced (1½ cups)

1 pint cherry tomatoes, halved (2 cups)

1 cup sliced green onions, with tops

1½ cups shredded sharp Cheddar cheese (6 ounces)(optional)

4 slices lean bacon, cooked and crumbled

For the dressing:

2 cups reduced-calorie mayonnaise

¼ cup each finely chopped fresh basil and parsley

2 tablespoons chopped chives or green onions

1 tablespoon chopped fresh dill or 1 teaspoon dried dill weed

1 tablespoon fresh lemon juice

¼ teaspoon black pepper

PREP TIME: 1 HR. / COOKING TIME: 20 MIN.
CHILLING TIME: 2 HR.

1 Half-fill a large saucepan with cold water and bring to a boil over high heat. Add the potatoes and cook for 10 minutes or until tender. Using a slotted spoon, transfer to a strainer, rinse with very cold water, drain, and place on a plate.

2 In the same saucepan, by the same method, cook the green beans, for 4 to 5 minutes, the corn for 1 minute, then the peas and the carrots for 30 seconds each. After cooking each vegetable, transfer to a separate plate and pat dry with paper towels.

3 In a clean 6-quart glass serving bowl, preferably with straight sides, layer the vegetables in the following order: lettuce, potatoes, red pepper, corn, green beans, carrots, celery, tomatoes, green onions, and peas.

4 To prepare the dressing: In a small bowl, stir together all of the dressing ingredients until well blended. Carefully spread over the salad and sprinkle with the cheese, if you wish. Cover and refrigerate for at least 2 hours. Before serving, garnish with the bacon. Makes 12 servings.

1 serving: Calories 219; Saturated Fat 5 g; Total Fat 8 g; Protein 9 g; Carbohydrate 30 g; Fiber 2 g; Sodium 345 mg; Cholesterol 34 mg

GAZPACHO SALAD

◆◆◆

In The Virginia Housewife *(1824), Mary Randolph offered the 19th-century American homemaker her recipe for a layered Spanish salad called Gaspacha. Our version is made with the same ingredients, but it's quickly tossed instead of layered.*

1½ pounds tomatoes, diced (3 cups)

1 cup chopped cucumbers

½ cup each chopped celery, red onion, and sweet green pepper

1 clove garlic, minced

2 slices whole-wheat or white bread, cubed and toasted (1 cup)

¼ cup minced parsley

For the dressing:

⅓ cup tomato-vegetable juice

2 tablespoons red wine vinegar or apple cider vinegar

1 tablespoon olive oil

1 teaspoon fresh lemon juice

½ teaspoon salt

⅛ to ¼ teaspoon ground red pepper (cayenne)

PREP TIME: 30 MIN.

1 In a large salad bowl, toss the tomatoes with the cucumbers, celery, onion, green pepper, and garlic. In a small bowl, whisk together all of the dressing ingredients. Immediately drizzle the dressing over the salad and toss until well coated. Sprinkle with the bread cubes and parsley and serve immediately. Makes 4 servings.

1 serving: Calories 123; Saturated Fat 1 g; Total Fat 5 g; Protein 4 g; Carbohydrate 20 g; Fiber 2 g; Sodium 461 mg; Cholesterol 0 mg

BUTTERMILK DRESSING

◆◆◆

1 cup low-fat buttermilk	½ cup reduced-fat sour cream
½ cup fruit-flavored vinegar, such as apple cider, raspberry, or blueberry	1 tablespoon vegetable oil
	½ teaspoon salt
	¼ teaspoon white pepper

PREP TIME: 5 MIN.

1 In a jar with a tight-fitting lid, place all of the ingredients. Cover tightly and shake until well blended, then refrigerate until serving time or for up to 5 days. Drizzle on fresh salad greens, coleslaw, carrot salad, or a salad of seafood, meat, or vegetables. This is also delicious on boiled potatoes or asparagus. Makes about 2 cups.

1 tablespoon: Calories 12; Saturated Fat 0 g; Total Fat 1 g; Protein 0 g; Carbohydrate 1 g; Fiber 0 g; Sodium 48 mg; Cholesterol 1 mg

◆

Ranch Country Dressing

Prepare as for Buttermilk Dressing, adding **¼ cup minced parsley, 3 tablespoons minced yellow onion, and 1 clove minced garlic.** Substitute **½ teaspoon black pepper** for the white pepper. This is a perfect serve-along for hot or cold roast beef or ham. Makes about 2⅓ cups. *1 tablespoon: Calories 10; Saturated Fat 0 g; Total Fat 1 g; Protein 0 g; Carbohydrate 1 g; Fiber 0 g; Sodium 41 mg; Cholesterol 1 mg*

Saucy Cucumber-Dill Dressing

Prepare as for Buttermilk Dressing, adding **½ cup grated peeled cucumber and 2 tablespoons finely chopped fresh dill or 2 teaspoons dried dill weed.** This is especially delicious with hot or cold seafood. Makes about 2½ cups. *1 tablespoon: Calories 10; Saturated Fat 0 g; Total Fat 1 g; Protein 0 g; Carbohydrate 1 g; Fiber 0 g; Sodium 38 mg; Cholesterol 1 mg*

RUSSIAN DRESSING

◆◆◆

Originating in America in the early 20th century, this dressing gets its name from the fact that all the early versions contained Russian caviar. With just a few additions, the recipe turns into Thousand Island Dressing, possibly first created in the Thousand Islands in the St. Lawrence River. One source suggests that it's so named because the bits and pieces resemble many islands in a sea of dressing.

½ cup reduced-calorie mayonnaise	2 tablespoons each minced sweet green pepper and drained pimientos
½ cup reduced-fat sour cream	1 tablespoon fresh lemon juice
¼ cup bottled chili sauce	¼ teaspoon each salt and black pepper
2 tablespoons red caviar (optional)	⅛ teaspoon ground red pepper (cayenne)
2 tablespoons minced chives or green onions	

PREP TIME: 15 MIN.

1 In a medium-size bowl, whisk together all of the ingredients until well blended. Cover and refrigerate until serving time or for up to 5 days. Drizzle over hamburgers, fish, vegetables, or a fresh green salad. Makes about 1½ cups.

1 tablespoon: Calories 14; Saturated Fat 0 g; Total Fat 1 g; Protein 0 g; Carbohydrate 2 g; Fiber 0 g; Sodium 89 mg; Cholesterol 3 mg

◆

Thousand Island Dressing

Prepare as for Russian Dressing, substituting **sweet red pepper** for the sweet green pepper. Add **¼ cup each drained and chopped dill pickle and minced parsley,** plus **1 peeled and chopped hard-cooked egg (page 363)** and **¼ teaspoon paprika.** Omit the caviar. Makes about 2 cups. *1 tablespoon: Calories 13; Saturated Fat 0 g; Total Fat 1 g; Protein 1 g; Carbohydrate 2 g; Fiber 0 g; Sodium 78 mg; Cholesterol 9 mg*

Russian Dressing whisked to perfection in America

GREEN GODDESS DRESSING
◆◆◆

¼ cup fresh parsley leaves	1 tablespoon fresh tarragon, or 1 teaspoon dried tarragon leaves
6 anchovy fillets, drained	1 cup reduced-calorie mayonnaise
6 chives, each about 5 inches long, or 3 green onions, with tops, trimmed and halved	½ cup plain low-fat yogurt
1 clove garlic	¼ cup tarragon vinegar

PREP TIME: 10 MIN.

1 In a food processor or blender, process the parsley, anchovies, chives, garlic, and tarragon until smooth. Add the mayonnaise, yogurt, and vinegar and process 1 minute more or until well blended. Cover and refrigerate for up to 5 days. Drizzle over fresh salad greens, chicken, turkey, crab, lobster, or shrimp. Makes about 2 cups.

1 tablespoon: Calories 12; Saturated Fat 0 g; Total Fat 1 g; Protein 1 g; Carbohydrate 1 g; Fiber 0 g; Sodium 68 mg; Cholesterol 4 mg

FARMHOUSE HORSERADISH CREAM
◆◆◆

4 ounces Neufchâtel cream cheese (½ cup)	2 tablespoons fresh lemon juice
½ cup reduced-fat sour cream	½ teaspoon paprika
2 tablespoons drained prepared horseradish	¼ teaspoon each salt and black pepper

PREP TIME: 8 MIN.

1 In a food processor or blender, place all of the ingredients. Process for 1 minute or until well blended. Cover and refrigerate until serving time or for up to 5 days. Drizzle over a salad of meat, seafood, or vegetables. It's also a wonderful sauce for grilled meat, roast beef or pork, and poached chicken or fish. Makes about 1½ cups.

1 tablespoon: Calories 19; Saturated Fat 1 g; Total Fat 2 g; Protein 1 g; Carbohydrate 1 g; Fiber 0 g; Sodium 63 mg; Cholesterol 5 mg

BLUE CHEESE DRESSING
◆◆◆

½ cup reduced-calorie mayonnaise	1 clove garlic, minced
½ cup low-fat yogurt	1 tablespoon white wine vinegar
¼ cup reduced-fat sour cream	⅛ teaspoon white pepper
2 tablespoons minced green onions	1 cup crumbled blue cheese (4 ounces)

PREP TIME: 12 MIN.

1 In a medium-size bowl, stir all of the ingredients until well blended. Cover and refrigerate for up to 5 days. Serve on mixed greens or a vegetable salad. This also makes a tasty serve-along with grilled beef steaks. Makes about 1½ cups.

1 tablespoon: Calories 28; Saturated Fat 1 g; Total Fat 2 g; Protein 2 g; Carbohydrate 1 g; Fiber 0 g; Sodium 99 mg; Cholesterol 6 mg

Made in America: This popular French Dressing, ready to toss on a fresh combination salad

COBB SALAD DRESSING

◆◆◆

Originally created for the Brown Derby Cobb Salad, this dressing makes the ideal topping for any meat or vegetable salad. We've adapted the original recipe, reducing the salt and oil while keeping the familiar flavors.

⅓ cup red wine vinegar

⅓ cup water

2 teaspoons fresh lemon juice

2 teaspoons salt

1 teaspoon black pepper

1 teaspoon Dijon mustard

1 teaspoon Worcestershire sauce

½ teaspoon sugar

1 small clove garlic, minced

⅔ cup salad oil

⅓ cup olive oil

PREP TIME: 15 MIN.

1 In a jar with a tight fitting lid, place the vinegar, water, lemon juice, salt, pepper, mustard, Worcestershire, sugar, and garlic. Cover tightly and shake until well blended.

2 Add both oils and continue shaking until well combined, refrigerate until ready to serve or for up to 4 weeks. Shake thoroughly again just before serving over the Brown Derby Cobb Salad (page 243). This dressing is also the perfect topping for chicken, meat, or vegetable salads. Makes about 1⅔ cups.

1 tablespoon: Calories 74; Saturated Fat 1 g; Total Fat 8 g; Protein 0 g; Carbohydrate 0 g; Fiber 0 g; Sodium 167 mg; Cholesterol 0 mg

OLD FASHIONED FRENCH DRESSING

To many Americans, French dressing means this thick orange version flavored with pimientos, rather than the simple vinaigrette of France. This particular one is low in oil, high in spice.

1 small all-purpose potato, peeled, cooked, drained, and diced (½ cup)	¼ cup red wine vinegar or apple cider vinegar
½ cup drained canned pimientos	3 tablespoons olive oil
⅓ cup white wine or water	2 tablespoons Dijon mustard
	¼ teaspoon each salt and black pepper

PREP TIME: 10 MIN. / COOKING TIME: 9 MIN.

1 In a food processor or blender, place all of the ingredients and process for 1 minute or until very smooth. Cover and refrigerate until serving time (will keep for up to 4 weeks). If the dressing thickens as it chills, stir in a little extra white wine or water. Drizzle over a vegetable, meat, or seafood salad; toss well. Makes about 1½ cups.

1 tablespoon: Calories 17; Saturated Fat 0 g; Total Fat 1 g; Protein 0 g; Carbohydrate 1 g; Fiber 0 g; Sodium 41 mg; Cholesterol 0 mg

ROASTED TOMATO VINAIGRETTE

Vinegar comes from the Latin word vinum *for wine and* acer *for sharp. Wine vinegars are still the best types for making vinaigrettes, though other varieties can be substituted.*

3 large ripe tomatoes (1½ pounds), roasted (page 360)	8 sprigs parsley
1 clove garlic	¼ cup each balsamic or red wine vinegar and olive oil
2 green onions, with tops	½ teaspoon each salt and black pepper

PREP TIME: 15 MIN. / COOKING TIME: 10 MIN.

1 When the roasted tomatoes are cool enough to handle, peel off the skins, quarter, and remove the seeds. You should have about 1½ cups.

2 Place the tomatoes and remaining ingredients in a food processor. Process for 3 minutes or until smooth; refrigerate until serving time (will keep for up to 4 weeks). Drizzle over vegetable, meat, or seafood salad. Makes about 1¾ cups.

1 tablespoon: Calories 8; Saturated Fat 0 g; Total Fat 0 g; Protein 0 g; Carbohydrate 2 g; Fiber 0 g; Sodium 41 mg; Cholesterol 0 mg

POPPY SEED DRESSING

2 large fresh peaches, peeled and pitted or 4 canned peach halves, drained	1 teaspoon dry mustard
½ cup sugar	½ teaspoon salt
½ cup apple juice	2 tablespoons vegetable oil (not olive oil)
⅓ cup apple cider vinegar	2 tablespoons poppy seeds
1 tablespoon chopped onion	

PREP TIME: 15 MIN.

1 In a food processor or electric blender, process the peaches for 30 seconds or until smooth. Add the sugar, apple juice, vinegar, onion, mustard, and salt; process 1 minute longer.

2 With the motor running, slowly add the oil, processing 1 minute longer or until thickened. Add the poppy seeds; process 30 seconds more or until well dispersed. Cover and refrigerate (not in the coldest part of the refrigerator) until serving time (will keep for up to 4 weeks). Drizzle over fresh fruits or greens. Makes about 2 cups.

1 tablespoon: Calories 26; Saturated Fat 0 g; Total Fat 1 g; Protein 0 g; Carbohydrate 4 g; Fiber 0 g; Sodium 34 mg; Cholesterol 0 mg

PICK OF
THE PANTRY

◆◆◆

Until well into the 19th century when commercial canning began, putting up food was a necessity. Hours were spent on warm summer days preserving homegrown vegetables and vine-ripened fruits. To help carry on this tradition, we've gathered blue-ribbon recipes from state and county fairs all across America. They include such irresistibles as Georgia Peach Preserves, Lime Sweet Pickles, End of Garden Relish, and Dilly Green Beans. Even if you don't have a garden, you can make these favorites with fresh produce from roadside stands, farmers' markets, and "pick your own" orchards.

But you don't have to do any canning to enjoy the pick of the pantry. We have seafood, pasta, and barbecue sauces that can easily be assembled any night of the week, plus great accompaniments, such as Cranberry Orange Conserve. We also feature flavored butters and syrups for pancakes and waffles, and fruit and fudge sauces to top desserts. Their fresh ingredients, just-right seasonings, and easy cooking techniques guarantee success. With these recipes you can treat family and friends to the works—homemade sauces, jellies, preserves, pickles, and relishes—all year long.

◆ Strawberry Pickin's ◆

It's a sunny Saturday in May at the Gizdich Ranch in Watsonville, California, south of San Francisco. The strawberry fields are bursting with some of the first ripe berries of the season. Families are now arriving for "pic-yor-sef" picking in the strawberry patch. Before they leave, most will visit the cider mill to see the apple pressing going on, enjoy a picnic under the shade of the old apple trees, take time for a slice of homemade pie in the bakery, stroll through the collectibles barn, and load up some fresh preserves to take home.

"My father-in-law started Gizdich Ranch 57 years ago," explains Nita Gizdich, "and it has been a family affair ever since. My two sons are taking over the farming and the rest of us are involved in the various activities.

"For over 31 years folks have been coming apple and berry picking. More than 50,000 visit us each year. We begin with strawberry picking in May, followed by Olallieberries (a kind of blackberry) and raspberries in June, then boysenberries in July. Next come the apple and pumpkin pickings, the bake-your-own apple contest, and the Mennonite apple butter festival in the fall."

Nita is an expert on picking, packing, and freezing berries. "Be sure to refrigerate berries as soon as you get them home, without washing or hulling them.

"If you can't eat them all, a great way to preserve them whole and fresh is what I call 'the natural pack freezing method.' Arrange a single layer of berries in a large flat pan that fits in your freezer. Freeze them for 15 to 30 minutes, then transfer to freezer containers or bags and return them to the freezer. They will keep for up to 6 months. Wash frozen berries just before using.

"When you're in our area, stop by for a visit," invites Nita. "You'll not only enjoy the day but you're also sure to take home many peaceful memories of this glorious place we call heaven."

STRAWBERRY PRESERVES
◆◆◆

This recipe made Evelyn Mounts a blue ribbon winner at the Oklahoma State Fair for 30 years. She found the original version in the Daily Oklahoman in 1941, credited to an Aunt Susan. Evelyn says you should not double the recipe. But it is so delicious, you might want to make several batches.

2 **heaping pints (5 cups) fresh ripe strawberries, hulled and washed, but not sliced**	4 **cups sugar** 1 **pint (2 cups) water**

PREP TIME: 30 MIN. / COOKING TIME: 45 MIN.
STANDING TIME: 24 HR.

1 In an 8-quart stainless steel or enameled stockpot, bring 1 pint of the strawberries, 2 cups of the sugar, and the water to a full rolling boil over high heat. Boil, uncovered, stirring occasionally, for 10 minutes (exactly!).

2 Remove from the heat, let stand until the bubbling stops, then gently stir in the remaining pint of strawberries and 2 cups of sugar. Boil over high heat, uncovered, stirring and skimming the surface often, 10 minutes longer or until the preserves begin to thicken and turn glossy.

3 Pour 1 inch deep into shallow pans. Let stand, uncovered, at room temperature for 24 hours or until the moisture has evaporated and the preserves have thickened to give you 4½ to 5 cups.

4 Sterilize 4 half-pint jelly jars (page 365). Spoon in the preserves, leaving a ½-inch head space; wipe the rims well and seal. Process in a boiling water bath (page 365) for 20 minutes, then let cool thoroughly and check the seals. Store in a cool, dark, dry place for up to 6 months. Makes 4 half-pints.

1 tablespoon: Calories 49 Saturated Fat 0 g; Total Fat 0 g; Protein 0 g; Carbohydrate 13 g; Fiber 0 g; Sodium 1 mg; Cholesterol 0 mg

Straight from the berry patch to your kitchen: Fresh, homemade Strawberry Preserves

GEORGIA PEACH PRESERVES

◆◆◆

7 **pounds fresh juicy, ripe peaches (about 25)**	2 **teaspoons whole cloves**
2 **cinnamon sticks, each 3 inches long, crushed**	7½ **to 8 cups sugar**
	¼ **cup fresh lemon juice**

PREP TIME: 30 MIN. / COOKING TIME: 48 MIN.

1 Peel, pit, and chop the peaches (you should have about 6 cups). In an 8-quart stainless steel or enameled stockpot, cook the peaches, uncovered, over moderate heat for 8 minutes, or until they are soft, stirring and mashing them constantly. While the peaches cook, tie up the cinnamon stick and cloves in a piece of cheesecloth.

2 Stir in the sugar and lemon juice, add the spice bag, and bring to a full rolling boil. Continue to boil, uncovered, stirring and skimming the surface often, for 25 to 30 minutes, or until a candy thermometer registers 218° to 220°F. and the preserves have thickened slightly and appear golden and glossy.

3 While the preserves cook, sterilize 8 half-pint jelly jars (page 365). Spoon in the preserves, leaving a ½-inch head space in each; wipe the rims well and seal. Process in a boiling water bath (page 365) for 10 minutes, then let cool thoroughly and check the seals. Store in a cool, dark, dry place for up to 6 months. Makes 8 half-pints.

1 tablespoon: Calories 27; Saturated Fat 0 g; Total Fat 0 g; Protein 0 g; Carbohydrate 7 g; Fiber 0 g; Sodium 0 mg; Cholesterol 0 mg

PEPPERMINT APPLE JELLY

◆◆◆

This refreshing pink apple jelly made Thomas A. Krentler from Troy, Michigan, a blue-ribbon winner at the Michigan State Fair in 1987. He first became interested in cooking in high school, when he was a school newspaper reporter; the home economics class was on his beat.

2 cups refrigerated or bottled apple juice	3 tablespoons fresh lemon juice
⅓ cup chopped fresh peppermint leaves or 1 tablespoon peppermint extract	¼ teaspoon unsalted butter
3½ cups sugar	2 drops red food coloring
	1 pouch (3 ounces) liquid pectin

PREP TIME: 15 MIN. / COOKING TIME: 22 MIN.
STANDING TIME: 10 MIN.

1 In a small saucepan, bring the apple juice to a boil; remove from the heat. Stir in the peppermint leaves, cover, and let stand for 10 minutes. Strain into an 8-quart stainless steel or enameled stockpot; discard the leaves.

2 Stir in the sugar, lemon juice, butter, and food coloring. Stirring constantly, bring to a full rolling boil over high heat. Add the pectin, all at once, and stir constantly until the mixture returns to a full rolling boil. Cook for 1 minute, stirring constantly and skimming the surface occasionally.

3 Meanwhile, sterilize 4 half-pint jelly jars (page 365). Pour in the jelly, leaving a ½-inch head space in each; wipe the rims well and seal.

4 Process the jelly in a boiling water bath (page 365) for 10 minutes. Let cool thoroughly, then check the seals. Store in a cool, dark, dry place for up to 6 months. Makes 4 half-pints.

1 tablespoon: Calories 48; Saturated Fat 0 g; Total Fat 0 g; Protein 0 g; Carbohydrate 13 g; Fiber 0 g; Sodium 3 mg; Cholesterol 0 mg

OREGON GRAPE JELLY

◆◆◆

From the Oregon State Fair comes this winning grape jelly, created by Mary Heinrichs, who has lived in Oregon all of her life. She often makes this jelly from the tiny clusters of wild grapeberries she finds on her grouse hunting trips in the mountains of Oregon. But Concord grapes work fine too.

3 quarts Concord grapes or wild grapeberries	1 box (1¾ ounces) granulated pectin
¼ cup fresh lemon juice	4½ cups sugar

PREP TIME: 20 MIN. / COOKING TIME: 19 MIN.

1 Crush the berries to extract the juice; you should have 3½ cups of berries and juice (if you don't, just add a little water). Strain into an 8-quart stainless steel or enameled stockpot; discard the skin, seeds, and pulp of the berries.

2 Stir in the lemon juice and pectin. Stirring constantly, bring the mixture to a full rolling boil over high heat. Add the sugar all at once, and stir constantly until the mixture returns to a full rolling boil. Cook for 1 minute, stirring constantly and skimming the surface occasionally.

3 Meanwhile, sterilize 6 half-pint jelly jars (page 365). Spoon in the jelly, leaving a ½-inch head space in each; wipe the rims well and seal.

4 Process the jelly in a boiling water bath (page 365) for 10 minutes. Let cool thoroughly, then check the seals. Store in a cool, dark, dry place for up to 6 months. Makes 6 half-pints.

1 tablespoon: Calories 43; Saturated Fat 0 g; Total Fat 0 g; Protein 0 g; Carbohydrate 12 g; Fiber 0 g; Sodium 1 mg; Cholesterol 0 mg

PINK GRAPEFRUIT MARMALADE

◆◆◆

The grapefruit was brought to Florida in the early 19th century, but gained little notice until the 1900's. Today, the United States (mainly Florida), produces at least three-fourths of the world's crop.

2 large or 3 small pink grapefruits	1 piece (2 inches long) fresh ginger, peeled and grated
2 cups cold water	4 cups sugar

PREP TIME: 20 MIN. / COOKING TIME: 1½ HR.

1 Peel and save the rinds from the grapefruit. Remove and discard the white pith from inside the rinds and around the fruit. Cut the rinds into thin julienne strips. Section the fruit, discarding the membranes and reserving all the juice. (You should have about 4 cups of fruit and juice.)

2 Half-fill a large saucepan with water, add the rind, and bring to a boil over high heat, then drain. Repeat this blanching twice, then transfer to an 8-quart stainless steel or enameled stockpot.

3 Stir in the grapefruit sections and juice, the 2 cups of water, and the ginger. Bring the mixture to a full rolling boil over high heat; boil, uncovered, stirring often, for 15 minutes. Add the sugar and boil, uncovered, stirring and skimming the surface often, for 25 to 30 minutes, or until a candy thermometer registers 218° to 220°F.

4 Meanwhile, sterilize 4 half-pint jelly jars (page 365). Spoon in the marmalade, leaving a ½-inch head space in each; wipe the rims well and seal. Process in a boiling water bath (page 365) for 10 minutes. Let cool thoroughly, then check the seals. Store in a cool, dark, dry place for up to 6 months. Makes 4 half-pints.

1 tablespoon: Calories 48; Saturated Fat 0 g; Total Fat 0 g; Protein 0 g; Carbohydrate 13 g; Fiber 0 g; Sodium 0 mg; Cholesterol 0 mg

Morning Wake-up Call: Hot tea, toast, and homemade Pink Grapefruit Marmalade

◆

Orange Marmalade

Set out **5 large oranges, 1 large lemon, 5 cups sugar,** and **4 cups cold water.** (Omit the ginger.) Prepare the oranges and lemon as in Step 1 for Pink Grapefruit Marmalade; omit the blanching in Step 2. Transfer the fruits, their juices, and rinds (you should have about 5 cups total) to the stockpot; stir in the sugar and water. Boil, as in Step 3, for 35 minutes or until a candy thermometer registers 218° to 220°F. Process as in Step 4. Store in a cool, dark, dry place for up to 6 months. Makes 6 half-pints. *1 tablespoon: Calories 41; Saturated Fat 0 g; Total Fat 0 g; Protein 0 g; Carbohydrate 11 g; Fiber 0 g; Sodium 0 mg; Cholesterol 0 mg*

A peck of cucumbers, all spiced up and ready for pickling

LIME SWEET PICKLES
♦♦♦

Evelyn Mounts has been entering (and often winning!) at the Oklahoma State Fair for more than 65 years. These pickles have brought her blue ribbons since 1958.

7	pounds firm pickling cucumbers, scrubbed and sliced ½ inch thick	8	cups sugar
1	gallon (16 cups) cold water	1	tablespoon pickling or Kosher salt
1	cup fresh lime juice	1	tablespoon celery seeds
2	quarts (8 cups) distilled white vinegar (5% acidity)	1½	teaspoons mustard seeds
		8	whole cloves
		1	cinnamon stick, 3 inches long, broken

PREP TIME: 30 MIN. / COOKING TIME: 45 MIN.
SOAKING TIME: 36 HR. / STANDING TIME: 2 WEEKS

1 In a 10-quart stainless steel or enameled stockpot, combine the cucumber slices, water, and lime juice. Cover loosely and let stand overnight; drain and rinse several times. Cover with fresh water, let soak 3 hours more, and rinse twice.

2 Drain the cucumbers well and return to the stockpot. Stir in the vinegar, sugar, and salt. Tie the celery and mustard seeds, cloves, and cinnamon stick in a cheesecloth bag; add to the stockpot (or put them in loose, if you like extra spicy pickles). Cover and soak overnight.

3 Bring the pickle mixture to a gentle boil, uncovered, over high heat; boil 20 to 35 minutes, depending on how crisp you like the pickles.

4 Meanwhile, sterilize 8 half-pint canning jars (page 365). Pack in the pickles and spoon in enough of the vinegar mixture to cover them, leaving a ½-inch head space. Add an extra teaspoon of mustard seeds for decoration to each jar if you wish. Wipe the rims well and seal. Process in a boiling water bath (page 365) for 10 minutes. Let cool thoroughly, then check the seals. Store in a cool, dark, dry place for at least 2 weeks before opening; they will keep for up to 6 months. The pickles are great to serve with Blue Ribbon Burgers (page 316). Makes 8 half-pints.

*2 tablespoons: Calories 102; Saturated Fat 0 g;
Total Fat 0 g; Protein 0 g; Carbohydrate 27 g; Fiber 0 g;
Sodium 102 mg; Cholesterol 0 mg*

CURRIED FRUIT MEDLEY
◆◆◆

This blend of dried and canned fruits makes the perfect accompaniment to roasted meats, such as Apricot-Glazed Pork Loin (page 105). It's also a simple hot dessert when topped with a little reduced-fat sour cream.

1 **can (16 ounces) pear halves in juice**	1½ **teaspoons curry powder**
1 **can (8 ounces) pineapple chunks in juice**	3 **cinnamon sticks, each 3 inches long**
1 **cup fresh orange juice**	1 **package (11 ounces) mixed dried fruit**
¼ **cup firmly packed brown sugar**	1 **can (11 ounces) Mandarin oranges in light syrup, drained**
3 **whole cloves**	

PREP TIME: 10 MIN. / COOKING TIME: 8 MIN.

1 Drain the pear halves, reserving ¾ cup of the juice and cut each pear half lengthwise into 3 pieces. Drain the pineapple chunks, reserving ⅓ cup of the juice. In a medium-size saucepan, combine the juices from the pears and pineapple with the orange juice, sugar, cloves, curry, and cinnamon sticks.

2 Stir over moderate heat until the sugar dissolves. Add the dried fruit and bring to a boil. Lower the heat and simmer for 5 minutes or until the fruit is plump and soft.

3 Remove from the heat and discard the cinnamon sticks and cloves. Gently stir in the pears, pineapple chunks, and Mandarin orange sections. Serve with roasted pork, chicken or turkey. Makes 5 cups.

½ cup: 160 Calories; Saturated Fat 0 g; Total Fat 0 g; Protein 1 g; Carbohydrate 38 g; Fiber 1 g; Sodium 12 mg; Cholesterol 0 mg

SPICY PICKLED PEACHES
◆◆◆

These peaches earned Mattie Lou Bynum a blue ribbon in the Georgia National Fair. They make the perfect serve-along for baked ham.

4 **cups sugar**	1 **teaspoon ground cinnamon**
3 **cups apple cider vinegar**	48 **whole cloves**
1 **tablespoon ground allspice**	24 **small fresh peaches, peeled (4 pounds)**

PREP TIME: 25 MIN. / COOKING TIME: 1¼ HR.
STANDING TIME: 2 WEEKS

1 In an 8-quart stainless steel or enameled stockpot, combine the sugar, vinegar, allspice, and cinnamon. Cook the mixture, uncovered, over moderately high heat for 15 minutes.

2 While the sugar mixture is cooking, insert 2 cloves in each peach. Drop 8 of the peaches into the boiling syrup and cook, uncovered, for 15 minutes. Meanwhile, sterilize 4 one-pint canning jars (page 365). With a slotted spoon, transfer 6 of the peaches to each jar. Repeat until all of the peaches have been processed. Spoon in enough of the hot syrup to cover the peaches completely, leaving a ½-inch head space; wipe the rims well and seal.

3 Process in a boiling water bath (page 365) for 10 minutes. Let cool thoroughly, then check the seals. Store in a cool, dark, dry place for at least 2 weeks before opening; they will keep for up to 6 months. These are wonderful with Honey Baked Ham (page 108). Makes 4 pints.

1 peach: Calories 154; Saturated Fat 0 g; Total Fat 0 g; Protein 1 g; Carbohydrate 43 g; Fiber 1 g; Sodium 1 mg; Cholesterol 0 mg

PICKLED ONIONS
◆◆◆

There are more than 70 varieties of onions native to North America. Look for the tiny white pearl onions to use for pickling.

4	pounds small white pearl onions	4	small dried red chili peppers or 1 teaspoon crushed red pepper flakes
½	cup pickling or kosher salt		
2	tablespoons mustard seeds	4	cups white vinegar
4	bay leaves	1	cup sugar

PREP TIME: 30 MIN. / COOKING TIME: 20 MIN.
SOAKING TIME: 24 HR. / STANDING TIME: 2 WEEKS

1 Half-fill a large saucepan with water and bring to a boil over high heat. Add the onions, return to a boil, and boil for 2 minutes, then rinse with cold water and peel, trimming off the ends as you go. In a large bowl, toss the onions and salt; cover with cold water. Cover loosely and let soak for 24 hours. Rinse several times and drain well.

2 Sterilize 4 one-pint canning jars (page 365). Pack in the onions and divide the mustard seeds, bay leaves, and chili peppers among them.

3 In a large stainless steel or enameled saucepan, bring the vinegar and sugar to a full rolling boil over high heat. Immediately pour over the onions, covering them completely and leaving a 1-inch head space. Gently run a knife around the inside of each jar to release any bubbles; wipe the rims well and seal.

4 Process in a boiling water bath (page 365) for 10 minutes. Let cool thoroughly, then check the seals. Store in a cool, dark, dry place for at least 2 weeks before opening; they will keep for up to 6 months. Makes 4 pints.

¼ cup: Calories 51; Saturated Fat 0 g; Total Fat 0 g; Protein 1 g; Carbohydrate 13 g; Fiber 0 g; Sodium 402 mg; Cholesterol 0 mg

DILLY GREEN BEANS
◆◆◆

2	pounds young slender green beans, washed, trimmed, and cut into 6-inch lengths	2	large clusters of dill or 2 teaspoons dill seeds
6	cloves garlic, halved	2½	cups apple cider or white vinegar
4	teaspoons pickling spices	2½	cups water
		¼	cup pickling or kosher salt

PREP TIME: 20 MIN. / COOKING TIME: 15 MIN.
STANDING TIME: 2 WEEKS

1 Sterilize 2 one-quart canning jars (page 365). Pack in the beans, trimming them to fit, if necessary, to allow a ½-inch head space in each jar. Divide the garlic, pickling spices, and dill between the jars.

2 In a large stainless steel or enameled saucepan, bring the vinegar, water, and salt to a full rolling boil over high heat. Immediately pour over the beans, covering them completely and leaving a 1-inch head space. Gently run a knife around the inside of each jar to release any bubbles; wipe the rims well and seal.

3 Process in a boiling water bath (page 365) for 10 minutes. Let cool thoroughly, then check the seals. Store in a cool, dark, dry place for at least 2 weeks before opening; they will keep for up to 6 months. Makes 2 quarts.

½ cup: Calories 22; Saturated Fat 0 g; Total Fat 0 g; Protein 1 g; Carbohydrate 7 g; Fiber 0 g; Sodium 404 mg; Cholesterol 0 mg

◆

Kirby Dills

In a large bowl, soak **10 firm kirby pickling cucumbers, 8 inches long,** in **6 cups water** and **½ cup pickling salt** for 24 hours. Rinse several times, then pack and process as in Dilly Green Beans, increasing the dill to **6 large clusters.** Makes 2 quarts. *1 pickle: Calories 45; Saturated Fat 0 g; Total Fat 1 g; Protein 2 g; Carbohydrate 14 g; Fiber 2 g; Sodium 650 mg; Cholesterol 0 mg*

PICKLED MUSHROOMS

Not until cultivated Parisian mushrooms were brought to this country at the end of the 19th century did Americans develop a love for these fungi. Pickling is now a favorite way to preserve them.

2 pounds button mushrooms, trimmed and washed	2 large cloves garlic, thinly sliced
3 cups water	4 bay leaves
2 tablespoons pickling or kosher salt	1 teaspoon whole cloves
3 cups apple cider or white vinegar	1 teaspoon black or green peppercorns
¼ cup extra virgin olive oil	4 small dried red chili peppers or 1 teaspoon crushed red pepper flakes

PREP TIME: 20 MIN. / COOKING TIME: 25 MIN.
STANDING TIME: 2 WEEKS

1 In a large stainless steel or enameled saucepan, combine the mushrooms, water, and salt. Bring to a boil over moderately high heat and simmer for 5 minutes. Rinse several times, then drain well. In the same saucepan, bring the vinegar and oil to a boil. Add the mushrooms, lower the heat, and simmer, uncovered, for 5 minutes.

2 While the mushrooms are simmering, sterilize 4 half-pint canning jars (page 365). Using a slotted spoon, pack in the mushrooms, reserving the vinegar mixture. Divide the remaining ingredients among the jars. Spoon in enough of the vinegar mixture to cover the mushrooms completely, leaving a 1-inch head space. Gently run a knife around the inside of each jar to release any bubbles; wipe the rims well and seal.

3 Process in a boiling water bath (page 365) for 10 minutes. Let cool thoroughly, then check the seals. Store in a cool, dark, dry place for at least 2 weeks before opening; they will keep for up to to 6 months. Makes 4 half-pints.

¼ cup: Calories 45; Saturated Fat 1 g; Total Fat 4 g; Protein 1 g; Carbohydrate 6 g; Fiber 1 g; Sodium 405 mg; Cholesterol 0 mg

Preserving the mushroom crop with vinegar and spice and all things nice

◆ Meet Me at the Fair! ◆

The day is warm and summery under the old hickory trees at the Iowa State Fair in Des Moines. Started in 1854, this fair is now one of the oldest and largest in the country. It was, in fact, the inspiration for Phil Stong's award winning novel, **"Meet Me at the Fair,"** plus Rodgers and Hammerstein's musical of the same name.

"Here inside the Family Center," explains Superintendent of Foods Arlette Hollister, "judges have been busy for days tasting more than 7,000 food entries. We always have plenty of standard cakes, pies, and jellies. But there are unique entries too: pioneer wedding cakes (each family member brings a layer), Depression cakes, green-tomato pies, and mud cakes (of chocolate), inspired by the great flood of 1993.

There's even been a blue ribbon for the ugliest cake (by a kid), decorated with flies, spiders, and bees (edible ones made of frosting, of course).

What makes a blue ribbon winner? Several state winners offer their tips: "When putting up foods like relishes, add something colorful, such as carrots or red peppers," advises Pat Hatch, the winner of over 400 blue ribbons at the Iowa State Fair. "For pickles, cut all cucumbers the same size, remove any seeds from other vegetables, and be sure to use only white vinegar (5% acidity)."

Gale Herrera, the Iowan winner for her Corn Relish, suggests: "Use the freshest corn and the brightest red peppers you can find!"

Evelyn Mounts, who has taken home more than 1,300 blue ribbons from the Oklahoma State Fair over the last 55 years, states: "When packing preserves, place each fruit individually, forming a ring at the bottom, then moving up the sides; pack them tightly in the center so the fruit does not move."

Such secrets bring home blue ribbons, year after year!

CORN RELISH
◆◆◆

In 1989, Gale Herrera and her husband moved to Altoona, Iowa, and Gale decided to enter the Iowa State Fair. She brought home a blue ribbon with this relish.

8 cups fresh corn kernels (about 12 ears)	1 medium-size yellow onion, chopped (1 cup)
2 cups cold water	2 tablespoons pickling or kosher salt
2 cups cider or distilled vinegar	2 teaspoons celery seeds
1 each extra large sweet green and red pepper, cored, seeded, and chopped (3 cups)	⅓ cup all-purpose flour
	2 tablespoons dry mustard
1½ cups sugar	1 teaspoon ground turmeric

PREP TIME: 30 MIN. / COOKING TIME: 47 MIN.

1 In an 8-quart stainless steel or enameled stockpot, bring the corn and 1½ cups of the water to a full rolling boil over moderately high heat. Boil gently, uncovered, for 12 minutes. Stir in the vinegar, peppers, sugar, onion, salt, and celery seeds and boil 15 minutes longer.

2 In a small bowl, blend the flour with the mustard and turmeric, then whisk in the remaining ½ cup of water until smooth. Stir this flour mixture into the corn mixture and cook, stirring constantly, for 5 minutes or until thickened, then cook 2 minutes longer.

3 Sterilize 5 one-pint canning jars (page 365). Spoon in the relish, leaving a ½-inch head space; wipe the rims well and seal.

4 Process the relish in a boiling water bath (page 365) for 10 minutes. Let cool thoroughly, then check the seals. Store in a cool, dark, dry place for up to 6 months. Makes 5 pints.

¼ cup: Calories 64; Saturated Fat 0 g; Total Fat 0 g; Protein 1 g; Carbohydrate 16 g; Fiber 0 g; Sodium 322 mg; Cholesterol 0 mg

Blue ribbon winners at the Iowa State Fair: End of Garden Relish and a fresh Corn Relish

END OF GARDEN RELISH

❖❖❖

Pat Hatch has been taking home blue ribbons from the Iowa State Fair for the last 10 years. This relish won her honors in 1989.

½ cup pickling or kosher salt

8 cups cold water

6 ounces fresh green beans, trimmed and chopped (1 cup)

2 stalks celery, chopped (1 cup)

1 small cucumber, unpeeled, chopped (1 cup)

1 medium-size yellow onion, chopped (1 cup)

1 large sweet green pepper, cored, seeded, and chopped (1 cup)

1 medium-size sweet red pepper, cored, seeded, and chopped (¾ cup)

½ cup chopped zucchini

2 cups sugar

2 cups apple cider vinegar

2 tablespoons mustard seeds

2 tablespoons ground turmeric

1 tablespoon celery seeds

PREP TIME: 45 MIN. / STANDING TIME: 12 HR.
COOKING TIME: 28 MIN.

1 In an 8-quart stainless steel or enameled stockpot, dissolve the salt in the water. Stir in the 7 vegetables, cover loosely, and let stand for 12 to 18 hours. Rinse several times, drain well, and return to the same stockpot.

2 Add the sugar, vinegar, and spices; bring to a full rolling boil over high heat. Boil gently, uncovered, for 15 minutes.

3 Meanwhile, sterilize 4 half-pint canning jars (page 365). Spoon in the relish, leaving a ½-inch head space; wipe the rims well and seal.

4 Process the relish in a boiling water bath (page 365) for 10 minutes. Let cool thoroughly, then check the seals. Store in a cool, dark, dry place for up to 6 months. Makes 4 half-pints.

*¼ cup: Calories 120; Saturated Fat 0 g;
Total Fat 1 g; Protein 1 g; Carbohydrate 32 g; Fiber 1 g;
Sodium 334 mg; Cholesterol 0 mg*

Cajun-spiced Shrimper's Sauce: Ready for dunking in freshly cooked shrimp

SHRIMPER'S SAUCE
◆ ◆ ◆

In the Carolina Low Country, shrimp boats have been bringing in the catch since Colonial days. Shrimpers are known for creating spicy sauces.

1 **can (14½ ounces) crushed tomatoes, drained**	1 **tablespoon sugar**
3 **tablespoons tomato paste**	½ **teaspoon Worcestershire sauce**
1½ **tablespoons each cider vinegar and prepared horseradish**	¼ **teaspoon salt**
	⅛ **teaspoon hot red pepper sauce**

PREP TIME: 10 MIN.

1 In a medium-size bowl, whisk together all the ingredients. Cover and refrigerate for up to 5 days. Spoon over cold cooked shrimp for a delicious shrimp cocktail, or serve as a dipping sauce for oysters or clams on the half-shell. This sauce is also perfect to serve on the side with broiled, steamed, or fried seafood or the fish of the day. Makes 1½ cups.

1 tablespoon: Calories 9; Saturated Fat 0 g; Total Fat 0 g; Protein 0 g; Carbohydrate 2 g; Fiber 0 g; Sodium 87 mg; Cholesterol 0 mg

TARTAR SAUCE

◆◆◆

When fried fish is on the menu in America, there are usually at least two bowls of sauce: the typical cocktail, or Shrimper's Sauce (opposite page), and this familiar mayonnaise-based variety, flavored with sweet pickles and capers.

½ cup reduced-fat sour cream	1 tablespoon chopped green onion
2 tablespoons reduced-calorie mayonnaise	4 teaspoons sweet pickles, diced
1 tablespoon capers, rinsed and patted dry	1 teaspoon fresh lemon juice
	⅛ teaspoon ground red pepper (cayenne)

PREP TIME: 10 MIN.

1 In a small bowl, whisk together the sour cream and mayonnaise, then stir in the remaining ingredients. Cover and refrigerate for up to 5 days. This sauce is a natural accompaniment for fried, baked, or broiled fish and seafood and is also a great topping for seafood salads. Makes ¾ cup.

1 tablespoon: Calories 17; Saturated Fat 0 g; Total Fat 1 g; Protein 0 g; Carbohydrate 2 g; Fiber 0 g; Sodium 46 mg; Cholesterol 3 mg

MARINARA SAUCE

◆◆◆

1 tablespoon olive oil	1 cup slivered fresh basil or minced parsley
1 medium-size yellow onion, finely chopped (1 cup)	¾ cup no-salt-added tomato paste
2 cloves garlic, minced	1 teaspoon sugar
5 pounds fresh plum tomatoes, chopped	1 teaspoon each dried oregano and thyme leaves, crumbled
2 cups no-salt-added tomato juice	1 bay leaf
½ cup Chicken Stock (page 74) or low-sodium chicken broth	½ teaspoon salt
	¼ teaspoon crushed red pepper flakes

PREP TIME: 15 MIN. / COOKING TIME: 40 MIN.

1 In a large nonstick saucepan, heat the oil over moderately high heat. Stir in the onion and garlic and sauté for 5 minutes or until tender.

2 Stir in the remaining ingredients and bring to a full boil. Lower the heat, cover, and simmer for 15 minutes; uncover and simmer 20 to 30 minutes more. Discard the bay leaf. Makes 8 cups, enough for 2 pounds cooked pasta (about 8 main-dish servings). May be frozen for up to 3 months.

¾ cup: Calories 84; Saturated Fat 0 g; Total Fat 2 g; Protein 3 g; Carbohydrate 16 g; Fiber 2 g; Sodium 287 mg; Cholesterol 0 mg

BOLOGNESE SAUCE

◆◆◆

1½ pounds lean ground beef or a mix of lean ground beef, veal, and pork	2 teaspoons olive oil
	8 ounces fresh mushrooms, sliced (3 cups)
2 cloves garlic, minced	1 recipe Marinara Sauce (this page)
½ teaspoon salt	⅓ cup minced parsley
¼ teaspoon black pepper	

PREP TIME: 30 MIN. / COOKING TIME: 55 MIN.

1 In a 12-inch nonstick skillet, sauté the beef, garlic, salt, and pepper over moderately high heat for 7 minutes or until browned. Using a slotted spoon, transfer to a plate. Add the oil to the drippings; sauté the mushrooms for 7 minutes or until tender. Transfer to the plate with the meat.

2 Assemble the Marinara Sauce. Just before simmering (Step 2), add the meat, mushrooms, and any juices that have collected. Add the parsley during the last 5 minutes. Makes 10 cups, enough for 3 pounds cooked pasta (12 main-dish servings). May be frozen for up to 2 months.

¾ cup: Calories 182; Saturated Fat 3 g; Total Fat 9 g; Protein 13 g; Carbohydrate 16 g; Fiber 2 g; Sodium 406 mg; Cholesterol 33 mg

TEXAS BARBECUE SAUCE

◆◆◆

This best-of-the-best barbecue sauce has been handed down for generations in Mancill Allen's family from Houston, Texas.

6 tablespoons unsalted butter or margarine	2 cups each ketchup and chili sauce
1½ cups each chopped onion and sweet red pepper	½ cup each molasses, and firmly packed light brown sugar
3 cloves garlic, minced	3 tablespoons each Worcestershire sauce and liquid smoke
1 tablespoon each chili powder and dry mustard	2 teaspoons hot pepper sauce, or to taste
1½ cups cider vinegar	

PREP TIME: 20 MIN. / COOKING TIME: 52 MIN.

1 In a large saucepan, melt the butter over moderate heat. Add the onion, red pepper, garlic, chili powder, and mustard; sauté for 5 minutes. Lower the heat, add the remaining ingredients, and simmer, uncovered, for 45 minutes. In a food processor or blender, process until smooth. Use on burgers, chops, or ribs. Refrigerate for up to 2 week;, freeze for up to 3 months. Makes 2 quarts.

2 tablespoons: Calories 42; Saturated Fat 1 g; Total Fat 1 g; Protein 0 g; Carbohydrate 8 g; Fiber 0 g; Sodium 189 mg; Cholesterol 3 mg

TANGY MUSTARD SAUCE

◆◆◆

Throughout the South, baked ham is often served with a creamy golden sauce made from powdered mustard seeds and heavy cream. Our version cuts back on the milkfat but not the flavor.

1 cup sugar	1 cup low-fat (1% milkfat) milk
¼ cup dry mustard	2 egg yolks, beaten
2 tablespoons all-purpose flour	1 cup cider vinegar
¼ teaspoon salt	2 tablespoons heavy cream (optional)

Fall Cooking Fest, a perfect time for canning fresh-cooked Chunky Cinnamon Applesauce

PREP TIME: 10 MIN. / COOKING TIME: 50 MIN.

1 In a medium-size bowl, sift together the sugar, mustard, flour, and salt. In a medium-size saucepan, heat the milk over moderate heat just until it begins to simmer. Gradually whisk in the sugar mixture, then the egg yolks, then the vinegar. Whisking constantly, return to a simmer.

2 Lower the heat and simmer, uncovered, whisking occasionally, for 45 minutes. Remove from the heat and whisk in the cream if you wish. Cover and refrigerate for up to 3 days. This sauce is wonderful with baked ham, roast beef, and corned beef. Makes 1⅔ cups.

1 tablespoon: Calories 44; Saturated Fat 0 g; Total Fat 1 g; Protein 1 g; Carbohydrate 9 g; Fiber 0 g; Sodium 25 mg; Cholesterol 16 mg

CHUNKY CINNAMON APPLESAUCE

◆◆◆

In New England, where apple orchards abound, applesauce is often referred to as apple sass. For this recipe, choose tart and juicy cooking apples, such as Cortlands, Granny Smiths, Jonathans, McIntoshes, or Winesaps, and leave them slightly chunky. If you prefer not to preserve the sauce, you can keep it in the refrigerator for up to 1 week.

6 pounds large tart cooking apples (about 14)	⅛ teaspoon ground cloves
1 cup cold water	4 cinnamon sticks, each 3-inches long, broken
1 cup firmly packed light brown sugar	1 tablespoon fresh lemon juice
1½ teaspoons ground cinnamon	

PREP TIME: 20 MIN. / COOKING TIME: 35 MIN.

1 Pare and core the apples, then cut them into 1-inch chunks. In a large stainless steel or enameled stockpot, bring the apples, water, sugar, cinnamon, cloves, and cinnamon sticks to a full rolling boil over moderate heat. Lower the heat, cover, and simmer, stirring often, for 10 minutes.

2 Remove the cover and cook, stirring often, 10 minutes longer or until the apples are very tender. Remove from the heat, discard the cinnamon sticks, and stir in the lemon juice.

3 Meanwhile, sterilize 4 one-pint canning jars (page 365). Spoon in the applesauce, leaving a ½-inch head space in each jar; wipe the rims well and seal.

4 Process in a boiling water bath (page 365) for 10 minutes. Let cool thoroughly, then check the seals. Store in a cool, dark, dry place for up to 6 months. Makes 4 pints.

½ cup: Calories 151; Saturated Fat 0 g; Total Fat 0 g; Protein 0 g; Carbohydrate 40 g; Fiber 1 g; Sodium 6 mg; Cholesterol 0 mg

APPLE BUTTER

◆◆◆

Eliza Leslie, in her 1848 edition of Directions for Cooking, *describes apple butter as "a compound of apples and cider boiled together till of the consistence of soft butter. It can only be made of sweet new cider fresh from the press,...[plus] some fine juicy apples." The recipe here won Anna Marie Hrdy a blue ribbon at the Oklahoma State Fair. It's perfect for gifts.*

6 pounds medium-size juicy, tart cooking apples, such as Winesap or Jonathan (about 18)	3 cups sugar
	1½ teaspoons ground cinnamon
	½ teaspoon ground cloves
2 quarts sweet apple cider	

PREP TIME: 30 MIN. / COOKING TIME: 1¾ HR.

1 Pare, core, and quarter the apples. In an 8-quart stainless steel or enameled stockpot, bring the cider to a boil over high heat. Add the apples; cook for 15 minutes or until tender; drain.

2 In a food processor, process the apples for 1 minute or until puréed, or press through a food mill (you should have about 3 quarts of pulp). Transfer to the same stockpot and stir over moderate heat for 15 minutes or until thick enough to hold up a spoon.

3 Add the sugar and spices and cook slowly, stirring frequently, for 1 hour or until very thick. Meanwhile sterilize 12 half-pint jelly jars (page 365). Spoon in the apple butter, leaving a ½-inch head space; wipe the rims well and seal.

4 Process in a boiling water bath (page 365) for 10 minutes. Let cool thoroughly, then check the seals. Store in a cool, dark, dry place for up to 6 months. Makes 12 half-pints.

1 tablespoon: Calories 25; Saturated Fat 0 g; Total Fat 0 g; Protein 0 g; Carbohydrate 6 g; Fiber 0 g; Sodium 0 mg; Cholesterol 0 mg

◆ Seven Sweets and Seven Sours ◆

During the 18th century, religious groups from the German Alps and Rhineland, among them the Moravians and Amish, settled into a new life in rural Pennsylvania. The Pennsylvania Dutch, as they became known, ate hearty food typical of the fare served on the farmlands back home.

Preserved vegetables and fruits were always part of their robust diet because of the unique custom known as "seven sweets and seven sours." It required that main courses be accompanied by seven different sweet foods, such as jelly, honey, spiced peaches, and apple butter, and seven tart condiments, such as pickles and relish. Only a table laden in this abundant manner was considered truly representative of their gracious hospitality.

CRANBERRY ORANGE CONSERVE

Thicker and chunkier than jams, conserves are made by mixing fruits, nuts, and sugars, then cooking them until they are thick enough to hold a spoon upright in the mixture.

- 2 large oranges
- 1 cinnamon stick, about 4 inches long, crushed
- 1 teaspoon whole cloves
- 4 cups cold water
- 1 tablespoon grated lemon rind
- 4 cups granulated sugar
- 2 cups firmly packed light brown sugar
- 2 pounds fresh whole cranberries, washed and stemmed (8 cups)
- 1 cup dark raisins
- 1 cup chopped walnuts, toasted (page 365)

PREP TIME: 30 MIN. / COOKING TIME: 1 HR.

1 Peel the oranges. Remove and discard the white pith from the rind and around the fruit. Coarsely chop the rind and cut the oranges into 1-inch pieces; place in a 6-quart stainless steel or enameled stockpot with any juice collected from the oranges. Tie up the cinnamon stick and cloves in cheesecloth and add them to the stockpot with the water and lemon rind.

2 Bring to a full rolling boil over high heat. Lower the heat; simmer, uncovered, stirring often, for 25 minutes, or until the rind is tender. Stir in the sugars, cranberries, and raisins; boil, stirring often, for 5 minutes. Add the nuts and continue simmering 10 minutes more, or until a candy thermometer registers 218° to 220°F.

3 Meanwhile, sterilize 10 half-pint jelly jars (page 365). Spoon in the conserve, leaving a ½-inch head space; wipe the rims well and seal.

4 Process in a boiling water bath (page 365) for 10 minutes. Let cool thoroughly, then check the seals. Store in a cool, dark, dry place for up to 6 months. Makes 10 half-pints.

¼ cup: Calories 157; Saturated Fat 0 g; Total Fat 2 g; Protein 1 g; Carbohydrate 37 g; Fiber 1 g; Sodium 5 mg; Cholesterol 0 mg

In 1663 in New England, cranberries [bounce berries] were tested for ripeness by their ability to bounce.

— The American Heritage Cookbook (1964)

CANDIED CRANBERRY SAUCE

❖❖❖

Whether cranberry sauce was served at the first Thanksgiving is questionable (due to conflicting accounts), but today it's a traditional holiday "must." And cranberry bogs abound, from Cape Cod in Massachusetts to the hills of Oregon.

2 cups cold water	½ teaspoon grated lemon rind
1 cup granulated sugar	½ teaspoon ground nutmeg
1½ cups firmly packed light brown sugar	¼ teaspoon ground cloves
24 ounces fresh whole cranberries, washed and stemmed (6 cups)	½ cup fresh orange juice
	¼ cup fresh lemon juice
2 teaspoons grated orange rind	2 teaspoons cornstarch
1 teaspoon ground cinnamon	3 cinnamon sticks, each 3 inches long

PREP TIME: 20 MIN. / COOKING TIME: 25 MIN.
CHILLING TIME: 1 HR.

1 In a large heavy stainless steel saucepan, bring the water and sugars to a boil over high heat; cook, stirring, for 5 minutes or until the sugar has dissolved. Stir in the cranberries, orange rind, cinnamon, lemon rind, nutmeg, and cloves.

2 Simmer for 3 minutes or until the berries begin to pop. Stir in the juices, cornstarch, and cinnamon sticks; bring to a boil. Lower the heat, cover, and simmer for 10 minutes. Transfer to a heatproof container; let cool. Discard the cinnamon sticks, then cover, and refrigerate for up to 1 week. Makes 5 cups.

¼ cup: Calories 119; Saturated Fat 0 g; Total Fat 0 g; Protein 0 g; Carbohydrate 31 g; Fiber 1 g; Sodium 6 mg; Cholesterol 0 mg

Candied Cranberry Sauce—just waiting for the roast turkey

DOWN HOME TRADITION

Chocolate has been around since the Aztecs ground cocoa beans into a powder to create a hot spiced drink that they called *xocolatl*, meaning "bitter water." But not until the Spanish sweetened the drink with sugar did the popularity of chocolate begin to grow. By the 19th century, Americans were enjoying chocolate from England and Switzerland, and even mass producing their own milk chocolate bars in Hershey, Pennsylvania. Gradually, the chocolate craze grew into American traditions: melt-in-your-mouth chocolate kisses, hearts for Valentine's Day, chocolate bunnies for Easter, and chocolate Santas at Christmas time, not to mention creamy hot fudge for ice cream sundaes.

◆ Hot Fudge Sauce ◆

½ cup heavy cream
3 tablespoons light corn syrup
2 tablespoons granulated sugar
2 tablespoons firmly packed dark brown sugar
⅛ teaspoon salt
1 cup (6 ounces) semisweet chocolate morsels
¼ cup unsalted butter (not margarine)
2 tablespoons vanilla extract

PREP TIME: 10 MIN. / COOKING TIME: 8 MIN.

1 In a medium-size heavy saucepan, bring the cream, corn syrup, both sugars, and the salt to a boil over moderate heat. Add the chocolate morsels and butter and stir constantly for about 5 minutes or until smooth.

2 Remove from the heat and stir in the vanilla. Serve over generous slices of Old Fashioned Pound Cake (page 330). Refrigerate any extra sauce in a covered container, then reheat before serving. Makes 1½ cups.

*3 tablespoons: Calories 261; Saturated Fat 7 g;
Total Fat 16 g; Protein 1 g; Carbohydrate 29 g; Fiber 0 g;
Sodium 61 mg; Cholesterol 37 mg*

DOUBLE CHOCOLATE SAUCE
◆◆◆

This contemporary sauce contains less fat than the traditional version. But it still has a double-rich chocolate taste, as it contains both cocoa and semisweet chocolate.

⅔ cup cold water
2 tablespoons unsweetened cocoa powder
2 squares (1 ounce each) semisweet chocolate
1 tablespoon unsalted butter (not margarine)
½ cup granulated sugar
½ cup firmly packed light brown sugar
3 tablespoons light corn syrup
1 tablespoon vanilla extract

PREP TIME: 10 MIN. / COOKING TIME: 15 MIN.

1 In a small bowl, whisk together ⅓ cup of the water with the cocoa. In a medium-size heavy saucepan, heat the semisweet chocolate and butter over low heat, stirring often, for 5 minutes or until melted.

2 Whisk in the cocoa mixture, the remaining ⅓ cup of water, both sugars, and the corn syrup and bring to a boil over moderate heat. Continue to boil, uncovered, for 7 minutes or until the sauce is reduced to 1½ cups.

3 Remove from the heat and stir in the vanilla. Serve immediately over ice cream sundaes or sections of Sour Cream Waffles (page 311), each topped with a small scoop of ice cream. Refrigerate any extra sauce in a covered container for up to 2 weeks; reheat over low heat before serving. Makes 1½ cups.

*3 tablespoons: Calories 179; Saturated Fat 1 g;
Total Fat 4 g; Protein 1 g; Carbohydrate 36 g; Fiber 0 g;
Sodium 12 mg; Cholesterol 4 mg*

Reminiscent of the 1940's: An old-fashioned banana split, topped with Butterscotch-Nut and Double Chocolate sauces

BUTTERSCOTCH-NUT SAUCE
◆◆◆

*This sauce gets its name from the fact
that it originated in Scotland.*

1 tablespoon all-purpose flour	2 tablespoons unsalted butter (not margarine)
¾ cup low-fat (1% milkfat) milk	⅛ teaspoon salt
1⅓ cups firmly packed light brown sugar	1 teaspoon vanilla extract
½ cup light corn syrup	1 cup pecans, toasted (page 365)
2 tablespoons cold water	

🕐 PREP TIME: 10 MIN. / COOKING TIME: 15 MIN.

1 Into a medium-size saucepan, measure the flour, then whisk in the milk until smooth. Bring to a boil over moderate heat; boil for 4 minutes, whisking constantly.

2 In a small saucepan, bring the sugar, corn syrup, water, butter, and salt to a boil over moderate heat and boil for 2 minutes. Gradually whisk this mixture into the milk mixture, return to a boil, and boil for 1 minute.

3 Remove from the heat and stir in the vanilla and nuts. Serve immediately over ice cream, Ruthie's Apple Pie (page 345), or Sunshine Cake (page 328). Refrigerate any extra sauce in a covered container for up to 1 week; reheat over low heat before serving. Makes 2 cups.

*3 tablespoons: Calories 246; Saturated Fat 2 g;
Total Fat 9 g; Protein 2 g; Carbohydrate 41 g; Fiber 0 g;
Sodium 55 mg; Cholesterol 7 mg*

Whipped and flavored butters: Scrumptious additions to muffins

HONEY 'N' SPICE BUTTER

◆◆◆

Often in the South, hot biscuits or other breads are served with a generous scoop of fluffy honey butter. It not only adds a hint of sweetness, but also makes the butter go farther.

½ cup (1 stick) unsalted butter (not margarine), at room temperature

3 tablespoons honey

¼ teaspoon grated lemon rind

¼ teaspoon each ground cinnamon and ginger

⅛ teaspoon ground allspice

1 teaspoon lemon juice

⅛ teaspoon salt

PREP TIME: 15 MIN.

1 In a medium-size bowl, with an electric mixer on high, beat the butter until creamy. Add the honey, lemon rind, cinnamon, ginger, and allspice and beat until well combined. Add the lemon juice and salt and beat 1 minute more or until well blended. Serve with Beth's Buttermilk Biscuits (page 306) or East Bay Jonnycakes (page 308). Makes about ¾ cup.

1 teaspoon: Calories 28; Saturated Fat 2 g; Total Fat 3 g; Protein 0 g; Carbohydrate 2 g; Fiber 0 g; Sodium 8 mg; Cholesterol 7 mg

STRAWBERRY BUTTER

◆◆◆

Fresh fruit combined with creamy butter makes a treat that is delightful with breads at breakfast or tea time.

½ cup fresh strawberries, washed and hulled

½ cup (1 stick) unsalted butter (not margarine), at room temperature

1 teaspoon confectioners sugar

1 teaspoon fresh lime juice

PREP TIME: 15 MIN.

1 In a food processor or blender, purée the strawberries. In a medium-size bowl, with an electric mixer on high, beat the butter until creamy. Add the sugar, lime juice, and strawberry purée and continue beating until the mixture is no longer separated and is well blended. Serve with hot Portland Popovers (page 310), Banana-Nut Bread (page 304) or Sally Lunn Bread (page 289). Makes about ⅔ cup.

1 teaspoon: Calories 26; Saturated Fat 2 g; Total Fat 3 g; Protein 0 g; Carbohydrate 0 g; Fiber 0 g; Sodium 0 mg; Cholesterol 8 mg

BLUEBERRY SYRUP

◆◆◆

In the 1950's, pancake houses began appearing all across America. A selection of flavored syrups has almost always been offered, inspiring cooks at home to experiment with new flavors.

1	quart fresh blueberries, washed and stemmed, or frozen blueberries, thawed (about 4½ cups)	2	cups sugar
		¼	cup light corn syrup
		3	tablespoons fresh lemon juice
1	cup cold water	½	teaspoon ground cinnamon
4	strips lemon zest, each 2 x ½ inch	¼	teaspoon ground allspice
6	whole cloves		

PREP TIME: 20 MIN. / COOKING TIME: 12 MIN.

1 In a food processor or blender, purée 3 cups of the blueberries. Pour into a medium-size saucepan along with the water, lemon zest, and cloves. Bring to a boil, lower the heat, and simmer, uncovered, for 3 minutes. Strain into a large heatproof bowl and discard the solids.

2 Return the purée to the saucepan with the sugar, corn syrup, lemon juice, cinnamon, and allspice. Bring to a boil and cook, uncovered, 3 minutes more. Remove from the heat and stir in the remaining 1 cup of blueberries. Serve over Flapjacks (page 309), Souffléd French Toast (page 310), or ice cream. Store in the refrigerator for up to 2 weeks. Reheat over low heat before serving. Makes about 4 cups.

3 tablespoons: Calories 143; Saturated Fat 0 g; Total Fat 0 g; Protein 1 g; Carbohydrate 38 g; Fiber 1 g; Sodium 5 mg; Cholesterol 0 mg

◆

Strawberry Syrup

Prepare as for Blueberry syrup, substituting **1 quart fresh or thawed frozen strawberries** for the blueberries. Makes about 4 cups. *3 tablespoons: Calories 124; Saturated Fat 0 g; Total Fat 0 g; Protein 1 g; Carbohydrate 33 g; Fiber 0 g; Sodium 2 mg; Cholesterol 0 mg*

RASPBERRY SAUCE

◆◆◆

With the introduction of the electric blender in the mid-20th century, this method of whirling up a dessert sauce from frozen berries became very popular. It's still a favorite today.

1	package (12 ounces) frozen dry-pack raspberries, thawed	¼	cup fresh orange juice
⅓	cup sugar	4	strips orange zest, each 2 x ½ inch

PREP TIME: 15 MIN. / COOKING TIME: 3 MIN.

1 In a food processor or blender, purée the raspberries. If you want a smooth sauce, line a strainer with cheesecloth and push through the purée, catching the juice in a bowl (you should have 1 cup of juice). Discard the solids and seeds.

2 In a small saucepan, bring all the remaining ingredients just to a boil over moderate heat. Strain into the raspberry purée. Serve the sauce at room temperature over Fresh Blueberry Waffles (page 311), Blueberry Batter Cakes (page 309), or slices of 1-2-3-4 Cake (page 336), or serve it chilled over ice cream. Refrigerate any extra sauce in a covered container for up to 2 weeks. Makes 1½ cups.

3 tablespoons: Calories 54; Saturated Fat 0 g; Total Fat 0 g; Protein 1 g; Carbohydrate 14 g; Fiber 1 g; Sodium 2 mg; Cholesterol 0 mg

◆

Cinnamon Peach Sauce

Prepare as for Raspberry Sauce, substituting **one 12-ounce package thawed, frozen, dry-pack peaches (preferably freestone),** and adding **two 3-inch cinnamon sticks, broken,** to the saucepan (Step 2). Makes 1½ cups. *3 tablespoons: Calories 52; Saturated Fat 0 g; Total Fat 0 g; Protein 0 g; Carbohydrate 14 g; Fiber 0 g; Sodium 0 mg; Cholesterol 0 mg*

FROM THE
BREAD BASKET

◆◆◆

Nothing says "down home" quite as much as bread baking in the oven. Indeed, at one time in America, creating a perfect loaf was considered an essential part of an accomplished homemaker's skills. Whether you're a pro or a novice at this task, there are ample opportunities in this chapter to try your hand at recapturing the heavenly aromas and homey memories of yesteryear.

For good health, start with Country Loaf or Rustic Whole-Wheat Round, made with such nutritious ingredients as whole-wheat flour, wheat germ, and nonfat milk. For a special occasion, shape up some sweet renditions, such as Monkey Bread, Sugarplum Wreath, or Cinnamon Rolls. When youngsters are around, roll out Crowd-Pleasin' Pizza or a batch of Honey-Glazed Doughnuts. Or if time is short, quickly stir up some Corn Pone or Hush Puppies from south of the Mason-Dixon Line. For a bit of nostalgia, try beating biscuits the way it used to be done—with a hammer! Or flip up some flapjacks. You'll find the rewards are many with our updated, health-conscious recipes that still feature the old-fashioned textures and flavors.

COUNTRY LOAF

◆◆◆

½ cup lukewarm low-fat (2% milkfat) milk (105° to 115°F)

2 packages (¼ ounce each) active dry yeast

6 teaspoons sugar

1¾ cups lukewarm water

½ cup non-fat dry milk

¼ cup wheat germ

4 tablespoons unsalted butter or margarine, melted

2 teaspoons salt

5 cups bread or all-purpose flour

PREP TIME: 30 MIN. / RISING TIME: 2 HR.
BAKING TIME: 35 MIN.

1 Into a large bowl, pour the low-fat milk; stir in the yeast and 1 teaspoon of the sugar. Let stand for 10 minutes or until foamy. In a medium-size bowl, combine the water, non-fat dry milk, wheat germ, 2 tablespoons of the butter, the salt, and the remaining 5 teaspoons of sugar; stir into the yeast mixture. Using a wooden spoon, beat in the flour, 1 cup at a time, until a soft dough forms.

2 Knead (page 364) on a lightly floured surface for 8 minutes or until the dough is smooth and elastic. Transfer the dough to a large buttered bowl, turning to coat with the butter. Cover loosely and let rise in a warm place for 1 hour or until doubled in size.

3 Lightly butter two 9" x 5" x 3" loaf pans or two 7-inch (1½-quart) soufflé dishes. Punch down the dough and knead gently on a lightly floured surface for 2 minutes. Shape into 2 loaves and place in the pans, seam-side-down. Cover and let rise for 1 hour more or until doubled in size.

4 Preheat the oven to 400°F. Brush the loaves with the remaining butter; bake for 35 minutes or until brown and the bread sounds hollow when tapped on the bottom. Turn onto a rack to cool and dust the tops with a little flour if you wish. Slice with a serrated knife. Makes 2 loaves.

One ¾-inch slice: Calories 137; Saturated Fat 2 g; Total Fat 3 g; Protein 4 g; Carbohydrate 24 g; Fiber 0 g; Sodium 218 mg; Cholesterol 6 mg

Old-fashioned homemade country bread, swirled with cinnamon and sugar and ready for enjoying

◆

Cinnamon Swirl

Prepare loaf pans and dough as for Country Loaf. Melt ¼ **cup unsalted butter or margarine**. In a cup, mix ½ **cup sugar** with **1 tablespoon ground cinnamon**. Halve the dough. Roll out 1 piece into a 9- x 15-inch rectangle. Brush with ½ of the butter, sprinkle with ½ of the sugar mixture, roll up jelly-roll-fashion. Repeat with the second piece. Let the loaves rise in pans for 1 hour; brush with the remaining butter as in Country Loaf. Bake at 375°F for 30 minutes. Makes 2 loaves. *One ¾-inch slice: Calories 176; Saturated Fat 3 g; Total Fat 5 g; Protein 4 g; Carbohydrate 29 g; Fiber 0 g; Sodium 218 mg; Cholesterol 13 mg*

RUSTIC WHOLE-WHEAT ROUND

◆◆◆

½ cup lukewarm low-fat (2% milkfat) milk (105° to 115°F)

2 packages (¼ ounce each) active dry yeast

6 teaspoons packed light brown sugar

1½ cups lukewarm water

½ cup non-fat dry milk

3 tablespoons light molasses

2 teaspoons salt

4 cups whole-wheat flour

2½ to 3 cups bread or all-purpose flour

2 tablespoons unsalted butter, melted

PREP TIME: 30 MIN. / RISING TIME: 2 HR.
BAKING TIME: 35 MIN.

1 Into a large bowl, pour the low-fat milk; stir in the yeast and 1 teaspoon of the sugar. Let stand for 10 minutes or until foamy. In a medium-size bowl, combine the water with the non-fat dry milk, molasses, the remaining 5 teaspoons of sugar, and salt; stir into the yeast mixture. Using a wooden spoon, beat in both of the flours, 1 cup at a time, until a soft dough forms.

2 Knead (page 364) on a lightly floured surface for 8 minutes or until the dough is smooth and elastic, then transfer to a large buttered bowl, turning to coat. Cover loosely and let rise in a warm place for 1 hour or until doubled in size.

3 Lightly butter two 7-inch (1½-quart) soufflé dishes. Punch down the dough and knead gently on a lightly floured surface for 2 minutes. Shape into 2 round loaves and place in the dishes, seam-side-down. Cover and let rise for 1 hour more or until doubled in size.

4 Preheat the oven to 400°F. Brush the loaves with the butter and bake for 35 minutes or until the bread sounds hollow when tapped on the bottom. Turn onto a rack to cool, and dust the tops with a little extra flour if you wish. Slice with a serrated knife. Makes 2 loaves.

One ¾-inch slice: Calories 201; Saturated Fat 1 g; Total Fat 2 g; Protein 7 g; Carbohydrate 40 g; Fiber 1 g; Sodium 285 mg; Cholesterol 5 mg

SALLY LUNN BREAD

◆◆◆

Sally Lunn sold golden, puffy tea breads on the streets of Bath, England, in the 18th century. Hers were made in tiny individual molds, but we've baked ours in a spectacular Bundt pan.

½ cup lukewarm low-fat (2% milkfat) milk (105° to 115°F)

½ cup lukewarm water

1 package (¼ ounce) active dry yeast

⅓ cup sugar

½ cup plus 2 table-spoons unsalted butter or margarine, at room temperature

1 teaspoon salt

3 large eggs

3½ to 4 cups all-purpose flour

PREP TIME: 30 MIN. / RISING TIME: 2 HR.
BAKING TIME: 40 MIN.

1 Into a small bowl, pour the low-fat milk and water, then stir in the yeast and 1 teaspoon of the sugar; let stand for 10 minutes or until foamy. In a large bowl, with an electric mixer on high, beat ½ cup of the butter until creamy. Add the remaining sugar and the salt, then the eggs one at a time, beating until light and fluffy.

2 Using a wooden spoon, beat in the flour, 1 cup at a time, alternately with the yeast mixture, until the dough is smooth and elastic. Transfer the dough to a large buttered bowl, turning to coat with the butter. Cover and let rise in a warm place for 1 hour or until doubled in size.

3 Butter a 9-inch nonstick Bundt or tube pan. Punch down the dough, beat with a spoon for 2 minutes, and transfer to the pan. Cover and let rise for 1 hour more or until doubled in size.

4 Preheat the oven to 350°F. In a small saucepan, melt the remaining 2 tablespoons of butter and brush on the top. Bake for 40 minutes or until golden. Turn onto a rack to cool. Makes one 9-inch Bundt or round loaf or 20 slices.

One ¾-inch slice: Calories 161; Saturated Fat 4 g; Total Fat 7 g; Protein 4 g; Carbohydrate 21 g; Fiber 0 g; Sodium 120 mg; Cholesterol 49 mg

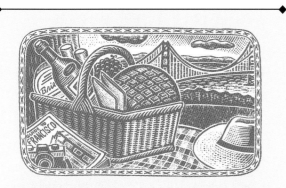

◆ Sourdough, from the City by the Bay ◆

"True sourdough begins with a starter of organic flour and water — no yeast at all," explains Steven Sullivan, baker extraordinaire of the Acme Bread Company near San Francisco. Because sourdough bread is naturally leavened, it takes longer to prepare, but that famous flavor the City by the Bay is known for is well worth the trouble. "Let the starter ferment for 2 to 3 days until nice and bubbly. Mix it with flour and water (see recipe below) to make the sponge, then add more flour, water, and salt for the dough.

"You need only ½ cup of starter to make 3 loaves, so you'll have plenty to use later. (This is the beauty of a good starter!). Refrigerate the extra in a covered container for up to 1 week. Use it for more bread, or discard half and replenish the rest (page 364). Within 3 hours, it's ready for baking or refrigerating again."

SAN FRANCISCO SOURDOUGH

◆◆◆

Here is a naturally leavened sourdough, made with a homemade starter, from baker Steven Sullivan of Berkeley, California.

For the starter:

1½ cups lukewarm water (105° to 115°F)

2 cups unbleached organic bread flour (often found in health food stores)

For the sponge and bread:

½ cup starter

10 cups unbleached organic bread flour

3 cups lukewarm water (105° to 115°F)

3½ teaspoons salt

PREP TIME: 45 MIN. / STARTER: 48 HR.
RISING TIME: 12 HR. / COOKING TIME: 2¼ HR.

1 To make the starter: In a medium-size bowl, stir ¾ cup of the water and 1 cup of the flour until smooth. Cover with a towel and set in a warm place for 2 days or until bubbly. Stir in the remaining ¾ cup of water and 1 cup of flour, cover, and let stand overnight before using in sourdough bread. Refrigerate leftover starter in a loosely covered container for up to 1 week.

2 To make the sponge: In a large bowl, combine the ½ cup of starter with ¼ cup each of the flour and water. Cover and let stand in a warm place for 2 hours. Stir in 3 cups of the flour and ¾ cup of the water until well blended. Cover and let rise for 4 to 6 hours or until spongy.

3 To make the bread: Into another large bowl, pour the remaining 2 cups of water. Add the sponge in pieces and let stand for 5 minutes or until softened. Stir in 6¼ cups of the remaining flour and the salt. Turn onto a floured board, cover, and let rest for 10 minutes. Knead (page 364) for 10 minutes or until smooth and elastic, adding the remaining ½ cup flour as needed. Transfer the dough to a large buttered bowl, turning to coat with the butter. Cover loosely and let rise in a warm place for 3 hours or until doubled in size.

4 Butter three 15½- x 14-inch baking sheets. Punch down the dough, divide into thirds, and shape each into an 8-inch round loaf. Place each loaf, smooth-side-up, on a baking sheet. Sprinkle with a little flour, cover, and let rise in a warm place for 3 to 4 hours or until doubled.

5 Preheat the oven to 475°F; place a pan of boiling water on the bottom rack. With a razor blade, make crisscrossed slashes in the top of each loaf. Lower the oven temperature to 400°F, and bake each loaf separately on the middle rack for 45 minutes or until golden. Makes 3 loaves.

One ¾-inch slice: Calories 196; Saturated Fat 0 g; Total Fat 1 g; Protein 6 g; Carbohydrate 39 g; Fiber 1 g; Sodium 313 mg; Cholesterol 0 mg

CHALLAH BREAD

◆◆◆

This bread is a Jewish tradition that assumes different shapes, depending upon the event for which it is served. On the Shabbat (Sabbath), it is braided; for Rosh Hashanah and Yom Kippur, it is shaped into round loaves.

¼	cup lukewarm low-fat (2% milkfat) milk (105° to 115°F)	3	tablespoons unsalted butter or margarine, melted
1	packet (¼ ounce) active dry yeast	1	teaspoon salt
2	tablespoons sugar	3	cups all-purpose flour
1	pinch saffron (optional)	1	large egg white
½	cup lukewarm water	1	tablespoon cold water
2	large eggs	2	tablespoons poppy seeds

PREP TIME: 30 MIN. / RISING TIME: 2 HR.
COOKING TIME: 30 MIN.

1 Into a large bowl, pour the milk, then stir in the yeast and 1 tablespoon of the sugar and let stand for 10 minutes or until foamy. Dissolve the saffron in the lukewarm water.

2 In a medium-size bowl, with an electric mixer set on high, beat the eggs until light yellow. Add the saffron water, butter, the remaining 1 tablespoon of sugar, and the salt, beating 1 minute longer, then stir into the milk mixture. Using a wooden spoon, beat in the flour, 1 cup at a time, until a soft dough forms.

3 Knead (page 364) for 8 minutes or until smooth and elastic. Transfer the dough to a large buttered bowl, turning to coat with the butter. Cover loosely and let rise in a warm place for 1 hour or until doubled in size.

4 Butter a 15½- x 14-inch baking sheet. Punch down the dough and divide into 3 equal pieces. On a lightly floured surface, roll out each piece into a 12- x 1-inch rope. Place the 3 ropes side-by-side on the baking sheet. Pinch the top ends together, braid, then tuck the ends under.

A braid of Jewish Challah: Ready for breaking and sharing with the family on the Shabbat

5 In a cup, whisk the egg white with the cold water and brush over the braid. Sprinkle with the poppy seeds. Cover and let rise for 1 hour more or until doubled in size.

6 Preheat the oven to 375°F. Bake for 30 minutes or until golden brown. (If the bread seems to be browning too quickly, lay a piece of foil loosely over the top.) Transfer to a rack to cool. Makes one 14- x 8-inch loaf.

One ¾-inch slice: Calories 209; Saturated Fat 3 g; Total Fat 6 g; Protein 6 g; Carbohydrate 32 g; Fiber 0 g; Sodium 236 mg; Cholesterol 53 mg

MINNESOTA LIMPA
◆◆◆

*Travel through the Swedish communities
in the Midwest and you're likely to find this
traditional country rye bread, flavored subtly
with orange and spices.*

2 cups cold water	¼ cup each honey and dark molasses
1 teaspoon each anise, caraway, and fennel seeds	1 to 2 tablespoons grated orange rind
2 packets (¼ ounce each) active dry yeast	2 teaspoons salt
	3 cups rye flour
3 tablespoons unsalted butter or margarine, at room temperature	1 cup light or dark raisins
	3 cups bread flour or all-purpose flour

PREP TIME: 45 MIN. / RISING TIME: 2 HR.
COOKING TIME: 35 MIN.

1 In a medium-size saucepan, bring 1 cup of the water and the anise, caraway, and fennel seeds to a boil over high heat. Lower the heat and simmer, uncovered, for 5 minutes. Pour into a large bowl, add the remaining 1 cup of water, and cool to lukewarm (105° to 115°F). Stir in the yeast and let stand for 10 minutes or until foamy.

2 Stir in the butter, honey, molasses, orange rind, and salt. Using an electric mixer set on low (preferably one equipped with a dough hook), beat in the rye flour, 1 cup at a time, until smooth.

3 Using a wooden spoon, stir in the raisins, then the bread flour, 1 cup at a time, beating until a stiff dough forms. Knead (page 364) for 8 minutes or until smooth and elastic. Transfer the dough to a large buttered bowl, turning to coat with the butter. Cover loosely and let rise in a warm place for 1 hour or until doubled in size.

4 Lightly butter a 15½- x 14-inch baking sheet. Punch down the dough and knead gently on a lightly floured surface for 2 minutes. Halve the dough, shape each half into a ball, then place the balls at opposite ends of the baking sheet, flatten-

Sweet Monkey Bread—A pull-apart ring for coffee hour or teatime, made by monkeying around with the dough

ing them slightly to form 5-inch rounds. Using a sharp knife, cut 3 slashes in each top; cover and let rise 1 hour more or until doubled in size.

5 Preheat the oven to 375°F. Bake the loaves for 35 minutes or until the tops are brown and the bottoms sound hollow when tapped. (If the bread seems to be browning too quickly, lay a piece of foil on top.) Transfer to a rack to cool. If you like a soft crust, brush the tops of the hot loaves with a little melted butter. Makes 2 loaves.

*One ¾-inch slice: Calories 228; Saturated Fat 1 g;
Total Fat 2 g; Protein 5 g; Carbohydrate 48 g; Fiber 0 g;
Sodium 271 mg; Cholesterol 5 mg*

MONKEY BREAD

◆◆◆

1½ cups lukewarm water
    (105° to 115°F)

2   packets (¼ ounce
    each) active dry yeast

3   tablespoons
    granulated sugar

½   cup nonfat dry milk

2   teaspoons salt

12 tablespoons
    (1½ sticks) unsalted
    butter (not
    margarine)

5   to 6 cups bread flour
    or all-purpose flour

⅓   cup firmly packed
    light brown sugar

⅓   cup honey

PREP TIME: 30 MIN. / RISING TIME: 2 HR.
COOKING TIME: 45 MIN. / STANDING TIME: 20 MIN.

1 In a large bowl, combine ½ cup of the water, the yeast, and 1 tablespoon of the granulated sugar; let stand for 10 minutes or until foamy. In a small bowl, combine the remaining 1 cup of water, the nonfat dry milk, the remaining 2 tablespoons of granulated sugar, the salt, and 2 tablespoons of the butter, then stir into the yeast mixture. Using a wooden spoon, beat in the flour, 1 cup at a time, until a soft dough forms.

2 Knead (page 364) for 8 minutes or until smooth and elastic. Transfer to a large buttered bowl, turning to coat with the butter. Cover loosely; let rise in a warm place for 1 hour or until doubled in size. Punch down the dough, knead gently for 2 minutes, then let rest for 10 minutes.

3 Butter a 10-inch tube pan. In a small saucepan, melt the remaining 10 tablespoons of butter and stir in the brown sugar and honey. Pull off golf-ball-size pieces of dough, dip in the butter mixture, and stack in the tube pan in circular layers. Brush the top with the remaining butter mixture; cover. Let rise 1 hour more or until doubled in size.

4 Preheat the oven to 375°F. Bake for 45 minutes to 1 hour or until set. Let the bread stand in the pan on a rack for 10 minutes, before turning out on the rack to cool. Makes 12 servings.

*1 serving: Calories 379; Saturated Fat 8 g;
Total Fat 13 g; Protein 7 g; Carbohydrate 59 g; Fiber 0 g;
Sodium 382 mg; Cholesterol 34 mg*

ANADAMA BREAD

◆◆◆

One of many tales attributes this bread to a New England sea captain's wife, who baked a delicious cornmeal and molasses bread. Supposedly, her gravestone reads: "Anna was a lovely bride, but Anna, damn 'er, up and died."

¾   cup low-fat
    (1% milkfat) milk

½   cup plus 1
    tablespoon yellow
    cornmeal

¼   cup molasses

2   tablespoons unsalted
    butter or margarine

1   teaspoon salt

¼   cup lukewarm water
    (105° to 115°F)

1   packet (¼ ounce)
    active dry yeast

1   teaspoon sugar

1   large egg, slightly
    beaten

3   cups all-purpose
    flour

PREP TIME: 30 MIN. / RISING TIME: 1¾ HR.
COOKING TIME: 45 MIN./ COOLING TIME: 10 MIN.

1 In a small saucepan, bring the milk just to a boil. Add the ½ cup of cornmeal, the molasses, butter, and salt; cool to lukewarm in a large bowl.

2 Meanwhile, in a cup, combine the water, yeast, and sugar; let stand for 10 minutes or until foamy, then stir into the cornmeal mixture. Beat in the egg and 1 cup of the flour, then the remaining flour until a soft dough forms.

3 Knead (page 364) for 5 minutes or until smooth and elastic. Transfer the dough to a buttered bowl, turning to coat with the butter. Cover loosely and let rise in a warm place for 1 hour or until doubled in size.

4 Butter a 9" x 5" x 3" loaf pan. Punch down the dough and knead gently for 2 minutes. Shape into a loaf, place in the pan, seam-side-down, and sprinkle with the remaining cornmeal. Cover; let rise for 45 minutes or until doubled. Preheat the oven to 350°F. Bake for 45 minutes. Cool in the pan on a rack for 10 minutes. Makes 1 loaf.

*One ¾-inch slice: Calories 225; Saturated Fat 2 g;
Total Fat 4 g; Protein 6 g; Carbohydrate 42 g; Fiber 0 g;
Sodium 231 mg; Cholesterol 29 mg*

Sugarplum Wreath

◆ ◆ ◆

Making wreaths for Christmas is a holiday tradition. This edible one makes a delicious way to celebrate Christmas morn.

½ cup lukewarm water (105° to 115°F)

2 packets (¼ ounce each) active dry yeast

2 tablespoons plus ⅓ cup granulated sugar

1½ cups lukewarm whole or low-fat (2% milkfat) milk

8 tablespoons unsalted butter (not margarine), at room temperature

2 large eggs, beaten

2 tablespoons grated orange rind

2 teaspoons salt

6 cups all-purpose flour

6 tablespoons unsalted butter (not margarine), melted

For the filling:

1 cup chopped red and green candied fruits (cherries and pineapple)

1 cup firmly packed light brown sugar

½ cup each pecans and golden raisins

1 tablespoon ground cinnamon

For the icing:

1¼ cups sifted confectioners sugar

2 tablespoons fresh orange juice

1 teaspoon vanilla extract

PREP TIME: 30 MIN. / RISING TIME: 2 HR.
COOKING TIME: 20 MIN. / COOLING TIME: 15 MIN.

---

1 In a large bowl, combine the water, yeast, and the 2 tablespoons of granulated sugar and let stand for 10 minutes or until foamy. In a medium-size bowl, combine the milk, the remaining ⅓ cup of sugar, the 8 tablespoons of the room temperature butter, the eggs, orange rind, and salt; stir into the yeast mixture.

2 Using a wooden spoon, beat in the flour, 1 cup at a time, until a soft dough forms. Knead (page 364) for 8 minutes or until smooth and elastic. Transfer the dough to a large buttered bowl, turning to coat with the butter; cover loosely. Let rise in a warm place for 1 hour or until the dough has doubled in size.

3 Lightly butter two 15½- x 14-inch baking sheets. For the filling: In a food processor or blender, process all the filling ingredients for 1 minute or just until finely chopped. Punch down the dough and divide into 2 equal pieces.

4 On a lightly floured surface, roll out each piece to a 20- x 15-inch rectangle, brush each with 3 tablespoons of the melted butter, and sprinkle with ½ of the filling, leaving a ½-inch border uncovered. Starting at a wide end, roll up each piece of dough jelly-roll-style. Lay each piece on a baking sheet, seam-side-down, and form into a ring, pinching the ends together.

5 Using scissors, cut at 1-inch intervals from the outside of the ring toward (but not through) the center. Twist each "petal" on its side to show the filling. Cover and let rise for 1 hour or until doubled in size.

6 Preheat the oven to 375°F. Brush each wreath with a little extra milk if you wish and bake for 20 minutes or just until lightly-browned. Meanwhile, make the icing by stirring all of the icing ingredients in a small bowl until smooth. Cool the wreaths on a rack for 15 minutes, then drizzle each with ½ of the icing. Decorate with candied red cherries and green gumdrop leaves (page 367) if you wish. Makes two 14-inch coffee cakes of 12 servings each.

---

1 serving: Calories 301; Saturated Fat 5 g; Total Fat 9 g; Protein 5 g; Carbohydrate 51 g; Fiber 0 g; Sodium 209 mg; Cholesterol 39 mg

◆

Orange Sunflower Coffee Cake

Prepare as for Sugarplum Wreath, substituting for the filling in Step 3 a mixture of **1 cup finely chopped toasted pecans, ½ cup each firmly packed light brown sugar and granulated sugar, 2 tablespoons grated orange rind, and 2 teaspoons ground cinnamon.** Shape, fill, bake, and glaze as directed. Makes two 14-inch coffee cakes of 12 servings each. *1 serving: Calories 305; Saturated Fat 7 g; Total Fat 12 g; Protein 5 g; Carbohydrate 44 g; Fiber 0 g; Sodium 193 mg; Cholesterol 46 mg*

*'Tis the season
for a holiday
gathering around
a Sugarplum Wreath*

CINNAMON ROLLS

◆◆◆

*During the Mississippi flood alert of 1993,
Sheriff Robert Nall from Quincy, Illinois, worked
the levees, hauling sandbags to hold back
the flood waters. Often, he arose at 4:00 a.m. to
bake these rolls for his crew.*

2½	cups all-purpose flour
⅓	cup granulated sugar
½	teaspoon salt
1	packet (¼ ounce) active dry yeast
½	cup (1 stick) plus 3 tablespoons unsalted butter or margarine

½	cup plus 3 tablespoons low-fat (2% milkfat) milk
2	tablespoons water
1	large egg, beaten
⅔	cup firmly packed light brown sugar
2	tablespoons ground cinnamon
1½	cups sifted confectioners sugar

PREP TIME: 30 MIN. / RISING TIME: 1¾ HR.
COOKING TIME: 15 MIN. / COOLING TIME: 5 MIN.

1 In a large bowl, combine the flour, granulated sugar, salt, and yeast. In a small saucepan, heat ½ cup each of the butter and milk with the water over moderate heat until very warm (120° to 130°F). Remove from the heat; whisk in the egg.

2 Using a wooden spoon, beat the milk mixture into the flour mixture until a soft dough forms. Knead (page 364) for 8 minutes or until smooth. Transfer the dough to a large buttered bowl, turning to coat with the butter; cover. Let rise in a warm place for 1 hour or until doubled.

3 Butter a 15½- x 14-inch baking sheet. In a cup, mix the brown sugar and cinnamon. Punch down the dough and roll out on a lightly floured surface into an 18- x 16-inch rectangle. Sprinkle with the sugar mixture. Starting at a narrow end, roll up the dough jelly-roll-style. Cut into 12 pieces, 1 inch thick; place cut-side-up on the baking sheet. Cover and let rise in a warm place 45 minutes more or until doubled in size.

4 Preheat the oven to 375°F. In a small saucepan, melt the remaining 3 tablespoons of butter over low heat and brush on the rolls. Bake for 15 minutes or until golden; cool on a rack for 5 minutes. Stir the confectioners sugar with the remaining 3 tablespoons of milk until smooth, then drizzle on the rolls. Makes 1 dozen rolls.

*1 roll: Calories 230; Saturated Fat 5 g;
Total Fat 8 g; Protein 3 g; Carbohydrate 37 g; Fiber 0 g;
Sodium 80 mg; Cholesterol 31 mg*

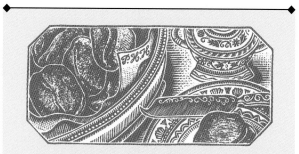

◆ A Delicious Mistake ◆

"The first Parker House rolls were a mistake," states Chef Joe Ribas of the Parker House Hotel in Boston. "One day in the late 1800's, a Chef Wood mixed up the dough for sweet rolls incorrectly. Instead of throwing it out, he baked some small rolls, and thus began a delicious tradition. Over the years, we have perfected their pocketbook shapes. The trick is to fold the circles of dough not quite in half, stretching the top half over the bottom, stopping just before the edges meet.

"We like to serve them hot from the oven. (On a busy day, we bake over 1,800!) If you wish to freeze them, do so right after shaping, then allow them to rise in a warm place before baking."

PARKER HOUSE ROLLS

◆ ◆ ◆

⅓ cup lukewarm water (105° to 115°F)	2 tablespoons nonfat dry milk
1 packet (¼ ounce) active dry yeast	7 tablespoons unsalted butter (not margarine), melted
4 tablespoons sugar	
1⅓ cups whole or low-fat (2% milkfat) milk	2 teaspoons salt
	4½ cups all-purpose flour

PREP TIME: 45 MIN. / RISING TIME: 1½ HR.
COOKING TIME: 10 MIN.

1 In a large bowl, combine the water, yeast, and 1 tablespoon of the sugar and let stand for 10 minutes or until foamy. Add the whole milk, nonfat dry milk, 4 tablespoons of the butter, the remaining 3 tablespoons of sugar, and the salt and stir until the dry milk has dissolved.

2 Stir in the flour, 1 cup at a time, beating until a soft dough forms. Knead (page 364) for 8 minutes or until smooth and elastic. Transfer the dough to a large buttered bowl, turning to coat with the butter. Cover loosely and let rise in a warm place for 1 hour or until doubled in size.

3 Preheat the oven to 375°F. Butter 2 large baking sheets. Punch down the dough and knead on a lightly floured surface for 1 minute. Halve the dough and roll out each half into a 12-inch circle, ¼ to ⅜ inch thick. Using a 2½-inch biscuit cutter, cut each piece into 15 rounds, re-rolling the scraps as you go.

4 With the back of a knife, make an indentation through the center of each circle. Fold almost in half to make pocket-like semicircles; place ½ inch apart on the baking sheets. Let rise for 30 minutes or until doubled in size. Bake for 10 minutes or just until lightly browned, then brush with the remaining butter Makes 2½ dozen rolls.

1 roll: Calories 108; Saturated Fat 2 g; Total Fat 3 g; Protein 3 g; Carbohydrate 17 g; Fiber 0 g; Sodium 150 mg; Cholesterol 9 mg

◆

Fan Tans

Butter 24 muffin cups. Prepare dough as for Parker House Rolls. Halve dough; roll each piece into an 8- x 16-inch rectangle, cut into five 16- x 1½-inch strips, stack, then cut the strips crosswise into 12 equal pieces. Place in muffin cups, cut-side-up. Brush with the melted butter. Let rise and bake as for Parker House Rolls. Makes 2 dozen.
1 roll: Calories 135; Saturated Fat 3 g; Total Fat 4 g; Protein 3 g; Carbohydrate 21 g; Fiber 0 g; Sodium 188 mg; Cholesterol 12 mg

Love Knots

Roll dough for Parker House Rolls into a rope, 24 x 2 inches; cut into twenty-four 1-inch pieces. Roll each piece into a slender 8-inch rope; tie in a simple knot. Brush with butter; let rise; bake as for Parker House Rolls. Makes 2½ dozen. *1 roll: Calories 108; Saturated Fat 2 g; Total Fat 3 g; Protein 3 g; Carbohydrate 17 g; Fiber 0 g; Sodium 150 mg; Cholesterol 9 mg*

POTATO ROLLS

◆◆◆

1 large baking potato, cooked and mashed (1 cup), reserving 1½ cups lukewarm cooking water (105° to 115°F)	1½ teaspoons salt
	2 large eggs, beaten
	4½ to 5½ cups all-purpose flour
2 packets (¼ ounce each) active dry yeast	2 tablespoons poppy seeds or sesame seeds
2 tablespoons sugar	**For the glaze:**
⅓ cup nonfat dry milk	1 large egg white
	1 teaspoon water

PREP TIME: 45 MIN. / RISING TIME: 1¾ HR.
COOKING TIME: 15 MIN.

1 In a large bowl, combine ½ cup of the potato cooking water, the yeast, and 1 tablespoon of the sugar; let stand for 10 minutes or until foamy. In a medium-size bowl, combine the remaining 1 cup of cooking water and 1 tablespoon of sugar, the nonfat dry milk, salt, and eggs. Stir in the mashed potatoes, then add this mixture to the yeast mixture and blend well.

2 Using a wooden spoon, stir in the flour, about 1 cup at a time, beating until a soft dough forms. Knead (page 364) for 8 minutes or until the dough is smooth and elastic. Transfer the dough to a large buttered bowl, turning to coat with the butter. Cover loosely and let rise in a warm place for 1 hour or until doubled in size.

3 Grease 2 large baking sheets. Punch down the dough and divide in half. Roll out each piece into a 20-inch log, about 2 inches in diameter, and cut into 12 equal pieces. Roll the pieces into 3-inch balls and place 2 inches apart on the baking sheets. Let rise 45 minutes longer or until doubled in size.

4 Preheat the oven to 400°F. To make the glaze: In a cup, whisk the egg white with the water. Brush on the tops of the rolls and sprinkle with the poppy seeds. Bake for 15 to 20 minutes or until golden brown. Makes 2 dozen rolls.

*1 roll: Calories 110; Saturated Fat 0 g;
Total Fat 1 g; Protein 4 g; Carbohydrate 21 g; Fiber 0 g;
Sodium 147 mg; Cholesterol 18 mg*

Three great rolls from just one dough: Parker House Rolls, Fan Tans and golden Love Knots

PIZZA CRUST

◆◆◆

Here's a homemade pizza dough that can be prepared in just 15 minutes. It makes enough for one extra-large or two standard-size pizzas.

1 cup lukewarm water (105° to 115°F)	3 cups all-purpose flour
1 packet (¼ ounce) active dry yeast	½ teaspoon salt
	2 tablespoons olive oil

PREP TIME: 15 MIN.

1 In a small bowl, stir together the water and yeast and let stand for 5 minutes or until foamy. In a large bowl, combine the flour and salt. Pour in the yeast mixture, drizzle on the oil, and beat with a wooden spoon until the mixture comes together in a soft dough.

2 Knead the dough (page 364) for 3 minutes or until smooth and elastic. Use to make All-American Pizza (page 187), Crowd Pleasin' Pizza (below), or your own favorite recipe. Makes sufficient dough for two 12-inch round pizzas or one 15- x 10-inch pizza, enough for 8 servings.

1 serving: Calories 203; Saturated Fat 1 g;
Total Fat 4 g; Protein 5 g; Carbohydrate 36 g; Fiber 0 g;
Sodium 135 mg; Cholesterol 0 mg

CROWD-PLEASIN' PIZZA

◆◆◆

1 recipe Pizza Crust (above)	2 tablespoons grated Parmesan cheese
2 tablespoons yellow cornmeal	2 plum tomatoes, thinly sliced (1 cup)
1 tablespoon olive oil	1 cup broccoli florets
1½ cups bottled marinara sauce	2 ounces pepperoni slices (optional)
2 cups shredded part-skim mozzarella cheese (8 ounces)	⅓ cup slivered fresh basil or 1 tablespoon dried basil leaves

Pan Pizza—plenty enough to please a hungry crowd

PREP TIME: 30 MIN. / COOKING TIME: 20 MIN.

1 Preheat the oven to 450°F. Prepare the dough. Sprinkle a 15½" x 10½" x 1" baking pan (or two 12-inch round pans) with the cornmeal. On a lightly floured surface, roll out the dough to a 17- x 12-inch rectangle (or two 14-inch circles).

2 Fit the dough into the pans and flute the edges. With your fingers, make small indentations (dimples) in the crust. Drizzle with the oil and top with the sauce. Bake for 10 minutes.

3 Remove from the oven, sprinkle with both of the cheeses, the tomatoes, broccoli, and the pepperoni if you wish, or add other favorite toppings. Sprinkle with the basil; bake 10 minutes longer. Makes 8 servings.

1 serving: Calories 343; Saturated Fat 4 g;
Total Fat 11 g; Protein 15 g; Carbohydrate 46 g; Fiber 1 g;
Sodium 422 mg; Cholesterol 17 mg

HAM AND CHEESE PIZZA ROLL

◆◆◆

From Josephine and Dennis Cieri of Hoboken, New Jersey, comes this rolled-up pizza. "It's great for a party . It can be served at room temperature, but is best when hot from the oven."

1 recipe Pizza Crust (opposite)
3 tablespoons olive oil
3 ounces thinly sliced ham (about 10 thin slices)
1 cup shredded sharp Cheddar cheese (4 ounces)

PREP TIME: 30 MIN. / COOKING TIME: 20 MIN.
COOLING TIME: 5 MIN.

1 Preheat the oven to 400°F and oil a 15½" x 14" x 1" baking sheet. Prepare the dough. On a lightly floured surface, roll out the dough into a 12- x 9-inch rectangle. Brush with the oil.

2 Lay the ham on the dough and sprinkle with the cheese, leaving a ½-inch border. Starting at a narrow end, roll up the dough jelly-roll-style. Using a sharp knife, make several slashes on top.

3 Bake for 20 minutes or until golden brown. Let the pan cool on a rack for 5 minutes. With a serrated knife, cut the roll into 1-inch slices. Serve with fresh greens tossed with Russian Dressing (page 260). Makes 8 servings.

1 serving: Calories 320; Saturated Fat 4 g; Total Fat 14 g; Protein 11 g; Carbohydrate 37 g; Fiber 0 g; Sodium 351 mg; Cholesterol 21 mg

As soon as one crosses the Mason-Dixon Line, hush puppies abound!

—John Shields
The Chesapeake Bay Cookbook

HUSH PUPPIES

◆◆◆

As one legend goes, during the Civil War, many cooks fried these bits of corn batter over a campfire. Then they tossed them to hungry dogs to stop their barking. These bites of fried bread soon became known as Hush Puppies.

2 cups yellow cornmeal
¼ cup all-purpose flour
1 teaspoon each baking powder, baking soda, and salt
⅓ cup finely chopped onion
1 large egg
1¼ cups low-fat buttermilk
Corn oil

PREP TIME: 15 MIN. / COOKING TIME: 10 MIN.

1 In a medium-size bowl, mix the cornmeal, flour, baking powder, baking soda, and salt, then stir in the onion. In a small bowl, whisk the egg and buttermilk. Add to the cornmeal mixture, all at once, and stir just until blended.

2 In a 12-inch skillet, heat 1 inch of the oil over medium heat to 365°F or until a 1-inch cube of bread browns in 30 seconds. Drop the batter by rounded teaspoonfuls into the hot oil. Cook for 2 to 3 minutes on each side or until golden brown. Drain on paper towels. Serve piping hot with Arkansas Slabs of Ribs (page 83). Makes 3 dozen Hush Puppies.

1 hush puppy: Calories 53; Saturated Fat 0 g; Total Fat 2 g; Protein 1 g; Carbohydrate 7 g; Fiber 1 g; Sodium 100 mg; Cholesterol 6 mg

◆

East Texas Hush Puppies

Prepare the batter as for Hush Puppies, adding **1 cup fresh or frozen corn kernels, 3 strips cooked bacon, crumbled, and 1 tablespoon minced jalapeño pepper** along with the onion in Step 1. Makes 3½ dozen Hush Puppies. *1 hush puppy: Calories 51; Saturated Fat 0 g; Total Fat 2 g; Protein 1 g; Carbohydrate 7 g; Fiber 0 g; Sodium 96 mg; Cholesterol 6 mg*

A spoonable bread made of corn and baked in a spider skillet

SPIDER SPOON BREAD

◆◆◆

During America's frontier days, a family's trusty iron frying pan often had legs that allowed it to set easily over coals; such a skillet was called a spider. But any heavy skillet works with this corn bread, also known as batter bread.

1 **cup sifted white or yellow cornmeal**	½ **cup unsalted butter or margarine**
¼ **cup all-purpose flour**	3 **large egg yolks**
3 **tablespoons sugar**	1½ **teaspoons baking powder**
1 **teaspoon salt**	1 **cup corn kernels**
4 **cups low-fat (2% milkfat) milk**	5 **large egg whites**

PREP TIME: 20 MIN. / COOKING TIME: 30 MIN.

1 Preheat the oven to 375°F. Grease a 12-inch cast iron or other heavy skillet (cover the handle of the second type with foil); heat in the oven.

2 Onto a piece of wax paper, mix the cornmeal, flour, sugar, and salt. In a medium-size saucepan, bring the milk and butter to a boil over moderate heat. Add the dry ingredients in a steady stream, whisking constantly. Remove from the heat and transfer to a large bowl to cool.

3 In a small bowl, with an electric mixer set on high, beat the egg yolks with the baking powder until thick and light yellow. Stir into the cornmeal mixture with the corn.

4 In a clean medium-size bowl, with clean beaters and the mixer set on high, beat the egg whites until stiff peaks form. Gently fold into the cornmeal mixture, then spoon into the hot skillet. Bake for 25 minutes or until puffy. Serve immediately, right from the skillet with Buttermilk Pecan Chicken (page 125). Makes 12 servings.

*1 serving: Calories 213; Saturated Fat 6 g;
Total Fat 11 g; Protein 7 g; Carbohydrate 22 g; Fiber 0 g;
Sodium 287 mg; Cholesterol 81 mg*

TEX-MEX CORN BREAD

Tex-Mex cooking may have begun along the Texas-Mexico border, but it fast became a favorite from coast to coast.

1¼ cups all-purpose flour	1 3-ounce jar roasted red peppers, drained and chopped
¾ cup yellow cornmeal	3 tablespoons each minced green onions and fresh or pickled jalapeño peppers with seeds
2 tablespoons sugar	
2 teaspoons baking powder	
1 teaspoon each baking soda and salt	1 cup fresh corn kernels (thawed if frozen)
1⅓ cups low-fat buttermilk	
1 large egg	3 tablespoons shredded Monterey Jack cheese
1 large egg white	
3 tablespoons vegetable shortening, melted	

PREP TIME: 30 MIN. / COOKING TIME: 20 MIN.

1 Preheat the oven to 425°F. Generously grease a 10-inch cast-iron skillet or other heavy skillet (cover the handle of the second type with foil) and place in the oven to heat.

2 In a large bowl, combine the flour, cornmeal, sugar, baking powder, baking soda, and salt. In a medium-size bowl, whisk the buttermilk, the egg and egg white, and shortening. Stir in the red peppers, green onions, and jalapeño peppers.

3 Pour the buttermilk mixture into the flour mixture all at once and stir just until blended. Fold in the corn, spoon the batter into the hot skillet, and sprinkle with the cheese. Bake for 20 minutes or until golden brown and a toothpick inserted in the center comes out clean. Serve immediately, straight from the skillet with Sespe Creek Chili (page 92). Makes 12 servings.

1 serving: Calories 268; Saturated Fat 2 g; Total Fat 6 g; Protein 8 g; Carbohydrate 46 g; Fiber 0 g; Sodium 392 mg; Cholesterol 27 mg

CORN PONE

In one part of the South, these corn sticks are known as Corn Pone; in other parts, Corn Dodgers. Most families have had a pan for baking them handed down generation after generation. If you don't have such a pan, bake the batter in a muffin pan instead.

2½ cups all-purpose flour	2 large eggs
1½ cups yellow cornmeal	2¼ cups low-fat buttermilk
½ cup sugar	¼ cup unsalted butter or margarine, melted
4 teaspoons baking powder	
1 teaspoon each baking soda and salt	¼ cup vegetable shortening, melted

PREP TIME: 20 MIN. / COOKING TIME: 12 MIN. FOR STICKS/MUFFINS OR 25 MIN. FOR BAKING PAN

1 Preheat the oven to 400°F. Grease a corn stick pan or 12 regular-size muffin cups, or one 12" x 8" x 3" baking pan; heat in the oven. In a large bowl, combine the flour, cornmeal, sugar, baking powder, baking soda, and salt.

2 In a medium-size bowl, with an electric mixer set on high, beat the eggs until light yellow. Reduce the speed to medium and blend in the buttermilk, butter, and shortening. Add to the flour mixture all at once and stir just until the flour disappears.

3 Spoon the batter into the hot pan. Bake the corn pone sticks or muffins for 12 to 15 minutes, the rectangular pan for 25 to 30 minutes or until golden and a toothpick inserted in the center comes out clean. Serve with Southern-Fried Steak (page 88). Makes 12 sticks or muffins or twelve 2½- x 3-inch servings.

1 corn pone stick: Calories 294; Saturated Fat 4 g; Total Fat 10 g; Protein 7 g; Carbohydrate 44 g; Fiber 0 g; Sodium 416 mg; Cholesterol 48 mg

BOSTON BROWN BREAD

◆◆◆

An old Puritan tradition couples the serving of this bread with Boston baked beans on the Sabbath.

1 cup all-purpose flour	1 cup low-fat buttermilk
1 cup rye flour	1 cup low-fat (2% milkfat) milk
1 cup yellow cornmeal	¾ cup dark molasses
2 teaspoons baking soda	1 cup dark raisins
1 teaspoon salt	1 cup chopped walnuts
1 teaspoon ground allspice	

PREP TIME: 20 MIN. / COOKING TIME: 1½ HR.
COOLING TIME: 10 MIN.

1 Butter 2 clean 12- to 16-ounce coffee cans. Completely line the insides with foil, leaving a 1-inch overhang; butter the foil. In a large bowl, mix both flours, the cornmeal, baking soda, salt, and allspice. Stir in both milks and the molasses until blended. Fold in the raisins and walnuts.

2 Evenly divide the batter between the 2 cans. Loosely cover the cans with plastic wrap, then tightly cover with foil. Place in an 8-quart stockpot, pour in enough boiling water to come halfway up the sides of the cans, and cover tightly.

3 Steam over low heat, (adding extra boiling water as needed) for 1½ hours or until a toothpick inserted in the center of the bread comes out clean. Using hot pads, carefully transfer the cans to a rack to cool for 10 minutes. Gently turn the cans upside down and lightly shake them as you ease the breads out in their foil liners. Carefully peel off the foil and serve with Boston Baked Beans (page 212). Makes 2 loaves.

One ¾-inch slice: Calories 222; Saturated Fat 1 g; Total Fat 5 g; Protein 5 g; Carbohydrate 41 g; Fiber 1 g; Sodium 265 mg; Cholesterol 2 mg

BISHOP'S BREAD

◆◆◆

On the American frontier in the 19th century, circuit-riding bishops would visit with families along their route. As the legend goes, when a bishop unexpectedly dropped by a parishioner's home one Sunday morning, his hostess created this bread from ingredients in the cupboard and named it in honor of her guest.

2 cups all-purpose flour	⅔ cup granulated sugar
1½ teaspoons each baking powder and ground cinnamon	⅓ cup firmly packed light brown sugar
½ teaspoon each salt, baking soda, and ground nutmeg	2 large eggs
	2 large egg whites
1½ cups each chopped mixed candied fruits and walnuts	¾ cup low-fat buttermilk
	1½ tablespoons grated orange rind
¼ cup unsalted butter or margarine, at room temperature	1 tablespoon grated lemon rind
	1 tablespoon vanilla extract

PREP TIME: 40 MIN. / COOKING TIME: 1 HR.
COOLING TIME: 5 MIN.

1 Preheat the oven to 350°F. Butter and flour a 9" x 5" x 3" loaf pan. Into a large bowl, sift the flour, baking powder, cinnamon, salt, baking soda, and nutmeg. Add the fruits and nuts; toss.

2 In a medium-size bowl, with an electric mixer set on high, beat the butter and 2 sugars on high until light and fluffy. Beat in the eggs and egg whites, the buttermilk, the orange and lemon rinds, and the vanilla. Add all at once to the flour mixture, stirring until well combined.

3 Spoon the batter into the pan and bake for 1 hour or until a toothpick inserted in the center comes out clean. Cool the bread in the pan on a rack for 5 minutes before removing. This bread freezes especially well. Makes one 9-inch loaf.

One ¾-inch slice: Calories 406; Saturated Fat 4 g; Total Fat 17 g; Protein 8 g; Carbohydrate 59 g; Fiber 1 g; Sodium 278 mg; Cholesterol 56 mg

Reminiscent of old New England: Freshly made Cranberry-Nut Bread

CRANBERRY-NUT BREAD

◆◆◆

*"When I ran our Soup du Jour restaurant
in Hopewell, New Jersey," states Frances Young,
"this was one of our favorite recipes. Its flavor
is even better the second day."*

2	cups all-purpose flour	1	small unpeeled orange, seeded and cut into small pieces
2	teaspoons baking powder	1½	cups coarsely chopped fresh or frozen cranberries
1	teaspoon salt		
½	teaspoon baking soda	1	cup sugar
¼	cup unsalted butter or margarine or vegetable shortening, at room temperature	1	large egg, beaten
		½	cup chopped walnuts

PREP TIME: 30 MIN. / COOKING TIME: 1 HR.
COOLING TIME: 5 MIN.

1 Preheat the oven to 350°F. Grease a 9" x 5" x 3" inch loaf pan. In a large bowl, sift together the flour, baking powder, salt, and baking soda. Using a pastry blender or 2 knives, cut in the butter until coarse crumbs form.

2 In a food processor or blender, process the orange pieces until almost smooth. Pour into a glass measuring cup and add boiling water to make 1 cup. Transfer to a medium-size bowl and mix with the cranberries, sugar, and egg.

3 Add this fruit mixture to the flour mixture all at once and stir just until blended. Fold in the walnuts and spoon into the pan. Bake for 1 hour. Cool the bread in the pan on a rack for 5 minutes before removing. Makes one 9-inch loaf.

*One ¾-inch slice: Calories 267; Saturated Fat 4 g;
Total Fat 9 g; Protein 4 g; Carbohydrate 43 g; Fiber 1 g;
Sodium 312 mg; Cholesterol 35 mg*

◆

Cranberry-Nut Muffins

Preheat the oven to 350°F. Butter 12 regular-size muffin cups or line with paper liners if you wish. Prepare the batter as for Cranberry-Nut Bread, then fill each muffin cup three-fourths full. Bake for 20 minutes or until set. Makes 1 dozen regular-size muffins. *1 muffin: Calories 222; Saturated Fat 3 g; Total Fat 8 g; Protein 4 g; Carbohydrate 36 g; Fiber 1 g; Sodium 260 mg; Cholesterol 29 mg*

BANANA-NUT BREAD

◆◆◆

Bananas were little known in North America until the late 19th century, when they appeared at the Philadelphia Centennial Exposition of 1876, wrapped in foil—yours for a dime!

2	cups all-purpose flour	2	tablespoons fresh lemon juice
1½	teaspoons baking powder	¼	cup unsalted butter or margarine, at room temperature
1	teaspoon ground cinnamon	⅔	cup granulated sugar
½	teaspoon baking soda	⅔	cup firmly packed light brown sugar
½	teaspoon salt	3	large eggs
¼	teaspoon each ground nutmeg and allspice	2	teaspoons vanilla
		⅓	cup low-fat buttermilk
4	large very ripe bananas (2 pounds)	⅔	cup chopped pecans, toasted (page 365)

PREP TIME: 30 MIN. / COOKING TIME: 1 HR.
COOLING TIME: 5 MIN.

1 Preheat the oven to 350°F. Grease a 9" x 5" x 3" loaf pan. Onto a piece of wax paper, sift the flour, baking powder, cinnamon, baking soda, salt, nutmeg, and allspice. In a medium-size bowl, using a potato masher, mash the bananas with the lemon juice (you should have about 3 cups.)

2 In a large bowl, with an electric mixer set on high, cream the butter. Add the granulated sugar, then ⅓ cup of the brown sugar, the eggs, one at a time, and the vanilla, beating until fluffy.

3 Using a wooden spoon, blend in the banana mixture. Stir in the flour mixture, alternately with the buttermilk just until the flour disappears; fold in the pecans. Spoon into the pan; sprinkle with the remaining brown sugar. Bake for 1 hour or until the center is set. Cool in the pan on a rack for 5 minutes before removing. Makes 1 loaf.

1 serving (for 12): Calories 377; Saturated Fat 4 g; Total Fat 11 g; Protein 4 g; Carbohydrate 70 g; Fiber 1 g; Sodium 233 mg; Cholesterol 14 mg

APPLE BRAN GEMS

◆◆◆

In 19th-century America, gems were made with whole-wheat or graham flour and baked in cast iron pans with rounded bottoms. Today's muffin pans work just as well.

1	cup wheat-bran dry cereal	1	cup chopped peeled baking apples, such as Rome Beauty
¾	cup low-fat (2% milkfat) milk	½	cup dark raisins
1	cup plus 2 tablespoons all-purpose flour	½	cup chopped walnuts (optional)
2	teaspoons baking powder	2	large eggs
½	teaspoon each salt and ground cinnamon	¼	cup vegetable oil
		⅓	cup firmly packed light brown sugar
		1	teaspoon vanilla extract

PREP TIME: 25 MIN. / COOKING TIME: 20 MIN.
COOLING TIME: 5 MIN.

1 Preheat the oven to 375°F. Grease 12 regular-size muffin cups or line with paper liners. In a small bowl, soak the bran cereal in the milk for 5 minutes or until softened.

2 Onto a piece of wax paper, sift the 1 cup of flour, the baking powder, salt, and cinnamon. On another piece of wax paper, toss the apples and raisins, plus the walnuts if you wish, with the remaining 2 tablespoons of flour.

3 In a large bowl, with an electric mixer set on high, beat the eggs, oil, sugar, and vanilla until light yellow. Using a wooden spoon, stir in the flour mixture, alternately with the bran mixture, just until blended. Fold in the apple mixture.

4 Fill each muffin cup almost full. Bake for 20 minutes or until golden. Cool in the pan on a rack for 5 minutes before removing them from the pan. Makes 1 dozen regular-size muffins.

1 muffin: Calories 170; Saturated Fat 1 g; Total Fat 6 g; Protein 4 g; Carbohydrate 27 g; Fiber 1 g; Sodium 203 mg; Cholesterol 37 mg

BLUEBERRY MUFFINS
◆◆◆

2 cups all-purpose flour

2 teaspoons baking powder

¼ teaspoon salt

2 tablespoons plus ⅔ cup sugar

½ teaspoon ground cinnamon

¼ teaspoon ground mace or nutmeg

½ cup unsalted butter or margarine, at room temperature

2 large eggs

1 teaspoon vanilla

3 cups fresh or dry-packed frozen and thawed blueberries, washed and stemmed

½ cup low-fat buttermilk

PREP TIME: 20 MIN. / COOKING TIME: 25 MIN. (REGULAR-SIZE) / COOLING TIME: 5 MIN.

1 Preheat the oven to 375°F. Grease 12 regular-size or 36 mini muffin cups or line with paper liners. Onto a piece of wax paper, sift the flour, baking powder, and salt. In a cup, mix 2 tablespoons of the sugar with the cinnamon and mace.

2 In a medium-size bowl, with an electric mixer set on high, beat the butter until creamy. Add the remaining ⅔ cup of sugar, then the eggs, one at a time, then the vanilla, beating until the mixture is light yellow and fluffy.

3 With a potato masher, mash 1 cup of the blueberries and stir them into the egg mixture with a wooden spoon. Using a wooden spoon, stir in the flour mixture, alternately with the buttermilk, just until blended. Fold in the remaining 2 cups of whole blueberries. Fill each muffin cup almost full, then sprinkle with the spiced sugar.

4 Bake for 25 minutes for regular-size or 15 minutes for mini muffins or until golden. Cool the muffins in the pan on a rack for 5 minutes before removing them. Serve with Strawberry Butter (page 284). Makes 1 dozen regular-size muffins or 3 dozen mini muffins.

1 regular-size muffin: Calories 234; Saturated Fat 5 g; Total Fat 9 g; Protein 4 g; Carbohydrate 35 g; Fiber 1 g; Sodium 124 mg; Cholesterol 58 mg

Children's tea time, with mini Mad Hatter Banana Muffins and tiny cups of hot chocolate

◆

Mad Hatter Banana Muffins

Prepare batter as for Blueberry Muffins, substituting ¾ **cup firmly packed light brown sugar** for the ⅔ cup granulated sugar and adding **1 teaspoon ground cinnamon** with the vanilla. Stir in **1½ cups ripe mashed bananas** instead of the berries, plus **1½ cups mini or regular-size chocolate chips**. Omit the spiced sugar topping. Bake in 3 dozen mini muffin cups for 15 minutes. Makes 3 dozen mini muffins. *1 mini muffin: Calories 112; Saturated Fat 2 g; Total Fat 5 g; Protein 2 g; Carbohydrate 16 g; Fiber 0 g; Sodium 48 mg; Cholesterol 21 mg*

Perfect for teatime:
Strawberry
Thumbprints, hot
from the oven

BETH'S BUTTERMILK BISCUITS

*Beth Allen's grandmother from
Gulfport, Mississippi, often made these biscuits
for breakfast, when the family gathered for holiday
visits. Although her grandmother never measured
anything, Beth has worked out the amounts of
ingredients to recreate the recipe.*

2 cups sifted all-purpose flour	⅓ cup solid vegetable shortening
1 tablespoon baking powder	2 tablespoons unsalted butter or margarine, at room temperature
1 teaspoon salt	
½ teaspoon baking soda	¾ cup low-fat buttermilk

PREP TIME: 20 MIN. / COOKING TIME: 12 MIN.

1 Preheat the oven to 450°F. In a large bowl, sift the flour, baking powder, salt, and baking soda. Using a pastry blender or 2 knives, cut in the shortening and butter until the mixture resembles coarse crumbs. Using a wooden spoon, stir in the buttermilk; mix just until a soft dough forms.

2 Knead (page 364) for 30 seconds on a lightly floured surface, then pat or roll into a 12-inch circle, ¾ inch thick. Using a 2-inch biscuit cutter (preferably a fluted one), cut into 18 biscuits, re-rolling the scraps of dough as you go.

3 Place 2 inches apart on an ungreased baking sheet; brush the tops with additional buttermilk, if you wish. Bake for 12 minutes or until golden brown. Makes 1½ dozen biscuits.

*1 biscuit: Calories 101; Saturated Fat 2 g;
Total Fat 5 g; Protein 2 g; Carbohydrate 11 g; Fiber 0 g;
Sodium 207 mg; Cholesterol 4 mg*

◆

Strawberry Thumbprints

Prepare the dough as for Beth's Buttermilk Biscuits. For each Thumbprint, pinch off about 1 rounded tablespoon of dough and roll in a ball; place balls 2 inches apart on a baking sheet. Using your thumb, make an indentation in the top of each and fill with about **1 teaspoon of strawberry jam**. Bake for 10 to 12 minutes or until lightly browned. Makes 2 dozen biscuits. *1 biscuit: Calories 93; Saturated Fat 1 g; Total Fat 4 g; Protein 1 g; Carbohydrate 13 g; Fiber 0 g; Sodium 156 mg; Cholesterol 3 mg*

BEATEN BISCUITS

Before cooks had baking powder, biscuit dough was beaten by hand, often as many as 500 strokes when company was coming. Our recipe includes a much easier food-processor method too.

2 cups all-purpose flour	½ cup cold hard butter, cut into small pieces
1 teaspoon salt	½ cup ice water

PREP TIME: 1 HR. (BY HAND) OR 20 MIN. (WITH FOOD PROCESSOR) / COOKING TIME: 30 MIN.

1 To beat biscuits by hand: In a large bowl, combine the flour and salt. Using your hands, work in the butter until coarse crumbs form. Add the ice water and stir with a fork just until a dough forms. Turn out on a lightly floured surface and beat with a hammer or mallet at least 200 times or until the dough blisters and becomes smooth and glossy.

2 To beat biscuits in a food processor: Put the flour and salt in the processor and spin the blade to aerate the mixture. While the processor is running, add the butter, then slowly pour in the ice water, processing until the dough forms a ball. Continue processing for about 2 minutes or until the dough becomes smooth and glossy.

3 To shape and bake the dough: Preheat the oven to 350°F. On a lightly floured surface, roll out the dough into a rectangle about ⅛ inch thick. Fold it over to make 2 equal layers. Cut with a 1½-inch biscuit cutter, re-rolling the scraps as you go. Arrange on an ungreased baking sheet. Using a fork, prick the top of each biscuit with 2 rows of holes. Bake for about 30 minutes or until golden brown. Serve with Honey Baked Ham (page 108). Makes 1½ dozen biscuits.

1 biscuit: Calories 98; Saturated Fat 3 g; Total Fat 6 g; Protein 2 g; Carbohydrate 11 g; Fiber 0 g; Sodium 120 mg; Cholesterol 15 mg

◆ Beating the Biscuits ◆

Back in the days of gracious plantation living, cooks in the deep South prided themselves on their beaten biscuits. When made right, they were light and flaky. Since baking powder was not yet available, air had to be beaten into the dough by hand to make the biscuits both light and tender.

Today, there are still many Southerners who carry on the beaten-biscuit tradition, but instead of beating the dough by hand, they use a hammer, a mallet, or even the flat side of an ax.

Evan Jones, in *American Food*, suggests using an electric food processor as a time-saving (and energy-saving!) way to beat the dough. "When baked and split, [the biscuits] should be crisply firm inside, similar to those made 200 years ago."

Once the dough is ready for shaping, folks who live in Virginia are likely to roll it out, then stamp it with a cutter. In Maryland, they roll each biscuit into a small ball, then flatten it slightly on the baking sheet. Finally, all the biscuits are pricked with the tines of a fork, just before baking.

Beaten biscuits may not be quite as high or flaky as the kind made with baking powder, but they are definitely just as delicious!

Our recipe includes both the hand method and the food-processor method; choose whichever you wish.

◆

Cheesy Biscuits

Prepare as for Beaten Biscuits, adding **1 cup of finely shredded sharp Cheddar cheese (4 ounces)** plus ½ **teaspoon crushed red pepper flakes** to the flour mixture. Sprinkle with paprika before baking. Makes 1½ dozen biscuits. *1 biscuit: Calories 124; Saturated Fat 5 g; Total Fat 8 g; Protein 3 g; Carbohydrate 11 g; Fiber 0 g; Sodium 159 mg; Cholesterol 21 mg*

DOWN HOME TRADITION

From the East Bay of Rhode Island across the state to the West Bay of Narragansett and in many villages between, the folks you meet seem to have their own views about jonnycakes. But one thing they do agree upon: breakfast in Rhode Island, especially in the spring, calls for a stack of these freshly baked griddle cakes made from corn. But are they Jonnycakes, Johnnycakes, or Journey Cakes? In the early days, they were called journey cakes, probably evolving from the fact that they are compact and travel well. Over the years, the names have changed. A state law dictates that only those cakes made from white cap flint corn, grown and stone-ground in Rhode Island, may be called jonnycakes (without the "h"). Made from any other meal they are known simply as johnnycakes. Just what does a jonnycake look and taste like? It all depends on where you go. Along the West Bay, they make them by scalding the meal with boiling water (no milk). These cakes bake up small, thick, and hearty, with a great corn flavor. Along the East Bay, the cakes are thin, lacy, almost crepe-like, with a mellow corn taste. To make this version, the inhabitants mix the corn meal with cold milk and keep the batter thin and rich, as in this recipe from Timothy McTague of Gray's Grist Mill in Adamsville, Rhode Island.

◆ East Bay Jonnycakes ◆

1 cup white cornmeal (preferably stone-ground)
½ teaspoon salt
¼ cup boiling water
½ cup whole milk
6 tablespoons heavy cream or whole milk

PREP TIME: 15 MIN. / COOKING TIME: 24 MIN.

---

1 In a medium-size bowl, combine the cornmeal with the salt, then stir in the water until dissolved. Whisk in the milk and cream until the mixture is smooth and creamy (it should be the consistency of a thick creamed soup). If the batter is too thick, add a little more cream.

2 Generously oil a nonstick griddle or a 12-inch nonstick or cast iron skillet and heat over moderately high heat. Or heat an electric griddle to 375°F. Using about 3 tablespoons of batter for each jonnycake, bake the cakes for 6 minutes on each side (it is unwise to rush a jonnycake). If you like them crisper, add a little more oil to the griddle. Serve hot with maple syrup. Makes twelve 3-inch cakes. For more jonnycakes, just double the recipe.

---

*1 jonnycake: Calories 69; Saturated Fat 2 g; Total Fat 4 g; Protein 1 g;
Carbohydrate 9 g; Fiber 0 g; Sodium 100 mg; Cholesterol 12 mg*

FLAPJACKS

◆◆◆

During the mid-19th century, Americans began to make griddle cakes with white flour instead of the traditional cornmeal. In the South these were called batter cakes; in the North, flapjacks; in logging camps, flannel cakes, possibly because their texture is similar to that of the loggers' flannel shirts.

1 cup all-purpose flour	¼ teaspoon salt
1 tablespoon sugar	1⅓ cups low-fat buttermilk
½ teaspoon baking powder	1 large egg
½ teaspoon baking soda	2 tablespoons vegetable oil

PREP TIME: 15 MIN. / COOKING TIME: 12 MIN.

1 In a medium-size bowl, mix the flour, sugar, baking powder, baking soda, and salt. In a small bowl, whisk the buttermilk, egg, and oil, then pour this liquid into the flour mixture. Using a wooden spoon, stir just until combined.

2 Heat a 12-inch nonstick griddle or skillet over moderate heat and brush with a little vegetable oil. Using about ¼ cup for each flapjack, pour the batter on the griddle; cook for 3 minutes or just until covered with bubbles. Flip over and cook 2 minutes more or until golden. Serve right off the griddle with Strawberry Syrup (page 285). Makes eight 4-inch flapjacks. For more flapjacks, just double the recipe.

1 flapjack: Calories 119; Saturated Fat 1 g; Total Fat 5 g; Protein 4 g; Carbohydrate 15 g; Fiber 0 g; Sodium 189 mg; Cholesterol 28 mg

◆

Blueberry Batter Cakes

Prepare batter as for Flapjacks, using **2 tablespoons of sugar**. Wash and stem **1 cup of fresh blueberries or frozen and thawed dry-pack blueberries.** Fold the berries into the batter and cook as directed in Step 2. Makes eight 4-inch batter cakes. *1 batter cake: 141 Calories; Saturated Fat 1 g; Total Fat 5 g; Protein 4 g; Carbohydrate 19 g; Fiber 0 g; Sodium 190 mg; Cholesterol 28 mg*

Hot and hearty Flapjacks, flipped up for breakfast

PORTLAND POPOVERS

•••

These hot breads resemble tiny Yorkshire puddings and get their name from the fact that the batter rises high, usually popping over the sides of the muffin cups during baking. Other names abound: whopovers, breakfast puffs, even puff popps in the deep South.

- 1 cup low-fat (2% milkfat) milk
- 2 large eggs
- ¼ teaspoon salt
- 2 tablespoons unsalted butter or margarine, at room temperature
- 1 cup sifted all-purpose flour

PREP TIME: 10 MIN. / COOKING TIME: 30 MIN.

1 Preheat the oven to 450°F. Grease 9 regular-size muffin cups well with butter or meat drippings; fill any remaining muffin cups with water. Place in the oven to heat. In a medium-size bowl, with an electric mixer set on high, beat the milk, eggs, salt, and butter until frothy.

2 Add the flour, beating just until smooth. Fill the 9 muffin cups ⅔ full. Bake for 20 minutes. Lower the heat to 350°F and bake 10 minutes longer or until golden and set. Serve immediately with Strawberry Preserves (page 266). Makes 9 popovers.

1 popover: Calories 105; Saturated Fat 2 g; Total Fat 5 g; Protein 4 g; Carbohydrate 12 g; Fiber 0 g; Sodium 87 mg; Cholesterol 57 mg

For successful popovers, preheat both the oven and the tins.

—from New England Cookery Book by Malabar Hornblower

SOUFFLÉD FRENCH TOAST

•••

In Creole Country, French toast, made from day-old bread, is known as pain perdu (lost bread). In Germany, it's called Nun's toast and in early American cookbooks, egg toast. To make it puffier, soak it overnight.

- 2 large oranges, peeled, sectioned, and seeded
- 2 large eggs
- 2 large egg whites
- ¼ cup low-fat (1% milkfat) milk
- 3 tablespoons granulated sugar
- 2 tablespoons orange-flavored liqueur, or 1 teaspoon orange extract
- 1 tablespoon finely grated orange rind
- 1 teaspoon vanilla extract
- ¼ teaspoon salt
- 8 slices challah, Portuguese bread, or French bread, 1 inch thick
- 2 tablespoons unsalted butter or margarine

For the topping:
Fresh berries, such as blueberries, raspberries, or strawberries
Sifted confectioners sugar
Maple syrup, warmed (optional)

PREP TIME: 25 MIN. / STANDING TIME: 30 MIN. COOKING TIME: 12 MIN.

1 In a food processor or blender, process the orange sections for 1 minute. Add the eggs, egg whites, milk, sugar, liqueur, orange rind, vanilla, and salt; process 1 minute longer.

2 In a shallow dish, arrange all the bread in a single layer. Pour over the egg mixture, cover with plastic wrap, refrigerate, and let stand for at least 30 minutes or overnight, turning once.

3 In a 12-inch nonstick skillet, melt 1 tablespoon of the butter over moderate heat. Cook 4 slices of the bread for 3 minutes on each side or until brown. Repeat with the remaining butter and bread. Top with the berries and confectioners sugar, also the syrup if you wish. Makes 8 slices.

1 slice: Calories 208; Saturated Fat 3 g; Total Fat 6 g; Protein 7 g; Carbohydrate 31 g; Fiber 0 g; Sodium 294 mg; Cholesterol 62 mg

Sour Cream Waffles

❖❖❖

*George Washington's mother was known
for her plantation breakfasts. They often featured
waffles, made from a rich cream batter and
topped with maple syrup and honey.*

1¾ cups all-purpose flour	3 large eggs, separated
2 tablespoons sugar	2 cups reduced-fat sour cream
1 tablespoon baking powder	1 cup low-fat (1% milkfat) milk
1 teaspoon baking soda	¼ cup unsalted butter (not margarine), melted
½ teaspoon salt	

PREP TIME: 20 MIN.
COOKING TIME: ABOUT 6 MIN. PER WAFFLE

1 Preheat a waffle iron. Into a large bowl, sift the flour, sugar, baking powder, baking soda, and salt. In a small bowl, with an electric mixer on high, beat the egg yolks, sour cream, and milk. Stir into the dry ingredients with the butter.

2 In a clean small bowl, with clean beaters and the electric mixer on high, beat the egg whites until stiff but not dry. Using a wire whisk, fold into the flour mixture just until the whites disappear. Bake the waffles according to the manufacturer's directions. If the batter becomes too thick, add a little more milk. Serve with a warm mixture of equal amounts of honey and maple syrup. Makes about 8 waffles.

*1 waffle: Calories 274; Saturated Fat 6 g;
Total Fat 12 g; Protein 8 g; Carbohydrate 33 g; Fiber 0 g;
Sodium 418 mg; Cholesterol 109 mg*

◆

Fresh Blueberry Waffles

Prepare as for Sour Cream Waffles, folding **1 cup washed fresh blueberries** and **1 teaspoon vanilla extract** into the batter just before folding in the egg whites. Makes about 8 waffles. *1 waffle : Calories 282; Saturated Fat 6 g; Total Fat 12 g; Protein 8 g; Carbohydrate 35 g; Fiber 1 g; Sodium 418 mg; Cholesterol 109 mg*

Golden Corn Waffles

Prepare as for Sour Cream Waffles, folding **½ cup shredded Cheddar cheese, ½ cup fresh or thawed, frozen corn kernels,** and **½ cup minced green onion** into the batter just before cooking. Makes about 8 waffles. *1 waffle: Calories 313; Saturated Fat 8 g; Total Fat 15 g; Protein 10 g; Carbohydrate 35 g; Fiber 0 g; Sodium 463 mg; Cholesterol 117 mg*

The all-American coffee break: Honey-Glazed Doughnuts and a mug of coffee

HONEY-GLAZED DOUGHNUTS

◆◆◆

Pilgrims had learned to make these "little nuts of fried dough" in Holland, but not with holes. The Pennsylvania Dutch are often credited with inventing the doughnut with a hole.

3½ cups all-purpose flour	1 cup sugar
4 teaspoons baking powder	¾ cup low-fat buttermilk
2 teaspoons ground cinnamon	Vegetable oil
½ teaspoon each baking soda, salt and ground nutmeg	**Glaze:**
	½ cup each honey, sugar, and water
2 large eggs	¼ cup fresh lemon juice
2 tablespoons unsalted butter, melted	½ teaspoon ground cinnamon

PREP TIME: 30 MIN. / CHILLING TIME: 1 HR.
COOKING TIME: 20 MIN.

1 Onto a piece of wax paper, sift the flour, baking powder, cinnamon, baking soda, salt, and nutmeg. In a large bowl, whisk the eggs, butter, and sugar until light yellow and frothy.

2 Add the flour mixture, 1 cup at a time, alternately with the buttermilk, stirring until a dough forms. Divide into 2 equal pieces and refrigerate for 1 hour.

3 On a lightly floured surface, roll out each piece of dough into a 12-inch circle, ½ inch thick. Using a 3-inch doughnut cutter, cut out a total of 16 doughnuts and holes, re-rolling the scraps (but not the holes) as you go.

4 In a deep 12-inch skillet, heat 1 inch of oil over moderately high heat to 360°F. or until a 1-inch cube of bread browns in 30 seconds. Cook doughnuts and holes in batches, turning once, for 3 minutes or until golden. Drain on paper towels.

5 To make the glaze: In a small saucepan, bring all of the ingredients to a simmer over moderately high heat. Cook, uncovered, for 5 minutes, then remove from the heat and keep warm. Using a fork, dip each warm doughnut into the glaze for a few seconds, then transfer to a rack to cool. Serve with mugs of coffee or Hot Chocolate (page 38). Makes 16 doughnuts and 16 holes.

1 doughnut and 1 hole: Calories 264; Saturated Fat 3 g; Total Fat 9 g; Protein 4 g; Carbohydrate 43 g; Fiber 0 g; Sodium 201 mg; Cholesterol 31 mg

APPLE FRITTERS

◆◆◆

For the apples:

4 large cooking apples, such as Granny Smith, peeled and cored

½ cup firmly packed light brown sugar

¼ cup apple brandy or apple cider

¼ cup fresh lemon juice

2 teaspoons vanilla

1 teaspoon ground cinnamon

Vegetable oil

Sifted confectioners sugar (optional)

For the batter:

1 cup all-purpose flour

1 teaspoon baking powder

¼ teaspoon salt

1 cup apple juice

1 tablespoon unsalted butter or margarine, at room temperature

1 large egg

1 large egg white

PREP TIME: 20 MIN. / STANDING TIME: 1 HR. COOKING TIME: 25 MIN.

1 To prepare the apples: Slice them crosswise into rings, ½ inch thick, being careful to keep them in rings; place in a large shallow glass dish. In a small bowl, whisk the brown sugar, brandy, lemon juice, vanilla, and cinnamon until blended; pour over the apples. Cover and let stand at room temperature for 1 hour, turning occasionally; drain on paper towels.

2 To make the batter: Meanwhile, in a food processor or blender, place all of the batter ingredients in the order listed, then process for 1 minute or until smooth. Refrigerate for 1 hour.

3 In a deep 12-inch skillet, heat 1 inch of oil over moderately high heat to 360°F or until a 1-inch cube of bread browns in 30 seconds. Using a long-handled fork, dip each apple ring into the batter, then slide it into the oil. Fry for 2 minutes on each side or until golden and crisp. Drain on a rack and sprinkle with confectioners sugar if you wish. Serve hot! Makes 2 dozen fritters.

1 fritter: Calories 109; Saturated Fat 1 g; Total Fat 6 g; Protein 1 g; Carbohydrate 13 g; Fiber 0 g; Sodium 43 mg; Cholesterol 10 mg

BEIGNETS

◆◆◆

Most visitors to New Orleans discover Beignets, rectangular doughnuts, cooked around the clock at the French Market coffeehouses. When they're piping hot, you'll find it's hard to eat just one.

½ cup lukewarm water (105° to 115°F)

1 packet (¼ ounce) active dry yeast

6 tablespoons granulated sugar

½ cup evaporated milk

1 large egg, beaten

½ teaspoon salt

2 tablespoons unsalted butter or margarine, at room temperature

3¾ cups all-purpose flour

1 cup vegetable oil

½ cup sifted confectioners sugar

PREP TIME: 30 MIN. / RISING TIME: 1 HR. STANDING TIME: 30 MIN. / COOKING TIME: 20 MIN.

1 In a large bowl, combine the water, yeast, and 2 tablespoons of the granulated sugar; let stand for 10 minutes or until foamy. Stir in the remaining sugar, milk, egg, salt, and butter until blended. Beat in the flour, about 1 cup at a time, until a soft dough forms. Cover and let rise in a warm place for 1 hour or until doubled in size.

2 On a lightly floured surface, roll out the dough, ⅛ inch thick. Using a sharp knife, cut into 2½- by 3½-inch rectangles.

3 In a large saucepan, heat the oil over moderately high heat to 350°F or until a 1-inch cube of bread browns in 45 seconds. Slide in the pieces of dough, about 3 at a time and cook for 30 seconds on each side, turning them over after they puff up. Using a slotted spoon, remove to paper towels to drain. Place the confectioners sugar in a strainer and dust each beignet lightly. These are best served hot. Serve with mugs of Café au Lait (coffee with hot milk). Makes 4 dozen beignets.

1 beignet: Calories 95; Saturated Fat 1 g; Total Fat 5 g; Protein 1 g; Carbohydrate 10 g; Fiber 0 g; Sodium 27 mg; Cholesterol 7 mg

BETWEEN THE BREAD

◆◆◆

The first sandwiches made in this country were simple affairs of meat and/or cheese between slabs of homemade bread. But cooks started improvising, and eventually there were toasted types with melted cheese in the middle; open-faced affairs, drenched with hot gravy; overstuffed renditions on rolls; and the creations now associated with America around the world: hotdogs and hamburgers.

In this chapter you'll find all of the above and more. The familiar recipes, gathered from many corners, will take you back in memory. A few examples: the Reuben, Sloppy Joe, Kentucky Hot Brown, Philly Cheese Steak, Monte Carlo, and Hero. These are the kinds of sandwiches that satisfy hearty appetites. But they're traditionally high in sodium and fat too. To bring them more in line with today's nutritional guidelines, we have chosen reduced-fat spreads and used them sparingly, selected the thinnest slices of meats and cheeses we could find and reduced their quantities. Still, we recommend that these sandwiches be enjoyed just now and then. They're the best of their tradition and well worth considering for a special day.

◆ The Great American Hamburger ◆

As all-American as the hamburger seems today, its name isn't American at all. Instead, it is named for the German city of Hamburg, where a form of beefsteak, pounded enough to break up the fibers and make it tender, became popular in the mid-19th century. By 1896, this dish had arrived in America.

Just a few years later, in 1902, Mrs. Sarah Tyson Rorer's *New Cook Book* described the Hamburg steak as "one put twice through a meat grinder and mixed with onion and pepper," not unlike our hamburger today.

History traces the origin of the ground meat version on a bun to Athens, Texas, in the late 19th century. As the story goes, Uncle Fletch Davis, a potter, found business slow. So he began selling sandwiches that consisted of a ground meat patty, set between two slices of home-made bread, topped off with hot mustard and a thick slice of Bermuda onion, and served with a big pickle on the side. In 1904, the townspeople sent Uncle Fletch to sell his sandwiches at the Louisiana Purchase Exposition in St. Louis. Thus, a long-lasting tradition was born.

Soon, the hamburger began appearing in a soft bun in diners and at stands along our highways and byways. Often, it was served with "the works"—ketchup, onions, pickles, and lettuce. Without its bun, this now popular meat started showing up in fancier restaurants, under the name of Salisbury Steak.

During the 1930's, Wimpy burgers became the rage, named for J. Wellington Wimpy, a beloved character in the Popeye comic strip who loved hamburgers. By the 1950's, the hamburger had become a truly American food, one that is now exported around the world.

BLUE RIBBON BURGERS

◆◆◆

This recipe won Jenell Hood the Grand Prize at the 1993 Uncle Fletch Davis Hamburger Cookoff in Athens, Texas. Her secret is to marinate the meat overnight, letting the flavors blend, then grill it over the coals. She serves these burgers up daily in her down-home restaurant, called Nana's Kitchen.

2 **pounds ground beef chuck or sirloin**	6 **hamburger buns**
2 **tablespoons Worcestershire sauce**	**Optional fixings:**
2 **teaspoons hot red pepper sauce**	**Pickled jalapeño peppers, sliced**
1 **teaspoon lemon pepper**	**Ripe tomatoes, sliced**
	Leaf lettuce
	Dill pickles, sliced

PREP TIME: 15 MIN. / MARINATING TIME: OVERNIGHT / COOKING TIME: 8 MIN.

1 In a medium-size bowl, mix the beef, Worcestershire, red pepper sauce, and lemon pepper until well blended. Form into six 6-inch patties, about 1½ inches thick. Cover with plastic wrap and refrigerate overnight.

2 Preheat the grill or broiler. Grill the patties over medium-hot coals or broil 4 inches from the heat for 4 minutes on each side for medium or until the burgers are the way you like them. Serve on buns with your favorite fixings and a helping of Steak Fries (page 230). Makes 6 burgers.

1 burger: Calories 405; Saturated Fat 8 g; Total Fat 20 g; Protein 32 g; Carbohydrate 21 g; Fiber 0 g; Sodium 376 mg; Cholesterol 94 mg.

◆

Barbecued Burgers

Prepare meat mixture as for Blue Ribbon Burgers, adding ½ **cup Texas Barbecue Sauce (page 278)** and ⅓ **cup minced red onion.** Marinate and cook as directed. Makes 6 burgers. *1 burger: Calories 435; Saturated Fat 8 g; Total Fat 21 g; Protein 32 g; Carbohydrate 27 g; Fiber 0 g; Sodium 471 mg; Cholesterol 96 mg*

A blue ribbon lunch, hot off the grill

SLOPPY JOES

◆ ◆ ◆

1 tablespoon vegetable oil	½ cup ketchup
1 medium-size yellow onion, finely chopped	1 teaspoon Worcestershire sauce
⅓ cup each finely chopped celery and sweet green pepper	½ teaspoon each salt and black pepper
1 pound lean ground beef	2 teaspoons white vinegar
1 can (14½ ounces) low-sodium stewed tomatoes, undrained	4 hamburger buns, split and toasted

PREP TIME: 20 MIN. / COOKING TIME: 14 MIN.

1 In a 12-inch nonstick skillet, heat the oil over moderately high heat. Add the onion, celery, and green pepper and sauté for 5 minutes or until tender. Stir in the beef and cook 4 minutes longer or until no longer pink.

2 Add the tomatoes with their juices, the ketchup, Worcestershire, salt, and black pepper. Cook, stirring often, 4 minutes more or until the flavors are well blended, then stir in the vinegar. Place the buns on individual plates and divide the meat mixture among them. Serve with Saratoga Chips (page 231). Makes 4 sandwiches.

1 sandwich: Calories 428; Saturated Fat 7 g;
Total Fat 20 g; Protein 26 g; Carbohydrate 37 g; Fiber 1 g;
Sodium 647 mg; Cholesterol 70 mg

◆

Texas Pulled Beef-wiches

Prepare as for Sloppy Joes, adding **1 to 2 teaspoons chili powder** with the onion mixture. Substitute **1 pound shredded cooked roast beef (about 3 cups)** for the ground beef and cook only 2 minutes longer, instead of 4 minutes, in Step 1. Makes 4 sandwiches. *1 sandwich: Calories 391; Saturated Fat 4 g; Total Fat 14 g; Protein 30 g; Carbohydrate 37 g; Fiber 1 g; Sodium 630 mg; Cholesterol 77 mg*

Hearty vittles for supper: An over-stuffed steak sandwich and Chopped Tomato Salad (page 256)

OMAHA STEAK SANDWICH

◆◆◆

In Nebraska, where the highways are lined with ranches and the eating is home-cooked and hearty, folks love their steaks. Such fare is frequently hot off the grill and served on an open-faced sandwich with a spicy chili sauce.

1 **pound boneless beef sirloin steak, 1 inch thick**	1 **tablespoon chopped cilantro or parsley**
¼ **cup steak sauce**	1 **clove garlic, minced**
1 **small tomato, diced (¾ cup)**	1 **teaspoon fresh lime juice**
2 **to 3 large fresh or pickled jalapeño peppers with seeds, finely chopped (2 to 3 tablespoons)**	¼ **teaspoon each salt and black pepper**
2 **tablespoons finely chopped red onion**	4 **French oblong rolls, split lengthwise, or slices of firm white bread, toasted and halved diagonally**

PREP TIME: 30 MIN. / COOKING TIME: 10 MIN.

1 Brush both sides of the steak with the sauce, place in a shallow dish and cover. Refrigerate for 30 minutes. Meanwhile, in a small bowl, mix the tomato, peppers, onion, cilantro, garlic, lime juice, salt, and pepper. Wrap the rolls in foil.

2 Preheat the grill or broiler. Grill the steak over medium-hot coals, or broil 4 to 5 inches from the heat, for 4 minutes on each side for medium-rare or until the steak is the way you like it. During the last 5 minutes, place the rolls alongside the steak to warm.

3 Slice the steak diagonally across the grain, ¼ inch thick. For each sandwich, stuff a roll with ¼ of the steak slices (or arrange the steak on top of 2 toast triangles). Add ¼ of the chili sauce. Serve with Chopped Tomato Salad (page 256) and Oven-Fried Onion Rings (page 225). Makes 4 sandwiches.

1 sandwich: Calories 304; Saturated Fat 4 g; Total Fat 11 g; Protein 29 g; Carbohydrate 19 g; Fiber 1 g; Sodium 588 mg; Cholesterol 76 mg

PHILLY CHEESE-STEAK SANDWICH

◆◆◆

To add variety to his menu at Pat's King of Steaks in Philadelphia in the 1930's, Pat Olivieri invented the cheese steak. This version comes from grandson Frank Olivieri, present owner with his father, who still serves every day to customers.

8	ounces boneless beef ribeye steak, 1½ inches thick
4	Italian rolls, split
3	tablespoons olive oil
2	extra-large yellow onions, peeled and slivered (about 3 cups)

1	each large sweet green and red pepper, cut in strips
4	ounces fresh mushrooms, sliced (1½ cups)
1	cup pasteurized process cheese spread, heated

PREP TIME: 20 MIN. / FREEZING TIME: 15 MIN.
COOKING TIME: 18 MIN.

1 Place the steak in the freezer for 15 minutes or just until firm. Using a very sharp knife, cut the meat across the grain into very thin slices. Preheat the oven to 350°F. Wrap the rolls in foil and place in the oven to warm.

2 On a nonstick griddle or in a 12-inch nonstick skillet, heat 1 tablespoon of the oil over moderately high heat. Add the onions and sauté for 8 minutes or until caramelized. Transfer to a bowl and cover to keep warm. Add 1 more tablespoon of oil, then the sweet peppers and mushrooms; sauté for 5 minutes or until soft; transfer to a plate and cover to keep warm.

3 Add the remaining tablespoon of oil to the skillet, then the beef, and cook, turning and flipping constantly, for 3 minutes or until the steak is sizzling and the way you like it. For each sandwich, stuff a roll with ¼ each of the steak slices, onions, and pepper mixture, then spoon on ¼ cup of the cheese. Makes 4 sandwiches.

1 sandwich: Calories 406,; Saturated Fat 7 g; Total Fat 22 g; Protein 22 g; Carbohydrate 31 g; Fiber 1 g; Sodium 565 mg; Cholesterol 54 mg

THE REUBEN

◆◆◆

One story traces the Reuben to a 1955 weekly poker game in Omaha, Nebraska. It was there that Reuben Kay often fixed a grilled sandwich of corned beef, Swiss cheese, and sauerkraut, piled between two slices of pumpernickel bread.

For the dressing:

¼	cup reduced-calorie mayonnaise
3	tablespoons minced celery
2	tablespoons bottled chili sauce
2	tablespoons minced pimiento
1	tablespoon minced green pepper

For the sandwiches:

8	slices pumpernickel or dark rye bread
10	ounces lean corned beef, thinly sliced
1½	cups shredded Swiss cheese (6 ounces)
1	cup sauerkraut, rinsed and drained well
2	tablespoons unsalted butter or margarine,

PREP TIME: 25 MIN. / COOKING TIME: 35 MIN.

1 Preheat the oven to 325°F. To make the dressing: In a small bowl, stir all of the dressing ingredients until well blended.

2 To make each Reuben: On a slice of bread, layer ⅛ of the corned beef, 3 tablespoons of the cheese, ¼ cup of the sauerkraut, 3 tablespoons of the dressing, ⅛ more of the corned beef, and 3 more tablespoons of the cheese; top with a second slice of bread.

3 In a 12-inch nonstick skillet, melt 1 tablespoon of the butter over moderate heat. Place 2 of the sandwiches in the skillet and cook for 8 minutes on each side or until heated through and the cheese has melted. Transfer to an ovenproof platter and keep warm in the oven. Repeat with the remaining tablespoon of butter and the other 2 sandwiches. Serve with Prayer Meeting Coleslaw (page 253). Makes 4 sandwiches.

1 sandwich: Calories 500; Saturated Fat 13 g; Total Fat 25 g; Protein 30 g; Carbohydrate 38 g; Fiber 1 g; Sodium 911 mg; Cholesterol 97 mg

KENTUCKY HOT BROWN

At Louisville's famous Brown Hotel in the 1920's, supper dances were popular affairs. When the band took a break around midnight, guests wanted something to eat. As the story goes, Chef Fred K. Schmidt created the open-faced Hot Brown for these occasions.

2 tablespoons unsalted butter or margarine	2 tablespoons heavy cream or evaporated skim milk, whipped (optional)
3 tablespoons all-purpose flour	
1¾ cups low-fat (1% milkfat) milk	4 slices white or whole-wheat bread, toasted
6 tablespoons grated Parmesan cheese	1 pound roasted turkey, thinly sliced
1 small egg, lightly beaten	4 slices bacon, cooked and drained
¼ teaspoon each salt and black pepper	

PREP TIME: 20 MIN. / COOKING TIME: 20 MIN.

1 Preheat the broiler. In a medium-size saucepan, melt the butter over moderate heat. Whisk in the flour and cook until bubbly. Whisk in the milk and cook for 4 minutes or until slightly thickened. Whisk in 3 tablespoons of the Parmesan cheese, the egg, salt, and pepper. Cook, stirring frequently, for 5 minutes or until thick, then fold in the cream if you wish.

2 Line each of 4 flameproof au gratin dishes with a slice of toast. For each sandwich, mound ¼ of the turkey on top of the toast, spoon on about ⅓ cup of the sauce, and sprinkle with ¼ of the remaining Parmesan. Broil, 6 inches from the heat, for 4 minutes or until bubbly and speckled brown. Top with a slice of bacon and serve immediately with Spicy Pickled Peaches (page 271). Makes 4 sandwiches.

1 sandwich: Calories 492 ; Saturated Fat 10 g; Total Fat 19 g; Protein 48 g; Carbohydrate 25 g; Fiber 0 g; Sodium 668 mg; Cholesterol 198 mg

PO' BOYS

In New Orleans, these over-stuffed sandwiches are called Po' Boys (poor boys), because, even if you don't have much to spend, you get a lot for your money!

½ cup reduced-calorie mayonnaise	4 white French or Italian rolls, each 8 inches long, split lengthwise
2 tablespoons hot red pepper sauce	
2 teaspoons fresh lemon juice	1 pound roast beef, thinly sliced
1 tablespoon minced parsley	¾ cup Beef Stock (page 74) or low-sodium beef broth
¼ teaspoon each salt and black pepper	2 small tomatoes, thinly sliced
	1 cup shredded lettuce

PREP TIME: 20 MIN. / COOKING TIME: 5 MIN.

1 Preheat the oven to 325°F. In a small bowl, mix the mayonnaise, red pepper sauce, lemon juice, parsley, salt, and pepper until blended; refrigerate. Wrap the rolls in foil and place in the oven to warm. Cut the roast beef into 5- x 2-inch strips.

2 In a large skillet, heat the beef stock over moderate heat. Add the beef and cook, turning constantly with a slotted spatula, for about 2 minutes or just until heated through.

3 For each sandwich, spread the cut sides of the top and bottom of a roll with the mayonnaise mixture. Layer ¼ of the beef slices on the bottom, drizzling some of the beef stock over each slice as you go. Top with ¼ of the tomato slices and ¼ of the lettuce, then cover with the top of the roll. Serve with Fourth of July Potato Salad (page 254). Makes 4 sandwiches.

1 sandwich: Calories 374; Saturated Fat 4 g; Total Fat 15 g; Protein 30 g; Carbohydrate 28 g; Fiber 1 g; Sodium 558 mg; Cholesterol 86 mg

MONTE CARLO

◆◆◆

This turkey and cheese sandwich is dipped in a batter like that used for French toast, then grilled until golden and crisp. Add slices of baked ham and the sandwich becomes the Monte Cristo.

8 slices firm white
  sandwich bread

4 teaspoons Dijon
  mustard

8 ounces roasted
  turkey, thinly sliced

8 ounces Swiss cheese,
  thinly sliced

2 tablespoons unsalted
  butter or margarine

For the batter:

2 large eggs

2 large egg whites

½ cup low-fat
  (1% milkfat) milk

¼ teaspoon salt

PREP TIME: 15 MIN. / COOKING TIME: 12 MIN.

1 For each sandwich, spread 1 side of 2 slices of bread with ½ teaspoon of mustard each. Top 1 slice with ¼ each of the turkey and cheese, then cover with the second slice, mustard-side-down, pressing down gently to close. In a medium-size bowl, whisk together all of the batter ingredients.

2 In a 12-inch skillet, melt the butter over moderately high heat. Dip each sandwich in the batter, turning it and allowing the batter to be absorbed. Cook the sandwiches for 3 minutes on each side or until golden brown and the cheese has melted. Serve immediately with Gazpacho Salad (page 259). Makes 4 sandwiches.

1 sandwich: Calories 543; Saturated Fat 15 g; Total Fat 27 g; Protein 44 g; Carbohydrate 29 g; Fiber 0 g; Sodium 769 mg; Cholesterol 225 mg

A Monte Carlo: The ultimate grilled sandwich, served with Gazpacho Salad (page 259)

DOWN HOME TRADITION

The hot dog craze in America can be traced back to our German settlers who, in the 19th century, introduced us to wienerwursts, or Vienna sausages. Years later, sausages from the German city of Frankfurt appeared inside long rolls at the St. Louis World's Fair of 1904. By the mid-20th century, people were attending wienie (or weenie) roasts, where guests cooked their own wienerwursts over an open fire. The idea of heating the rolls and adding condiments was the creation of a chef at the New York Polo Grounds. His vendors could be heard crying: "Red hots...get your red hots here!" Then Tad Doorman, a sports cartoonist, created a dachshund with a body resembling a sausage, giving birth to the nickname of hot dog. Soon, hot dog stands began appearing across America. One concession at Coney Island, New York, became so well known for its franks that people began calling the popular sandwich "The Coney Island."

◆ Coney Island Chili Dog ◆

¼ pound ground beef round
1 large yellow onion, chopped (1 cup)
1 can (15 ounces) chili without beans
2 tablespoons bottled chili sauce
2 tablespoons minced parsley
½ cup pasteurized process cheese spread
4 beef hot dogs (4 ounces each)
4 hot-dog buns, split on the side
4 teaspoons prepared mustard, or to taste

PREP TIME: 15 MIN. / COOKING TIME: 20 MIN.

1 Preheat the grill or broiler. To make the chili: In a 10-inch nonstick skillet, sauté the beef and ½ cup of the onion over moderately high heat for 10 minutes or until well browned. Stir in the chili, chili sauce, and parsley and heat for 5 minutes or until hot.

2 In a small saucepan, stir the cheese spread over moderately high heat for 5 minutes or until creamy. Meanwhile, grill or broil the hot dogs, turning occasionally, for 7 minutes, until they are browned the way you like them. During the last 3 minutes, warm the buns alongside the hot dogs.

3 For each chili dog, place a hot dog in a bun and spread with ¼ each of the mustard and chili mixture. Sprinkle with ¼ each of the cheese and the remaining onion. Serve with Oven Fries (page 231). Makes 4 chili dogs.

1 chili dog: Calories 561; Saturated Fat 10 g; Total Fat 38 g; Protein 24 g; Carbohydrate 33 g; Fiber 0 g; Sodium 1718 mg; Cholesterol 54 mg

Seventh-inning stretch at the ballpark: Time for a frank with all the trimmings

BALLPARK FRANKS
◆◆◆

To cut down on fat, this recipe calls for chicken franks, omits the chili, and uses a pepper relish instead of cheese.

1 tablespoon vegetable oil	1 tablespoon light brown sugar
1 large yellow onion, chopped (1 cup)	2 teaspoons white wine vinegar
1 medium-size sweet green pepper, cored, seeded, and chopped (1 cup)	¼ teaspoon salt
	1 tablespoon minced parsley
1 medium-size sweet red pepper, cored, seeded, and chopped (1 cup)	4 chicken or all-beef hot dogs
	4 hot-dog buns, split on top
3 tablespoons water	4 teaspoons prepared mustard

PREP TIME: 15 MIN. / COOKING TIME: 17 MIN.

1 Preheat the grill or broiler. To make the pepper relish: In a 12-inch skillet, heat the oil over moderate heat; sauté the onion and sweet peppers for 5 minutes or until tender. Stir in the water, sugar, vinegar, and salt. Lower the heat, cover, and simmer for 5 minutes, then stir in the parsley.

2 Grill or broil the hot dogs, turning, for about 7 minutes or until browned on all sides. During the last 3 minutes, warm the buns alongside. For each Ballpark Frank, place a hot dog in a bun, spread with 1 teaspoon of mustard, and top with ¼ of the relish. Serve with Lime Sweet Pickles (page 270) and orange drink. Makes 4 franks.

1 frank: Calories 304; Saturated Fat 4 g;
Total Fat 15 g; Protein 10 g; Carbohydrate 33 g; Fiber 1 g;
Sodium 950 mg; Cholesterol 46 mg

RUTHIE'S CLUB SANDWICH

◆◆◆

*Some people contend that the club
sandwich was first served in the two-decker
club cars on the streamliner trains of the late 19th
century. Others trace it to casinos and private
men's clubs. Though the original versions had
only two slices of bread and no cheese, this
one, from Ruthie and Moe's Diner in
Cleveland, Ohio, has the works!*

1	**jar (7 ounces) roasted sweet red peppers, rinsed and well drained**
⅓	**cup reduced-calorie mayonnaise**
¼	**teaspoon black pepper**
⅛	**teaspoon salt, or to taste (optional)**
12	**slices white or light rye bread**
4	**deli slices Bavarian ham (¾ ounce each)**
4	**thin deli slices Swiss cheese (¾ ounce each)**
1	**cup shredded curly leaf lettuce**
4	**thin slices roasted breast of turkey (¾ ounce each)**
8	**slices bacon, cooked and drained**
2	**medium-size ripe tomatoes, thinly sliced (2 cups)**

PREP TIME: 20 MIN. / COOKING TIME: 10 MIN.

1 In a food processor or blender, purée the
sweet red peppers for 30 seconds or just until
smooth, but not liquified. In a small bowl, mix the
peppers with the mayonnaise, black pepper, and
salt if using. Toast the bread on both sides until
light golden.

2 For each sandwich, spread the top side of
1 slice of toast with about 1 tablespoon of the
pepper-mayonnaise mixture. Layer with ¼ each
of the ham, cheese, and lettuce.

3 Spread both sides of a second slice of toast
with the pepper-mayonnaise mixture; place
on top of the lettuce. Top with ¼ of the turkey,
2 slices of the bacon, and ¼ of the tomatoes.

4 Spread 1 side of a third slice of toast with the
mayonnaise and place mayonnaise-side-down
on top of the tomatoes. Secure with toothpicks.

**The old-fashioned club sandwich—made a little
healthier by using very thin slices of meats and cheese**

Using a serrated knife, slice the sandwich diagonally into 4 triangles. Serve with Saratoga Chips
(page 231). Makes 4 sandwiches.

*1 sandwich: Calories 489; Saturated Fat 6 g;
Total Fat 20 g; Protein 29 g; Carbohydrate 46 g; Fiber 1 g;
Sodium 875 mg; Cholesterol 64 mg*

◆

Dagwood Sandwich

Prepare as for Ruthie's Club Sandwich, adding
**¾ ounce each thin deli slices of bologna, salami,
and American cheese and 4 dill pickles, thinly
sliced.** Add the bologna and pickles to the first
layer (Step 2); the salami and American cheese to
the second layer (Step 3). Makes 4 sandwiches.
*1 sandwich: Calories 750; Saturated Fat 15 g; Total Fat
44 g; Protein 38 g; Carbohydrate 45 g; Fiber 1 g; Sodium
1555 mg; Cholesterol 106 mg*

MUFFULETTA

At the turn of the 20th century, the Italians living in New Orleans created their own version of a meal-in-a-sandwich, from cold meats, cheeses, and a spiced olive salad. To lower the sodium, use fewer olives and fresh vegetables instead of pickled ones.

For the olive salad:

- 1 jar (12 ounces) pickled anitpasto vegetables, rinsed and well drained or 2 cups diced mixed fresh vegetables
- ⅓ cup pimento stuffed green olives, chopped
- ¼ cup kalamata or other black olives, pitted and chopped
- 2 tablespoons olive oil
- 2 tablespoons minced parsley
- 1 clove garlic, minced
- ½ teaspoon dried oregano leaves

For the sandwich:

- 1 round loaf (1 pound) Italian bread
- 4 thin deli slices provolone cheese (¾ ounce each)
- 4 thin deli slices salami (¾ ounce each)
- 4 thin deli slices baked ham (¾ ounce each)
- 2 cups shredded romaine lettuce

PREP TIME: 30 MIN.

1 To make the olive salad: In a medium-size bowl, combine the vegetables, green olives, kalamata olives, oil, parsley, garlic, and oregano.

2 Using a serrated knife, halve the bread horizontally. Scoop out the center of the bread leaving a 1-inch shell. (Reserve the center for bread crumbs for later use.)

3 Fill the bottom half with ½ of the olive mixture. Then layer on the cheese, salami, ham, lettuce, and the remaining olive salad. Cover with the top of the bread. Secure with long toothpicks and cut into quarters. Makes 4 small or 2 large sandwiches.

1 sandwich (for 4): Calories 623; Saturated Fat 7 g; Total Fat 21 g; Protein 27 g; Carbohydrate 77 g; Fiber 1 g; Sodium 1624 mg; Cholesterol 42 mg

THE HERO

This sandwich goes by various names: grinder, hoagie, submarine, wedge, and of course, hero. But whatever it's called, almost always it's made with a loaf of Italian bread, piled high with meats and cheese and drizzled with a spicy dressing.

- ¼ cup olive oil
- ¼ cup white wine vinegar
- 1 teaspoon dried Italian herb seasoning
- ½ teaspoon crushed red pepper flakes
- ⅛ teaspoon salt, or to taste (optional)
- 1 18-inch loaf Italian bread (2 pounds), split lengthwise
- 2 plum tomatoes, sliced (1 cup)
- 4 thin deli slices salami (¾ ounce each)
- 4 thin deli slices provolone cheese (½ ounce each)
- 4 thin deli slices baked ham (¾ ounce each)
- 8 ounces thin deli slices roasted breast of turkey
- ⅔ cup bottled pickled antipasto vegetables, rinsed and well drained
- 1 cup shredded romaine lettuce

PREP TIME: 30 MIN.

1 In a small bowl, mix the oil, vinegar, Italian seasoning, crushed red pepper, and salt. Brush about half of the mixture on the insides of both the top and bottom of the bread.

2 Line the bottom with the tomato slices, then layer on the salami, cheese, ham, and turkey, sprinkling the slices with the remaining vinegar-oil mixture as you go. Top with the vegetables, then the lettuce, and cover with the top of the bread. Secure with toothpicks; slice diagonally into 6 equal pieces. Makes 6 sandwiches.

1 sandwich: Calories 689; Saturated Fat 5 g; Total Fat 17 g; Protein 36 g; Carbohydrate 91 g; Fiber 1 g; Sodium 974 mg; Cholesterol 58 mg

HOMESPUN DESSERTS

◆◆◆

More than a few desserts have grown up with America. Pumpkin pie, for instance, was included at early Thanksgiving celebrations; pound cake was brought here by the English colonists; and koekjes (cookies) were popularized by Dutch settlers. Quite a few sweet customs developed from the bounty of fresh fruits found here: Strawberry shortcake is one; apple pie and blueberry buckle are two others. Americans invented the pineapple upside-down cake and peanut butter cookies. And though chocolate can't claim to be all-American, several desserts made with it are—chocolate chip cookies, Mississippi mud cake, and chocolate pudding, being three delicious examples.

This collection also includes such regional favorites as Missouri Scripture Cake, New York Cheesecake, and Shortnin' Bread from the Deep South. Along the way we've lowered fat and calories, in some cases by decreasing egg yolks and increasing the whites, in others by judicious use of low-fat milk, reduced-fat cream cheese, or fruit juice. But in the end, scrumptiousness has prevailed, and the homemade goodness of down-home desserts can be savored with every tempting bite.

SUNSHINE CAKE

◆◆◆

*From the Sunshine State of Florida comes
this golden-glow sponge cake that's light, high, and
flavorful with lemon, lime, and orange.*

1½ cups sifted cake flour	2 teaspoons each grated lemon, lime, and orange rind
½ teaspoon salt	10 large egg whites
7 large egg yolks	1 teaspoon cream of tartar
1¾ cups sugar	
3 tablespoons fresh orange juice	Assorted fresh berries (optional)

PREP TIME: 30 MIN. / COOKING TIME: 35 MIN.
COOLING TIME: 4 HR.

1 Preheat the oven to 350°F and set out an un-greased 10-inch tube pan. Onto a piece of wax paper, sift the flour and salt. In a large bowl, with an electric mixer on high, beat the egg yolks for 5 minutes or until thick and light yellow. Gradually add 1 cup of the sugar and beat 5 minutes longer. Blend in the orange juice and the lemon, lime, and orange rinds.

2 In another clean large bowl, with clean beaters and the mixer on high, beat the egg whites and cream of tartar until soft peaks form. Beat in the remaining ¾ cup of sugar until stiff peaks form. Gently fold ⅓ of the beaten whites into the yolk mixture, then add all of the flour mixture, and finally the remaining whites.

3 Spoon the batter into the pan and bake for 35 minutes or until a toothpick inserted in the center comes out clean (page 364). Immediately invert the pan and cool the cake for 4 to 6 hours, before turning out onto a serving plate. Serve with fresh berries if you wish. Makes 16 servings.

*1 serving: Calories 154; Saturated Fat 1 g;
Total Fat 2 g; Protein 4 g; Carbohydrate 30 g; Fiber 0 g;
Sodium 119 mg; Cholesterol 93 mg*

COCONUT CHIFFON CAKE

◆◆◆

2 cups sifted cake flour	1 teaspoon coconut extract
1¼ cups sugar	8 large egg whites
1 tablespoon baking powder	For the frosting:
¾ teaspoon salt	1 cup heavy cream
5 large egg yolks	2 tablespoons sifted confectioners sugar
½ cup vegetable oil	1 can (3½ ounces) angel flake coconut, lightly toasted
½ cup cold water	
1 tablespoon vanilla extract	

PREP TIME: 30 MIN. / COOKING TIME: 30 MIN.
COOLING TIME: 2 HR.

1 Preheat the oven to 325°F. Butter and flour three 9-inch round cake pans; line the bottoms with wax paper. Onto wax paper, sift the flour, ½ cup of the sugar, the baking powder, and salt.

2 In a large bowl, with an electric mixer on high, beat the egg yolks for 5 minutes or until thick. Add the oil, water, vanilla, and coconut extract; beat 3 minutes longer or until well blended.

3 In another clean large bowl, with clean beaters and the mixer on high, beat the egg whites until soft peaks form. Beat in the remaining ¾ cup of sugar until stiff peaks form.

4 Gently fold ⅓ of the egg whites into the yolk mixture, then fold in all the flour mixture and finally the remaining whites. Spoon into the pans. Bake for 30 minutes or until a toothpick inserted in the center comes out clean (page 364). Cool in the pans on racks for 5 minutes. Turn out onto the racks, peel off the paper, and cool completely.

5 To make the frosting: In a small bowl, with the mixer on high, beat the cream and sugar until stiff peaks form. Spread the cream between the layers, on the sides, and on top, sprinkling with the coconut as you go. Makes 16 servings.

*1 serving: Calories 284; Saturated Fat 8 g;
Total Fat 16 g; Protein 4 g; Carbohydrate 31 g; Fiber 0 g;
Sodium 214 mg; Cholesterol 87 mg*

Scarlet's delectable
orange cake,
ready to enjoy with
afternoon tea

SCARLET'S ORANGE CAKE

◆◆◆

1 cup blanched almonds	⅔ cup vegetable oil
2 cups granulated sugar	½ cup fresh orange juice
2¼ cups sifted all-purpose flour	1 tablespoon grated orange rind
1 tablespoon baking powder	7 large egg whites
1¼ teaspoons ground cinnamon	**For the glazes:**
½ teaspoon each baking soda and salt	2 cups sifted confectioners sugar
4 large egg yolks	1 cup orange juice
	2 teaspoons grated orange rind

PREP TIME: 30 MIN. / COOKING TIME: 1 HR.
COOLING TIME: 1 HR.

1 Preheat the oven to 325°F. Butter and flour a 10-inch Bundt or tube pan. In a food processor, process the almonds with ½ cup of the granulated sugar until finely ground. Onto a piece of wax paper, sift the flour, baking powder, cinnamon, baking soda, and salt, then toss with the almond mixture.

2 In a large bowl, with an electric mixer on high, beat the egg yolks for 5 minutes or until thick and light yellow.

3 Gradually add the oil, 1 cup of the sugar, the orange juice, and the rind. In another clean large bowl, with clean beaters and the mixer on high, beat the egg whites until soft peaks form. Beat in the remaining ½ cup of sugar until stiff.

4 Fold ⅓ of the egg whites into the yolk mixture, then all the flour mixture and remaining whites. Spoon into the pan. Bake for 1 hour or until a toothpick inserted in the center comes out with moist crumbs (page 364). Transfer to a rack.

5 To make the glazes: While the cake bakes, in a small bowl, stir together 1¾ cups of the confectioners sugar and 3 tablespoons of the orange juice; set aside. In a small saucepan, bring the remaining orange juice and ¼ cup of confectioners sugar and the rind to a simmer over moderate heat.

6 As soon as the cake comes out of the oven, pierce it all over with a toothpick, then drizzle with the hot glaze, letting it soak in. Leave the cake in the pan for 30 minutes. Turn out onto a serving plate and cool 30 minutes more. Drizzle with the cold glaze. Makes 24 servings.

1 serving: Calories 230; Saturated Fat 2 g;
Total Fat 9 g; Protein 4 g; Carbohydrate 36 g; Fiber 0 g;
Sodium 121 mg; Cholesterol 36 mg

Pat-a-cake,
pat-a-cake,
baker's man,
Bake me
a cake
as fast as
you can.

—*Pat-a-Cake
Nursery Rhyme
(Anonymous)*

DOWN HOME TRADITION

Many American cookbooks from the 18th and 19th centuries included a recipe for a homemade pound cake. To quote Eliza Leslie's *Directions for Cookery* (1848): "Sift a pound of the finest flour, and powder a pound of loaf-sugar...cut in a pound of fresh butter...beat ten eggs as light as possible...put in a deep tin pan with straight sides...bake in a moderate oven from two to three hours. Flavour the icing with an essence of lemon, or with extract of roses." Another writer of those times, Mary Randolph, suggested flavoring the cake batter, instead of the frosting, in her popular cookbook, *The Virginia House-Wife* (1826). She wrote: "Add some grated lemon peel, a nutmeg, and a gill of brandy." Through the years, this cake has been varied in many ways, but this old-fashioned recipe is still used by many families, especially throughout the Deep South.

◆ Old-Fashioned Pound Cake ◆

1 pound (4 cups) sifted all-purpose flour

1 teaspoon ground cinnamon

½ teaspoon ground nutmeg

1 pound (4 sticks) unsalted butter,
at room temperature

1 pound granulated sugar (2 cups)

1 pound eggs (8 large)

2 tablespoons brandy or 1 teaspoon brandy extract

2 tablespoons sifted confectioners sugar

PREP TIME: 20 MIN. / COOKING TIME: 1 HR. 20 MIN. / COOLING TIME: 1 HR.

1 Preheat the oven to 325°F and butter and flour a 10-inch tube pan. Onto a piece of wax paper, sift the flour, cinnamon, and nutmeg.

2 In a large bowl, with an electric mixer on high, cream the butter with the granulated sugar until light yellow and fluffy. Add the eggs, 1 at a time, beating well after each addition, then blend in the brandy.

3 Using a wooden spoon, beat in the flour mixture, ⅓ at a time. Spoon the batter into the pan and bake for 1 hour and 20 minutes or until a toothpick inserted in the center comes out clean (page 364). Cool the cake in the pan on a rack for 10 minutes, before turning out onto the rack to cool. Dust the top with the confectioners sugar. Makes 24 servings.

*1 serving: Calories 306; Saturated Fat 7 g; Total Fat 17 g; Protein 4 g;
Carbohydrate 35 g; Fiber 0 g; Sodium 24 mg; Cholesterol 113 mg*

SOUR CREAM POUND CAKE

◆◆◆

3 cups sifted all-purpose flour	1 tablespoon vanilla extract
½ teaspoon each baking soda and salt	1 cup reduced-fat sour cream
1 cup (2 sticks) unsalted butter, at room temperature	2 teaspoons grated lemon rind
2 cups sugar	7 large egg whites
4 large egg yolks	1 recipe Pecan Praline Glaze (page 342)

PREP TIME: 30 MIN. / COOKING TIME: 1 HR. 20 MIN.
COOLING TIME: 1 HR.

1 Preheat the oven to 325°F and butter and flour a 10-inch tube pan. Onto a piece of wax paper, sift the flour, baking soda, and salt.

2 In a large bowl, with an electric mixer on high, cream the butter with the sugar until light yellow. Add the egg yolks, 1 at a time, beating well after each addition; blend in the vanilla.

3 Beat in the flour mixture, ⅓ at a time, alternating with the sour cream and beginning and ending with the flour. Stir in the lemon rind. In a clean medium-size bowl, with clean beaters and the mixer on high, beat the 7 egg whites until stiff peaks form. Fold ⅓ of the whites into the flour mixture, then gently fold in the remaining whites.

4 Spoon the batter into the pan. Bake for 1 hour and 20 minutes or until a toothpick inserted in the center comes out clean (page 364). Cool the cake in the pan on a rack for 10 minutes, before turning out onto the rack. Drizzle the glaze over the cooled cake. Makes 24 servings.

*1 serving: Calories 201; Saturated Fat 5 g;
Total Fat 11 g; Protein 3 g; Carbohydrate 25 g; Fiber 0 g;
Sodium 62 mg; Cholesterol 45 mg*

◆

Happy Clown Cake

Make 2 recipes Sour Cream Pound Cake, dividing the batter, ⅓ in a 9-inch round cake pan and ⅔ in a 13" x 9" x 3" baking pan. After baking and

**Happy Clown Cake—all dressed up for
the party and ready to wish you a Happy Birthday!**

cooling, use a serrated knife to level the top of each cake. From the 13- x 9-inch cake, cut pieces as shown in the right diagram on page 365. On a large board or baking sheet, arrange the pieces and round cake, top-side-up, as shown in the left diagram. Frost with 3 recipes of Cream Cheese Frosting (page 343), reserving ¼ cup of frosting. To make the nose, color the ¼ cup of frosting with red food coloring and use to frost a chocolate-marshmallow or other ball-shaped cookie. For the hair, color 1 cup sweetened flaked coconut with orange food coloring. Use assorted candies to create the mouth and eyes and decorate the hat, pompom, and tie. Makes 42 servings. *1 serving: Calories 389; Saturated Fat 11 g; Total Fat 21 g; Protein 5 g; Carbohydrate 55 g; Fiber 0 g; Sodium 141 mg; Cholesterol 82 mg*

A treasured
Southern tradition:
Homemade
Hummingbird Cake
chock full of bananas
and pineapple

CARROT CAKE

♦♦♦

3 cups sifted all-purpose flour	1 tablespoon vanilla extract
1 tablespoon each baking soda and pumpkin pie spice	2 cups golden raisins
1 teaspoon salt	1 cup cinnamon applesauce
¾ pound carrots, peeled	1 cup chopped walnuts, toasted (page 365) (optional)
3 large eggs	
3 large egg whites	1 recipe Cream Cheese Frosting (page 343)
¾ cup vegetable oil	
3 cups sugar	2 cups angel flake coconut, toasted (page 365) (optional)
½ cup reduced-fat sour cream	

⏱ PREP TIME: 30 MIN. / COOKING TIME: 35 MIN.
COOLING TIME: 1 HR.

1 Preheat the oven to 325°F. Butter and flour three 9-inch round cake pans; line the bottoms with wax paper. Onto a piece of wax paper, sift the flour, baking soda, pumpkin pie spice, and salt.

2 Grate ½ of the carrots to make 1½ cups; slice the remainder. In a small saucepan of boiling water, cook the sliced carrots for 5 minutes; drain. In a food processor, purée to make ¾ cup.

3 In a large bowl, with an electric mixer on high, beat the eggs and egg whites for 5 minutes or until light yellow and slightly thickened. Add the oil, sugar, carrot purée, sour cream, and vanilla, beating 3 minutes longer or until fluffy. With a wooden spoon, stir in the flour mixture, then fold in the grated carrots, raisins, and applesauce, plus the walnuts if you wish.

4 Spoon the batter into the pans and bake for 35 minutes or until a toothpick inserted in the center comes out with moist crumbs. Cool the cake in the pans on racks for 5 minutes. Turn out onto the racks, peel off the paper, and cool completely.

5 While the cake cools, make the frosting. Ice the cake between the layers, on the sides, and on top, sprinkling as you go with the coconut if you wish. Makes 16 servings.

*1 serving: Calories 401; Saturated Fat 6 g;
Total Fat 14 g; Protein 4 g; Carbohydrate 67 g; Fiber 0 g;
Sodium 257 mg; Cholesterol 46 mg*

HUMMINGBIRD CAKE
◆◆◆

This Southern cake comes from The Eseeola Lodge in Linville, North Carolina. We've cut the oil in half by increasing the quantity of bananas.

3 cups sifted all-purpose flour	3 large bananas, mashed (2¼ cups)
2 cups sugar	1 can (8 ounces) crushed pineapple in juice, undrained
1½ teaspoons ground cinnamon	1 recipe Cream Cheese Frosting (page 343)
1 teaspoon each baking soda and salt	1 cup chopped pecans, toasted (page 365)
3 large eggs	
¾ cup vegetable oil	
1½ teaspoons vanilla extract	

PREP TIME: 20 MIN. / COOKING TIME: 25 MIN.
COOLING TIME: 1 HR.

1 Preheat the oven to 325°F. Butter and flour three 9-inch round cake pans; line the bottoms with wax paper. Onto a piece of wax paper, sift the flour, sugar, cinnamon, baking soda, and salt.

2 In a medium-size bowl, using an electric mixer on high, beat the eggs until light yellow and fluffy; beat in the oil and vanilla. Using a wooden spoon, stir in the bananas with the pineapple and its juice until well blended.

3 Stir in the flour mixture just until the flour disappears; divide the batter evenly among the pans. Bake for 25 minutes or until a toothpick inserted in the center comes out with moist crumbs (page 364). Cool the cake in the pans on racks for 5 minutes. Turn out onto the racks, peel off the wax paper, and cool completely.

4 While the cake cools, make the frosting. Ice the cake between the layers, on the sides, and on top, sprinkling as you go with the pecans. Makes 24 servings.

1 serving: Calories 364; Saturated Fat 6 g;
Total Fat 17 g; Protein 4 g; Carbohydrate 52 g; Fiber 0 g;
Sodium 171 mg; Cholesterol 45 mg

MYSTERY CAKE
◆◆◆

This spicy cake, which first became popular in the early 20th century, is known as the Mystery Cake, because most people who eat it are unable to guess its secret ingredient of tomato soup.

2 cups sifted all-purpose flour	¼ cup unsalted butter or margarine, at room temperature
2 teaspoons baking powder	1 cup sugar
1 teaspoon each ground cinnamon and nutmeg	1 large egg
¼ teaspoon ground cloves	2 large egg whites
1 cup condensed low-sodium tomato soup, undiluted	1 cup low-fat (2% milkfat) milk
1 teaspoon baking soda	1 cup golden raisins
	1 cup chopped walnuts
	1 recipe Cream Cheese Frosting (page 343)

PREP TIME: 20 MIN. / COOKING TIME: 35 MIN.
COOLING TIME: 1 HR.

1 Preheat the oven to 350°F and butter and flour a 13" x 9" x 3" baking pan. Onto a piece of wax paper, sift the flour, baking powder, cinnamon, nutmeg, and cloves. In a cup, blend the tomato soup and baking soda.

2 In a medium-size bowl, with an electric mixer on high, beat the butter and sugar until light yellow. Add the egg and egg whites and beat until fluffy. Using a wooden spoon, stir in the tomato soup mixture. Add the flour mixture, ⅓ at a time, alternating with the milk, just until blended. Fold in the raisins and walnuts and spread in the pan.

3 Bake for 35 minutes or until golden and a toothpick inserted in the center comes out with moist crumbs (page 364). Cool the cake in the pan on a rack for 10 minutes, before turning out onto the rack to cool. Make the frosting; ice the top and sides of the cake. Makes 20 servings.

1 serving: Calories 340; Saturated Fat 7 g;
Total Fat 15 g; Protein 5 g; Carbohydrate 51 g; Fiber 1 g;
Sodium 148 mg; Cholesterol 41 mg

MISSISSIPPI MUD CAKE

The name of this cake was inspired by the richly colored mud on the banks of the Mississippi River. We've removed some of the fat by substituting a glaze for the standard rich frosting.

1½ cups sifted all-purpose flour	½ cup chopped pecans, toasted (page 365)
½ cup unsweetened cocoa powder	For the chocolate glaze:
¼ teaspoon salt	½ cup sifted confectioners sugar
1 cup (2 sticks) unsalted butter or margarine, at room temperature	2 tablespoons unsweetened cocoa powder, sifted
1¾ cups granulated sugar	1 tablespoon melted butter
4 large eggs	3 teaspoons low-fat (1% milkfat) milk
2 teaspoons vanilla extract	¼ teaspoon vanilla extract

PREP TIME: 30 MIN. / COOKING TIME: 45 MIN.
COOLING TIME: 1 HR.

1 Preheat the oven to 350°F and butter and flour a 9-inch Bundt or tube pan. Onto a piece of wax paper, sift the flour, cocoa, and salt.

2 In a large bowl, with an electric mixer on high, cream the butter and granulated sugar until light yellow. Beat in the eggs, 1 at a time, then blend in the vanilla and beat 1 minute more.

3 Stir in the flour mixture just until the flour disappears. Spoon the batter into the pan and sprinkle the pecans on top. Bake for 45 minutes or until a toothpick inserted in the center comes out with moist crumbs. Cool in the pan on a rack for 10 minutes, then turn out onto the rack to cool.

4 To make the glaze: In a small bowl, mix all of the ingredients until smooth, adding more milk, if necessary, to make a flowing mixture. Drizzle over the cooled cake. Makes 16 servings.

1 serving: Calories 299; Saturated Fat 9 g; Total Fat 17 g; Protein 4 g; Carbohydrate 34 g; Fiber 0 g; Sodium 53 mg; Cholesterol 88 mg

CRAZY MIXED-UP CAKE

This very easy chocolate cake is mixed right in the pan. We've cut fat from the traditional recipe by using low-fat milk and cocoa instead of baking chocolate.

1½ cups all-purpose flour	⅓ cup vegetable oil
1 cup firmly packed light brown sugar	1 tablespoon white vinegar
¼ cup unsweetened cocoa powder, sifted	2 teaspoons vanilla extract
1 teaspoon baking soda	1 cup low-fat (1% milkfat) milk
½ teaspoon salt	2 tablespoons sifted confectioners sugar

PREP TIME: 5 MIN. / COOKING TIME: 30 MIN.
COOLING TIME: 15 MIN.

1 Preheat the oven to 350°F and grease and flour an 8-inch square pan. Combine the flour, brown sugar, cocoa, baking soda, and salt in the pan, then shake the pan to level the ingredients.

2 Using the back of a spoon or 2 clean fingers, make 3 holes in the dry ingredients. Pour the oil in one hole, the vinegar in another, and the vanilla in the third. Pour the milk over the top and mix with a fork until well blended.

3 Bake for 30 minutes or until a toothpick inserted in the center comes out with moist crumbs (page 364). Cool the cake in the pan on a rack for 15 minutes. Dust with confectioners sugar, then serve right from the pan. Makes 12 servings.

1 serving: Calories 198; Saturated Fat 1 g; Total Fat 7 g; Protein 3 g; Carbohydrate 32 g; Fiber 0 g; Sodium 174 mg; Cholesterol 1 mg

A taste of the 1940's—mayonnaise baked up into a yummy chocolate cake

CHOCOLATE MAYONNAISE CAKE

◆◆◆

Because mayonnaise contains egg yolks, oil, and lemon juice, it makes the perfect beginning for a cake batter.

2 cups sifted all-purpose flour	1 cup reduced-calorie mayonnaise
⅔ cup unsweetened cocoa powder	1⅓ cups cold water
1¼ teaspoons baking soda	**For the chocolate frosting:**
¼ teaspoon baking powder	12 ounces semisweet chocolate chips
3 large eggs	1 cup reduced-fat sour cream
1⅔ cups sugar	½ teaspoon vanilla extract
1 teaspoon vanilla extract	2 squares (1 ounce each) semisweet chocolate, melted

PREP TIME: 20 MIN. / COOKING TIME: 30 MIN.
COOLING TIME: 15 MIN.

1 Preheat the oven to 350°F. Butter and flour two 9-inch round cake pans; line the bottoms with wax paper. Onto a piece of wax paper, sift the flour, cocoa, baking soda, and baking powder.

2 In a large bowl, with an electric mixer on high, beat the eggs, sugar, and vanilla for 3 minutes or until fluffy. Reduce the speed to low and blend in the mayonnaise.

3 Using a wooden spoon, stir the flour mixture into the egg mixture, ⅓ at a time, alternating with the water and beginning and ending with the flour. Divide the batter evenly between the pans and bake for 30 minutes or until a toothpick inserted in the center comes out with moist crumbs (page 364). Cool the cake in the pan on a rack for 10 minutes. Turn out onto the rack, peel off the paper, and let stand 5 minutes more.

4 While the cake cools, make the frosting: In a small saucepan, stir the chocolate chips over moderately-low heat until melted. Remove from the heat and stir in the sour cream and vanilla. Ice the cake between the layers, on the sides, and on top with the chocolate frosting, then drizzle with the melted chocolate. Makes 16 servings.

*1 serving: Calories 289; Saturated Fat 2 g;
Total Fat 14 g; Protein 5 g; Carbohydrate 41 g; Fiber 0 g;
Sodium 218 mg; Cholesterol 43 mg*

1-2-3-4 CAKE

◆◆◆

The name of this cake, famous in the late 1900's, refers to its ingredients: 1 cup of butter, 2 cups of sugar, 3 cups of flour, and 4 eggs.

3 cups sifted all-purpose flour	1 cup (2 sticks) unsalted butter or margarine, at room temperature
1 tablespoon baking powder	
½ teaspoon salt	2 cups granulated sugar
1 cup low-fat (1% milkfat) milk	4 large eggs
1 tablespoon vanilla extract	1 tablespoon sifted confectioners sugar

PREP TIME: 30 MIN. / COOKING TIME: 1 HR.
COOLING TIME: 1 HR.

1 Preheat the oven to 350°F and butter and flour a 10-inch tube pan. Onto a piece of wax paper, sift the flour, baking powder, and salt. In a cup, stir the milk and vanilla.

2 In a large bowl, with an electric mixer on high, cream the butter and granulated sugar until light yellow and fluffy. Add the eggs, 2 at a time, beating well after each addition.

3 Using a wooden spoon, stir in the flour mixture, ⅓ at a time, alternating with the milk and beginning and ending with the flour. Spoon the batter into the pan and bake for 1 hour or until a toothpick inserted in the center comes out clean (page 364). Cool the cake in the pan on a rack for 10 minutes before turning out onto the rack to cool. Dust the top with the confectioners sugar. Makes 16 servings.

1 serving: Calories 203; Saturated Fat 5 g; Total Fat 9 g; Protein 3 g; Carbohydrate 28 g; Fiber 0 g; Sodium 103 mg; Cholesterol 58 mg

MISSOURI SCRIPTURE CAKE

◆◆◆

Actually a variation of the 1-2-3-4 Cake, this one gets its name from many of its ingredients, which are mentioned in the scriptures. It makes a wonderful fruitcake for the holidays.

2 cups white raisins (I Samuel 30:12)	1 recipe 1-2-3-4 Cake (this page)
1 cup each red and green candied cherries, halved	1½ teaspoons each allspice, ground cinnamon and nutmeg (I Kings 10:2)
1 cup finely chopped dried figs (I Samuel 30:12)	1 cup slivered almonds, toasted (Numbers 17:8)
1 cup brandy (preferably peach) or fresh orange juice	1 tablespoon honey (Exodus 16:31)

PREP TIME: 30 MIN. / SOAKING TIME: 15 MIN.
COOKING TIME: 1¼ HR. / COOLING TIME: 1 HR.

1 Preheat the oven to 350°F and butter and flour a 10-inch tube pan. In a medium-size bowl, soak the raisins, cherries, and figs in the brandy for 15 minutes. Prepare the cake batter, folding the soaked fruits, any brandy left in the bowl, and the remaining ingredients into the batter as directed in Step 3. Spoon into the pan.

2 Bake for 1¼ hours or until a toothpick inserted in the center comes out with moist crumbs (page 364). If the top seems to be browning too fast, lay a piece of foil loosely over it. Cool the cake in the pan on a rack for 10 minutes before turning out onto the rack to cool. If you wish, wrap the cake in a cloth sprinkled with peach brandy, place in an airtight can, and let mellow for a day before serving. Makes 24 servings.

1 serving: Calories 346; Saturated Fat 6 g; Total Fat 12 g; Protein 5 g; Carbohydrate 53 g; Fiber 1 g; Sodium 133 mg; Cholesterol 58 mg

LADY BALTIMORE CAKE

◆◆◆

In Charleston, South Carolina, in the 19th century, there was a Lady Baltimore Tea Room, which very likely served this cake. It's made with the whites of eggs; the leftover yolks were often used the next day to make a sponge cake called Lord Baltimore.

4	cups sifted all-purpose flour
4	teaspoons baking powder
½	teaspoon salt
1	cup (2 sticks) unsalted butter (not margarine), at room temperature
2	cups sugar
1	tablespoon vanilla extract
1½	cups low-fat (2% milkfat) milk

8	large egg whites
1	recipe Orange Sea Foam Frosting (page 343)

For the filling:

1	cup chopped pecans
1	cup finely chopped dried figs
½	cup finely chopped pitted dates
½	cup dark raisins
¼	cup Grand Marnier, brandy or orange juice

PREP TIME: 30 MIN. / COOKING TIME: 20 MIN.
COOLING TIME: 1 HR.

1 Preheat the oven to 350°F. Butter and flour three 9-inch round pans and line the bottoms with wax paper. Onto a piece of wax paper, sift the flour, baking powder, and salt.

2 In a medium-size bowl, with an electric mixer on high, cream the butter until fluffy. Add 1½ cups of the sugar and the vanilla, then beat 2 minutes more. Using a rubber spatula, fold in the flour mixture, ⅓ at a time, alternating with the milk and beginning and ending with the flour.

3 In a clean large bowl, with clean beaters and the mixer on high, beat the egg whites until soft peaks form. Beat in the remaining ½ cup of sugar until stiff. Fold into the butter mixture. Bake for 20 minutes or until a toothpick inserted in the center comes out clean (page 364). Cool in the pans on racks for 5 minutes. Turn out onto the racks, peel off the paper, and cool completely.

A slice of stately Southern heritage: Lady Baltimore Cake swirled with a delicate orange frosting

4 While the cake cools, make the frosting and set aside. In a medium-size bowl, mix all of the filling ingredients and fold ½ of the frosting into the filling. Assemble the cake on a serving plate, spreading the filling between the layers and the remaining frosting on the sides and on top. Makes 16 servings.

1 serving: Calories 376; Saturated Fat 6 g; Total Fat 12 g; Protein 5 g; Carbohydrate 56 g; Fiber 0 g; Sodium 135 mg; Cholesterol 23 mg

Fresh plums from the orchard, ready for brunch inside a hot kuchen

PLUM KUCHEN
◆◆◆

1½	cups sifted all-purpose flour	1	teaspoon grated lemon rind
1½	teaspoons baking powder	½	teaspoon ground nutmeg
1	teaspoon ground cinnamon	2	large eggs
½	cup (1 stick) cold unsalted butter or margarine	½	cup low-fat buttermilk
1¼	cups firmly packed light brown sugar	8	large purple plums, halved and pitted

PREP TIME: 30 MIN. / COOKING TIME: 45 MIN.
COOLING TIME: 5 MIN.

1 Preheat the oven to 350°F; butter and flour a 9-inch round springform pan. In a large bowl, stir the flour, baking powder, and ½ teaspoon of the cinnamon. Using a pastry blender or 2 knives, cut in the butter until coarse crumbs form. Stir in 1 cup of the sugar and the lemon rind. For the topping, remove 2 tablespoons of this mixture to a small bowl; stir in the remaining ¼ cup of sugar and ½ teaspoon of cinnamon, and the nutmeg.

2 In a medium-size bowl, with an electric mixer on high, beat the eggs and buttermilk until light yellow and frothy. Using a wooden spoon, stir this mixture into the flour mixture just until the flour disappears, then spoon into the pan.

3 Arrange the plums, cut-side-down, on top and sprinkle with the topping. Bake for 45 minutes or until a toothpick inserted in the center comes out with moist crumbs (page 364). Let cool in the pan for 5 minutes before transferring to a platter. This is best served warm. Makes 9 servings.

1 serving: Calories 336; Saturated Fat 7 g; Total Fat 13 g; Protein 4 g; Carbohydrate 53 g; Fiber 1 g; Sodium 94 mg; Cholesterol 77 mg

◆

Fresh Peach Kuchen

Prepare and bake as for Plum Kuchen, substituting for the plums **8 medium-size peaches,** peeled, quartered, and pitted. Makes 9 servings. *1 serving: Calories 337; Saturated Fat 7 g; Total Fat 13 g; Protein 5 g; Carbohydrate 54 g; Fiber 1 g; Sodium 94 mg; Cholesterol 77 mg*

BLUEBERRY BUCKLE
♦♦♦

Here is a homey coffee cake that "buckles" while baking. This particular recipe comes from Rachel Gray of Princeton, New Jersey, who frequently bakes it for weekend brunches.

2	cups sifted all-purpose flour
2	teaspoons baking powder
½	teaspoon salt
¼	cup (½ stick) unsalted butter or margarine, at room temperature
¾	cup sugar
1	large egg
½	cup low-fat (2% milkfat) milk

2½	cups fresh blueberries, stemmed, or frozen blueberries, thawed and drained

For the topping:

½	cup sugar
⅓	cup sifted all-purpose flour
½	teaspoon ground cinnamon
¼	cup (½ stick) unsalted butter or margarine, at room temperature

PREP TIME: 20 MIN. / COOKING TIME: 40 MIN.

1 Preheat the oven to 350°F; butter and flour a 10-inch round springform pan. Onto a piece of wax paper, sift the flour, baking powder, and salt.

2 In a medium-size bowl, with an electric mixer on high, cream the butter, sugar, and egg. Add the milk and beat until light yellow and fluffy. Stir in the flour mixture, then fold in the blueberries and spread in the pan.

3 In a small bowl, mix the topping ingredients with your fingers until blended, then sprinkle on top of the batter. Press four fingers about half way down into the batter, in 3 or 4 places, until the batter looks bumpy.

4 Bake for 40 minutes or until golden and a toothpick inserted in the center comes out with moist crumbs (page 364). This is best served warm, right from the pan. Makes 12 servings.

1 serving: Calories 257; Saturated Fat 6 g; Total Fat 9 g; Protein 4 g; Carbohydrate 42 g; Fiber 1 g; Sodium 158 mg; Cholesterol 41 mg

CINNAMON FLOP
♦♦♦

All around America in the mid-1950's, morning coffee with friends often meant pieces of this cinnamon-swirl coffee cake, hot from the oven.

For the streusel:

½	cup firmly packed light brown sugar
½	cup finely chopped pecans
1	tablespoon cinnamon

For the flop:

2½	cups all-purpose flour
1	tablespoon baking powder

¾	teaspoon salt
6	tablespoons (¾ stick) unsalted butter, melted
1	cup granulated sugar
1	large egg
1	large egg white
1	cup low-fat (2% milkfat) milk

PREP TIME: 20 MIN. / COOKING TIME: 25 MIN.

1 Preheat the oven to 350°F; butter and flour a 13" x 9" x 3" pan. In a small bowl, mix the brown sugar, pecans, and cinnamon until blended. In another small bowl, mix together the flour, baking powder, and salt.

2 In a medium-size bowl, with an electric mixer on medium, cream the butter and sugar until light yellow. Add the egg and egg white and beat 2 minutes more or until fluffy. Stir in the flour mixture, ⅓ at a time, alternating with the milk and beginning and ending with the flour.

3 Spread ½ of the batter in the pan; sprinkle with ½ of the streusel; repeat with the remaining batter and streusel. Using a knife, cut through the batter several times, creating swirls.

4 Bake for 25 to 30 minutes or until a toothpick inserted in the center comes out with moist crumbs (page 364). Cut into 3-inch squares. This is best served warm. Makes 12 servings.

1 serving: Calories 293; Saturated Fat 4 g; Total Fat 10 g; Protein 5 g; Carbohydrate 47 g; Fiber 0 g; Sodium 240 mg; Cholesterol 36 mg

NEW YORK CHEESECAKE

◆◆◆

*We've cut some of the fat from this creamy
cheesecake by using reduced-fat versions
of cream cheese and sour cream.*

For the crust:
1½ cups gingersnap
   crumbs
6 tablespoons
   (¾ stick) unsalted
   butter or margarine,
   melted

For the filling:
4 packages (8 ounces
   each) Neufchâtel
   cream cheese, at
   room temperature
1 cup sugar

2 large eggs
2 large egg whites
1 tablespoon vanilla
   extract
2 teaspoons grated
   lemon rind

For the topping:
1 cup reduced-fat sour
   cream
1 tablespoon sugar
2 teaspoons vanilla
   extract

PREP TIME: 20 MIN. / COOKING TIME: 1 HR. 10 MIN.
COOLING TIME: 4¾ HR.

1 Preheat the oven to 325°F. To make the crust:
In a 9-inch springform pan, mix the crumbs
and butter. Press evenly in the bottom of the pan
and half-way up the sides.

2 To make the filling: In a large bowl, with an
electric mixer on medium, beat the cream
cheese and sugar until smooth. Add the eggs, egg
whites, vanilla, and lemon rind. Beat, scraping the
sides of the bowl occasionally, for 5 minutes or
until creamy. Pour into the crust. Bake for 1 hour,
then cool in the pan on a rack for 10 minutes.

3 While the cake cools, make the topping. Mix
the topping ingredients in a small bowl, then
spread on top of the cake. Return the cake to the
oven and bake 10 minutes more or until the topping is set. Turn off the oven, leaving the door
ajar, and let the cake stand in the oven for 30 minutes. Cover and refrigerate for at least 4 hours.
Makes 16 servings.

*1 serving: Calories 312; Saturated Fat 12 g;
Total Fat 22 g; Protein 8 g; Carbohydrate 23 g; Fiber 0 g;
Sodium 291 mg; Cholesterol 86 mg*

PINEAPPLE UPSIDE-DOWN CAKE

◆◆◆

2¼ cups sifted cake
   flour
2½ teaspoons baking
   powder
½ teaspoon baking
   soda
¼ teaspoon salt
¾ cup (1½ sticks)
   unsalted butter or
   margarine
½ cup firmly packed
   light brown sugar

2 cans (8 ounces each)
   pineapple slices
   packed in juice
4 large candied
   cherries, halved
15 large walnut halves
   (optional)
1 cup granulated sugar
3 large eggs
2 teaspoons vanilla
   extract
⅔ cup reduced-fat sour
   cream

PREP TIME: 20 MIN. / COOKING TIME: 30 MIN.
COOLING TIME: 10 MIN.

1 Preheat the oven to 325°F. Onto a piece of wax
paper, sift the flour, baking powder, baking
soda, and salt. In a 10-inch skillet, preferably cast
iron, melt ¼ cup of the butter over moderate heat.
Stir in the brown sugar; remove from the heat.

2 Arrange the pineapple in the skillet (reserving
the juice) and place half of a cherry, cut-side-
up, in the center of each. Arrange the nuts, flat-
side-up, around the pineapple rings if you wish.

3 In a large bowl, with an electric mixer on
high, cream the remaining ½ cup of butter
with the granulated sugar until light and fluffy.
Beat in the eggs, 1 at a time, then 3 tablespoons of
the reserved pineapple juice and the vanilla.

4 Using a wooden spoon, stir in the flour mixture, ⅓ at a time, alternating with the sour
cream and beginning and ending with the flour.
Carefully spoon the batter over the fruit. Wrap
the skillet handle with foil; bake for 30 minutes or
until a toothpick inserted in the center comes out
clean (page 364). Cool in the pan on a rack for
10 minutes, then place a serving platter on top
and turn upside down. Makes 12 servings.

*1 serving: Calories 324; Saturated Fat 8 g;
Total Fat 13 g; Protein 4 g; Carbohydrate 49 g; Fiber 0 g;
Sodium 175 mg; Cholesterol 83 mg*

Pineapple Upside-Down Cake — bottom side up and ready for serving

PEANUT BUTTER AND CHOCOLATE CUPCAKES
◆◆◆

The all-American favorite — peanut butter — is mated here with chocolate. Children of all ages seem to love this combination.

2¼	cups sifted all-purpose flour
1	tablespoon baking powder
½	teaspoon salt
¾	cup (1½ sticks) unsalted butter or margarine, at room temperature
1½	cups granulated sugar
3	large eggs
2	large egg whites

¾	cup creamy peanut butter
2	teaspoons vanilla extract
⅔	cup low-fat (1% milkfat) milk
½	cup mini chocolate chips
½	cup finely chopped peanuts, toasted (page 365) (optional)

PREP TIME: 30 MIN. / COOKING TIME: 20 MIN.
COOLING TIME: 30 MIN.

1 Preheat the oven to 350°F and butter and flour 18 regular-size muffin tins (or line with paper liners if you wish). Onto a piece of wax paper, sift the flour, baking powder, and salt.

2 In a large bowl, with an electric mixer on high, cream the butter and granulated sugar until light yellow and fluffy. Add the eggs, then the egg whites, beating well after each addition. Beat in the peanut butter and vanilla.

3 Using a wooden spoon, beat in the flour mixture, ⅓ at a time, alternating with the milk and beginning and ending with the flour. Spoon the batter into the cups, filling them almost full. Sprinkle each cupcake with about 1 teaspoon of the chocolate chips, then the peanuts if you wish.

4 Bake for 20 minutes, or until a toothpick inserted in the center comes out clean (page 364). Transfer the cupcakes to a rack to cool for 30 minutes. Makes 18 regular-size cupcakes.

1 regular-size cupcake: Calories 287; Saturated Fat 7 g; Total Fat 16 g; Protein 6 g; Carbohydrate 33 g; Fiber 0 g; Sodium 189 mg; Cholesterol 57 mg

A bowlful of creamy Caramel-Nut Frosting, ready to swirl on your favorite cake

CREAMY FUDGE FROSTING

◆◆◆

4 squares (1 ounce each) unsweetened chocolate	⅔ cup low-fat milk
	5 cups sifted confectioners sugar
2 tablespoons unsalted butter	1 tablespoon vanilla extract

PREP TIME: 20 MIN. / COOKING TIME: 5 MIN.

1 In a small heavy saucepan, stir the chocolate, butter, and milk over low heat until the chocolate melts. Cool to lukewarm, then pour into a medium-size bowl; stir in the sugar and vanilla. Using an electric mixer on high, beat for about 10 minutes or until thick enough to spread. Makes about 2½ cups of frosting or enough to fill and frost a 2-layer, 9-inch round cake, a 13" x 9" x 2" oblong cake, or 2 dozen regular-size cupcakes.

2 tablespoons frosting: Calories 140; Saturated Fat 1 g; Total Fat 4 g; Protein 14 g; Carbohydrate 27 g; Fiber 0 g; Sodium 5 mg; Cholesterol 4 mg

PECAN PRALINE GLAZE

◆◆◆

2 cups firmly packed light brown sugar	⅓ cup sifted confectioners sugar
½ cup (1 stick) unsalted butter (not margarine	1 cup chopped pecans, toasted (page 365)
⅓ cup half-and-half or evaporated milk	1 tablespoon vanilla extract

PREP TIME: 15 MIN. / COOKING TIME: 7 MIN.

1 In a small heavy saucepan, stir the brown sugar, butter, and half-and-half over moderate heat for 5 minutes or until the mixture comes to a full boil. Boil for 3 minutes, then remove from the heat and stir in the confectioners sugar, pecans, and vanilla. Immediately drizzle over the top of Sour Cream Pound Cake (page 331) or any other cake baked in a 9- or10-inch Bundt or tube pan. Makes about 2 cups.

4 teaspoons glaze: Calories 143; Saturated Fat 3 g; Total Fat 7 g; Protein 1 g; Carbohydrate 20 g; Fiber 0 g; Sodium 7 mg; Cholesterol 12 mg

CARAMEL-NUT FROSTING

◆◆◆

2½	cups sifted confectioners sugar
¼	teaspoon salt
1	cup firmly packed light brown sugar
¼	cup whole milk

3	tablespoons unsalted butter (not margarine), at room temperature
¼	cup fresh orange juice
¾	cup finely chopped pecans, toasted (page 365)

PREP TIME: 15 MIN. / COOKING TIME: 10 MIN.
COOLING TIME: 15 MIN.

1 Onto a piece of wax paper, sift the confectioners sugar and salt. In a small heavy saucepan, bring the brown sugar, milk, and butter to a boil over moderately high heat, then continue to boil, without stirring, for 5 minutes. Pour into a heatproof bowl and quickly stir in the confectioners sugar mixture and orange juice.

2 With an electric mixer on high, beat for 10 minutes or until fluffy. Stir in the pecans. Makes about 2 cups or enough to fill and frost a 2-layer, 9-inch round cake, a 13" x 9" x 2" oblong cake, or 1½ dozen regular-size cupcakes.

2 tablespoons frosting: Calories 171; Saturated Fat 2 g; Total Fat 6 g; Protein 1 g; Carbohydrate 31 g; Fiber 0 g; Sodium 40 mg; Cholesterol 7 mg

ORANGE SEA FOAM FROSTING

◆◆◆

1¼	cups sugar
¼	cup cold water
3	large egg whites

1	teaspoon grated orange rind
1	teaspoon vanilla extract

PREP TIME: 15 MIN. / COOKING TIME: 10 MIN.

1 In a medium-size heavy saucepan, stir the sugar and water over high heat until a candy thermometer reaches 240°F or ½ teaspoon dropped in a saucer of cold water forms a soft ball.

2 In a clean large bowl, with an electric mixer on high, beat the egg whites until soft peaks form. Slowly add the hot syrup, then the orange rind and vanilla, beating constantly for about 5 minutes or until stiff peaks form. Makes about 2½ cups of frosting or enough to fill and frost a 2-layer, 9-inch round cake, a 13" x 9" x 2" oblong cake, or 2 dozen regular-size cupcakes.

2 tablespoons frosting: Calories 48; Saturated Fat 0 g; Total Fat 0 g; Protein 0 g; Carbohydrate 12 g; Fiber 0 g; Sodium 9 mg; Cholesterol 0 mg

CREAM CHEESE FROSTING

◆◆◆

8	ounces Neufchâtel cream cheese, at room temperature
½	cup (1 stick) unsalted butter (not margarine), at room temperature
1	box (16 ounces) confectioners sugar, sifted (4½ cups)

1	to 2 tablespoons reduced-fat sour cream
1	teaspoon vanilla extract
1	teaspoon grated lemon rind (optional)

PREP TIME: 15 MIN.

1 In a small bowl, with an electric mixer on high, beat the cream cheese and butter until creamy. Turn the speed to medium and gradually beat in the sugar, about 1 cup at a time, just until blended and fluffy. Do not overbeat, as the frosting can become too soft.

2 Using a wooden spoon, stir in the sour cream, vanilla, and lemon rind. Makes about 3 cups or enough to fill and frost a 3-layer, 9-inch round cake, a 13" x 9" x 2" oblong cake, or 2½ dozen regular-size cupcakes.

2 tablespoons frosting: Calories 135; Saturated Fat 4 g; Total Fat 6 g; Protein 1 g; Carbohydrate 19 g; Fiber 0 g; Sodium 39 mg; Cholesterol 19 mg

VERY CHERRY PIE

In the Midwest, cherry pie is a favorite, perhaps stemming from the fact that cherry trees grow in so many back yards there.

1 recipe Single Pie Crust (page 368)	¼ cup cornstarch
¼ teaspoon baking powder	2 teaspoons ground cinnamon
¾ cup plus 3 tablespoons sugar	2 tablespoons unsalted butter or margarine
3 pounds sour red cherries, stemmed and pitted, or 3 cans (1 pound each) pitted sour red cherries in juice, drained (8 cups)	¾ teaspoon almond extract
	1 large egg white
	1 teaspoon water

PREP TIME: 45 MIN. / COOKING TIME: 37 MIN.
COOLING TIME: 1¼ HR.

1 Preheat the oven to 400°F. Make the crust, adding the baking powder and 2 tablespoons of the sugar to the flour; refrigerate for 30 minutes.

2 Meanwhile, make the filling: In a large saucepan, bring the cherries, the ¾ cup of sugar, the cornstarch, and cinnamon to a boil over moderately high heat. Lower the heat and cook, stirring constantly, for 2 minutes or until thickened. Stir in the butter and almond extract; cool for 15 minutes.

3 Roll out the dough into a 16-inch circle and fit into a deep-dish 9-inch pie plate, letting the edges hang over. Spoon in the filling, mounding it high in the center. Bring the edges of the dough toward the center, leaving some fruit exposed.

4 In a cup, whisk the egg white and water, then brush on the dough and sprinkle with the remaining sugar. Bake for 30 minutes or until golden. Cool for at least 1 hour. Makes 9 servings.

1 serving: Calories 441; Saturated Fat 7 g; Total Fat 15 g; Protein 4 g; Carbohydrate 73 g; Fiber 0 g; Sodium 58 mg; Cholesterol 25 mg

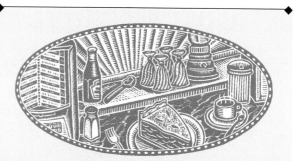

◆ Dinner at the Diner ◆

"**O**ne Diner Club on white and a big slice of Ruthie's apple pie," says the man sitting at the end of the counter. "He's a regular," explains owner Moe Helman, of Ruthie and Moe's Diner in Cleveland, Ohio. "Many of our customers come in knowing just what they want."

As you drive up to Ruthie and Moe's, you can imagine yourself back in the 1940's. The 55-year old diner is an authentic design by Jerry O'Mahony, a leading diner manufacturer in the early 1900's. It resembles the streamlined dining cars of the era: black and white tile floor, rounded windows, a green marble counter, black stools with shiny rims, and sleek stainless steel walls, giving an Art Deco feeling all around.

"We feature daily home-made specials, such as our own Chicken Waldorf Salad or Ruthie's meat loaf," Moe explains. "Plus, there are the expected diner foods (all homemade), such as stacks of pancakes, hot off the grill, burgers any way you like them, tuna melts, chili, and hot turkey sandwiches.

"Most customers leave room for a slice of Ruthie's carrot cake (we serve over 6,000 slices a year!) or pie, or one of her fabulous, freshly baked brownies. They go away full and happy, promising to diet some other day!"

Cherry Lattice Pie

Mix the crust as for Very Cherry Pie, dividing the dough into 2 pieces consisting of ⅔ and ⅓; chill. Use the larger piece to line a 9-inch pie plate (not a deep dish one). Prepare the filling as directed and use to fill the pie. With the remaining dough, prepare a lattice crust (page 369); glaze and bake as directed in Step 4. Makes 9 servings. *1 serving: Calories 441; Saturated Fat 7 g; Total Fat 15 g; Protein 4 g; Carbohydrate 73 g; Fiber 0 g; Sodium 58 mg; Cholesterol 25 mg*

RUTHIE'S APPLE PIE

◆◆◆

Ruthie Helman serves this pie almost every day at her diner in Cleveland. Her pastry is made with ½ pound of butter, but we've substituted our healthier crust instead.

1	recipe Double Pie Crust (page 368)	⅔	cup each packed light brown sugar and all-purpose flour
5	pounds Granny Smith apples	1	teaspoon salt
2	tablespoons fresh lemon juice	2	tablespoons ground cinnamon
1¼	cups granulated sugar	1½	teaspoons pumpkin pie spice

PREP TIME: 1 HR. / COOKING TIME: 45 MIN.
COOLING TIME: 1 HR.

1 Preheat the oven to 425°F. Make the crust, roll out ½, and fit it into a deep-dish 10-inch pie plate, letting the edge hang over 1-inch.

2 Peel, core, and slice the apples ¼ inch thick. In a large bowl, toss them with the lemon juice. Onto a piece of wax paper, sift both sugars, the flour, salt, cinnamon, and pumpkin pie spice, then toss with the apples. Spoon into the pie crust, mounding the apples high in the center.

3 Roll out the remaining dough to make the top crust and cut out 3 openings in the shape of an apple (page 369). Place on top of the pie and flute the edges (page 368). If you wish, re-roll the scraps of dough, cut out leaf-shapes (page 369), and set them in clusters on top of the pie.

4 Bake for 20 minutes; lower the temperature to 375°F and bake 25 minutes longer or until the apples are tender when tested with a fork. Let the pie cool on a rack for at least 1 hour before serving. Makes 10 servings.

1 serving: Calories 625; Saturated Fat 9 g; Total Fat 21 g; Protein 6 g; Carbohydrate 109 g; Fiber 2 g; Sodium 271 mg; Cholesterol 25 mg

Fresh apple pie— the way it's made at Ruthie and Moe's Diner—ready for slicing

BERRY-PEACH PIE IN A BAG

◆◆◆

From a pantry shop in the village of Glen Haven, high in the Rockie Mountains, came this idea of baking a pie in a bag. The overflowing juices collect in the bag instead of the oven.

1	recipe Single Pie Crust (page 368)	1	teaspoon vanilla extract
3	pounds fresh peaches, peeled pitted and sliced ½ inch thick, or frozen peaches, thawed and drained (about 6 cups)		**For the topping:**
		½	cup all-purpose flour
		½	cup firmly packed light brown sugar
		2	tablespoons unsalted butter or margarine, at room temperature
1	cup fresh blueberries, stemmed, or frozen blueberries, thawed and drained	½	teaspoon ground cinnamon
			Optional serve-along:
½	cup granulated sugar		Reduced-fat sour cream or low-fat vanilla ice cream
2	tablespoons all-purpose flour		

PREP TIME: 45 MIN. / COOKING TIME: 1 HR.
COOLING TIME: 30 MIN.

1 Preheat the oven to 400°F. Make the pie crust, fit into a 9-inch pie plate, and flute the edges (page 368). In a large bowl, toss the peaches, berries, sugar, flour, and vanilla. Spoon into the crust, mounding the fruit high in the center.

2 To make the topping: In a small bowl, work all of the ingredients with your fingers until coarse crumbs form. Sprinkle evenly over the fruit, completely covering the top of the pie.

3 Slide the pie into a large, heavy brown paper bag, staple closed, and place on a baking sheet. Bake for 1 hour, then transfer to a rack. Using scissors, carefully cut open the bag, standing away from the steam. Cool for at least 30 minutes. Serve with the sour cream or ice cream if you wish. Makes 9 servings.

*1 serving: Calories 389; Saturated Fat 6 g;
Total Fat 14 g; Protein 5 g; Carbohydrate 21 g; Fiber 1 g;
Sodium 36 mg; Cholesterol 21 mg*

PECAN PIE

◆◆◆

In the South, where pecan groves are plentiful, recipes for this pie are handed down from generation to generation. Older recipes were often made with sorghum instead of the milder-flavored corn syrup used today.

1	recipe Single Pie Crust (page 368)	2	tablespoons unsalted butter (not margarine), melted
3	large eggs		
½	cup firmly packed light brown sugar	2	tablespoons all-purpose flour
½	cup light or dark corn syrup	1	teaspoon vanilla extract
½	cup molasses	1½	cups pecan halves, toasted (page 365)

PREP TIME: 45 MIN. / COOKING TIME: 35 MIN.
COOLING TIME: 1 HR.

1 Preheat the oven to 375°F. Make the pie crust, fit into a 9-inch pie plate, and flute the edges (page 368). In a large bowl, with an electric mixer on medium, beat the eggs, sugar, corn syrup, molasses, butter, flour, and vanilla for 1 minute or just until blended and frothy. Stir in 1 cup of the nuts; pour into the crust, distributing the nuts evenly.

2 Arrange the remaining pecan halves, with rounded-sides-up, around the edge. Bake for 35 minutes or until golden-brown and puffy. Cool on a rack for at least 1 hour before serving. Makes 10 servings.

*1 serving: Calories 458; Saturated Fat 6 g;
Total Fat 25 g; Protein 6 g; Carbohydrate 55 g; Fiber 0 g;
Sodium 65 mg; Cholesterol 83 mg*

Hurrah for the fun!
Is the turkey done?
Hurrah for the pumpkin pie!

—by Lydia Marie Child

Giving thanks—for family, friends, and homemade Pumpkin Pie!

PUMPKIN PIE

◆◆◆

Ever since pumpkin pie was served at the second Thanksgiving in 1623, this spicy custard pie has been a traditional holiday treat.

1 recipe Single Pie Crust (page 368)	½ cup firmly packed dark brown sugar
1½ cups cooked fresh or canned pumpkin purée	¼ cup maple syrup
¾ cup evaporated whole milk	2 tablespoons unsalted butter or margarine, at room temperature
2 large egg yolks	2 teaspoons pumpkin pie spice
	3 large egg whites

 PREP TIME: 45 MIN. / COOKING TIME: 40 MIN.
    COOLING TIME: 1 HR.

1 Preheat the oven to 375°F. Make the pie crust, fit into a 9-inch pie plate, and make a rope edge (page 368).

2 In a large bowl, with an electric mixer on medium, beat the pumpkin purée, milk, egg yolks, sugar, syrup, butter, and pumpkin pie spice. In a clean medium-size bowl, with clean beaters and the mixer on high, beat the egg whites until stiff but not dry. Fold the egg whites into the pumpkin mixture; pour into the crust.

3 Bake for 40 minutes or until a knife inserted in the center comes out clean. Cool on a rack for 1 hour before serving. Makes 9 servings.

1 serving: Calories 345; Saturated Fat 8 g; Total Fat 17 g; Protein 7 g; Carbohydrate 44 g; Fiber 1 g; Sodium 88 mg; Cholesterol 74 mg

◆

Sweet Potato Pie

Mix and bake as for Pumpkin Pie, substituting **1½ cups fresh, cooked or canned sweet potato purée** for the pumpkin. Makes 9 servings. *1 serving: Calories 374; Saturated Fat 8 g; Total Fat 17 g; Protein 7 g; Carbohydrate 50 g; Fiber 0 g; Sodium 118 mg; Cholesterol 75 mg*

A fresh Strawberry-Almond Tart, filled with a light custard cream... It's the berries!

STRAWBERRY-ALMOND TART

❖❖❖

Elegant and inviting, this tart seems to say: "Company's coming!"

For the crust:

1¾	cups all-purpose flour
¼	cup ground almonds
¼	cup each unsalted butter or margarine and vegetable shortening
¼	cup confectioners sugar
4	to 5 tablespoon iced water

For the filling:

½	cup granulated sugar
4	teaspoons cornstarch
1	cup each low-fat (2% milkfat) milk and half-and-half
1	large egg
2	large egg yolks
1	teaspoon each almond and vanilla extracts
5	cups strawberries, hulled and halved or whole raspberries, hulled
⅓	cup red currant jelly
¼	cup sliced almonds, toasted (page 365)

PREP TIME: 45 MIN. / COOKING TIME: 20 MIN.
CHILLING TIME: 1½ HR.

1 To make the crust: Preheat the oven to 400°F. In a medium-size bowl, mix the flour, almonds, butter, shortening and confectioners sugar with your fingers until coarse crumbs form. Add enough water to form a dough. Press into the bottom and up the sides of a 12-inch tart pan with a removable bottom. Chill for 30 minutes. Fill with pie weights or dried beans and blind-bake for 10 minutes (page 368). Remove the weights and bake 8 minutes more or until light brown.

2 Meanwhile, make the filling: In a medium-size saucepan, mix the sugar and cornstarch. Whisk in the milk and half-and-half and cook, whisking, over moderately high heat for about 5 minutes or until the mixture boils and thickens.

3 Meanwhile, in a medium-size bowl, with an electric mixer on high, beat the egg and egg yolks until light yellow and thick. Stir about 1 cup of the hot milk mixture into the eggs, then return this mixture to the saucepan. Whisking constantly, cook for 3 minutes or until thickened (do not boil). Remove from the heat, stir in the almond and vanilla extracts, and pour into the tart shell. Cool for 30 minutes.

4 Arrange the berries decoratively in circles on top of the custard. In a small saucepan, warm the jelly over low heat, then carefully brush over the strawberries. Sprinkle with the toasted almonds and refrigerate for at least 1 hour before serving. Makes 10 servings.

1 serving: Calories 294; Saturated Fat 4 g; Total Fat 11 g; Protein 6 g; Carbohydrate 45 g; Fiber 1 g; Sodium 24 mg; Cholesterol 79 mg

COCONUT CREAM PIE

◆◆◆

1	recipe Single Pie Crust (page 368)	2⅔	cups low-fat (2 % milkfat) milk
1⅔	cups sugar	4	large eggs, separated
3	tablespoons cornstarch	1½	cups shredded coconut
2	tablespoons all-purpose flour	3	tablespoons unsalted butter (not margarine)
¼	teaspoon salt	1	tablespoon vanilla extract

PREP TIME: 45 MIN. / COOKING TIME: 35 MIN.
COOLING TIME: 3 HR.

1 Fit the crust in a 9-inch deep-dish pie plate; blind-bake for 10 minutes (page 368). Reduce the oven to 350°F. In a medium-size saucepan, mix ⅔ cup of the sugar with the cornstarch, flour, and salt, then whisk in the milk. Cook, whisking occasionally, over moderately high heat for about 5 minutes or until the mixture boils and thickens.

2 Meanwhile, in a medium-size bowl, with an electric mixer on high, beat the egg yolks until light yellow and thick. Stir about 1 cup of the hot milk mixture into the egg yolks, then return this mixture with 1¼ cups of the coconut to the saucepan. Cook, stirring constantly, for 3 minutes or until thickened (do not boil). Remove from the heat, stir in the butter and vanilla, and pour into the pie shell. Cool for 30 minutes.

3 In a clean large bowl, with clean beaters and the mixer on high, beat the egg whites until stiff peaks form. Gradually add the remaining sugar, beating 3 minutes more or until glossy. Swirl the meringue on the pie and sprinkle with the remaining ¼ cup of coconut. Bake for 25 minutes or until the meringue is light-golden. Cool on a rack for about 30 minutes, then chill for at least 2 hours. Makes 9 servings.

1 serving: Calories 533; Saturated Fat 14 g; Total Fat 26 g; Protein 8 g; Carbohydrate 70 g; Fiber 0 g; Sodium 196 mg; Cholesterol 129 mg

LEMON MERINGUE PIE

◆◆◆

1	recipe Single Pie Crust (page 368)	1¾	cups cold water
2¼	cups plus 1 tablespoon sugar	2	teaspoons grated lemon rind
½	cup cornstarch	4	large eggs, separated
		⅔	cup lemon juice

PREP TIME: 45 MIN. / COOKING TIME: 32 MIN.
COOLING TIME: 3 HR.

1 Fit the crust in a 9-inch deep-dish pie plate and blind-bake for 10 minutes (page 368). Reduce the oven to 350°F. In a medium-size saucepan, mix 1¼ cups of the sugar, the cornstarch, water, and lemon rind. Stir over moderately high heat for about 5 minutes or until thick.

2 Meanwhile, in a medium-size bowl, with an electric mixer on high, beat the egg yolks until thick. Stir about 1 cup of the hot sugar mixture into the egg yolks, then return to the saucepan. Cook, whisking constantly, for 3 minutes or until thickened (do not boil). Stir in the lemon juice and pour into the pie shell. Cool for 30 minutes.

3 In a clean large bowl, with clean beaters and the mixer on high, beat the egg whites until stiff. Gradually add 1 cup of the remaining sugar, beating 3 minutes more or until glossy. Swirl the meringue on the pie; sprinkle with the remaining sugar. Bake for 25 minutes or until golden. Cool for 30 minutes; chill for 2 hours. Makes 9 servings.

1 serving: Calories 413; Saturated Fat 5 g; Total Fat 13 g; Protein 6 g; Carbohydrate 70 g; Fiber 0 g; Sodium 61 mg; Cholesterol 109 mg

◆

Key Lime Pie

Prepare as for Lemon Meringue Pie, using only ⅔ **cup sugar** in the filling. Substitute **1 cup sweetened condensed milk and ¾ cup water** for the water, **fresh lime juice and grated lime rind** for the lemon juice and rind. Makes 9 servings. *1 serving: Calories 478; Saturated Fat 7 g; Total Fat 16 g; Protein 8 g; Carbohydrate 78 g; Fiber 0 g; Sodium 103 mg; Cholesterol 120 mg*

DIXIE STRAWBERRY SHORTCAKE

Summertime means strawberry shortcake time! This one comes from the Deep South, where biscuits are used instead of cake. We've cut the fat by replacing the cream in the biscuits with buttermilk and extending the topping with reduced-fat sour cream. You can cut calories even more by using the light topping recipe on page 365.

2	quarts ripe strawberries, hulled	1	cup heavy cream
1	recipe Beth's Buttermilk Biscuits (page 306)	1	tablespoon vanilla extract
		¼	teaspoon ground cinnamon
4	tablespoons sugar	1	cup reduced-fat sour cream
1	large egg, beaten		

PREP TIME: 30 MIN. / COOKING TIME: 12 MIN.

1 Preheat the oven to 450°F. Using a food processor or blender, purée 1 cup of the berries and pour into a serving bowl. Slice the remaining berries; toss with the purée and set aside.

2 Prepare the dough, sifting 2 tablespoons of the sugar with the flour and adding the beaten egg with the buttermilk. Pat out the dough to 1½ inches thick; cut with a 3½-inch round cutter (preferably fluted) into 6 shortcakes, re-rolling the scraps as you go. Bake on an ungreased baking sheet for 12 minutes or until golden and puffy.

3 While the biscuits bake, in a clean medium-size bowl, with an electric mixer on high, beat the heavy cream until frothy. Add the remaining sugar, the vanilla, and cinnamon, beating until stiff, then fold in the sour cream. To serve, split the hot biscuits and generously layer with berries and cream, inside and on top. Makes 6 servings.

1 shortcake: Calories 426; Saturated Fat 12 g; Total Fat 26 g; Protein 6 g; Carbohydrate 45 g; Fiber 1 g; Sodium 396 mg; Cholesterol 56 mg

Dixie Strawberry Shortcake—a buttery, sweetened biscuit, laden with juicy berries and luscious cream

The table was laid with sweet cakes and short cakes, ginger cakes and crumbling crullers, and the whole family of cakes.

—from The Legend of Sleepy Hollow by Washington Irving

VELVETY CHOCOLATE PUDDING

◆◆◆

Creamy chocolate puddings are what many childhood memories are made of. This one is lighter in fat, but still rich in dark chocolate taste.

1	cup sugar	4	large eggs
¼	cup cornstarch	2	teaspoons unsalted butter
½	teaspoon salt	1	tablespoon vanilla extract
3	cups low-fat (1% milkfat) milk		
4	squares (1 ounce each) semisweet chocolate, melted		

 PREP TIME: 20 MIN. / COOKING TIME: 8 MIN.

1 In a large heavy saucepan, mix the sugar, cornstarch, and salt, then whisk in the milk. Cook, whisking occasionally, over moderately high heat for about 5 minutes or until the mixture boils and thickens. Blend in the chocolate.

2 In a medium-size bowl, with an electric mixer on high, beat the eggs until thick. Stir about 1 cup of the hot chocolate mixture into the eggs, then return to the saucepan. Cook, whisking, for 3 minutes or until thick and smooth (do not boil). Remove from the heat and stir in the butter and vanilla. Serve warm or chilled. Makes 9 servings.

1 serving: Calories 263; Saturated Fat 2 g; Total Fat 9 g; Protein 7 g; Carbohydrate 41 g; Fiber 0 g; Sodium 212 mg; Cholesterol 113 mg

◆

Chocolate Meringue Pie

Prepare and blind-bake a 9-inch deep-dish Single Pie Crust (page 368). Reduce the oven to 350°F. Prepare Velvety Chocolate Pudding, using **7 tablespoons cornstarch** and the **4 egg yolks**; pour into the shell. In a clean large bowl, with the mixer on high, beat the **4 egg whites** with 1 **cup sugar** until glossy, then swirl on the pie. Bake for 25 minutes. Cool; chill for 2 hours. Makes 9 servings. *1 serving: Calories 516; Saturated Fat 6 g; Total Fat 19 g; Protein 9 g; Carbohydrate 81 g; Fiber 0 g; Sodium 220 mg; Cholesterol 114 mg*

LEMON PUDDING CAKE

◆◆◆

Pudding cakes became popular in the 1950's. Made from one simple batter, they go into the oven as a pudding and come out as a cake, with a pudding sauce on the bottom.

2	large eggs, separated	2	teaspoons grated lemon rind
¼	teaspoon salt	2	tablespoons unsalted butter or margarine, melted
¾	cup granulated sugar		
1¾	cups low-fat (1% milkfat) milk	1	pint fresh raspberries or blueberries, washed and stemmed (optional)
⅓	cup all-purpose flour		
⅓	cup fresh lemon juice		

PREP TIME: 20 MIN. / COOKING TIME: 40 MIN.
COOLING TIME: 5 MIN.

1 Preheat the oven to 350°F and butter a 9-inch square or a 2-quart shallow baking dish. In a clean medium-size bowl, with clean beaters and an electric mixer on high, beat the egg whites and salt until soft peaks form. Gradually add ½ cup of the sugar and beat until stiff peaks form.

2 In a large bowl, with an electric mixer on high, beat the egg yolks until light yellow and thick. Add the remaining ¼ cup of sugar, then the milk, and beat until fluffy. Using a wooden spoon, stir in the flour, lemon juice, lemon rind, and butter until well blended.

3 Fold in the egg whites just until they disappear, then spoon the batter into the baking dish. Bake for 40 minutes or until golden and puffy on top. Cool in the dish on a rack for 5 minutes. To serve, scoop the hot cake into individual serving dishes, then spoon some of the pudding sauce on top. Sprinkle generously with fresh berries if you wish. Makes 6 servings.

1 serving: Calories 210; Saturated Fat 4 g; Total Fat 7 g; Protein 5 g; Carbohydrate 34 g; Fiber 0 g; Sodium147 mg; Cholesterol 85 mg

In the 1897 catalog of Sears, Roebuck and Company, this rich chocolate cookie made its debut—and it has truly been a down-home American favorite ever since. These are fudgey and slightly moist inside.

◆ Chocolate Fudge Brownies ◆

1½ cups (3 sticks) unsalted butter
(not margarine)

7 squares (1 ounce each) unsweetened chocolate

2¼ cups sifted all-purpose flour

1½ teaspoons salt

4 cups coarsely chopped walnuts

6 large eggs

3 cups sugar

1½ tablespoons vanilla extract

36 walnut halves (optional)

PREP TIME: 20 MIN. / COOKING TIME: 35 MIN.
COOLING TIME: 15 MIN.

1 Preheat the oven to 325°F and butter a 15½" x 10½" x 2" baking pan. In a small saucepan, melt the butter and chocolate over low heat; cool. Onto a piece of wax paper, sift the flour and salt, then toss with the nuts.

2 In a large bowl, with an electric mixer on high, beat the eggs just until foamy. Add the sugar, then the cooled chocolate mixture and vanilla, and beat just until blended.

3 Stir in the flour mixture just until it disappears, then spoon into the pan; top with the walnut halves if you wish. Bake for 35 minutes or just until set and a toothpick inserted in the center comes out almost clean (page 364). Let cool in the pan for 15 minutes; cut into 2- x 1½-inch bars. Makes 3½ dozen.

1 brownie: Calories 242; Saturated Fat 5 g; Total Fat 17 g; Protein 4 g; Carbohydrate 22 g; Fiber 1 g; Sodium 88 mg; Cholesterol 49 mg

DOUBLE DUTCH BROWNIES
◆◆◆

This recipe, with much less fat, comes from the family of Maurine Ryan in Cheyenne, Wyoming.

2 cups sifted all-purpose flour

2 cups granulated sugar

1 teaspoon baking soda

1 cup (2 sticks) unsalted butter (not margarine)

1 cup water

¼ cup unsweetened cocoa powder

2 large eggs, beaten

½ cup low-fat buttermilk

1 tablespoon vanilla extract

For the frosting:

¼ cup (½ stick) butter (not margarine)

¼ cup unsweetened cocoa powder

6 tablespoons low-fat buttermilk

1 pound sifted confectioners sugar (4½ cups)

2 teaspoons vanilla extract

1 cup chopped walnuts

PREP TIME: 20 MIN. / COOKING TIME: 15 MIN.
COOLING TIME: 1 HR.

1 Preheat the oven to 400°F and butter a 15½" x 10½" x 2" baking pan. In a large bowl, sift the flour, sugar, and baking soda.

2 In a small saucepan, bring the butter, water, and cocoa to a boil over moderate heat. Pour over the flour mixture, whisking until smooth, Blend in the eggs, buttermilk, and vanilla. Pour into the pan. Bake for 15 minutes or just until the top springs back when lightly touched.

3 Meanwhile, make the frosting: In a medium-size heavy saucepan, over moderate heat, stir the butter, cocoa, and buttermilk for 4 minutes or just until the mixture begins to bubble. Remove from the heat and stir in the remaining ingredients. When the brownies come out of the oven, immediately spread the frosting on top. Cool in the pan on a rack for at least 1 hour, then cut into 2- x 1½-inch bars. Makes 3½ dozen brownies.

1 brownie: Calories 172; Saturated Fat 4 g; Total Fat 8 g; Protein 2 g; Carbohydrate 24 g; Fiber 0 g; Sodium 33 mg; Cholesterol 26 mg

Cookie-and-milk break: Blonde brownies, filled with polka dots of chocolate and bits of walnuts

POLKA DOT SQUARES

◆◆◆

After chocolate chip cookies became popular in the 1930's, other cookies made with similar ingredients began appearing. This one resembles a blonde brownie with chocolate scattered throughout.

2	cups sifted all-purpose flour	½	cup firmly packed light brown sugar
1½	teaspoons baking powder	2	large eggs
1	teaspoon ground cinnamon	⅓	cup low-fat buttermilk
½	teaspoon salt	1	tablespoon vanilla extract
1	cup (2 sticks) unsalted butter or margarine, at room temperature	6	ounces semisweet chocolate chips (1 cup)
¾	cup granulated sugar	¾	cup finely chopped walnuts, toasted (page 365)

PREP TIME: 15 MIN. / COOKING TIME: 25 MIN.
COOLING TIME: 10 MIN.

1 Preheat the oven to 375°F and butter a 13" x 9" x 2" baking pan. Onto a piece of wax paper, sift the flour, baking powder, cinnamon, and salt.

2 In a large bowl with an electric mixer on high, cream the butter with both sugars until light yellow. Add the eggs, one at a time, then the buttermilk and vanilla, and beat until light and fluffy.

3 Using a wooden spoon, stir in the flour mixture just until the flour disappears; fold in the chocolate chips and walnuts. Spread in the pan and bake for 25 minutes or until a toothpick inserted in the center comes out almost clean (page 364). Let cool in the pan on a rack for 10 minutes; cut into 2-inch squares. Makes 2 dozen cookies.

1 cookie: Calories 213 ; Saturated Fat 5 g;
Total Fat 13 g; Protein 3 g; Carbohydrate 24 g; Fiber 0 g;
Sodium 77 mg; Cholesterol 40 mg

School's out...time for Chunky Toll House Cookies and Peanut Butter Cookies from the cookie jar

CHUNKY TOLL HOUSE COOKIES
◆◆◆

The old Toll House Inn, built in 1709 near Whitman, Massachusetts, was once a half-way stop for people traveling from Boston to New Bedford. In the 1930's, Ruth Graves Whitman and her husband began the tradition there of providing a home-away-from-home, serving great meals, which included the famous Toll House Cookies. We've made the old recipe a bit better for you by adding rolled oats.

¾ cup sifted all-purpose flour	6 tablespoons firmly packed light brown sugar
½ teaspoon baking soda	1 large egg
½ teaspoon salt	1½ teaspoons vanilla extract
½ cup uncooked old-fashioned oats	½ teaspoon hot water
½ cup (1 stick) unsalted butter or margarine, at room temperature	6 ounces semisweet chocolate chips (1 cup)
6 tablespoons granulated sugar	½ cup chopped pecans

PREP TIME: 15 MIN. / COOKING TIME: 10 MIN.
COOLING TIME: 10 MIN.

1 Preheat the oven to 375°F; butter 2 baking sheets. Onto a piece of wax paper, sift the flour, baking soda, and salt, then toss with the oats. In a large bowl, with an electric mixer on high, beat the butter with both of the sugars until creamy.

2 Blend in the egg, then the vanilla and water and beat for 3 minutes or until light yellow and fluffy. Using a wooden spoon, stir in the flour mixture just until it disappears, then fold in the chocolate chips and pecans.

3 Drop by rounded teaspoonfuls, 2 inches apart, onto the baking sheets. Bake for 10 minutes or until light brown. Let cool on the baking sheets for 2 minutes; with a spatula, transfer to racks. Store in an airtight container for up to 2 weeks or in the freezer for up to 3 months. Makes about 30 cookies. For more, double the recipe.

*1 cookie: Calories 111 ; Saturated Fat 2 g;
Total Fat 7 g; Protein 2 g; Carbohydrate 13 g; Fiber 0 g;
Sodium 53 mg; Cholesterol 16 mg*

PEANUT BUTTER COOKIES

◆◆◆

At the St. Louis World's Fair in 1904, the doctor who had recently invented peanut butter promoted it as a health food. Today it's one of America's favorite foods, especially when used to make these popular cookies.

1¾ cups sifted all-purpose flour	¾ cup (1½ sticks) unsalted butter (not margarine), at room temperature
⅓ cup nonfat dry milk powder	
2 teaspoons baking powder	¾ cup firmly packed light brown sugar
1 cup chunky peanut butter	1 large egg
	2 teaspoons vanilla extract

PREP TIME: 30 MIN. / COOKING TIME: 10 MIN.
COOLING TIME: 10 MIN.

1 Preheat the oven to 350°F and butter 2 baking sheets. Onto a piece of wax paper, sift the flour, dry milk powder, and baking powder.

2 In a large bowl, with an electric mixer on high, beat the peanut butter and butter until creamy. Add the sugar, then the egg and vanilla, and continue beating until light and fluffy.

3 Using a wooden spoon, stir in the flour mixture just until the flour disappears. Shape the dough into 1-inch balls; place them 2 inches apart on the baking sheets. Using a fork, lightly press a crisscross design on the top of each cookie.

4 Bake for 10 minutes or just until golden but not brown. Let cool on the baking sheets for 2 minutes; with a spatula, transfer to racks to cool. These cookies keep well in an airtight container for up to 2 weeks or in the freezer for up to 3 months. Makes about 4 dozen 2-inch cookies. For more cookies, just double the recipe.

1 cookie: Calories 91; Saturated Fat 3 g;
Total Fat 6 g; Protein 2 g; Carbohydrate 8 g; Fiber 0 g;
Sodium 45 mg; Cholesterol 13 mg

LEMON BARS

◆◆◆

This recipe, with its shortbread crust and tart, lemony filling, is a cross between a cookie and a little pie.

For the crust:

1½ cups sifted all-purpose flour	¼ cup sifted all-purpose flour
½ cup sifted confectioners sugar	1 teaspoon baking powder
¾ cup plus (1½ sticks) unsalted butter or margarine, at room temperature	4 large eggs
	⅓ cup fresh lemon juice

For the filling:

2 cups granulated sugar	2 teaspoons grated lemon rind
	2 tablespoons sifted confectioners sugar

PREP TIME: 20 MIN. / COOKING TIME: 35 MIN.
COOLING TIME: 10 MIN.

1 To make the crust: Preheat the oven to 350°F and butter a 13" x 9" x 2" baking pan. In a medium-size bowl, mix the flour with the confectioners sugar, then work in the butter with your fingers until a dough forms. Press in the bottom of the pan and bake for 10 minutes.

2 Meanwhile, make the filling: Onto a piece of wax paper, sift the granulated sugar, flour, and baking powder. In a medium-size bowl, whisk the eggs until thick, then blend in the sugar mixture, the lemon juice, and rind. Spread over the hot crust and immediately return to the oven. Bake 25 minutes longer or until set.

3 Let cool in the pan for 10 minutes, then dust with the 2 tablespoons of confectioners sugar and cut into 2- x 1½-inch bars. With a spatula, transfer to racks to cool. Store the cookies in an airtight container in the refrigerator for up to 1 week; do not freeze. Makes 3 dozen cookies.

1 cookie:: Calories 112; Saturated Fat 3 g;
Total Fat 5 g; Protein 1 g; Carbohydrate 17 g; Fiber 0 g;
Sodium 17 mg; Cholesterol 35 mg

GINGERBREAD PEOPLE

◆ ◆ ◆

*Here's a taste of Victorian Christmases past,
when families hung cookies on their
holiday tree. To make holes for hanging,
pierce the top of each cookie with a skewer
as soon as it comes out of the oven.*

4 cups sifted all-purpose flour	1 cup molasses
1 tablespoon ground cinnamon	1 tablespoon cold water
2 teaspoons baking powder	**Optional decorations:**
1½ teaspoons each ground ginger and ground cloves	Currants for eyes
	Strips of candied cherries for smiles
1 teaspoon each baking soda, ground nutmeg, and salt	Red hot cinnamon candies for buttons
1 cup (2 sticks) unsalted butter (not margarine), at room temperature	**For the icing:**
	2½ cups sifted confectioners sugar
1 cup granulated sugar	½ teaspoon vanilla extract
2 large eggs, separated	3 to 4 tablespoons cold water
	Assorted food colors

🕐 PREP TIME: 1 HR. / CHILLING TIME: 1 HR.
COOKING TIME: 8 MIN. / COOLING TIME: 10 MIN.

1 Onto a piece of wax paper, sift 3½ cups of the flour, the cinnamon, baking powder, ginger, cloves, baking soda, nutmeg, and salt. In a large bowl, with an electric mixer on high, cream the butter and sugar until light yellow and fluffy. Beat in the egg yolks, one at time, then the molasses. Using a wooden spoon, stir in the flour mixture. Cover and refrigerate the dough for at least 1 hour or overnight.

2 Preheat the oven to 350°F; butter 3 baking sheets. On a pastry cloth or board, sprinkle ¼ cup of the remaining flour and roll out half of the dough, ¼ inch thick. With cookie cutters, cut out gingerbread people; with a spatula, transfer them to the baking sheets. Decorate with currants, cherries, and cinnamon candies if you wish.

◆ Cookie Cut-ups ◆

"**A** good recipe takes you only halfway toward making great sugar cookies," advises professional baker Elizabeth Vernon, from Akron, Ohio. "It's the cutting, rolling and baking that really count." Elizabeth should know. Her creations sell out daily at her family's West Point Market, and are often seen at historical restorations, too.

Elizabeth suggests: "When mixing the dough, set aside about ½ cup of the flour to use for rolling out the cookies, instead of adding extra flour, which can make them tough. Roll out dough ⅛ to ¼ inch thick (no thinner); dip the cutter in flour before cutting out each cookie; bake the cookies until the edges just begin to brown—no longer."

3 In a cup, whisk the egg whites with the water. Bake the cookies for 5 minutes, then brush lightly with the egg whites; bake 2 to 3 minutes more. Let cool on the baking sheets for 2 minutes;, with a spatula, transfer to racks to cool. Repeat with the remaining dough and flour.

4 To make the icing: In a small bowl, stir the sugar with the vanilla, then add enough water to make a stiff icing. Divide into small cups and color as you wish. When the cookies are cold, pipe out designs, such as smiling faces, zigzags, bow ties for men, and aprons for women. If using different colors of icing, let one color dry before piping the next. Store cookies in an airtight container for up to 2 weeks; do not freeze, as the icing could crack. Makes about 4 dozen cookies.

*1 cookie: Calories 127; Saturated Fat 3 g;
Total Fat 4 g; Protein 1 g; Carbohydrate 21 g; Fiber 0 g;
Sodium 80 mg; Cholesterol 20 mg*

SUGAR COOKIES

◆◆◆

In the 19th century, sugar cookies were favorites for the holidays and were often lavishly decorated. Frequently, the name of a family member or friend was written in icing.

3 cups all-purpose flour	1 cup granulated sugar
2 teaspoons baking powder	2 large eggs
¼ teaspoon salt	2 teaspoons vanilla extract
1 cup (2 sticks) unsalted butter or margarine, at room temperature	2 teaspoons grated lemon rind
	Multi-colored sugar sprinkles (optional)

PREP TIME: 45 MIN. / CHILLING TIME: 2 HR.
COOKING TIME: 8 MIN. / COOLING TIME: 10 MIN.

1 Onto a piece of wax paper, sift 2½ cups of the flour, the baking powder, and salt. In a large bowl, with an electric mixer on high, cream the butter and sugar until light yellow and fluffy.

2 Beat in the eggs, one at a time, then the vanilla and lemon rind. Using a wooden spoon, stir in the flour mixture. Divide into 3 equal pieces, wrap in plastic wrap, and refrigerate for at least 2 hours or until thoroughly chilled.

3 Preheat the oven to 350°F; butter 3 baking sheets. On a surface lightly floured with about ⅓ of the remaining ½ cup of flour, roll out 1 piece of dough, ¼ inch thick, and cut into shapes with cookie cutters.

4 With a spatula, transfer to the baking sheets, sprinkle with the sugar if you wish, and bake for 8 minutes or just until the edges start to brown. Let cool on the baking sheets for 2 minutes, then transfer to racks to cool. Repeat with the remaining dough. Decorate as desired, using the icing for Gingerbread People (opposite page). Store in an airtight container, but do not freeze frosted cookies. Makes about 6 dozen cookies.

1 cookie: Calories 54; Saturated Fat 2 g; Total Fat 3 g; Protein 1 g; Carbohydrate 7 g; Fiber 0 g; Sodium 19 mg; Cholesterol 13 mg

The gingerbread cookie crowd — dressed up in their Sunday best and ready to wish every one happy holidays!

PECAN ICE BOX COOKIES

◆◆◆

For homebaked cookies on the
spur of the moment, just slice and bake.

1½ cups sifted all-purpose flour	⅔ cup firmly packed light brown sugar
¾ teaspoon ground cinnamon	⅓ cup granulated sugar
½ teaspoon baking soda	1 large egg
¼ teaspoon salt	2 teaspoons vanilla extract
½ cup (1 stick) unsalted butter (not margarine), at room temperature	¾ cup finely chopped pecans or walnuts, toasted (page 365)

PREP TIME: 20 MIN. / CHILLING TIME: 2 HR.
COOKING TIME: 8 MIN.

1 Onto a piece of wax paper, sift the flour, cinnamon, baking soda, and salt. In a large bowl with an electric mixer on high, cream the butter with both sugars until light and fluffy.

2 Add the egg and vanilla; beat for 3 minutes or until light and fluffy. Stir in the flour mixture just until the flour disappears; stir in the pecans.

3 Turn the dough onto a lightly floured surface; shape into a 14- x 1½-inch log. Wrap tightly in plastic wrap and refrigerate for at least 2 hours. (It will keep in the refrigerator for up to 1 week, in the freezer for up to 1 month.)

4 To bake the cookies: Preheat the oven to 400°F. Using a sharp knife, slice the chilled or frozen dough ¼ inch thick, and place slices ½ inch apart on ungreased baking sheets. Bake chilled dough for 8 minutes (frozen dough for 10 minutes) or until crisp and very lightly browned. Let cool on the baking sheets for 2 minutes, then transfer to racks to cool. Makes about 8 dozen cookies. For more, just double the recipe.

1 cookie: Calories 30; Saturated Fat 1 g;
Total Fat 2 g; Protein 0 g; Carbohydrate 4 g; Fiber 0 g;
Sodium 11 mg; Cholesterol 5 mg

A basketful of Snowballs—covered with sugar "snow" and gift-wrapped for traveling to a favorite friend

◆

Chocolate Pinwheels

Prepare dough as for Pecan Ice Box Cookies and divide into 2 equal pieces. Into ½ of the dough, beat **1 square (1 ounce) melted semisweet chocolate.** On a lightly floured surface, roll out each piece into a 14- x 10-inch rectangle. Carefully lay the chocolate dough on top of the vanilla dough. Starting at one wide end, roll up the dough tightly into a 14- x 1½-inch log. Chill and bake as directed. Makes about 8 dozen cookies.
1 cookie: Calories 31; Saturated Fat 1 g; Total Fat 2 g; Protein 0 g; Carbohydrate 4 g; Fiber 0 g; Sodium 11 mg; Cholesterol 5 mg

SNOWBALLS
◆◆◆

This version of one of America's favorite cookies, comes from Jean Dittrich of Mansfield, Ohio, who often serves them when entertaining friends.

2 cups sifted all-purpose flour	1 tablespoon vanilla extract
¾ teaspoon salt	1 cup finely chopped pecans
1 cup (2 sticks) unsalted butter or margarine	¾ cup sifted confectioners sugar
½ cup granulated sugar	

PREP TIME: 45 MIN. / COOKING TIME: 25 MIN.
COOLING TIME: 15 MIN.

1 Preheat the oven to 325°F; butter 2 baking sheets. Onto a piece of wax paper, sift the flour and salt. In a medium-size bowl, with an electric mixer on high, cream the butter and granulated sugar until light and fluffy; blend in the vanilla.

2 Using a wooden spoon, stir in the flour mixture, then the pecans. Dust your hands with a little of the confectioners sugar and roll the dough into 1-inch balls. Place 2 inches apart on the baking sheets and bake for 25 minutes or just until light brown. Transfer to racks to cool for 15 minutes, then roll in the confectioners sugar. These cookies keep well in an airtight container for up to 2 weeks; do not freeze them. Makes about 4 dozen cookies. For more, just double the recipe.

*1 cookie: Calories 81; Saturated Fat 3 g;
Total Fat 6 g; Protein 1 g; Carbohydrate 8 g; Fiber 0 g;
Sodium 33 mg; Cholesterol 11 mg*

◆
Black-eyed Susans

Prepare and roll dough into balls as for Snowballs; place on baking sheets. Press a **chocolate candy kiss**, flat side down, in the center of each cookie, flattening the dough slightly. Bake as directed. Makes about 4 dozen cookies. *1 cookie: Calories 105; Saturated Fat 4 g; Total Fat 7 g; Protein 1 g; Carbohydrate 11 g; Fiber 0 g; Sodium 38 mg; Cholesterol 11 mg*

SHORTENIN' BREAD
◆◆◆

Replacing some of the flour with cornstarch gives these cookies a smoother texture.

1 cup plus 2 tablespoons sifted all-purpose flour	¾ cup (1½ sticks) unsalted butter (not margarine), at room temperature
½ cup cornstarch	
½ cup firmly packed light brown sugar	1 tablespoon granulated sugar

PREP TIME: 20 MIN. / CHILLING TIME: 20 MIN.
COOKING TIME: 40 MIN. / COOLING TIME: 10 MIN.

1 Preheat the oven to 350°F; butter an 8-inch square baking pan. Onto a piece of wax paper, sift the flour and cornstarch. In a medium-size bowl, with an electric mixer on high, cream the brown sugar and butter until light and fluffy. Using a wooden spoon, stir in the flour mixture. Spread the dough in the pan; chill for 20 minutes.

2 Using the back of a knife, mark the dough into 2- x 1¼-inch bars, prick gently with a fork, and sprinkle with the granulated sugar. Bake for 40 minutes or until golden and crisp. Let cool in the pan for 10 minutes; cut into 24 bars and transfer to racks to cool. These cookies keep well in an airtight container for up to 2 weeks or in the freezer for up to 3 months. Makes 2 dozen cookies. For more, just double the recipe.

*1 cookie: Calories 103; Saturated Fat 4 g;
Total Fat 6 g; Protein 1 g; Carbohydrate 12 g; Fiber 0 g;
Sodium 3 mg; Cholesterol 17 mg*

◆
Petticoat Tails

Prepare dough as for Shortenin' Bread; chill for 20 minutes. On a lightly floured surface, roll out dough ½ inch thick; cut into rounds with a 1½-inch cookie or biscuit cutter, preferably fluted. Bake on buttered baking sheets for 10 minutes or until golden. Makes 2 dozen cookies. *1 cookie: Calories 103; Saturated Fat 4 g; Total Fat 6 g; Protein 1 g; Carbohydrate 12 g; Fiber 0 g; Sodium 3 mg; Cholesterol 17 mg.*

BACK TO BASICS

◆◆◆

Many of our mothers and grandmothers seemed to know always how to do the correct things with food, like how to cook an egg perfectly or bake wonderfully flaky pie crust. Here, we've collected some of their knowledge, then updated it to reflect today's technology. So that you have a handy reference, we've selected especially those techniques that you probably don't do every day, such as trussing chicken, shucking clams, and kneading bread. We've also included charts that tell you how much to buy per serving for fresh foods, and what to substitute if you're missing a recipe ingredient. And for the look of it all, we've added some simple but effective garnishes.

Cooking corn on the cob

Remove the husks and silks from the corn. Line a large skillet with a few husks; lay the corn on top. Add **1 inch of cold water** and sprinkle with **2 tablespoons of sugar.** Bring to a full boil, cover, and cook, turning once, for 2 minutes, or until the corn is the way you like it. Serve immediately.

Blanching fresh vegetables for salads

Cooking fresh vegetables briefly in boiling water (called blanching) brings out their best color and flavor, especially important for salads. Bring a large saucepan of cold water to a rolling boil over high heat. Add a little salt if you wish, then the vegetables—one type at a time—and boil just until their color brightens but they are still crisp. Snow peas need only a few seconds; green beans, about 1 minute; broccoli florets, 2 to 3 minutes. Using a slotted spoon, transfer vegetables to a bowl of ice water and swish them around for a few moments, then drain.

Roasting sweet peppers or tomatoes

Preheat the broiler. On a baking sheet, arrange whole sweet peppers or unskinned tomatoes. Set under the broiler, 6 inches from the heat. Broil, turning frequently, about 3 minutes for tomatoes, 10 minutes for peppers, or until their skins are black. Using tongs, transfer to a clean paper bag, close tightly, and let stand for about 10 minutes or until cool enough to handle. Pull off the skins with your fingers.

Roasting garlic

Preheat the oven to 350°F. Peel away the white papery skin and the colored skins from **as many garlic cloves as you need.** Place the cloves on **a piece of foil, about 11 x 8 inches.** Sprinkle with **a little virgin olive oil, fresh or dried thyme leaves, coarse salt,** and **black pepper.** Fold the long edges of the foil tightly together and twist the ends, making a foil packet. Place directly on the oven rack and bake for 8 to 10 minutes or until the garlic is soft.

Pitting olives

Put an olive on a cutting board. Place the flat edge of a chef's knife or a pancake turner over the olive, then hit it gently with your fist to lightly smash the olive. Pick out the pit.

Making homemade mashed potatoes

Half-fill a large saucepan with water and bring to a boil over high heat. Peel **2 pounds of Idaho russets, Yukon Gold, Yellow Finn, or all-purpose potatoes**. Cut them into chunks, slide them into the boiling water, and return to a simmer. Cook, uncovered, for 15 minutes or until tender, then drain and return to the pan. In a small saucepan, bring **½ cup low-fat (1% milkfat) milk, 2 tablespoons of unsalted butter or margarine, ½ teaspoon salt,** and **¼ teaspoon black pepper** just to a simmer. Using an electric mixer on medium or a hand potato masher, mash the hot potatoes, while slowly adding the milk mixture, until everything comes together. (Leave a few lumps for texture.) For an extra touch, stir in **¼ cup minced green onion or parsley or grated Parmesan.** Makes 6 to 8 servings (page 125).

Making sweet potato puffs in orange cups

1 Cut **3 fresh oranges** in half crosswise and scoop out the fruit. In a large bowl, place **3 pounds of peeled, cooked hot sweet potatoes**. Add **¼ cup each of low-fat (1% milkfat) milk and fresh orange juice, 3 tablespoons dark brown sugar, 2 tablespoons unsalted butter or margarine, 1½ teaspoons grated orange rind,**

¾ **teaspoon salt, ½ teaspoon each black pepper and ground cinnamon,** and ¼ **teaspoon each ground ginger and nutmeg**. With an electric mixer on medium, beat for 3 minutes or until almost smooth. Using a pastry bag fitted with a large fluted tip, pipe the potatoes into the orange cups (or use a small spoon). Broil 6 inches from the heat for 5 minutes or until puffy and golden brown. Makes 6 puffs (page 108).

Peeling tomatoes easily

1 Half-fill a large saucepan with water and bring to a boil. Core the tomatoes. With a sharp pointed knife, mark a shallow X on the bottom of each one. Drop the tomatoes into the water for 15 to 30 seconds. Using a slotted spoon, transfer to ice water, then peel off the skin with the knife or your fingers, starting at the X.

Preparing tomatoes for stuffing

Cut the tomatoes in half crosswise. Gently squeeze or poke out the seeds, then sprinkle the cavities lightly with salt. Turn upside down on paper towels for 30 minutes to drain out the excess liquid.

Soaking and cooking dried beans

Before dried beans are cooked (except lentils and split peas), they must first be soaked. Sort

and rinse them, picking out any broken beans or stones. To soak overnight, place the beans in a bowl and cover with cold water. To quick-soak, place beans in a large saucepan or Dutch oven, fill with cold water to cover by 2 inches, and bring to a boil over high heat. Turn off the heat, cover, and let stand for 1 hour. Drain and rinse the beans and return to the saucepan with cold water to cover. Add seasonings that you like, such as **chopped onion, minced garlic, bay leaves,** and **cracked pepper**, then bring to a boil. Lower the heat, cover, and cook for the time suggested on the package or until tender. Add **salt to taste** halfway through the cooking time; when added at the beginning, salt can make beans less tender. Don't allow them to boil or they may break apart.

Making oven-baked croutons

Preheat the oven to 350°F. Brush **4 slices of whole-wheat, rye, or white bread** (with or without the crusts, your choice) with **2 tablespoons olive oil**. Cut into cubes and spread on an ungreased baking sheet. Bake uncovered, turning frequently, for 20 minutes, or until nicely browned and crisp all over. **For Pepper Croutons,** mix ¼ **teaspoon salt** and ½ **teaspoon black pepper** into the oil. **For Garlic Croutons,** mix **2 minced cloves of garlic** into the oil. **For Parsley-Cheese Croutons,** mix **2 tablespoons each minced parsley and grated Parmesan** in a cup. After toasting, toss the croutons with the parsley mixture, then bake 5 minutes longer. For extra-special croutons, use the ingredients for all 3 variations.

Shucking oysters

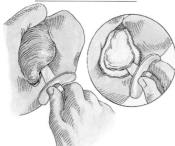

1 In the palm of one hand, hold an oyster, flat-side-up, over a bowl to catch the liquor. (Protect your hand with an oven mitt or folded washcloth.) Push the tip of an oyster knife between the shells near the hinge and work it back and forth until the oyster opens. Cut the muscle and hinge that hold the shells together, then lift off the top shell. Run the knife under the oyster, freeing it from the bottom shell.

2 To open a large oyster, wrap it in a towel, flat-side-up, and brace it on a hard, flat surface,

Shucking clams

1 Holding a clam in the palm of one hand, insert a clam knife near the hinge and slide it around toward the opposite side until the clam pops open. Snap off the top shell. Run knife under the clam to free it from the bottom shell.

Boiling shrimp

Half-fill a large saucepan with water. Add **salt if you wish**, plus **whole peppercorns and pickling spices or shrimp boil** (available in many supermarkets). Bring to a boil over high heat, then slide in **the shrimp**. If you have already peeled them, add **some shells for extra flavor**. Return to a boil and simmer for about 3 minutes for medium-size, unshelled shrimp, 5 minutes for jumbo or just until pink. (If shelled, they may need slightly less time.) Transfer to a colander, then rinse with cold water to stop the cooking.

Peeling and deveining shrimp

1 Peel off the outer shell of the shrimp, ring by ring, leaving the tail on if you wish.

2 Using the tip of a paring knife, cut a shallow slit along the curved outside edge. Holding the shrimp under cold water, scrape out the vein with the knife or pull it out with your fingers.

Poaching fresh fish fillets

Lay the fish in a single layer in a poacher or large deep skillet. Pour in enough boiling water to completely cover the fish by ½ inch. For each quart of water,

add **1 teaspoon salt** and **3 tablespoons fresh lemon juice or wine vinegar, or 1 cup white wine**. Bring to a simmer. Keeping the water barely simmering (if it boils, the fish may fall apart), cook the fish for 6 to 8 minutes. It should feel springy when done. With a slotted spatula, transfer immediately to warm plates.

Boning a whole round fish

1 With a sharp knife, enlarge the slit along the bottom of the fish between the head and the tail.

2 Slide the knife between the ribs and flesh to free them, then along both sides of the backbone, to free the bony cage.

3 Using kitchen shears, cut the backbone at both ends and lift it out, leaving a boneless, fleshy cavity for stuffing as in Cajun Stuffed Snapper (page 147).

Stuffing and trussing a chicken, turkey, or goose

1 Wash the bird, inside and out, and pat dry. Stuff the neck cavity, fold the neck skin over, and secure with skewers. Stuff the body cavity. Fold the skin over the opening and sew (as shown above) or skewer closed.

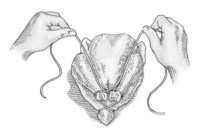

2 With the breast side up, lift the wings up and push the tips under the bird so the wings lie flat. Center a 3- to 4-foot length of string under the tail. Cross the string, bring it around the legs, and cross it again. Pull the ends under the breast bone and back toward the wings.

3 Turn the chicken over. Pull the string snugly against the wings and tie a knot.

Pounding meat and poultry cutlets

Lay meat or poultry on a board and whack it with a meat pounder or the bottom of a heavy skillet. If a recipe calls for it to be very thin, such as for Chicken-Fried Steaks (page 89) or Veal Cordon Bleu (page 114), place it between two pieces of wax paper and keep pounding until you obtain the desired thickness.

Poaching chicken breasts

Half-fill a large, deep skillet with chicken stock (page 74) or low-sodium chicken broth. Add **4 sprigs of parsley, 1 sprig each fresh rosemary and thyme, 1 teaspoon black peppercorns,** and **1 bay leaf.** Bring to a boil, then add **boneless, skinless chicken breast halves** in a single layer. Cover, lower the heat, and simmer for 15 minutes or until the chicken is no longer pink in the center. Remove with a slotted spoon.

Preparing a board for planking

To plank a steak (page 80) or a trout (page 148), use a planking board (thick piece of hardwood), found in specialty cookware shops, or a cutting board that's at least 1 inch thick. To prepare the board, soak it for 30 minutes in water, pat it lightly with paper towels, then coat it well with olive or vegetable oil. Cover all or most of the board with food, then cover any still exposed areas with small pieces of foil.

Making perfect dumplings

To make dumplings that are light, not tough or chewy, avoid overworking the dough. When adding the liquid, stir just until the flour disappears—no more. On a very lightly floured surface, roll out the dough quickly, then cut out the dumplings and slide them into simmering (not boiling) liquid. They are cooked when they look puffy and cake-like (usually after about 5 minutes) and when cutting one open reveals an inside that's firm but not doughy.

Making a white sauce

	Thin	All-purpose	Thick
Milk (1%)	1 cup	1 cup	1 cup
Butter	2 tsp	1 Tbsp	4 tsp
Flour	1 Tbsp	1½ Tbsp	2 Tbsp

In a small saucepan, heat the milk over moderate heat. In a separate saucepan, melt the butter over low heat. Using a wooden spoon, stir in the flour; cook for 3 minutes or until bubbly to eliminate the raw floury taste. Gradually whisk in the hot liquid and cook, whisking, for 2 minutes or until thickened. Season to taste.

Hard cooking eggs

Put the eggs in a saucepan, preferably in a single layer, cover completely with cold water, and bring just to a boil over high heat (the eggs should barely jiggle). Adjust the heat to the lowest setting possible and simmer, uncovered, for 15 minutes. Quickly transfer the eggs to a pan or bowl filled with cold water and leave them until cool. This gentle way of cooking helps keep the shells from cracking (especially important when making Easter eggs!) and the yolks from becoming rubbery. Dousing them in cold water makes the shells easier to peel.

Flour basics

Flours vary according to content of gluten (the elastic protein that holds dough together) and these differences can affect your success with a recipe. To make sure you are using the right flour, read the label for gluten content. The greatest amount is found in **bread flour** (around 14 grams per cup); this gives yeast-leavened bread a nice springy texture. **All-purpose flour** has about 10 grams per cup, making it better for yeast coffee cakes, gravies, pie crusts, and quick breads (the kind leavened with baking powder and/or eggs). **Cake, or pastry, flour** has the least amount of gluten (about 2 grams per cup); it's best for delicate cakes. Whenever a recipe calls for sifted flour, you should sift the flour first, then measure it; otherwise, you will end up with more flour than is needed. When measuring, scoop the flour into the measuring cup and level it off gently—don't pack it down.

Kneading and proofing yeast bread

1 Kneading yeast breads is what gives them a light and elastic texture. To start, shape the dough into a ball with lightly floured fingers. Place it on a lightly floured board, marble slab, or work surface. Using your fingertips, pull up the dough on the far side and fold it back toward you.

2 Using the heel(s) of one or both hands, press down and away from you with a rolling movement, pushing firmly but not too hard. Give the dough a quarter turn and repeat the process, again and again, until the dough is smooth and elastic, usually 8 to 10 minutes. If the dough sticks too much to the board or your hands, add just a bit of flour—not too much, or the bread will be dry.

3 Place the dough in a buttered bowl and turn it over to coat with the butter. Cover and place it in a warm place (about 85°F) to rise for the time indicated in the recipe (usually 1 to 2 hours) or until doubled in size. Be sure it's away from drafts. An oven that has been heated briefly then turned off is suitable. To test the dough, press 2 fingers into it, ½ inch deep, as shown. If the dents remain, the dough is ready.

Replenishing sourdough starter

If you have been saving sourdough starter in the refrigerator, you must replenish it every 7 days as follows: Discard about half. Into the remaining half, stir **1 cup unbleached organic bread flour** and **1 cup tepid water (105° to 115°F)**. Let stand at room temperature for 3 hours before using. If you do not use all of it, refrigerate the remainder in a loosely covered container as before.

Deciding when a cake is done

After a cake has baked the minimum time indicated, insert a toothpick in the center. If the recipe calls for a clean toothpick test, nothing should adhere; a moist-crumb test, a few crumbs should cling to the pick; an almost clean test (as for brownies), a little moist batter should adhere.

Grating lemon, orange or lime rind

Lay a piece of parchment paper, wax paper, or plastic wrap over the fine-hole side of a metal grater. Grate a few strokes with the fruit, just until the pith (bitter white part) begins to appear, then move to a new spot on the fruit. The zest (colored part of the rind) will collect on the paper.

Making citrus julienne

Using a zester, remove small strips of the colored zest from an orange, lemon, or lime, taking care not to get any bitter pith. Or, using a vegetable peeler, remove larger pieces, then cut them into thin strips (julienne). Drop the strips into boiling water for about 30 seconds. With a slotted spoon, remove to paper towels to drain.

Canning

Appropriate jars for canning are the heat tempered types that can be sealed with dome lids and bands. **To sterilize jars** for foods that will be processed in them for 10 minutes or longer, wash the jars in hot soapy water, rinse, and keep hot. Or put them through the short wash cycle in your dishwasher and leave them, without opening the door, until ready to fill. When food will be processed in jars for less than 10 minutes, place the empty jars, right-side-up, plus lids and bands, on a rack in a canner or stockpot. Cover with water, bring to a rolling boil, and boil for 10 minutes. Keep them in the hot water until time to use. **To fill jars,** drain them, one at a time, and fill with the hot food, packing firmly to within ½ inch of the jar top for jams and jellies; 1 inch for vegetables and relishes. To remove air bubbles, run a thin spatula around the inside edge of each jar. Wipe the jar top clean and put the lid on. Tightly screw the metal band over the lid. **To process in a water bath,** place the jars on a rack in a canner or stockpot (they should not touch the sides) and fill with enough hot water to cover the jars by 2 inches. Cover the canner, bring to a full boil over high heat, and start timing the processing. Boil gently and steadily for the time given in the recipe, adding more boiling water if needed to keep the jars covered. With long-handled tongs, transfer the jars to a surface covered with a towel. Let cool for 12 hours, then check each seal by pressing down on the lid; it should stay down. If any do not, reprocess them.

Toasting nuts and coconut

Toasting nuts intensifies their rich flavor. Preheat the oven to 350°F. Spread the nuts on an ungreased baking sheet and toast them, stirring every 3 minutes or so, until brown but not burned. Toast whole blanched or unblanched almonds for about 20 minutes; pecan halves, walnut halves, and slivered almonds, about 15 minutes; sliced almonds and chopped nuts, about 10 minutes. **To toast coconut,** preheat the oven to 350°F. Spread either flaked or shredded coconut in a shallow pan and bake, tossing now and then, for 10 minutes or until crispy and golden brown.

Unmolding a gelatin salad

To unmold a gelatin salad (page 256) or a mousse (page 246), first be sure it is thoroughly set. Dip the mold into very hot water for a few seconds. Loosen the edges of the salad with the tip of a knife. Holding a serving plate over the top of the mold, quickly flip it over; shake it gently, if necessary, until the salad slides out onto the plate. Chill until serving time.

Making a lighter topping

Instead of whipping heavy cream for desserts, you can make a lighter topping with milk. In a medium-size freezer-safe bowl, pour **1 cup whole milk or evaporated skim milk.** Place in the freezer until very cold and ice crystals appear. Using an electric mixer on high, beat until thick and foamy. Beat in **1 tablespoon superfine or confectioners sugar** and **½ teaspoon vanilla extract.** Serve immediately.

Diagram for clown cake (page 331)

For the face, use the round cake. With a serrated knife, cut the hat, hair, and tie from the 13- x 9-inch cake, using the diagram, far right, as an approximate guide (the cake will have shrunk a bit while baking). Arrange all the pieces as shown, right, using some of the extra cake, if needed, to fill in any gaps.

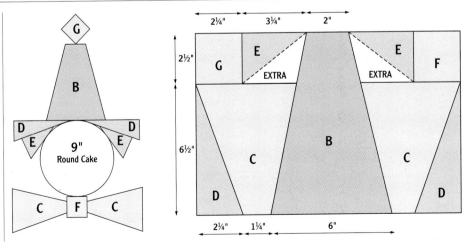

GREAT GARNISHES

❖❖❖

You can dress up your foods in simple ways before taking them to the table. For example, stack hot muffins in a napkin-lined basket, then add a cluster or two of fresh strawberries and mint leaves; toss a salad with its dressing, then arrange a few more of its most colorful ingredients in the center; surround a roast on a platter with its vegetables instead of serving them in a separate bowl. For other special effects, try your hand at some of these easy extras.

Ham rose

1 From a thin piece of ham ($\frac{1}{16}$ to $\frac{1}{8}$ inch thick), cut a strip, $1\frac{1}{2}$ x 6 inches. Starting at one narrow end, roll up a tight cylinder for the center.

2 Continue forming circles of "petals," loosely draping the ham and pinching the bottom edges of the rose together as you go. Secure with a toothpick.

Green onion fans

1 Trim off the root of each onion and all but 3 inches of the green top. On a cutting board, insert the pointed end of a sharp knife into the top of the white part, then gently pull it through the green part. Repeat several times, cutting narrow strips.

2 Place the onions in a bowl of ice water for about 2 hours or until the tops fan out and curl, then drain (page 15).

Fluted mushroom flower

1 With a paring knife, cut out a gently curved wedge, about $\frac{1}{4}$-inch wide, as shown. Continue around the mushroom, making 8 to 10 petals. To serve uncooked, dip in lemon juice (to prevent discoloration); to serve them cooked, sauté in a little butter. They're perfect with steaks (page 80).

Radish flowers

1 **Radish peonies** (page 206): Using a sharp pointed knife, trim off the root end of each radish; make 5 or 6 narrow slices from root to stem, not cutting all the way through. Make a quarter turn and cut 5 or 6 perpendicular slices, keeping the radish intact. Proceed to Step 3 below.

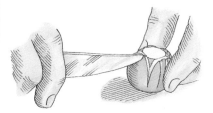

2 **Radish daisies** (page 206): Trim off the root end of each radish, then cut 4 petals from root to stem, taking care not to cut all the way through the bottom. Cut each petal into 3 sections. Proceed to Step 3 below.

3 Place radish flowers in a bowl of ice water for about 2 hours or until they open, then drain. Use Italian parsley for the leaves.

Carrot tulips & curls

1 **Carrot tulips** (page 206): Peel a carrot, leaving it whole. Starting about 2 inches from the pointed end, angle a sharp knife toward the center, making a petal about ½ inch wide. Continue around the carrot, making 3 to 5 petals, then twist off the end. Repeat at 2-inch intervals. Proceed to Step 3, below.

2 **Carrot curls** (page 68): Peel 1 or 2 large long carrots. Using a vegetable peeler, cut long thin wide strips of carrot. Starting at the narrow end, roll up the strips tightly, then pack them snugly in a small, flat-bottomed dish, so they cannot unroll.

3 Place **tulips** in a bowl of ice water for about 4 hours or until they open, then drain. Use Italian parsley for leaves. Cover **curls** with ice water for 4 to 6 hours. Drain and gently unroll each curl like a spring.

Cobwebs for soup

1 For 6 bowls of soup: In a cup, mix **2 tablespoons of reduced-fat sour cream or yogurt** and **2 tablespoons of low-fat milk.** Using a small spoon, place a large drop of the mixture in the center of a bowl of soup. Starting from the center, make a spiral with the spoon, going around 3 or 4 times.

2 With a knife, drag from the center to the edge 4 times, cutting the circles into fourths.

3 Starting midway between 2 points of a section, drag from the outside to the center. Repeat with the other 3 sections, creating a star burst (page 71). If you make a mistake, stir the cobweb into the soup and begin again.

Gumdrop flowers & leaves for cakes

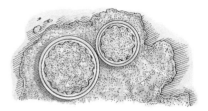

1 Preheat the oven to 325°F In a heatproof bowl, soften several large gumdrops of one color in the oven for 2 to 3 minutes; press them together to form a ball of dough. On a heavily sugared surface, roll out, ⅛ to ¼ inch thick. To prevent sticking, sugar the surface and the dough as you go. **For flowers,** use 2 fluted cutters, 1 and 1¾ inches in diameter, to cut out circles (an equal number of each size).

2 Place a small circle on top of a larger one; from underneath, pinch in the center to form petals. Secure with a toothpick. Place in mini muffin cups to harden.

3 **To make leaves** (page 295), from cardboard cut out a pattern for holly or another leaf. Lay it on green gumdrop dough and trace around with a sharp pointed knife. Arrange on top of a cake.

PIE PERFECT
◆◆◆

Single Pie Crust (enough for one 8- or 9-inch regular or deep-dish pie): In a large bowl, stir **2 cups all-purpose flour** and ½ **teaspoon salt.** Using a pastry blender or 2 knives, cut in ¼ **cup each very cold unsalted butter or margarine (cut in pieces) and very cold vegetable shortening.** Add ⅓ **cup ice water** and stir just until the mixture comes together. Work the dough as little as possible: the larger the pieces of shortening and butter that remain, the flakier the crust will be. Wrap the dough in plastic wrap and chill for at least 30 minutes or until firm. Chilling not only lets the dough relax, but also firms up the fat. Roll out and shape. Bake at 425°F, 10 minutes for a partially baked crust, or 20 minutes for a fully baked one.

Double Pie Crust (enough for one 8- or 9-inch regular or deep dish pie): Make dough as for Single Pie Crust, using **3 cups all-purpose flour,** ¾ **teaspoon salt,** ⅓ **cup each very cold unsalted butter or margarine (cut in pieces) and vegetable shortening,** plus ½ **cup ice water.**

Rolling out the dough

1 If possible, work in a cool room, so the dough won't become sticky as you roll it out. (It's tough to roll out pie crusts in 95°F weather!) Lightly dust a marble slab or wooden pastry board with flour. (Marble is best because it stays cool and keeps the dough colder.) Lightly dust your rolling pin with flour too.

2 Using even strokes, roll from the center outward, ¼ to ⅜ inch thick, keeping an even thickness and turning every couple of strokes to prevent sticking. Work quickly. If the dough starts to stick, dust the underside with flour. For a regular 9-inch bottom crust, roll out a 12-inch circle; for a deep-dish 9-inch bottom crust, a 13- to 14-inch circle, depending on the depth of your plate; for a top crust, an 11-inch circle. You'll need at least a 1-inch overhang all the way around. **Tip:** If you wish to make crusts ahead of time, roll them out, wrap them individually in several sheets of plastic wrap, then freeze them flat for up to 3 months. Defrost them in the refrigerator before using.

Shaping the crust

1 To transfer a crust easily to a pie plate, loosely roll it on the rolling pin, then unroll it over the plate, as shown above. Gently fit it in place, pressing out any air bubbles. Avoid stretching the dough, as this causes shrinkage during baking. For a single crust, roll and tuck extra pastry under the edge of the crust, forming a double stand-up edge, then flute and trim. For a double crust pie, after filling the pie, add the top crust, tuck the edges of both crusts under to form one stand-up edge, then flute and trim.

2 **For a fluted edge** (page 345): Put the thumb of one hand on the inside edge of the crust. Push slightly outward toward the edge, while pinching with the thumb and index finger of your other hand on the outside edge of the crust. Repeat all around, leaving ½ inch between flutes.

3 **For a rope edge** (page 347): Pinch the pastry edge between the thumb and knuckle of your index finger, at a 45° angle. Repeat all the way around, placing your thumb each time in the indention just left by your knuckle.

Prebaking a crust (blind baking)

When a recipe calls for a partially baked or pre-baked bottom crust, shape it, then prick the bottom and sides all over with the tines of a fork. Line the crust with foil and fill with pie weights, dried beans, or uncooked rice. Bake at 425°F for 6 minutes, then gently lift out the foil and weights and return the crust to the oven. For a partially baked crust, bake 4 minutes more. For a fully baked crust, bake 8 to 10 minutes more or just until lightly browned.

Glazing a pie

In a small bowl, whisk **1 large egg white** with **1 tablespoon of water** until frothy. Use this mixture to stick together the edges of top and bottom crusts, to stick other pastry decorations on a top crust, and to glaze the top crust. When making a fruit pie, sprinkle **about 1 tablespoon of sugar** over the glaze just before baking.

Down-home decorations

1 **Cluster of apples** for Ruthie's Apple Pie (page 345): Cut out 2 cardboard patterns: 1, an apple, about 3 inches high; the other, a leaf, 1½ inches long (both with stems). Roll out the top crust, ¼ to ⅜ inch thick. Using a sharp knife, cut out 3 apples and carefully remove the dough, leaving 3 apple holes; save the trimmings.

2 **Apple leaves:** Roll out the trimmings, ½ inch thick. Cut around the leaf pattern 8 or 10 times. With the tip of the knife, mark veins on each leaf. Lightly pinch the ends of the leaves to make them curl. Place in clusters on the crust. Glaze before baking.

1 **Old-fashioned braid** for any double crust pie: Roll out the trimmings into a strip 18 x 1½ inches and ½ inch thick. Cut 3 strips, ½-inch wide. Starting in the center, braid out to each end.

2 Carefully, place the braid in a circle on the top of the pie, about 1 inch in from the fluted edge. Pinch the ends of the braid together and seal with a glaze (above left). Decorate the center with a diamond flower (below).

3 **Diamond flower:** Roll out the trimmings. Using a sharp, pointed knife, cut out 5 diamond-shaped pieces about 2 inches long by 1 inch wide; place in a circle on the pie, with all tips meeting at the center. To make the center, cut out a 4- by ¼-inch strip of pastry, roll into a tight coil, and place flat-side-up where the points of the diamonds meet. Brush with the glaze and sprinkle with the sugar before baking.

Lattice top

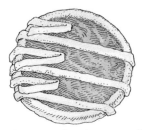

1 Make a single pie crust, dividing the dough into ⅔ and ⅓. Roll out and fit the larger piece in a pie plate, leaving a 1-inch overhang. Roll out the smaller piece in a circle that will fit the top of the pie. Using a sharp knife or fluted pastry wheel, cut it into 1-inch strips. Lay 6 strips evenly across the pie; fold back every other strip.

2 At center of pie, place one remaining strip perpendicular to the others; reset the folded strips.

3 Fold back the alternate strips, lay down a second crosswise strip, and reset the folded ones. Repeat until a lattice covers the entire top of the pie, then seal and trim the edges. Glaze if you wish.

◆ From the Bean Pot ◆

DRIED BEANS	UNCOOKED WEIGHT	AMOUNT UNCOOKED	AMOUNT COOKED
Black-eyed peas	1 pound	2½ cups	6 cups
Great northern beans	1 pound	2½ cups	6 cups
Kidney beans, pinto beans	1 pound	2½ cups	6 cups
Lentils, split peas	1 pound	2¼ cups	5 cups
Lima beans (baby)	1 pound	2½ cups	6 cups
Navy beans, pea beans	1 pound	2 cups	6 cups

◆ At the Cheese & Dairy Bar ◆

DAIRY ITEMS	AMOUNT	EQUIVALENT
Butter or margarine	4 ounces (1 stick)	½ cup or 8 tablespoons
Cream, heavy	½ pint (1 cup)	2 cups whipped
Cream, sour	½ pint	1 cup
Cheese, Cheddar	4 ounces	1 cup shredded
Cheese, cottage	8 ounces	1 cup
Cheese, cream	3 ounces	6 tablespoons
Milk, evaporated	14½-ounce can	1⅔ cups

◆ The Baker's Corner ◆

	MARKET WEIGHT	AMOUNT
All-purpose flour and bread flour	1 pound	3½ cups unsifted 4 cups sifted
Cake flour	1 pound	4½ cups sifted
Bread crumbs	1 slice fresh, soft 1 slice dried or toasted	½ cup ¼ cup ground
Brown sugar	1 pound	2¼ cups firmly packed
Confectioners sugar	1 pound	4 cups unsifted 4½ cups sifted
Granulated sugar	1 pound	2 cups

◆ In the Egg Basket ◆

	1 EGG	12 EGGS
Large whole egg(s)	3 tablespoons	2¼ cups
Large egg white(s)	2 tablespoons	1½ cups
Large egg yolk(s)	1 tablespoon	¾ cup

◆ At the Fruit Stand ◆

	MARKET WEIGHT	AMOUNT
Apples	1 pound (3 medium)	peeled, cored, and sliced, 3 cups
Bananas	1 pound (3 medium)	sliced, 2⅓ cups mashed, 1½ cups
Blueberries	1 dry pint	whole, 2 to 2⅓ cups
Bing cherries	1 pound	halved and pitted, 1½ cups
Cranberries	10-ounce bag	whole, 3 cups
Grapefruit	1 medium	sections, 1 cup
Grapes with seeds	1 pound	seeded and halved, 2 cups
Seedless grapes	1 pound	whole, 2½ cups
Lemons	1 medium	juice, 3 tablespoons; grated rind, 1 tablespoon
Limes	1 medium	juice, 2 tablespoons; grated rind, 1 tablespoon
Oranges	1 medium	juice, ⅓ cup; grated rind, 2 tablespoons
Peaches	1 pound (4 medium)	peeled and sliced, 2 cups
Pears	1 pound (4 medium)	peeled, cored, and sliced, 2 cups
Pineapple	2 pounds (1 medium)	chunks, 3 cups
Plums	1 pound (8 medium)	sliced, 2 cups
Raspberries	½ pint	whole, 1 cup
Strawberries	1 pint	hulled and sliced, 2 cups

◆ At the Vegetable Stand ◆

	MARKET WEIGHT	AMOUNT
Asparagus	1 pound (20 medium-thick stalks)	trimmed and cut up, 2½ cups uncooked, 2 cups cooked
Beets	1 pound (6 medium)	sliced, 2 cups cooked
Broccoli	1 pound	trimmed and cut up, 4 cups uncooked, 2 cups cooked
Brussels sprouts	1 pound (2 pint cartons)	trimmed, 4 cups uncooked, 3½ cups cooked
Cabbage (all types)	1 pound (1 small head)	shredded, 4 cups uncooked, 2 cups cooked
Carrots	1 pound (5 or 6 large) 1 large	shredded, 3 cups; sliced or chopped, 2½ cups sliced or chopped, ½ cup
Cauliflower	1½ pounds (1 small head)	trimmed and cut up, 4 cups uncooked, 2 cups cooked
Celery	1 pound (2 bunches) 1 stalk	chopped, 4½ cups uncooked, 2 cups cooked chopped, ½ cup uncooked
Corn on the cob	1 large ear	uncooked kernels, ¾ cup; cooked kernels, ½ cup
Cucumber	6 ounces (1 small)	seeded and sliced, ¾ cup; chopped with seeds, 1 cup
Eggplant	1 pound (1 medium)	sliced or diced, 4 cups
Green beans	1 pound	trimmed and cut up, 3 cups uncooked, 2½ cups cooked
Green onions	white part only white and green parts	sliced or chopped, 1 tablespoon sliced or chopped, 2 tablespoons
Greens (collard, mustard, turnip)	1 pound	whole leaves, 6 cups uncooked, 2 cups cooked
Lettuce	1 pound (1 small head)	torn or shredded, 4 cups
Mushrooms	8 ounces	sliced, 3 cups uncooked, 1 cup cooked
Nuts (almonds)	1 pound in shell 4 ounces shelled	nutmeats, 1¼ cups chopped, ¾ cup
Nuts (pecans, walnuts)	1 pound in shell 4 ounces shelled	nutmeats, 2 cups chopped, 1 cup
Okra	1 pound	sliced, 4 cups uncooked or cooked
Onions (white, yellow)	4 ounces (1 small) 6 ounces (1 medium) 8 ounces (1 large)	chopped, ½ cup chopped, ¾ cup chopped, 1 cup
Parsnips	1 pound (4 medium)	cut into chunks, 2¾ cups uncooked or cooked
Green peas	1 pound in pods	shelled, 1 cup uncooked or cooked
Peppers (sweet green, red, yellow)	4 ounces (1 small) 6 ounces (1 medium) 8 ounces (1 large)	chopped, ½ cup chopped, ¾ cup chopped, 1 cup
Potatoes (white)	1 pound (3 medium)	sliced and cooked, 2¼ cups; cooked and mashed, 1¾ cups
Potatoes (sweet, yams)	1 pound (2 medium)	sliced and cooked, 2¼ cups; cooked and mashed, 1¾ cups
Pumpkin	1 pound	cooked and puréed, 1 cup
Shallot	1 small	minced, 1 tablespoon
Spinach	1 pound	whole leaves, 6 cups uncooked, 1 to 1½ cups cooked
Summer squash	1 pound (3 medium)	trimmed and sliced, 3¼ cups uncooked, 3 cups cooked
Tomatoes	1 pound (3 medium) 6 ounces (1 medium)	cored and chopped, 3 cups uncooked, 1½ cups cooked cored and chopped, 1 cup
Zucchini	1 pound (2 medium)	trimmed and sliced, 3¼ cups uncooked, 3 cups cooked

• At the Fishmonger's •

How much fish to buy for each serving

1 pound whole or drawn (gutted) fresh fish

8 ounces pan-dressed fish (cleaned, without head or fins)

6 to 8 ounces fish steaks

4 to 6 ounces fish fillets

Seafood to buy when what you want isn't available

FISH AND SHELLFISH	SUBSTITUTE WITH
Black sea bass or sea bass	Grouper, halibut, snapper, tilefish, mahimahi
Bluefish	Mackerel, lake trout
Catfish	Brook trout
Cod	Flounder, haddock, scrod
Flounder (flatfish)	Halibut, sole, turbot
Grouper (sea bass family)	Halibut, snapper, walleye pike, tilefish
Haddock (cod family)	Cod, flounder
Halibut	Grouper, cod, snapper, turbot
Lobster	Monkfish, crab legs
Mahimahi (dolphinfish)	Snapper, sea trout, swordfish
Mussels	Clams
Oysters	Clams, mussels
Pike	Cod, snapper
Pompano	Yellowtail flounder, snapper, kingfish
Snapper	Grouper, halibut, tilefish
Swordfish	Shark, mahimahi
Trout	Pink salmon, whiting
Tuna	Mahimahi, shark, swordfish

Clams and Oysters

Look for closed shells, with no cracks or chips.

1 pint shucked Cherrystone clams = 20 to 24 in liquor

1 pint shucked oysters (extra-select) = about 20 in liquor

7½-ounce can minced clams = ½ cup drained

How much crab to buy for each serving

1 to 1½ pound(s) live blue crabs or Dungeness crabs in the shell

8 ounces crab legs, cooked (2 to 3 legs)

3 to 4 ounces cooked crabmeat (pick through it for shells)

1½ pounds live crab in the shell = 1 cup cooked crabmeat

How much lobster to buy for each serving

1 whole live lobster in the shell (1 to 1½ pounds)

1 uncooked lobster tail in the shell (8 ounces)

3 to 4 ounces cooked lobster meat

1 pound live lobster in the shell = 1 cup cooked lobster meat

How many scallops to buy for each serving

4 ounces shelled uncooked scallops

1 pound bay scallops = 70 to 90 scallops

1 pound sea scallops = 20 to 30 scallops

How much shrimp to buy for each serving

6 ounces raw shrimp in the shell

4 ounces uncooked and shelled shrimp

3 ounces cooked and shelled shrimp

2 pounds unshelled raw shrimp = 1 pound after shelling

12 ounces raw shrimp in the shell = 1 cup cooked and shelled

4½ ounces canned shrimp = 1 cup drained shrimp

Shrimp Countdown

Jumbo shrimp = 10 to 12 per pound

Large shrimp = 18 to 22 per pound

Medium shrimp = 25 to 30 per pound

Small shrimp = 35 to 50 per pound

• At the Butcher Shop •

The color of meat to look for

Freshly cut beef: bright cherry red

Vacuum-packed beef: purplish red

Veal: light pink

Pork: grayish pink

Vacuum-packed pork: purplish red

Lamb: pinkish red

How much meat to buy for each serving

4 to 5 ounces boneless roast (Yields 3 to 4 ounces of cooked meat.)

6 to 8 ounces bone-in cuts (roasts, steaks, chops)

12 ounces to 1 pound very boney cuts (spareribs, beef ribs)

How much uncooked poultry to buy for each serving

4 ounces boneless, skinless chicken breast or thigh

6 ounces chicken breast with bone

8 ounces chicken thighs or legs with bone

1 pound whole chicken, duck, or turkey

◆ A Great Cup of Coffee ◆

◆ Buy the freshest coffee you can find, preferably in small amounts.

◆ If you have a grinder, buy whole coffee beans and grind them as you need them. (Keeps fresher this way.)

◆ Store coffee in an airtight container in the refrigerator or freezer.

◆ Keep your coffee maker sparkling clean by following the manufacturer's directions.

◆ Start with cold water and the proper grind for your coffee maker.

◆ Serve freshly made coffee whenever possible. If you must let it stand, pour it into an insulated thermal pot.

◆ Try 2 level tablespoons per ¾ cup of water for each cup of coffee, then experiment to suit your taste.

◆ A Pot of Perfect Rice ◆

Measure rice and water carefully (see chart as a guide), but also check amounts suggested on the package. If you want rice that is softer and moister, use a little more water; for a firmer rice, use slightly less water. While it cooks, no peeking, as this lets out steam and the rice may dry out before it's fully cooked.

1 CUP RICE	WATER	COOKED
Long-grain white	2 cups	3 cups
Long-grain converted white	2½ cups	4 cups
Instant white	1 cup	2 cups
Long-grain brown	2½ cups	3 cups
Wild rice	3 cups	4 cups

◆ Substitutions ◆

IF YOU DON'T HAVE THIS	USE THIS
Baking powder, 1 teaspoon	½ teaspoon cream of tartar + ¼ teaspoon baking soda
Buttermilk, 1 cup	1 cup yogurt or 1 tablespoon vinegar + enough low-fat milk to make 1 cup (Let stand for 5 minutes before using.)
Cake flour, 1 cup, sifted	1 cup minus 2 tablespoons sifted all-purpose flour
Chocolate (semisweet), 1 square (1 ounce)	3 tablespoons semisweet chocolate chips or 1 square (1 ounce) unsweetened chocolate + 1 tablespoon sugar
Chocolate (unsweetened), 1 square (1 ounce)	3 tablespoons unsweetened cocoa powder + 1 tablespoon butter, margarine, or oil
Cornstarch (for thickening), 1 tablespoon	2 tablespoons all-purpose flour
Garlic, 1 clove, minced	⅛ teaspoon garlic powder
Fresh herbs, chopped, 1 tablespoon	1 teaspoon dried herbs (Crumble them.)
Honey, 1 cup	1¼ cups sugar + ¼ cup liquid from recipe
Lemon juice, 1 teaspoon	¼ teaspoon cider vinegar
Milk (low-fat), 1 cup	½ cup skim evaporated milk + ½ cup water
Onion, 1 small, chopped	1 teaspoon dried onion powder
Pumpkin pie spice, 1 teaspoon	½ teaspoon ground cinnamon + ¼ teaspoon each ground ginger and allspice + ⅛ teaspoon ground nutmeg
Sour cream (reduced-fat dairy), 1 cup	1 cup low-fat yogurt (in baking)

◆ Measurement Equivalents ◆

Pinch or dash = less than ⅛ teaspoon
3 teaspoons = 1 tablespoon
2 tablespoons liquid = 1 fluid ounce
4 tablespoons = ¼ cup
5 tablespoons + 1 teaspoon = ⅓ cup

10 tablespoons + 2 teaspoons = ⅔ cup
1 cup liquid = 8 fluid ounces
2 cups = 1 pint
½ of ¼ cup = 2 tablespoons
½ of ⅓ cup = 2 tablespoons + 2 teaspoons

½ of ¾ cup = ¼ cup + 2 tablespoons
⅓ of ¼ cup = 1 tablespoon + 1 teaspoon
⅓ of ⅓ cup = 1 tablespoon + 2⅓ teaspoons
⅓ of ½ cup = 2 tablespoons + 2 teaspoons
⅓ of ⅔ cup = 3 tablespoons + 1⅔ teaspoons

ACKNOWLEDGMENTS & INDEX

◆ Our thanks to ◆

Food Stylist, Delores Custer (**Pages 78–115**); Prop Stylists: Adrienne Abseck (**Pages 12–81, 114–141**); Francine Matalon-Degni (**Pages 82–113**); Photographers: Tom Eckerle (**Pages 208-209**); Fabri/Gruppo Editoriale (**Pages 188–189**); Joshua Greene (**Pages 116–117, 144–145**); Spencer Jones (**Pages 314–315**); C.R. Pleasant/FPG (**Pages 286–287**); Michael Skott (**Pages 10–11, 46–47, 76–77, 168–169, 238–239, 264–265, 326–327**)

Grateful acknowledgment is made to the following sources for permission to use or adapt their recipes.

AMERICAN FOOD by Evan Jones and Judith B. Jones, "Beaten Biscuits," Copyright © 1974, 1975, 1981, 1990 by Evan Jones and Judith B. Jones. Published by Overlook Press. SAN FRANCISCO ENCORE by The Junior League of San Francisco, Golden Gate "Avocado Dip" (original title, "Layered Mexican Delight"), Copyright © 1986 by the Junior League of San Francisco. Used by permission of Doubleday, a division of Bantam Doubleday Dell Publishing Group, Inc.

The editors are grateful to the following for their courtesy in lending items for photography. Items not listed are privately owned.

Pages 13 & 27: Tiles—*Country Floors, Inc., NYC.* **Page 63:** Tureen, soup bowl, underliner, and glass—*Pierre Deux, NYC.* **Page 95:** Table—*The Bombay Company, NYC;* lace table runner and napkins—*White Linen, Schodack Landing, NY;* serving dish—*Oneida Silversmiths, Oneida, NY;* "Lavinia" plates—*Royal Worcester, Moorestown, NJ;* salad bowl—*Dalzell-Viking, New Martinsville, WV.* **Page 96:** Tiles—*Country Floors, Inc.;* knife—*Spyderco, Inc., Golden, CO.* **Page 99:** "Chelsea Wicker" platter—*Spode, Moorestown, NJ;* glasses—*Dalzell-Viking.* **Page 108:** Table and chair—*The Bombay Company;* tablecloth and napkins—*White Linen;* "English Garden" plates—*Royal Worcester;* flatware and crystal—*Oneida Silversmiths, Oneida, N.Y..* **Page 111:** Table—*Grange, NYC.* **Page 113:** Tiles—*Country Floors, Inc.;* knife—*Spyderco, Inc.* **Page 114:** "Neptune" wine glass and "White Open Lace" plate—*Royal Copenhagen, NYC;* napkin—*Anichini, Inc., Turnbridge, Vt.* **Page 118:** Blanket—*Pier 1 Imports Inc., NYC.* **Page 121:** Skillet—*Le Creuset USA.* **Page 125:** Curtain and napkin—*Country Curtains, Stockbridge, MA;* plate—*Pier 1 Imports Inc.;* chicken salt and pepper shakers—*Somethin' Else, NYC.* **Page 132:** Picnic basket—*Basketville, Putney, VT;* quilt—*Somethin' Else, NYC;* salt and pepper shakers—*Pier 1 Imports Inc.* **Page 135:** "Neptune" wine glass—*Royal Copenhagen.* **Page 140:** Wallpaper—*Janovic/Plaza, NYC.* **Page143:** Blue Canton tureen/stand and platter—*Mottahedeh & Co., Inc., Stratford, CT.;* tablecloth and napkin—*Anichini, Inc.* **Page 147:** Tiles—*Country Floors, Inc.* **Page 149:** Plates—*Pier 1 Imports Inc.* **Page 151:** Fish platter—*Williams-Sonoma;* towel—*Le Jacquard Français.* **Page 152:** Plate and glass—*Waterford Wedgwood USA Inc.;* tablecloth—*Le Jacquard Français.* **Page161:** Cupboard—*ABC Carpet and Home, NYC.* **Page 163:** Tablecloth—*Le Jacquard Français.* **Page 164:** Platter—*Waterford Wedgwood USA Inc.* **Page 174:** Coffee pot, cup, and saucer—*Waterford Wedgwood USA Inc.* **Page 177:** Plate, cup, and saucer—*Williams-Sonoma;* flatware—*Jean Couzon, Inc., NYC.* **Page 181:** Quiche dish—*Jacques Jugeat, Inc.*

Page 182: Fondue pot and forks—*Le Creuset of America;* plate—*Jacques Jugeat, Inc.;* glass—*Williams-Sonoma.* **Page 185:** Fiestaware plates, bowls, and pitcher—*Homer Laughlin China Co., NYC.* **Page 186:** Skillet—*Chantal Cookware Corp.* **Page 194:** Heart towel—*Le Jacquard Français;* Orrefors pitcher—*Royal Copenhagen/Georg Jensen Silversmiths.* **Page 197:** Plate—*Williams-Sonoma.* **Page 199:** Bowl, and underliner—*Williams-Sonoma;* flatware—*Royal Copenhagen/Georg Jensen Silversmiths.* **Page 201:** Plate and placemat—*Williams-Sonoma.* **Page 205:** Platter—*Royal Copenhagen/Georg Jensen Silversmiths.* **Page 210:** Knife—*Jean Couzon, Inc.* **Page 212:** Bean pot/bowls—*Williams-Sonoma.* **Page 214:** Vegetable bowl—*Spode.* **Page 218:** Griddle—*Le Creuset USA.* **Page 227:** Skillet—*Chantal Cookware Corp./Williams-Sonoma.* **Pages 228:** Baskets, glasses, napkin, and napkin ring—*Pier 1 Imports Inc.* **Page 245:** Table—*Pier 1 Imports Inc.* **Page 252:** Plates and cups—*Pier 1 Imports Inc.* **Page 258:** Cabbage plates—*Williams-Sonoma;* serving spoon—*Pottery Barn;* candlesticks—*Pier 1 Imports Inc.* **Page 261:** Bowls, mortar, and pestle—*Williams-Sonoma;* towel—*Le Jacquard Français.* **Page 262:** Sauceboat—*Pottery Barn;* scoop—*Williams-Sonoma.* **Page 270:** Napkins—*Pottery Barn.* **Page 281:** Wallpaper—*Janovic/Plaza.* **Page 284:** Basket—*Pier 1 Imports Inc.;* tablecloth—*Le Jacquard Français;* butter crocks—*Williams-Sonoma.* **Page 288:** Tablecloth and napkins—*Pier 1 Imports Inc.* **Page 292:** Teapot—*William Wayne & Company, NYC.* **Page 295:** Tablecloth, napkin ring, and gift boxes—*Pier 1 Imports Inc.* **Page 298:** Tablecloth, pizza cutter, and spatula—*Williams-Sonoma.* **Page 312:** Basket and napkin—*Pier 1 Imports Inc.* **Page 332:** Plate, cup, and saucer—*Spode;* wallpaper—*Janovic/Plaza., NYC.* **Pages 337 and 338:** Plates, cup and saucer—*Royal Worcester.*

◆Index◆

A

B

Page numbers in *italic* type refer to illustrations.

Page numbers in *italic* type refer to illustrations.

Page numbers in *italic* type refer to illustrations.

Page numbers in *italic* type refer to illustrations.

Page numbers in *italic* type refer to illustrations.